THE HANDBOOK OF RESEARCH ON TOP MANAGEMENT TEAMS

The Handbook of Research on Top Management Teams

Edited by

Mason A. Carpenter

University of Wisconsin–Madison, USA

Edward Elgar
Cheltenham, UK • Northampton, MA, USA

© Mason A. Carpenter 2011

Published by
Edward Elgar Publishing Limited
The Lypiatts
15 Lansdown Road
Cheltenham
Glos GL50 2JA
UK

Edward Elgar Publishing, Inc.
William Pratt House
9 Dewey Court
Northampton
Massachusetts 01060
USA

A catalogue record for this book
is available from the British Library

Library of Congress Control Number: 2010929035

ISBN 978 1 84844 660 1 (cased)

Typeset by Servis Filmsetting Ltd, Stockport, Cheshire
Printed and bound by MPG Books Group, UK

Contents

v

PART IV   HOW EXECUTIVE ACTIONS AFFECT STRATEGY,
          RIVALRY, AND ENTREPRENEURSHIP

PART V   THE CONTEXT SURROUNDING CHANGES IN THE
         EXECUTIVE SUITE

Contributors

Allen C. Amason, Associate Professor and Chair of the Management Department at the University of Georgia, earned his PhD from the University of South Carolina in 1993. His research focuses on strategy and strategic decision making and his work has been published in a variety of outlets like the *Academy of Management Journal*, the *Journal of Management*, the *Journal of Management Studies* and the *Journal of Business Venturing*. He is currently Associate Editor of the *Journal of Management Studies* and is a past Associate Editor of the *Journal of Management*. He has also served on the boards of the *Academy of Management Journal* and the *Journal of Management*. Professor Amason's teaching and consulting focus on strategic management, strategic decision making, and top management processes. He is an award-winning educator and has worked with numerous organizations including Exide Technologies, Rosetta Marketing, Johnson and Johnson, Computer Associates, Novartis, Tenet Healthcare, Nortel, and Advanced Micro Devices.

Ted Baker is an Associate Professor in the Management, Innovation and Entrepreneurship Department at the North Carolina State University College of Management, where he is Executive Director of the Center for Entrepreneurship and Technology Commercialization. He earned his PhD (Sociology) from UNC-Chapel Hill and his MBA from the University of Chicago. The first half of his adult life was spent in leadership roles in a variety of entrepreneurial ventures. His current research focuses on entrepreneurship under resource constraints (for example, in the informal settlements around Cape Town, South Africa and in the textiles industry in the American South) and in particular on bricolage and improvization as constructs useful for understanding resourceful behavior. He serves on the editorial boards of *Academy of Management Review*, *Administrative Science Quarterly*, *Journal of Business Venturing*, *Journal of Management Studies*, and *Strategic Entrepreneurship Journal*.

Joseph B. Beck is an Associate Professor of Management in the John L. Grove College of Business at Shippensburg University, having received his PhD in Strategy from the Paul Merage School of Business at University of California, Irvine, in June 2010. He received an MBA from the University of Oregon in 2003. His research investigates issues related to corporate scope and corporate governance, encompassing elements of international expansion as well as expansion through innovation. His dissertation research focuses on the linkage between the theoretical determinants of corporate scope and strategic outcomes such as corporate divestment, as well as research into the relationship between external governance mechanisms and CEO dismissal.

Christine M. Beckman, Associate Professor of Organization and Management, joined the faculty of the Paul Merage School of Business at University of California, Irvine, in 1999, after receiving her PhD from Stanford University. She is a Chancellor's Fellow and the Associate Director for The Don Beall Center for Innovation and Entrepreneurship. She was a visiting faculty member at the Haas School of Business at UC Berkeley in 2008–09. Her research focuses on how the social structures within which firms are embedded shape organizational actions and learning. She examines how the diversity and heterogeneity of social structure in various guises – networks, affiliations, team diversity, and internal labor markets – affect outcomes. Her work has focused on both established and emerging companies. She sits on the editorial boards of *Administrative Science Quarterly*, *Organization Science*, and *Strategic Organization* and has published in the top management and sociology journals.

M. Diane Burton is an Associate Professor in the School of Industrial and Labor Relations at Cornell University. Prior to joining the Cornell faculty in 2009, she was an Associate Professor of Management at the MIT Sloan School of Management. Professor Burton began her academic career at the Harvard Business School teaching leadership and organizational behavior. She earned her PhD in Sociology at Stanford University. Professor Burton studies employment relations and organizational change in entrepreneurial companies. Her work has been published in the *American Sociological Review*, the *American Journal of Sociology*, and *Organization Science*. Professor Burton is a Senior Editor of *Organization Science* and is a past Associate Editor of *Management Science*. She also serves on the editorial boards of *Administrative Science Quarterly*, *Journal of Business Venturing*, and *Strategic Entrepreneurship Journal*. A native of Pittsburgh, Pennsylvania, Professor Burton earned an undergraduate degree at Carnegie Mellon University, and an MEd from Harvard University Graduate School of Education.

Albert A. Cannella Jr. is Koerner Chair in Strategy and Entrepreneurship at Tulane University. He received his PhD from Columbia University in 1991. He serves on the editorial review boards of *Academy of Management Journal*, *Academy of Management Review*, *Journal of Management*, *Administrative Science Quarterly*, *Entrepreneurship Theory and Practice*, and *Strategic Management Journal*. His research interests focus on executives, entrepreneurship, and competitive dynamics.

Mason A. Carpenter is the M. Keith Weikel Professor in Leadership and the Pyle-Bascom Professor of Business Leadership in the Wisconsin School of Business at the University of Wisconsin–Madison. He joined the UW–Madison in 1997 after receiving his PhD from the University of Texas at Austin. Professor Carpenter studies corporate governance, top management teams, social networks, and the strategic management of global start-ups. He is Associate Editor of the *Academy of Management Review*, and serves on the editorial board of the *Strategic Management Journal*. His work has been published in *Academy of Management Journal*, *Academy of Management Review*, *Strategic Management Journal*, *Journal of Management*, and elsewhere. Professor Carpenter is an award-winning teacher who also works to integrate experiential and behavioral perspectives of strategic management into the classroom through positions on the Business Policy and Strategy (BPS) and Strategic Management Society Executive committees, Doctoral and New Faculty BPS consortia, and the widely used BPS Strategy Teaching Toolkit. He is a California native, and earned his BS in finance and economics from Humboldt State University and University of Copenhagen, Denmark, MBA from

California State University at Bakersfield, and enology diploma from the University of Bordeaux II, France.

Kevin D. Clark is the Senior Associate Dean at the Villanova School of Business, Philadelphia where he is also a Research Associate of that school's Innovation, Creativity, and Entrepreneurship (ICE) Center and the Center for Global Leadership. His research has been published in the *Academy of Management Journal, Organizational Dynamics*, and the *Leadership Review* and focuses primarily on the role of the top management team in creating competitive advantage through strategic decision-making processes, the development and use of relational networks, and the facilitation of knowledge creation and innovation. He has also investigated the use of strategic human resource systems as applied to executive teams, the role of the leader in calibrating team process, and the micro-factors that contribute to the persistent wage gap in white collar professions. Future research plans involve a comparative study of executive teams in the People's Republic of China and the Republic of Italy.

Walter J. Ferrier (PhD University of Maryland) is a Gatton Endowed Associate Professor of Management in the Gatton College of Business and Economics at the University of Kentucky. He recently served as a Visiting Professor at the Helsinki University of Technology in Finland. His research interests lie mainly in the areas of dynamic competitive interaction, strategic leadership, and the structure of interorganizational networks. His research has been published in the *Academy of Management Journal, Academy of Management Review, Strategic Management Journal, Managerial and Decision Economics*, and others. He won the *Academy of Management Journal*'s "Best Paper Award" for his research on competitive interaction published in 1999. He also served as a guest editor for *Information Systems Research* for a special issue on "Digital Systems and Competition."

Yan Gong is an Assistant Professor of Strategy at the Paul Merage School of Business at the University of California, Irvine. He received his PhD in Management from the University of Wisconsin–Madison. His research focuses on capabilities, routines, and unexpected events in entrepreneurial firms. His current research explores dynamic paths of how new firms develop routines and capabilities, and how they respond to surprise events in entrepreneurial processes. His research has appeared in the *Academy of Management Review, Handbook of Organizational Routines*, and *Frontiers of Entrepreneurship Research*.

Scott D. Graffin is an Assistant Professor at the University of Georgia's Terry College of Business. He received his PhD in Strategic Management and Organization Theory from the University of Wisconsin–Madison. His research interests include corporate governance, and the impact of reputation, status, and the financial press on organization outcomes. Broadly, his work suggests that third-party assessments, such as reports by the financial press and certification contests, represent external governance mechanisms that influence the perceived quality of organizations and executives. Scott's research has been published in the *Academy of Management Journal, Organization Science, Strategic Organization*, and other outlets. A native of Waukesha, Wisconsin, Professor Graffin earned an undergraduate degree at University of Wisconsin–Madison, and an MBA from the University of Wisconsin, Oshkosh.

Ciaran Heavey is currently an Assistant Professor/Lecturer of Strategy at the Quinn School of Business, University College Dublin. He received his PhD in Management from the University of Connecticut in 2009. His research interests span strategy and entrepreneurship and include such topics as top management teams, organizational ambidexterity, and corporate entrepreneurship and have been published in the *Strategic Management Journal*, the *Journal of Management Studies*, and *Advances in Global Leadership*.

Margaret Hughes-Morgan (PhD University of Kentucky) is an Assistant Professor of Strategy at the Eli Broad College of Business at Michigan State University. Her research interests lie mainly in the areas of dynamic competitive interaction, top management teams, and investor psychology. She is a member of the Academy of Management and the Strategic Management Society. She has eight years of work experience on Wall Street where her most recent position was a Director for the United Bank of Switzerland. She specializes in analysis of biotechnology and pharmaceutical stocks.

M. Nesij Huvaj is a PhD student in Management at the University of Connecticut. The central themes of his research interests are strategic leadership and entrepreneurship, with particular emphasis on governance, innovation, and new ventures.

Carla D. Jones is an Assistant Professor at the Bauer College of Business, University of Houston. She received her PhD from the W.P. Carey School of Business at Arizona State University. She is a member of the Academy of Management, and the Strategic Management Society. Her primary research interests are organizational executives (upper echelons) and competitive dynamics. She also researches organizational leaders (the CEO, the executive team, and the board of directors) and their influence on organizational outcomes. Related interests include the effects of organizational structure and ownership on corporate governance.

Giuseppe (Joe) Labianca (PhD Penn State University) is a Gatton Endowed Associate Professor of Management at the University of Kentucky's Gatton College of Business and Economics. He was previously on faculty at Emory's Goizueta Business School and Tulane's Freeman School of Business. His main research stream involves examining organizational behavior from a social network perspective, including recent work on network approaches to interpersonal conflict, groups, gossip, organizational justice, job satisfaction, and interpersonal control. His work has appeared in *Science*, the *Academy of Management Journal*, the *Academy of Management Review*, *Harvard Business Review*, *Organization Science*, and elsewhere. He is currently serving on the editorial board of *Organization Science* and as an Executive Committee member of the Academy of Management's Organization and Management Theory (OMT) Division. He recently won the OMT Division's Best Paper Award, Goizueta's Alumni Award for Excellence in Research, and the University of Kentucky Alumni Association's Great Teacher Award.

Peggy M. Lee is an Associate Professor at the W.P. Carey School of Business, Arizona State University. She has been a Visiting Professor at the McCombs School of Business, University of Texas at Austin and an Assistant Professor at the Goizueta Business School, Emory University. She received her doctorate from the Kenan-Flagler Business School, University of North Carolina at Chapel Hill. Her research focuses on corporate governance issues with a focus on the relationship between managers and shareholders. Her work has been published in the *Academy of Management Journal*, the *Strategic Management Journal, Organization Science*, and the *Journal of Financial Economics*, among others. She has served on the executive committees of the Business Policy and Strategy Group of the Academy of Management and the Competitive Strategy Group of the Strategic Management Society. She currently serves on the editorial boards of the *Strategic Management Journal* and the *Journal of Management*.

Patrick G. Maggitti is Assistant Professor of Strategic Management and Entrepreneurship and the Carmen and Sharon Danella Director of the Center for Innovation, Creativity, and Entrepreneurship (ICE Center) at the Villanova School of Business. His research interests focus on dynamic processes including innovation, entrepreneurship, decision making, search behavior, and market- and non-market-based competition. He has published in several journals including the *Academy of Management Journal, Academy of Management Executive, Employment Relations Today*, and *Leadership Review*. Dr. Maggitti has also been a chief executive officer and board member in the steel and mining industries where he founded two successful companies.

Jeffrey A. Martin is an Assistant Professor of Management in the Culverhouse College of Commerce at the University of Alabama. Prior to joining the Alabama faculty in 2010, he was an Assistant Professor of Management at the McCombs School of Business at The University of Texas at Austin. Professor Martin received his PhD in Management Science and Engineering from Stanford University in 2002. Professor Martin's research involves the programmatic study of organization and strategy in highly dynamic markets. An important theme in his work is a behavioral approach to the micro-foundations of dynamic capabilities. Professor Martin is conducting research in two different but complementary organizational settings that together build a more complete depiction of how dynamic capabilities originate and operate: multi-business organizations competing in high-tech product markets and the formation of new promising ventures. His paper (with Eisenhardt) "Dynamic Capabilities: What are they?" won the Dan and Mary Lou Schendel Best Paper Award for the *Strategic Management Journal* 2007.

Anne S. Miner is the Ford Motor Company Distinguished Chair in Management and Human Resources at the University of Wisconsin–Madison, where she is the Executive Director for the Initiative for Studies in Transformational Entrepreneurship and the Executive Director for the Strategic Management in the Life and Engineering Sciences. Her current research focuses on organizational entrepreneurial learning, learning from success and recovery experiences, and learning from failure. She has received several grants from the National Science Foundation, has served on the editorial boards of *Administrative Science Quarterly, American Sociological Review*, and *Academy of*

Management Review, and has been honored as the Distinguished Scholar of the Year for the Academy of Management division of technology and innovation management.

Ann C. Mooney is an Associate Professor at the Wesley J. Howe School of Technology Management at Stevens Institute of Technology. She received her PhD and MBA from The University of Georgia, and is a CPA. Mooney teaches Organizational Behavior and Strategic Management courses, and her research interests center on conflict and strategic decision-making practices of top executives and boards of directors. Mooney has published articles in a variety of journals including *The Academy of Management Review*, *Strategic Organization*, *The Journal of Management Studies*, and *The Academy of Management Perspectives*, and has received numerous teaching and research awards, including several Best Paper awards and a Women in International Science Collaboration award from the AAAS and NSF. Mooney consulted for Coopers and Lybrand and Arthur Andersen prior to her career in academia. As a professor, she has served as an independent consultant and professional facilitator for several Fortune 500 companies.

Jay O'Toole is a doctoral candidate at the University of Wisconsin–Madison. His current research focuses on founding top management teams, organizational entrepreneurial learning, and genealogical transfer of organizational routines. He has received several competitive research awards from the University of Wisconsin–Madison and his papers have been presented at the annual meetings of the Academy of Management as well as entrepreneurship research conferences such as the Smith Entrepreneurship Research Conference.

Suzanne J. Peterson is an Assistant Professor of Organizational Behavior and Management at the W.P. Carey School of Business at Arizona State University where she teaches graduate courses in leadership and organizational behavior. She holds degrees from the University of Southern California (BA) and The University of Nebraska (MBA, PhD). Her research interests include leadership dynamics surrounding executives, authentic leadership, positive organizational behavior, and most recently, the neuroscientific origins of leadership. Her work has appeared in business and psychology journals such as the *Journal of Applied Psychology*, *Personnel Psychology*, *Journal of Organizational Behavior*, and the *Journal of Management*. Before entering academia, Dr. Peterson worked as a change management consultant for Accenture.

Smriti Prabhakar is a PhD student in Management at the University of Connecticut. Her current research interests are in the area of strategic alliance portfolio, strategic entrepreneurship, and top management teams.

Wm. Gerard (Gerry) Sanders is Professor of Strategic Management at the Jones Graduate School of Business at Rice University. He was previously on the faculty of the Marriott School of Management at Brigham Young University. He earned a PhD in Strategic Management from The University of Texas at Austin in 1996. Professor Sanders' research is focused on the interpart of corporate governance and executive leadership, with a particular interest in their effects on firm strategy and performance. His research has been published in leading management journals. His work on the effects of stock option pay has been featured in major news outlets such as the *New York Times, The Economist, Business Week, CFO*, and on National Public Radio's Marketplace. Professor Sanders is currently an Associate Editor of the *Academy of Management Journal*.

Andrew Sangster is a Professor of Management and Organizational Development at Touro University, teaching strategic management, organizational behavior, and research methods. He is also the director of the Management and I/O Psychology graduate programs there. Prior to his academic career he was an executive in the aerospace and computer industries. He holds a PhD in Strategic Management from the Drucker School of the Claremont Graduate University, and an MS in Finance from the University of Southern California. Professor Sangster's research focuses on a number of behavioral aspects of business strategy development and implementation. One of these is the relationship between executives' enduring dispositions and strategy formation and implementation (as in this *Handbook*). He also studies the strategic effects of working coalitions with respect to decision biases, social embedding, agency considerations, and their interactions. He is a reviewer for the *Academic of Management Journal*.

Zeki Simsek is an Associate Professor and Ackerman Scholar at the Business School of University of Connecticut. Professor Simsek's current research deals with theory and evidence at the interface of strategic leadership and entrepreneurship. He has authored papers on this topic in journals such as *Academy of Management Journal, Strategic Management Journal, Journal of Applied Psychology, Journal of Management Studies, Journal of Management, Organizational Research Methods*, and others. He teaches a PhD seminar on Strategic Entrepreneurship, an MBA course on Venturing and Value Creation, and an award-winning undergraduate course on Venture Planning, Management, and Growth. He currently serves on the editorial boards of *Academy of Management Journal, Strategic Entrepreneurship Journal, Entrepreneurship Theory and Practice, Venture Capital: An International Journal of Entrepreneurial Finance, Journal of Management Studies*, and *Organizational Research Methods*.

Alexander D. Stajkovic is the Procter & Gamble Bascom Associate Professor of Organizational Behavior at the University of Wisconsin–Madison. Alex was a visiting scholar at Stanford University (psychology department) in 2007–08. He received a distinguished research award in 2007 (UW–Madison), and two excellence in teaching awards (in 2005 at UW–Madison, and in 1998 at UC–Irvine). Alex's research focuses on motivation and leadership, which has been published in premier psychology and management journals such as *Psychological Bulletin, Journal of Applied Psychology, Academy of Management Journal*, and *Personnel Psychology*. Alex serves on the Editorial Boards of *Journal of Applied Psychology* (contributing editor), *Organizational Behavior and Human Decision Processes, Organizational Dynamics*, and *South African Journal of Human Resource Management*, and is a member of the Advisory Council of the *Harvard Business Review*. Alex is one of the most cited management scholars of his career age. He received both his MA and PhD degrees from the University of Nebraska at Lincoln in Organizational Behavior.

Anja Tuschke is Professor of Strategic Management at the Munich School of Management at Ludwig-Maximilians-University in Munich, Germany. Prior to joining the Munich

School of Management in 2007, she was Professor of Organizational Behavior and Director at the Institute of Organization and Human Resource Management at the University of Bern in Switzerland. The research interests of Professor Tuschke revolve around the link between strategic management, corporate governance, and performance. She is particularly interested in how social networks, top management characteristics, and governance mechanisms affect strategic choice and performance. Her work has been published in top management journals such as *Academy of Management Journal* and *Strategic Management Journal*. Professor Tuschke serves on the editorial boards of *Strategic Management Journal* and *Business and Research*.

Andrew Ward is the James T. Kane Associate Professor of Management and Associate Dean at the College of Business and Economics at Lehigh University. He was formerly on the faculty at the University of Georgia's Terry College of Business and Emory University's Goizueta Business School. He received his PhD from The Wharton School of the University of Pennsylvania. Ward conducts research on reputations, networks, CEO successions, CEO compensation, the roles and concerns of the chief executive officer, CEO/board relations, leadership, and corporate governance. His work has been published in numerous journals including *Administrative Science Quarterly*, *Organization Science*, and *Strategic Organization*, and he currently serves on the editorial review board of *Strategic Management Journal*. Ward is also the author of two books, *Firing Back* (Harvard Business School Press, 2007) and *The Leadership Lifecycle* (Palgrave Macmillan, 2003).

Margarethe F. Wiersema holds the Dean's Professorship in Strategic Management at the Paul Merage School of Business, University of California, Irvine. She has an MBA and PhD from the Ross School of Business at the University of Michigan. Professor Wiersema is internationally recognized as one of the leading experts on corporate strategy and CEO succession and replacement. The recipient of numerous awards for excellence in research and teaching, Professor Wiersema was awarded the 2006 Distinguished PhD Alumni Award from the Ross School of Business at the University of Michigan. She has published her research in the *Harvard Business Review*, *Strategic Management Journal*, the *Academy of Management Journal*, and *Administrative Science Quarterly*. Her research is widely acknowledged by over 1500 citations and she has been quoted by the *New York Times*, *The Financial Times*, *The Economist*, *Fortune*, *Business Week*, and the *Washington Post*. Professor Wiersema is an elected member of the board of directors of the Strategic Management Society and serves as Associate Editor of the *Strategic Management Journal*, the premier journal in the strategy field and serves on the editorial boards of the *Academy of Management Review*, *Organization Science*, and the *California Management Review*.

Yan (Anthea) Zhang holds the Jones School Distinguished Associate Professor of Management at the Jesse H. Jones Graduate School of Business at Rice University. Her research areas include CEO succession, corporate governance, high-technology entrepreneurship in China, and foreign direct investment in/from emerging markets. Her work has been published in *Academy of Management Journal*, *Strategic Management Journal*, *Journal of International Business Studies*, and *Journal of Management*. Her research has been widely cited by prominent business media outlets including *The Economist, USA Today, Business Week, New York Times*, and *Financial Times*. She serves on the editorial review board of *Academy of Management Journal* and *Strategic Management Journal*, and is a consulting editor of *Management and Organization Review*. She is the representative-at-large of the Corporate Strategy and Corporate Governance Interest Group of Strategic Management Society and the representative-at-large of the Americas of the International Association of Chinese Management Research.

Zhen Zhang is an Assistant Professor of Management in the W.P. Carey School of Business at Arizona State University. He earned his PhD in Human Resources and Industrial Relations at the University of Minnesota. His research focuses on leadership process and development, the biological basis of organizational behavior, the inter-part between organizational behavior and entrepreneurship, and research methods. His work has appeared or is forthcoming in several journals including *Journal of Applied Psychology, Personnel Psychology, Organizational Behavior and Human Decision Processes*, the *Leadership Quarterly, Journal of Business Venturing, Psychological Methods*, and *Organizational Research Methods*.

Introduction
Mason A. Carpenter

It is nearly impossible to open an edition of the *Economist*, *Wall Street Journal*, *Financial Times*, *Business Week*, *Fast Company*, or other business press outlet without seeing mention of the exploits, excesses, strengths, or failings of a Chief Executive Officer (CEO), her or his management team, or board of directors. Similarly, almost every issue of our top academic journals like *Administrative Science Quarterly*, *Academy of Management Journal*, *Academy of Management Review*, and *Strategic Management Journal* has an article or more about top management teams (TMTs) and the upper echelons – TMT and upper echelons are the collective terms for research concerning executives, TMTs, and their boards of directors. Whether due to actual causal or reciprocal relationships between executives and organizational outcomes, or simply our romance with leadership, most people perceive there to be a real relationship between leaders and features of their organizations, including firm performance.

While decades ago there was disagreement as to whether top managers mattered or not, there is ample cumulative evidence today from management (Carpenter et al., 2004), psychology (Peterson et al., 2003), and financial economics (Bertrand and Schoar, 2003), that executive effects on organizational outcomes are both statistically and practically significant. As a result, the emphasis of TMT research has shifted from questions about *if managers matter*, to questions about *under what conditions they matter*. Importantly, some of the new research exploring the upper echelons highlights when, where, and how senior executives contribute to innovation, accounting and stock market performance, and firm survival; at the same time there is ample research showing how TMTs seek to game the system through impression management or unethical or illegal business practices. Therefore, it is fairly safe to say that not all TMT research is laudatory, and that we are in fact learning a great deal about the good, bad, and ugly of upper echelons' effects.

MOTIVATION FOR THE *HANDBOOK*

The primary motivation for the *Handbook* is to articulate and stake out new research directions about the upper echelon – executives, TMTs, and their boards. The guiding premise of this area of research is that organizations are a reflection of their executives, TMTs, and boards of directors (though see Mooney and Amason in Chapter 2 for a different spin on this), which collectively comprises their strategic leadership. Credit for this premise is often given to Hambrick and Mason's (1984) seminal theory paper on the upper echelons perspective. When I and colleagues reviewed the upper echelons literature for the *Journal of Management* in 2004, Hambrick and Mason (1984) had racked up well over 500 ISI citations (Carpenter et al., 2004); my cite count for Hambrick and Mason (1984) as of the date I'm writing this introductory chapter (mid-2010, just six years later) is an astonishing 1057 in ISI, and a Google Scholar citation count of over

2500! Thus, interest in the upper echelons shows no signs of slowing down. Indeed, our review and others have chronicled and documented the dramatic growth of research in and around the spirit of the upper echelons perspective (see, for instance, additional comprehensive reviews in Finkelstein and Hambrick, 1996, and Finkelstein et al., 2009).

As Finkelstein et al. (2009) note inside the front book-jacket cover of their indispensible and authoritative tome on strategic leadership:

> in order to understand why organizations do the things they do, or perform the way they do, we need to deeply comprehend the people at the top – their experiences, abilities, values, social connections, aspirations, and other human features. The actions – or inactions – of a relatively small number of key people at the apex of an organization can dramatically affect organizational outcomes.

It is in the spirit of elaborating on that description that the chapters of the *Handbook* have been written and compiled.

Beyond this topical description of what the *Handbook* covers, it is important to also note that a secondary motivation for this collection is to let the *Handbook* authors aggressively lay out new research avenues related to executives, top management teams, and boards of directors. It is true that most published empirical and theoretical articles sound out new research directions, or at least they should. This is also the objective of recent review pieces like Carpenter et al. (2004) and Finkelstein et al. (2009). In the case of the *Handbook*, however, I gave authors greater license and the "stretch goal" to talk about the research implications of their chapter for future work in pretty expansive terms – implications for their own work and, perhaps most importantly, the innovative and game-changing work of others. As a result, I hope you will agree that the *Handbook*'s authors have identified and staked out some really important and novel new ground.

ORGANIZATION OF THE *HANDBOOK*

Given the researchers' common interest in top executives, the 15 chapters in the *Handbook* are all somewhat interrelated, though at the same time there are clusters of the chapters that are organized into five respective parts: (I) Definitions of top management teams, (II) Personalities and profiles of top executives, (III), TMT experience and strategy, (IV) How executive actions affect strategy, rivalry, and entrepreneurship, and (V) The context surrounding changes in the executive suite (see Table 0.1). I review each of the parts and chapters briefly below.

Top Management Teams Defined

The *Handbook* opens with three chapters on top management team definition. Two of the papers are conceptual (Jones and Cannella; Beckman and Burton), and the third is empirical (Mooney and Amason). Chapter 1 (Jones and Cannella) builds on the seminal work of Thompson (1967), wherein he established that top managers are responsible for setting the strategic direction of the firm. As such, Jones and Cannella argue that the TMT is the most appropriate level of analysis to use when studying firm outcomes. Their work expands the upper echelons discussion by dissecting the TMT; specifically, they

Table 0.1   *A summary of the parts of the book and authors by part*

Definitions of Top Management Teams	Personalities and Profiles of Top Executives	TMT Experiance and Strategy	How Executive Actions Affect Strategy, Rivalry, and Entrepreneurship	The Context Surrounding Changes in the Executive Suite
Jones & Cannella Mooney & Amason Beckman & Burton	Sangster Stajkovic, Carpenter, & Graffin Peterson & Zhang Clark & Maggitti	Miner, Gong, Baker, & O'Toole Sanders & Tuschke	Martin Hughes-Morgan, Ferrier, & Labianca Simsek, Heavey, Prabhakar, & Huvaj	Ward, Amason, Lee, & Graffin Zhang Beck & Wiersema

distinguish the role of the CEO from other non-CEO TMT members. At the same time, they develop a clearer sense of which executives participate in strategic decision making. Their goal, based on the contention that more accurately identifying the executives who are included in the TMT will strengthen the explanatory power of the upper echelons perspective, is to develop theory to improve the ability to predict executive involvement in strategic decision making based on the decision context.

Chapter 2 (Mooney and Amason) also draws on Thompson (1967) to revisit the definition of the TMT. They note that Thompson introduced the notion that an inner circle of top management team members exists, and that the CEO relies heavily on this small group when making strategic decisions. Although much research has been done examining top management teams, Mooney and Amason are among the first to give explicit research attention to executive inner circles. In their chapter, the authors argue and find empirical evidence that some but not all TMT members are involved in strategic decision making. These results support the idea that an inner circle indeed exists. Mooney and Amason also explore how the CEO selects the inner circle and present competing theoretical arguments of similarity/attraction and information processing. Moreover, their data suggests that CEOs have a tendency to select inner circle members that share similar characteristics and experiences as the CEO. Importantly, they conclude that their evidence suggests that, rather than the organization being a reflection of its TMT (Hambrick and Mason, 1984), the organization may more appropriately be a reflection of an inner circle of the TMT, who in turn reflect the CEO.

Chapter 3 (Beckman and Burton) takes a different tack by exploring the temporal determinants of TMT composition. The authors note that TMTs continuously morph as the definition of top management roles evolve and as individual executives come and go, yet these structural and temporal dynamics have received limited direct attention from scholars who study top management team demography. This is surprising given that many of the oft-studied demographic characteristics of teams – age, tenure, experience – change over time. In their chapter, Beckman and Burton illustrate how attention to organizational structure and a broader understanding of time and change open new research avenues. They demonstrate how individual mobility and top management team role definitions are subject to temporal and historical forces that influence our ability to make inferences and accumulate knowledge across research studies. Beyond conceptual arguments they illustrate their points using functional and tenure heterogeneity as two examples. Beckman and Burton conclude their chapter with an agenda for longitudinal top management team research that distinguishes roles from individual incumbents and incorporates an understanding of time and change.

Executive Personalities and Profiles

Those who study top management teams using demographic characteristics and other executive data available through archival sources are familiar with the oft-mentioned caveat that future research should go inside the black box. A number of my own published studies, for instance, state something like this:

> As a result, by following the norms of upper echelons research we have "black-boxed" important underlying processes and causal mechanisms and ignored other characteristics that may have been pertinent to our arguments. Research is still needed to further illuminate the nature of the relationships between TMT characteristics and the actual cognitions and behaviors of upper echelon executives. (Carpenter and Fredrickson, 2001, p. 543)

This caveat is an essential limitation and commonplace feature of the TMT research landscape.

However, the chapters in this part need no such caveat in their discussion sections. In fact, the novelty common to all four chapters is that they provide valuable exemplars of empirical work that does go into the hard-to-access black box of executive teams to help us better understand executive personalities, profiles, and their consequences. Two of the chapters (4 and 5) look at the psychological profiles of individual executives, while two of the chapters consider TMT profiles (6 and 7).

In Chapter 4, for instance, Sangster studies the personality profiles of US top executives (the head of a business and that person's direct reports). He finds important personality differences across businesses, and between these top executives and the US population as a whole. Top executives materially differ from the average citizen on four out of the five dimensions of personality (openness, conscientiousness, extraversion, agreeableness, and neuroticism – the Big Five Factor Model). Moreover, for at least one dimension of personality, top management is more homogeneous than the citizenry, as a whole. Though four out of five dimensions of personality differentiate top executives from the US norm, the fifth dimension differentiates top management teams from each other. Sangster concludes by noting that his study's findings imply the need to understand one's competitors not only in terms of their technology and physical capital, but also in terms of their human and psychological capital.

Stajkovic, Carpenter, and Graffin (Chapter 5) develop a theoretical framework that links charismatic leadership to the extensiveness of an executive's social networks, and then predicts that such network extensiveness can subsequently be related to an individual's motivation to set challenging personal career goals. This chapter complements Sangster's in the sense that they link psychological and social capital (i.e., managers' social networks) both theoretically and empirically. To assess the generalizability and boundary conditions of their theory, they test it in two samples of senior managers: one from the United States (an individualistic culture) and the second from China (a collectivistic culture). In the first part of the study, Stajkovic and colleagues find that charismatic leadership is positively related to social network extensiveness and that culture moderates this relationship. In the second part, they find that social network extensiveness is positively related to the setting of challenging career goals. This latter finding held up in both the individualistic and the collectivistic cultures. The authors note that TMT research either ignores managerial social networks or assumes they are the primary explanatory mechanism, and conclude by calling for research that looks at the possible causal and reciprocal relationships between executive personality and social network extensiveness and structure.

The research in Chapter 6 shifts attention from individual executives to the level of the TMT. Peterson and Zhang draw on a sample of 67 TMTs to examine the associations between TMT members' collective psychological characteristics and business unit performance. More specifically, the authors tested whether TMT members' collective core self-evaluations (comprised of self-esteem, generalized self-efficacy, locus of control, and emotional stability) and psychological capital (comprised of hope, optimism, task-specific self-efficacy, and resilience) predicted business unit performance. Their results revealed that TMT collective psychological capital was positively associated with business unit performance but TMT collective core self-evaluation was not. In addition, transformational leadership of the TMT leaders moderated the relationship between TMT collective psychological capital and unit performance. When levels of transformational leadership were high, the relationship between collective TMT psychological capital and unit performance was stronger than when levels of transformational leadership were low. Peterson and Zhang conclude their chapter by discussing the theoretical and practical implications of these results, highlighting the importance of studying TMT-level psychological characteristics.

Chapter 7 (Clark and Maggitti) emphasizes the fact that TMTs are charged with making critical strategic decisions. Often these decisions carry long-lasting implications for the health of the firm and they are made under time pressure and in conditions of novelty and ambiguity. TMT researchers continue to make strides to overcome the unique methodological challenges they face. In their chapter, Clark and Maggitti discuss some of these challenges and issues involved in overcoming them. To illustrate, the authors present a dual-method study of TMT confidence and strategic decision-making outcomes. Using data collected from an intensive field study of TMTs, they employ a positivist theory-testing approach to establish the importance of top management team potency (confidence) followed by an inductive outlier analysis in the discussion part that was used to develop propositions concerning functional vs. dysfunctional potency. Clark and Maggitti conclude the chapter with a proposed research agenda for further articulating the role of TMT confidence. They also discuss the need for continued improvement in TMT research methodology.

TMT Experience and Strategy

The two *Handbook* chapters in this part, one based on a novel field study setting and the other drawing on career histories of Chinese corporate elites, address questions related to the sources of executive experience. One of the most-cited papers in the area of executive effects is Hambrick and Mason's (1984) upper echelons perspective. They theorized that prior experience of TMT members affects organizational strategies because it shapes their fields of vision, selective perceptions, and interpretation of environmental and organizational stimuli. The two chapters in this part both contribute to Hambrick and Mason's seminal perspective on the role and effects of experience in predicting executive choices and behaviors.

For instance, the authors of Chapter 8 (Miner, Gong, Baker, and O'Toole), open their chapter with the observation that important research has, consistent with the upper echelons perspective (Hambrick and Mason, 1984), theorized that prior TMT experiences affect organization strategies through the development of executive perceptions and cognitive filters of environmental and organizational stimuli. Based on inductive field research on founding TMTs, the authors advance an additional causal pathway by which TMT prior experience shapes later firm actions and outcomes: the impact of exposure to pre-existing organizational routines. Miner and colleagues first present an inductive study of founding top management teams, which suggests that they import and re-deploy organizational routines based on their experience in prior firms and with advisor networks. Specifically, the teams they study (1) automatically import routines from their prior experience, (2) selectively import routines, (3) re-deploy prior routines for new purpose, (4) recombine routines from diverse prior organizations, and (5) recombine routines from informal advisory networks. The authors go on to generalize to argue that TMT experience in ongoing organizations will also affect organizational strategy through routine-based processes, and that this offers an important but relatively unexplored causal path in the TMT literature. Their chapter illustrates how the routines approach would provide an alternative account for some important prior TMT research results, and they then offer six testable propositions grounded in their framework. The authors show how testing these propositions will help explore the relative and joint impact of cognitive or routine-based processes, and the impact of different routine-based processes on key outcomes such as speed of change. Consistent with the spirit of the *Handbook*, the authors note that their paper is exploratory, and invite others to probe whether and how the additional causal pathway has useful theoretical or managerial implications.

The authors of Chapter 9 similarly break new ground by helping us to better understand how career histories build up accumulated experiences to affect executive choice. Specifically, Sanders and Tuschke use detailed career histories of members of the Chinese corporate elite to study how formative experiences affect the propensity of Chinese firms to adopt western-styled corporate governance reform. They identify forms of western experiences and government positions and work experiences as formative in affecting the values and mindsets of the corporate elite and their propensity to adopt corporate governance changes (e.g., adding independent directors to the board). In doing so, they first account for the possible path dependency of these formative experiences as well as the mutual selection process that may match firms with top leaders with certain backgrounds. Consistent with their expectations, Sanders and Tuschke find that greater levels of government experiences within the corporate elite is positively associated with firms following the directive of the central government to add more independent directors to their boards. However, contrary to their expectations, they found that greater levels of western experience were negatively associated with such changes. Sanders and Tuschke's work, resonating with some of the observations made by Beckman and Burton, suggests that a viable and intriguing avenue for future research is to turn attention to the developmental pathways that senior managers follow.

Consequences of Executive Action

Whereas the prior part of the *Handbook* considered sources of executive experience, this part looks at how such experience might affect different organizational outcomes. Chapter 10 (Martin) helps us understand how executive leadership groups provide firms with a form of dynamic managerial capability, Chapter 11 (Hughes-Morgan, Ferrier, and Labianca) shows how TMT characteristics and competitive behaviors jointly affect firm performance, and Chapter 12 (Simsek, Heavey, Prabhakar, and Huvaj) consider how strategic leadership might play out in an emerging context they describe as strategic entrepreneurship.

Martin's chapter (Chapter 10) is developed from a broader research program of organization and strategy in highly dynamic markets. He draws on recent empirical studies of cross-business collaboration and dynamic managerial capabilities, along with novel incentive and demographic data, to develop a practice theory of executive leadership groups. In addition, a practice theory lens is used to add greater understanding to the emerging conceptualization of dynamic managerial capabilities. Specifically, Martin's chapter describes how the system of organizational relationships within executive leadership groups creates affordances and constraints in the resource actions they sense, formulate, and ultimately take. Overall, his chapter considers inertia and adaptability to be two sides of the same coin, rather than distinct attributes of particular structures, processes, or individual agency in executive leadership groups.

In Chapter 11, Hughes-Morgan, Ferrier, and Labianca integrate core ideas from upper echelons research with competitive dynamics. Their chapter summarizes their study of how a firm's stock market performance is jointly influenced by its top-level human capital and the pattern of competitive behavior the firm carries out against rivals. More specifically, they drew a sample of Fortune 500 firms that carried out nearly 2000 competitive actions over a seven-year time period and tested the interaction between a composite measure of TMT heterogeneity and three characteristics of the firm's competitive strategy – strategic complexity, strategic volume, and strategic heterogeneity – on monthly stock returns and firm-specific unsystematic risk. Owing to the firm's higher stock returns and lower levels of stock risk, their findings provide strong evidence that investors value the "fit" between TMT experiential and cognitive breadth and how the firm maneuvers in the marketplace. Thus, their chapter suggests that the complex, dynamic relationships among managerial capabilities, competitive strategy, and stock-market-based performance cannot be disentangled from one another.

In the third chapter of this part of the book (Chapter 12), Simsek and colleagues introduce and develop the notion of strategic entrepreneurship (SE), defined as entrepreneurial action with a strategic perspective. They argue that SE has emerged as an exciting construct for strategic management and entrepreneurship researchers. Although strategic leaders (SL) including CEOs, TMTs, and boards of directors play a pivotal role in SE behaviors and outcomes, there has to date been no systematic thematization of the

SL–SE nexus in terms of central constructs, research evidence, and an overall conceptual framework. Toward that end, the authors first adopt a typological perspective of SE, articulating and juxtaposing its advantage-seeking and opportunity-seeking dimensions to yield four archetypal forms – refinement, replication, rejuvenation, and revolution. Using these four forms, they then undertake a comprehensive review of previous studies dealing with the nexus of SL–SE, over a 30-year period (1978–2008), spanning 12 management journals. Synthesizing their typology and review, Simsek and colleagues develop a conceptual framework and trace the implications of this framework for future research directions.

The Context Surrounding Executive Succession

The final part of the *Handbook* brings us full circle in the study of executives, TMTs, and boards to consider executive succession. For instance, in Chapter 13, Ward, Amason, Lee, and Graffin argue that organizations hire chief executives, in part, to assume the symbolic responsibility for organizational performance. Essentially, in the view they espouse, new CEOs agree either to perform up to expectations or to become scapegoats should performance fall short. This implicit agreement works like an insurance policy, whereby the CEO provides the board protection against adverse selection and the board provides the CEO premium payments commensurate with the risk underwritten. Thus, the compensation paid to a new CEO should relate directly to the performance expectations for which the chief executive is assuming responsibility. Ward and colleagues test this proposition by looking at the compensation of new CEOs in the Fortune 500 from 1995 to 2002, and new head football coaches in NCAA Division I schools from 1998 to 2004.

An essential part of the chapter by Ward and colleagues is the introduction of the Expectations Index (EI) construct. Investment opportunity set is a term used to describe the present value of a firm's future investment options. That present value reflects the return potential of the investments, as well as the likelihood of realizing those returns successfully. In other words, the investment opportunity set should reflect the performance expectations of key stakeholders, such as the board who are aware of the investments being made by the firm to develop and capitalize upon future options. As such, the authors term this construct the EI. Over time, EI is the present value of the future returns, if the firm makes the right decisions and executes as necessary to realize the potential of those opportunities. Their results support their hypotheses that an organization's EI predicts CEOs' fixed compensation, the gap between CEO pay and that of other top managers, and the proportion of total compensation that is guaranteed.

In Chapter 14, Zhang helps us better understand the domain of research evaluating the entire spectrum of a CEO's tenure, including before he or she joins the firm and after she or he has departed it. She opens the chapter by reiterating how the question of "how do CEOs matter?" has attracted significant scholarly attention in the past decades. In her view, most studies on this topic have focused on what happens when CEO leadership changes: either when a CEO is newly appointed or when a CEO leaves office. Recent studies have also examined how the length of CEO tenure in office can affect organizational outcomes such as strategy and performance. In her chapter, Zhang goes on to review recent developments in this literature and develops an agenda for CEO leadership research. Specifically, she divides a CEO's career into five major stages and identifies key issues at each of the stages: (1) appointing a new CEO, (2) taking charge, (3) tenure as CEO, (4) departure, and (5) post-departure. More importantly, she discusses the connections between these stages; that is, what happens in an earlier stage can affect what happens in a later stage. With this evolutionary and holistic perspective, her chapter can help us better understand the impact of a CEO on the firm that he or she leads and the impact of the firm on the CEO.

In our closing chapter of this part and the *Handbook*, Beck and Wiersema (Chapter 15) note the significant increase in the frequency of CEO dismissal (involuntary turnover), not just in the US, but in Germany, France, and Japan as well. Previous theoretical models of CEO dismissal have focused on board expectations, perceptions, and attributes, while empirical investigations have largely focused on the role of poor firm performance. However, in order to better understand CEO dismissal, the authors argue that it is necessary to broaden the conceptualization of the firm's governance context in our model of CEO dismissal, specifically taking into account the role of both internal and external monitors of the firm. In this chapter, Beck and Wiersema propose an integrated model of CEO dismissal that acknowledges the role of the firm's broader governance context, thus arriving at a better understanding of the conditions that lead to CEO dismissal. In particular they examine investment analysts and institutional investors: important external constituents who, in their respective roles as information intermediaries and informed investors with sizeable holdings, have a powerful influence on how the board evaluates the CEO. In the case of institutional investors, these external constituents have become directly involved in the monitoring role of the board itself. In developing their framework, Beck and Wiersema incorporate prior empirical work in both the finance and management literatures on the contextual conditions surrounding CEO dismissal. Their revised model of CEO dismissal demonstrates that the financial community, as represented by investment analysts and institutional investors, has multiple paths of influence connecting it to the board, and thus to the CEO dismissal decision.

THEMES IN RESEARCH ON EXECUTIVES, TOP MANAGEMENT TEAMS, AND BOARDS

Even if you are new to the study of TMTs, I hope that it is apparent to you that the chapters of the *Handbook* fit readily into the larger set of research themes you would expect to see on executives, top management teams, and boards of directors. The broader upper echelons research themes are summarized in Table 0.2, and the interparts of the respective chapters with these themes are summarized in Table 0.3. Each of the papers is identified with a primary research theme, and one or more secondary themes. For instance, Jones and Cannella are primarily concerned with *who* to include in theoretical and empirical conceptualizations of the TMT, though their chapter also has important implications for research on TMTs, changes in TMT composition, and executive compensation.

While the *Handbook*'s chapters collectively mirror the full spectrum of TMT research, our treatment is in no way exhaustive. However, the chapters do touch on those themes and topics that are state of the art; areas where we both know the most, but also about which we need to know much more. At the same time, future TMT research is likely to

Table 0.2 *A list of TMT research themes*

Top Executives	Individual Differences	Team and Team Member Differences	Changes in Team Composition	Boards of Directors	Executive Compensation
Examples:	Examples:	Examples:	Examples:	Examples:	Examples:
Definitions	How do they	Teams versus groups	Determinants	Roles of boards	Determinants
Who are they?	affect	Who comprises the	Consequences	Structure	Consequences
What do they do?	executive	top team?	Succession	Composition	Structure
Do they matter?	action?	Differences in power	processes	Consequences of	Economic,
Under what	Psychological	Team member and	CEO change	board structure	political,
conditions do	differences	CEO interaction	Executive change	and composition	and social
they matter?	Demographic	Determinants of team	Board of director		explanations
Romance of	differences	characteristics	change		Distribution
leadership	Consequences	Team processes			
	of individual	Consequences of			
	executive	team composition			
	characteristics				

Table 0.3 Treatment of the TMT research themes by our authors

Section/Chapter	Top Executives	Individual Differences	Team and Team Member Differences	Changes in Team Composition	Boards of Directors	Executive Compensation
I. DEFINITIONS OF TOP MANAGEMENT TEAMS						
1. Jones & Cannella	Primary	Primary	Secondary	Secondary		Secondary
2. Mooney & Amason	Primary	Primary	Secondary	Secondary		
3. Beckman & Burton	Primary	Secondary		Secondary		
II. PERSONALITIES AND PROFILES OF TOP EXECUTIVES						
4. Sangster		Primary	Primary			
5. Stajkovic, Carpenter, & Graffin		Primary	Primary			
6. Peterson & Zhang		Secondary	Primary			
7. Clark & Maggitti		Secondary	Primary			
III. TMT EXPERIENCE AND STRATEGY						
8. Miner, Gong, Baker, & O'Toole			Primary	Secondary		
9. Sanders & Tuschke			Primary	Secondary	Secondary	Secondary
IV. HOW EXECUTIVE ACTIONS AFFECT STRATEGY, RIVALRY, AND ENTREPRENEURSHIP						
10. Martin		Secondary	Primary	Secondary		Secondary
11. Hughes-Morgan, Ferrier, & Labianca			Primary	Secondary		
12. Simsek, Heavey, Prabhakar, & Huvaj			Primary			Secondary
V. THE CONTEXT SURROUNDING CHANGES IN THE EXECUTIVE SUITE						
13. Ward, Amason, Lee, & Graffin				Secondary	Secondary	Primary
14. Zhang				Primary	Secondary	
15. Beck & Wiersema				Primary	Secondary	Secondary

ferret out blind spots in our current map of research themes. It is unlikely though that future research will lead us to discard the entire set of themes we have covered in the *Handbook*, and in my humble view no TMT researcher should embark on work in our area without first consulting it.

ACKNOWLEDGMENTS

Michele Yoder provided invaluable assistance in helping me review and organize the chapters in the *Handbook*. I am indebted to the *Handbook*'s authors for delivering their work as promised in terms of quality. I also want to acknowledge the intellectual motivation and inspiration for this *Handbook* provided by Bert Cannella, Syd Finkelstein, and Don Hambrick – I hope readers consider this *Handbook* to be the other bookend partnering Cannella et al. (2009). Finally, I want to thank Jim Fredrickson for getting me into this business, and my wife Lisa for providing early stage angel funding for a new career without compare.

REFERENCES

Bertrand, M. and Schoar, A. (2003). Managing with style: The effect of managers on firm policies. *Quarterly Journal of Economics*, **118**(4), 1169–208.
Carpenter, M.A. and Fredrickson, J.W. (2001). Top management teams, global strategic posture, and the moderating role of uncertainty. *Academy of Management Journal*, **44**(3), 533–45.
Carpenter, M.A., Geletkanycz, M.A., and Sanders, W.G. (2004). The upper echelons research revisited: Antecedents, elements, and consequences of top management team composition. *Journal of Management*, **30**(6), 749–78.
Finkelstein, S. and Hambrick, D.C. (1996). *Strategic leadership: Top executives and their effects on organizations.* St Paul, MN: West Publishing.
Finkelstein, S., Hambrick, D.C., and Cannella, A.A. (2009). *Strategic leadership: Theory and research on executives, top management teams, and boards.* New York, NY: Oxford University Press.
Hambrick, D.C. and Mason, P.A. (1984). Upper echelons: The organization as a reflection of its top managers. *Academy of Management Review*, **9**(2), 193–206.
Peterson, R.S., Smith, D.B., Martorana, P.V., and Owens, P.D. (2003). The impact of chief executive officer personality on top management team dynamics: One mechanism by which leadership affects organizational performance. *Journal of Applied Psychology*, **88**(5), 795–808.
Thompson, J.D. (1967). *Organizations in action.* New York, NY: McGraw-Hill.

PART I

DEFINITIONS OF TOP MANAGEMENT TEAMS

1 Alternate configurations in strategic decision making

Carla D. Jones and Albert A. Cannella Jr.

Since Thompson first established the idea in 1967, it seems widely accepted among organizational researchers that top management teams (TMTs) are charged with setting the strategic direction of their organizations (Thompson, 1967). This assumption seems to especially characterize scholars in the upper echelons tradition (i.e., Hambrick and Mason, 1984; Carpenter et al., 2004; Finkelstein et al., 2009). However, a careful review of the upper echelons literature highlights three issues that we take up in this chapter. First, while the general notion of what a TMT is and what its responsibilities are seems widely accepted, persistent questions remain regarding the concept of a unitary TMT. Rather, there seems to be a growing belief in the notion of a variety of executive teams emerging around specific strategic issues (Roberto, 2003). Put differently, subsets of executives coalesce around strategic issues that need resolution, raising questions about the existence of a unitary TMT. This complicates the study of TMTs, as we lack a clear sense of which executives comprise the TMT and the extent to which the TMT's composition depends on the strategic decision under consideration. Second, since Hambrick and Mason argued strongly that the TMT is the appropriate level of analysis for studying strategic decisions (in an article published in 1984), most empirical researchers have actually emphasized the Chief Executive Officer (CEO) alone when studying strategic decisions. While there are good empirical reasons for doing this, it does undercut the widely held assumption that the TMT is the appropriate level of analysis for studies of organizational decision making. Finally, despite calls for considering the role of individual executive power when modeling strategic decisions at the TMT level, most TMT studies still fall short of fully specifying the CEO's role with respect to the TMT (see, for example, Carpenter et al., 2004; Finkelstein et al., 2009). Put differently, most TMT research empirically treats the CEO as another regular team member, when theory suggests that the reality is substantially different.

It is important to begin with some definitions of terms. In the upper echelons literature, the term "TMT" traditionally refers to the CEO and some set of other top executives (i.e., vice-presidents and above) who report directly to the CEO. Our use of the term TMT will conform to this tradition. For our study, a TMT refers to a CEO and other executives who together comprise the "dominant coalition" (Thompson, 1967) and are charged with strategic decision making for the organization. Because we do not view the CEO as just another TMT member, we will use the term executive management team (EMT) to refer to non-CEO executives (of any rank) who are part of the TMT. There are instances when members of the board are included in strategic decision making. Our theory development will incorporate the use of directors in strategic decision making, depending on CEO characteristics and the decision context. Members of the board who participate in strategic decision making are counted as members of the EMT. Therefore, the TMT is comprised of the CEO and the EMT.

Upper echelons research assumes that the process of strategic decision making is critical to organizations, yet we know very little about the factors that determine which executives are included in strategic decision making and the dynamics that exist among those who comprise TMTs. Researchers typically assume that these executives work together in a team-like fashion to determine the strategic direction of the firm. Most widely held views of "teams" (the broader concept) include the notion that teams consist of two or more persons who interact with one another in such a way that each person influences and is influenced by each other person (Shaw, 1981). A few additional characteristics extend the team definition: two or more persons who come into contact for a purpose (Mills, 1976); the presence of interdependence among team members (Lewin, 1951); and a set of individuals who share a common fate (Fiedler, 1967). Teams of different structures vary along these dimensions in ways that can sharply affect team functioning. For instance, executives may hold diverse perspectives – a fact that presents both benefits (i.e., more complete understandings and creativity) and challenges (i.e., problems of communication, cohesion, and speed of decision making) in reaching consensus (Cannella et al., 2008). The topic of team dynamics and team interactions are complex subjects often approached with primary data (i.e., Gully et al., 2002). However, much of the research on TMTs is accomplished using archival data. Thus, researchers often have little ability to assess the extent to which individual members contribute to the group (i.e., who is on the TMT and the various roles served by team members) and the extent to which the group, once identified, exhibits team-like behavior. Our chapter represents an attempt to push the debate forward regarding TMT emergence and decision making to better understand who is involved in decision making and whether the decision makers comprising the team are static or change across decision contexts (see, for example, Roberto, 2003). Our research challenges some common underlying assumptions, hopefully leading to a better understanding of the contributors to the decision process and their unique roles.

Our approach attempts to build upon the special and unique role of the CEO as the most powerful individual in an organization (Rajagopalan, 1996; Rajagopalan and Datta, 1996). As the head of the organization, the CEO has the ability to both directly and indirectly influence the strategic decision-making process. CEOs' direct influence on the decision process is manifest through the determination of which issues rise to the level of TMT consideration, the framing of the decision situation, including the presumed effects the decision may have on the organization, and CEOs' preferences regarding the alternatives developed and selected. The CEO's indirect influence is multi-faceted. The CEO is instrumental in determining which executives serve on the team and the power that the team can exercise. Mooney and Amason discuss this in greater detail in their chapter on the inner circle (Chapter 2). Further, the CEO at least potentially determines how the decision process will unfold – how the issue will be discussed, in how much detail, and weighted by what factors. One reason for the dominance of strategic decision-making studies that rely on CEO data alone is that it is easier to gather data on a single very high-level individual than on the multiple executives that might make up a TMT. However, as the discussion above indicates, the CEO also likely has a very disproportionate impact on strategic decision making relative to other executives.

Our chapter is outlined as follows: we inspect TMT strategic decision making by examining the contributors to the process. We start by separating the CEO from other executives in order to assess the direct impact of the power and influence associated with the office. We then consider particular members of the EMT to develop a better understanding of the unique contributions from various executives and directors who are affiliated with an organization. We consider the contributions of the EMT, members of the executive team, and finally, the board of directors. In each section, we develop propositions to identify the contributors and capture the dynamics of each combination's influence on decision making.

THEORY DEVELOPMENT

We focus specifically on the context of strategic decision making, limiting our consideration to high-level decisions that normally fall within the scope of top management (Hambrick and Mason, 1984). Strategic decisions require the attention of the executives due to unique decision characteristics. These decisions involve non-routine situations that require adjustments to resource allocations to better meet the demands of the external environment. Strategic decisions are important due to the scope of their impact or the long-term implications that are associated with decision outcomes. Ultimately, the goal of strategic decision making is to align a firm's resources with environmental opportunities and constraints (Thompson, 1967). A fundamental assumption of the upper echelons literature is that strategic decisions set the course for the entire organization, so it seems important to understand which executives are involved in the decision-making process and what their roles are.

Theory about executive involvement in strategic decision making suggests that involvement depends on the magnitude of importance associated with the decision and the number of areas that the decision impacts (Vroom and Jago, 1988). The inclusion of multiple contributors to a decision process presents both potential costs and benefits to the firm. On one hand, the involvement of multiple contributors is linked to at least the potential for higher-quality decision making (Hollenbeck et al., 1995). Decisions that derive from the effective use of inputs from multiple sources follow from access to more information as well as unique insights (ibid.). It is easy to perceive the benefits of an inclusive approach in business organizations, as all parties who may be affected by the decisions can be party to the decision process. Of course, involvement from diverse group members also complicates group functioning, and may not lead to better ultimate decisions (Jackson, 1992; Cannella et al., 2008). Because different individuals and subunits can easily have conflicting interests with respect to any given decision, the resulting intransigence can lead to decision paralysis if the decision-making body is too inclusive.

Our lack of understanding regarding which executives contribute to strategic decision making further complicates our ability to determine where the boundaries of TMTs lie. In the section below, we develop theory to more clearly identify members of the TMT and how the influence of different members is exercised.

Executive Involvement in Strategic Decision Making

The upper echelons literature, which links executive characteristics to organizational outcomes, depends heavily on identifying the set of executives who influence organizational outcomes. Researchers using the upper echelons lens have used a variety of definitions to identify the TMT; however, there is no universally accepted approach for identifying TMT members.

Researchers have used a host of terms to refer to the executive members of an organization. Cyert and March (1963) coined the term "dominant coalition" to refer to the entire team of the firm's top decision makers. Other researchers have defined the top management team as "those individuals at the highest level of management – the chairman, vice chairmen, CEO, president, and chief financial and operating officers (CFO and COO) – as well as the next highest level as identified in the *Dun and Bradstreet Reference Book of Corporate Managements*" (Ferrier, 2001, p. 867). The empirical boundaries of the TMT, reflected in the empirical choices made by researchers, range from all inclusive – all officers (Wagner et al., 1984) to highly restricted – only inside directors (Finkelstein and Hambrick, 1990) – to more mid-range alternatives like all executives above the vice-president level (Chaganti and Sambharya, 1987; Murray, 1989; Michel and Hambrick, 1992; Hambrick et al., 1996). Another convenient way to identify TMTs is to use the five highest-paid executives, as identified in the company's annual proxy statements.

The variety and heterogeneity in empirical choices regarding the boundaries of the TMT raise important questions for furthering our understanding about strategic decision making. The TMT, as we have already explained, is widely considered to be (at least in theory) the most critical unit of analysis for studying strategic decision making. Most researchers agree that studying the entire team of contributing individuals will increase the ability to both understand and predict strategic decisions relative to focusing solely on the CEO (Hambrick and Mason, 1984). However, without clearly establishing the boundaries of the TMT, it is difficult to see how further progress can be made. A small group of researchers has been able to match executives with specific decisions. For example, in a rare study, Amason (1996) linked specific executives to specific organizational outcomes. Amason operationalized the top management team as *only* those executives who participated in the decision process. This study was accomplished using a small company, which provided much easier access to decision makers. For most strategy researchers, especially those using archival data, the inability to clearly define who participates in what decisions weakens the ability to directly link executive characteristics to organizational outcomes. As we will describe below, we adopt a flexible approach to identification of the TMT – one that permits membership to at least partially change with the decision setting. In this approach, each decision is considered by a "team" whose membership is flexibly determined by the decision to be made.

The difficulties of solidifying whose influences should be considered in decision making have led researchers to rely more heavily on the influence of the CEO. Empirically, it is easier to obtain data and test the influences of one individual rather than include a non-uniform set of executives. Additionally, there is a certain intrigue to the CEO position, thus encouraging emphasis on that position alone (e.g., Sanders, 2001; Crossland and Hambrick, 2007; Sanders and Hambrick, 2007). So, while most broader theories suggest that there is important benefit in considering all of the primary parties to a decision, the bulk of existing empirical work has focused on the CEO alone. Finally, as we will describe below, the CEO has a powerful impact on what decisions are considered, who serves, and how the decision is framed.

CEO Influence on Strategic Decision Making

The CEO is typically the most powerful individual in an organization (Rajagopalan, 1996; Rajagopalan and Datta, 1996). The CEO's unique position, power, and experience allow for both direct and indirect influence over strategic decision making. The direct influence is manifest in the CEO's individual preferences and inclinations about the decision itself – which decisions rise to a level of importance that leads them to be considered, the strategic priorities that set the context in which decisions are evaluated, and which alternatives are preferred or discounted ceteris paribus. The indirect influence is manifest in the selection of those who will be involved in decision making as well as in the structuring of their interactions, and the setting of parameters within which the decision is to be made (Cannella and Holcomb, 2005). In sum, the CEO's perception of the issue influences the decision process through his or her influence on choice of issues to be resolved, on framing the issues, on determining which executives will be involved in developing solutions, and how the decision processes will unfold (Pitcher and Smith, 2001).

There are likely two primary avenues that issues travel on as they reach the attention of the TMT. The first avenue involves the EMT. Here, non-CEO members of the TMT are exposed to numerous stimuli. These executives, limited by bounded rationality, are likely to notice certain stimuli and ignore others, and this process derives from their individual experience, values, and personalities (Dearborn and Simon, 1958; Hambrick and Mason, 1984; Walsh, 1988). Put differently, members of the EMT both notice stimuli and filter stimuli based on their dispositional make-up (Kahneman and Tversky, 1979). For example, EMT members (non-CEO members of the TMT) are more likely to notice stimuli that draw upon or impact their areas of expertise and/or specific areas of responsibility (Dearborn and Simon, 1958). Stimuli subsequently turn into issues of concern that are brought to the attention of the CEO and other senior executives in the firm. However, because the issue was first noticed by a specific member of the executive group, when it is presented to others (the CEO included) its positioning (or framing) is probably strongly influenced by the EMT member who brings it forward (Cannella and Holcomb, 2005). The notion that the EMT member who brings an issue forward will also likely champion a specific framing of it is implicit in upper echelons theory. Other members of the TMT and perhaps even the CEO may "accept" the framing of the individual who brought forth the issue. Here, the individual who brought the issue to the team's attention is implicitly considered to be an "expert" with increased standing regarding the resolution of the issue. On the other hand, if there are conflicts in framing the issue, it is likely to be the CEO who ultimately determines the overall framing, the level of importance, and the subsequent resources that will be extended to resolve the issue. These are extensions of the strategic agenda, which is clearly under the purview of the CEO.

The second avenue that issues can travel through in order to reach the attention of the TMT involves the CEO. We can assume the CEO is exposed to a different range of stimuli than other members of the TMT, due to his/her duties dealing with both internal and external constituents and stakeholders. The same processes of noticing and framing that we described for TMT members also apply directly to the CEO. However, the CEO holds significantly more power and influence than do members of the EMT. Thus, framing offered by the CEO may be such that other members of the TMT simply accept it without significant discussion. Further, not all issues that are raised by EMT members ultimately end up on the TMT agenda. Should the CEO believe that an issue deserves consideration, it is fair to say that it will be considered. The CEO also has the power to determine which executives are involved in analyzing the situation, deciding whether or not a response is appropriate, and if so, the process used to develop that response (Dutton and Jackson, 1987; Dutton and Ashford, 1993). As CEOs are made aware of issues that require organizational attention – either through their own noticing, or through the raising of the issues by other executives, their perceptions about the issue will shape how the decision making proceeds from there. That is, the CEO's perceptions of an issue will affect which other executives are involved in the decision process, how the issue is framed, and what resources are brought to bear. In our view, EMT involvement takes place at the CEO's discretion.[1] The CEO may involve others for a host of reasons, ranging from an attempt to broaden the perspectives considered, to securing specialized resources, to co-opting one or more powerful stakeholders.

The CEO's perception of the decision context influences who should be involved in the decision process (Hickson, 1989; Roberto, 2003). Strategic issues may require expertise or resources that extend beyond the arbitrary boundaries of TMTs as perceived by empirical researchers, even to extend beyond the organization's executives. In this event, the search for expertise may not be limited to in-house executives, but could potentially extend to members of the board (Pfeffer and Salancik, 1978; Finkelstein, 1997) when outside directors have insights or experiences that can supplement the resources of the TMT. In some instances, powerful suppliers or buyers might also be involved.

CEO perceptions and the capacity to determine which executives participate in strategic decision making position the CEO as the architect of the entire decision process. Whether the process involves many perspectives and extensive debate or whether decisions are based solely on the CEO's perspective depends mainly on the CEO and his or her preferences and inclinations. In a later section, we will consider how the CEO's personality affects his or her preferences and inclinations with respect to a TMT.

The Strategic Decision Process

Strategic decision making at the TMT level involves three broad factors that jointly influence the strategic decision process: (1) the perspective of the decision makers; (2) the organizational context; and (3) the environment (Schneider and De Meyer, 1991). Our knowledge regarding the strategic decision-making process and the elements that contribute to it are still in the early stages (Papadakis et al., 1998). Researchers have attempted to gain insights by studying the potential influences and antecedents of decision making (Pettigrew, 1992). Yet, questions remain about whether the managerial factors, the organizational context, or the environmental context have the greatest influence on decision making (ibid.). We do not discount the influence of the other elements of the process, but focus the bulk of our attention on the managerial factors.

The role of managerial choice influences many aspects of the strategic decision process. For example, the initial determination of whether an issue is viewed as an opportunity or a threat has traditionally been viewed as determined by the CEO, perhaps in conjunction with other executives. Further, the initial framing has an important impact on the entire decision process (Mintzberg et al., 1976; Billings et al., 1980; Fredrickson, 1985; Dutton and Ashford, 1993). The behavioral component of decision making is often perceived as driven by the CEO and reflective of his or her characteristics (Cyert and March, 1963; Child, 1972). Our earlier discussion of how issues are noticed and brought to the TMT's attention, however, weakens this notion. Extensions to the idea of executive or managerial choice and its impact on decision making have developed as bodies of literature focusing on upper echelons or the top management team (Hambrick and Mason, 1984; Miller and Toulouse, 1986). The main focus of this literature is to examine the influence of top managers (Finkelstein and Hambrick, 1990). Our interest builds on this previous work to determine who among the top managers are involved in making strategic decisions and if executive involvement depends on the decision context. In addition, we highlight the CEO's role in influencing the entire decision process.

Recently, Papadakis (2006) studied the influence of the CEO and the TMT separately, and called for future research that integrates the influence of both entities. A large number of authors have argued that considering the TMT as a unitary group will yield stronger predictive relationships than considering the CEO separately (Hambrick and Mason, 1984; Gupta, 1988; Bantel and Jackson, 1989; Murray, 1989; Finkelstein, 1992; Papadakis and Barwise, 2002). Our research incorporates the views of both perspectives. We argue that both the CEO and the TMT play important roles in the decision process. Our concern is that the CEO should not be treated as a regular TMT member, and that the other decision makers involved should be clearly identified.

Organizational Decision Context

Few studies of the decision process have examined the organizational context of decision making. These studies have incorporated aspects of the internal environment or characteristics in order to gauge the resources available for response. Internal factors that determine an organization's ability to respond can be linked to formal planning systems, firm performance, firm size, and firm ownership. For example, Sinha (1990) examined the relationship between internal planning systems and the decision process, and concluded that formal planning systems are only one avenue for planning and that much of the actual planning takes place outside of a formal planning process. Corporate performance is another common factor used to gauge the organizational context of decision making. The relationship between firm performance and strategic decision processes requires further investigation as some researchers have found that superior performance leads to a minimization of the decision process (Cyert and March, 1963; Fredrickson, 1985). Others have found a positive relationship between performance and (comprehensive) strategic decision processes (Smith et al., 1988). Performance measures are used to capture the presence of organizational slack, as excess resources allow firms the opportunity for suboptimal decision processes (Bourgeois, 1981).

Environmental Decision Context

The environmental factors perspective considers influence from factors external to the organization. Decision making within the organization takes place in the context of opportunities, threats, stability, and crises. Some scholars who subscribe to the environmental perspective consider that managers have very little influence on organizational strategic direction (Hannan and Freeman, 1977). Environmental considerations allow scholars to examine what is taking place in the environment that may impact the decision process. The evidence in support of this view is not strong, but leads to the conclusion that environmental factors add to uncertainty in strategic decision making (Dess and Rasheed, 1991; Rajagopalan et al., 1993; Sharfman and Dean, 1997).

PROPOSITION DEVELOPMENT

The CEO is in a position to exert more influence on the strategic decision process than any other person or entity in the firm (Hickson et al., 1986, 1989). The influence of the CEO plays an integral role in establishing the dynamics for strategic decision making. Many aspects of CEO power have been advanced in the strategy literature. An early framework of CEO power was developed by French and Raven (1958). More recently, Finkelstein (1992) developed a model of CEO power that incorporated both objective and perceptual measures of power. These measures of structural, ownership, prestige, and expert power have been tested jointly to reflect the multi-dimensional nature of power (Finkelstein, 1992).

Structural power is based on the formal role of an executive held within an organization (Hambrick, 1981; Finkelstein, 1992). This form of power is also represented and enhanced by an executive's influence over other managers and the board of directors. Structural power derives from formal titles and compensation; more titles and higher compensation are associated with higher structural power. A very common approach for capturing the CEO's structural power is the issue of duality – whether the CEO is also the board chair. High levels of structural power give the CEO more control over the strategic decision process by enhancing his or her capacity to select the issues that receive attention as well as to select the executives who will take part in the specific decision's analysis (Finkelstein and D'Aveni, 1994). CEOs who also hold the position of chair of the board (representing duality) have very high levels of structural power, leading to unity of command, which has been shown to be very beneficial in times of uncertainty (e.g., Brockmann et al., 2004).

Duality represents the case of a CEO who embodies extreme structural power (Rechner and Dalton, 1991). The CEO is the highest-ranking leader of the organization and as the chair has the ability to set the agenda for the board of directors (Finkelstein et al., 2009). Additionally, duality also likely enhances the CEO's influence in nominating new outside directors for the board. The CEO with high structural power has a greater capacity to fill the board with executives who support his or her direction and thereby effectively limiting the opportunity for opposition to his or her desired strategic direction. This influence is likely to be observed in terms of enhanced capacity to determine which strategic issues are focused upon, and how the decision process is framed. This leads us to offer our first proposition:

Proposition 1a: CEOs with high structural power will be associated with lower EMT and director involvement in strategic decision making.

Absent duality, the CEO's structural power is weaker, and he or she is likely in a situation that demands the sharing of significant structural power with whoever is the chair of the board. Almost by definition, this power sharing will reduce the discretion of the CEO to select strategic issues and control the overall strategic agenda, as the chair is likely to be an active participant in setting a strategic agenda and identifying key strategic issues. The chair's formal duties involve setting the strategic agenda and offering advice on resource availability and allocation (Finkelstein et al., 2009). Additionally, when a separate chair exists and plays a prominent role in setting the strategic direction, it is also more likely that other board members may be involved in decision making.

When separate executives hold the office of CEO and chair of the board, there is a greater opportunity to involve other executives in the decision-making process (Finkelstein and D'Aveni, 1994; Sanders and Carpenter, 1998). The opportunity for shared decision responsibility motivates involvement from other executives and direc tors. Additionally, joint decision making has a greater chance of taking place given that the CEO is more likely to be held accountable by the board (Harrison et al., 1988). One of the potential benefits of having a greater number of contributors is the potential for enriched decision making that leverages the skills and resources of those involved:

Proposition 1b: CEOs with low structural power will be associated with higher board chair and outside director involvement in strategic decision making.

Proposition 1c: CEOs with low structural power will be associated with more collaborative decision-making processes.

Ownership power represents founder status and significant voting influence. CEOs with high levels of ownership are potentially more interest-aligned with shareholders, which serves to limit the likelihood that they will act in an opportunistic manner (Finkelstein, 1992; Fischer and Pollock, 2004). A high level of ownership may also create more of a stewardship perspective for the CEO, thereby creating greater alignment with the broader interests of the firm.

CEOs with high levels of ownership have their wealth aligned with the success of the firm. High levels of ownership are widely believed to encourage CEOs to make strategic decisions that promote high growth and returns (Ang et al., 2000; De Miguel et al., 2004). In this context, CEOs are more likely to act in ways that benefit the firm and thereby benefit themselves without having to be monitored by the board (Walsh and Seward, 1990).

CEOs with high ownership power are more able to promote only executives who share their views, thereby limiting dissent (and by extension, limiting breadth of views brought to bear). By having greater control over director selection, the CEO with high ownership power may be able to create a board who is more supportive of his or her leadership. This might be particularly true in the case of family ownership (Lester and Cannella, 2006; Miller et al., 2007). A supportive board, that is largely nominated/selected by the CEO, is likely to act in a "hands off" manner, allowing the CEO to set the strategic direction of the firm without raising serious questions or challenges (Finkelstein et al., 2009):

Proposition 2a: CEOs with high ownership power will be associated with less collaborative decision-making processes.

Other non-CEO executives can hold high levels of stock ownership, though their ownership percentages seldom rise to the level of the CEO's. However, executives with higher levels of ownership do have a greater stake in the success of the firm, leading us to predict that such executives will likely be more involved in determining and implementing the strategic direction of the firm than those with lesser ownership. High levels of ownership suggest that there is a significant "downside" to risks taken that turn out badly, in contrast to high levels of stock options, which have a severely limited downside (Sanders, 2001). Stock ownership (again, in opposition to stock options – see Devers et al., 2006) is likely to encourage more careful risk-taking and longer-term perspectives. Both of these issues would seem to lead to the involvement of more individuals in the decision process and a more thorough vetting of the alternatives before a decision is made:

Proposition 2b: High ownership power among EMT members will be associated with more collaborative decision-making processes.

Prestige power derives, as its name implies, from prestige, which is defined as "having status" (D'Aveni, 1990; Brockmann et al., 2004). Typically, prestige emanates from affiliations that a CEO maintains external to the firm, and these are often captured through outside directorships. Additionally, however, prestige power arises from being a member of an elite social or country club, as such affiliations provide a firm with organizational legitimacy (D'Aveni, 1990) and access to more centrally placed players in the business community (Granovetter, 1982). For example, Lester and colleagues showed that Initial Public Offering (IPO) firms with prestigious directors achieved higher initial valuations than those with less prestigious directors (Certo, 2003). Prestige can also be derived from exclusive education, which also indicates access to elite networks and from participation on various boards, which indicates access to other elite executives (D'Aveni, 1990; Finkelstein, 1992). Having connections to other elite networks signals that the CEO is likely to be better able to use his or her external connections for the benefit of the firm (Selznick, 1957; Finkelstein, 1992).

Having access to elite educational networks also implies that a CEO will be able to draw upon information that will be useful in times of uncertainty (D'Aveni, 1990; Burt, 1992; Finkelstein, 1992). As opposed to "bonding" network connections (Adler and Kwon, 2002) these "bridging" connections provide access to unique information or resources. Any such resources that can be exchanged among trusted members enhance the value of having access to the network.

While the CEO typically has the highest level of prestige power in the firm, such power is not exclusive to the CEO. Non-CEO executives can have prestige, and it can be considered a characteristic of an entire TMT rather than linked to a particular individual (Finkelstein, 1992; Pfeffer, 1983). Whether at the individual or team level, prestige implies access to resources. To the extent that non-CEO executives have high prestige power, they will also be in the position to access networks and resources to respond to external uncertainty:

Proposition 3: High prestige power among EMT members will be associated with more collaborative decision-making processes.

The last form of power presented by Finkelstein (1992) is expert power. There are at least two ways that an executive can develop expertise power: (1) experience dealing with uncertainties in a corporate environment (e.g., numerous years of work experience in a particular industry); and (2) functional experience gained over a significant amount of time by working in one functional area. Both signals of expertise translate to the ability to develop strategic responses to environmental uncertainties. Experiential knowledge (functional or industry) facilitates the opportunity to maneuver around uncertainties based on previous experience (Bach and Smith, 2007).

Executives who reach the level of CEO have typically had many years of experience in general management as opposed to specializing in one functional area (Hambrick, 1981). In the case of CEOs, expertise power is more closely aligned by measuring industry experience which can be used to gauge experience handling uncertainties. Many researchers have used industry experience as a gauge to measure the ability to deal with environmental uncertainty. Pitcher and Smith (2001) linked industry experience to firm performance and were able to show that CEOs with greater industry experience achieved higher firm performance than those with less industry experience. The authors interpreted the evidence as supporting the notion that CEOs with greater experience were better able to respond to the changing needs of the industry.

Non-CEO executives are likely to have developed significant expert power. Although many high-level executives have accumulated years of experience in general management, their careers often begin with experience in a specific functional area. Additionally, many top executives are clearly experts in narrow areas (e.g., Chief Financial Officers or Executive VP of Manufacturing). Expert power can be very useful in resolving uncertainties that require specific functional insights. Its source arises from the individual's capacity to resolve ongoing uncertainties that arise from a firm's external environment. Executives who are able to respond and reduce the impact of uncertainties encountered by a firm are more likely to be viewed as highly valued resources and are accorded higher power (Pfeffer, 1981).

The two sources of expert power (broad general management experience and narrow functional experience) are complimentary. It is likely that CEOs with more general management experience will call upon executives who have deeper functional experience to develop strategies and to deal with environmental uncertainties. The pool of executives who have greater functional experience is not limited to those executives who are employees of the focal firm, but might also include experts external to the firm (e.g., outside directors). The needs of the firm will dictate whether the CEO draws on in-house talent (e.g., EMT) or reaches outside of the organization to involve other functional experts:

Proposition 4a: CEOs with high expert power will be associated with lower EMT and director involvement in strategic decision making, and this effect will be stronger when the decision context reflects the area of the CEO's expertise.

Proposition 4b: EMT members with high expert power are more likely to be involved in decision situations that relate closely to their specific functional areas.

Proposition 4c: EMT members with high expert power are more likely to be strongly influential in decision situations that relate closely to their specific functional areas.

The Influence of CEO Personality on Decision-making Configurations

In addition to the positional characteristics of the CEO, it is important to consider how leaders' personality characteristics influence organizational outcomes. The characteristics or personality of the CEO determines the extent to which others are involved in the decision process (Simsek et al., 2005). Simsek and colleagues concluded that specific characteristics of the CEO (i.e., collectivist orientation) represent a greater percentage of the variance than firm-level or team-level variance in those same characteristics. This study provides the foundation for our theory of the relationship between CEO personality characteristics and decision processes. We draw from the Five Factor Model of personality to examine how personality characteristics influence the CEO's approach to strategic decision making. The Five Factor Model or Big Five personality dimensions incorporate neuroticism, extraversion, openness to experience, agreeableness, and conscientiousness. Sangster reveals how a sample of top executives in the US score on the Big Five dimensions.

The first dimension, extraversion consists of two main components – ambition and sociability (Hogan, 1986). The second dimension, emotional stability (or neuroticism) is associated with the extent to which the person is angry, anxious, embarrassed, or emotional (Borgatta, 1964; Conley, 1985). The third dimension, agreeableness is associated with being likable or friendly (Goldberg, 1981). The fourth dimension, conscientiousness, is associated with conformity or dependability (Hogan, 1983). The last dimension, openness to experience, has received much attention. This dimension reflects the extent to which the person prefers familiar routines to new experiences, and also reflects the person's range of interests. Additionally, openness has been associated with intelligence, imagination, and broad-mindedness (Digman, 1990). Judge and Bono (2000) found extraversion, agreeableness, and openness to new experience to be traits that benefit long-term team development and cohesion.

Not all of the five factors of personality directly influence whether a CEO will be more amenable to involving executives of the firm or members of the board of directors in decision making. We posit that the primary factors that influence leadership style and the involvement of other executives are extraversion, openness to experience, and agreeableness. Our predictions are based on the CEO's profile with respect to these three factors.

The core dimension of extraversion is positive emotionality (Watson and Clark, 1997). Extraverts exhibit and express positive emotions. This positive disposition is more likely to be associated with leaders who are inspirational. Subordinates are more likely to follow a leader who displays characteristics such as positive affect and ambition:

Proposition 5a: CEOs who rate highly on extraversion will be associated with higher EMT and director involvement in strategic decision making.

Openness to experience represents individuals' tendency to be creative, resourceful, and insightful (John and Sanjay, 1999). Individuals high on this trait exhibit more flexible attitudes and are more likely to embrace divergent thinking (McCrae, 1994). Judge and Bono (2000) found that openness to experience was associated with transformational leadership. Individuals are more likely to commit themselves and their resources to support leaders who exhibit openness to experience:

Proposition 5b: CEOs who rate highly on openness to experience will be associated with higher EMT and director involvement in strategic decision making.

The last of the Big Five personality factors that we discuss is agreeableness. Persons with this factor tend to be cooperative, trusting, gentle, and kind (Graziano and Eisenberg, 1997). CEOs high on agreeableness might involve other executives to create an opportunity for development and to leverage the expertise of those others. Agreeableness is also associated with modesty, kindness, trustworthiness, and consideration; these traits build upon the CEO's ability to serve as a role model. Lastly, agreeable leaders are not likely to be passive leaders:

Proposition 5c: CEOs who are high on agreeableness will be associated with higher EMT and director involvement in strategic decision making.

Influence of the External Environment on Decision Configurations

Environmental influences are an important factor in determining the type of resources that may be helpful in developing or changing firm strategy. Environmental stability represents the extent to which a firm's environment is complex, uncertain, and prone to strategic change (Huber and McDaniel, 1986). The stability of the external environment is a key factor in determining whether internal (the EMT) or external (the board) resources are required. In stable environments the key is to implement existing strategies, while unstable environments require that new strategies be developed. Dess and Beard (1984) and Keats and Hitt (1988) considered three facets of environmental stability (munificence, dynamism, and complexity). Our theory applies to each of these dimensions. We chose the term "uncertainty" because we believe it reflects all three of these dimensions. Put differently, high uncertainty is associated with environments that are characterized by high dynamism, or high complexity, or low munificence.

The EMT and the board provide different resources for strategic decision making. The EMT or internal executives of the focal firm have greater insight regarding firm-specific knowledge (Castanias and Helfat, 1991, 2001). Members of the EMT are great resources for providing specific types of expertise and links to external entities, but the strongest resource they provide is based on their (internal) firm-specific experience.

The external members of the board, those directors who are not executives of the focal firm, are better equipped to provide the essential resources to deal with external contingencies (Pfeffer and Salancik, 1978). These members serve as links to the external environment by providing a heterogeneous set of skills and resources, in addition to serving as communication channels between the focal firm and external organizations.

Essentially, the EMT and the board provide heterogeneous sets of resources, thus the potential value of one resource relative to the other is influenced by the context of the firm (i.e., the external environment). When a firm operates in a stable environment or is able to maintain the status quo, members of the EMT are better positioned to influence the strategic decision process. In this context, the EMT has the best insight in determining how firm-specific knowledge can be used to strengthen the firm's position. The ability to maintain the status quo is better handled by the executives of the firm. This leads to the following proposition:

Proposition 6a: CEOs are more likely to involve members of the EMT in strategic decision making when the firm's external environment is more stable.

As change takes place in the environment, firms often have to alter their corporate strategy. A change in resource availability may influence firm strategy; these changes may contribute to creating uncertainty in the environment. The firm's ability to respond to uncertain environments depends on linkages to desired resources. The firm's board, in particular the outside directors, are in the best position to assist with setting the required strategic change (Mizruchi, 1983; Boeker and Goodstein, 1991).

Resource dependence theory suggests that boards of directors are used for managing external dependencies (Pfeffer and Salancik, 1978) and reducing environmental uncertainty (Pfeffer, 1972). In an unstable environment, the future success of a firm depends on the ability of the firm's leaders (mainly, the CEO) to develop new alternatives that realign an organization's resources with the changing environment (Tushman and Anderson, 1986; Haleblian and Finkelstein, 1993). CEOs are more likely to depend on the linkages provided by the board in times of environmental change. The board is better positioned to either provide or link the firm to a heterogeneous set of resources that can be used develop a new strategy. External members of the board of directors offer the best set of resources that can be used in the strategic decision process; external directors have insights regarding the focal firm and can co-opt relationships with other firms (Pfeffer and Salancik, 1978). As such:

Proposition 6b: CEOs are more likely to involve members of the board of directors in strategic decision making when the firm's external environment is more uncertain.

Extant literature that examines board composition considers the changing dynamics or needs of the firm in relation to the uncertainty or external dependencies (Pfeffer and Salancik, 1978). However, the disposition of the CEO is another factor of influence regarding whether directors will be used. Our theory suggests that CEO disposition acts as a mediator of the board's ability to fulfill its role as resource providers. In particular, an additional factor that determines whether the CEO uses the board or the EMT may be more heavily influenced by the CEO than previously considered. As such, we propose the following interaction effects:

Proposition 7a: CEO personality characteristics will be more influential in decision processes in more stable environments than in less stable environments.

Proposition 7b: Given a less stable external environment, the CEO's use of the board of directors will depend on his/her personality characteristics (i.e., extraversion, openness to experience, and agreeableness).

DISCUSSION

Our purpose in this chapter was to extend the upper echelons perspective by offering a more rigorous set of rules for linking specific executives to decision outcomes. We started by dissecting the TMT. We parse out the CEO (office of) in an effort to improve our understanding of the influence the CEO holds over the strategic decision process. We offer theory that predicts how CEO influence impacts decision making. Next we determine which executives comprise the TMT. Researchers have long connected executives to organizational outcomes without being able to clearly distinguish which executives were involved in the process. Our "model" identifies the most likely executives who would influence the decision process. We make the connection between specific executives and organizational outcomes in an effort to develop a better framework. Finally, we offer theory to better understand executive influence and involvement based on the decision context.

Our theorizing develops a more complete framework toward understanding the influence of executives on organizational decision making. We enhance the predictability of the upper echelons perspective by developing more concrete links between decision makers and organizational outcomes. Most of the research to date examines the influence of the TMT as a group of equals. We debate this point in that the CEO is integral to shaping and controlling the decision process. The CEO has the ability to determine both who participates in the process and how the process evolves. To this extent, the CEO cannot be "just" another member of the TMT. The framework developed here also helps to explain performance results observed in previous research. Our theorizing predicts that not all who are considered members of the upper echelon are included in decision making. To this end, our theory helps to improve the predictive power of the upper echelons perspective. Previously, researchers have used several different ways to determine or identify members of the upper echelons and subsequently link them to decision outcomes. By more succinctly identifying which executives participate in decision making, we should greatly improve the explanatory power of the relationship linking firm executives to organizational outcomes.

According to Hambrick and Mason (1984), the definition of the TMT is of utmost importance. Conceptually, strategy researchers agree on the TMT concept. We broadly recognize the TMT as executives at a strategic level, yet our empirical definition of the TMT is much less concrete: Tihanyi et al. (2000) identify the TMT as all employees who are executive vice-presidents and above; Boeker (1997) used all of the CEO's direct reports; Ferrier (2001) used the top five highest paid executives; Papadakis and Barwise (2002) and Simons et al. (1999) were able to survey the CEO and use those executives whom the chief executive identified. Most empirical definitions are the result of convenience sampling. We believe there is much to be gained (we can improve the amount of variance explained) by connecting decision contexts to specific decision makers. This chapter is an initial attempt to refine the upper echelons perspective.

By more fully developing the relationship between executives and organizational outcomes that is currently under-represented in the literature, we can offer a roadmap for future research. Understandably, the need to use more defined definition of the TMT would shed light on how the EMT works together. The more that is learned regarding the team, the greater potential we have to track the influence of each executive individually. Overall, the field would benefit from greater investment in both theory and empirical studies. The importance of using specific decision contexts and being able to link them to key executives would provide opportunities that we have previously not explored.

To date when research involving the TMT is discussed we also have to mention the "black box" and how so much of what takes place is unknown. However, we should not underestimate the value of reducing the surface area of the "black box." Each new discovery about the executive team helps researchers to gain insights that previously were unknown. Eventually, we will no longer have a need to refer to the "black box" to cover the unknowns, but will be able to offer roadmaps for the discoveries that have added to our existing frameworks.

Some of the milestones that firms face as they navigate the life cycle adjustments, competitive interactions, and search for limited resources are common occurrences. We can use these occasions to examine decision contributors and decision processes among firms in an industry. The insights gained through future research should be used to help researchers create theories predicting how executives influence team dynamics and team functioning. Since our empirical examinations have centered on the influence of the CEO, we can more succinctly gauge how the CEO influences strategic decision making. Building on the work of Simons et al. (1999) we can predict how executive teams might be structured as a function of the CEO's Big Five personality traits. In a related vein, in Chapter 6 of this volume, Peterson and Zhang explore the effects of TMT psychological characteristics, specifically core self-evaluations and psychological capital, as moderated by transformational leadership.

Using our insights regarding the influence of CEO personality, we can make stronger predictions linking CEO characteristics to decision contexts. Our main concern should be focused on making strong predictions and developing testable hypotheses that examine CEO influence on the EMT (all of the potential non-CEO executives who might be involved in decision making). Our quest to link executives to specific roles in the decision process will allow us to understand decision characteristics that are influenced by both individual characteristics and executive group decision making.

NOTE

1. We recognize that this assumption is a bit restrictive. We can easily imagine that some decisions may fall into traditional categories, and therefore might be framed historically, limiting the CEO's discretion a bit. In other cases, the presence of strong expertise in a particular area might hamper the CEO's discretion surrounding issues that fall into the heavy expertise area. We leave these situations for future theory development.

REFERENCES

Adler, P.S. and Kwon, S.-W. (2002). Social capital: Prospects for a new concept. *Academy of Management Review*, **27**(1), 17–40.

Amason, A.C. (1996). Distinguishing the effects of functional and dysfunctional conflict on strategic decision-making: Resolving a paradox for top management teams. *Academy of Management Journal*, **39**(1), 123–48.

Ang, J.S., Cole, R.A., and Lin, J.W. (2000). Agency costs and ownership structure. *Journal of Finance*, **55**(1), 81–106.

Bach, S.B. and Smith, A.D. (2007). Are powerful CEOs beneficial to post-IPO survival in high technology industries? An empirical investigation. *Journal of High Technology Management Research*, **18**(1), 31–42.

Bantel, K.A. and Jackson, S.E. (1989). Top management and innovations in banking: Does the composition of the top team make a difference? *Strategic Management Journal*, **10**(S1), 107–24.

Billings, R.S., Milburn, T.W., and Schaalman, M.L. (1980). A model of crisis perception: A theoretical and empirical analysis. *Administrative Science Quarterly*, **25**(2), 300–316.

Boeker, W. (1997). Strategic change: The influence of managerial characteristics and organizational growth. *Academy of Management Journal*, **40**(1), 152–70.

Boeker, W. and Goodstein, J. (1991). Organizational performance and adaptation: Effects of environment and performance on changes in board composition. *Academy of Management Journal*, **34**(4), 805–26.

Borgatta, E.F. (1964). The structure of personality characteristics. *Behavioral Science*, **9**(1), 8–17.

Bourgeois, L.J., III (1981). On the measurement of organizational slack. *Academy of Management Review*, **6**(1), 29–39.

Brockmann, E.N., Hoffman, J.J., Dawley, D.D., and Fornaciari, C.J. (2004). The impact of CEO duality and prestige on a bankrupt organization. *Journal of Managerial Issues*, **16**(2), 178–96.

Burt, R.S. (1992). *Structural holes: The social structure of competition*. Cambridge, MA: Harvard University Press.

Cannella, A.A., Jr. and Holcomb, T.R. (2005). A multilevel analysis of the upper-echelons model. In A. Dansereau and F.J. Yammarino (eds), *Research in multi-level issues* (Vol. 4). Oxford, UK: Elsevier Ltd, pp. 197–237.

Cannella, A.A., Jr., Park, J.H., and Lee, H.U. (2008). Top management team functional background diversity and firm performance: Examining the roles of team member co-location and environmental uncertainty. *Academy of Management Journal*, **51**(4), 768–84.

Carpenter, M.A., Geletkanycz, M.A., and Sanders, W.G. (2004). The upper echelons research revisited: Antecedents, elements, and consequences of top management team composition. *Journal of Management*, **30**(6), 749–78.

Castanias, R.P. and Helfat, C.E. (1991). Managerial resources and rents. *Journal of Management*, **17**(1), 155–71.

Castanias, R.P. and Helfat, C.E. (2001). The managerial rents model: Theory and empirical analysis. *Journal of Management*, **27**(6), 661–78.

Certo, S.T. (2003). Influencing initial public offering investors with prestige: Signaling with board structures. *Academy of Management Review*, **28**(3), 432–46.

Chaganti, R. and Sambharya, R. (1987). Strategic orientation and characteristics of upper management. *Strategic Management Journal*, **8**(4), 393–401.

Child, J. (1972). Organization structure, environment and performance: The role of strategic choice. *Sociology*, **6**(1), 1–22.

Conley, J.J. (1985). Longitudinal stability of personality traits: A multitrait- multimethod- multioccasion analysis. *Journal of Personality and Social Psychology*, **49**(5), 1266–82.

Crossland, C. and Hambrick, D.C. (2007). How national systems influence executive discretion: A study of CEO effects in three countries. *Strategic Management Journal*, **28**(8), 767–89.

Cyert, R.M. and March, J.G. (1963). *A behavioral theory of the firm*. Englewood Cliffs, NJ: Prentice-Hall.

D'Aveni, R.A. (1990). Top managerial prestige and organizational bankruptcy. *Organization Science*, **1**(2), 121–42.

Dearborn, D.W.C. and Simon, H.A. (1958). Selective perception: A note on the departmental affiliations of executives. *Sociometry*, **21**(2), 144–50.

De Miguel, A., Pindado, J., and de la Torre, C. (2004). Ownership structure and firm value: New evidence from Spain. *Strategic Management Journal*, **25**(12), 1199–207.

Dess, G.G. and Beard, D.W. (1984). Dimensions of organizational task environments. *Administrative Science Quarterly*, **29**(1), 52–73.

Dess, G.G. and Rasheed, A. (1991). Conceptualizing and measuring organizational environments: A critique and suggestions. *Journal of Management*, **17**(4), 701–10.

Devers, C.E., Holcomb, T.R., Holmes, R.M., Jr., and Cannella, A.A., Jr. (2006). Inside the black box: The contrasting effects of TMT long-term incentives on interest alignment. Paper presented at the Academy of Management Best Papers Proceedings, Atlanta, GA.

Digman, J.M. (1990). Personality structure: Emergence of the five-factor model. *Annual Review of Psychology*, **41**(1), 417–40.

Dutton, J.E. and Ashford, S.J. (1993). Selling issues to top management. *Academy of Management Review*, **18**(3), 397–428.

Dutton, J.E. and Jackson, S.E. (1987). Categorizing strategic issues: Links to organizational action. *Academy of Management Review*, **12**(1), 76–90.

Ferrier, W.J. (2001). Navigating the competitive landscape: The drivers and consequences of competitive aggressiveness. *Academy of Management Journal*, **44**(4), 858–77.

Fiedler, F.E. (1967). *A theory of leadership effectiveness*. New York, NY: McGraw-Hill.

Finkelstein, S. (1992). Power in top management teams: Dimensions, measurement, and validation. *Academy of Management Journal*, **35**(3), 505–38.

Finkelstein, S. (1997). Interindustry merger patterns and resource dependence: A replication and extension of Pfeffer (1972). *Strategic Management Journal*, **18**(10), 787–810.

Finkelstein, S. and D'Aveni, R.A. (1994). CEO duality as a double-edged sword: How boards of directors balance entrenchment avoidance and unity of command. *Academy of Management Journal*, **37**(5), 1079–108.

Finkelstein, S. and Hambrick, D.C. (1990). Top management team tenure and organizational outcomes: The moderating role of managerial discretion. *Administrative Science Quarterly*, **35**(3), 484–503.

Finkelstein, S., Hambrick, D.C., and Cannella, A.A., Jr. (2009). *Strategic leadership: Theory and research on executives, top management teams, and boards* (Vol. 2). Oxford, UK: Oxford University Press.

Fischer, H.M. and Pollock, T.G. (2004). Effects of social capital and power on surviving transformational change: The case of initial public offerings. *Academy of Management Journal*, **47**(4), 463–81.

Fredrickson, J.W. (1985). Effects of decision motive and organizational performance level on strategic decision processes. *Academy of Management Journal*, **28**(4), 821–43.

French, J. and Raven, B. (1958). The bases of social power. In D. Cartwright (ed.), *Studies in social power*. Ann Arbor, MI: Institute for Social Research, pp. 150–67.

Goldberg, L.R. (1981). Language and individual differences: The search for universals in personality lexicons. In L. Wheeler (ed.), *Review of personality and social psychology* (Vol. 2). Beverly Hills, CA: Sage, pp. 141–66.

Granovetter, M. (1982). The strength of weak ties: A network theory revisited. In P.V. Marsden and N. Lin (eds), *Social structure and network analysis*. Thousand Oaks, CA: Sage, pp. 105–30.

Graziano, W.G. and Eisenberg, N.H. (1997). Agreeableness: A dimension of personality. In R. Hogan, J. Johnson and S. Briggs (eds), *Handbook of personality psychology*. San Diego, CA: Academic Press, pp. 795–824.

Gully, S.M., Incalcaterra, K.A., Joshi, A., and Beaubien, J.M. (2002). A meta-analysis of team-efficacy, potency, and performance: Interdependence and level of analysis as moderators of observed relationships. *Journal of Applied Psychology*, **87**(5), 819–32.

Gupta, A.K. (1988). Contingency perspectives on strategic leadership: Current knowledge and future research directions. In D.C. Hambrick (ed.), *The executive effect: Concepts and methods for studying top managers*. Greenwich, CT: JAI Press, pp. 141–78.

Haleblian, J. and Finkelstein, S. (1993). Top management team size, CEO dominance, and firm performance: The moderating roles of environmental turbulence and discretion. *Academy of Management Journal*, **36**(4), 844–86.

Hambrick, D.C. (1981). Environment, strategy and power within top management teams. *Administrative Science Quarterly*, **26**(2), 253–76.

Hambrick, D.C. and Mason, P. (1984). Upper echelons: The organization as a reflection of its top managers. *Academy of Management Review*, **9**(2), 193–206.

Hambrick, D.C., Cho, T.S., and Chen, M.J. (1996). The influence of top management team heterogeneity on firms' competitive moves. *Administrative Science Quarterly*, **41**(4), 659–84.

Hannan, M.T. and Freeman, J.H. (1977). The population ecology of organizations. *American Journal of Sociology*, **82**(5), 929–64.

Harrison, J.R., Torres, D.L., and Kukalis, S. (1988). The changing of the guard: Turnover and structural change in the top-management positions. *Administrative Science Quarterly*, **33**(2), 211–32.

Hickson, D.J., Butler, R.J., Cray, D., Mallory, G.R., and Wilson, D.C. (1986). *Top decisions: Strategic decision-making in organizations*. San Francisco, CA: Jossey-Bass.

Hickson, D.J., Butler, R.J., Cray, D., Mallory, G.R., and Wilson, D.C. (1989). Decision and organization: Processes of strategic decision-making and their explanation. *Public Administration*, **67**(4), 373–90.

Hogan, R. (1983). A socioanalytic theory of personality. In M.M. Page (ed.), *Personality – current theory and research: Nebraska symposium on motivation*. Lincoln, NE: University of Nebraska Press.

Hogan, R. (1986). *Manual for the Hogan Personality Inventory*. Minneapolis, MN: National Computer Systems.

Hollenbeck, J.R., Ilgen, D.R., Sego, D.J., Hedlund, J., Major, D.A., and Phillips, J. (1995). The multi-level theory of team decision-making: Decision performance in teams incorporating distributed expertise. *Journal of Applied Psychology*, **80**(2), 292–316.

Huber, G.P. and McDaniel, R.R. (1986). The decision-making paradigm of organizational design. *Management Science*, **32**(5), 572–89.

Jackson, S.E. (1992). Consequence of group composition for the interpersonal dynamics of strategic issue processing. In P. Shrivastava, A.S. Huff and J. Dutton (eds), *Advances in strategic management* (Vol. 8). Greenwich, CT: JAI Press, pp. 345–82.

John, O.P. and Sanjay, S. (1999). The big-five trait taxonomy: History, measurement and theoretical perspectives. In L.A. Pervin and O.P. John (eds), *Handbook of personality: Theory and research* (2nd edition). New York, NY: Guilford, pp. 102–38.

Judge, T.A. and Bono, J.E. (2000). Five-factor model of personality and transformational leadership. *Journal of Applied Psychology*, **85**(5), 751–65.

Kahneman, D. and Tversky, A. (1979). Prospect theory: Analysis of decision-making under risk. *Econometrica*, **47**(2), 263–92.

Keats, B.W. and Hitt, M.A. (1988). A causal model of linkages among environmental dimensions, macro organizational characteristics, and performance. *Academy of Management Journal*, **31**(3), 570–98.

Lester, R.H. and Cannella, A.A., Jr. (2006). Interorganizational familiness: How family firms use interlocking directorates to build community-level social capital. *Entrepreneurship Theory and Practice*, **30**(6), 755–75.

Lewin, K. (1951). Intention, will and need. In D. Rapaport (ed.), *Organization and pathology of thought: Selected sources*. New York, NY: Columbia University Press, pp. 95–153.

McCrae, R.R. (1994). Openness to experience: Expanding the boundaries of factor V. *European Journal of Personality*, **8**(4), 251–72.

Michel, J.G. and Hambrick, D.C. (1992). Diversification posture and top management team characteristics. *Academy of Management Journal*, **35**(3), 9–37.

Miller, D. and Toulouse, J.M. (1986). Chief executive personality and corporate strategy and structure in small firms. *Management Science*, **32**(1), 1389–409.

Miller, D., Le Breton-Miller, I., Lester, R.H., and Cannella, A.A., Jr. (2007). Are family firms really superior performers? *Journal of Corporate Finance*, **13**(5), 829–58.

Mills, T.M. (1976). *The sociology of small groups*. Englewood Cliffs, NJ: Prentice-Hall.

Mintzberg, H., Raisinghani, D., and Theoret, A. (1976). The structure of unstructured decision processes. *Administrative Science Quarterly*, **21**(2), 246–75.

Mizruchi, M.S. (1983). Who controls whom? An examination of the relation between management and board of directors in large American corporations. *Academy of Management Review*, **8**(3), 426–35.

Murray, A.I. (1989). Top management group heterogeneity and firm performance. *Strategic Management Journal*, **10**(S1), 125–41.

Papadakis, V. (2006). Do CEOs shape the process of making strategic decisions? Evidence from Greece. *Management Decision*, **44**(3), 367–94.

Papadakis, V.M. and Barwise, P. (2002). How much do CEOs and top managers matter in strategic decision-making? *British Journal of Management*, **13**(1), 83–95.

Papadakis, V.M., Lioukas, S., and Chambers, D. (1998). Strategic decision-making processes: The role of management and context. *Strategic Management Journal*, **19**(2), 115–47.

Pettigrew, A.M. (1992). On studying managerial elites. *Strategic Management Journal*, **13**(S2), 163–82.

Pfeffer, J. (1972). Size and composition of corporate boards of directors: The organization and its environment. *Administrative Science Quarterly*, **17**(2), 218–29.

Pfeffer, J. (1981). *Power in organizations*. Boston, MA: Pitman.

Pfeffer, J. (1983). Organizational demography. In L.L. Cummings and B.M. Staw (eds), *Research in organizational behavior* (Vol. 5). Greenwich, CT: JAI Press, pp. 299–357.

Pfeffer, J. and Salancik, G.R. (1978). *The external control of organizations: A resource dependence perspective*. New York, NY: Harper & Row.

Pitcher, P. and Smith, A.D. (2001). Top management team heterogeneity: Personality, power, and proxies. *Organization Science*, **12**(1), 1–18.

Rajagopalan, N. (1996). Strategic orientations, incentive plan adoptions, and firm performance: Evidence from electric utility firms. *Strategic Management Journal*, **18**(10), 761–85.

Rajagopalan, N. and Datta, D.K. (1996). CEO characteristics: Does industry matter? *Academy of Management Journal*, **39**(1), 197–215.

Rajagopalan, N., Rasheed, A.M.A., and Datta, D.K. (1993). Strategic decision processes: Critical review and future directions. *Journal of Management*, **19**(2), 349–84.

Rechner, P.L. and Dalton, D.R. (1991). CEO duality and organizational performance: A longitudinal analysis. *Strategic Management Journal*, **12**(2), 155–60.

Roberto, M.A. (2003). The stable core and dynamic periphery in top management teams. *Management Decision*, **41**(2), 120–31.

Sanders, W.G. (2001). Behavioral responses of CEOs to stock ownership and stock option pay. *Academy of Management Journal*, **44**(3), 477–92.

Sanders, W.G. and Carpenter, M.A. (1998). Internationalization and firm governance: The roles of CEO compensation, top team composition, and board structure. *Academy of Management Journal*, **41**(2), 158–78.

Sanders, W.G. and Hambrick, D.C. (2007). Swinging for the fences: The effects of CEO stock options on company risk-taking and performance. *Academy of Management Journal*, **50**(5), 1055–78.

Schneider, S.C. and De Meyer, A. (1991). Interpreting and responding to strategic issues: The impact of national culture. *Strategic Management Journal*, **12**(4), 307–20.

Selznick, P. (1957). *Leadership in administration: A sociological interpretation*. New York, NY: Harper & Row.

Sharfman, M.P. and Dean, J.W., Jr. (1997). Flexibility in strategic decision making: Informational and ideological perspectives. *Journal of Management Studies*, **34**(2), 191–217.

Shaw, M.E. (1981). *Group dynamics*. New York, NY: McGraw-Hill.

Simons, T., Pelled, L.H., and Smith, K.A. (1999). Making use of difference: Diversity, debate, and decision comprehensiveness in top management teams. *Academy of Management Journal*, **42**(6), 662–73.

Simsek, Z., Veiga, J., Lubatkin, M., and Dino, R.N. (2005). Modeling the multilevel determinants of top management team behavioral integration. *Academy of Management Journal*, **48**(1), 69–84.

Sinha, D.K. (1990). The contribution of formal planning to decisions. *Strategic Management Journal*, **11**(6), 479–92.

Smith, K.G., Gannon, M.J., Grimm, C.M., and Mitchell, T.R. (1988). Decision-making behavior in smaller entrepreneurial and larger professionally managed firms. *Journal of Business Venturing*, **3**(3), 223–32.

Thompson, J.D. (1967). *Organizations in action: Social science bases of administrative theory*. New York, NY: McGraw-Hill.

Tihanyi, L., Ellstrand, A.E., Daily, C.M. and Dalton, D.R. (2000). Composition of the top management team and firm international diversification. *Journal of Management*, **26**(6), 1157–77.

Tushman, M.L. and Anderson, P. (1986). Technological discontinuities and organizational environments. *Administrative Science Quarterly*, **31**(3), 439–65.

Vroom, V.H. and Jago, A.G. (1988). *The new leadership: Managing participation in organizations*. Englewood Cliffs, NJ: Prentice Hall.

Wagner, W.G., Pfeffer, J., and O'Reilly, C.A., III (1984). Organizational demography and turnover in top-management groups. *Administrative Science Quarterly*, **29**(1), 74–92.

Walsh, J.P. (1988). Selectivity and selective perception: An investigation of managers' belief structures and information processing. *Academy of Management Journal*, **31**, 873–96.

Walsh, J.P. and Seward, J.K. (1990). On the efficiency of internal and external corporate control mechanisms. *Academy of Management Review*, **15**(3), 421–58.

Watson, D. and Clark, L.A. (1997). Measurement and mismeasurement of mood: Recurrent and emergent issues. *Journal of Personality Assessment*, **68**(2), 267–96.

2 In search of the CEO's inner circle and how it is formed

Ann C. Mooney and Allen C. Amason

Researchers have conducted hundreds of studies seeking to improve the understanding of how top management teams (TMTs) function and contribute to strategic decisions and organizational outcomes (for review, see Finkelstein and Hambrick, 1996; Finkelstein et al., 2009). Although much has been learned from this work, it still remains that numerous TMT studies have been inconclusive, offering mixed or non-significant findings.

We believe a key to advancing TMT research lies in a more careful consideration of who is actually making the decisions and why. Researchers have indirectly tried to address this issue by adopting varying conceptualizations of the TMT based on assumptions of who in the organization makes strategic decisions. For example, researchers have identified the TMT as the Chief Executive Officer (CEO) and his or her direct reports (Fredrickson and Iaquinto, 1985; Sutcliffe, 1994), inside board members (Finkelstein, 1992), and the group of managers with titles above the rank of vice-president (Cannella and Hambrick, 1993; Cannella et al., 2008). Few researchers, however, have given the identification of the TMT more than cursory attention, and have provided little more than a quick notation in the methods section. Yet, who makes the decisions matters. Indeed, researchers have found that alternate definitions of the TMT significantly influence research findings (Flatt, 1992; Carpenter and Fredrickson, 2001).

In this chapter, we offer a different approach to this issue. Specifically, we remove the assumption that the TMT should approximate the strategic decision-making group. Based on our experience with top teams, we see that firms refer to a certain group of executives as the top management team and that these executives identify themselves as being part of the TMT and will even meet as a team. Consistent with Hambrick (1994), however, we have found that not all team members are equally engaged in strategic decision making. Rather, what seems to happen is that the true strategic decisions are being made by a smaller group of top executives handpicked by the CEO.

We argue that it is this smaller group, referred to as the "inner circle" by Thompson (1967, p. 140), that should be the focus of TMT research. The full top management team exists and plays a role inside firms, but in terms of strategic decision making we argue that its purpose lies mainly in being the reservoir from which the CEO selects the inner circle.[1]

Despite the decades that have passed since Thompson's (1967) work, research offers little guidance on inner circles. Moreover, we know even less about how inner circles are selected. In this chapter, we will examine inner circles and address two main research questions. First, we will examine whether inner circles do indeed exist. We will pursue this question by reviewing the literature and our own experience with top teams, as well as with an empirical test of 40 top management teams. Second, we will explore how executives are selected into the inner circle. Individuals promoted or hired into top executive positions go through a relatively formal and time-consuming selection process over which the CEO may only have limited control due to factors such as board oversight. Conversely, we argue that executives who are on "the inside" are granted that status by the CEO, for reasons that the CEO need not make clear. Indeed, because the inner circle is informal, there are no stated criteria for membership and no formal reporting of its members or activities. Thus, the CEO has much latitude in selecting these individuals. As we will discuss and empirically test, we argue that the CEO's selection of inner circle members is based largely on the CEO's assessment of how similar or different the executive is from the CEO.

Taken together, this research suggests that rather than the nature of the firm being a reflection of its top management (Hambrick and Mason, 1984), it may more significantly be a reflection of the inner circle of top management. Moreover, the firm may also strongly reflect the CEO since it is the CEO who selects inner circle members.

THEORY

The Dominant Coalition

The upper echelon perspective evolved out of the behavioral theory of the firm (Cyert and March, 1963). Behavioral theory differed from the classical economic view (Coase, 1937) in a number of important ways. One was that the management and goal-setting activities of the firm were the result of coalition behavior. Another was that the members of the various coalitions had different individual interests, perspectives, and priorities. As a result, key decisions emerged from a negotiation process, where managers sought to have their own priorities and interests addressed. In light of this, the goals and strategies of a firm could be seen as reflecting the interests and tendencies of those managers in the dominant coalition (Hambrick and Mason, 1984).

Focus on a dominant coalition sparked interest in the process of strategic decision making. One study by Mintzberg et al. (1976) described the process by which unstructured and complex decisions were actually made. Among the findings of this study was the observation that strategic decisions emerged from an irregular and non-linear process. Even important decisions ran into unanticipated roadblocks and interruptions. Nevertheless, they still followed discernible patterns.

For example, decisions were initiated through the identification or diagnosis of a problem. They also involved a choice from among a set of alternatives. These two basic structures had substantial implication for the upper echelon view. For example, problem identification and the diagnosis and framing of issues are influenced by characteristics of the managers involved and the conditions under which those managers function (Dutton et al., 1983; Thomas and McDaniel, 1990; Julian and Ofori-Dankwa, 2008). Furthermore, the way an issue is diagnosed and framed affects the mechanics of subsequent decision making and the outcomes of decisions (Dutton and Jackson, 1987).

The selection of alternatives is also influenced by the interests and biases of the decision makers. Child (1972) observed that the focus of early organizational research was on the many constraints guiding decision making. The result was an analytical process where actual decision makers were largely irrelevant and outcomes were determined by a calculating process, driven by the "economic and administrative exigencies" of the situation (ibid., p. 16). Focusing on a dominant coalition, whose members had different perspectives and biases even though they had shared interests, introduced a new type of variance. If decision making was a function of the decision makers, then each dominant coalition would assess its alternatives differently and make decisions based on its own unique blend of preferences, experiences, and beliefs (Child, 1972). In other words, each coalition could face the same exact circumstances and yet produce very different decisions.

Thus, TMTs came to be seen as a unique and powerful source of influence in the strategic process. And, as the anecdotal and empirical evidence suggested, some teams simply performed better in this role than others. For example, some teams were just better at innovation (Bantel and Jackson, 1989), while others were better suited to diversification (Jensen and Zajac, 2004; Marlin et al., 2004).

The Top Management Team and the Inner Circle

Over the years, a variety of different pictures of the upper echelon emerged. Hambrick and Mason (1984) originally described the TMT as the firm's "officers" (p. 196). However, as the TMT was later operationalized, a number of different definitions evolved. Some defined the TMT as the top levels of management, including the chair and CEO, along with the next tier of managers (Weirsema and Bantel, 1992; Carpenter and Fredrickson, 2001). Others saw the TMT as the inside board members (Finkelstein, 1992; Haleblian and Finkelstein, 1993), as the CEO and those reporting directly to the CEO (Fredrickson and Iaquinto, 1985; Sutcliffe, 1994) or as the group of managers with titles above the rank of vice-president (Cannella and Hambrick, 1993; Cannella et al., 2008). Still others adopted a different approach, allowing the CEO to identify the team members based upon actual involvement in the strategic process (Amason, 1996; Colbert et al., 2008).

Across these different definitions was a common assumption, that the managers included in the top management team actually exercised some influence over strategic decision making. After all, it made no sense to define the TMT to include managers irrelevant to the strategic process. Rather, research on the TMT sought to better connect management action to firm outcomes. So, it made sense to focus on those managers whose actions were most influential and connected to firm performance.

The distinction between the full TMT and a smaller group that exists within the TMT was noted first by Thompson (1967) who labeled the smaller group the "inner circle" (p. 140). The emergence of an inner circle is subtle and informal, designed to the increase efficiency and speed in decision making. Rather than involve the entire coalition, a CEO may simply consult with a few key people, getting quickly to the pulse of the top group and listening intently to a limited set of trusted advisors. Given the size of the TMT in most large organizations, along with the breadth of tasks and responsibilities with which this group must deal, it is rare that the full TMT would gather often to collectively identify strategic issues and make strategic decisions (Hambrick, 1994; Roberto, 2003). Rather, it is more likely that the CEO, informed by the members of the coalition but in concert with a small subset of the larger group, makes the most important decisions.

This is consistent with the process reported by Allison (1971) in his description of the Executive Committee during the Cuban Missile Crisis. While the full committee consisted of 15 top officials, Kennedy consulted most often with and listened most carefully to just three people. Those three – the Attorney General, the Secretary of Defense, and the Special Counsel – exercised much more influence over the policy and decisions than did the others. In reality, it was this inner circle that drove the process and the outcomes that emerged from it.

We found the same dynamic at a company we will call TechnoCo. This firm, a publicly held, multi-billion-dollar high-technology manufacturing firm, had a TMT of 14 top executives. This TMT included the C-level executives, such as the CEO, Chief Operating Officer (COO), and Chief Financial Officer (CFO), the vice-presidents of areas like sales, operations, and corporate affairs, as well as the general managers of various semi-autonomous business units. The group referred to themselves as the top management team and used the term often. They also met often, either in person or through a virtual audio/video system that created the illusion of being around a single table. These meetings, however, were rarely strategic in nature; they were mostly information-sharing sessions, with little real interaction. Within the group of 14 was a subset of four, one of whom was the CEO. The other three were the COO and two vice-presidents. These three often met informally with the CEO and were recognized by the rest of the TMT as the "greatest among equals." These three had the ear of the CEO; their objections could override suggestions from the rest of the team and their philosophies were often repeated by the CEO in the explanation of his decisions. It was clear to the rest of the team that this group was an inner circle, with much more access and influence than the rest.

These brief examples illustrate how we suspect TMTs most often work. As reported throughout the literature, TMTs consist of diverse sets of managers, brought together to represent different interests and expertise from across the firm. That breadth enables better information sharing, which facilitates better decisions and more efficient implementation. However, that breadth may also slow decision processing, creating conflict and diluting focus. As a result, the leader, most typically the CEO, develops a smaller and stable inner circle of trusted advisors (Roberto, 2003; Arendt et al., 2005). This inner circle indentifies the key issues, sets the broad directions, and makes the hard choices. This smaller group can then present a unified front to the rest of the TMT, which facilitates consensus and buy-in and builds momentum for implementation.

Getting on the Inside

The process by which managers come into the inner circle is subtle, informal, and subjective. Indeed, there is no reason for a CEO to openly state that some managers are more important or influential than others. At the same time, the CEO has a vested interest in getting the best counsel. Thus, a number of factors likely come into play. The CEO's shared experience with another manager, for example, may be a key. A shared set of values about the business, the industry, or the way issues should be approached and addressed could be another. A CEO may recognize key talents possessed by a member of the TMT or may simply find some managers easier to connect with than others. It could simply be that there are some members of the TMT that the CEO trusts more than others. All of these factors, alone or in combination, could affect which managers are most closely involved in specific strategic decisions.

In the case of the Cuban Missile Crisis (Allison, 1971), the connection between the

President and the members of his inner circle was clear. The Attorney General was Robert Kennedy, brother to the President and a trusted political ally. The Secretary of Defense was Robert McNamara, a respected intellectual, with a reputation for independent thinking, who shared a strong bond of common values and purpose with the President and his brother. The final member of the group was Theodore Sorensen, Special Counsel to and speechwriter for the President; it was Sorensen who wrote the President's famous inaugural address. Early in the crisis these three individuals emerged as the "triple alliance" on whose advice the President would most heavily lean and against whose judgments the President would test the input and ideas of the other members of the Executive Committee (ibid., p. 203).

At TechnoCo the connections were similarly clear. The CEO and two members of the inner circle had shared a long tenure, both at TechnoCo and a previous firm. They had worked together at the previous firm and followed the CEO soon after he accepted this new job. The other member of the inner circle was not connected by tenure but by a common passion for competition. Both shared a similar view of the industry, a similar us-against-the-world outlook, and held a similar view on TechnoCo's position and strategy. Together, these four were very similar in terms of their outlook on the industry, priorities for the firm, and strategic imperatives. While they often disagreed, they did so privately and with an assurance of openness and trust. When before the rest of the TMT, they typically worked together, pushing a common agenda and articulating a common view.

Given these examples and the literature supporting the notion, it seems likely that most CEOs would cultivate an inner circle within the TMT. The members of that inner circle would be key managers, whose experiences, connections, and values served to elevate them in the eyes of the CEO. Two familiar theoretical perspectives suggest how this inner circle might develop. First, similarity/attraction (Byrne, 1971) speaks to the comfort and familiarity of the connection between a CEO and the members of the inner circle. Second, information processing (Galbraith, 1973) speaks to the need for CEOs to supplement their own understanding with specific skills or expertise, as necessary to insure good outcomes.

Similarity/attraction and the inner circle
The similarity/attraction paradigm provides a simple and yet powerful explanation of how a top manager might come to the inner circle. In essence, people are attracted to others like themselves (Byrne, 1971). That attraction can occur across a range of characteristics, including attitudes, values, and demographic variables and can reflect both affective and cognitive mechanisms (Moss et al., 1975).

In terms of affect, similarity may improve the sense of identity an individual feels as well as the cohesion of the group (O'Reilly et al., 1989). It may also help to limit the level of disaffection or personal friction ignited by disagreement (Pelled, 1996). In terms of cognition and information processing, similarity may influence an individual's communication patterns as well as the formality and openness of the relationships within a team (Zenger and Lawrence, 1989; Smith et al., 1994). Given these strong and pervasive affects, dissimilarity within teams has been associated with decreased information exchange, increased personal tension and friction, as well as greater turnover, stress, and dissatisfaction (Tsui and O'Reilly, 1989).

At the same time, there are important benefits of dissimilarity (Jackson, 1992). Research suggests dissimilar teams are able to process more complex information and to better consider multiple alternatives in parallel. They are able to better test underlying assumptions, to stimulate more creative and unorthodox thinking, and to encourage commitment and consensus once a decision is reached. As a result, heterogeneity among the membership and the inclusion of multiple and diverse perspectives within the TMT has become an accepted idea and practice.

Given the range of potentially positive and negative outcomes that can result from dissimilarity among top management (Hambrick et al., 1996), it makes sense that a CEO would seek to gain the benefits while avoiding the costs. One way of doing that would be to have a large and diverse TMT but to also have a smaller, more familiar inner circle. Roberto (2003) describes such a structure, where membership in the "dominant coalition is rather fluid, typically consisting of a stable core group combined with a dynamic periphery" (p. 123). Given the pervasiveness of the similarity/attraction phenomenon and the importance to the CEO of listening especially to those opinions in which he or she puts the greatest trust, it makes sense that the inner circle would consist of managers who are similar to the CEO in terms of experience and perspective.

In support of this thinking is the research on relational demography (Tsui and O'Reilly, 1989). The relational demography view offers two insights of particular importance here. First, similarity has strong effects at the dyadic level. While typically used as a team-level construct, similarity can have powerful influence on the way individuals see and relate to one another on a one-to-one basis. Second, those dyadic effects appear to transcend the effects of formal position. As a result, a manager may behave differently toward one subordinate than another based on their demographic similarity. Tsui and O'Reilly (1989) explain that demographic similarity is "associated with attitudinal and value similarity, which may enhance interpersonal attraction and increased frequency of communication" (p. 420). This attraction between manager and subordinate translates into better attitudes towards, and perceptions and evaluations of subordinates by the supervisors. Stated plainly, sharing some key characteristics with the CEO can serve to elevate a subordinate in the eyes of that CEO.

As seen in the examples above, CEOs will feel more comfortable with those with whom they share basic characteristics. That comfort will translate into more frequent communication and greater affinity. Thus, according to the similarity/attraction perspective, those managers who share basic demographics and experiential similarity with the CEO should be more likely to be included in the inner circle and so to be more involved in strategic decision making. On the other hand, those managers who differ from the CEO in terms of basic demography and experience should be less likely to be included in the inner circle and so less involved in strategic decision making.

Information processing and the inner circle
Research offers another rationale by which managers are included in the inner circle. The information-processing perspective (Galbraith, 1973) explains why CEOs may intentionally seek out dissimilarity. To understand, recall that TMTs face substantial ambiguity and issues of substantial importance (Mintzberg et al., 1976). Their complex tasks necessitate complex information-processing capability (Galbraith, 1973). Diverse skills and experiences can facilitate information processing (Haleblian and Finkelstein,

1993). Similarity/attraction effects then may serve to limit the ability of a team to deal with highly complex issues effectively. As a result, CEOs may purposefully seek out those who can span specific boundaries or offer specific skills and abilities.

A CEO whose inner circle has too little breadth could easily become isolated from parts of the organization or from certain points of view. While familiar and comfortable in the short term, such isolation could, over time, lead to poorer decisions and limited ability to motivate and lead across the breadth of the organization. Too much similarity could create a self-replicating momentum, where managers gain access to the inner circle by espousing values and views similar to the CEO. Those managers would then affirm the opinions, calculations, and judgments of the CEO, reinforcing the insular nature of the inner circle and restricting access even further for those outside the group. Indeed, a number of studies were conducted on decision-making techniques, such as dialectical inquiry and devil's advocacy, designed to counter the effects of premature consensus and inadequate examination of assumptions and biases (Schwenk, 1989; Schweiger et al., 1989). Introducing some dissimilarity when developing the inner circle could facilitate better decision making by interjecting a measure of balance and scrutiny.

AN EMPIRICAL TEST OF THE INNER CIRCLE

Given that decades have passed since Thompson (1967) introduced the notion of the inner circle and that strong theoretical and anecdotal evidence supports its existence, it is surprising that with the exception of Roberto (2003) we know of no empirical research on the phenomenon. Thus, we conducted an empirical test of inner circles. The study focused on two basic research questions. The first was a relatively simple one and was focused on the question of whether an inner circle indeed exists. Provided evidence was found for the existence of inner circles, we then pursued a second research question that was more complex and focused on the manner by which the CEO selects individuals for the inner circle.

Our study focused on the top management teams of 40 public firms. We included these top management teams in our study because the CEOs of these firms responded to our survey. Specifically, we mailed surveys and made follow-up phone calls to 200 CEOs randomly selected from the database of the Chief Executive Leadership Institute, a non-profit leadership development organization that holds CEO conferences and other special events. The 40 firms reflected a usable response rate of 20 percent.

In the survey, we asked the CEO to record those individuals who were involved in a specific strategic decision. Concurrently, we reviewed the SEC (US Securities & Exchange Commission) filings for the 40 firms who responded to the survey, and recorded all non-CEO executives who were listed as being part of the top management team (335 executives).

Recall that our first research question focused on whether an inner circle exists. Based on our review of the literature and our own experience with top management teams, we expected that an inner circle would exist and that it would represent a subgroup of the top management team. Consistent with our expectations, the CEO of all 40 firms reported that a smaller subset of the top management team was engaged in strategic decision making. The CEO, on average, identified 4.6 individuals as being involved in strategic decision making in contrast to the average TMT size (as reported in the SEC filings) of 9.4. Moreover, nearly all – 182 out of 184 executives – listed by the CEO were also listed in the SEC filings, showing that the CEO drew his or her inner circle members from top management (versus selecting inner circle members from lower ranks of the firm, or outside the firm).

Our second research question focused on how the CEO selects his or her inner circle. As discussed above, the similarity/attraction and information processing perspectives both suggest that the CEO selects inner circle members based on judgments about the characteristics of top managers, that is, potential inner circle members, vis-à-vis characteristics of the CEO. The two perspectives, however, present competing predictions about how those judgments are made. The similarity/attraction perspective (Byrne, 1971) supports a CEO selecting individuals with whom he or she has the most in common, as such commonalities have been shown to promote more frequent communication, greater affinity, and an improved ease in interacting and working together. The information-processing perspective (Galbraith, 1973) supports a CEO selecting individuals who offer different skills and experiences than the CEO. Based on this perspective, CEOs would seek out such differences because they provide greater cognitive breadth, which improves the ability to make complex decisions.

To test these theoretical perspectives, we collected data from the firm's SEC filings[2] on common demographic and experiential characteristics, including age, job and firm tenure, gender, board membership, and functional experience. We then calculated how similar or different TMT members were from the CEO along these characteristics. For age, job tenure, and firm tenure, we followed Tsui and O'Reilly's (1989) approach and squared the absolute value of the differences between the CEO's score and the TMT member's score. For gender, board membership, and functional specialty, we included dummy codes. For gender, a "1" meant the TMT member was a different gender from the CEO, and a "0" meant they were the same gender. For board membership, a "1" meant the TMT member did not sit on the board of directors (BOD) with the CEO, and a "0" meant they both sat on the board. For functional experience, a "1" meant the TMT member and the CEO did not have any functional experiences in common, and a "0" meant they had at least one functional experience in common.[3] Using ANOVA (analysis of variants), we then compared these CEO–TMT member difference measures above across two groups – those top managers who were included in the inner circle with those managers who were not included in the inner circle (see Table 2.1 for results).

Our results provided evidence that CEOs have a tendency to select inner circle members who are similar to themselves. That is, the inner circle members in our study shared significantly more in common with the CEO than the top management team members outside the inner circle. Specifically, we found that inner circle members were significantly more similar to the CEO than other TMT members in four of the six characteristics we examined – job tenure, firm tenure, board membership, and gender. We did not find support that the inner circle members are significantly more similar or different than the CEO for the other two characteristics we examined – age and functional experience.

Table 2.1   Results of ANOVA test

	Means	F
Squared age difference	Inner circle: 118.9	1.12
	Outside circle: 101.8	
Squared job tenure difference	Inner circle: 22.4	3.42*
	Outside circle: 36.8	
Squared firm tenure difference	Inner circle: 69.6	5.89*
	Outside circle: 128.3	
Gender difference	Inner circle: 0.08	5.01*
	Outside circle: 0.17	
Membership on BOD difference	Inner circle: 0.03	5.04*
	Outside circle: 0.08	
Functional experience difference	Inner circle: 0.24	0.82
	Outside circle: 20	

Note: * $p < 0.05$.

Source: Authors' research.

DISCUSSION AND FUTURE RESEARCH

Our point in this paper is simple; the TMT is typically not the core, strategic decision-making body that it is often thought to be. Rather, a smaller, more intimate group with close connections to the CEO forms an inner circle, within the TMT, exercising immediate and direct influence over strategic decision making and directing the course of the firm overall. This view complements Hambrick's (1994) contention that TMTs could be more accurately called top management groups. Moreover, viewing the TMT in this way, as a relatively large group of managers, representing the range of top offices in the organization, with a smaller, inner circle of closely knit individuals, is consistent with theorizing by Thompson (1967) and with observations offered by Allison (1971).

This picture of the TMT was confirmed by our data. Across the 40 firms, the actual strategic decision-making groups were substantially smaller, averaging 4.6 members, than the full TMTs, which averaged 9.4 members, suggesting that an inner circle exists. Moreover, our data suggests that TMT members are more likely to get into the inner circle when they share much in common with the CEO. Indeed, team members who made it to the inner circle were significantly more similar to the CEO than other TMT members in terms of age, gender, job tenure, firm tenure, and board membership. These patterns are consistent with the similarity/attraction affect identified by Byrne (1971) and Roberto (2003).

Despite our findings, we suspect that the information-processing perspective (Galbraith, 1973) plays a role in explaining how CEOs select TMT members to be in his or her inner circle. Recall that the information-processing perspective emphasizes the importance of including the strongest cognitive capabilities in the decision-making group, due to the complexity of strategic decisions. This perspective then would lead to CEOs being inclined to consult TMT members with different backgrounds and expertise as such differences would broaden the cognitive capabilities of the inner circle. Although we didn't find any support for this approach, a more nuanced examination of inner circles, especially with a larger sample size, might yield interesting findings.

In particular, we suspect that there are certain conditions that might weaken the tendency for CEOs to select like-minded inner circle members, and consider information-processing demands. These conditions, or moderators, fall into four main areas – the nature of the CEO, the firm, the board, and the industry. For example, CEOs who are newer to a firm might be more apt to seek diverse talents and backgrounds as they lack the requisite firm knowledge to make informed strategic decisions. This is consistent with Keck and Tushman (1993) who found that a CEO's newness in the firm resulted in more diverse top management teams.

With regard to the nature of the firm, it seems likely that CEOs of firms that have performed poorly would be more motivated to compose a diverse inner circle in the hopes that such diversity will lead to different, more effective decision-making processes. CEOs with boards that are more vigilant should also be more motivated to select diverse inner circles members as those CEOs would need to justify to the board more thoroughly the decisions that were made and the decision processes that were followed.

Finally, we suspect that the nature of the industry might impact a CEO's selection of the inner circle. For example, CEOs in industries with high product differentiability and unstable demand seem more likely to confront more complex issues for which they may not have adequate cognitive wherewithal. As a result, it seems plausible that the CEO would include a more diverse group of managers in the decision-making process.

We omitted these moderating conditions from the empirical test presented in this chapter due to inadequate data, but encourage researchers to explore these in future research. We also encourage future research to consider the nature of the decision to glean how inner circles function across decision contexts. Roberto (2003) found that there was an inner circle that made most decisions (he referred to this as the "stable core") and that this group was often supplemented with other TMT members on a decision-specific basis (he referred to this as the "dynamic periphery"). Reconsidering Roberto's research in light of our findings, it may be that the CEO selects the inner circle based on similarity/attraction forces, and supplements this group if needed based more on the information-processing needs of the decisions that must be made.

Future research should also explore more fully the consequences of inner circles. As Hambrick (1994) notes, TMTs are not really teams at all, at least not in the traditional sense. It may well be that they never function as a team, all at once, making a key strategic decision. Yet, they are the reservoir from which the actual, inner circle of decision makers is drawn. Each CEO draws from the ranks of top management, that core group of trusted advisors that he or she will rely on most heavily. While this inner circle may function as a team, its business is often conducted out of sight and its processes are often difficult to observe and measure. So, we focus on the full TMT. It should come as no surprise then that this team often functions in a way that is inconsistent with our expectations.

For example, consider Bantel and Jackson's (1989) study relating TMTs to innovations in the banking industry. While all 198 of the TMTs in their sample were defined and measured in the same way, not all of those TMTs were similarly involved in actual strategic decision making. Indeed, it is very likely that a different subset of each of those

198 teams made the decisions that led to the measured outcomes. Each team had its own CEO, with his or her own background, interests, and biases. And each team likely had its own inner circle, which was a reflection of the interests, biases, and backgrounds of the different CEOs. Thus, by focusing on the entire team, Bantel and Jackson (1989) introduced into their analysis a source of statistical noise that actually obfuscated the effect that they were attempting to document and measure. The same would be true of many other TMT studies as well.

A stronger understanding of inner circles may provide greater opportunity to those seeking to connect managerial actions to firm outcomes. That is, inner circles may represent one more avenue by which CEO priorities and values are translated into outcomes at the organizational level. For example, a CEO who relies on an inner circle made up of like-minded individuals may be more able to push his or her agenda through than a CEO who seeks council from a diverse set of advisors. On the other hand, relying on a like-minded inner circle might be good in that it helps improve the speed and efficiency of decision making and may improve the communication of strategic decisions, which can lead to stronger strategy implementation (Guth and MacMillan, 1986). To tease out these effects, we encourage research to also consider the intermediate effects of inner circle membership on decisions process like social integration (O'Reilly et al., 1989) and task and relationship conflict (Amason, 1996).

Understanding the inner circle may also give new insights into the sources of dysfunction within TMTs. As described in the examples above, the recognition of an inner circle may serve to demotivate those other managers in the TMT. Those other managers may be less assertive, less connected to organizational issues outside of their own areas, and less willing to take risks as necessary to advance their own ideas and or to address issues they see as problematic.

We also believe our findings might offer interesting insights into gender issues in TMTs. Recall that the inner circles we examined were comprised of executives who were more likely to be the same gender as the CEO than those executives outside the inner circle. Given that in 2009, 485 of the Fortune 500 firms were run by a male CEO,[4] it isn't a stretch to conclude based on our results that those CEOs may be forming inner circles that are predominantly male. This possibility calls into question whether women, who have made such progress in attaining top management positions, are really performing key roles in directing firms than heretofore believed, which may have important consequences for not only the advancement of women but the outcomes of those firms.

CONCLUSIONS

Although modest, these findings are exciting and we hope that others will share our enthusiasm for this line of inquiry. Perhaps the TMT is not the key strategic actor that many have thought. Perhaps instead, the TMT represents the bench strength or potential energy of the firm's top management, who, to stay with the analogy, are fully effective only when catalyzed by a CEO and a set of circumstances to which they are especially fit.

Research on inner circles might also help to help explain how CEOs influence firm outcomes. It has always been surprising to us as TMT researchers that the press and business community continue to focus predominantly on the CEO rather than on the

TMT, given all we've learned from TMT research. For example, in a two-year period, we counted a total of 640 articles that were published on either CEOs or upper echelons/ TMTs in the *Wall Street Journal*, the *Financial Times*, and *Business Week*. Of these articles, 589 or 92 percent focused on the CEO alone, while only 51 or 8 percent focused on the top management team. If the firm is truly a reflection of its TMT, then why do so many still pay so much attention to just the CEO? One possible answer to that question is this: the CEO is singularly important because it is the CEO who cultivates and empowers that inner circle of decision makers who actually do guide the firm. For example, consider again Allison's (1971) description of the Cuban Missile Crisis. Certainly Robert Kennedy, Robert McNamara, and Theodore Sorensen were among the most significant actors within the Executive Committee. Their inputs and concerns guided the President's thinking and shaped the policy that emerged from his office. Yet, none of these men would have exercised such influence had President Kennedy not appointed them to their offices and then chosen to listen to them above the others. In understanding that the CEO selects those managers who will exercise the most immediate and meaningful decision-making authority, we begin to see the top management team in a somewhat different light.

ACKNOWLEDGMENTS

The authors would like to thank Jeff Sonnenfeld and the Chief Executive Leadership Institute for their help in collecting data.

NOTES

1. See Jones and Cannella in Chapter 1 for an alternative viewpoint on strategic decision making and TMT configurations.
2. In some cases (<10 percent), the bios included in the SEC filings did not provide us the data we needed. We then turned to alternate sources, including *Who's Who in Finance and Industry; Standard & Poor's Register of Corporations, Directors, and Executives; Dun & Bradstreet's Reference Book of Corporate Managements*; and the firm's website.
3. Note that we determined functional experience by listing all functional area(s) with which the TMT member and CEO had experience by using eight functional area codes (General Administrative; Marketing; Finance; Engineering and R&D; Operations and Manufacturing; Information Systems; Human Resources; Legal). We reviewed bios from the most recent as well as all past SEC filings.
4. http://money.cnn.com/magazines/fortune/fortune500/2009/womenceos/, accessed 14 July 2010.

REFERENCES

Allison, G.T. (1971). *The essence of decision: Explaining the Cuban Missile Crisis*. Boston, MA: Little Brown.
Amason, A.C. (1996). Distinguishing the effects of functional and dysfunctional conflict on strategic decision making: Resolving a paradox for top management teams. *Academy of Management Journal*, **39**(1), 123–48.
Arendt, L.A., Priem, R.L., and Ndofor, H.A. (2005). A CEO-adviser model of strategic decision making. *Journal of Management*, **31**(5), 680–99.
Bantel, K. and Jackson, S. (1989). Top management and innovations in banking: Does the composition of the top team make a difference? *Strategic Management Journal*, **10**(S1), 107–24.
Byrne, D. (1971). The ubiquitous relationship: Attitude similarity and attraction. *Human Relations*, **24**(3), 201–7.

Cannella, A.A. and Hambrick, D.C. (1993). Effects of executive departures on the performance of acquired firms. *Strategic Management Journal*, **14**(S), 137–52.

Cannella A.A., Park, J.H., and Lee, H.U. (2008). Top management team functional background diversity and firm performance: Examining the roles of team member colocation and environmental uncertainty. *Academy of Management Journal*, **51**(4), 768–84.

Carpenter, M.A. and Fredrickson, J.W. (2001). Top management teams, global strategic posture, and the moderating role of uncertainty. *Academy of Management Journal*, **44**(3), 533–45.

Child, J. (1972). Organizational structure, environment, and performance: The role of strategic choice. *Sociology*, **6**(1), 1–22.

Coase, R. (1937). The nature of the firm. *Economica*, **4**(16), 386–405.

Colbert, A.E., Kristof-Brown, A.L., Bradley, B.H., and Barrick, M.R. (2008). CEO transformational leadership: The role of goal importance congruence in top management teams. *Academy of Management Journal*, **51**(1), 81–96.

Cyert, R.M. and March, J.G. (1963). *The behavioral theory of the firm*. Cambridge, MA: Blackwell Business.

Dutton, J.E. and Jackson, S.E. (1987). Categorizing strategic issues: Links to organizational action. *Academy of Management Review*, **12**(1), 76–90.

Dutton, J.E., Fahey, L., and Narayanan, V.K. (1983). Toward understanding strategic issue diagnosis. *Strategic Management Journal*, **4**(4), 43–60.

Finkelstein, S. (1992). Power in top management teams: Dimensions, measurement, and validation. *Academy of Management Journal*, **35**(3), 505–38.

Finkelstein, S. and Hambrick, D.C. (1996). *Strategic leadership: Top executives and their effects on organizations*. Minneapolis/St. Paul: West Educational Publishing.

Finkelstein, S., Hambrick, D.C., and Cannella, A. (2009). *Strategic leadership: Theory and research on executives, top management teams, and boards*, Oxford, UK: Oxford University Press.

Flatt, S. (1993). A longitudinal study in organizational innovativeness: How top management team demography influences organizational innovation. PhD dissertation. Berkeley: University of California.

Fredrickson, J.W. and Iaquinto, A.L. (1985). Inertia and creeping rationality in strategic decision processes. *Academy of Management Journal*, **32**(3), 516–42.

Galbraith, J. (1973). *Designing complex organizations*. Reading, MA: Addison-Wesley.

Guth, W. and MacMillan, I. (1986). Strategy implementation versus middle management self-interest. *Strategic Management Journal*, **7**(4), 313–27.

Haleblian, J. and Finkelstein, S. (1993). Top management team size, CEO dominance, and firm performance. *Academy of Management Journal*, **36**(4), 844–63.

Hambrick, D.C. (1994). Top management groups: A conceptual integration and reconsideration of the "team" label. In B.M. Staw and L.L. Cummings (eds), *Research in organizational behavior*. Greenwich, CT: JAI Press, pp. 171–214.

Hambrick, D.C. and Mason, P.A. (1984). Upper echelons: The organization as a reflection of its top managers. *Academy of Management Review*, **9**(2), 193–206.

Hambrick, D.C., Cho, T.S., and Chen, M.J. (1996). The influence of top management team heterogeneity on firms' competitive moves. *Administrative Science Quarterly*, **41**(4), 659–84.

Jackson, S.E. (1992). Consequence of group composition for the interpersonal dynamics of strategic issue processing. *Advances in Strategic Management*, **8**, 345–82.

Jensen, M. and Zajac, E.J. (2004). Corporate elites and corporate strategy: How demographic preferences and structural position shape the scope of the firm. *Strategic Management Journal*, **25**(6), 507–24.

Julian, S.D. and Ofori-Dankwa, J.C. (2008). Toward an integrative cartography of two strategic issue diagnosis frameworks. *Strategic Management Journal*, **29**(1), 963–84.

Keck, S. and Tushman, M. (1993). Environmental and organizational context and executive team structure. *Academy of Management Journal*, **36**(6), 1314–44.

Marlin, D., Lamont, B.T., and Geiger, S.W. (2004). Diversification strategy and top management team fit. *Journal of Managerial Issues*, **16**(3), 361–81.

Mintzberg, H., Raisinghani, D., and Theoret, A. (1976). The structure of unstructured decision processes. *Administrative Science Quarterly*, **21**(2), 246–75.

Moss, M.K., Byrne, D., Baskett, G.D., and Sachs, D.H. (1975). Informational versus affective determinants of interpersonal attraction. *Journal of Social Psychology*, **95**, 39–53.

O'Reilly, C.A., Caldwell, D.F., and Barnett, W.P. (1989). Work group demography, social integration, and turnover. *Administrative Science Quarterly*, **34**(1), 21–37.

Pelled, L.H. (1996). Demographic diversity, conflict, and work group outcomes: An intervening process theory. *Organization Science*, **7**(6), 615–31.

Roberto, M.A. (2003). The stable core and the dynamic periphery in top management teams. *Management Decision*, **41**(2), 120–31.

Schweiger, D.M., Sandberg, W.R., and Ragan, J.W. (1986). Group approaches for improving strategic decision making: A comparative analysis of dialectical inquiry, devil's advocacy and consensus. *Academy of Management Journal*, **29**(1), 51–71.

Schwenk, C. (1989). A meta-analysis on the comparative effectiveness of devil's advocacy and dialectical inquiry. *Strategic Management Journal*, **10**(3), 303–6.

Smith, K.G., Smith, K.A., Olian, J.D., Sims, Jr., H.P., O'Bannon, D.P., and Scully, J.A. (1994). Top management team demography and process: The role of social integration and communication. *Administrative Science Quarterly*, **39**(3), 412–38.

Sutcliffe, K. (1994). What executives notice: Accurate perceptions in top management teams. *Academy of Management Journal*, **37**(5), 1360–78.

Thomas, J. and McDaniel, R. (1990). Interpreting strategic issues: Effects of strategic and the information processing structure of top management teams. *Academy of Management Journal*, **33**(2), 286–306.

Thompson, J.D. (1967). *Organizations in action*. New York, NY: McGraw-Hill.

Tsui, A. and O'Reilly, C.A. (1989). Beyond simple demographic effects: The importance of relational demography in superior-subordinate dyads. *Academy of Management Journal*, **32**(2), 402–23.

Wiersema, M.F. and Bantel, K.A. (1992). Top management team demography and corporate strategic change. *Academy of Management Journal*, **35**(1), 91–121.

Zenger T.R. and Lawrence, B.S. (1989). Organizational demography: The differential esffects of age and tenure distributions on technical communication. *Academy of Management Journal*, **32**(2), 353–76.

3 Bringing organizational demography back in: time, change, and structure in top management team research

Christine M. Beckman and M. Diane Burton

Organizational scholars have achieved broad consensus on two facts: the era of the loyal "organization man" is over, and traditional large bureaucracies are being replaced by new organizational forms. Commentators in both the popular press and the scholarly literature have documented the myriad ways that jobs at all levels are less secure and how both organizations and employees are less loyal (cf., Cappelli, 1999; Osterman, 1999). These changes in the nature of the employment relationship are particularly visible in the executive ranks. The promotions and ousters of corporate leaders that are core to academic theories of governance and motivation are chronicled in the press in colorful detail. Executive tenure has declined and executive mobility is facilitated by professional executive search firms (Khurana, 2002). At the same time, we see widespread change in how organizations are designed and managed (Barley, 1992; Guillen, 1994); and in different eras, different organizational forms dominate (e.g., functional, divisional, and matrix forms; see Chandler, 1962; Davis et al., 1994; Shenhav, 2000; Zuckerman, 2000). We have seen the rise (Fligstein, 1987) and fall (Davis, 2009) of financial capitalism, and the emergence of new executive roles such as the Chief Operating Officer (COO) (Hambrick and Cannella, 2004) and the Chief Financial Officer (CFO) (Zorn, 2004; Zorn et al., 2004). Given the known game of musical chairs in the executive suite as people come and go, and the extensive changes in organizational structures that change the chairs drawn up to the table, it is surprising that most scholarship on top management team (TMT) demography is cross-sectional in nature and implicitly treats the TMT as a stable entity.

In the 25 years following the publication of Hambrick and Mason's (1984) "Upper echelon theory" and Pfeffer's (1983) "Organizational demography," TMT research has been one of the most vibrant research areas in organizational studies. Researchers have conducted an impressive array of studies linking TMT characteristics to such factors as organizational performance, strategic change, and turnover. Despite these vigorous efforts, attempts to synthesize the cumulative wisdom have been unproductive. The findings are often contradictory, the methods and measures inconsistent, and the theoretical underpinnings poorly specified (Finkelstein and Hambrick, 1996; Jackson et al., 2003; Carpenter et al., 2004; Cannella et al., 2008; Nielsen, 2009).

There have been many excellent reviews of the broader TMT literature: Williams and O'Reilly (1998) reviewed over 80 articles published between 1959 and 1997 on organizational demography and diversity (not TMT demography in particular); Jackson et al. (2003) reviewed 63 articles on workplace diversity published between 1997 and 2002; Carpenter et al. (2004) identified 31 TMT articles that build on upper echelons theory between 1996 and 2003; Nielsen (2009) reviewed 60 articles on TMT heterogeneity published between 1984 and 2005. All of these reviews document the vibrancy of the research area as well as the conflicting findings. We do not attempt a comprehensive review. Instead, we highlight features of the TMT literature that are barriers to accumulation and synthesis: it combines two perspectives on TMTs that are in many ways incommensurate and in doing so conflate roles and individuals; and it relies on cross-sectional methods and static analyses in a setting that is necessarily dynamic and sensitive to historical context.

In brief, TMT research embodies two distinct traditions: one focused on top managers as a team of strategic leaders and the other focused on top management demographics as a reflection of an organization. Important, but largely unstated, differences in the units of analysis and the mechanisms of interest exist across these two traditions. The strategic leadership perspective is rooted in psychology and managerial behavior and emphasizes the individual and group levels of analysis. The demographic perspective is rooted in sociology and organization studies and emphasizes the organizational level of analysis. These different traditions draw on different underlying theories (e.g., social cohesion vs. human capital) and are often focused at a different level of analysis (e.g., team vs. firm). For example, the strategic leadership perspective centers on group processes while the demographic perspective concentrates on the structural conditions that shape team interactions. From at least the mid-1990s the strategic leadership perspective has dominated, and as a result the field has lost sight of two important considerations: structure and temporal dynamics.

Advancing our understanding of top management teams and organizations requires that we give renewed attention to the sociological perspective. Doing so forces us to consider both the antecedents of TMT composition as well as the consequences. It demands that we recognize that as the world changes, firms change and teams change. It also reminds us that strong causal inferences are impossible from cross-sectional research. It suggests that role structures are distinct from individual executives. Refocusing away from individual interactions towards structure and context allows us to better incorporate the lessons of change from the broader field of organization studies. The path to developing a deep understanding of TMTs and organizations is a research agenda that (1) considers structural roles beyond individual incumbents, (2) attends to historical time and context, and (3) acknowledges and examines when roles and the individuals occupying those roles change. In this chapter we outline such a research agenda and articulate the need for historically contextualized analyses and longitudinal research designs. Our agenda points to new questions to ask about TMT structure (e.g., how does the duration of a job shape the tenure of an individual in that job? and do team structures predict role interdependence?) and calls into question some key areas of TMT research (i.e., methodological problems and exogenous antecedents to tenure and functional heterogeneity). We conclude by illustrating important areas for future research.

TWO TRADITIONS OF TMT RESEARCH

Current understandings of top management teams and organizations embody two very different conceptualizations of the phenomena. In the strategic leadership tradition, top management teams represent collective leadership responsible for determining and executing organizational strategy and driving organizational performance (i.e., Finkelstein et al., 2009). In the organizational demography tradition, top management teams are a visible representation of the organizational workforce and a convenient proxy for otherwise unobservable characteristics of human resources and culture (i.e., Sørensen, 2000). These alternative conceptualizations tend to focus attention on different features of top management teams and organizations. Where strategic leadership has emphasized individual discretion and personality, organizational demography has attended to industry and labor market characteristics. These alternative conceptualizations also yield different interpretations of the same top management team features. Where the strategic leadership perspective sees cognition and interpersonal processes, the organizational demography perspective sees mobility and structure. More generally, where the strategic leadership perspective sees opportunity and transformation, the organizational demography perspective sees inertia and constraint. These differences aren't surprising as the strategic leadership perspective evolved from an interest in managerial characteristics to focus on Chief Executive Officers (CEOs) and multi-person teams; in contrast, organizational demography emerged from interest in organizational populations. But theoretical and empirical progress within both traditions has brought them into overlapping territory. We must now explicitly examine the intersection and integrate across the traditions. We begin by reexamining the common roots for both traditions.

Both Pfeffer (1983) and Hambrick and Mason (1984), in their early formulations of organizational demography and upper echelons theory, argued that background characteristics can be used to predict behavior. Hambrick and Mason (1984) argued that organizational outcomes (such as innovation and growth), as well as strategic actions, are shaped by background characteristics of managers and top management teams in particular. These background characteristics were seen as indicators of the cognitions and values of boundedly rational executives. Pfeffer (1983) went further and argued that demographic composition may predict outcomes better than intervening constructs. This approach of emphasizing the background characteristics was methodologically appealing, even if somewhat noisy (Hambrick and Mason, 1984), and resulted in a flurry of research. The resulting large body of empirical research linked aggregate measures of team composition (e.g., functional heterogeneity, age diversity, tenure diversity) to firm-level outcomes.

More than a decade later, Lawrence (1997) argued it was important to open the "black box" and understand the processes by which demographic composition matters. She and other scholars suggested that the direct effects of composition on strategic choices are not likely to be robust and instead advocated the need to examine the intermediate processes (Finkelstein et al., 2009). As a result, the upper echelons perspective has increasingly moved towards examining social psychological processes and individual perceptions and beliefs and links demographic variables with team-level variables such as cohesion, consensus, social integration, and cognitive heterogeneity (Jackson et al., 2003; Finkelstein et al., 2009; Nielsen, 2009). This move required going inside organizations and directly asking executive teams about their attitudes, information sharing, communication frequency, conflict, and commitment. The top management team has, in large part, been treated as just another kind of small group. Although valuable insights come from these micro-theories, it is time to close the "black box." The primary focus on internal processes effectively eliminated from examination the historical and structural factors that are antecedents of TMT composition, ignored major shifts and trends in the organizational world, and clouded our ability to see what is distinctive about TMTs.

Although the bulk of TMT research relies on micro-level social psychological theories for explanation, some scholars persist with a more macro-level demographic perspective, a perspective that comes from a broad tradition in sociology that studies populations and population change. This macro-level perspective relies on patterns of data, rather than focusing on individuals, and focuses attention on events such as entrances and exits. More importantly, this perspective examines both the causes and consequences of demographic distributions. As one example, Carroll and Harrison (1998) argue for focusing on a global macro-concept (in their case, culture) that can explain demographic patterns. Using a computer simulation, they demonstrate that using the global concept of culture can explain differences in tenure heterogeneity. This example documents one way to draw inferences from demographic data without resorting to social psychological theories.

Why do we focus on "simplistic" demographic variables when scholars decry that we do not need "yet another study that examines the main effect of TMT demographic effects on another organizational outcome" (Carpenter et al., 2004, p. 770)? Beyond parsimony and easy measurement, there are important empirical and theoretical insights that come from the demographic tradition.

First, TMT demography offers a window into organizations. The structure of the TMT can be a stand-in for the structure of the organization. Is it hierarchical? Is it diverse? We see by the titles and backgrounds of TMT members what functions are valued (Fligstein, 1987); by the promotion and tenure patterns whether time in the organization is an asset or a detriment (Dencker, 2009); and we receive some insight into organizational stratification by race and gender by looking at the composition of the TMT (Broschak et al., 1998). As titles change and new roles emerge, we see shifting managerial ideologies. By treating the TMT as representing the organization, we begin to address how and why the characteristics of organizations are changing over time. By emphasizing the top management team as a "team," and focusing on the group processes and individual attributes of team members, we lose sight of inequality and discrimination in organizations. The level of hierarchy and heterogeneity in a TMT is not only relevant because of how it affects decision-making processes in teams but also because it reflects inequality and diversity in the organization. The fact that the vast majority of TMT demography studies predict organizational-level outcomes may suggest that leaders influence strategic actions (Jackson et al., 2003). But it also suggests that TMTs are a microcosm of the organization and provide insights about both the organization as a whole and about organizational processes.

Second, as the link to population studies suggests, and key scholars have acknowledged, organizational demography allows us to connect the organization with the larger context in which it is embedded. Williams and O'Reilly (1998) begin their review with an example and acknowledgment of the changing nature of teams over the last 50 years. Changes in demographic diversity, they argue, are critical to understanding workplaces today; indeed, one explanation for the mixed findings is that the firms themselves look demographically different than when Hambrick and Mason (1984) first wrote. In the field of demography writ large, researchers collect annual surveys to track this constant flux. Surprisingly, we do not see the TMT literature examining what happens within the larger population and labor market constraints and how these influence organizational dynamics. Yet labor market changes, as well as changes in organizational forms, shape mobility within and thus the demography of organizations (Haveman and Cohen, 1994).

Third, the broader demographic tradition explores the factors that influence demographic distributions and their consequences. Despite numerous calls, our understanding of the antecedents of TMT demography remain limited (Pettigrew, 1992; Lawrence, 1997; Williams and O'Reilly, 1998; Hambrick, 2007). While TMT scholars have made some progress in considering context – for example, there is considerable evidence that heterogeneous TMTs are more successful in turbulent environments (e.g., Eisenhardt and Schoonhoven, 1990; Keck, 1997; Certo et al., 2006) – this research generally considers context as an important moderator of demographic effects and has involved largely static considerations of the effects of industry and environmental context (Jackson et al., 2003). However, both industries and environments change over time and this raises important questions for TMT scholars. For example, how does a team change from that which is successful in the dynamic, fast-paced environment of a start-up to one that can effectively lead in a period of more industry- and firm-level stability? To say that a firm requires a heterogeneous team in a dynamic environment does not help us understand how firms come to have heterogeneous teams. Our own research on 170 high-technology companies suggests that the answers to these questions are both considerable and complex. For example, despite a need to do so, some firms find it difficult to broaden the experience of the TMT. The personnel decisions and structural choices made early in a firm's life have long-lasting influences on the recruitment and retention of new TMT members (Burton and Beckman, 2007; Beckman and Burton, 2008; see also Boone et al., 2004). As another recent example, Cho and Hambrick (2006) study US airlines in the period before and after deregulation. They find that shifts in the structural composition of the TMT towards "output-oriented" functions after deregulation have performance consequences. They look at changes in structural composition; however, they do not focus on what leads to compositional change. Thus, we need to better understand the sources and consequences of demographic shifts within organizations. Without such an understanding, our ability to make causal predictions and practical suggestions to managers about how to hire the most appropriate TMT is somewhat limited given path-dependent and structural factors that restrict demographic diversity and change.

The final reason to resurrect the demographic tradition recognizes that demographers have pioneered longitudinal methods and dynamic analyses. It is only through longitudinal research that the types of insights described above are possible, but the bulk of the TMT literature is cross-sectional (25 percent of the 60 articles reviewed by Nielsen were longitudinal; only two – Boeker and Wiltbank (2005) and Boone et al. (2004) – examined antecedents). We are not the first to call for temporal-based or dynamic models in TMT research (Jackson et al., 2003; Carpenter et al., 2004); however, these calls have been embedded in a longer list of critiques and largely gone unheeded. We demonstrate why this focus is essential to TMT research by offering examples of mis-specification and confusion that result from this lack of attention to change and time. By explaining the problems of existing research and the potential rewards of incorporating change and structure, we encourage more scholars to take up the call. Zhang, for instance, in Chapter 14 of this volume, has done so by proposing a model of CEO tenure that encompasses five distinct stages.

Using demographic measures, and conducting longitudinal data analyses, not only allows for different types of analyses than are possible with data from inside the teams themselves but also opens new types of research questions. In recognizing the analytical distinction between structure (roles) and incumbents (individuals) and acknowledging when roles and individuals are likely to shift and change, we can begin to disentangle person and situation effects on outcomes. By attending to historical context we can draw boundary conditions on empirical findings and begin to accumulate knowledge over time about the elusive relationship between top managers and organizational performance.

REDISCOVERING STRUCTURE AND ROLES

Structure deserves more prominence in the TMT literature. Just as organizational designs vary within any given context, the roles that comprise the top management team also vary. According to Hambrick (1994, p. 178; italics original), "The *structure* of a top group refers to the roles of members and the relationships among those roles." Roles reflect organizational design choices made by top managers and in many cases by founders. They signal how the organization is structured. The roles that report directly to the CEO are an indication of the functions or business units believed to be most important to organizational performance. These roles give clues as to where power resides and how decisions are made. Individuals may have more influence in one role than another in that same role, but it is important to consider the positional or structural sources of influence.

We must conceptualize the TMT as a set of individuals *and* roles. Consider the relationship between individuals and roles with a more general example: two hypothetical firms that are the same age and size, have the same number of executives reporting to the CEO, and have TMTs of middle-aged white men with the same age and tenure distribution. Firm A is organized in a functional structure and Firm B is organized in a divisional structure by region (Figure 3.1).

The top managers of Firm A occupy different functional roles and will likely have different functional backgrounds from each other. The top managers of Firm B, with the possible exception of the Executive Vice-President (EVP) of Finance and Administration, will all be general managers and may or may not have different functional backgrounds. The top managers of Firm A will be collaborating as functional experts for the benefit of the firm overall; the regionally focused top managers of Firm B will be competing for corporate resources that are managed by the CEO and the EVP of Finance and Administration to benefit their region. This simple illustration highlights how structure matters to both TMT composition and group process. It is clear that in some structures TMT roles are set up to operate largely independently and the interactions that occur are likely to be competitive rather than collaborative (e.g., business units); whereas in others the TMT roles explicitly demand coordination and cooperation (e.g., functional structure). Relatedly, the organizational structure influences the likelihood that the top management team is comprised of general managers or functional specialists. In other words, this structure has implications for the interdependence across the roles as well as the profiles of executives likely to hold those positions. Task or role interdependence has been considered an important structural consideration (Finkelstein et al., 2009), but most researchers fail to see how task interdependence is a consequence of rather than a

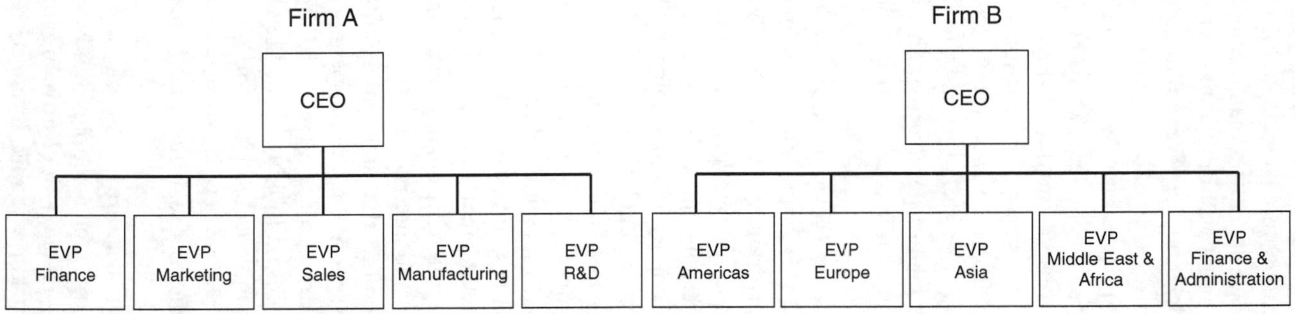

Firm A

CEO

EVP Finance | EVP Marketing | EVP Sales | EVP Manufacturing | EVP R&D

Firm B

CEO

EVP Americas | EVP Europe | EVP Asia | EVP Middle East & Africa | EVP Finance & Administration

Figure 3.1   A functional structure (Firm A) and a divisional structure (Firm B)

measure of structure and how comparing top management team functioning across these structural archetypes is an apples-to-oranges comparison.

In our longitudinal study of TMTs in high-technology start-ups, we demonstrate how roles (structure) and incumbents (individuals) are analytically distinct and evolve differently. We find that firms benefit when the top management team is comprised of both broadly experienced individuals and a well-differentiated role structure. But individuals and structures do not have parallel influence. We find that although broadly experienced individuals can build team structures around them, firms whose functional roles are held by individuals without the relevant experience are less likely to ever attract the experienced individuals subsequently needed and less likely to develop well-differentiated role structures. We document negative individual and organizational consequences when there is a mismatch between the experiences of individuals and the particular roles they hold (Burton and Beckman, 2007; Beckman and Burton, 2008). Our work highlights how individuals and roles have distinct effects, yet they need to be considered in conjunction rather than in isolation because the relationship between them is complex. Unfortunately, the existing TMT literature largely confounds the roles and experiences of individuals (Bunderson and Sutcliffe, 2002).

This simple highlighting of structural roles in contrast to individual incumbents illuminates one of the puzzles in the TMT literature: mixed findings in the relationship between TMT heterogeneity and firm performance. Does TMT heterogeneity have a positive or negative effect on firm performance? While a number of scholars have attempted to account for differences in the external context (Keck, 1997; Carpenter, 2002; Joshi and Roh, 2009) and the interpersonal context (Cannella et al., 2008), little attention has been devoted to organizational structure. But for top management teams, organizational structure in large part determines task interdependence and the concomitant likelihood of and the need for interaction among senior executives. As we describe above, structure influences the likelihood that these interactions are cooperative or competitive in nature. Most importantly, for TMTs, structure is antecedent to both process and task interdependence. Thus, an important first step in synthesizing the TMT performance literature is to acknowledge these differences in organizational structure and account for them in research design, analysis, and interpretation.

But perhaps more radically, the fact that structure is antecedent to both and easy to measure is yet another reason to ignore the lure of opening the black box and return to pure demography. Examining group processes and individual cognitions has provided new insights, but the exclusive focus on looking inside the black box has obscured other useful research approaches. A simple examination of job titles, rather than collecting complicated measurements of group process, reveals the interdependence between roles without measuring interdependence per se. Thus, we advocate a return to simple demographic measures.

One of the dangers of ignoring structure is that scholars mis-specify the relationship between composition and outcome. For example, Bunderson and Sutcliffe (2002) find that intrapersonal diversity is associated with positive organizational outcomes. Because they ignore structure, we do not know if this finding is because diverse experience is performance enhancing (as they conclude). Or is it because the people with diverse experiences are more likely to be in TMT structures with performance benefits (e.g., organizations that have divisional structures rather than functional structures)? Or is it because people with diverse experiences are more likely to be in certain roles (such as strategic planning or business development), and the existence of these roles on the TMT is associated with higher performances? As these questions imply, structure is a source of unobserved heterogeneity in the extant TMT literature; and it is a source of heterogeneity easy to miss because the exact shape of its influence is changing over time as structures evolve. More attention to structure and time will allow us to better specify the causal mechanisms by which TMTs influence firms and to unpack the mixed findings that currently confound structure and experience.

Separating roles and incumbents also raises the question as to whether there are differences in the aggregate characteristics of incumbents for different positions. For example, are marketing executives more diverse – in age, gender, race, functional and educational background – than finance executives? Again, there is evidence suggesting the answer is likely to be yes. For example, in our study of high-technology start-ups, we find people in finance and HR roles disproportionally bring narrow but functionally relevant prior experience to the role; whereas, people in general management, business development, strategic planning, and service and support tend to have broader prior functional experiences (Burton and Beckman, 2007, p. 250). Although this work aggregates across individuals, it speaks to both the variation in normative expectations for different roles as well as the likelihood that an individual in any given role will have a broad or narrow functional background.

In addition to analytically separating individuals and roles, we must examine how both individuals and roles change over time. This will allow us to understand mixed findings, to explore the impact of time and change in TMT research, and most importantly, it will open new territory for TMT researchers.

ROLE STRUCTURES AND CHANGE

There is growing evidence that TMT role structures change over time. Scholars have documented dramatic shifts in organizational structure (Hayes and Abernathy, 1980; Fligstein, 1987), the emergence of new executive roles (Hambrick and Cannella, 2004; Zorn, 2004), and the rise and fall of particular functions (Fligstein, 1987; Nath and Majahan, 2008). For example, in a study of the 100 largest US firms between 1919 and 1979, Fligstein (1987) demonstrates how the dominant structural form shifted multiple times from a holding company, to a functionally organized firm, to a multidivisional organization of related products, to a multidivisional organization that is global and includes unrelated product divisions. Zorn (2004) illustrates the emergence and diffusion of the CFO position between 1964 and 2000. In 1964, none of the largest publicly traded US firms had a CFO; in 2000, the position had been adopted by more than 80 percent of these firms. Moreover, he documents how change in accounting rules and disclosure obligations in 1979 accelerated the rate at which major corporations added the CFO role to their TMTs to the point where "CFO positions have become firmly entrenched at the top" (p. 362). Hambrick and Cannella (2004) similarly investigate the relatively recent phenomenon of the COO position. Not surprisingly, the propensity to have the COO role on the TMT is strongly correlated with firm size. But more interesting is the fact that the propensity to have the COO role varies dramatically by industry; as Hambrick and

Cannella describe, "perhaps industries develop inclinations, conventions, or traditions that take them in the direction of having COOs or not; but the incidence is not rooted in any discernible contextual conditions" (p. 971). This suggests further analysis is needed: differences across industries may be a function of complex structural and historical patterns and has implications for understanding TMT heterogeneity across industries.

There is also evidence that the roles within a firm are shaped by the prestige of certain functions within a firm or industry. For example, Nath and Majahan (2008) find that 97 percent of the large firms they sampled had a CFO whereas approximately 40 percent of the firms had a Chief Marketing Officer (CMO). The presence of a marketing officer was related to industry, firm size, and strategy with small, diversified firms less likely to have a CMO and firms pursuing an innovation or branding strategy more likely.

All of these studies reveal how different functional roles are represented on the top management team in different contexts and how TMT roles have changed throughout historical time. These major compositional shifts are largely unaccounted for in attempts to synthesize the cumulative findings of the TMT literature. Over the many decades of research, the dominant TMT structures have changed. New positions have emerged, others have faded, and this has consequences for the interdependence among team members, the functional background characteristics of TMT members, the group processes that result, and the expected influence of the TMT. It is not surprising, then, that looking simply at TMT functional diversity collapsed across time fails to demonstrate clear patterns. The structure of these teams is likely to be different across time.

INDIVIDUAL TEAM MEMBERS AND CHANGE

Just as role structures vary by context and across historical time, we also know that the characteristics of the labor force and the rates at which individuals change jobs vary by context and over time. For example, we know that increasing numbers of women and minorities in the workplace are changing organizational demography. We also know that promotion rates and turnover rates vary over time.

The growing numbers of women and minorities in the labor force have implications throughout the organizational hierarchy; for example, there is evidence that having women at higher organizational levels increases the promotion of women beneath them in the organization (Broschak et al., 1998). Yet we also know that the proportion of women (and minorities) that have become part of the TMT and senior leadership of firms is still a small minority (Daily et al., 1999). But by recognizing broader trends, we can anticipate that these types of compositional differences are likely future topics of inquiry for TMT research.

More relevant immediately is the well-documented finding that both promotion rates and turnover rates vary over time. While industrial relations scholars tie shorter job durations and increasing mobility to the overall demise of the internal labor market (Cappelli, 1999; Osterman, 1999), organizational ecologists emphasize population dynamics such as the number and type of competitor organizations (Sørensen, 1999) as well as organizational growth, decline, founding, failure, and merger (Haveman and Cohen, 1994). For example, Haveman (1995), in a study of the savings and loan industry, finds that the rates of individual entry and exit into organizations change as new organizations are formed in the environment, or as existing organizations merge with one another. Boeker and Wiltbank (2005) add that important external stakeholders, such as venture capital owners and board members, increase the rate of top management changes. The broad insight from this burgeoning literature is that exogenous forces impact individual mobility. This work offers a more realistic sense of how top management team composition is shaped by the context in which it is embedded. As firms emerge, grow, die, merge, and compete with one another, the composition of the top management team is impacted.

Why are these exogenously determined mobility processes relevant for TMT research? Because at an extreme they imply that the composition of the TMT may be an artifact of other factors, and, at a minimum, they highlight how attempts to generalize the relationship between TMT composition and organizational outcomes across time and context is fraught with complexity. If we are to understand the relationship between top management team characteristics and organizational outcomes, we must also consider both the individual and organizational mechanisms that contribute to composition. There are a multitude of factors that influence individual job duration. Individuals have different tendencies to stay and go: some people are job hoppers whereas others are loyal soldiers. But we also know that the baseline propensities for individuals to change jobs changes over time such that the longer you are in a job, the less likely you are to leave it. To further complicate the picture, we also know that there are firm-level strategic and political factors associated with executive turnover as well as industry and environmental factors shaping the likelihood of team entrances and exits (Thornton and Ocasio, 1999). Moreover, the disruptive or beneficial effects of entrances versus exits likely differ, and these differences are shaped by whether the new team member is an insider or an outsider and whether the addition or replacement was anticipated versus sudden. Clearly, a nuanced understanding of top management team mobility and change demand attention to time and context. But in addition, we must also disaggregate the effects of team entrances and exits (e.g., the impact of a new addition or a replacement to a team should be considered separately from the loss of a team member) and recognize the causes of entrances and exits (e.g., as the result of individual mobility or structural role shifts).

ROLES, INDIVIDUAL MOBILITY, AND CHANGE IN THE CONTEXT OF TMT DEMOGRAPHY RESEARCH

Thus far, we have explained the importance of differentiating roles from individuals, and we have explored how both roles and individuals change over time. In order to more fully illustrate the implications of these shifts for TMT research, we turn to two hallmark compositional attributes of TMTs that are studied in the research literature: tenure heterogeneity and functional heterogeneity. Indeed, it is these two dimensions that have yielded much of the corpus of inconsistent findings. We use these two types of heterogeneity as exemplars of the problems that arise from conflating roles and individuals and from ignoring time and change.

To begin, however, we must note that the literature has tended to treat both functional heterogeneity and tenure heterogeneity as instantiations of "task-oriented heterogeneity" (Joshi and Roh, 2009, p. 612; indeed, Finkelstein et al., 2009 discuss heterogeneity as an overall construct rather than distinguish between cognitive, education, function, or tenure heterogeneity). Thus, the underlying logic for both tends to be the same – that diversity brings greater knowledge and resources, which is associated with quality decisions, but also brings more conflict and disruption, which can interfere with implementation (Finkelstein et al., 2009). Relying on Harrison and Klein's (2007) insightful typology, we can see that most TMT scholars are simultaneously invoking "variety" and "separation" arguments that have opposite effects on performance. Variety is beneficial and performance-enhancing because it provides unique information and experience; separation is harmful because it reduces cohesiveness and results in in-group and out-group categorizations. Given that different measures capture separation and variety, but scholars often fail to recognize the implications of these differences, it is not surprising that the research on the relationship between TMT heterogeneity and performance is inconclusive.

In addition to matching measures and constructs, the field would benefit from considering individual executives as distinct from structural roles. Current studies of tenure heterogeneity focus on top management team members, ignoring structural roles. But considering the arrival of new roles, the duration of existing roles, and the variability in the length of time that roles have been considered part of the TMT offers a window into how much the organizational structure has changed over time and offers a different lens on tenure heterogeneity and performance. Similarly, considering the functional role structure, comparing role structures across firms, and linking structural factors to outcomes offers a different lens on functional heterogeneity. As Bunderson and Sutcliffe (2002) pointed out, current studies of functional heterogeneity contain different operational measures that have substantively different meanings. Although they did not explicitly point to the separation of roles from individuals, the distinctions between the concept of "functional assignment diversity," "functional background diversity," "dominant function diversity," and "interpersonal diversity" they point out are a step in this direction. In general, functional assignment diversity refers to the assigned roles on the team (e.g., VP of sales, COO, CFO). Functional background diversity refers to all the functional experiences that individuals bring with them to a particular role (e.g., a COO with an engineering background and a general management background). Dominant function diversity refers to the function in which individuals have spent the majority of their careers (e.g., a COO with mostly general management experience). Functional assignment diversity is a measure of team structure; dominant function and functional background diversity are both measures of individual experience. We advocate going even further and explicitly treating roles as entities worthy of study independent of the executive who holds the role. This approach extends ideas about "idiosyncratic jobs" to the organizational level (Miner, 1991) and reiterates the need to understand how and when roles are added or eliminated, the duration of roles, the characteristics of vacant or difficult-to-fill roles, and how this relates to outcomes.

Of course, function, tenure, individuals, and roles necessarily interact in ways that may be difficult to disentangle. An example will serve to illuminate this complexity. We calculate the Blau Index (a frequently used measure for functional heterogeneity) for different individual and role combinations. Consider a five-person TMT where we are measuring functional heterogeneity across five functions (general management, engineering, sales/marketing, finance, and operations) in a young technology start-up. Imagine the role structure for this team includes five "chief" roles: CEO, CTO (Chief

Technology Officer), CMO, CFO, and COO. The functional assignment diversity score for this role structure using the Blau Index is 0.8. The measures of functional background diversity are only the same across roles and individuals if all of the executives only have experience in their respective functional specialties. Now consider several variations on the backgrounds of the incumbents in this role structure in order to illustrate the differences between role structures and individual experience. If all of the executives have also held general management positions (i.e., had run a small company or a division within a large company) in addition to their functional experience, the Blau Index is zero. If all five team members do not have functional experience but have engineering backgrounds, with no prior senior executive experience, the Blau Index is also zero. All team members have engineering backgrounds and nothing else. Thus, the functional diversity of the team with functional experience and shared senior management experience are considered to be the same as the team with only engineering backgrounds.[1] Both are considered less diverse than a team with functional experience alone (demonstrating the problem between dominant function and functional background diversity). If all of the executives had prior experience in all five of the functions that are being measured – an unlikely, but not impossible scenario of generalist executives – then the Blau Index is again zero. This example makes salient both the analytic problems with the Blau measurement, and the differences you see in functional heterogeneity when you are interested in structure vs. individuals.

Finally, separating roles from individuals' forces scholars to consider how teams change by virtue of roles being added or reconfigured in contrast to how they change by virtue of individuals being replaced. Consider a corporate reorganization, where roles are recreated and individuals moved to different positions: this may result in changes in task interdependence but not changes in interpersonal interaction. Role reconfigurations among the same set of individual incumbents might impact the functional assignment heterogeneity but neither the functional background heterogeneity nor the individual-level tenure distribution. Replacing a person in an existing role is only an interpersonal disruption (it changes the tenure distribution but not the functional assignment distribution and perhaps not the functional background diversity). In contrast, the addition of a new TMT role (with a new hire) has the potential to affect task interdependence as well as interpersonal interactions (it will change the tenure distribution and the functional diversity measures). Here we begin to see that the relationship between functional and tenure heterogeneity; in particular, we see that they will not necessarily move in parallel.[2] By differentiating roles from individuals, it becomes even more apparent that tenure heterogeneity and functional heterogeneity must be disentangled.

The second set of issues to discuss with respect to tenure and functional heterogeneity involves the role of time and change. Both exemplars serve to demonstrate the importance of macro-level changes as well as micro-level inertia. Since Pfeffer's original treatise (1983), tenure heterogeneity has been a staple in TMT demography research. The spirit of the original argument was concerned with the distributional characteristics of team tenure; however, many scholars have considered only the average tenure or the coefficient of variation. Both measures mask the differential effects of team entrances and exits. Both also obscure the effects of team growth. The impact of entrances and exits need to be considered in the local and historical context (why are these changes happening?) as well as over time (what are the patterns of entrances and exits?).[3]

Disentangling entrances and exits as the components of tenure heterogeneity begins to address some of these conceptual problems, and it also leads to a better understanding of some antecedents to TMT composition and change. As we note above, individuals move between organizations with frequency and for a wide variety of reasons. These differing reasons for individual mobility call into question inferences derived from observed tenure heterogeneity effects. For example, the most frequently cited studies that find positive effects for tenure heterogeneity are studying high uncertainty or entrepreneurial contexts (Eisenhardt and Schoonhoven, 1990; Virany et al., 1992; Keck and Tushman, 1993). These are the contexts where firms are often experiencing rapid firm and team growth, which results in multiple entrances to the TMT. As a consequence, tenure heterogeneity increases. The positive effect on firm performance, then, may stem from the entrances and growth that firms are experiencing rather than tenure heterogeneity per se. This calls into question the causal logic of research on tenure heterogeneity and suggests, at the very least, that longitudinal analyses of entrances and exits are necessary. This also speaks to the larger issue of how the addition of new roles and individual entrances and exits are subject to what Haveman (1995) describes as the "demographic metabolism" of organizational populations.

There are similar macro-level changes happening over time with regard to functional heterogeneity (e.g., new roles emerge, Zorn, 2004) but here we want to highlight the firm-level path-dependent processes also at work that keep the functional experience and structure of a firm relatively stable over time. We expect similar firm-level path dependence with regard to the tenure of particular roles (Miner, 1991). There is convincing evidence across a variety of studies that functional heterogeneity is subject to path-dependent processes within organizations. At organizational founding, the amount and types of functional experience on the founding team are subject to environmental and external forces. Stinchcombe (1965) first proposed the idea of environmental imprinting in which firms will reflect the concerns and resources of the time of its founding. These external influences can be labor market conditions (Stinchcombe, 1965), the availability of air travel (Marquis, 2003), or the existing technology (Tripsas, 2009). These external forces will shape the functional experiences of individuals chosen to represent the firm. Internally, organizational imprints are shaped by the prior functional experiences and affiliations of the early TMT members (Burton et al., 2002; Phillips, 2005; Beckman, 2006; Burton and Beckman, 2007).

Once the imprint occurs, the expected functional backgrounds of individuals and role structures have staying power. Indeed, the initial founding team experiences and structures predict how the TMT will evolve over time (Beckman and Burton, 2008). An individual's functional experience at founding predicts TMT functional experience at later points in time (and, similarly, founding functional structures predict TMT functional structures at later points in time). Even when conditions such as declining performance suggest that the team needs new skills (Boone et al., 2004), firms tend to bring in new managers demographically similar to those that remain. This persistence of functional and demographic experience is consistent with a larger literature on homosocial reproduction, so it should not be surprising that TMT members tend to be demographically similar to one another. It is interesting, and perhaps counterintuitive, to note that we find more path dependence in the experiences of individuals in a role than in the role structures themselves. In our work (Burton and Beckman, 2007; Beckman and Burton,

2008), we find that when the functional experience of an executive differs from the functional experience of the person who created the role, higher turnover results; further, the initial role structure predicts how additional structures will be added. However, the role structure does not attract an individual with the relevant experience unless the initial role incumbent also had the relevant experience. Taken together, this suggests that path dependence may operate differently for and across roles and individuals within a firm. That said, firms that begin with functional heterogeneity (of both individuals and roles) are likely to maintain that heterogeneity over time. History is an important antecedent to TMT composition.

In addition to these initial functional choices being persistent, they have important consequences for firms. Organizational imprints shape the adoption of various formal structures as well as bureaucratization (Baron et al., 1999a). Boeker (1988) first demonstrated that the strategy of semiconductor firms was related to the functional background of the founder. In our work, we find initial functional structures, experiences, and affiliations have a lasting effect on individuals, teams, and firms. For example, Beckman and Burton (2008) demonstrate that founding team functional structures predict the important firm milestone of going public, even after controlling for subsequent changes to the team from the founding period (see also Beckman, 2006; Beckman et al., 2007). However, despite the persistence of functional heterogeneity and their consequences, this does not mean that the influence of functional heterogeneity will necessarily be the same over time. This is where we again see the relationship between function and tenure.

In fact, there is little evidence that functional diversity at a point in time will not differ based on elapsed time. How long does it take to understand how another person thinks or to learn what another person knows? At what point does individual expertise get absorbed into the collective intelligence of the group? As anyone who has been a member of an organizational group knows, there is an interaction between time/tenure and functional diversity, yet few scholars consider this interaction. It seems obvious that functional diversity among a newly formed team likely operates differently than functional diversity among a team that has worked together for a number of years. The tension between diversity as informational variety and social separation is vivid as we consider functional composition and tenure over time.

Taken together, this suggests that, because of path dependence and the ability for team members to incorporate the knowledge and expertise of other group members, analysts may be over-attributing the influence of the current top management team on performance. Suggesting that team composition is subject to path-dependent processes is not to negate the significance of managerial choice and agency, but it does allow or perhaps requires us to ask different questions about top management teams themselves. Putting aside history to focus on the present, as most TMT research does, creates misspecification and perhaps misdiagnosis of the causal relationship. We do not want to focus on "a 'snapshot' explanation for what should be seen as a moving picture" (Pierson, 2000, p. 263) because focusing on temporal patterns allows us to consider the source of social outcomes. By focusing on path dependence, we can identify the sources of stability and change, and understand when and what types of TMTs are more conducive to path-dependent processes. If we can understand the processes by which path dependence occurs, we can explicate the sources of heterogeneity and the mechanisms of inertia and ultimately better understand drivers of performance.

In summary, we use function and tenure heterogeneity as examples to demonstrate that: (1) roles and individuals should be separated; (2) roles and individuals are subject to macro-level change over time; (3) roles and individuals are subject to micro-level change and inertia within the firm. The extension of sociological work into TMT research writ large would suggest that the impact of demography on organizational outcomes may sometimes be driven by larger population-level dynamics rarely included in the models and other times be driven by historical exigencies embedded in the firm structure and resistant to change. The tendency in the extant TMT literature has been to aggregate these distinct demographic attributes (e.g., tenure and function, roles, and individuals) – which are differentially influenced by history and context – into the same category of "task-oriented diversity." This inappropriate aggregation is why meta-analyses and syntheses have difficulty reaching convincing conclusions.

NEW RESEARCH QUESTIONS

We end with three suggestions for future research on TMTs – research that would help us address some of the questions we have raised in this chapter and advance TMT research. First, we reiterate that tenure heterogeneity needs to be understood longitudinally as a pattern of entrances and exits. In our work on entrepreneurial teams, we find that team entrance results in positive outcomes for firms (such as obtaining venture capital and going public more quickly). Team exits, to the contrary, have negative consequences (Beckman et al., 2007; but see Tushman and Rosenkopf, 1996). The distinction between entrances and exits allows us to better understand what we think is lost and gained through team change, whether it be variety and information, shared knowledge, or cohesion. Furthermore, a consideration of team entrances and exits raises additional questions. Is it patterned? Do executives arrive randomly, or do they come and go in groups? Does individual versus collective turnover matter? In their simulation, Carroll and Harrison (1998) model turnover events incrementally. As a result, their simulation has "lumpy" changes (where multiple turnover events occur simultaneously) only infrequently. Given contagion effects, this assumption may not be valid. Longitudinal data allows us to examine these assumptions empirically and then examine the consequences of those patterns. For instance, it may be easier to change multiple team members simultaneously because together they will renegotiate job boundaries. But this will be true only if roles are enforced by contemporaneous team members rather than existing structures, processes, and systems. These types of examinations will help us further disentangle the influence of individuals from structure.

Second, differentiating TMT roles and incumbents opens the study of TMT *vacancies* as a potentially fruitful topic of inquiry. For example, are there performance consequences of leaving a position vacant versus naming an "acting" or interim executive? (Zhang also asks this question in Chapter 14.) If our research is any indication, the imprinting of a position by a temporary role holder may have negative repercussions for the person who steps in to permanently assume that role (Burton and Beckman, 2007). Of course, this choice itself might reveal something about the firm or team. To consider truly exogenously driven vacancies, economists have recently taken advantage of accidental deaths of star scientists as an exogenous shock to working groups and find subsequent performance declines (Oettl, 2009; Azoulay et al., 2010). Another innovative identification strategy is seen in research on networks and hiring (Fernandez and Fernandez-Mateo, 2006) where new TMT members could be compared with the available choice set of potential TMT members. Who else was considered and how and why was this TMT member chosen over other possibilities? Both approaches allow scholars to draw causal inferences by isolating mechanisms of change.

Finally, we highlight one of our early, and largely unaddressed, conjectures: we can study the TMT as a microcosm of the broader organization. Is this true? There is evidence that diversity among leaders contributes to diversity throughout (and across) the organization(s) (Beckman and Phillips, 2005; Baron et al., 2007). To what extent does hierarchy among the leadership ranks reveal hierarchy throughout the organization? If TMT studies took on this question it would change the focus from organizational consequences to organizational dynamics, structures, and processes. This could be a fruitful area of research and add to our broader understanding of organizational functioning.

SUMMARY AND CONCLUSION

Our primary goal in this chapter has been to revitalize the demographic approach to TMTs and to advocate research avenues that do not require "opening the black box." Most TMT researchers are driven by questions of organizational strategy and performance but have been lulled into viewing these phenomena only through the lens of individual action. This has led us to ignore what makes a top management team different than other teams. The field as a whole has largely ignored structure and proceeded with only minimal concern for broader environmental and contextual factors that operate on TMTs and organizations. By attending to organizational structure and how it changes over historical time and context, we advocate a return to some of the simple demographic measures first proposed in the field – a stance that puts us in opposition with much of the current literature.

We argue that TMT structures are often antecedent to the processes hypothesized to impact organizational outcomes in the traditional TMT literature. In addition, founding composition and structure has a lasting impact on the firm. More importantly, taking structure into account reveals that compositional characteristics of top managers are not a random happening. TMT members are the result of a deliberate selection process – both in terms of which roles are represented in the innermost circle and in terms of the particular incumbents who occupy the roles. TMT members are likely to have very different experiences depending on the organizational structure. While organizational structural choices might plausibly be uncorrelated with age, gender, race, or tenure (although we doubt it), they are almost certainly correlated with functional background. Thus, even scholars who are only interested in individual factors ignore structure at their peril. Considering an individual's functional background without attention to his or her structural role is akin to considering an athlete's height without attention to whether the sport is basketball or hockey. As a first step, TMT scholars must consider roles and incumbents as distinct and separable.

In addition to bringing structure back to the table, and separating individuals from roles, we highlight the importance of taking into account changing labor market conditions as well as shifting preferences for corporate structures. These macro-level factors clearly influence both the TMT roles and the characteristics of role incumbents. In fact, a challenge for the field is rejecting the claim that the relationship between TMT composition and outcomes is the spurious product of macro-level factors. Doing so requires a research design that eliminates causal ambiguity and also allows for careful controls. In our own work, we've studied entrepreneurial firms longitudinally from inception. This is a step in the right direction, but we do not claim to account for all sources of unobserved heterogeneity.

We discussed a range of macro-level forces that shape managerial discretion and executive cognitions, with the intent of tempering the strategic leadership view. These include both temporal processes and contextual factors such as the legal environment (Davis et al., 1994; Zorn et al., 2004; Davis, 2009), external stakeholders (Zuckerman, 2000), and founding conditions (Baron et al., 1999a, 1999b). While many TMT scholars are interested in an array of organizational and environmental contingencies, from both the strategic leadership and the demographic perspectives, we are not the first to point out that this research has not gone far enough (Jackson et al., 2003). Most studies in this vein use a pooled cross-sectional design. Scholars have included variables such as environmental uncertainty, industry structure, organizational age, and the size of the firm to understand the determinants of TMT characteristics (Finkelstein et al., 2009) without considering that these variables also change. This overall lack of attention to contextual factors may be a key reason why conflicting results are found across studies (Triandis, 1995; Jackson et al., 2003; but see Cho and Hambrick, 2006). That said, a few studies are moving in the right direction. Jensen and Zajac (2004) begin to consider macro-level contextual factors in their study of how corporate governance and TMT characteristics interact. Joshi and Roh (2009) do an admirable job of linking occupational demography to teams (although they explicitly exclude TMTs!). Furthermore, there is evidence that different organizational settings have various constituents who shape the TMT composition (Boeker and Wiltbank, 2005). These approaches, which take context into account as either explanatory variables or as theoretical boundary conditions, offer compelling models for future studies.

In addition to understanding how the external context affects TMTs, we need to consider how historical context shapes the TMT. Although it is true, as strategic leadership scholars argue, that managerial discretion may be limited by contemporaneous environmental, organizational, and individual factors (Finkelstein et al., 2009), we find it more useful to consider managerial action as shaped by historical processes. The industry structure, organizational culture, and personal characteristics of managers certainly influence managerial discretion. But to include them as concurrent variables to be controlled ignores the fact that industry, culture, and managerial experience are embedded in the history of the firm and are changing over time.

For those of us who are teachers as well as scholars, the question becomes, where is the best place for intervention and diagnosis? Should we measure individual characteristics or organizational history and context? We argue that understanding the history of the field, the organization, and the TMT is a more fruitful diagnostic tool than measuring individual characteristics because, outside the experimental setting, selection decisions are driven by macro-level changes in roles, as well as organizational histories and cultures. The strategic leadership tradition overstates the importance of individual factors and does not give enough attention to the historical constraints and structural choices that influence TMT composition. In fact, our research suggests that even when individuals with the needed experience are chosen for a particular organizational position (e.g., a professional HR person hired into a VP of HR position), they are more likely to leave if those experiences do not fit with the history of the organization (Burton and Beckman, 2007). These findings should give us pause and suggests a rationale for appreciating that organizational selection decisions are subject to idiosyncratic firm-level considerations.

By attending to path-dependent processes that shape TMT composition, we better specify the points of leverage for affecting change. If we understand sources of inertia (such as homophily resulting in stable functional representation over time) and mechanisms of heterogeneity (such as external and temporal changes in the environment; or perhaps internal opportunities for learning and reconsideration), we can better understand the role of managerial agency and identify the opportunities for re-directing or interrupting path-dependent processes. Considering these path-dependent processes also begins to illuminate the pressing questions about antecedents of TMT composition (Pettigrew, 1992; Lawrence, 1997; Hambrick, 2007). Simply put, we know that macro-level changes and environmental pressures shape the emergence and death of executive roles. In addition, TMTs are artifacts of the decisions and individuals of early organizational members. Yet, we need to better understand what factors are endogenous to TMT change and composition as well as what factors are exogenous. Together this would help us better understand the antecedents of TMT composition.

All of this requires that TMT researchers separate individuals from their positions, gather longitudinal data, and use modeling strategies that are designed to account for change and time. This will allow us to understand how roles, and the individuals in those roles, evolve and change over time as a result of macro-level changes and firm-level path dependencies. Such an agenda provides enormous opportunities for another quarter-century of vibrant research.

NOTES

1. The Teachman's Index, another commonly used measure, gives similar values.
2. To further complicate matters, the amount of "overlap" depends on how broadly or narrowly functions are described, the period of time over which experiences are aggregated, and the number of people on the team.
3. Sørensen (2002) and Harrison and Carroll (2006) carefully describe the problems with the coefficient of variation as a measure of tenure heterogeneity (which are as complex as the problems we note with the Blau Index above). Their commentary is similar to the general commentary about all measures of diversity made by Harrison and Klein (2007): there are distinct conceptualizations that invoke different underlying processes but the theories and measures are often unclear as to which are being invoked.

REFERENCES

Azoulay, P., Zivin, J.G., and Wang, J. (2010). Superstar extinction. *Quarterly Journal of Economics*, **125**(2), 549–89.

Barley, S.R. (1992). Design and devotion: Surges of rational and normative ideologies of control in managerial discourse. *Administrative Science Quarterly*, **37**(3), 363–99.

Baron, J.N., Burton, M.D., and Hannan, M.T. (1999a). Engineering bureaucracy: The genesis of formal policies, positions, and structures in high-technology firms. *Journal of Law, Economics, and Organization,* **15**(1), 1–41.

Baron, J.N., Hannan, M.T., and Burton, M.D. (1999b). Building the iron cage: Determinants of managerial intensity in the early years of organizations. *American Sociological Review,* **64**(4), 527–47.

Baron, J.N., Hannan, M.T., Hsu, G., and Koçak, O. (2007). In the company of women: Gender inequality and the logic of bureaucracy in start-up firms. *Work and Occupations,* **34**(1), 35–66.

Beckman, C.M. (2006). The influence of founding team company affiliations on firm behavior. *Academy of Management Journal,* **49**(4), 741–58.

Beckman, C.M. and Burton, M.D. (2008). Founding the future: Path dependence in the evolution of top management teams from founding to IPO. *Organization Science,* **19**(1), 3–24.

Beckman, C.M. and Phillips, D.J. (2005). Interorganizational determinants of promotion: Client leadership and promotion of women attorneys. *American Sociological Review,* **70**(4), 678–701.

Beckman, C.M., Burton, M.D., and O'Reilly, C. III. (2007). Early teams: The impact of team demography on VC financing and going public. *Journal of Business Venturing,* **22**(2), 147–73.

Boeker, W. (1988). Organizational origins: Entrepreneurial and environmental imprinting at time of founding. In G.R. Carroll (ed.), *Ecological models of organizations.* Cambridge, MA: Ballinger, pp. 33–51.

Boeker, W. and Wiltbank, R. (2005). New venture evolution and managerial capabilities. *Organization Science,* **16**(2), 123–33.

Boone, C., Van Olffen, W., Van Witteloostuijn, A., and De Brabander, B. (2004). The genesis of top management team diversity: Selective turnover among top management teams in Dutch newspaper publishing, 1970–1994. *Academy of Management Journal,* **47**(5), 633–56.

Broschak, J., Cohen, L., and Haveman, H. (1998). And then there were more? The effect of organizational sex composition on the hiring and promotion of managers. *American Sociological Review,* **63**(5), 711–27.

Bunderson, J.S. and Sutcliffe, K.M. (2002). Comparing alternative conceptualizations of functional diversity in management teams: Process and performance effects. *Academy of Management Journal,* **45**(5), 875–933.

Burton, M.D. and Beckman, C.M. (2007). Leaving a legacy: Position imprints and successor turnover in young firms. *American Sociological Review,* **72**(2), 239–66.

Burton, M.D., Sørensen, J., and Beckman, C.M. (2002). Coming from good stock: Career histories and new venture formation. In *Research in the sociology of organizations* (Volume: Social structure and organizations revisited). Oxford: JAI Press, pp. 229–62.

Cannella Jr., A.A, Park, J., and Lee, H. (2008). Top management team functional background diversity and firm performance: Examining the roles of team colocation and environmental uncertainty. *Academy of Management Journal,* **51**(4), 768–84.

Cappelli, P. (1999). *The new deal at work: Managing the market-based employment relationship.* Boston, MA: Harvard Business School Press.

Carpenter, M.A. (2002). The implications of strategy and social context for the relationship between top management team heterogeneity and firm performance. *Strategic Management Journal,* **23**(3), 275–84.

Carpenter, M.A., Geletkanycz, M.A., and Sanders, W.G. (2004). Upper echelons research revisited: Antecedents, elements and consequences of top management team composition. *Journal of Management,* **30**(6), 749–78.

Carroll, G.R. and Harrison, J.R. (1998). Organizational demography and culture: Insights from a formal model and simulation. *Administrative Science Quarterly,* **43**(3), 637–67.

Certo, S.T., Lester, R.H., Dalton, C.M., and Dalton, D.R. (2006). Top management teams, strategy and financial performance: A meta-analytic examination. *Journal of Management Studies,* **43**(4), 813–39.

Chandler, A.D. (1962). *Strategy and structure: Chapters in the history of the American industrial enterprise.* Cambridge, MA: MIT Press.

Cho, T.S. and Hambrick, D. (2006). Attention patterns as mediators between top management team characteristics and strategic change: The case of airline deregulation. *Organization Science,* **17**(4), 453–69.

Daily, C.M., Certo, S.T., and Dalton, D.R. (1999). A decade of corporate women: Some progress in the boardroom, none in the executive suite. *Strategic Management Journal,* **20**(1), 93–9.

Davis, G. (2009). *Managed by the markets: How finance reshaped America.* Oxford: Oxford University Press.

Davis, G.F., Diekmann, K.A., and Tinsley, C.H. (1994). The decline and fall of the conglomerate firm in the 1980s: The de-institutionalization of an organizational form. *American Sociological Review,* **59**(4), 547–70.

Dencker, J.C. (2009). Relative bargaining power, corporate restructuring and managerial incentives. *Administrative Science Quarterly,* **54**(3), 453–85.

Eisenhardt, K. and Schoonhoven, C.B. (1990). Organizational growth: Linking founding team strategy, environment, and growth among U.S. semiconductor ventures, 1978–1988. *Administrative Science Quarterly,* **35**(3), 504–29.

Fernandez, R.M. and Fernandez-Mateo, I. (2006). Networks, race and hiring. *American Sociological Review,* **71**(1), 42–71.

Finkelstein, S. and Hambrick, D.C. (1996). *Strategic leadership: Top executives and their effects on organizations.* St. Paul, MN: South-Western College Publishing.

Finkelstein, S., Hambrick, D.C., and Cannella Jr., A.A. (2009). *Strategic leadership: Theory and research on executives, top management teams and boards.* Oxford: Oxford University Press.

Fligstein, N. (1987). The intraorganizational power struggle: Rise of financial personnel to top leadership in large corporations, 1919–1979. *American Sociological Review*, **52**(1), 44–58.

Guillen, M.F. (1994). *Models of management: Work, authority and organization in a comparative perspective.* Chicago, IL: University of Chicago Press.

Hambrick, D.C. (1994). Top management groups: A conceptual integration and reconsideration of the "team" label. *Research in Organizational Behavior*, **16**(3), 171–213.

Hambrick, D.C. (2007). Upper echelons theory: An update. *Academy of Management Review*, **32**(2), 334–43.

Hambrick, D.C. and Cannella Jr., A.A. (2004). CEOs who have COOs: Contingency analysis of an unexplored structural form. *Strategic Management Journal*, **25**(10), 959–79.

Hambrick, D.C. and Mason, P.A. (1984). Upper echelons: The organization as a reflection of its top managers. *Academy of Management Review*, **9**(1), 193–206.

Harrison, D.A. and Klein, K.J. (2007). What's the difference? Diversity constructs as separation, variety, or disparity in organizations. *Academy of Management Review*, **32**(4), 1199–228.

Harrison, J.R. and Carroll, G. (2006). *Culture and demography in organizations.* Princeton, NJ: Princeton University Press.

Haveman, H.A. (1995). The demographic metabolism of organizations: Industry dynamics, turnover, and tenure distributions. *Administrative Science Quarterly*, **40**(4), 586–618.

Haveman, H.A. and Cohen, L.E. (1994). The ecological dynamics of careers: The impact of organizational founding, dissolution, and merger on job mobility. *American Journal of Sociology*, **100**(1), 153–95.

Hayes, R.H. and Abernathy, W.J. (1980). Managing our way to economic decline. *Harvard Business Review*, **58**(4), 67–77.

Jackson, S.E., Joshi, A., and Erhardt, N.L. (2003). Recent research on team and organizational diversity: SWOT analysis and implications. *Journal of Management*, **29**(6), 801–30.

Jensen, M. and Zajac, E.J. (2004). Corporate elites and corporate strategy: How demographic preferences and structural position shape the scope of the firm. *Strategic Management Journal*, **25**(6), 507–24.

Joshi, A. and Roh, H. (2009). The role of context in work team diversity research: A meta-analytic review. *Academy of Management Journal*, **52**(3), 599–627.

Keck, S. (1997). Top management team structure: Differential effects by environmental context. *Organization Science*, **8**(2), 143–56.

Keck, S. and Tushman, M. (1993). Environmental and organization context and executive team characteristics. *Academy of Management Journal*, **36**(6), 1314–44.

Khurana, R. (2002). *Searching for a corporate savior: The irrational quest for charismatic CEOs.* Princeton, NJ: Princeton University Press.

Lawrence, B.S. (1997). The "black box" of organizational demography. *Organization Science*, **8**(1), 1–22.

Marquis, C. (2003). The pressure of the past: Network imprinting in intercorporate communities. *Administrative Science Quarterly*, **48**(4), 655–89.

McKelvey, B. (1982). *Organizational systematics: Taxonomy, evolution, classification.* Berkeley, CA: University of California Press.

Miner, A.S. (1991). Organizational evolution and the social ecology of jobs. *American Sociological Review*, **56**(6), 772–85.

Nath, P. and Majahan, V. (2008). Chief marketing officers: A study of their presence in firms' top management teams. *Journal of Marketing*, **72**(1), 65–81.

Nielsen, S. (2009). Top management team diversity: A review of theories and methodologies. *International Journal of Management Reviews*, 1–19, available at: http://www3.interscience.wiley.com/journal/120125469/issue; accessed 14 July 2010.

Oettl, A. (2009). Productivity and helpfulness: A new taxonomy for star scientists. Mimeo: Georgia Institute of Technology unpublished doctoral dissertation.

Osterman, P. (1999). *Securing prosperity: The American labor market: How it has changed and what to do about it.* Princeton, NJ: Princeton University Press.

Pettigrew, A. (1992). On studying managerial elites. *Strategic Management Journal*, **13**(S2), 163–82.

Pfeffer, J. (1983). Organizational demography. In L.L. Cummings and B. Staw (eds), *Research in organizational behavior* (Vol. 5). Greenwich, CT: JAI Press, pp. 299–357.

Phillips, D.J. (2005). Organizational genealogies and the persistence of gender inequality: The case of Silicon Valley law firms. *Administrative Science Quarterly*, **50**(3), 440–72.

Pierson, P. (2000). Increasing returns, path dependence and the study of politics. *The American Political Science Review*, **94**(2), 251–67.

Shenhav Y.A. (2000). *Manufacturing rationality: The engineering foundations of the managerial revolution.* Oxford: Oxford University Press.

Sørensen, J.B. (1999). Executive migration and interorganizational competition. *Social Science Research*, **28**(3), 289–315.

Sørensen, J.B. (2000). The longitudinal effects of group tenure composition on turnover. *American Sociological Review*, **65**(2), 298–310.

Sørensen, J.B. (2002). The use and misuse of the coefficient of variation in organizational demography research. *Sociological Methods and Research*, **30**(4), 475–91.

Stinchcombe, A.L. (1965). Social structure and organizations. In J.G. March (ed.), *Handbook of organizations.* Chicago, IL: Rand McNally, pp. 142–93.

Thornton, P.H. and Ocasio, W. (1999). Institutional logics and the historical contingency of power in organizations: Executive succession in the higher education publishing industry, 1958–1990. *American Journal of Sociology*, **105**(3), 801–43.

Triandis, H.C. (1995). The importance of contexts in studies of diversity. In S.E. Jackson and M.N. Ruderman (eds), *Diversity in workteams: Research paradigms for a changing workplace.* Washington, DC: American Psychological Association, pp. 225–33.

Tripsas, M. (2009). Technology, identity, and inertia through the lens of "The Digital Photography Company." *Organization Science*, **20**(2), 441–60.

Tushman, M. and Rosenkopf, L. (1996). Executive succession, strategic reorientation and performance growth: A longitudinal study in the U.S. cement industry in stable environments. *Management Science*, **42**(7), 939–53.

Virany, B., Tushman, M., and Romanelli, E. (1992). Executive succession and organization outcomes in turbulent environments: An organization learning approach. *Organization Science*, **3**(1), 72–91.

Williams, K.Y. and O'Reilly, C.A. (1998). Demography and diversity in organizations: A review of 40 years of research. In B.M. Staw and L.L. Cummings (eds), *Research in organizational behavior* (Vol. 20). Greenwich, CT: JAI Press, pp. 77–140.

Zorn, D.M. (2004). Here a chief, there a chief: The rise of the CFO in the American firm. *American Sociological Review*, **69**(3), 345–64.

Zorn, D., Dobbin. F., Dierkes, J., and Kwok, M. (2004). Managing investors: How financial markets reshaped the American firm. In K.K. Cetina and A. Preda (eds), *The sociology of financial markets.* London: Oxford University Press, pp. 269–89.

Zuckerman, E.W. (2000). Focusing the corporate product: Securities analysts and de-diversification. *Administrative Science Quarterly*, **45**(3), 591–619.

PART II

PERSONALITIES AND PROFILES OF TOP EXECUTIVES

4 The personality profile of US top executives
Andrew Sangster

Scant research has been done on the personality profiles of *top* management: that is, the head of a business unit and his or her direct reports (Van Eynde and Tucker, 1996; Halikias and Panayotopoulou, 2003). If members of top management have an asymmetrically large effect on firm outcomes, and if behavior is a function of an individual's enduring dispositions (i.e., his or her personality), it becomes particularly important to understand the ways in which these individuals differ from the adult norm (if, in fact, they do), and whether, and in what way, they differ among themselves. This study attempts to correct some of this deficiency in the literature by focusing specifically on the personality profiles of top management.

There is, of course, a plethora of studies on personality, both normal (Allport and Odbert, 1936; Goldberg, 1981; Costa and McCrae, 1990) and abnormal (Hathaway and McKinley, 1951; Butcher and Spielberger, 1995; DSM-IV-TR, 2000). There are numerous studies of the population as a whole, studies contrasting US personality norms with those of other countries (McCrae and Costa, 1997b; Salgado, 1997), and studies of various subpopulations by occupation (Furnham and Stringfield, 1993; Gailbreath et al., 1997; Judge et al., 1999), and various other demographics (Collins and Gleaves, 1998). There are, not surprisingly, a number of studies on the personalities of managers in general (O'Connor et al., 1992; Gardner and Martinko, 1996; Carr, 2006), and of entrepreneurs (Fraboni and Saltstone, 1990; Malach-Pines et al., 2002; Zhao and Seibert, 2006). But management at the very top has been largely neglected, perhaps because of the difficulty of studying this population.

A key premise of this study is that these top executives have personalities that are materially different from that of the population as whole. Moreover, these executives have some characteristics that make them personality-wise more homogeneous than the general population, and yet other personality characteristics that distinguish one top management team (TMT) from another. First, in this "tri-morphic" personality characterization of TMTs, personality tends to differentiate these TMT members from the general population: a heteromorphic effect. Second, within top management echelons individuals have some personality dimensions that tend to make them alike: an isomorphic effect. Finally, some TMT member personality dimensions differentiate one TMT from another: a polymorphic effect.

Personality heteromorphism with respect to the population as a whole can have important implications for top management selection and organizational performance. It implies that not everyone has an equal chance of attaining such top positions. It also has implications on the performance of organizations, which will be addressed later. One mechanism through which it may affect performance is strategic decision making; Jones and Cannella develop propositions regarding the effect of CEO personality traits on strategic decision making in Chapter 1.

Greater personality isomorphism within top executive ranks (as compared with the general population) could be a double-edged sword. It could represent a beneficial adaptation to the rigors of such high positions. But it can be argued that such isomorphism might not be an adaptation to the competitive environment, but to other organizational imperatives that are maladaptive to the organization's environment.

Furthermore, it can be argued that personality polymorphism across TMTs could represent an environmental adaptation. If so, such differences in personality distributions could be beneficial because they could focus a firm on certain modes of acting upon opportunities, and reacting to environmental threats. They could also be detrimental should an environmental change make these TMT characteristics maladaptive, causing opportunities to be lost, and threats to be ignored or inappropriately addressed.

If personality effects are an important factor in policy-making, then knowledge of these personality effects furthers our understanding of how and when a variety of management theories contribute to the successes or failures of firms. If there are TMT member personality profile differences across firms, it raises the question of whether some executive personalities have a better fit with certain environments. Top executive personality differences suggest that these personality effects within an organization may create organizational "antennae" that are directional: an organization is both finely tuned to perceive and react to certain environmental stimuli, and mistuned to perceive and react to other environmental changes. Because human personality is mostly stable in adulthood (Costa and McCrae, 1988, 1997, 2006; McCrae et al., 1999, 2004), and because it could have an effect upon strategic choice, it may not be easy for an organization to remedy its "blindsidedness." Top executives have a disproportionate influence on organizational policy, making their personality profiles of special interest, and making the study of this influential population worth its inherent difficulties.

HYPOTHESIS DEVELOPMENT

Historical Perspective

Research interest in the importance of executive characteristics upon leadership has waxed and waned, and then waxed again over time. In the early parts of the last century, the "great man" approach to leadership held considerable sway. Leaders, so the theory implied, could not so much be trained by business schools or businesses themselves as they could be selected for their leadership nature (Bass, 1990). In such an approach it was natural to assume that personality, or enduring traits of the potential leader, should play an important role. As first behavioral psychology and then cognitive psychology and the humanist school influenced management and leadership thinking, trait-dominated approaches lost favor, and, cognitive, affective, and environmentally and situationally contingent theories of management came to the fore (McGregor, 1960; Fiedler, 1972; House and Mitchell, 1974; Blake and Mouton, 1978; Hersey and Blanchard, 1995). This view of trait importance culminated in Stogdill's (1948) analysis that traits do not have a bearing on leadership. More recently, however, it has become evident that a leader's traits are one of several important factors that need to be understood (Saunders and Stanton, 1976; Howell et al., 1990; Fitting, 1991; Kirkpatrick and Locke, 1991). For example, personality seems to play a more important role in decision making when the decision maker is under stress (Soltan, 1995). Hence, I first investigate what, if anything, separates the personalities of top executives from those of the US adult norm.

Personality Model Determination

There are a number of models of personality that have been used in personality studies. In business, the most frequently used model is still the four-factor Jungian model of personality (Jung [1923] 1971) because of the extensive use of the Myers-Briggs Type Indicator (MBTI) as an instrument (Myers and McCaulley, 1985). Tens of thousands of managers have taken this test. The Jungian model has some intuitive appeal in management studies because of the relationship of some of its dimensions to specific aspects of leadership. In the Jungian model, the sensing/intuition dimension represents modes of gathering data while the thinking/feeling dimension relates to modes of decision making. In contrast, more recent theory, based on a lexical foundation and factor-analytic studies, suggests that these dimensions have a somewhat less direct meaning in terms of leadership. The sensing/intuition dimension does capture some established routines (openness to new experiences), but the thinking/feeling dimension shows no relationship to the utilization of facts. Thinking types do not seem to be more analytical, and feeling types do not tend to have outbursts (Schweiger, 1985). The sensing/intuition dimension has more to do with the amount of information a person prefers, not its type, and the thinking/feeling dimension has more to do with a preference for developing interpersonal warmth (agreeableness) as opposed to a dichotomy of using logic versus one's feelings for decision making (McCrae and Costa, 1989a).

There are other models and scales of normal personality in recent use. Two-dimensional personality models exist that view these dimensions superimposed on a "circumplex" where points along the circumference of a circle identify important personality aspects (Leary, 1957; Wiggins, 1995; McAdams, 1997). The California Psychological Inventory (CPI) uses 20 scales (Groth-Marnat, 1990), but these scales have considerable overlap (Anastasi, 1988). And, of course, the Minnesota Multiphasic Personality Inventory (MMPI) is routinely used to assess personality abnormalities in clinical settings. None of these models, however, provide a comprehensive and truly dimensional model of normal personality as the Jungian model does.

In order to use a comprehensive model of normal personality with orthogonal factors that improves content validity over the Jungian model, the Five Factor Model (the Big Five) was used in this study. Based on observable traits that can reveal one's enduring and underlying dispositions (Costa and McCrae, 1990), the five orthogonal factors of the Big Five have been replicated in numerous factor-analytic studies (McCrae and Costa, 1989b; McCrae et al., 1993; Wiggins and Trapnell, 1997). The Five Factor Model appears to be culturally independent (McCrae and Costa, 1997b), and has reasonable stability in adulthood (Costa and McCrae, 1997, 2006; McCrae et al., 1999). A number of studies have also shown that some of the models noted above are effectively subsumed by the Five Factor Model (Costa et al., 1986; McCrae and Costa, 1989b; Trull et al., 1995).

Executive Differences from the US Population

As noted earlier, there is scant research on the personality characteristics of top executives. Hence, clues to their characteristics must come from less direct sources. Managers in general report that they believe their personalities to be different from the norm (Carr, 2006). A number of studies have theorized or found important differences between entrepreneurs and the US norm (Gartner, 1985; Winslow and Solomon, 1989; Aldridge, 1997; Miner, 1997), and between entrepreneurs and managers (Aldridge, 1997; Malach-Pines et al., 2002). There are also a number of studies that observed personality differences across professions in general (Barrick and Mount, 1991; Barrick et al., 2003), and personality uniqueness for particular professions such as accounting (Satava, 1996), executive recruiters (Dykeman and Dykeman, 1996), creative types (King et al., 1996), army personnel (Gailbreath et al., 1997), and salespeople and managers (Barrick and Mount, 1991). Some meta-analyses have found correlations between leadership and personality traits (e.g., Judge et al., 2002). Other recent studies have focused on what might moderate the relationship between personality and performance (Barrick et al., 2005, 2007). What little evidence exists for top executives includes a study that found personality uniqueness for hospital CEOs (Van Eynde and Tucker, 1996), and health care executives (O'Connor et al., 1992). Moreover, top managers have scored differently from the adult norm on an associated concept of emotional intelligence (Van der Zee and Wabeke, 2004).

Heteromorphic effects between top executives and the population in general would exist if the selection process for top positions was, in part, a selection by one or more enduring traits of the individual. Reaching a top executive position is a process of repetitive selection as the individual advances to one of these positions. A complex mix of skills (ability to lead, organizational, technical, political, social, etc.) is required. Though the requisite skills have been acquired through education and experience, a person's intrinsic characteristics play an important role in an individual's ability and desire to acquire the requisite capabilities. Personality, as a stable characteristic of an individual in adulthood, is one of those intrinsic characteristics. Therefore, since the skills of a top executive are very unique, and since they are, in part, founded upon the individual's personality, a top executive's personality will set this individual apart from the population as a whole.

In order to understand potential differences at the individual personality factor level, I first examine the available evidence with respect to neuroticism. Evidence suggests that high self-esteem individuals are twice as likely to take the risks necessary for top management decision-making (Josephs, 1990). There is also evidence that success, as measured by income, is inversely related to neuroticism (Judge et al., 1999). Moreover, dominating negotiating styles, though not necessarily a desirable TMT trait, have been inversely related to neuroticism (Antonioni, 1998). Perhaps more importantly, high levels of neuroticism can interfere with effective interpersonal functioning. Neuroticism, therefore, will interfere with a number of the requisite capabilities of a top executive and will be negatively correlated with membership in these ranks:

Hypothesis 1: US top executives' personalities will exhibit lower neuroticism than that of the adult norm.

As much as neuroticism inversely predicted income-based success, extroversion positively predicted it (Judge et al., 1999). Moreover, high extroversion seems to separate business leaders from entrepreneurs (Aldridge, 1997). Since executive positions are less constrained by upper management oversight because of their position in the hierarchy, and are therefore relatively more autonomous, it is noteworthy that extroversion has been found to be a better predictor of success in more autonomous jobs (Barrick and Mount, 1993). Extroversion, not surprisingly, has been found to predict sales and managerial success (Barrick and Mount, 1991):

Hypothesis 2: US top executives' personalities will exhibit higher extroversion than that of the adult norm.

Individuals who are open to experience tend to enjoy – and therefore seek out – variety in their experiences (McCrae and Costa, 1997a). Those low in openness find these same activities discomforting, and tend to have a world view that emphasizes staying close to one's roots. It seems reasonable that strategic thinking should benefit from openness, and, therefore, top executives might have an overabundance of more open individuals. Divergent thinking has been associated with those higher in openness (McCrae, 1987). In some firms, particularly large firms, the path to a top executive position entails demonstrating competence in a succession of diverse managerial jobs, requiring an ability to assimilate a wide variety of knowledge, requiring a wide range of organizing and coordinating abilities, requiring broad problem-solving abilities, and so forth. This process can result in the promotion of those with more divergent thinking propensities, giving personalities that are more open an advantage in securing top executive level positions:

Hypothesis 3: US top executives' personalities will exhibit higher openness to experience than that of the adult norm.

Agreeable individuals put high value in generating warm relationships with those they associate with (Graziano and Eisenberg, 1997). They are most comfortable when there is group consensus. Conversely, those with low agreeableness are not particularly worried about dissension. Not surprisingly, agreeable leaders have been shown to prefer participative management styles (Stevens and Ash, 2001). Agreeable personalities are associated with integrative means of dealing with conflict (Antonioni, 1998). Superior job performance has been linked with agreeableness with greater validity when there was high job autonomy (Barrick and Mount, 1993). Agreeableness, therefore, will be a desirable personality dimension in engineering one's path to top management, and, once there, for success in the relatively autonomous characteristics of a top management position:

Hypothesis 4: US top executives' personalities will exhibit higher agreeableness than that of the adult norm.

Finally, conscientiousness has been linked to higher performance motivation (Wright, 2003). Though personality traits are highly longitudinally stable in adulthood, there is some drift over time, and in the case of conscientiousness, it tends to increase somewhat with age (McCrae et al., 1999, 2004). Conscientiousness has been linked to superior task performance when mediated by performance expectancy and goal choice (Gellatly, 1996). Like extroversion, conscientiousness is a more valid predictor of higher performance in more autonomous jobs (Barrick and Mount, 1993). Hence, the relative autonomy of top management positions will result in higher conscientiousness in these executives when compared with the population as a whole:

> *Hypothesis 5:* US top executives' personalities will exhibit higher conscientiousness than that of the adult norm.

Executive Group Personality Characteristics

Personality isomorphism within organizations
Neither people nor organizations are neutral about personality. There is substantial evidence of an important bi-directional selection process. Groups select, recognize, and promote people based on personality characteristics. Conversely, people choose and avoid situations (social, education, occupational) based on personality.

Extroverts are more likely than introverts to seek situations that involve intimacy, competition, and assertion. Extroverts seek situations that involve more social activities (Emmons et al., 1986). "Individuals attempt to identify and selectively enter those situations that encourage and reinforce the expression of their own particular attributes" (Ickes et al., 1997, p. 175). Moreover, when people enter personally incongruent situations they often attempt to alter the situation (Ickes et al., 1997). It should also be noted that people seem to differ on how disparate a situation they can handle. Some people appear to be able to change their responses to incongruent situations more than others are able to change them. "High self-monitors" adopt different characteristics to deal with situational incongruencies more than "low self-monitors" do (ibid., p. 179).

If individuals choose to enter and spend time inside groups that encourage the exposition of their natural traits, a logical corollary is that groups would reciprocally tend to select and retain those that supported group attitudes. Strategic postures, once established, encourage the selection, retention, and promotion of individuals with distinct personality attributes (Thomas and Moss, 1995). Decision makers often take advice from advisers who have the same MBTI typing as they do on sensing/intuiting and thinking/feeling scales (cf., Five Factor openness and agreeableness dimensions) (Hunt et al., 1989).

In attraction, selection, and attrition theory (ATA) (Schneider, 1987) acculturation is not only socialization but also the tendency of organizations to select and reject members based on (perhaps unconscious) personality similarities. Therefore, organizations tend to have modal personalities. A very large study using archival MBTI data (13 000 managers from 142 organizations) shows support for this theory (Schneider et al., 1998). It found that there were significant differences in modal personality across organizations and even across industries.

The evidence that people tend to select groups, and groups tend to select members based on perceived personality similarities suggests that those in top executive positions have greater personality homogeneity than the US population has. There is a tendency to sameness, or isomorphism, of personalities within policy-making bodies:

Hypothesis 6: Top executives' personalities will display isomorphism (i.e., show less variance) on at least one dimension of personality when compared with the distribution of personality traits for the population as a whole.

Personality sameness tends to create uniform ways of looking at situations (Schaubroeck and Lam, 2002). When well adapted to the business unit's circumstances, this uniform way of addressing the environment can facilitate rapid exploitation of new opportunities or rapid response to threats. On the other hand, "groupthink" may well be exacerbated by personality isomorphism. "Groupthink" is predicated upon a "concurrency seeking tendency" (Janis and Mann, 1977). Commitment to a course of action may similarly be exacerbated. It is partly a function of group pressure and one's need for self-justification (Staw, 1981). A lack of variation in executive personalities might limit executive search for effective strategies or strategic responses, causing opportunities to be missed.

Environmental effects upon the collective personality of groups
Although personality isomorphism might exist within top executive ranks, it does not necessarily follow that heterogeneity cannot exist across policy-making bodies. In fact, situational pressures should have a divergent effect. For example, bargaining in cooperative settings has been argued to have a personality component (Boone et al., 1999). Innovative thinking has been connected to openness (positively), and agreeableness and conscientiousness (negatively) (Patterson, 2000). One would expect different policy-making bodies not to exhibit all the same personality characteristics. Whether these bodies are in the same firm or in different firms, as long as they need to react to significantly different environments, situational differences should cause the policy-making bodies to exhibit different personality clustering characteristics.

Environmentally contingent theory has a long history in management studies. Organizational structure has been found to be a function of environmental stability (Lawrence and Lorsch, 1967; Miles et al., 1978). Organizational culture formation has been conceptualized as an adaptation to the external environment (Schein, 1992). Even the use of systems theory to explain organizational adaptation implies an external environmental imperative (Katz and Kahn, 1966).

Business policy formulation, an important function of TMTs, is inherently an exercise in aligning long-term plans with the environment: effecting environmental change where possible and desirable, accommodating where the environment cannot be changed. The notion of cost leader vs. product differentiator vs. niche player (Porter, 1980) is a way of conceptualizing effective environmental adaptations. The value chain (Porter, 1985) is a technique for analyzing the value created by an organizational entity in the environment of interest. The resource-based view (Dierickx et al., 1989; Barney, 1991; Wernerfeldt, 1995) makes environmental isolation foundational for competitive advantage. And transaction cost economics relates certain external market conditions to vertical and horizontal integration strategies (Coase, 1952; Williamson, 1985).[1]

Therefore, if strategy is frequently an external adaptation exercise, one would expect that any characteristics of personality that predispose an individual to prefer certain strategies would be reflected in the personality centroid (i.e., the personality dimensions' central tendencies) of the policy-making group. We should expect that the personality clusters within policy-making groups would be contingent upon environmental forces.

Personality clusters can be one aspect of organizational adaptation, along with TMT skill sets, organizational structure, organizational culture, and numerous other organizational attributes. Different businesses will tend to have different personality centroids:

> *Hypothesis 7:* Business unit TMTs will display personality centroid polymorphism in that the centroids of the personality dimensions of policy-making groups will differ from each other on at least one dimension of personality.

METHODOLOGY

Sample

All members of participating top executive teams, selected from for-profit institutions, were tested in this study. The executive teams were composed of the heads of business units and all their direct reports. Business unit executive teams were selected as the level in an organizational hierarchy to study because a business unit addresses a single market. Therefore, the selected executive teams are the organizational members most responsible for the policy formation and the results of their businesses. In firms with only a single business unit, this meant that the chief executive and his or her staff were the individuals studied. In large multi-business firms the management teams studied were the heads of business units and their staffs.

The study consisted of 71 participants in seven different businesses. The studied businesses ranged in revenue from a few hundred million dollars per annum to several billion dollars per annum. Profits ranged from several tens of millions to hundreds of millions of dollars per annum. Employees ranged from approximately 800 to approximately 8000. Firm participation was solicited from the Fortune 100 companies, from a representative sampling of established medium-sized businesses, and from the Fortune 100 Fastest Growing Companies (Fortune, 1999). Business classifications represented in this study included plastics manufacturing, healthcare delivery, space vehicle components, military aerospace products, computers, and computer peripherals. Geographically, the executives studied all worked in the Midwest or Western areas of the United States (Michigan to California).

Instrumentation

All participants completed the Five Factor Inventory (NEO-FFI) instrument for normal personality assessment (Costa and McCrae, 1992). In order to minimize response bias, individual responses were collected without the respondent's identification attached. Additionally, business unit confidentiality was given to respondents to the extent that the study would not reveal the names of the business units participating, merely a general characterization of the units in the study. Because TMTs would most likely be highly male in composition, gender demographic data was not collected in order to assure female participants that they would not self-identify, potentially causing response bias.[2]

Since personality was assessed with the Five Factor Model of personality, the NEO-FFI instrument was most appropriate for this study. The NEO-FFI is an abbreviated form of the NEO-PI-R[3] (NEO Personality Inventory – Revised). It is a 60-question Likert-scaled instrument that has established validity and reliability for obtaining the five personality dimensions of the Five Factor Model. It was chosen because completion of the entire questionnaire was deemed paramount, and it was anticipated that the time a TMT could spend completing the instrument would be limited. Scoring the NEO-FFI results in values for each of the five factors. Retest reliability of the NEO-PI-R has been performed over six years resulting in stability coefficients of from 0.68 to 0.83, and, in another study, over seven years resulting in coefficients of from 0.68 to 0.81 (all reliability and validity information cited in this subsection is referenced in Costa and McCrae, 1992). Convergent validity has been assessed on the NEO-PI-R by comparing its scores to scores of similar constructs in other instruments including the MMPI, the Profile of Mode States, and the Personality Research Form. Discriminant validity has been assessed by pairing the NEO-PI-R with the 300-item Adjective Check List (Gough and Heilbrun, 1983). After selection of the seven highest adjective correlates for each of the NEO-PI-R facets, results showed a consistent discriminative pattern in the facet scales. Results from tests of the shorter NEO-FFI correlate well with results from the NEO-PI-R, with very little degradation in validity measures. In one large study, the NEO-FFI's five factors correlated with their NEO-PI-R equivalents as follows: 0.93(*N*), 0.90(*E*), 0.94(*O*), 0.88(*A*), and 0.89(*C*). Coefficient alphas were 0.90, 0.78, 0.76, 0.86, and 0.90 respectively.

RESULTS

Analysis

Hypotheses 1 through 5 assert that top executive personality factor means will differ from the corresponding factor of the US adult norm. This was operationalized with a Multivariate Analysis of Variance (MANOVA), thereby avoiding any elevation of Type I error:

$$H_0: \begin{Bmatrix} \bar{x}_{NT} \\ \bar{x}_{ET} \\ \bar{x}_{OT} \\ \bar{x}_{AT} \\ \bar{x}_{CT} \end{Bmatrix} = \begin{Bmatrix} \bar{x}_{NUS} \\ \bar{x}_{EUS} \\ \bar{x}_{OUS} \\ \bar{x}_{AUS} \\ \bar{x}_{CUS} \end{Bmatrix} \tag{4.1}$$

$$H_A: \text{ at least one set is significantly different than the rest}$$

where: $\bar{x}_{Pi}$ is the mean of the *P*th personality factor for the *i*th group, and where a group state is either *T* (top executives) or US (the adult norm). Hypotheses 1 through 5 were assessed from the underlying ANOVAs in the above formulation.

Hypothesis 6 asserts that the top executives' personalities will display less variance, on at least one dimension of personality, than the population as a whole. Hence, if the variance of at least one of the distributions of the five personality dimensions for the executives collectively is significantly different – and smaller – than the equivalent variance for the population as a whole, Hypothesis 6 can be accepted. In order to test this hypothesis the distribution of the US population for each personality dimension was obtained from those reported in Costa and McCrae (1992) for the NEO-FFI. The significance of the differences in variances was tested utilizing an F-test of the variance ratios with a Bonferroni correction applied to account for the five tests (one for each personality dimension).

Hypothesis 7 implies that, for at least one personality dimension, the mean of that personality dimension will differ across business units. This was operationalized with a second MANOVA formulation as follows:

$$
H_0: \quad \begin{Bmatrix} \bar{x}_{N1} \\ \bar{x}_{E1} \\ \bar{x}_{O1} \\ \bar{x}_{A1} \\ \bar{x}_{C1} \end{Bmatrix} = \begin{Bmatrix} \bar{x}_{N2} \\ \bar{x}_{E2} \\ \bar{x}_{O2} \\ \bar{x}_{A2} \\ \bar{x}_{C2} \end{Bmatrix} = \{\ldots\} = \begin{Bmatrix} \bar{x}_{Nn} \\ \bar{x}_{En} \\ \bar{x}_{On} \\ \bar{x}_{An} \\ \bar{x}_{Cn} \end{Bmatrix} \tag{4.2}
$$

$H_A:$ *at least one set is significantly different than the rest*

where: $\bar{x}_{Pi}$ is the mean of the Pth personality factor for the ith TMT,
where TMT is a top management team $[1 \leq TMT \leq n]$, and
where n is the total number of business units in the study.

Personality means and standard deviations for the business units (BU) in the study, for the sample as a whole, and for the US population are provided in Table 4.1.[4]

Personality Heteromorphism – Top Executives vs. the Adult Norms

MANOVA results showed that TMT personalities were significantly different from the adult norms in four of the five personality dimensions (Table 4.2). Moreover, values of

Table 4.1   Personality data (means and standard deviations)

	N		E		O		A		C	
BU	Mean	S.D.	Mean	S.D.	Mean	S.D.	Mean	S.D.	Mean	S.D.
A	11.03	5.52	34.50	3.98	30.40	5.72	32.70	3.95	37.20	4.05
B	16.27	5.00	30.36	4.97	28.18	7.29	29.27	4.31	36.36	6.34
C	13.85	5.73	32.00	6.14	29.92	5.51	34.31	5.19	36.69	5.57
D	9.40	4.38	35.20	5.29	30.78	5.19	37.30	5.06	39.78	4.55
E	11.70	6.91	34.10	6.72	30.20	5.27	34.80	4.16	38.10	2.81
F	12.43	5.35	31.43	6.40	24.86	5.05	30.57	5.91	39.14	3.93
G	10.70	4.45	33.00	4.19	32.00	4.78	33.40	3.44	36.00	6.31
All BU	12.35	5.60	32.93	5.47	29.66	5.74	33.30	5.04	37.46	5.00
US pop	19.03	7.45	27.71	5.62	27.02	5.61	32.85	4.79	34.58	5.75
d[a]	−0.99		0.94		0.47		0.09		0.53	

Note: a. Cohen's *d*: Business units (BUs) vs. US population.

Source: Author's research.

Table 4.2   MANOVA comparison of top executives with US norm

Personality Factor	Omnibus Statistics (p)	Mean Square	F Statistic[a]	Significance (p)	η_p^2	Adjusted R^2
Wilks' Lambda	0.015 (0.000)	–	–	–	–	–
Pillai's Trace	0.985 (0.000)	–	–	–	–	–
Roy's Largest Root	67.192 (0.000)	–	–	–	–	–
N	–	1771.719	39.002	0.000	0.189	0.184
E	–	1075.576	34.943	0.000	0.173	0.168
O	–	285.133	8.888	0.003	0.051	0.045
A	–	6.241	0.259	0.611	0.002	0.000
C	–	340.447	11.459	0.001	0.064	0.059

Note: a. Corrected model (df, corrected total = 168).

Source: Author's research.

partial eta squared (η_p^2) and adjusted R^2 showed moderate effects for both neuroticism and extroversion, and lesser but important effect sizes for openness and conscientiousness. These effect sizes are supported by the data in Table 4.1 as well. Table 4.1 shows that the top executive neuroticism mean was about one standard deviation lower, and the top executive extroversion mean was about one standard deviation higher than the adult norm. Top executive openness and top executive conscientiousness are both about one-half a standard deviation higher than the adult norm. In the MANOVA formulation Box's M was significant, but sample sizes were not dramatically different, and all omnibus significance statistics (including Pillai's Trace) were significant at $p < 0.001$. Neuroticism displayed an unequal error variance (Levene's F of 4.876, $p = 0.029$), but Pillai's Trace was significant ($p < 0.001$), providing corroboration of the overall significance of the personality centroid differences.

The associated ANOVAs showed ample significance ($p \leq 0.001$ in all cases) for neuroticism, extroversion, openness, and conscientiousness. Effect sizes (see Table 4.2) were low to modest for these variables. Hence, Hypotheses 1, 2, 3, and 5 were upheld. On the other hand, it is clear from Table 4.2 that Hypothesis 4 cannot be upheld.

Personality Isomorphism Within Top Executive Ranks

Hypothesis 6 implies that the distributions of TMT member personality dimensions should have lower variances than the equivalent dimensions of the US population. As an examination of Table 4.1 shows, most teams did have lower variances in neuroticism, extroversion, and conscientiousness. However, an F-test of the variance ratios for unequal variances revealed that only neuroticism had a significantly lower variance than the corresponding personality factor for the adult population (Table 4.3). Neuroticism is significant after applying a Bonferroni correction for the five personality factors.

Hence, Hypothesis 6.can be upheld, but top executive personality sameness, relative to the US population, can be said to be valid only for neuroticism.

Table 4.3   Variance comparison of top executives vs. adult norm

Personality Factor	F Ratio	F Significance (p)[a]	Levene F	Levene Significance (p)
N	0.57	0.01	5.01	0.03
E	0.95	0.81	0.11	0.75
O	1.05	0.82	0.00	0.99
A	1.11	0.64	0.11	0.74
C	0.76	0.22	1.74	0.19

Note: a. Before Bonferroni correction.

Source: Author's research.

Table 4.4   MANOVA comparison of business units

Personality Factor	Omnibus Statistics (p)	Mean Square	F Statistic[a]	Significance (p)	η_p^2	Adjusted R^2
Wilks' Lambda	0.568 (0.270)	–	–	–	–	–
Pillai's Trace	0.485 (0.221)	–	–	–	–	–
Roy's Largest Root	0.464 (0.000)	–	–	–	–	–
N	–	49.099	1.67	0.14	0.137	0.055
E	–	27.381	0.91	0.49	0.080	0.007
O	–	43.467	1.35	0.25	0.115	0.030
A	–	69.351	3.23	0.01	0.236	0.163
C	–	19.191	0.75	0.61	0.067	0.022

Note: a. Corrected model (df, corrected total = 69).

Source: Author's research.

Personality Polymorphism Across Business Units

Hypothesis 7 sought to determine if TMT personality centroids differed across business units. MANOVA tests performed across executive teams showed that that was in fact the case: agreeableness was significantly different across the management teams ($p < 0.01$) (Table 4.4). Post hoc tests showed that this was attributable to six pair-wise significant business unit comparisons (Tukey's LSD) (Table 4.5). Box's *M* showed no unequal variance issues as did Levene tests on each factor. No other personality factor displayed a difference across business units. Overall, the Wilks and Pillai statistics were not significant, while Roy's Root did show significance ($p < 0.001$), which was not surprising given that significance of the individual personality dimensions was limited to one of the five dimensions.

The effect size of the agreeableness result is sufficiently large to imply that it has importance to practice ($\eta_p^2 = 0.24$). As can be deduced from Table 4.1, the difference between

Table 4.5 Significance of pairwise differences across BUs: agreeableness[a]

	Business Unit A		Business Unit B		Business Unit C		Business Unit D		Business Unit E		Business Unit F	
	Diff.	p	Diff.	p	Diff.	p	Diff.	p	Diff.	p	Diff.	p
Business Unit A												
Business Unit B	−3.43	0.10										
Business Unit C	1.61	0.41	5.03	0.01								
Business Unit D	4.63	0.03	8.06	0.00	3.03	0.14						
Business Unit E	2.10	0.31	5.53	0.01	0.49	0.80	−2.53	0.24				
Business Unit F	−2.13	0.35	1.30	0.56	−3.74	0.09	−6.76	0.01	−4.23	0.07		
Business Unit G	0.70	0.74	4.13	0.05	−0.91	0.64	−3.93	0.07	−1.40	0.50	2.83	0.22

Note: a. Tukey's LSD.

Source: Author's research.

the team with the highest agreeableness score and the one with the lowest score is 8.03 (or 1.59 standard deviations). That interval spans the 23rd to the 83rd percentiles of the US population (i.e., 60 percent of the distribution of the population). Hence, Hypothesis 7 – that personality characteristics *across* business units would exhibit polymorphic properties – was supported.

DISCUSSION

There is strong evidence in this study of the heteromorphic nature of top executive personality with respect to the population as a whole. Top executives are substantially different from the average person. They are much lower in neuroticism and much higher in extroversion. They are also somewhat higher than the average person in openness and conscientiousness. It appears that the repetitive selection process that results in one attaining a top management position entails (perhaps unconscious) selection by personality. This has profound implications for the prospects of individuals in attaining one of these relatively rare positions. It has implications on the way that firms and even academic institutions explain and prepare employees for a likely and rewarding career path. It is less clear that personality is connected with top executive performance. This study attests to who gets to these positions based on personality, but it cannot say that these personalities necessarily make the most effective top executives. Further study in this area is needed. Certain personality characteristics might lead to superior executive functioning, but they might just as likely be associated with top management inertia in the face of environmental changes. Organizations can some-times adapt; organizations can also learn superstitiously and suboptimally (Cyert and March, 1963).

This study also found that top executives have less variance in their personality distribution than the adult norm: relative to the adult norm, they tend to sameness (isomorphism). This is in line with research that shows that social organizations tend to select those like themselves. But the constricted variance was limited to neuroticism; no other dimension of personality showed any significant tendency to be different in variance from the adult norm. This suggests that the iterative selection process neces-sary to reach a top management position is not a conscious or subconscious process to select only those with same limited range of enduring characteristics *overall*. Although top executives have dramatically different personalities from the adult norm *on average*, the range is not also restricted – except with respect to neuroticism. This may represent a realization by TMTs that neuroticism is a special case that needs special management. In the same vein, it may suggest that, outside of neuroticism, restricting the personality range is either not desirable – variance is a good adaptation – or it is not sufficiently desirable to outweigh the many other selection criteria for a TMT position. Here again further study should be illuminating. We might better understand how executive teams function (resolve conflict, reach consensus, reach out for support, etc.) had we a better understanding of why four out of five of the TMT personality dimensions are offset dramatically from the adult norm, while at the same time four out of five of these dimen-sions are not range restricted.

Lastly, personality polymorphism was observed across TMTs: agreeableness differ-entiated one team from another. The fact that agreeableness did not differentiate top executives, as a whole, from the adult population, but that it did differentiate TMTs from each other is noteworthy. It suggests that agreeableness is the principal way in which personality becomes an environment adaptation (and not a top management selection criterion, as are the other personality dimensions).

The study findings imply the need to understand one's competitors not only in terms of their technology and physical capital, but also in terms of their human capital. Admittedly, trying to understand the personality effects of a competitor's TMT is dif-ficult, and possibly error-prone. Examining a competitor's past actions and reactions to circumstances provides some indirect clues.

The articles in the *Handbook* demonstrate that TMT research yields valuable insights. It is worth noting that much of the literature of business strategy concerns itself with the nature of the environment and the nature of the firm's resources, but much less with how the behavior of the firm's key individuals affect strategy creation and its implementation. This article suggests that TMT personality centroids might explain some aspects of policy making and its implementation. Further investigation in this area could illuminate connections between TMT agreeableness (which this research suggests needs further study) and adaptability to certain types of environmental changes. Findings from such research might illuminate better any TMT-based effects linked to "creative destruction" (Schumpeter, 1942) – which should be immensely valuable to theory and practice. More generally, our understanding of personality and other behavioral influences on business policy would benefit from increased TMT research.

NOTES

1. For a classification of the various forms of strategic fit, see Venkatraman and Camillus (1984).
2. For example, respondents were instructed not to fill in gender in the NEO-FFI.
3. NEO-PI-R is a trademark of Psychological Resources, Inc.
4. US population statistics were computed from NEO-FFI distribution data in Costa and McCrae (1992).

REFERENCES

Aldridge, J.H., Jr. (1997). An occupational personality profile of the male entrepreneur as assessed by the 16PF fifth edition. Unpublished doctoral dissertation, Cleveland State University.

Allport, G.W. and Odbert, H.S. (1936). *Personality: A psychological interpretation*. New York, NY: Holt.

Anastasi, A. (1988). *Psychological testing*. New York, NY: Macmillan Publishing Co., Inc.

Antonioni, D. (1998). Relationship between the big five personality factors and conflict management styles. *International Journal of Conflict Management*, 9(4), 336–55.

Barney, J. (1991). Firm resources and sustained competitive advantage. *Journal of Management*, 17(1), 99–120.

Barrick, M.R. and Mount, M.K. (1991). The big five personality dimensions and job performance: A meta-analysis. *Personnel Psychology*, 44(1), 1–26.

Barrick, M.R. and Mount, M.K. (1993). Autonomy as a moderator of the relationships between the big five. *Journal of Applied Psychology*, 78(1), 111–18.

Barrick, M.R., Mount, M.K., and Gupta, R. (2003). Meta-analysis of the relationship between the five-factor model of personality and Holland's occupational types. *Personnel Psychology*, 56(1), 45–74.

Barrick, M.R., Parks, L., and Mount, M.K. (2005). Self-monitoring as a moderator of the relationships between personality traits and performance. *Personnel Psychology*, 58(3), 745–67.

Barrick, M.R., Bradley, B.H., Kristof-Brown, A.L., and Colbert, A.E. (2007). The moderating role of top management team interdependence: Implications for real team and working groups. *Academy of Management Journal*, 50(3), 544–57.

Bass, B.M. (1990). *Bass and Stogdill's handbook of leadership*. New York, NY: The Free Press.

Blake, R.R. and Mouton, J.S. (1978). *The new managerial grid*. Houston, TX: Gulf.

Boone, C., de Brabander, B., and van Witteloostuijn, A. (1999). The impact of personality on behavior in five prisoner's dilemma games. *Journal of Economic Psychology*, 20(3), 343–77.

Butcher, J.N. and Spielberger, C.D. (eds) (1995). *Advances in personality assessment* (Vol. 10). Hillsdale, NJ: Lawrence Erlbaum Associates Publishers.

Carr, M. (2006). How managers and non-managers differ in their MBTI personality type. *People Management*, 12(9), 48.

Coase, R.H. (1952). The nature of the firm. In G.J. Stigler and K.E. Boulding (eds), *Readings in price theory*. Homewood, IL: Richard D. Irwin, Inc.

Collins, J.M. and Gleaves, D.H. (1998). Race, job applicants, and the five-factor model of personality: Implications for black psychology, industrial/organizational psychology, and the five-factor theory. *Journal of Applied Psychology*, 83(4), 531–44.

Costa Jr., P.T. and McCrae, R.R. (1988). Personality in adulthood: A six-year longitudinal study of self-reports and spouse ratings on the NEO personality inventory. *Journal of Personality and Social Psychology*, 54(5), 853–63.

Costa Jr., P.T. and McCrae, R.R. (1990). Personality in adulthood: Emerging lives, enduring dispositions. In *Handbook of personality psychology*. New York, NY: Guilford Press.

Costa Jr., P.T. and McCrae, R.R. (1992). *Professional manual: Revised NEO personality inventory and NEO five-factor inventory*. Odessa, FL: Psychological Assessment Resources, Inc.

Costa Jr., P.T. and McCrae, R.R. (1997). Longitudinal stability of adult personality. In R. Hogan, J. Johnson, and S. Briggs (eds), *Handbook of personality psychology*. San Diego, CA: Academic Press, Inc, pp. 269–92.

Costa Jr., P.T. and McCrae, R.R. (2006). Age changes in personality and their origins: Comment on Roberts, Walton, and Viechtbauer (2006). *Psychological Bulletin*, 132(1), 26–8.

Costa Jr., P.T., Busch, C.M., Zonderman, A.B., and McCrae, R.R. (1986). Correlations of MMPI factor scales with measures of the five factor model of personality. *Journal of Personality Assessment*, 50(4), 640–50.

Cyert, R.M. and March, J.G. (1963). *A behavioral theory of the firm* (2nd edition). Cambridge, MA: Blackwell Publishers.

Dierickx, I., Cool, K., and Barney, J.B. (1989). Asset stock accumulation and sustainability of competitive advantage. *Management Science*, 35(12), 1504–14.

DSM-IV-TR (2000). *Diagnostic and statistical manual of mental disorders* (Vol. IV-TR). Washington, DC: American Psychiatric Association.

Dykeman, C. and Dykeman, J.J. (1996). Big-five personality profile of executive search recruiters. *Journal of Employment Counseling*, **33**(2), 77–86.

Emmons, R.A., Diener, E., and Larsen, R.J. (1986). Choice and avoidance of everyday situations and affect congruence: Two models of reciprocal interactionism. *Journal of Personality and Social Psychology*, **51**(4), 815–26.

Fiedler, F.E. (1972). How do you make leaders more effective? New answers to an old puzzle. In *Organizational dynamics*. Amsterdam: Elsevier Science, Ltd, pp. 1–18.

Fitting, E.A. (1991). Personality type and its influence on the decision-making process in an organizational setting (Jungian). Unpublished PhD dissertation, Stanford University, Palo Alto, CA.

Fortune (1999). Fortune's one hundred fastest-growing companies. *Fortune*, **140**, 90–102.

Fraboni, M. and Saltstone, R. (1990). First and second generation entrepreneur typologies: Dimensions of personality. *Journal of Social Behavior & Personality*, **5**(3), 105–13.

Furnham, A. and Stringfield, P. (1993). Personality and occupational behavior: Myers-Briggs type indicator correlates of managerial practices in two cultures. *Human Relations*, **46**(7), 827–48.

Gailbreath, R.D., Wagner, S.L., Moffett III, R.G., and Hein, M.B. (1997). Homogeneity in behavior preference among U.S. army leaders. *Group Dynamics: Theory, Research, and Practice*, **1**, 222–30.

Gardner, W.L. and Martinko, M.J. (1996). Using the Myers-Briggs type indicator to study managers: A literature review and research agenda. *Journal of Management*, **22**(1), 45–83.

Gartner, W.B. (1985). A conceptual framework for describing the phenomenon of new venture creation. *Academy of Management Review*, **10**(4), 696–706.

Gellatly, I.R. (1996). Conscientiousness and task performance: Test of a cognitive process model. *Journal of Applied Psychology*, **81**(5), 474–82.

Goldberg, L.R. (1981). Language and individual differences: The search for universals in personality lexicons. In L. Wheeler (ed.), *Review of personality and social psychology* (Vol. 2). Beverly Hills, CA: Sage Publications, pp. 141–65.

Gough, H.G. and Heilbrun Jr., A.B. (1983). *Adjective check list manual*. Palo Alto, CA: Consulting Psychologists Press.

Graziano, W. and Eisenberg, N.H. (1997). Agreeableness: A dimension of personality. In R. Hogan, J. Johnson, and S. Briggs (eds), *Handbook of personality psychology*. San Diego, CA: Academic Press, Inc, pp. 795–825.

Groth-Marnat, G. (1990). *Handbook of psychological assessment*. New York, NY: John Wiley and Sons, Inc.

Halikias, J. and Panayotopoulou, L. (2003). Chief executive personality and export involvement. *Management Decision*, **41**(4), 340–49.

Hathaway, S.R. and McKinley, J.C. (1951). *Minnesota multiphasic personality inventory manual (revised)*. San Antonio, TX: Psychological Corporation.

Hersey, P. and Blanchard, K.H. (1995). Situational leadership. In J.T. Wren (ed.), *The leader's companion: Insights on leadership through the ages*. New York, NY: The Free Press, pp. 207–11.

House, R.J. and Mitchell, T.R. (1974). Path–goal theory of leadership. *Journal of Contemporary Business*, **3**(Fall), 81–97.

Howell, J.P., Bowen, D.E., Dorfman, P.W., Kerr, S., and Podsakoff, P.M. (1990). Substitutes for leadership: Effective alternatives to ineffective leadership. In *Organizational Dynamics* (Vol. 19). Amsterdam: Elsevier Science, Ltd.

Hunt, R.G., Krzystofiak, F.J., Meindl, J.R., and Yousry, A.M. (1989). Cognitive style and decision making. *Organizational Behavior and Human Decision Processes*, **44**(3), 436–53.

Ickes, W., Snyder, M., and Garcia, S. (1997). Personality influences on the choice of situations. In R. Hogan, J. Johnson, and S. Briggs (eds), *Handbook of personality psychology*. San Diego, CA: Academic Press.

Janis, I.L. and Mann, L. (1977). *Decision making: A psychological analysis of conflict, choice, and commitment*. New York, NY: The Free Press.

Josephs, R.A. (1990). The threat of risky decision-making to self-esteem (prospect theory). Unpublished doctoral dissertation, University of Michigan.

Judge, T.A., Higgins, C.A., and Thoresen, C.J. (1999). The big five personality traits, general mental ability, and career success across the life span. *Personnel Psychology*, **52**(3), 621–52.

Judge, T.A., Bono, J.E., Ilies, R., and Gerhardt, M.W. (2002). Personality and leadership: A qualitative and quantitative review. *Journal of Applied Psychology*, **87**(4), 765–80.

Jung, G.C. [1923] (1971). *Psychological types* (H. G. r. R. F. C. H. Baynes, Trans.). Princeton, NJ: Princeton University Press.

Katz, D. and Kahn, R.L. (1966). *The social psychology of organizations*. New York, NY: John Wiley and Sons, Inc.

King, L.A., Walker, L.M., and Broyles, S.J. (1996). Creativity and the five factor model. *Journal of Research in Personality*, **30**(2), 189–203.

Kirkpatrick, S.A. and Locke, E.A. (1991). Leadership: Do traits matter? *Academy of Management Executive*, **5**(2), 48–60.

Lawrence, P.R. and Lorsch, J.W. (1967). Differentiation and integration in complex organizations. *Administrative Science Quarterly*, **12**(1), 1–47.

Leary, T. (1957). *Interpersonal diagnosis of personality*. New York, NY: Ronald Press.

Malach-Pines, A., Sadeh, A., Dvir, D., and Yafe-Yanai, O. (2002). Entrepreneurs and managers: Similar yet different. *International Journal of Organizational Analysis*, **10**(2), 172–90.

McAdams, D.P. (1997). A conceptual history of personality psychology. In R. Hogan, J. Johnson and S. Briggs (eds), *Handbook of personality psychology*. San Diego, CA: Academic Press, Inc, pp. 3–39.

McCrae, R.R. (1987). Creativity, divergent thinking, and openness to experience. *Journal of Personality and Social Psychology*, **52**(6), 1258–65.

McCrae, R.R. and Costa Jr., P.T. (1989a). Reinterpreting the Myers-Briggs type Indicator from the perspective of the five-factor model of personality. *Journal of Personality*, **57**(1), 17–40.

McCrae, R.R. and Costa Jr., P.T. (1989b). The structure of interpersonal traits: Wiggins' circumplex and the five-factor model. *Journal of Personality and Social Psychology*, **56**(4), 586–95.

McCrae, R.R. and Costa, Jr. P.T. (1997a). Conceptions and correlates of openness to experience. In R. Hogan, J. Johnson, and S. Briggs (eds), *Handbook of personality psychology*. San Diego, CA: Academic Press, Inc, pp. 826–48.

McCrae, R.R. and Costa Jr., P.T. (1997b). Personality trait structure as a human universal. *American Psychologist*, **52**(5), 509–16.

McCrae, R.R., Costa Jr., P.T., and Piedmont, R.L. (1993). Folk concepts, natural language, and psychological constructs: The California psychological inventory and the five-factor model. *Journal of Personality*, **61**(1), 1–16.

McCrae, R.R., Costa Jr., P.T., Hrebickova, M., and Urbanek, T. (2004). Age differences in personality traits across cultures: Self-report and observer perspectives. *European Journal of Personality*, **18**(2), 143–57.

McCrae, R.R., Costa Jr., P.T., Pedroso de Lima, M., and Simoes, A. (1999). Age differences in personality across the adult life span: Parallels in five cultures. *Developmental Psychology*, **35**(2), 466–77.

McGregor, D. (1960). *The human side of enterprise*. New York, NY: McGraw-Hill, Inc.

Miles, R.E., Snow, C.C., Meyer, A.D., and Coleman, H.J., Jr. (1978). Organizational strategy, structure, and process. *Academy of Management Review*, 546–62.

Miner, J.B. (1997). *A psychological typology of successful entrepreneurs*. Westport, CT: Quorum Books.

Myers, I.B. and McCaulley, M.H. (1985). *Manual: A guide to the development and use of the Myers-Briggs type indicator*. Palo Alto, CA: Consulting Psychologists Press.

O'Connor, S.J., Shewchuk, R.M., and Raab, D.J. (1992). Patterns of psychological type among health care executives. *Hospital & Health Services Administration*, **37**(4), 431–47.

Patterson, F. (2000). Great minds don't think alike? Person-level predictors of innovation at work. In C.L. Cooper and I.T. Robertson (eds), *International review of industrial and organizational psychology* (Vol. 17). Chichester, UK: John Wiley and Sons, pp. 115–44.

Porter, M.E. (1980). *Competitive strategy: Techniques for analyzing industries and competitors*. New York, NY: The Free Press.

Porter, M.E. (1985). *Competitive advantage: Creating and sustaining superior performance*. New York, NY: The Free Press.

Salgado, J.F. (1997). The five factor model of personality and job performance in the European Community. *Journal of Applied Psychology*, **82**(1), 30–43.

Satava, D. (1996). Personality types of CPAs: National vs. local firms. *Journal of Personality Type*, **36**, 36–41.

Saunders, G.B. and Stanton, J.L. (1976). Personality as influencing factor in decision making. *Organizational Behavior and Human Performance*, **15**(2), 241–57.

Schaubroeck, J. and Lam, S.S.K. (2002). How similarity to peers and supervisor influences organizational advancement in different cultures. *Academy of Management Journal*, **45**, 1120–36.

Schein, E.H. (1992). *Organizational culture and leadership*. San Francisco, CA: Jossey-Bass Publishers.

Schneider, B. (1987). The people make the place. *Personnel Psychology*, **40**(3), 437–54.

Schneider, B., Smith, D.B., Taylor, S., and Fleenor, J. (1998). Personality and organizations: A test of the homogeneity of personality hypothesis. *Journal of Applied Psychology*, **83**(3), 462–70.

Schumpeter, J.A. (1942). *Capitalism, socialism and democracy*. London, UK: Harper and Row.

Schweiger, D.M. (1985). Measuring managerial cognitive styles: On the logical validity of the Myers-Briggs type indicator. *Journal of Business Research*, **13**(4), 315–28.

Soltan, G.A.G. (1995). Decision-making under stress: A case study of the Iraqi behavior during the Gulf crisis. Unpublished doctoral dissertation, Northern Illinois University.

Staw, B.M. (1981). The escalation of commitment to a course of action. *Academy of Management Review*, **6**(4), 577–87.

Stevens, C.D. and Ash, R.A. (2001). Selecting employees for fit: Personality and preferred managerial style. *Journal of Managerial Issues*, **13**(4), 500–517.

Stogdill, R.M. (1948). Personal factors associated with leadership: A survey of the literature. *Journal of Psychology*, **25**(1), 37–71.

Thomas, A.S. and Moss, S.E. (1995). A theoretical examination of the role of personality in research on strategic process. *Psychological Reports*, **76**, 403–17.

Trull, T.J., Useda, J.D., Costa, P.T., and McCrae, R.R. (1995). Comparison of the MMPI-2, personality psychopathology five (PSY-5), the NEO-PI and the NEO-PI-R. *Psychological Assessment*, **7**(4), 508–16.

Van der Zee, K. and Wabeke, R. (2004). Is trait-emotional intelligence simply or more than just a trait? *European Journal of Personality*, **18**(4), 243–67.

Van Eynde, D.F. and Tucker, S.L. (1996). Personality patterns of health care and industry CEOs: Similarities and differences. *Health Care Management Review*, **21**(2), 87–95.

Venkatraman, N. and Camillus, J.C. (1984). Exploring the concept of "fit" in strategic management. *Academy of Management Review*, **9**(3), 513–25.

Wernerfeldt, B. (1995). The resource-based view of the firm: Ten years after. *Strategic Management Journal*, **16**(3), 171–85.

Wiggins, J.S. (1995). *Interpersonal adjectives scales: Professional manual*. Odessa, FL: Psychological Assessment Resources.

Wiggins, J.S. and Trapnell, P.D. (1997). Personality structure: The return of the big five. In R. Hogan, J. Johnson, and S. Briggs (eds), *Handbook of personality psychology*. San Diego, CA: Academic Press, Inc, pp. 737–65.

Williamson, O.E. (1985). *The economic institutions of capitalism*. New York, NY: The Free Press.

Winslow, E.K. and Solomon, G.T. (1989). Further development of a descriptive profile of entrepreneurs. *Journal of Creative Behavior*, **23**(2), 149–61.

Wright, T.A. (2003). What every manager should know: Does personality help drive employee motivation? *The Academy of Management Executive*, **17**(2), 131–3.

Zhao, H. and Seibert, S.E. (2006). The big five personality dimensions and entrepreneurial status: A meta-analytical review. *Journal of Applied Psychology*, **91**(2), 259–71.

5 Charismatic leadership, social networks, and goal setting among US and Chinese executives

Alexander D. Stajkovic, Mason A. Carpenter, and Scott D. Graffin

We integrate three widely studied theories, from three management disciplines, which have not seen such integration in the literature. We integrate theories of charismatic leadership (leadership field), social networks (strategy), and goal setting (organizational behavior) to propose that: (1) charismatic leaders tend to attract more followers; (2) as a result, they will be able to form more extensive social networks; (3) those leaders with more extensive social networks will exhibit higher career aspiration operationalized through the setting of challenging career goals; (4) charismatic leadership would not directly lead to setting of more challenging goals without the aid (mediation) of one's social network, and (5) these relationships may vary across national cultures. Using cross-cultural samples of executives from the US and China, we find a positive relationship between a leader's charisma and the size of his/her social network, which then positively relates to that leader's setting of challenging career goals (see Figure 5.1).

These new insights (further elaborated below) would not have been possible without the theory integration process. That is, while social network theory frequently makes an economics-based argument that networks are formed mostly because people want to gain some material/financial benefit from it, no arguments are made that networks may be formed also because people are psychologically attracted to the charismatic leadership. Also, there is no linking in the present literature of social networks potentially being

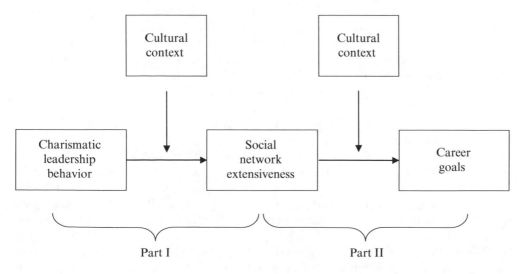

Figure 5.1   Conceptual models examined in Parts I and II of our study

useful to setting challenging goals. We believe that these insights represent particular novelties of our theory integration process.

For instance, the notion that charismatic leaders attract others has been at the heart of the charisma construct since it was introduced (Weber, 1947). Charisma is a personal attractiveness that enables one to influence others; a social network is an extended group of people with similar interests or concerns who interact and remain in informal contact for mutual assistance/support. Our theory integration process leads us to suggest that the charismatic ability of a leader to attract others is related to the extensiveness of his/her social network. While intuitive, this link has not been considered in the study of social networks. Previous networks research has typically sought to answer a question of *why someone builds* a social network (Mizruchi and Galaskiewicz, 1993). From such work we have learned that people tend to form social networks based on the material and social gains they believe the network will offer (Granovetter, 1973; Burt, 1997).

However, scant research has examined the question of *why others contribute* their time, effort, and affection to the person trying to form the social network – why do people choose to become part of that social network? Resource dependence (Pfeffer and Salancik, 1978) and homophily perspectives (Kanter, 1977) provide only partial answers to this "reverse" question. While charisma and social networks have been examined widely in their own right, practically no research has related these two important constructs. For instance, out of 340 studies on leadership conducted in the past 100 years, and with the exception of Pastor et al. (2002), we found no research that linked these two constructs in any setting.[1]

Social networks have been found to be positively related to numerous outcomes such as career success (Gabbay and Zuckerman, 1998), job search and success (Granovetter, 1973; Lin and Dumin, 1996; Burt, 1997), and one's health (Cohen et al., 2003). However, no research has suggested that there may be psychological motivational *processes* through which social networks lead to outcomes for individuals. We suggest that the more extensive social network a leader has, the more challenging goals (desired end states) he or she is likely to pursue. Using an election setting as an example, voting results capture expressed preferences – the more supporters a candidate has, the more he or she can try to do. We connect the two theories and suggest that such supporter breadth, in the form of network extensiveness, allows the candidate to set more challenging goals. At work, the more supporters a CEO has on the board of directors or the more contacts a manager has to draw upon for support, the more likely they are to try to set challenging goals.

Research has not made a bridge between social networks to motivational variables, and yet goal setting is one of the most researched motivational mechanisms through which people impact desired outcomes (Locke and Latham, 1990, 2002). As Locke and Latham assert: "The evidence is overwhelming that goal setting affects performance across tasks, setting, subjects, countries, criteria, and time spans. . . Few if any theories . . . can claim such consistent and wide-ranging support" (1990, p. 46). Indeed, Miner (2003) reports that, out of 73 management theories, organizational behavior professors rank goal-setting theory as number one in importance. In their book, Locke and Latham (1990, p. 133) note that "most goal-setting studies have focused on the effects of the assigned goals," and call for more research on self-set goals. And yet, based on our review of four existing meta-analyses on goals and a reference search based on Locke and Latham (1990, 2002), we did not find a single study that linked social networks and goals of any kind.

One explanation for this research gap is that charismatic leadership, social networks, and goal setting have been studied widely, but in research considering each topic, independently. We reviewed 914 studies on social networks and found none that links charismatic leadership and goals to networks. In this work, we show how these three prominent theories could be integrated to provide new insight and knowledge that would not be possible without the integration process. In addition, we also propose that these relationships may work differently in different national cultural contexts (Burt, 1992; Conger and Kanungo, 1998). Thus, another aspect of the integrated theoretical framework we propose is the incorporation of national culture (i.e., individualistic culture in the US sample, and collectivistic in China sample) as a moderator. This allows us to simultaneously explore the generalizability and boundary conditions of our proposed integration.

THEORETICAL BACKGROUND

In this section, we present the integration of charismatic leadership, social networks, and goal setting for new insights. We first describe each theory and construct on their own, and then conceptually integrate them to develop new theory insights and hypotheses.

Charisma

Charisma was introduced as a construct by Weber (1947). Weber saw charisma as a unique "revolutionary force" in terms of its effect on others that is possessed by a person who has "specific gifts of body and mind" (Weber [1925] 1968, p. 1112). He defined charismatic people as those who "reveal a transcendent mission or course of action which may be in itself appealing to the potential followers, but which is acted upon because the followers believe their leader is extraordinarily gifted" (Weber, 1947, p. 358). Indeed, charisma in the Greek language means "gift," and the idea of describing someone who is gifted with powerful influence on others is pervasive in most, if not all, definitions of charisma, including lexical ones. Synonyms for charisma include terms such as allure, charm, fascination, magnetism, mystique, and panache. Weber (1947) saw charisma as a personality trait: a stable and inborn psychological disposition.

Charismatic leadership

More recent conceptualizations define charisma in behavioral terms (House, 1977; Sashkin, 1988; Shamir et al., 1993). Such charismatic behaviors are more widely known as charismatic leadership (House, 1977; Conger and Kanungo, 1994; Yukl, 1999). In their comprehensive book on this topic, Conger and Kanungo (1998) state that charisma is based on both the leader's behavior and the way in which such behavior is interpreted and acted upon by others – that is, a leader exhibits certain behaviors, and people in a given context perceive whether those behaviors are charismatic or not. Thus, the attribution of charisma to a leader by others is based on the interaction between the leader's behaviors and the context in which those behaviors take place (ibid.). This behavioral view is the prevalent way of defining charismatic leadership in contemporary research.

Conger and Kanungo (ibid.) define charismatic leadership as consisting of five sets of behaviors: vision articulation, risk taking, unconventional behaviors, sensitivity to environment, and sensitivity toward others' needs. Vision articulation deals with developing a view that challenges the status quo and then communicating it to others. Crafting and articulating a vision has long been recognized as a charismatic attribute (Conger, 1985; Shamir et al., 1993; Conger and Kanungo, 1998). Risk taking represents behaviors with uncertain outcomes, where the leader's actions may increase his/her risk of being fired, demoted, or the loss of status (Conger and Kanungo, 1998). By engaging in such behaviors, charismatic leaders demonstrate their convictions and thus serve as a role model for the vision they espouse. The unconventional behaviors are unexpected and can surprise others. By engaging in them, charismatic leaders demonstrate their convictions and thus serve as a role model for the vision they espouse. These three sets of behaviors just described are defined by Conger and Kanungo (ibid.) as being more person-oriented, in that the leader engages in them based on his/her own ideals and convictions and not necessarily on collective conclusions derived from collaboration with others.

Sensitivity to the environment involves assessing the environmental constraints of the firm. Sensitivity to others' needs serves a dual purpose. First, it allows the leader to assess the affinities of members of the group. This allows the leader to better understand where the organization may have advantages and plan accordingly. Second, such analysis will also help increase the buy-in of followers. When leaders engage in this type of behavior, followers may feel that the leader's actions are meant to serve them and the organization as a whole rather than simply serving the leader (Hollander, 1958). Conger and Kanungo (ibid.) define these two sets of behaviors as more group oriented; they represent the assessment process that leaders engage in to better understand opportunities, which increases the buy-in of members around the leader.

Social Networks

While social networks can operate at higher levels of analysis (e.g., Dubini and Aldrich, 1991; Liebeskind et al., 1996; Uzzi, 1999), we emphasize them at the individual level of analysis. This is consistent with the idea that "networks are constructed when . . . humans interact" (Salancik, 1995, p. 345). A network of social ties provides value to its members by giving them access to the various resources that are present in that network (Seibert et al., 2001; Adler and Kwon, 2002). Not all social networks are the same. They vary in their attributes, which in turn determine network extensiveness. We focus on the following elements of social network extensiveness (SNE) because of their prevalent attention in the social networks literature (cf., Wasserman and Faust, 1994; Athanassiou and Nigh, 1999): number of network ties, structural holes/number of weak ties, demographic/gender similarity, and network ties to senior colleagues.

Number of ties
Ceteris paribus, larger networks provide more resources than smaller networks (Burt, 1992). Simply, large networks can provide more information, advice, or support than small networks. While a larger network can provide ample resources, at some point the

returns from additional social ties begin to diminish; moreover, redundant contacts may add little new information and come at a cost of time spent nurturing them (ibid.).

Structural holes/weak ties

The concepts of both structural holes and weak ties emphasize the importance of new information from distant sources. A structural hole is a term used to describe the separation between unique (non-redundant) contacts (ibid.). As a result of the hole between them, the two contacts provide network benefits that are to some degree likely more additive than overlapping. Weak ties capture a conceptually similar idea. Granovetter (1973) suggests that access, via weak ties, to different groups of individuals can provide unique informational benefits over those of strong ties. Granovetter concludes that information spread using weak ties will traverse greater social distance.

Similarity of tied actors

Demographic similarity between a focal actor and his or her network ties can have an impact on the information that is shared between the two. Research shows that demographic similarity tends to increase interpersonal trust (Kanter, 1977), which in turn fosters the value that network contacts place on the information they receive through the contact. A more favorable attitude toward each other based on demographic similarity may upwardly bias the evaluation of network contacts (Judge and Ferris, 1993), making it more likely the contacts will positively view the focal actor and be more likely to provide referral benefits.

Number of senior ties

Typically, contacts who are more senior in organizations tend to have access to resources (e.g., employment opportunities) and information sooner than less senior individuals. Greater seniority within an organization also increases the weight of a referral given by such a person. For instance, DeGraff and Flap (1988) found that the higher the occupational prestige of the contact person one used to find a job, the better the job the focal actor received. Lin et al. (1981) also found that the occupation status of a network contact had a positive effect on job status attained by the focal actor who used that contact. Therefore, number of senior ties is expected to be a positive indicator of network extensiveness.

Goal Setting

Goals are regulators of behavior and are defined as desired end states (Locke and Latham, 2002). Reviewed in detail elsewhere (Locke and Latham, 1990), goal-setting theory states that specific and difficult goals lead to better performance outcomes than goals that are non-specific, easy, or both. In goal-setting theory, goals need conscious activation and can be assigned, self-set, or participatively set. Goal commitment helps people persevere in their goal-related pursuits, especially when faced with obstacles, and is studied mostly in conjunction with assigned goals (Klein et al., 1999). The positive effects of goals on performance have been shown across different tasks, settings, samples, and cultures (Tubbs, 1986; Mento et al., 1987; Kyllo and Landers, 1995; Locke and Latham, 2002).

Beyond the summary of goal setting provided by Locke and Latham (1990), new studies include the relationship between goals and task strategies (Locke, 2000); the role of learning goals when participants need to find strategies for new, complex tasks (Seijts and Latham, 2001); the relationship between goals and risk (Knight et al., 2001); the role of goals as mediators of personality traits and incentives (Locke, 2001); the relationship between goals and goal orientation (VandeWalle et al., 2001); the relations of goals to small venture growth (Baum et al., 2001); and interactive relationships between conscious and subconscious goals in affecting performance (see Stajkovic et al., 2006; Latham et al., 2010).

THEORY INTEGRATION

Integrating Charismatic Leadership and Social Networks

We suggest that part of the reason people join a social network is because they are attracted to the charismatic behaviors of the leader building a network. Charismatic leadership has not been linked specifically to the extensiveness of social networks, but the notion that it can lead to the formation of social groups has been suggested indirectly. Meindl (1990) argued that charisma produces highly romanticized and contagious effects among people. He also used the metaphor of "catching a cold" to describe the spread of charismatic effects (Meindl, 1993). Klein and House (1998) described the same infatuation with charismatic people and their influence on others as a "raging fire" spreading to "followers." The influence stems from behaviors and how they are perceived, and not from a formal position of power legitimated by some rules (Conger and Kanungo, 1987).

The more specific question is, what do charismatic leaders actually do to attract others to them? Conger and Kanungo (1998) tried to answer it by proposing five sets of behaviors that may attract others to charismatic individuals. While we described these behaviors earlier, the underlying premise is that people are attracted to those who have ideas that challenge the status quo and who are linked to uncertainty. As Pastor et al. (2002, p. 412) note, "A wealth of basic social psychological research indicates that individual judgments are generally more open to the influence of others when they are tied to uncertainty and ambiguity." Flynn and Staw (2004) provide more evidence for this effect: charismatic leadership behaviors attracted more financial support from outsiders, and this was heightened during economic crises. Several studies have asserted this overall attraction effect of charisma to be generally applicable (Bass, 1997; Dorfman et al., 2004). Based on this evidence, we believe that the five described charismatic behaviors lead to SNE – that is, the more a person is perceived to be exhibiting charismatic leadership behaviors, the more extensive his or her social network will be:

Hypothesis 1: Charismatic leadership is positively related to social network extensiveness.

A moderating role of culture in the relationship between charisma and social networks

We are also interested in whether national culture, as a contextual variable, moderates the effects of charisma on social network extensiveness. Conger (1999, p. 164), for instance notes: "Cultural variables are a crucial dimension of context. Because different cultures have different beliefs, values, and modes of articulation and so on, leadership effectiveness and attributions of charismatic leadership should vary across cultural contexts." Culture is defined as "distinctive environments . . . about which members share meaning and values, resulting in . . . pattern of common affective, attitudinal, and behavioral orientation that is transmitted across generations and that differentiates collectivities from one another" (House et al., 1997, p. 540). Simply, culture helps us interpret and attach meaning to our experiences (Erez and Earley, 1993). Although there are many variations across cultures in terms of variables (Hofstede, 1980; House and Javidan, 2004), organizational research is often conducted under the assumption that theoretical constructs are culturally universal (Adler, 2002).

Research has identified individualism/collectivism (I/C) as one of the key culture characteristics (Hofstede, 1980; Smith et al., 1996; Triandis, 2004). In individualistic cultures, members' identities are formed by personal choices and achievements; in collectivistic cultures, identity is predominantly a function of the groups to which members belong (Hofstede, 1980). We propose that I/C moderates the link between charismatic leadership behaviors and SNE. That is, if charismatic behaviors are perceived as congruent with I/C cultural expectations, then they will lead to more extensive social networks.

Individualism can be viewed as:

> the inherent separateness of distinct persons. . . Achieving the cultural goal of independence requires construing oneself as an individual whose behavior is organized and made meaningful primarily by reference to one's own internal repertoire of thoughts, feelings, and actions, rather than by reference to the thoughts, feelings, and actions of others. (Markus and Kitayama, 1991, p. 226)

In an individualistic culture, "everyone is expected to look after himself or herself or her immediate family" (Hofstede, 1991, p. 51). In such cultures people tend to see themselves primarily as unique individuals, and they use their personal achievements to define their identity (Adler, 2002). Those people view themselves as autonomous and seek ways to express their uniqueness, and tend to place an emphasis on behaviors that distinguish one from the group (Geertz, 1975; Hofstede, 1980).

In a collectivistic culture, people stress their connectedness to each other. People see themselves as a part of a social relationship and believe that their behavior is determined by, and is contingent upon, what they perceive to be the thoughts, feelings, and actions of others in the group relationship (Markus and Kitayama, 1991). They assign great importance to the inferences made about the nature of their relationship with other members of a group. As a result, members of a collectivistic culture emphasize group maintenance activities (Bass et al., 1979; Fukuda, 1983; Bolon and Crain, 1985; Ivancevich et al., 1986).

We theorize that I/C will frame expectations as to the leadership behaviors seen as being charismatic. We reason that Conger and Kanungo's (1998) person-related charismatic behaviors (i.e., vision articulation, risk taking, and unconventional behaviors) will be perceived as charismatic in individualistic cultures. In contrast, we theorize that what Conger and Kanungo (ibid.) define as group-related charismatic behaviors (i.e., sensitivity to the environment and sensitivity toward others' needs) will be perceived as charismatic in a collectivistic culture. In summary, behaviors viewed as congruent with I/C expectations will attract more followers.

As discussed above, each of the person-centered charismatic behaviors shares a common thread: they differentiate one individual from others (ibid.). Since individualistic cultures stress members' individual character, they are more likely to respond positively to behaviors that emphasize individual characteristics because such responses are culturally congruent. However, focus on individual actions and attributes may be incongruent with the undercurrents defining a collectivistic culture. In such contexts, leaders who try to distinguish themselves from the group may be viewed as a threat to the group's harmony and well-being. Collectivistic cultures perceive that a leader who puts their own interests ahead of the group is acting selfishly (Ho, 1978; Yamaguchi, 1994); decisions are made at the group level, and adverse reactions may follow behaviors that violate this *natural* state (Hofstede, 1980; House, 1996).

Group-centered charismatic behaviors also have the underlying characteristic that they focus on the well-being of others (Conger and Kanungo, 1998). In a collectivistic environment, "maintaining a connection to others will mean being constantly aware of others and focusing on their needs, desires, and goals" (Markus and Kitayama, 1991, p. 229). Thus, behaviors that are oriented toward a group and maintain harmony are likely to be perceived as congruent with cultural norms of collectivism. However, in an individualistic culture, group-centered behaviors may be perceived differently. As Markus and Kitayama wrote, "This responsiveness is fostered not so much for the sake of responsiveness itself. Rather, social responsiveness often, if not always, derives from the need to strategically determine the best way to express or assert the internal attributes of the self" (ibid., p. 226). This view permeates US organizations; a supervisor who frequently makes sure that work is done may be seen as a "father figure" in a collectivistic culture but as mistrustful in an individualistic culture (Smith and Peterson, 1988). Based on this evidence reviewed and theory integration proposed we offer these moderation hypotheses:

Hypothesis 2: In an individualistic culture, person-centered charismatic leadership is positively related to SNE, and group-centered is not.

Hypothesis 3: In a collectivistic culture, group-centered charismatic leadership is positively related to SNE, and person-centered is not.

Integrating Social Networks and Goal Setting

As we previously noted, social networks have been shown to impact various tangible outcomes. However, does social network impact motivational variables that psychologically motivate us to succeed? Does it impact goals one sets for him/herself? We emphasize goals because, from a practical standpoint, goal-directed behavior is one of the major features of a Western way of thinking. Specifically, Bourgeois states that the formulation of goals is "so fundamental to the Western way of thinking that the circumvention of the 'set a goal and then take action' idea is considered a violation of the rational model" (1980, p. 228). As we noted earlier, organizational behavior researchers view goal-setting theory as important to our understanding of human action (Miner, 2003), and research supporting for the effectiveness of goals is strong and consistent.

We believe there is a connection between social networks and goal setting that has been unexplored in the previous research, and suggest two underlying mechanisms. First, social ties provide network members information about themselves, others, and their social environment. Larger social networks offer more information, and a greater variety of it. Both goal-setting theory (Locke and Latham, 1990) and behavioral decision theory (Cyert and March, 1963) suggest that individuals are more likely to set challenging goals when they think that they have a great deal of information about their environment. Such information from a social network is likely to include indications as to what is possible, given the circumstances, regarding one's career prospects, or at least what is considered an easy versus difficult career goal (Wasserman and Faust, 1994). The availability of more and varied information may raise people's awareness of potential opportunities and allow them to set more informed and challenging personal goals. Such informational benefits from social networks include awareness of job opportunities (Granovetter, 1974) or receipt of useful information from good sources (Lin, 1988; Burt, 1992).

The second mechanism by which social networks may impact individuals to set higher career goals is by providing direct and indirect access to the resources of others (Pfeffer and Salancik, 1978; Burt, 1992). Through others, network membership gives its members additional sources of power, influence, and ability to take action. As Coleman (1988, p. 100) notes, network ties "come about through changes in the relations among persons that facilitate actions" (see also Lin, 1988). Thus, access to others' resources, and their utilization, may encourage and facilitate individuals to set more challenging career goals. Based on this rationale, we offer this hypothesis:

Hypothesis 4: Social network extensiveness is positively related to setting challenging career goals.

A moderating role of culture in the relationship between social networks and goals

The majority of research on social networks and goals has been done in individualistic cultures (Welsh et al., 1993; House and Aditya, 1997; Adler, 2002), and that is the research background we drew upon in the development of Hypothesis 4. While the majority of these studies have taken place in individualistic cultures, there are reasons to believe they will also apply in collectivistic ones. In this section we argue that the relationship between SNE and setting career goals will be equally reflected in both individualistic and collectivistic cultures.

In a collectivist culture, members of one's group take on great importance. Explicit boundaries are often drawn around an individual's referent group (Kim, 1994) and only the needs of others who are identified as being part of the group are perceived to be important (Markus and Kitayama, 1991). As a result, members perceived as being part of the in-group receive a more favorable evaluation by other members of the in-group (Tajfel and Turner, 1986; Gomez et al., 2000), are given more generous rewards (Hui et al., 1991), and are seen as more equitable and fair than members of the out-group (Leung and Bond, 1984). This research also suggests that as the size of a group grows, members will have access to more and varied resources, and this in turn may spur their achievement aspirations. Moreover, in China, the definition of the word for man, *jen*, includes a component for both the individual and the individual's place in society (Hofstede, 1980), illustrating that individuals in this cultural context perceive the fate of the group as intertwined with their definition of self. Our theory suggests that such social network importance and psychological connection to the very perceptions of oneself will have an influence on what a person tries to do in his/her career.

Again, much of this research was developed and tested mainly in the US. However, sufficient evidence exists to suggest that social network ties will also have a favorable impact on individuals in a collectivistic cultural context as the increase in network ties expands the number of others to whom an individual will be socially beholden, and who can help him/her in career pursuits. Thus, we offer the following:

> *Hypothesis 5:* SNE is positively related to setting of difficult and specific career goals in both individualistic and collectivistic cultures.

METHOD

Laboratory Experiment

We tested Hypothesis 1 in a laboratory experiment and with executives. The laboratory experiment was conducted to verify causality between charisma and SNE. The subjects were 37 undergraduate (56.6 percent female; average age 21.51 years, S.D. = 1.04) business students at a large university. Class credit was given for participation. This experiment was one-way analysis of variance (ANOVA), with the treatment manipulating leadership charismatic and noncharismatic behaviors. Participants were assigned randomly to one of the two treatment conditions.

Treatment manipulation

Leadership behaviors were manipulated by two scenarios (available from the authors). We developed the scenarios based on Conger and Kanungo's (1998) theory of charismatic leadership, and Kirkpatrick and Locke's (1996) study that experimentally manipulated charismatic leadership. The charisma scenario incorporated all focal charismatic behaviors (e.g., vision, challenging the status quo, unconventional actions, and focus on the environment and employees). The no-charisma scenario replaced these particular behavior descriptions with more noncharismatic ones. Regarding the demeanor of the leader, in both scenarios we incorporated charismatic leadership demeanor (e.g., captivating voice, eye contact) that was experimentally manipulated in the Kirkpatrick and Locke (1996) study.

Dependent variable

The dependent variable was a four-item scale we developed to capture effects of leadership charismatic behaviors. The content of each item was congruent with the theory described earlier: specific items about joining a leader's social network (based on our theory, and related to that of Meindl, 1990), excitement (Klein and House, 1998), increased level of feeling good (Shamir et al., 1993), and willingness to pursue the vision (Meindl, 1993).

Study with Executives

This study was conducted using 129 middle-to-high-level managers. One sample was from the US ($n = 80$), and represents an individualistic culture. The other sample was from China ($n = 49$), and represents a collectivistic culture. This sample selection was based on past research showing the US to be an individualistic culture, and China to be a collectivistic culture (Hofstede, 1980; Smith et al., 1996; House and Javidan, 2004; Triandis, 2004). The two samples were similar in terms of basic demographics. The average age of managers was 36.6 (US) and 34.7 (China), 35 percent (US) and 36 percent (China) were females, and the average industry tenure was 11.4 (US) and 8.5 (China). The educational levels across the two samples were similar; all managers were enrolled in executive MBA programs at the time of the study. The managers from the US were part of an executive MBA program at a US business school. The managers from China were part of the joint executive MBA program of this US school and one of the leading universities in China. Participation in the study was voluntary, and no participation credits were offered.

Measures

We used covariance structure analysis where exogenous and endogenous constructs are latent. Thus, we used structural equation modeling (SEM) where latent constructs are indicated by observed variables or indicators (Bollen, 1989). Multiple indicators are recommended to gauge the underlying constructs. We describe our measures as indicators in the context of SEM.

Charismatic leadership
The first exogenous latent construct (ξ_1), charismatic leadership, was measured using the validated Conger and Kanungo (1998) scale. It was indicated by five manifest variables (or subscales): vision articulation (λ_{x1}), taking personal risk (λ_{x2}), unconventional behaviors (λ_{x3}), sensitivity to the environment (λ_{x4}), and sensitivity to member needs (λ_{x5}). Internal consistencies for the entire scale (all five indicators) were acceptable (Nunnally, 1978): $\alpha = 0.80$ for the entire sample; $\alpha = 0.81$ for the US sample only, and $\alpha = 0.77$ for the Chinese sample only. Consistent with our moderation hypotheses, we also examined charisma as person-oriented charismatic leadership behaviors, and group-related charismatic leadership behaviors (per Conger and Kanungo, 1998). The former latent construct (ξ_{1p}) was indicated by the three manifest variables: vision articulation (λ_{x1}), taking personal risk (λ_{x2}), and unconventional behaviors (λ_{x3}). The latter latent construct (ξ_{1g}) was indicated by two manifest variables: sensitivity to the environment (λ_{x4}) and sensitivity to member needs (λ_{x5}). Internal consistencies for ξ_{1p} were $\alpha = 0.85$ for the entire sample; $\alpha = 0.89$ for the US sample only, and $\alpha = 0.75$ for the Chinese sample only. For ξ_{1g} they were $\alpha = 0.66$ for the entire sample; $\alpha = 0.69$ for the US sample only, and $\alpha = 0.61$ for the Chinese sample only.

Social network extensiveness
Representing the first endogenous construct in the model (η_1), this latent construct was measured at an individual level of analysis by four manifest variables: network size or

number of ties (λ_{y1}), number of weak ties (λ_{y2}), number of more senior ties (λ_{y3}), and gender similarity of ties (λ_{y4}). We collected these data by using a network-grid survey designed for this study. Study participants were asked to map out their network on a grid, followed by questions requiring numeric answers about the four indicators described previously. Social network ties were defined for the participants in the beginning of the survey as "a set of relationships that help one advance professionally, get things done, and develop professionally." The questions regarding social ties focused on existing ones: "If you look back over the last two to three years, who are the people with whom you have. . ." We framed the question in this fashion to capture network ties that have been in existence rather than ties one wanted to have in the future. Participants also recorded actual names of ties.

Goals

As defined by goal-setting theory (Locke and Latham, 1990), we measured the self-set career goals (CG) endogenous construct by the two main attributes of goals: goal difficulty and goal specificity; these data were collected from a career goal survey designed for this study.[2]

Specifically, as part of a seven-page goal-setting exercise, study participants were asked to envision themselves five years from now, write a short story about their anticipated career achievements, ultimately derive their five-year career goal, state it in one sentence, and explain it in a two-page write-up. They were also asked questions about goal-related covariates (described below). Goals were defined for study participants in the beginning of the survey as "a desired end-state that is something that we wish to achieve at some point in the future." The questions' emphasis in this goal-setting survey was on the future – setting a five-year career goal.

An example of a story where participants were asked to envision what might be said about them at work five years from now is provided below. The text summarizes how one participant hoped his CEO might describe his career achievements in a speech in his honor:

> If you think back . . . when Brian arrived at XYZ we had an outdated in-house computer system, balancing was done manually by pencil and paper, employees were afraid to make suggestions or take initiative. Brian "softened" yet "strengthened" Office Services. We all know Brian is rather conservative and likes saving a buck. By always looking out for our owners' interests, he had the idea to look at alternative health plans. Brian was the one who brought us the idea of self-insurance. It is estimated that our self-insurance plan saves the company $75 000 a year. Brian did take a chance and convince the board of directors that interest rates were going to drop, when experts were predicting just the opposite. By staying with variable interest rates, we have saved over $850 000 over the three years. These two ideas alone have saved us over $1 million. Brian brings humor to the workplace. I don't think I have ever seen him lose his temper. His calm demeanor encourages employees to approach him with new ideas and even occasional problems.

Participants were then asked to boil their story down to one major career goal. Based on the preceding account, the person's goal was "to be XYZ's President of Education and Innovation."

Goal difficulty and goal specificity were rated by two raters on a scale of 1 (very easy/not specific) to 9 (very difficult/very specific). Both raters were graduate students familiar with the goal-setting literature, and the second (but not first) rater was blind to the hypotheses. We calculated interclass correlations ($ICC_{2,1}$) to estimate interrater reliability (Shrout and Fleiss, 1979). These reliabilities were adjusted by the Spearman-Brown prophecy formula to reflect that two raters were used. After the initial coding, the $ICC_{2,1}$ value for goal difficulty was 0.78 and for goal specificity was 0.78 for the combined sample. ICC values above 0.75 are considered to represent good interrater reliability (Landis and Koch, 1977). Because the remaining unreliability can still bias the results, the two raters discussed their coding for each case for which their scores differed by more than three points. After discussing these cases, the raters individually decided whether or not to adjust their ratings. The ICCs based on new coding were 0.87 for goal difficulty and 0.87 for goal specificity, indicating good interrater reliability (Nunnally, 1978). However, due to a high degree of collinearity between the two coders' ratings of goal difficulty and goal specificity, we averaged the two coders' ratings and used average goal difficulty and average goal specificity as the two indicators of goal level. We initially considered allowing the error terms to correlate, however, research (e.g., Williams and Hazer, 1986; Landis et al., 2009) suggests that may be inappropriate. Given such research recommendations, we fixed the indicator loadings of average goal difficulty and average goal specificity to the square-root of the reliability of each indicator (ibid.).

Analyses

We estimated the models by SEM (Bollen, 1989) using the sample covariance matrix as input. Parameters were estimated using a maximum likelihood procedure. The *t*-values for structural paths were calculated as cov [*x*, *y*]/standard error (Bollen, 1989). By SEM (LISREL 8.5), we tested the hypotheses, estimated the models' goodness-of-fit, and compared nested models. These fit indexes are shown for each model: the chi-squared statistic, the root-mean square error of approximation (RMSEA), the comparative fit index (CFI), and the incremental fit index (IFI). To test for changes in the fit of nested models we used both the chi-squared statistic and the Bayesian information criterion (BIC; Raftery, 1986). The BIC is based on Bayesian theory for posterior tests that provides a penalized change in model fit that takes into account the size of the sample(s) being tested. A negative BIC indicates superior fit, and in comparisons of nested models, those with more negative BIC are preferred (Hauser and Wong, 1989).

RESULTS

Laboratory Experiment

The Chronbach's alpha for the dependent variable was $\alpha = 0.94$. Items and descriptive statistics for each item are presented in Table 5.1.

The one-way ANOVA showed that study participants perceived the leader in the first condition (mean = 25.61, SE = 0.97) to have exhibited significantly more charismatic behaviors than the leader in the second (mean = 17.47, SE = 0.99) scenario/condition, $F(1, 36) = 34.61, p < 0.01, \eta^2$ (partial eta squared) = 0.49 (49 percent of the variation in this outcome measure was accounted for by the intervention, indicating a strong effect

Table 5.1   Descriptive statistics for lab study

Dependent Variable Items	Treatment Condition	Estimated Marginal Mean	Standard Error	95% Confidence Interval Lower	95% Confidence Interval Upper	Percentage Mean Difference
1. If a leader like this had a social network, I would like to be part of it	Charisma	5.56	0.236	5.08	6.04	130
	No charisma	2.42	0.230	1.96	2.89	
2. From the above speech, it appears that it may be exciting to work for this leader	Charisma	5.72	0.213	5.29	6.15	193.3
	No charisma	1.95	0.207	1.53	2.37	
3. I would feel good around this leader	Charisma	5.72	0.230	5.26	6.19	97.24
	No charisma	2.90	0.224	2.44	3.35	
4. If I were an employee of this leader, I would like to join him/her in a pursuit of this vision	Charisma	5.23	0.253	4.77	5.79	47.5
	No charisma	3.56	0.246	3.08	4.08	
All four items combined into one score	Charisma	22.28	0.739	20.78	23.78	124
	No charisma	10.84	0.719	9.38	12.30	

Source: Authors' calculations.

magnitude; Cohen, 1988). This analysis used a six-item (one or each one of the key charismatic behaviors discussed above) scale ($\alpha = 0.67$) that we developed for a treatment manipulation check (available from the authors). Each item on this scale was drawn from Conger and Kanungo's (1998) charismatic leadership scale.

The second set of analyses showed the effects of treatment on the dependent variable. The charismatic condition produced the highest relative means on each of the four scale items used as a separate outcome measure. Specifically, several one-way ANOVAs indicated that participants in the leadership charismatic behaviors condition expressed a notably stronger desire to join this leader's social network, $F(1, 36) = 90.62, p < 0.01, \eta^2 = 0.72$, felt that it would be more exciting to work for this leader, $F(1, 36) = 161.42, p < 0.01, \eta^2 = 0.82$, thought they would feel better around this leader, $F(1, 36) = 77.44, p < 0.01, \eta^2 = 0.69$, and were more willing to pursue the vision, $F(1, 36) = 23.20, p < 0.01, \eta^2 = 0.40$. If the overall score of this scale was used as an outcome measure instead of each item, the results were equally strong indicating a significantly greater overall attachment to the charismatic leader, $F(1, 36) = 122.94, p < 0.01, \eta^2 = 0.78$

Study with Executives

Table 5.2 shows the correlation matrix and descriptive statistics. An advantage of SEM is that the models testing each hypothesis can be re-created with the respective correlation

Table 5.2   Descriptive statistics and correlations for the estimated model – combined sample for field study

	Mean	S.D.	1	2	3	4	5	6	7	8	9	10	11	12	13
1. Charismatic SE	18.79	2.63	–												
2. Charismatic STO	14.31	2.18	0.29	–											
3. Charismatic VA	32.28	4.57	0.31	0.09	–										
4. Charismatic PR	12.19	2.65	0.19	0.07	0.47	–									
5. Charismatic UB	11.60	2.76	0.04	0.08	0.51	0.32	–								
6. Network size	12.84	5.53	0.11	0.18	0.16	0.14	0.14	–							
7. Contacts – more senior	4.81	3.11	0.11	0.08	0.04	-0.03	0.16	0.56	–						
8. Contacts – different firm	4.71	4.52	0.07	0.04	0.17	0.09	0.15	0.57	0.37	–					
9. Contacts – same gender	8.73	5.25	0.13	0.09	0.19	0.14	0.11	0.77	0.55	0.53	–				
10. Rater A – goal specificity	6.20	2.60	0.02	-0.01	0.02	0.18	-0.08	0.26	0.13	0.08	0.26	–			
11. Rater A – goal difficulty	5.77	2.36	0.02	-0.06	0.11	0.24	-0.01	0.32	0.15	0.16	0.34	0.91	–		
12. Rater B – goal specificity	5.67	2.50	-0.06	-0.10	0.13	0.30	0.13	0.18	0.02	0.03	0.15	0.77	0.77	–	
13. Rater B – goal difficulty	5.55	2.57	0.02	-0.10	0.06	0.31	0.08	0.23	0.06	0.13	0.21	0.74	0.77	0.87	–

Note: $n = 129$. Correlations greater than 0.17 are significant at $p < 0.05$ and correlations greater than 0.21 are significant at $p < 0.01$ (two-tailed). Abbreviations for the charisma indicators are defined as follows: SE = sensitivity to environment, STO = sensitivity toward others, VA = vision articulation, PR = personal risk, UB = unconventional behavior.

Source: Authors' calculation.

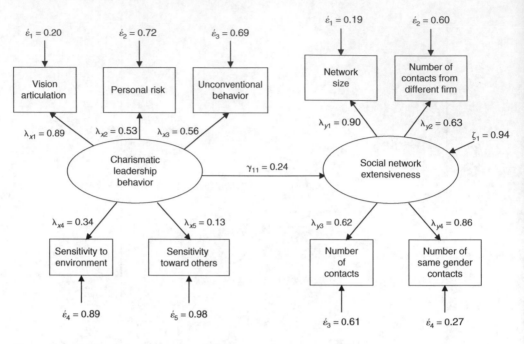

Note: Completely standardized path coefficients.

Source: Authors' calculations.

Figure 5.2   The estimated model – full sample (US and Chinese managers)

matrix (Shook et al., 2004). The correlation matrices for the US and Chinese subsamples are omitted from this chapter but are available upon request from the authors. The test of Hypothesis 1 is reported in Figure 5.2. Results show that in the combined sample charismatic leadership behavior is positively related to SNE ($\gamma_{11} = 0.24$, $t = 1.97$, $p < 0.05$). This result provides support for Hypothesis 1, and goodness-of-fit indexes of χ^2 (26 df) $= 30.46$, $p > 0.20$, BIC $= -95.9$, RMSEA $= 0.04$, CFI $= 0.98$, IFI $= 0.98$ indicate that the data fit the model well. Kline (1998) proposes values for these indexes as representing good fit to the data: RMSEA < 0.10, CFI > 0.90, and IFI > 0.90. The χ^2 test for the sensitivity of the χ^2 model fit index to sample size also shows good model fit ($\chi^2/\text{df} = 1.17 < 3$). It is suggested that these values be < 3 (the lower the value, the less sensitivity to sample size; Bollen, 1989).

Figure 5.3 shows the estimates used to test Hypothesis 2. In an individualistic culture (US sample) person-related charismatic leadership behavior is positively related to SNE ($\gamma_{11} = 0.38$, $t = 3.22$, $p < 0.01$), and group-related charismatic leadership behavior is not ($\gamma_{12} = -0.10$, $t = -0.38$, n.s.). This pattern of relationships provides support for Hypothesis 2. This model produced the following fit indexes: chi-squared (χ^2) statistic (25 df) $= 25.3$, $p > 0.40$, BIC $= -84.3$, RMSEA $= 0.01$, CFI $= 0.99$, IFI $= 0.99$, which show the data fit the model very well. Again, following Kline (1998) and Bollen (1989), the test for the sensitivity of the χ^2 fit index to sample size also showed that the model fits the data well ($\chi^2/\text{df} = 1.01 < 3$).

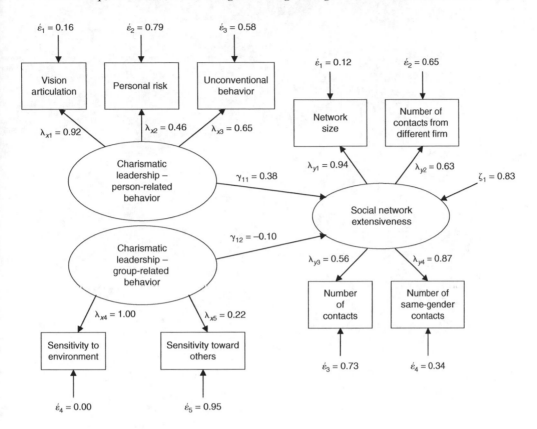

Note: Completely standardized path coefficients.

Source: Authors' calculations.

Figure 5.3 The estimated model – individualistic culture (US sample)

To further substantiate the support for Hypothesis 2, we compared the fit of nested models. We fixed the link between group-related charismatic leadership behaviors (γ_{12}) and SNE to zero (Figure 5.4, Model A) and compared it with the model in which this parameter is freed (original model). The χ^2 index showed that the revised model (γ_{12} fixed to zero) provides better fit to the data than the original model (χ^2 change = 0.90, 1 df, $p >$ 0.30). The BIC statistic (−87.7, improvement of 3.2) also provides positive evidence that the revised model is more parsimonious (Raftery, 1986). These comparisons of nested models suggest that group-related charismatic leadership behaviors have little to do with SNE in the individualistic cultural context and are actually "hurting" the model fit. Thus, we estimated a final model that included only person-related charismatic leadership behaviors and SNE (Figure 5.4, Model B). This model produced a χ^2 statistic (13 df) of 9.2, $p > 0.75$, RMSEA = 0.00, CFI = 1.00, IFI = 1.00. Per model fit criteria provided by Kline (1998), these values show an excellent fit of the model to the data.

Figure 5.5 shows the estimates used to test Hypothesis 3. In a collectivistic culture (Chinese sample), group-related charismatic leadership behavior is positively related to

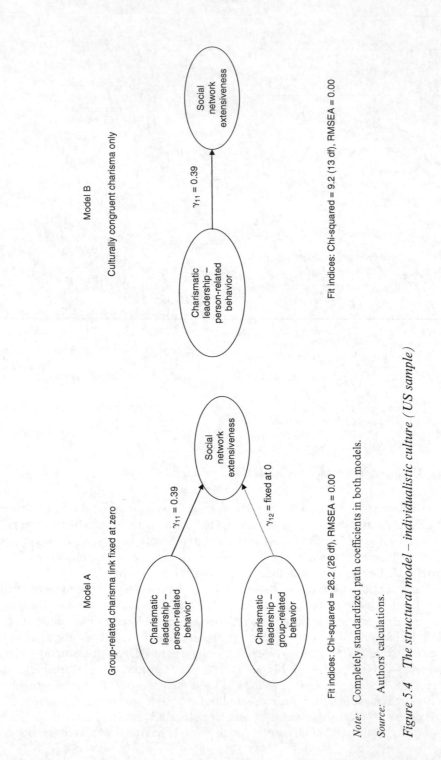

Model A

Group-related charisma link fixed at zero

$\gamma_{11} = 0.39$

γ_{12} = fixed at 0

Charismatic leadership – person-related behavior

Charismatic leadership – group-related behavior

Social network extensiveness

Fit indices: Chi-squared = 26.2 (26 df), RMSEA = 0.00

Model B

Culturally congruent charisma only

$\gamma_{11} = 0.39$

Charismatic leadership – person-related behavior

Social network extensiveness

Fit indices: Chi-squared = 9.2 (13 df), RMSEA = 0.00

Note: Completely standardized path coefficients in both models.

Source: Authors' calculations.

Figure 5.4 The structural model – individualistic culture (US sample)

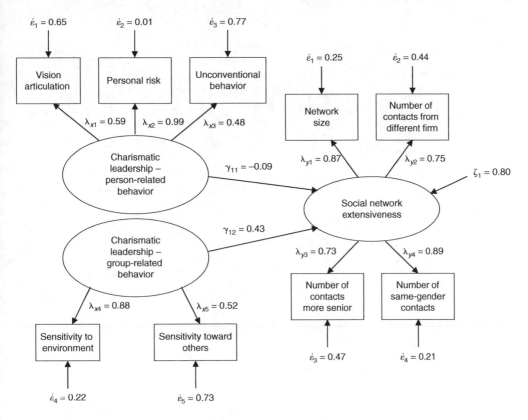

$\dot{\varepsilon}_1 = 0.65$ $\dot{\varepsilon}_2 = 0.01$ $\dot{\varepsilon}_3 = 0.77$

$\dot{\varepsilon}_1 = 0.25$ $\dot{\varepsilon}_2 = 0.44$

Vision articulation   Personal risk   Unconventional behavior

Network size   Number of contacts from different firm

$\lambda_{x1} = 0.59$ $\lambda_{x2} = 0.99$ $\lambda_{x3} = 0.48$

Charismatic leadership – person-related behavior

$\gamma_{11} = -0.09$

$\lambda_{y1} = 0.87$ $\lambda_{y2} = 0.75$

$\zeta_1 = 0.80$

Social network extensiveness

$\gamma_{12} = 0.43$

Charismatic leadership – group-related behavior

$\lambda_{y3} = 0.73$ $\lambda_{y4} = 0.89$

$\lambda_{x4} = 0.88$ $\lambda_{x5} = 0.52$

Number of contacts more senior   Number of same-gender contacts

Sensitivity to environment   Sensitivity toward others

$\dot{\varepsilon}_3 = 0.47$ $\dot{\varepsilon}_4 = 0.21$

$\dot{\varepsilon}_4 = 0.22$ $\dot{\varepsilon}_5 = 0.73$

Note: Completely standardized path coefficients.

Source: Authors' calculations.

Figure 5.5   The estimated model – collectivistic culture (China sample)

SNE ($\gamma_{12} = 0.43$, $t = 2.24$, $p \leq 0.01$), and person-related charismatic behavior is not ($\gamma_{11} = -0.09$, $t = -0.63$, n.s.), which supports Hypothesis 3. This model produced the following fit indexes: χ^2 (25 df) = 35.3, $p > 0.05$, BIC = −62.0, RMSEA = 0.09, CFI = 0.91, IFI = 0.91, which show an acceptable fit of the data to the model (Kline, 1998). The test for the sensitivity of the χ^2 model fit index to sample size also showed that our model fits the data (χ^2/df = 1.41 < 3).

To further substantiate the support for Hypothesis 3, we statistically compared the fit of nested models – that is, we fixed the link between person-related charismatic leadership behaviors (γ_{11}) and SNE to zero (Figure 5.6, Model A) and compared it with the model in which this parameter is freed (original model). The χ^2 index indicated that the revised model (γ_{11} fixed to zero) provides a better fit to the data than the original model (χ^2 change = 0.28, 1 df, $p > 0.50$). The BIC statistic (−65.6, improvement of 3.6) also provides positive evidence that the revised model is more parsimonious. These comparisons of nested models show that person-related charismatic leadership behaviors have little to do with SNE in a collectivistic cultural context, and it is detracting from the model

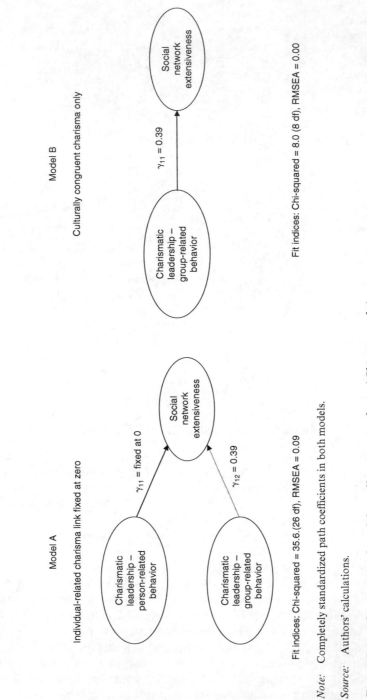

Model A

Individual-related charisma link fixed at zero

Model B

Culturally congruent charisma only

γ_{11} = fixed at 0

γ_{12} = 0.39

γ_{11} = 0.39

Fit indices: Chi-squared = 35.6 (26 df), RMSEA = 0.09

Fit indices: Chi-squared = 8.0 (8 df), RMSEA = 0.00

Note: Completely standardized path coefficients in both models.

Source: Authors' calculations.

Figure 5.6 The structural model – collectivistic culture (China sample)

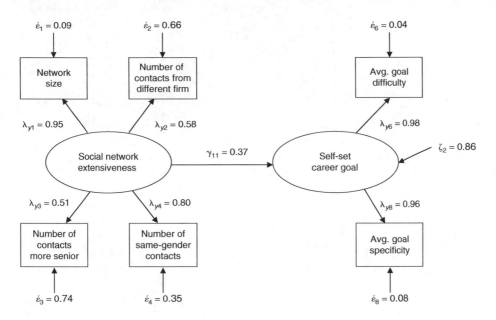

Note: Completely standardized path coefficients. Goal difficulty and goal specificity were coded by two raters and averaged.

Source: Authors' calculations.

Figure 5.7   The estimated model – individualistic culture (US sample)

fit. Therefore, we estimated a final model that included only group-related charismatic leadership behaviors and SNE (Figure 5.6, Model B). This model produced a χ^2 statistic (8 df) of 8.0, $p > 0.40$, RMSEA = 0.00, CFI = 1.00, IFI = 1.00. Again, per criteria provided by Kline (1998), these values show an excellent fit of the model to the data.

These results provide evidence that I/C moderates the relationship between charismatic leadership and SNE. In our US sample of managers, culturally congruent person-related charismatic leadership behaviors were positively related to SNE (17 percent of variance explained). Culturally incongruent group-related charismatic leadership behaviors were not related to SNE. In a sample of managers from China, culturally congruent group-related charismatic leadership behaviors were positively related to SNE (20 percent of variance explained). Culturally incongruent person-related charismatic leadership behaviors were not related to SNE.

To test Hypotheses 4 and 5, the relationship between SNE and SSCG, γ_{11}, was estimated in the US and China samples. As shown in Figure 5.7, in the US sample there was a positive relation between SNE and SSCG ($\gamma_{11} = 0.37$, $t = 3.22$, $p < 0.01$). This model produced these goodness-of-fit indexes: χ^2 (9 df) = 14.5, $p > 0.10$, RMSEA = 0.08, CFI = 0.97, and IFI = 0.97, indicating good model fit. The χ^2 test for the sensitivity of the χ^2 model fit index to sample size indicated good model fit (χ^2/df = 1.61 < 3).

As shown in Figure 5.8, in the collectivistic sample there was also a positive relation between SNE and SSCG ($\gamma_{11} = 0.32$, $t = 2.39$, $p < 0.01$). This model produced these goodness-of-fit indexes: χ^2 (9 df) = 8.35, $p > 0.45$, RMSEA = 0.00, CFI = 1.00, and IFI

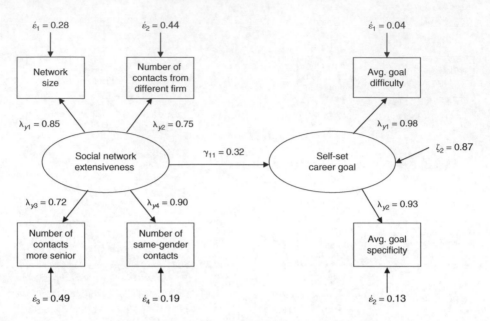

$\acute{\varepsilon}_1 = 0.28$ $\acute{\varepsilon}_2 = 0.44$ $\acute{\varepsilon}_1 = 0.04$

Network size

Number of contacts from different firm

Avg. goal difficulty

$\lambda_{y1} = 0.85$ $\lambda_{y2} = 0.75$ $\lambda_{y1} = 0.98$

Social network extensiveness

$\gamma_{11} = 0.32$

Self-set career goal

$\zeta_2 = 0.87$

$\lambda_{y3} = 0.72$ $\lambda_{y4} = 0.90$ $\lambda_{y2} = 0.93$

Number of contacts more senior

Number of same-gender contacts

Avg. goal specificity

$\acute{\varepsilon}_3 = 0.49$ $\acute{\varepsilon}_4 = 0.19$ $\acute{\varepsilon}_2 = 0.13$

Note: Completely standardized path coefficients. Goal difficulty and goal specificity were coded by two raters and averaged.

Source: Authors' calculations.

Figure 5.8   The estimated model – collectivistic culture (China sample)

= 1.00, indicating again that the model fits the data well. The χ^2 test for the sensitivity of the χ^2 model fit index to sample size also indicated a good model fit ($\chi^2/\text{df} = 0.93 <$ 3). These two sets of results both provide support for Hypotheses 4 and 5. Our results show that SNE is positively related to SSCG in both individualistic and collectivistic cultures. SNE explained 14 percent of variance in SSCG in an individualistic culture and 13 percent of variance in SSCG in a collectivistic culture. These findings suggest that social networks help managers set challenging and specific career goals.

DISCUSSION

We hope that the present research will stimulate development of integrated, meta-theories of management. Such integration here has contributed new insights with regard to relationships among charismatic leadership, social networks, and career goals. Charismatic leaders had more extensive social networks, and the networks positively influenced the leader's setting of challenging career goals. However, these relationships can vary across national cultures, depending on the I/C context. Another contribution is the methodological breadth (Aguinis et al., 2009) of this research. To test our hypotheses we used experimental design and ANOVA, SEM, regression, and path analysis.

The new insights and knowledge generated by the present research would not have been possible without utilizing the theory integration process. Charismatic leadership has been related to many different outcomes at both individual and organizational levels in past research (Howell and Frost, 1989; House et al., 1991; Shamir et al., 1993; Barling et al., 1996) but not to social networks. Social networks have also been related to numerous criteria (Granovetter, 1973; Wasserman and Faust, 1994; Adler and Kwon, 2002) but not to motivational outcomes such as goals. Goals have been mostly examined as an assigned intervention, and more research on antecedents of self-set goals has been repeatedly called for (Locke and Latham, 1990, 2002). Integrating these three theories offers a new contribution to each and hopefully an effort toward the development of more integrated management theories.

For instance, aside from resource dependence and homophily arguments, the networks literature has largely ignored the question of why people would choose to join another's network, and the answer to this question is an essential underpinning of social network characteristics in the first place. Past research has suggested that access to social capital may indeed be unevenly distributed among focal actors (Wasserman and Faust, 1994). However, such research has not offered an individual-level explanation of this phenomenon (i.e., the role of characteristics like charisma). Our first hypothesis supports Weber's notion that a charismatic's influence on others exists when the "specific gifts of body and mind [charismatic behaviors]" ([1925] 1968, p. 1112) are acknowledged by others as a reason "for their participation in an extraordinary programme of action" (Dow, 1978, p. 83, e.g., joining the charismatic leader's social network). We also found a boundary condition for this relationship; whether leadership behaviors are perceived as charismatic or not depends on the cultural context in which they are observed. If they are congruent with cultural expectations associated with I/C, they seem to lead to more extensive network ties. If behaviors are seen as incongruent with these cultural expectations, then they explain no variance in the extensiveness of one's social network.

Limitations

First, one concern relates to model specification. If charisma impacts SNE, which then relates to SSCG, does charisma directly impact SSCG? While we theorized that charisma attracts others, as reflected by SNE, it is not immediately clear how one's charisma would directly contribute to the setting of challenging goals. We attempt to address this model specification question empirically by using the same type and sequence of analyses as described in the previous parts of our study. Figures 5.9 and 5.10 show the complete results, including model fit indexes for the US and Chinese samples. When the relations among all three constructs are tested together in one model, our results between charisma and SNE and between SNE and SSCG are replicated. However, direct relations between charisma and SSCG are not found in either sample. When we compared nested models (γ_{21} fixed to zero in both samples), the data showed better fit of models without the direct link between charisma and SSCG, as compared with those with this link.

These findings indicate that, in our samples, the relationship between charisma and SSCG exists only through SNE; in analytical terms, this suggests that social networks fully mediate the relationship between charisma and the difficulty of self-set career goals. It is possible that charismatic individuals have high aspirations due to the unusual nature of their personalities, or the valence they attach to some outcomes. They may be inclined to set high goals regardless of (or in the absence of) the social support or

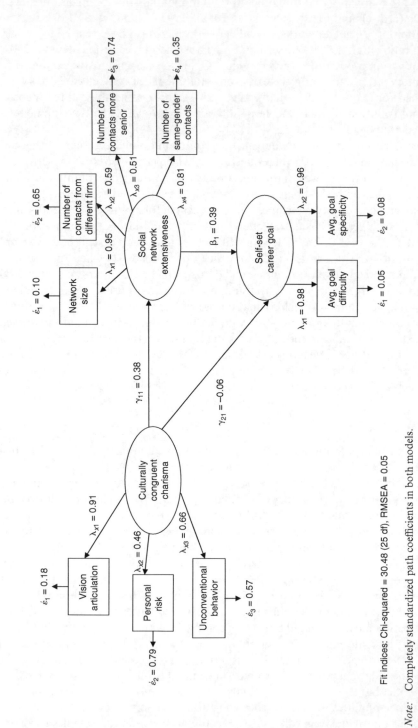

Note: Completely standardized path coefficients in both models.

Source: Authors' calculations.

Figure 5.9 *All three constructs – individualistic culture (US sample)*

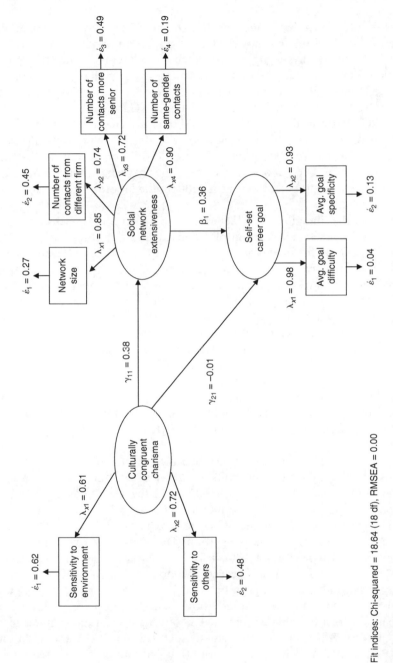

Fit indices: Chi-squared = 18.64 (18 df), RMSEA = 0.00

Note: Completely standardized path coefficients in both models. To save space, only structural links are shown.

Source: Authors' calculations.

Figure 5.10 All three constructs – collectivistic culture (China sample)

information about the environment. However, the results shown in Figures 5.9 and 5.10 do not appear to support such an alternative theoretical framework. Future research may examine these possibilities.

Second, there is a concern regarding the direction of causality in our model. Hypothesis 1 states that charismatic behaviors attract others, and not that others make leaders charismatic. Conceptually, engaging in charismatic behaviors is typically defined as a characteristic of some individuals that does not necessarily change from day to day (Weber, 1947; House, 1977). Historical accounts frequently suggest that charismatic behaviors of leaders such as Martin Luther King Jr. (Gardner, 1995) or John F. Kennedy (Dallek, 2003) attracted others to them and their policies, and not necessarily that others made them charismatic. Also, even if some leaders have notable followings (e.g., US businessman Ross Perot during the 1992 elections) it does not mean that they will be seen as charismatic. Direction of causality from charisma to social networks has also been addressed and supported experimentally in the laboratory experiment we performed.

Hypothesis 4 posits the direction of influence from SNE to SSCG. Schwab (1999) offers several criteria for assessing direction of influence, and our study satisfies these three criteria as follows: first, the predictor and criterion (SNE and SSCG) were related. Second, the variation in the predictor preceded the variation in the criterion. Our measures focused on a networks-to-goals temporal sequence. As described, the network survey asked about the past (i.e., "If you look back over the last two to three years. . ."), and the goal survey focused on the future (i.e., a five-year career goal, where goals were defined as an end state to "achieve at some point in the future"). Third, we tested an alternative charisma-goals-to-networks model (we included charisma here because reversing only the two latent constructs would produce identical results). We found a worse fit ($\chi^2 = 54.27$, RMSEA = 0.07 in the US sample, and $\chi^2 = 37.22$, RMSEA = 0.07 in the Chinese sample) of the alternative model when compared with the charisma-to-networks-to-goals model. Future research could examine the dynamics of charismatic behaviors and the potential feedback loop between SNE and self-set goals that may unfold over time.

Third, although our sample from China included high-level leaders (e.g., heads of major institutions), it had only 49 participants. While it is difficult to obtain a large sample of high-level managers in other countries (and in the US as well), we call for future research based on more study participants from China. Statistically, our sample from China did not seem to be an issue regarding statistical power. Cohen (1988) states that to find a medium effect size in the population (ES = r = 0.30) with 10 percent likelihood of committing a type II error (beta = 0.90) at one-tailed significance level of 0.05 (á = 0.05), 93 study participants are needed. We obtained greater effect size magnitudes for the hypothesized relationships in the models we tested (e.g., 0.39, 0.43) with 53 percent of the suggested sample size. In addition, we also conducted path analyses (because fewer parameters are estimated, parameter-to-sample-size ratio requires fewer participants) in place of SEM and found virtually identical results. These additional analyses suggest that concerns over type II errors (false negative) may be reasonably ruled out in our study.

Fourth, we were concerned that our data came from one source, the study participants, and took precautions to minimize the issues potentially associated with common method variance (CMV). SEM helps deal with random measurement error, though it is also important to address other potential sources of systematic measurement error (Campbell and Fiske, 1959; Podsakoff et al., 2003). For instance, it is not likely that a consistency motive was present (i.e., participants try to maintain consistency between their attitudes and beliefs) in their responses that dealt with their behaviors (charisma) and those of others (SNE). Also, we are reasonably certain that the participants did not have an implicit theory of what we were trying to do. Our data collection instruments were intermingled among many other scales that were part of an overall personality assessment administered as part of executive management training classes, and the classes were conducted in different semesters and countries. This fits with suggestions of Podsakoff et al. (2003) to use a cover story to make it appear that the measurement of variables is not connected. There is no evidence that social desirability had contributed to CMV, nor can we find evidence to suggest that the measurement of our variables triggered affective reactions that would bias the results in a certain direction.

Finally, consistent with prior literature, in our theory we distinguish between charismatic behaviors and network extensiveness. These constructs are both conceptually distinct and analytically separable. At the same time, we also want to be clear that charisma is inherently social. In other words, at the limit, charisma is unattainable without a network. That is, while we cleanly separated charisma and social networks conceptually and empirically, the fact remains that charisma requires a social network context in some shape or form. For instance, if one were to take a different approach and model charisma as a function of network extensiveness, where the latter is fit as a spline, the resulting step function would probably reveal sharp drops in charisma as extensiveness drops off, especially if the number of ties loads particularly well. Future research might consider these intriguing implications.

Other Research Directions and Practical Implications

This research may give rise to several new research avenues and practical implications. For instance, the resource dependence view (Pfeffer and Salancik, 1978) suggests that organizations may increase chances of survival by either decreasing their dependence on other organizations or increasing the dependence of other organizations on them. One of the ways the latter can be accomplished is through coalition building (Thompson, 1967; Yan and Gray, 1994; Flynn and Staw, 2004). We found that leaders who engage in charismatic behaviors have more extensive networks of social ties than less charismatic managers. This implies an important research question as to whether charismatic leaders may be more effective in terms of coalition building and, as such, more helpful to an organization's survival and prosperity.

Neo-institutional theory is similarly concerned with organizational survival, and suggests that organizations can establish and maintain legitimacy with regulators, outside stakeholders, shareholders, customers, and the like (Di Maggio and Powell, 1983). It seems to us that the influence of charismatic leaders in building social networks may be helpful here, too. It has been said that we live in a network-based economy (Miles and Snow, 1995; Powell et al., 1996; Flynn and Staw, 2004), where many organizations depend on and relate to each other, and where alliances and joint ventures are frequent ways of doing business. The skills of charismatic leaders in building social networks (attracting others) may be instrumental in helping companies compete in today's globally interconnected economy. This assertion too provides an opportunity for new research.

While the above suggestions seem reasonably clear, they are not necessarily aligned conceptually in the somewhat divided micro–macro worlds of management disciplines. The issue is whether organizational behavior is the product of collective entities, or largely individuals when they are managers/leaders. Our theory integration process in this work may help with this subject that lies at the heart of the debate as to whether certain theoretical perspectives offer under- or over-socialized views of organizations and organizational behavior. We suggest that individuals with certain characteristics (charisma) can and do wield influence, and that a psychological perspective contributes to the understanding of what is going on in the larger organizational setting (Child, 1972; Staw and Sutton, 1992). As Flynn and Staw (2004, p. 325) note: "Of all the psychological theories that can help explain organization–environment relations, models of charismatic leadership may be among the most useful." Our findings add to their argument, and we hope spur research that further illuminates the settings in which charisma is effective.

For instance, how does charismatic leadership influence network formation over time? Answers to this research question would add to our understanding of the influence of leadership behaviors on organization- and interorganizational-level outcomes (House and Podsakoff, 1994; Conger, 1999). Regarding this topic, Conger wrote that leadership scholars "have made few attempts to understand leadership at the larger organizational level" (1999, p. 161). The majority of previous studies have linked leadership behaviors to follower satisfaction (Lowe et al., 1996), follower self-assurance (Smith, 1982), or reduced conflict among followers (Howell and Frost, 1989). Our results here take the next step in suggesting that the extent to which a leader's behaviors attract followers may also allow that leader to set higher career goals. Future longitudinal research could examine whether higher leader goals then lead to more followers being attracted to the leader. This potential feedback loop may help explain why some leaders are able to implement large organizational change by first building social coalitions.

Hoppe recently quoted Geert Hofstede, a doyen of cross-cultural research, as suggesting, "Understanding the biggest differences in the mindsets between people from different countries helps enormously in interpreting what's going on" (Hoppe, 2004, p. 79). In their recent (2004) global project entitled "GLOBE," House, Javidan, and hundreds of colleagues unequivocally suggest that the need for a better understanding of cultural impact on leadership has never been greater. This is because we are faced with unprecedented globalization and growing interdependencies among nations. As a result, there is a growing need for managers who can understand and work successfully in cross-cultural environments (Dorfman et al., 2004). We feel that our findings may have implications for the design of studies that afford us a better understanding of what is going on in different cultures and effectively dealing with the differences and similarities.

If firms plan to send managers abroad, the following suggestion could be deduced from our findings: modeling culturally congruent charismatic behaviors seems to help build coalitions. To reverse the correlates, Dorfman et al. suggest that "we know little about the effect of leadership that violates culturally endorsed norms" (2004, p. 670).

We found that culturally incongruent charismatic behaviors will likely have no effect on building social network ties. This finding is important for US executives given that they tend to think that management styles that are effective at home translate well across cultures, and such is not always the case (Welsh et al., 1993; Trompenaars, 1998).

Further on, the positive benefit in terms of SSCG associated with having social network ties seems to endure in both individualistic and collectivistic samples of managers. Given this finding, a broad implication for firms may be to encourage employees to actively network with one another. Organizations could potentially employ formal mentoring programs to ensure that employees at different levels interact. They can also encourage informal interaction between employees through the use of social gatherings and other related events. The bottom line seems to be that the larger one's social network, the more likely that one will set high career goals.

While the goal-performance implication is appealing, we know very little about the extent to which people pursue self-set career goals in the future. Goal research states that we need to be committed (psychologically attached) to goals for them to work (Locke and Latham, 1990; Seijts and Latham, 2001). Thus, we developed an SSCG commitment scale to examine how likely the managers in our study are to stick to their goals down the road (see Appendix for items, reliabilities, and confirmatory factor analysis). The mean response of 6.30 on this scale (anchored 1, not at all to 7, absolutely) indicates that managers in our study, based on the items, seemed to have valued their career goal, thought of it as important, and were willing to pursue it. Longitudinal research is needed to show if such attachment plays out in actual goal pursuit.

One other variable that comes to mind for goal-setting is network closure. In a closed network, there may be added pressure to set difficult goals. Burt (2005, pp. 77–8), for instance, discusses brokerage as a "forcing function." This is entirely consistent with our theory, but closure can also induce pressure. Specifically, brokerage might be more likely to induce more stringent generalist goals, while closure would likely force tougher goals aimed at improvement. Thus, future research can consider how network closure affects the nature of goals beyond their level of difficulty.

Finally, there are several methodological approaches that we believe could have potential for future new discoveries facilitated by the properties of these methods. First, in the above suggestions for future research, we call frequently for longitudinal research, and believe that using Hierarchical Linear Modeling (HLM) would show great potential. In case of the theory we proposed in this study, HLM would allow for both modeling time and levels of analysis, that is, leaders (Level 2), nested within social networks (Level 3), who are setting and adjusting career goals over time as their careers unfold (Level 1). Few other approaches allow for modeling time, while at the same time partialing the within-person and between-person variance. Second, we also call for the increased use of meta-analytic structural equation modeling. That is, each of the theories we integrated in this work has been widely examined on their own. Thus, such literature would provide enough evidence for a comprehensive and most current meta-analysis of each topic. Then, structural equation modeling can be used to examine the covariance matrix based on the meta-analytic findings. Albeit complex, we believe this combined approach would bring the increased reliability to the findings, and would offer results based on cumulative data.

CONCLUSION

We suggest that integrating theories in the field of management is likely to provide a better understanding of the complexity of human action and interaction in organizations. The present research offers new contributions and suggests new research avenues in the management literature that could not have been possible without the theory integration process. By drawing from the three prominent theories of charismatic leadership, social networks, and goal setting we hope to have provided an initial step in the direction of developing more integrated theories of management with broader research and practical implications.

ACKNOWLEDGMENTS

We thank Barry Gerhart, Edwin A. Locke, and participants in the Wisconsin Research Seminar Series for their comments on earlier versions of this manuscript. The Center for International Business Education and Research (CIBER) at UW–Madison provided research support for this project.

NOTES

1. This list, with the exception of Pastor et al. (2002), and descriptions of studies were compiled by Bruce Avolio and associates at the Gallup Leadership Institute at the University of Nebraska, Lincoln. Avolio and associates used the following criteria for their list: (1) the study must have been conducted in the last 100 years, (2) it must have investigated leadership effects on followers, (3) the leadership intervention must have been manipulated, (4) and the assignment method was either random or non-random. This list is available upon request, with permission from Avolio and associates.
2. There are no standardized measures of self-set goals; E.A. Locke (personal communication) provided us with advice on the design of this survey.

REFERENCES

Adler, N.J. (2002). *International dimensions of organizational behavior.* Cincinnati, OH: Thomson South Western.
Adler, P. and Kwon, S. (2002). Social capital: Prospects for a new concept. *Academy of Management Review*, **27**(1), 17–40.
Aguinis, H., Pierce, C.A., Bosco, F.A., and Muslin, I.S. (2009). First decade of *Organizational Research Methods. Organizational Research Methods*, **12**(1), 69–112.
Attanassiou, N. and Nigh, D. (1999). The impact of U.S. company internationalization on management team advice networks: A tacit knowledge perspective. *Strategic Management Journal*, **20**(1), 83–92.
Barling, J., Weber, T., and Kelloway, E.K. (1996). Effects of transformational leadership training on attitudinal and financial outcomes: A field experiment. *Journal of Applied Psychology*, **81**(6), 827–32.
Bass, B.M. (1997). Does the transactional–transformational leadership paradigm transcend organizational and national boundaries? *American Psychologist*, **52**(2), 130–39.
Bass, B.M., Burger, P.C., Doktor, R., and Barrett, G.V. (1979). *Assessment of managers: An international comparison.* New York, NY: Free Press.
Baum, J.R., Locke, E.A., and Smith, K.E. (2001). A multidimensional model of venture growth. *Academy of Management Journal*, **44**(2), 292–303.
Bollen, K.A. (1989). *Structural equations with latent variables.* New York, NY: John Wiley and Sons.
Bolon, D.S. and Crain, C.R. (1985). Decisions sequence: A recurring theme in comparing American and Japanese management. Academy of Management Proceedings: San Diego, CA.
Bourgeois, L.J. (1980). Performance and consensus. *Strategic Management Journal*, **1**(3), 227–48.

Burt, R.S. (1992). *Structural holes: The social structure of competition.* Cambridge, MA: Harvard University Press.

Burt, R.S. (1997). The contingent value of social capital. *Administrative Science Quarterly*, **42**(2), 339–65.

Burt, R.S. (2005). *Brokerage and closure: An introduction to social capital.* Oxford: Oxford University Press.

Campbell, D.T. and Fiske, D. (1959). Convergent and discriminant validation by multitrait-multimethod matrix. *Psychological Bulletin*, **56**(2), 81–105.

Child, J. (1972). Organizational structure, environment, and performance: The role of strategic choice. *Sociology*, **6**(1), 1–22.

Cohen, D.A., Mason, K., Bedimo, A., and Scribner, R. (2003). Neighborhood physical conditions and health. *American Journal of Public Health*, **93**(3), 467–71.

Cohen, J. (1988), *Statistical power analysis for behavioral sciences* (2nd edition). Hillsdale, NJ: Lawrence Erlbaum.

Coleman, J.S. (1988). Social capital in the creation of human capital. *American Journal of Sociology*, **94**, S95–S120.

Conger, J.A. (1985). Charismatic leadership in business: An exploration study. Unpublished doctoral dissertation, Harvard University.

Conger, J.A. (1999). Charismatic and transformation leadership in organizations: An insider's perspective on these developing streams of research. *Leadership Quarterly*, **10**(4), 145–79.

Conger, J.A. and Kanungo, R.N. (1987). Toward a behavioral theory of charismatic leadership in organizational settings. *Academy of Management Journal*, **12**(4), 637–47.

Conger, J.A. and Kanungo, R.N. (1994). Charismatic leaderships in organizations: Perceived behavior attributes and their measurement. *Journal of Organizational Behavior*, **15**(5), 439–52.

Conger, J.A. and Kanungo, R.N. (1998). *Charismatic leadership in organizations.* Thousand Oaks, CA: Sage.

Cyert, R.R. and March, J.G. (1963). *A behavioral theory of the firm.* Upper Saddle River, NJ: Prentice Hall.

Dallek, R. (2003). *An unfinished life: John F. Kennedy, 1917–1963.* New York, NY: Little, Brown and Company.

DeGraaf, N.D. and Flap, H.D. (1988). With a little help from my friends: Social resources as an explanation of occupational status and income in West Germany, the Netherlands, and the United States. *Social Forces*, **67**(2), 452–72.

DiMaggio, P.J. and Powell, W.W. (1983). The iron cage revisited: Institutional isomorphism and collective rationality in organizational fields. *Annual Sociological Review*, **48**(2), 147–60.

Dorfman, P.W., Hanges, P.J., and Brodbeck, F.C. (2004). Leadership and cultural variation: The identification of culturally endorsed profiles. In R.J. House, P.J. Hanges, M. Javidan, P.W. Dorfman, and V. Gupta (eds), *Culture, leadership, and organizations: The GLOBE study of 62 societies.* Thousand Oaks, CA: Sage, pp. 669–720.

Dow, T.E. (1978). Analysis of Weber's work on charisma. *British Journal of Sociology*, **29**(1), 83–93.

Dubini, P. and Aldrich, H. (1991). Personal and extended networks are central to the entrepreneurial process. *Journal of Business Venturing*, **6**(5), 305–13.

Erez, M. and Earley, P.C. (1993). *Culture, self-identity, and work.* New York, NY: Oxford University Press.

Flynn, F.J. and Staw, B.M. (2004). Lend me your wallets: The effect of charismatic leadership on external support for an organization. *Strategic Management Journal*, **25**(4), 309–30.

Fukuda, J.K. (1983). Japanese and Chinese management practices: Uncovering the differences. *Mid-Atlantic Journal of Business*, **21**(2), 35–44.

Gabbay, S.M. and Zuckerman, E.W. (1998). Social capital and opportunity in corporate R&D. *Social Science Research*, **27**(2), 189–217.

Gardner, H. (1995). *Leading minds: An anatomy of leadership.* New York, NY: Basic Books.

Geertz, C. (1975). On the nature of anthropological understanding. *American Scientist*, **63**, 47–53.

Gomez, C., Shapiro, D.L., and Kirkman, B.L. (2000). The impact of collectivism and in-group/out-group membership on the evaluation generosity of team members. *Academy of Management Journal*, **43**(6), 1097–106.

Granovetter, M.S. (1973). The strength of weak ties. *American Journal of Sociology*, **78**(6), 1360–80.

Granovetter, M.S. (1974). *Getting a job: A study of contacts and careers.* Cambridge, MA: Harvard University Press.

Hauser, R.M. and Wong. R.S.-K. (1989). Sibling resemblance and intersibling effects on educational attainment. *Sociology of Education*, **62**(3), 149–71.

Ho, D.Y.F. (1978). Psychosocial implications of collectivism: With special reference to the Chinese case and Maoist dialectics. Presented at the Fourth Congress of Cross-cultural Psychology, Munich.

Hofstede, G. (1980). *Culture's consequences.* London: Sage.

Hofstede, G. (1991). *Cultures and organizations: Software of the mind.* London: McGraw-Hill.

Hollander, E.P. (1958). Conformity, status, and idiosyncrasy credit. *Psychological Review*, **65**(2), 117–27.

Hollenbeck, J.R., Klein, H.J., O'Leary, A.M., and Wright, P.M. (1989). Investigation of the construct validity of a self-report measure of goal commitment. *Journal of Applied Psychology*, **74**(6), 951–6.

Hoppe, M.H. (2004). An interview with Geert Hofstede. *Academy of Management Executive*, **18**(1), 75–9.
House, R.J. (1977). A 1976 theory of charismatic leadership. In J. Hunt and L.L. Larson (eds), *Leadership: The cutting edge*. Carbondale, IL: Southern Illinois University Press, pp. 189–207.
House, R.J. (1996). Path-goal theory of leadership: Lessons, legacy, and a reformulated theory. *Leadership Quarterly*, **7**(3), 323–52.
House, R.J. and Aditya, R.N. (1997). The social scientific study of leadership: Quo vadis? *Journal of Management*, **23**(3), 409–73.
House, R.J. and Javidan, M. (2004). Overview of GLOBE. In R.J. House, P.J. Hanges, M. Javidan, P.W. Dorfman, and V. Gupta (eds), *Culture, leadership, and organizations: The GLOBE study of 62 societies*. Thousand Oaks, CA: Sage, pp. 9–28.
House, R.J. and Podsakoff, P.M. (1994). Leadership effectiveness: Past perspectives and future directions for research. In J. Greenberg (ed.), *Organizational behavior: The state of the science*. Hillsdale, NJ: Erlbaum, pp. 45–82.
House, R.J., Spangler, W.D., and Woycke, J. (1991). Personality and charisma in the U.S. presidency: A psychological theory of leadership effectiveness. *Administrative Science Quarterly*, **36**(3), 364–96.
House, R.J., Wright, N.S., and Aditya, R.N. (1997). Cross-cultural research on organizational leadership: A critical analysis and a proposed theory. In P.C. Earley and M. Erez (eds), *New perspectives on international industrial/organizational psychology*. San Francisco, CA: New Lexington Press, pp. 535–625.
Howell, J.M. and Frost, P.J. (1989). A laboratory study of charismatic leadership. *Organizational Behavior and Human Decision Process*, **43**(2), 243–69.
Hui, C.H., Triandis, H.C., and Lee, C. (1991). Cultural differences in reward allocation: Is collectivism the explanation? *British Journal of Social Psychology*, **30**(2), 145–57.
Ivancevich, J.M., Schweiger, D.M., and Ragan, J.W. (1986). Employee stress, health, and attitudes: A comparison of American, Indian, and Japanese managers. Academy of Management Proceedings: Chicago, IL.
Judge, T.A. and Ferris, G.R. (1993). Social context of performance evaluation decisions. *Academy of Management Journal*, **36**(1), 80–105.
Kanter, R.M. (1977). *Men and women of the corporation*. New York, NY: Basic Books.
Kim, U. (1994). Individualism and collectivism: Conceptual clarification and elaboration. In U. Kim, H.C. Triandis, C. Kagitsibasi, S.C. Chio, and G. Yoon (eds), *Individualism and collectivism: Theory, method, and applications*. Thousand Oaks, CA: Sage Publications.
Kirkpatrick, S. and Locke, E.A. (1996). Direct and indirect effects of three core charismatic leadership components on performance and attitudes. *Journal of Applied Psychology*, **81**(1), 36–51.
Klein, H.J., Wesson, M.J., Hollenbeck, J.R., and Alge, B.J. (1999). Goal commitment and the goal-setting process: Conceptual clarification and empirical synthesis. *Journal of Applied Psychology*, **84**(6), 885–96.
Klein, K.J. and House, R.J. (1998). Further thoughts on fire: Charismatic leadership and levels of analysis. In F. Dansereau and F.J. Yammarino (eds), *Leadership: The multiple-level approaches*. Stamford, CT: JAI Press, pp. 45–52.
Kline, R.B. (1998). *Principles and practice of structural equation modeling*. New York, NY: Guilford Press.
Knight, D., Durham, C., and Locke, E.A. (2001). The relationship of team goals, incentives, and efficacy to strategic risk, tactical implementation and performance. *Academy of Management Journal*, **44**(2), 326–38.
Kyllo, L.B. and Landers, D.M. (1995). Goal setting in sport and exercise: A research synthesis to resolve the controversy. *Journal of Sport and Exercise Psychology*, **17**(2), 117–37.
Landis, J. and Koch, G. (1977). The measurement of observer agreement for categorical data. *Biometrics*, **33**(1), 671–9.
Landis, R.S., Edwards, B.D., and Cortina, J.M. (2009). On the practice of allowing correlated residuals among indicators in structural equation modeling. In C.E. Lance and R.J. Vandenberg (eds), *Statistical and methodological myths and urban legends*. New York, NY: Routledge, pp. 193–212.
Latham, G.P., Stajkovio, A.D., and Locke, E.A. (2010). The relevance and viability of subconscious goals in the workplace. *Journal of Management*, **36**(1), 234–55.
Leung, K. and Bond, M.H. (1984). The impact of cultural collectivism on reward allocation. *Journal of Personality and Social Psychology*, **47**(4), 793–804.
Liebeskind, J.P., Oliver, A.L., Zucker, L.G., and Brewer, M.B. (1996). Social networks, learning, and flexibility: Sourcing scientific knowledge in new biotechnology firms. *Organization Science*, **7**(4), 429–42.
Lin, N. (1988). Social resources and social mobility: A structural theory of status attainment. In R. Beiger (ed.), *Social mobility and social structure*. Cambridge: Cambridge University Press, pp. 120–46.
Lin, N. and Dumin, M. (1996). Access to occupations through social ties. *Social Networks*, **8**(4), 365–85.
Lin, N., Ensel, W.M., and Vaughn, J.C. (1981). Social resources and strength of ties: Structural factors in occupational status attainment. *American Sociological Review*, **46**(4), 393–405.
Locke, E.A. (2000). Motivation, cognition and action: An analysis of studies of task goals and knowledge. *Applied Psychology: An International Review*, **49**(3), 408–29.
Locke, E.A. (2001). Self-set goals and self-efficacy as mediators of incentives and personality. In M. Erez,

U. Kleinbeck, and H. Thierry (eds), *Work motivation in the context of a globalizing economy.* Mahwah, NJ: Lawrence Erlbaum, pp. 13–26.

Locke, E.A. and Latham, G. (1990). *A theory of goal-setting and task performance.* Englewood Cliffs, NJ: Prentice Hall.

Locke, E.A. and Latham, G. (2002). Building a practically useful theory of goal setting and task motivation: A 35-year odyssey. *American Psychologist*, **57**(9), 705–17.

Lowe, K.B., Kroeck, K.D., and Sivasubramaniam, N. (1996). Effectiveness correlates of transformational and transactional leadership: A meta-analytic review of the MLQ literature. *Leadership Quarterly*, **7**(3), 385–425.

Markus, H.R. and Kitayama, S. (1991). Culture and the self: Implications for cognition, emotion and motivation. *Psychological Review*, **98**(2), 224–53.

Meindl, J.R. (1990). On leadership: An alternative to the conventional wisdom. In B.M. Staw and L.L. Cummings (eds), *Research in organizational behavior* (Vol. 12). Greenwich, CT: JAI, pp. 159–203.

Meindl, J.R. (1993). Reinventing leadership: A radical social-psychological approach. In K. Murnighan (ed.), *Social psychology in organizations: Advances in theory and research.* Englewood Cliffs, NJ: Prentice-Hall, pp. 89–118.

Mento, A.J., Steel, R.P., and Karren, R. (1987). A meta-analytic study of the effects of goal setting on task performance: 1966–1984. *Organizational Behavior and Human Decision Processes*, **39**(1), 52–83.

Miles, R.E. and Snow, C.C. (1995). The new network firm: A spherical structure built on a human investment philosophy. *Organizational Dynamics*, **23**(4), 4–18.

Miner, J. (2003). The rated importance, scientific validity and practical usefulness of organizational behavior theories: A quantitative review. *Academy of Management Learning and Education*, **2**(3), 250–68.

Mizruchi, M.S. and Galaskiewicz, J. (1993). Networks of interorganizational relations. *Sociological Methods and Research*, **22**(1), 46–70.

Nunnally, J. (1978). *Psychometric theory* (2nd edition). New York, NY: McGraw-Hill.

Pastor, J.-C., Meindl, J.R., and Mayo, M.C. (2002). A network effects model of charisma attributions. *Academy of Management Journal*, **45**(2), 410–20.

Pfeffer, J. and Salancik, G.R. (1978). *The external control of organization: A resource-dependence perspective.* New York, NY: Harper and Row.

Podsakoff, P.M., MacKenzie, S.B., Lee, J.-Y., and Podsakoff, N.P. (2003). Common method biases in behavioral research: A critical review of the literature and recommended remedies. *Journal of Applied Psychology*, **88**(5), 879–903.

Powell, W., Koput, K., and Smith-Doerr, L. (1996). Interorganizational collaboration and the locus of innovation: Networks of learning in biotechnology. *Administrative Science Quarterly*, **41**(1), 116–45.

Raftery, A.E. (1986). Choosing models for cross-classifications. *American Sociological Review*, **51**(1), 145–6.

Salancik, G.R. (1995). WANTED: A good network theory of organization. *Administrative Science Quarterly*, **40**(2), 345–9.

Sashkin, M. (1988). The visionary leader. In J. Conger and R. Kanungo (eds), *Charismatic leadership: The elusive factor in organizational effectiveness.* San Francisco, CA: Jossey-Bass, pp. 122–60.

Schwab, D.P. (1999). *Research methods for organizational studies.* Mahwah, NJ: Erlbaum.

Seibert, S.M., Kraimer, M.L., and Liden, R.C. (2001). A social capital theory on career success. *Academy of Management Journal*, **44**(2), 219–37.

Seijts, G.H. and Latham, G.P. (2001). The effect of distal learning, outcome, and proximal goals on a moderately complex task. *Journal of Organizational Behavior*, **22**(3), 291–307.

Shamir, B., House, R.J., and Arthur, M. (1993). The motivational effects of charismatic leadership. *Organizational Science*, **4**, 577–94.

Shook, C.L., Ketchen, Jr., D.J., Hult, G.T.M., and Kacmar, M. (2004). An assessment of the use of structural equation modeling in strategic management research. *Strategic Management Journal*, **25**(4), 397–404.

Shrout, P. and Fleiss, J. (1979). Intraclass correlations: Uses in assessing rate reliability. *Psychological Bulletin*, **86**(2), 420–28.

Smith, B.J. (1982). An initial test to a theory of charismatic leadership based on the responses of subordinates. Unpublished doctoral dissertation, University of Toronto.

Smith, P.B. and Peterson, M.F. (1988). *Leadership, organizations, and culture.* London: Sage.

Smith, P.B., Dugan, S., and Trompenaars, F. (1996). National culture and the values of organizational employees. *Journal of Cross-cultural Psychology*, **27**(2), 231–64.

Stajkovic, A.D., Locke, E.A., and Blair, E.S. (2006). A first examination of the relationships between primed subconscious goals, assigned conscious goals, and task performance. *Journal of Applied Psychology*, **91**(5), 1171–80.

Staw, B.M. and Sutton, R.I. (1992). Macro organizational psychology. In J.K. Murnighan (ed.), *Social psychology in organizations: Advances in theory and research.* Englewood Cliffs, NJ: Prentice Hall, pp. 350–84.

Tajfel, H. and Turner, J.C. (1986). The social identity theory of intergroup behavior. In S. Worchel and W.G. Austin (eds), *Psychology of intergroup relations* (2nd edition). Chicago, IL: Nelson-Hall, pp. 7–24.

Thompson, J.D. (1967). *Organizations in action*. New York, NY: McGraw-Hill.
Triandis, H.C. (2004). The many dimensions of culture. *Academy of Management Executive*, **18**(1), 88–93.
Trompenaars, A. (1998). *Riding the waves of culture* (2nd edition). New York, NY: McGraw-Hill.
Tubbs, M.E. (1986). Goal setting: A meta-analytic examination of the empirical evidence. *Journal of Applied Psychology*, **71**(3), 474–83.
Uzzi, B. (1999). Embeddedness in the making of financial capital: How social relations and networks benefit firms seeking financing. *American Sociological Review*, **64**(4), 481–505.
VandeWalle, D., Cron, W.L., and Slocum, J.W. (2001). The role of goal orientation following performance feedback. *Journal of Applied Psychology*, **86**(4), 629–40.
Wasserman, S. and Faust, K. (1994). *Social network analysis: Methods and applications*. Cambridge: Cambridge University Press.
Weber, M. (1947). *The theory of social and economic organization*. Translated by A.M. Henderson and T. Parson, NY: Free Press.
Weber, M. [1925] (1968). *Economy and society*. New York, NY: Bedminister.
Welsh, D.H.B., Luthans, F., and Sommer, S.M. (1993). Managing Russian factory workers: The impact of the U.S.-based behavioral and participative techniques. *Academy of Management Journal*, **36**(1), 58–79.
Williams, L.J. and Hazer, J.T. (1986). Antecedents and consequences of satisfaction and commitment in turnover models: A reanalysis using latent variable structural equation models. *Journal of Applied Psychology*, **71**(2), 219–31.
Yamaguchi, S. (1994). Empirical evidence on collectivism among the Japanese. In U. Kim, H.C. Triandis, C. Kagitcibasi, S.C. Choi, and G. Yoon (eds), *Individualism and collectivism: Theory, method, and applications*. Newbury Park, CA: Sage, pp. 175–88.
Yan, A. and Gray, B. (1994). Bargaining power, management control and performance in United States – China joint ventures: A comparative case study. *Academy of Management Journal*, **37**(6), 1478–517.
Yukl, G. (1999). An evaluation of conceptual weaknesses in transformational and charismatic leadership theories. *Leadership Quarterly*, **10**(2), 285–305.

APPENDIX 5A

Given that "most goal setting studies have focused on the effects of the assigned goals" (Locke and Latham, 1990, p. 133), goal commitment has typically been assessed for assigned goals (Klein et al., 1999), and measures of goal commitment for assigned goals may not be relevant for self-set goals. For instance, one of the measures of goal commitment has four items (Hollenbeck et al., 1989, p. 953), and three of those four seem to be inconsistent with the logic of self-set goals: "It's hard to take this goal seriously," "It's unrealistic for me to expect to reach this goal," and "Quite frankly, I don't care if I achieve this goal or not." Thus, we developed a scale for this research tailored to assess managers' commitment to their self-set goals. We assessed goal commitment as a check of psychological attachment of study participants to their SSCG. The scale was developed for this research and has three items. The number of items was based on suggestions by Hollenbeck et al. (ibid., p. 951) that are relevant to the purposes of our analysis:

> In those cases in which a measure of goal commitment is to be used as a check rather than as a central construct of interest, length becomes an issue. There is a limit to how long a questionnaire can be, and measures of checks cannot be allowed to interfere with the measurement of more central constructs. For this reason it is also important to generate a measure of goal commitment . . . *with a minimum number of items.* [Emphasis added]

Goal-setting theory suggests that valence about a goal and perceived goal importance are good indicators of goal commitment (Locke and Latham, 1990). Hollenbeck et al. further suggest that "goal commitment also implies an unwillingness to change or abandon goals over time" (1989, p. 954). Thus, our three items ($\alpha = 0.74$) assessed managers' valence about their goal ("I value this five-year career goal"), the importance of this goal to them ("This five-year career is really important to me"), and if they really wanted to pursue this career goal for the next five years ("I want to live my life for the next five years in pursuit of this goal") on a scale of 1 (not at all) to 7 (absolutely). In the confirmatory factor analysis we performed, each of the three items had good and statistically significant factor loadings (see Figure 5A.1 for the values of all the estimates).

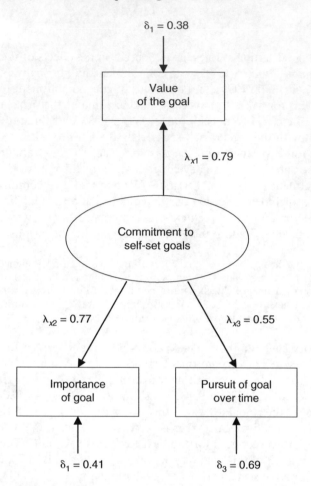

Note: Completely standardized path coefficients. $N = 115$. Φ set to 1. The t-value for $\lambda_1 = 5.96, p < 0.01$; $\lambda_2 = 5.85, p < 0.01$; $\lambda_3 = 4.40, p < 0.01$. In case of confirmatory factor analysis, lambdas are interpreted as regression coefficients (Bollen, 1989). Similar results were obtained when samples from the United States and China were run separately.

Source: Authors' calculations.

Figure 5A.1   Confirmatory factor analysis of commitment to self-set goals scale (combined sample)

6 Examining the relationships between top management team psychological characteristics, transformational leadership, and business unit performance

Suzanne J. Peterson and Zhen Zhang

The upper echelons theory suggests that an organization's strategic choices and subsequent performance are reflections of the characteristics of its top executives, and especially its top management team (TMT; Hambrick and Mason, 1984; Carpenter et al., 2004). Many studies in this area have typically used TMT characteristics such as functional background, education level, age, and tenure to examine their effects on firm performance (e.g., Finkelstein and Hambrick, 1996; Certo et al., 2006; Cannella et al., 2008). Considerably less research has focused on the psychological characteristics of executives, and several authors in this volume seek to remedy that lack. Jones and Cannella develop propositions linking CEO Big Five characteristics to TMT involvement in strategic decision making in Chapter 1, while Sangster, in Chapter 4, reports results of Big Five tests for a sample of US executives. According to Finkelstein and Hambrick (1996), the lack of such research is primarily because assessment of psychological constructs is often problematic due to the difficulty in attaining data from executive samples.

In contrast, Priem et al. (1999) argued that a focus on psychological constructs in TMT research is important as these constructs are more directly linked to behavior than the distal demographic characteristics used as proxies. In fact, research on teams lower in the organizational hierarchy shows significant personality effects in work groups (Moynihan and Peterson, 2001), pointing to the importance of studying other deep-level composition variables in TMTs. While recent research has examined various psychological characteristics of executives such as trait positive affect (Barsade et al., 2000), locus of control (Boone et al., 2000; Boone and Hendriks, 2009), emotional stability (Peterson et al., 2003), hubris (Hayward and Hambrick, 1997), and overconfidence (Simon and Houghton, 2003; Forbes, 2005) among others, many of these studies may have suffered from a lack of conceptual grounding or methodological concerns. Indeed, Hiller and Hambrick (2005, p. 298) noted that:

> The few attempts to explore executive self-potency have involved an array of disconnected concepts, including those that address only narrow slices of overall self-assessment; colloquial concepts, that despite intuitive appeal, lack rigorous psychological and methodological grounding; psychopathological concepts that are difficult to operationalize beyond clinical settings; and constructs that describe executive self-concept only on a post hoc basis.

In response to this gap, in Chapter 7, Clark and Maggitti disaggregate executive confidence and study its effects on strategic decision making. Recently, researchers have also identified and validated two broadly defined, higher-order constructs that have the potential to advance theory and research in the area of executive self-assessment. Specifically, as developed by Judge and colleagues (2002b) and first introduced into the strategic management literature by Hiller and Hambrick (2005), the concept of core self-evaluation refers to a dispositional trait that defines how individuals evaluate themselves and their relationship with the environment. Core self-evaluation is conceptualized to be a higher-order construct, which combines four well-researched, but previously unconnected concepts: self-esteem, generalized self-efficacy, locus of control, and emotional stability (Judge et al., 2002b). At around the same time, Luthans and colleagues introduced the higher-order construct of psychological capital to describe an individual's positive motivational state that encompasses four other well-known psychological resources: hope, task-specific self-efficacy, optimism, and resilience (Luthans et al., 2007a). While core self-evaluations and psychological capital share some conceptual overlap, they are considered both theoretically and empirically distinct (Luthans et al., 2007b) – the primary difference being that core self-evaluation is a generalized trait or globalized view of oneself and psychological capital is a more specific appraisal of one's circumstances and probability for success based on motivation and effort.

Although several studies have applied both the core self-evaluation and psychological capital concepts, the majority have focused solely on the individual level of analysis and/ or have not considered top executive samples. In particular, empirical research has yet to consider the impact of TMT-level core self-evaluations or psychological capital on organizational outcomes. Given that previous research has demonstrated that both constructs are positively related to individual performance and lower-level team performance (e.g., Erez and Judge, 2001; Luthans et al., 2005, 2007b; Walumbwa et al., 2009), a natural next step in this area of research is to investigate whether these effects hold at higher levels of analysis, namely at the TMT level. Further, because it is becoming increasingly apparent that long-term organizational success is largely based on the combined capacity of the members of TMTs (Carpenter et al., 2004), such an investigation will extend the upper echelons perspective by going beyond focusing on top executives' functional characteristics to include their psychological characteristics. As such, in the present study, our primary purpose is to explore the relationship between collective core self-evaluations and psychological capital among TMT members and performance for the team as a whole.

A secondary purpose of this study is to explore the conditions under which TMT collective psychological characteristics (i.e., psychological capital and core self-evaluations) may be more or less predictive of organizational performance. Given the uncertainty associated with today's business environment, there are increasing expectations on TMTs' most senior leaders to build confidence and instill motivation and commitment to organizational objectives in order to build on the sustained success of the TMTs. As such, transformational leadership may constitute a potent moderator of the TMT members' psychological characteristics and team outcomes. Transformational leaders inspire followers (i.e., fellow TMT members) to transcend self-interest and to become more effective in pursuing collective goals (Bass et al., 2003). Studies have found transformational leadership to be positively associated with subordinate performance at the individual and organizational level, leading researchers such as Bass (1998) to conclude that "transformational leadership at the top of the organization is likely to be needed for commitment to extend to the organization as a whole" (p. 19). Given this perspective, the second purpose of the present study is to determine if transformational leadership is capable of moderating the relationships between TMT collective psychological capital, core self-evaluation, and TMT performance.

Our study seeks to contribute to three literatures. First, we extend previous research to provide a theoretical framework for examining the impact of executive psychological characteristics on outcomes of interest to the field of strategic management (i.e., organizational performance). By going beyond the demographic proxies of top management teams (Priem et al., 1999), this study answers the call for research that examines "richer measures" of the upper echelons (Carpenter et al., 2004, p. 772). Second, this study is the first to provide evidence of the effects of core self-evaluations and psychological capital at the TMT level. We also extend previous efforts to better understand when (i.e., the conditions under which) both core self-evaluations and psychological capital have more or less positive effects on outcomes of interest. Finally, with respect to transformational leadership, we investigate the interactive effects of leadership style and team psychological characteristics in the TMT environment. These aims are of theoretical and practical importance. For example, adding theoretically grounded, validated psychological constructs to the exploration of executive self-assessment would provide additional insights into the upper echelons perspective. In addition, if transformational leadership were identified as a means whereby the TMT members' psychological characteristics could be more predictive of performance, organizations could emphasize efforts to develop this form of leadership.

We begin by defining and reviewing the extant research and theory relevant to the effects of core self-evaluation and psychological capital on organizational performance. We then develop our hypotheses regarding whether the collective core self-evaluations and psychological capital of TMT members will impact the team's business unit performance. We present additional hypotheses regarding the moderating role of transformational leadership in these relationships. Finally, we present the data and analysis and discuss the result of our study testing these hypotheses in 67 top management teams.

THEORY DEVELOPMENT

Core Self-evaluation

Core self-evaluation (CSE) refers to an enduring evaluation of oneself as an individual (Judge et al., 1999b). Numerous studies based on a variety of samples have indicated that CSE is the common core, or central factor of four extensively studied psychological characteristics: self-esteem, generalized self-efficacy, locus of control, and emotional stability (cf. Judge and Bono, 2001). Because CSE is at the core, or captures the intersection of four psychological traits, it is important to briefly review these components to better understand CSE:

- *Self-esteem* represents an individual's global evaluation of self-worth (Baumeister et al., 1996). Self-esteem is important in the workplace because it has been shown to be related to various outcomes in non-executive samples, including openness to change (Wanberg and Banas, 2000) and organizational commitment (Hui and Lee, 2000).

- *Generalized self-efficacy* refers to one's overall belief in his or her capabilities to execute and perform well across situations (Gist and Mitchell, 1992). Generalized self-efficacy differs from the more commonly studied task-specific self-efficacy (to be discussed later), which focuses on an individual's confidence level in a specific domain. Research has indicated that generalized self-efficacy is positively related to job performance and organizational commitment in non-executive samples (Gardner and Pierce, 1998).
- *Locus of control* is the belief one holds about control over life's events (Rotter, 1954). Those with an internal locus of control believe that they control what happens to them, while those with an external locus of control believe that what happens to them is driven by factors outside of their control. Locus of control has been widely studied in non-executive samples and research has indicated its positive association with outcomes such as job performance (Colquitt et al., 2000) and acceptance of organizational change (Wanberg and Banas, 2000).
- *Emotional stability* refers to one's tendency to worry, fear, stress, and feelings of helplessness (Costa and McCrae, 1992). Therefore, a person low on emotional stability will feel these things commonly and strongly, whereas a person high on emotional stability will lack these feelings. Research has generally confirmed that emotional stability is positively associated to job performance (Ployhart et al., 2001), career success (Judge et al., 1999a), and leadership emergence (Judge et al., 2002a) in non-executive samples.

A myriad of studies exist that examine the self-esteem, self-efficacy, locus of control, and emotional stability independently. In addition, the number of studies that consider CSE as a unitary construct has grown considerably in the last decade. Importantly, meta-analytic results suggest that the four component variables clearly load on the CSE factor (Judge et al., 2002b). Theoretically, it is expected that while each variable is unique in certain ways, there is considerable overlap or a common core. Thus, CSE does not encompass the entirety of all four constructs. Rather, it represents a significant and common core of the four component traits. In addition to the evidence of CSE as a core construct, empirical research has consistently demonstrated that CSE is a better predictor of workplace outcomes than any of the four traits alone. For example, CSE has been shown to be more strongly related to job performance and satisfaction, motivation, stress, and other personality measures than are the four individual traits (Erez and Judge, 2001; Judge et al., 2002b, 2003).

Psychological Capital

Similar to CSE, psychological capital (PsyCap) is also a broad, higher-order, psychological construct. However, whereas CSE is essentially an evaluation of one's self-concept, PsyCap is an assessment of one's motivational propensity to accomplish goals and succeed. More specifically, PsyCap is an individual's positive psychological state of development characterized by four psychological resources: task-specific self-efficacy (confidence to take on and put in the necessary effort to succeed at specific tasks), hope (one's ability to persevere toward a goal), optimism (a positive expectation about succeeding now and in the future), and resilience (being able to sustain and bounce back to attain success when beset by problems and adversity) (Luthans et al., 2007a). The term psychological capital was used to build on the distinction that has been made between economic, social, and intellectual capital, highlighting these positive psychological resources as being important to individual, group, and organizational effectiveness. We more clearly define each component and its relationship to work outcomes below:

- *Task-specific self-efficacy* is "an individual's conviction (or confidence) about his or her abilities to mobilize the motivation, cognitive resources, and courses of action necessary to successfully execute a specific task within a given context" (Stajkovic and Luthans, 1998, p. 66). As noted above, task-specific efficacy differs from generalized or global self-efficacy, which is a part of CSE. For example, regarding task-specific self-efficacy, a person may be very confident in his or her abilities to implement a strategic plan, but may lack confidence in his or her decision-making ability. In contrast, generalized self-efficacy would suggest that this person is either generally confident or generally not confident about his or her abilities regardless of the specific task at hand. Task-specific self-efficacy in non-executive samples has been found to be strongly correlated with work-related performance (Stajkovic and Luthans, 1998; Bandura and Locke, 2003).
- *Hope* refers to an individual's positive motivational state that is based on a combined sense of successful (1) agency (goal-directed energy) and (2) pathways (planning to meet goals) (Snyder et al., 1991). Thus, hopeful individuals have both a sense of agency or willpower, or determination to achieve their goals. In addition, those who are hopeful are skilled at proactively designing alternative pathways and contingency plans to achieve their goals when they face obstacles and blockages. Research supports hope's impact on individual job performance (Peterson and Byron, 2008), organizational profitability (Adams et al., 2002), and the profitability of their units (Peterson and Luthans, 2003; Peterson et al., 2009).
- *Optimism.* Carver and Scheier (2002, p. 231) note "optimists are people who expect good things to happen to them; pessimists are people who expect bad things to happen to them" and the difference between the two is not trivial as optimists "differ in how they approach problems and challenges and differ in the manner and success with which they cope with adversity." Seligman (1998) uses an attribution framework (i.e., explanatory style) to define optimism whereby optimists make internal, stable, and global causal attributions of positive events and external, unstable, and specific attributions of negative events. For example, an optimist might attribute success at work to their hard work and abilities (internal explanation) and failures to a difficult environment, a temporary setback, or a mistake (external explanation). In contrast, a pessimist would think the opposite. He or she might attribute success to luck, for example, for whatever reason we had a great quarter (external explanation) and failures to personal shortcomings, for example, I'm just not a great manager (internal explanation). Optimism has also been shown to be related to performance across a variety of non-executive samples (Seligman and Schulman, 1986; Wunderley et al., 1998; Schulman, 1999; Chemers et al., 2000).

- *Resilience* is "the positive psychological capacity to rebound, to 'bounce back' from adversity, uncertainty, conflict, failure or even positive change, progress and increased responsibility" (Luthans, 2002, p. 702; also see Luthans et al., 2006; Youssef and Luthans, 2007). Resilient individuals possess "a staunch acceptance of reality; a deep belief, often buttressed by strongly held values, that life is meaningful; and an uncanny ability to improvise" (Coutu, 2002, p. 48). Research indicates that resilience in non-executives samples has been shown to be positively related to job performance (Coutu, 2002; Harland et al., 2005; Luthans et al., 2005).

Although the four PsyCap resources have each received considerable research attention in the psychological literature, recent theory and empirical research suggests that combining them into a higher-order construct results in a common synergistic capacity considered representative of "one's positive appraisal of circumstances and probability for success based on motivated effort and perseverance" (Luthans et al., 2007b, p. 550). Supporting this claim, Stajkovic (2006) argued, "that the four constructs share a common confidence core that exists at a higher level of abstraction" (p. 1212). Importantly, empirical research consistently supports that the four positive resources of hope, optimism, efficacy, and resilience do indeed load on the higher-order construct of PsyCap. Moreover, evidence suggests that the PsyCap higher-order factor is more predictive of variety of job behaviors and outcomes than are the four component resources (Luthans et al., 2007b).

Differentiating Core Self-evaluation and Psychological Capital

As we briefly discussed in the introduction, while CSE and PsyCap appear to be similar constructs, a key distinguishing factor is that PsyCap is conceptualized to be state-like and open to development and intervention, whereas CSE is more fixed and trait-like. To more clearly distinguish the difference between trait-like and state-like constructs we refer to previous work suggesting that states and traits are not independent, dichotomous constructs, but instead fall along a continuum (Luthans et al., 2007a, 2008; also see Chen et al., 2000). Specifically, the positions of a state–trait continuum would be: (1) at one extreme would be relatively "pure states," which are momentary and very changeable such as pleasure, moods, and happiness; (2) next would be "state-like" constructs, which are more malleable and open to development, representing the positive psychological resources found in PsyCap; (3) then would be "trait-like" constructs, which are more fixed and difficult to change, such as personalities and strengths (e.g., Big Five personality dimensions and core self-evaluations); and (4) would be the opposite extreme of relatively "pure traits," which are fixed and very difficult to change (e.g., intelligence and talents). In other words, PsyCap is conceptualized to be more stable than states such as moods or emotions, but not as fixed as core self-evaluations.

Recent evidence supports the state-like and trait-like distinction between PsyCap, CSE, and other pure states such as emotions (Luthans et al., 2007b; Avey et al., 2010). Specifically, after correcting for internal consistency reliability, the corrected test–retest reliabilities show CSE measures (0.87) had relatively high stability versus PsyCap (0.52) and the positive emotions measure (0.46) (see Luthans et al., 2007b). This knowledge combined with findings suggesting that psychological capital is developable through an online training exercise (see Luthans et al., 2008) serves as a basis for proposing that PsyCap is open to change and development while CSE is not.

TMT Collective Core Self-evaluation and Team Performance

According to previous research (see Gibson, 1999, 2001; Kozlowski and Klein, 2000), team-level capability beliefs may originate with individual team members, but will be strengthened by interpersonal interactions and ultimately emerge as collective phenomena. Indeed, the notion of team-level capability beliefs is not a new concept. For example, researchers have advanced the construct of team efficacy and team potency as a team's (as opposed to an individual's) perception of its capability to perform well on a given task or across tasks (Zaccaro et al., 1995; Knight et al., 2001; Gully et al., 2002; Lee et al., 2002). Despite precedents for examining individual constructs at the team level, previous work has yet to consider CSE at the group or team level. We believe individual-level CSE and team-level CSE represent conceptually (and empirically) distinct phenomena. These two constructs are likely to have distinct construct functions in terms of both antecedents and outcomes. For example, while individual CSE may predict individual motivation and work behaviors, team CSE is more likely to predict collective team outcomes (e.g., team performance).

We define team collective core self-evaluation as a team's fundamental and positive evaluation that it holds about itself as a group. Based on research conducted at the individual level of analysis, we expect that the collective CSE of TMT members should have a positive effect on the team's performance. More specifically, research at the individual level has indicated that when CSE is high, job performance is positively affected (Judge and Bono, 2001). Judge et al. (1998) argue that the reason for the performance impact is because those high in CSE are motivated to perform their jobs. Since motivation is a major factor in better job performance, it makes sense that individuals with positive self-evaluations will perform their work at a higher level, due to increased sense of self-worth or confidence in their abilities. In support of this idea, Erez and Judge (2001) found that CSEs were linked to motivation and that motivation mediated part of the relationship between CSEs and job performance.

While these ideas have yet to be tested at the executive and TMT level of analysis, we expect that the combined motivational effect of a TMT having a high CSE should contribute to the team's overall performance. Indeed, Hiller and Hambrick (2005) proposed that CEO core self-evaluation may have implications for strategic decision making organizational performance. Hence, we extend their work by explicitly testing whether the TMT's collective combination of high self-esteem (the team generally feel good about who they are and believe they deserve success), generalized self-efficacy (the team are collectively confident in their abilities to do most anything put in front of them) emotional stability (the team stay cool under pressure), and an internal locus of control (the team have a shared belief that they control their own outcomes and make their own success) will be beneficial to the team. Overall, we suggest that when a team's shared CSE is high, their motivation to pursue collective goals and objectives will be higher, resulting in documented performance gains:

Hypothesis 1: TMT collective core self-evaluation is positively associated with business unit performance.

TMT Psychological Capital and Team Performance

Unlike CSE, which to date has not been examined as a team-level construct, research is emerging that examines PsyCap as a collective phenomenon. According to Walumbwa et al. (2009), collective psychological capital represents "the *group's shared* psychological state of development that is characterized by [hope, efficacy, optimism, and resilience]" (p. 3; italics original). In other words, collective psychological capital is a team's shared positive appraisal of their circumstances and probability for success under those circumstances based on their combined motivated effort and perseverance. In their work, Walumbwa et al. (2009) found significant group-level variation in PsyCap, indicating that PsyCap may indeed be a group-level phenomenon. In addition, Walumbwa et al. (2009) revealed that team-level PsyCap was a significant predictor of group citizenship behavior and team performance.

We expect that a positive association between TMT collective PsyCap and business unit performance will exist due to the combined motivational impact of each individual member in the TMT. That is, when TMT members have a strong collective positive psychological state of development, they should be more willing to work hard and to persist in the face of challenges and adversity (Larson and LaFasto, 1989), believing that their efforts will eventually pay off in the form of successful outcomes. Indeed, as Bandura (1997) has argued for team collective self-efficacy, we believe that collective PsyCap is "the product of the interactive and coordinative dynamics of its members; interactive dynamics create an emergent property that is more than the sum of the individual's attributes" (ibid., pp. 477–8).

Collective PsyCap should play an important role in performance especially when members have to rely on each other to accomplish goals as is typically the case in TMTs (Colbert et al., 2008). Moreover, when faced with obstacles, TMTs with higher levels of collective PsyCap should be more likely to work together to persist in trying to solve problems because of their shared mental persistence and commitment to goals. In addition, high PsyCap TMTs should be more confident about their tasks, engage in their work, and set out on a path they believe will lead to effective performance (West et al., 2009). That is, because of the synergistic effect of the four PsyCap resources, we expect *hopeful* teams to be highly motivated to set and achieve collective goals and to be eagerly focused on eliminating obstacles to goal attainment. *Efficacious* teams will display a high level of confidence in the team's ability to achieve the goals. As such, they will put forth the requisite effort and persistence needed to achieve them. Teams marked by *optimism* will use positive language to express their outlook for the future – they will tend to focus on their likelihood of success rather than potential for failure. Finally, *resilience* will allow teams to bounce back quickly when uncertainty or adversity strikes. In particular, they will focus on coping with problems directly rather than being depressed by them. Overall, high PsyCap should contribute to the feeling that the team is capable of tackling whatever it faces. Based on this reasoning, we suggest the following hypothesis:

Hypothesis 2: TMT collective psychological capital is positively associated with business unit performance.

In summary, we expect both the TMT's collective CSE and PsyCap to demonstrate a positive relationship with business unit performance. Collective CSE represents the TMT's combined level of positive and enduring self-views. Collective PsyCap is characterized by the TMT's shared positive appraisal of the team's ability to accomplish the goals in front of them. Both CSE and PsyCap should be integral factors in contributing to the collective motivation and performance of the TMT. We now turn to a discussion of potential moderators of these relationships. In particular, we consider whether leaders of the TMT who display transformational leadership behaviors will contribute to higher TMT performance gains than leaders of TMTs who do not.

Transformational Leadership as a Moderator

As Avolio and Bass (2004) contend, transformational leaders act as role models, provide inspirational motivation and intellectual stimulation, and show individualized consideration. They are assumed to facilitate team performance by directing followers' collective optimism, efficacy, and identification with the team toward the team's objectives (Bass and Riggio, 2006). Despite the large body of studies documenting the positive effects of transformational leadership on numerous important outcomes (Judge and Piccolo, 2004), the majority of past research has focused on the individual level (Judge et al., 2002a). This is somewhat curious because many scholars have suggested that "leadership may have its most important consequences for teams and thus a focus on the team level is also important" (Lim and Ployhart, 2004, p. 610). Several scholars have thus called for shifting the focus from the leadership of individuals to the leadership of teams (Lim and Ployhart, 2004; Chen et al., 2007).

While the number of studies that examine the impact of transformational leadership on teams is growing (Bass et al., 2003; Lim and Ployhart, 2004; Schaubroeck et al., 2007; Kearney and Gebert, 2009), studies examining the impact of transformational leadership on TMT performance is scant. A notable exception is Colbert et al. (2008) who found that CEO transformational leadership was positively related to organizational performance as mediated through TMT members' goal congruence. More work in this area is much needed given the relevance of this type of leadership to TMTs. For example, Morgeson (2005) suggested that due to the influence and decision-making authority that leaders of TMTs have, leadership may be especially important to this population. More specifically, Pawar and Eastman (1997) suggested that the generally positively impact of transformational leadership, which has been observed at lower levels of the managerial hierarchy, will also be observed at higher levels. Similarly, Agle et al. (2006), suggested that transformational CEOs will influence firm performance because of their ability to overcome the inertial forces that impair firms from successfully adapting a dynamic environment.

Further, little research exists that examines whether the relationship of team psychological characteristics with team performance varies depending upon levels of transformational leadership. A recent study by Peterson et al. (2009) linked hope and optimism to transformational and firm performance, suggesting that this is a relationship worth exploring.

However, further work is needed. Although we have hypothesized that TMT members' collective CSE and PsyCap will have positive effects on team performance, we also expect that TMT leaders may play a moderating role in these relationships. Teams must learn to work together in such a way that the positive resources brought into the teams by each member are fully utilized toward meeting collective objective and goals. Leaders are likely to play a key role in facilitating this process (Hogan and Kaiser, 2005). In particular, transformational leaders will likely play a larger role than other types of leaders because transformational leaders emphasize the collective rather than individual interests (Shamir et al., 1993; Waldman and Yammarino, 1999). Because of this collective focus, followers of transformational leaders (in this case, TMT members) are likely to band together their common goals. In addition, transformational leaders are known for their strong abilities to communicate a common vision and goals. As such, followers should have a common understanding of goals. As noted by Colbert et al. (2008, p.84), "a shared understanding of the importance of specific organizational goals among TMT members is likely the first step toward successful organization performance on those goals."

Based on this discussion, we examine the moderating role played by transformational leadership in the TMT psychological characteristics–performance relationship. In particular, we test whether the relationship between TMT collective CSE and PsyCap, and TMT performance varies depending upon the level of transformational leadership. Based upon transformational leadership theory, we expect that TMT leaders' transformational leadership can enhance the positive effect of TMT psychological characteristics on team performance:

Hypothesis 3a: Transformational leadership will moderate the positive effect of TMT core self-evaluation on business unit performance such that the effect is stronger for TMTs with high levels of transformational leadership than for TMTs with low levels of transformational leadership.

Hypothesis 3b: Transformational leadership will moderate the positive effect of TMT psychological capital on business unit performance such that the effect is stronger for TMTs with high levels of transformational leadership than for TMTs with low levels of transformational leadership.

Figure 6.1 shows the hypothesized model for this study.

METHOD

Participants and Procedures

Participants of the current study are from TMTs that are in charge of strategic business units (SBUs) of a large US conglomerate. In this context, a top management team consists of a leader (the President of the SBU) and two or more team members (with the titles of Vice-Presidents of the unit) who are collectively responsible for managing the work force in a particular region (i.e., a county or a metropolitan area). We recognize that our definition differs from the traditional TMT definition, which involves only

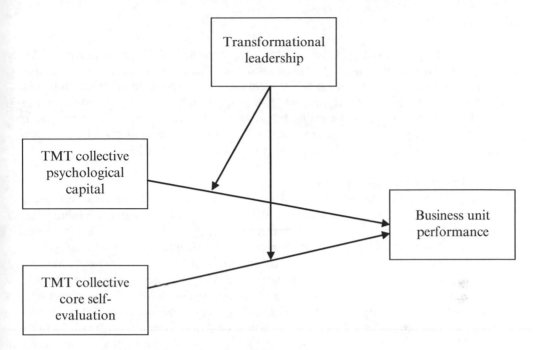

Figure 6.1   The proposed conceptual model

C-level executives. However, each SBU in our sample represents a different business and operates virtually independent of the others, and the teams in charge are comprised of the most senior-level executives in that business. These teams are directly involved in the strategic decisions involving their business and the leaders and the members in these teams have interdependent tasks and are jointly responsible for the SBUs' overall performance. As such, for our study's purpose, we refer to these senior teams as TMTs. The number of TMT members is directly related to the size of the SBU – smaller SBUs may only have three members while large SBUs have up to eight. The average number of employees working in each SBU is roughly 500.

Survey data on TMT collective psychological characteristics and TMT members' and leaders' demographic information were collected on-site at the annual company meeting where all regional TMTs attended. Business unit performance was collected from company records. Of the 82 TMTs that received the surveys, we were able to obtain adequate responses from 67 teams (67 TMT leaders, i.e., Presidents and 244 members, i.e., Vice-Presidents). The number of TMT member responses (excluding the leader) ranged from two to six, with a mean of 3.64 (S.D. = 1.26) members per team. Among the 67 TMT leader respondents, 89.6 percent were male, 97.0 percent were Caucasian, 50.7 percent had bachelor's degrees and 43.3 percent had graduate degrees. Leader respondents have an average age of 45.78 (S.D. = 5.38) and an average tenure of 5.67 (S.D. = 3.20) in the current job role. Among the 244 TMT member respondents, 82.4 percent were male, 90.6 percent were Caucasian, 68.9 percent had bachelor's degrees and 20.1 percent had graduate degrees. TMT member respondents have an average age of 45.95 (S.D. = 6.16) and an average tenure of 5.38 (S.D. =3.23) in the current job role.

Measures

The level of analysis was at the team level for hypothesis testing. When measuring TMT collective psychological characteristics, we used TMT members' self-reported measures on psychological capital and core self-evaluations. Transformational leadership was measured as TMT members' ratings on their respective leader (i.e., President of the SBU). For all the measures, we examined inter-member reliability (ICC_1 and ICC_2), F-values in one-way analysis of variance, and within-group agreement index ($r_{wg(j)}$; James et al., 1984) before aggregating individuals' responses to the TMT level.

TMT collective psychological capital

To assess TMT collective psychological capital we used the 24-item Psychological Capital Questionnaire (PCQ; Luthans et al., 2007b). TMT members (excluding the leader) rated the degree to which they agreed with each of the items on a Five-point Likert scale (1 = strongly disagree, 5 = strongly agree). Sample items include the following: (1) task-specific efficacy: "I feel confident in representing my work area in meetings with management" and "I feel confident helping to set targets/goals in my work area"; (2) hope: "Right now I see myself as being pretty successful at work" and "If I should find myself in a jam at work, I could think of many ways to get out of it"; (3) resilience: "When I have a setback at work, I have trouble recovering from it, moving on" and "I usually take stressful things at work in my stride"; and (4) optimism: "I always look on the bright side of things regarding my job" and "If something can go wrong for me work-wise, it will." The individual-level reliability coefficient was 0.98. We obtained support for aggregating this variable to the team level (ICC_1 = 0.16, ICC_2 = 0.40, $F(66, 177)$ = 1.67, $p < 0.01$). The median $r_{wg(j)}$ value with a uniform expected variance distribution was 0.98.

TMT collective core self-evaluation

We used Judge et al.'s (2003) measure to assess TMT collective core self-evaluation. TMT members (excluding the leader) rated the degree to which they agree with each of the 12 items on a Five-point Likert scale (1 = strongly disagree, 5 = strongly agree). Example items include (1) generalized efficacy: "I am confident I get the success I deserve in life"; (2) self-esteem: "Overall, I am satisfied with myself"; (3) emotional stability: "I am capable of coping with most of my problems"; and (4) locus of control: "I determine what will happen in my life." The individual-level reliability coefficient was 0.96. Support was found for aggregating this variable to the team level (ICC_1 = 0.18, ICC_2 = 0.45, $F(66, 177)$ = 1.81, $p < 0.001$). The median $r_{wg(j)}$ value with a uniform expected variance distribution was 0.96.

Transformational leadership

The TMT leader's transformational leadership was measured using the 20-item Multifactor Leadership Questionnaire (MLQ form 5x, Short; Bass and Avolio, 1995). TMT members (excluding the leader) rated the frequency that the leader exhibited the four components of transformational leadership: idealized influence, inspirational motivation, intellectual stimulation, and individualized consideration. Respondents responded to items using a Five-point Likert scale (1 = not at all, 5 = frequently, if not always). The individual-level reliability coefficient was 0.98. Support was obtained for aggregating this variable to the team level (ICC$_1$ = 0.63, ICC$_2$ = 0.86, $F(66, 177)$ = 7.18, $p < 0.001$). The median r$_{wg(j)}$ value with a uniform expected variance distribution was 0.99.

Business unit performance

We obtained business unit performance data based on company records for the first two quarters of 2009. Business unit performance was a composite of two performance measures: (1) the number of sales opportunities generated by the unit (mean = 185, S.D. = 75), and (2) the natural log of the unit's sales revenue (before the natural log, mean = 2.14 million dollars, S.D. = 4.18 million dollars). The two variables were correlated at $r = 0.80$ ($p < 0.01$, $n = 67$) and were standardized to form a composite variable representing business unit performance. Number of sales opportunities is a somewhat unique way that each SBU is evaluated in this particular organization. Because of the typically long sales cycle, SBUs are required to report "viable" opportunities in their pipeline. An opportunity is considered viable when a formal presentation has been given to the client or customer and a letter of understanding (LOU) has been signed by the client indicating that they intend to do business. While the LOU does not guarantee the business, it is a sign of the team performing well enough to get opportunities downstream.

Controls

The TMT members' and leaders' tenure in TMTs were shown to influence team processes and, ultimately, business unit performance (e.g., Ancona and Caldwell, 1992; Carpenter, 2002). Therefore, we controlled for the average team tenure in the analysis. As Becker (2005) has shown, the inclusion of unnecessary control variables in analysis can lead to lower statistical power as well as potential biased estimates. Given the current sample size, we only controlled for average team tenure.

Analysis

We first conducted individual-level omnibus confirmatory factor analyses (CFAs) to ascertain that members' reported psychological capital, core self-evaluations, and transformational leadership were distinct constructs. We then tested our team-level hypotheses using hierarchical regressions. In order to reduce multicollinearity, variables were mean-centered before we calculated interaction terms for moderation testing.

RESULTS

Table 6.1 presents means, standard deviations, and intercorrelations for all TMT-level variables. As shown in Table 6.1, TMT collective psychological capital ($r = 0.34$, $p < 0.01$) and transformational leadership ($r = 0.48$, $p < 0.001$) are significantly related to business unit performance. TMT collective core self-evaluation was not significantly related to unit performance ($r = 0.12$, n.s.).

Omnibus confirmatory factor analysis on the three TMT member-reported scales

Table 6.1   Mean, standard deviations, and intercorrelations of study variables

Variable	M	SD	1	2	3	4	5
1. Average TMT tenure	5.44	1.93	–				
2. TMT collective psychological capital	3.54	0.53	0.17	–			
3. TMT collective core self-evaluation	3.49	0.56	−0.01	0.52***	–		
4. Transformational leadership	3.21	0.80	0.18	0.46***	0.28*	–	
5. Business unit performance	0.00	0.95	0.19	0.34**	0.12	0.48***	–

Note: $N = 67$. Average TMT tenure was based on reports from TMT members and the leader. The two TMT collective psychological measures and transformational leadership were based on TMT members' reports only. * $p < 0.05$, ** $p < 0.01$, *** $p < 0.001$.

suggested a better fit for the proposed three-factor model, in comparison with two-factor or single-factor models. In order to reach an optimal ratio of sample size and number of items in CFAs, we randomly grouped the items into four-item parcels for core self-evaluation (three parcels), psychological capital (six parcels), and transformational leadership (five parcels), respectively. The three-factor model shows acceptable fit with $\chi^2(74, n = 235) = 281.72$, $p < 0.001$, CFI = 0.96, TLI = 0.95, SRMR = 0.02, and RMSEA = 0.06. The two-factor models and the single-factor model had significant worse fit, with CFIs and TLIs in the 0.45 to 0.81 range and SRMRs and RMSEAs in the 0.12 to 0.28 range.

Table 6.2 presents the results for hypothesis testing. Hypotheses 1 and 2 suggested that TMT collective psychological capital and core self-evaluation would be positively related to unit performance. Supporting Hypothesis 1, TMT collective psychological capital was positively related to unit performance (unstandardized coefficient $B = 0.64$, $p < 0.05$). Hypothesis 2 was not supported in that TMT collective core self-evaluation was not significantly related to unit performance. In support of Hypothesis 3, transformational leadership moderated the relationship between TMT collective psychological capital and unit performance ($B = 0.64$, $p < 0.05$). We did not find any significant moderating effect of transformational leadership on the relationship between TMT collective core self-evaluation and unit performance, failing to support Hypothesis 4.

To better interpret the moderating effect of transformational leadership, we present a graph (Figure 6.2) showing the TMT collective psychological capital–unit performance relationship under high vs. low levels of transformational leadership (i.e., one S.D. above and below the mean value of transformational leadership). As Figure 6.2 shows, when transformational leadership is high, TMT collective psychological capital is strongly and positively related to unit performance. In contrast, when transformational leadership is low, TMT collective psychological capital is not related to unit performance (simple slope was not significant).

Table 6.2 Regression results for main effects and moderating effects

Variable	Unit Performance	
	Main effect	Moderating effect
Constant	−0.34	−0.35
Average TMT tenure	0.06	0.04
TMT collective psychological capital (PsyCap)	0.64*	0.37
TMT collective core self-evaluation (CSE)	−0.11	−0.16
Transformational leadership (TFL)		0.43**
PsyCap × TFL		0.64*
CSE × TFL		−0.14
Adj-R^2	0.10	0.26
Δ Adj-R^2		0.16

Note: N = 67. Unstandardized coefficients are reported. * $p < 0.05$, ** $p < 0.01$.

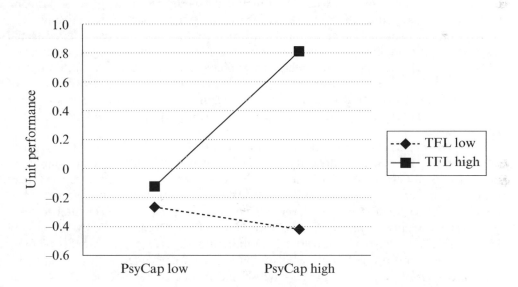

Figure 6.2 The moderating effect of transformational leadership (TFL) on the relationship between TMT collective psychological capital (PsyCap) and unit performance. Unit performance is an average of two standardized variables for the strategic business unit

DISCUSSION

This study represents one of the first theoretically grounded empirical investigations of the impact of executives' psychological characteristics on organizational-level outcomes. It makes a unique contribution by integrating the previously validated constructs of CSE and PsyCap, which to date have primarily been studied in the organizational behavior literature (see Hiller and Hambrick, 2005, for an exception), into the strategic management literature. Within TMTs, we used survey data and objective indicators of unit performance to explore the direct effects of TMT collective CSE and collective PsyCap on the performance of the business units led by the TMT. We also examined transformational leadership as a moderator of these relationships. Results based on 67 TMTs were mixed and in some cases surprising. While we expected both TMT collective CSE and collective PsyCap to be positively related to business unit performance, our results indicated that only TMTs' collective PsyCap was positively related to business unit performance. Collective CSE was *not* significantly related to business unit performance. Results further indicated that the relationship between the TMTs' collective PsyCap and business unit performance was enhanced when the TMT was led by a transformational leader. These results offer several theoretical and practical implications.

Theoretical Implications

First, our results have implications for the upper echelons perspective. Our work goes beyond the examination of executives' functional characteristics to provide a strong theoretical and systematic framework for investigating the impact of executive psychological characteristics on organizational performance. Past research has pointed to the importance of studying psychological characteristics of executives (e.g., Priem et al., 1999) but has also recognized the difficulties and challenges associated with this area of inquiry (see Finkelstein and Hambrick, 1996). Hence, we add to the growing body of work on TMTs by introducing and empirically testing the impact of two theoretically grounded constructs with valid measurement, CSE and PsyCap, on TMT business unit performance.

Similarly, our study has implications for the study of diversity in TMTs, namely deep-level (e.g., personality) diversity (see Harrison and Klein, 2007). While our study did not look at CSE or PsyCap differences between TMT members, future work may want to consider this within-team diversity. While functional diversity is assumed to be a good thing for TMTs, deep-level diversity is assumed to be detrimental to team effectiveness because it may trigger relationship conflict. Recent work by Boone and Hendriks (2009) supports this idea. The authors found performance benefits of functional background diversity but negative consequences associated with diversity with regard to locus-of-control. Future research should expand this line of inquiry to include comparing PsyCap and CSE diversity to other deep-level diversity variables or to functional diversity.

In addition, our study contributes to the respective literatures surrounding CSE and PsyCap. While previous research has consistently demonstrated the positive influence of these constructs on individual and lower-level team performance, the impact of CSE and PysCap on TMT and organizational performance has yet to be examined until now. Because results from one level of analysis do not always translate to other levels (Kozlowski and Klein, 2000), it is important to determine if previous CSE and PsyCap performance effects generalize from the individual to the TMT level of analysis. Our results indicated that, at least where PsyCap is concerned, the positive effects of individual PsyCap on performance tend to translate to the TMT level. Specifically, in line with recent speculation (see West et al., 2009) that a team's overall sense of positivity should hold the potential to influence team members, their interactions, and their performance, our findings support this importance of considering executives' PsyCap as a potential predictor of TMT team and organizational performance.

Further, while there is precedent for various psychological constructs such as personality (e.g., Barrick et al., 1998; LePine et al., 2000) to be operationalized at the team level, research has yet to consider CSE as a team-level construct and has only begun to do so for PsyCap (e.g., Walumbwa et al., 2009; West et al., 2009). Given the importance of team-based collaboration for organizational performance (Gully et al., 2002; Cannella et al., 2008; Colbert et al., 2008), focusing on the identification of team-level constructs that may elicit team effectiveness is becoming increasingly important. Our study represents the most comprehensive examination to date that considers team representations of CSE and PsyCap and applies them directly to team-level outcomes. More specifically, our findings demonstrate that PsyCap applied to the team level, collective PsyCap, can contribute to TMT business unit performance. We suggest that a team's shared belief in its collective ability to perform certain tasks (task-specific efficacy), its expectations regarding the likelihood of positive outcomes (optimism), its focus on jointly setting goals, pursuing goals and overcoming obstacles to goal attainment (hope), and its ability to bounce back from setbacks, conflict, or failure (resilience) will propel the team to more actively engage in their work and proactively interact with each other toward the successful completion of team goals. In other words, a team high in collective PsyCap should be more motivated, directed, and effective at achieving success.

However, while we also expected TMT collective CSE to be positively related to business unit performance, our data did not support this expectation. According to Judge and Bono (2001) and based on their findings at the individual level of analysis, higher CSE should equate with higher levels of performance. As such, we expected similar findings when we aggregated CSE to the team level. After all, it certainly seems probable to think that a TMT whose members all have high CSE should outperform those with a lower aggregated CSE. Hiller and Hambrick (2005) offer some insight as to why this might not be the case. Specifically the authors suggested that when executive CSE is too high (i.e., hyper-CSE), this may be equated with hubris, and could lead executives to take on risky initiatives or to make decision too quickly. In other words, executives with overly high levels of CSE may think so highly of themselves that they fail to conduct adequate data analysis before making strategic decisions or choices. Instead, Hiller and Hambrick argue that those with a slightly lower CSE, who have more self-doubt, may behave more reliably over time. While our study's results did not indicate that a TMT's collective CSE was unusually high compared with what would be expected for executives (see Hiller and Hambrick, 2005), this explanation provides some evidence of the proposition put forth by the authors.

Finally, this study is the first we know of that examines the conditions under which both CSE and PsyCap have more or less positive effects on organizational-level performance. In particular, we focused on transformational leadership, arguably the most popular form of leadership (Bass and Riggio, 2006), as a moderator of the relationship. Our results demonstrated that transformational leadership did enhance the impact of TMT collective PsyCap on the team's business unit performance. Given the already large body of work that supports that transformational leadership can positively impact follower attitudes, motivation, and individual, group, and organizational perform-ance (Judge and Piccolo, 2004), our work adds to these findings by suggesting that the relationship between a TMT's collective PsyCap and performance will be even stronger when the leader of that team displays transformational leadership behavior. Perhaps because transformational leaders are already focused on collective interests and common goals (Shamir et al., 1993), they represent a natural condition to influence the relation-ship between collective constructs and team outcomes. In addition, due to the fact that recent research has found transformational leaders to be high on the dimensions of PsyCap themselves (see Peterson et al., 2009), it may also be that their positivity is "cas-cading" or "trickling down" to followers (e.g., Bass et al., 1987; Aryee et al., 2007).

Practical Implications

This study also has practical implications for executives, TMTs, and organizations. Given that our findings suggest that a TMT with a high collective PsyCap might outperform its lower PsyCap counterparts, professionals in the executive development arena may want to consider integrating PsyCap into how they approach and develop their executives. Because PsyCap has been shown to be open to development and interventions aimed at increasing PsyCap are emerging (see Luthans et al., 2008), discovering new ways to apply PsyCap development to executives may prove worthwhile. Whether this is through executive coaching or executive education, leveraging positivity could prove to have an ROI (return on investment). In addition, because positivity is thought to be contagious (Quinn, 2000), executive PsyCap may "rub off" on others. For example, when employees are around hopeful and optimistic executives, they tend to be more hopeful and opti-mistic themselves. After all, few employees would desire to be led by an executive team known as being pessimistic, fearing failure, and lacking confidence in their abilities. Such negativity can have ripple effects across the organizations. With respect to the leader's level of PsyCap, when immediate supervisors demonstrate higher positive PsyCap, we would expect their followers to mimic the same behavior such that these positive supervi-sor states are transferred to their followers (Yammarino et al., 2008).

Regarding CSE, while we did not find the hypothesized effects here, we certainly think CSE is a valuable disposition. Our results suggest that the relationship between TMT CSE and business unit performance was positive – just not significant. Clearly, CSE is something worth considering and selecting for in organizations. Our results simply imply that caution should be used in terms of potentially confusing what is an optimal level of CSE with hyper-CSE, hubris, or narcissism, which may be less desirable. Given CSE's trait-like nature, it is not expected to change much. As such, CSE has more implications for selection of executives than it does for development.

Finally, regarding transformational leadership, our results provide additional support for developing executives toward this form of leadership. Not only do our results support what others have found – that transformational leaders can impact the bottom line, but they can augment the impact of psychological characteristics. By communicating a clear collective vision of the future, by modeling appropriate behaviors and positivity them-selves (see Peterson et al., 2009), transformational leaders should only enhance the effects of PsyCap on business unit performance. In other words, transformational leaders will endorse and encourage collective optimism, hope, efficacy, and resilience in the teams they lead. As such, organizations should continue to develop this type of leadership in executives.

Future Research Directions

It is our hope that this study stimulates researchers to continue down the path of exploring executive and TMT psychological characteristics. First and foremost, future studies should go beyond our somewhat limited definition of TMTs to include traditional TMTs. While the challenges associated with gathering psychological data from executives in general, and conventional TMTs in particular, remain, given our results indicating that the combined PsyCap of these teams' members may contribute to the organization's bottom line, this area of research seems promising. Not only should researchers attempt to replicate our findings regarding the positive impact of PsyCap in different executive contexts and in conventional TMTs, but a study that compares the impact of functional characteristics and PsyCap on TMT outcomes could be especially illuminating. Such work would allow researchers to better understand the relative predictive power of functional versus psychological characteristics.

In addition, future work needs to go beyond the examination of the direct relationship between PsyCap and performance to examine the underlying processes involved in this relationship. Our work here stops short of examining why the relationship between PsyCap and TMT business unit performance might exist. Researchers interested in executive psychological characteristics in general, and in PsyCap in particular, would benefit from a more solid understanding of the mediating processes involved in the relationship between PsyCap and outcomes of interest to executives and TMTs.

Further, researchers should pay particular attention to CSE in executives in an attempt to further understand this relationship. Specifically, we urge researchers to examine why we did not garner the expected results in this study. We expected collective CSE in TMTs to be positively related to TMT performance, yet this relationship was not significant. It is certainly possible that when it comes to CSE, more is not necessary better (see Hiller and Hambrick, 2005). Instead, perhaps the relationship between CSE in executives and their performance is curvilinear, suggesting that there may be an optimal level of CSE. It is also possible that certain contextual or moderating factors not explored here are influencing this relationship. Future work should explicitly examine these possibilities.

Our work should also interest researchers focused on the state–trait distinction. As discussed earlier, an important differentiator for PsyCap is that it is thought to be state-like – open to development and change while CSE is considered trait-like or fixed and dispositional in nature. Given that we did not find the same results for PsyCap (a state-like variable) and CSE (a trait-like variable), future work should consider why states versus traits may have a differential relationship or impact on performance.

Finally, our work has implications for future work on transformational leadership theory in general. In this study, we have extended transformational leadership theory by investigating the interactive effects of transformational leadership and team psychological characteristics in the TMT setting. Previous research found that transformational leadership was a moderator of the relationship between age, nationality, and educational background diversity with team outcomes (Kearney and Gilbert, 2009). However, we do not know of any research that examined the moderating effects of transformational leadership on relationships between psychological characteristics and team outcomes. While our results are promising for advocates of transformational leadership as they suggest that transformational leaders augment the relationship between psychological characteristics (i.e., PsyCap) and team outcomes, additional efforts down this line of inquiry are necessary. Specifically, researchers should investigate whether transformational leadership serves as a moderator between other psychological characteristics beyond PsyCap and team-level outcomes. That is, are hopeful, optimistic, confident, and resilient teams (high collective PsyCap teams) especially susceptible to transformational leaders or, given transformational leaders' emphasis on collective interest and goals (Shamir et al., 1993), is it likely that transformational leaders will impact many relationships involving team-level constructs? Additional empirical work is needed to explore these ideas.

CONCLUSIONS

This study shows the importance of TMT collective psychological capital and transformational leadership in their interactively influencing business unit performance. Organizations aiming to provide positive interventions in executive development can utilize the findings to design more effective TMT training programs that target at enhancing TMT members' collective self-views with regard to goals at work, and to develop transformational leadership that can help reap the performance benefits of such programs.

ACKNOWLEDGMENT

We want to thank Natalie Miller, an MBA student from Arizona State University who helped with data entry for this project.

REFERENCES

Adams, V.H., Snyder, C.R., Rand, K.L., King, E.A., Sigmon, D.R., and Pulvers, K.M. (2002). Hope in the workplace. In R. Giacolone and C. Jurkiewicz (eds), *Handbook of workplace spirituality and organizational performance*. New York, NY: Sharpe, pp. 367–77.
Agle, B.R., Nagarajan, N.J., Sonnenfeld, J.A., and Srinivasan, D. (2006). Does CEO charisma matter? An empirical analysis of the relationships among organizational performance, environmental uncertainty, and top management team perceptions of CEO charisma. *Academy of Management Journal*, 49(1), 161–74.
Ancona, D. and Caldwell, D.F. (1992). Demography and design: Predictors of new product team performance. *Organization Science*, 35(3), 321–41.
Aryee, S., Chen, Z., Sun, L., and Debrah, Y. (2007). Antecedents and outcomes of abusive supervision: Test of a trickle-down model. *Journal of Applied Psychology*, 92(1), 191–201.
Avey, J.B., Luthans, F., and Youssef, C.M. (2010). The additive value of positive psychological capital in predicting work attitudes and behaviors. *Journal of Management*, 36(2), 430–52.
Avolio, B.J. and Bass, B.M. (2004). *Multifactor leadership questionnaire*. Menlo Park, CA: Mind Garden.
Bandura, A. (1997). *Self-efficacy: The exercise of control*. New York, NY: Freeman.
Bandura, A. and Locke, E. (2003). Negative self-efficacy and goal effects revisited. *Journal of Applied Psychology*, 88(1), 87–99.
Barrick, M.R., Stewart, G.L., Neubert, M., and Mount, M.K. (1998). Relating member ability and personality to work team processes and team effectiveness. *Journal of Applied Psychology*, 83(3), 377–91.
Barsade, S.G., Ward, A.J., Turner, J.D.F., and Sonnenfeld, J.A. (2000). To your heart's content: A model of affective diversity in top management teams. *Administrative Science Quarterly*, 45(4), 802–36.

Bass, B.M. (1998). *Transformational leadership: Industry, military, and educational impact.* Mahwah, NJ: Erlbaum.

Bass, B.M. and Avolio, B.J. (1995). *MLQ Multifactor leadership questionnaire: (Form 5x-Short).* Redwood City, CA: Mind Garden.

Bass, B.M. and Riggio, R.E. (2006). *Transformational leadership.* Mahwah, NJ: Lawrence Erlbaum Associates.

Bass, B.M., Avolio, B.J., and Goodheim, L. (1987). Biography and the assessment of transformational leadership at the world-class level. *Journal of Management*, **13**(1), 7–19.

Bass, B.M., Avolio, B.J., Jung, D.I., and Berson, Y. (2003). Predicting unit performance by assessing transformational and transactional leadership. *Journal of Applied Psychology*, **88**(2), 207–18.

Baumeister, R., Smart, L., and Boden, J. (1996). Relation of threatened egotism to violence and aggression: The dark side of self-esteem. *Psychological Review*, **103**(1), 5–33.

Becker, T.E. (2005). Potential problems in the statistical control of variables in organizational research: A qualitative analysis with recommendations. *Organizational Research Methods*, **8**(3), 274–89.

Boone, C. and Hendriks, W. (2009). Top management team diversity and firm performance: Moderators of functional-background and locus-of-control diversity. *Management Science*, **55**(2), 165–80.

Boone, C., De Brabander, B., and Hellemans, J. (2000). Research note: CEO locus of control and small firm performance. *Organization Studies*, **21**(3), 641–6.

Cannella, A.A., Park, J.H., and Lee, H.U. (2008). Top management team functional background diversity and firm performance: Examining the roles of team member colocation and environmental uncertainty. *Academy of Management Journal*, **51**(4), 768–84.

Carpenter, M.A. (2002). The implications of strategy and social context for the relationship between top management team heterogeneity and firm performance. *Strategic Management Journal*, **23**(3), 275–84.

Carpenter, M.A., Geletkanycz, M.A., and Sanders, W.G. (2004). The upper echelons research revisited: The antecedents, elements, and consequences of top management team composition. *Journal of Management*, **30**(6), 749–78.

Carver, C.S. and Scheier, M.S. (2002). Optimism. In C.R. Snyder and S.J. Lopez (eds), *Handbook of positive psychology.* Oxford, UK: Oxford University Press, pp. 231–43.

Certo, S.T., Lester, R.H., Dalton, C.M., and Dalton, D.R. (2006). Top management teams, strategy and financial performance: A meta-analytic examination. *Journal of Management Studies*, **43**(4), 813–39.

Chemers, M.M., Watson, C.B., and May, S.T. (2000). Dispositional affect and leadership effectiveness: A comparison of self-esteem, optimism, and efficacy. *Personality and Social Psychology Bulletin*, **26**(3), 267–77.

Chen, G., Gully, S.M., Whiteman, J.A., and Kilcullen, R.N. (2000). Examination of relationships among trait-like individual differences, state-like individual differences, and learning performance. *Journal of Applied Psychology*, **85**(6), 835–47.

Chen, G., Kirkman, B., Kanfer, R., Allen, D., and Rosen, B. (2007). A multilevel study of leadership, empowerment, and performance in teams. *Journal of Applied Psychology*, **92**(2), 331–46.

Colbert, A.E., Kristof-Brown, A.L., Bradley, B.H., and Barrick, M.R. (2008). CEO transformational leadership: The role of goal importance congruence in top management teams. *Academy of Management Journal*, **51**(1), 81–96.

Colquitt, J.A., LePine, J.A., and Noe, R. (2000). Toward an integrative theory of training motivation: A meta-analytic path analysis of 20 years of research. *Journal of Applied Psychology*, **85**(5), 678–707.

Costa, P.T. and McCrae, R.R. (1992). *Revised NEO personality inventory and NEO five-factor inventory.* Odessa, FL: Psychological Assessment Resources.

Coutu, D.L. (2002). How resilience works. *Harvard Business Review*, **80**(5), 45–55.

Erez, A. and Judge, T.A. (2001). Relationship of core self-evaluations to goal setting, motivation, and performance. *Journal of Applied Psychology*, **86**(6), 1270–79.

Finkelstein, S. and Hambrick, D.C. (1996). *Strategic leadership: Top executives and their effects on organizations.* St. Paul, MN: West.

Forbes, D.P. (2005). Are some entrepreneurs more overconfident than others? *Journal of Business Venturing*, **20**(5), 623–40.

Gardner, D.G. and Pierce, J.L. (1998). Self-esteem and self-efficacy within the organizational context: An empirical examination. *Group and Organization Management*, **23**(1), 48–70.

Gibson, C.B. (1999). Do they do what they believe they can? Group efficacy and group effectiveness across tasks and cultures. *Academy of Management Journal*, **42**(2), 138–52.

Gibson, C.B. (2001). From knowledge accumulation to accommodation: Cycles of collective cognition in work groups. *Journal of Organizational Behavior*, **22**(2), 121–34.

Gist, M.E. and Mitchell, T.R. (1992). Self-efficacy: A theoretical analysis of its determinants and malleability. *Academy of Management Review*, **17**(2), 183–211.

Gully, S.M., Incalcaterra, K.A., Joshi, A., and Beaubien, J.M. (2002). A meta-analysis of team-efficacy, potency, and performance: Interdependence and level of analysis as moderators of observed relationships. *Journal of Applied Psychology*, **87**(5), 819–32.

Hambrick, D.C. and Mason, P.A. (1984). Upper echelons: The organization as a reflection of its top managers. *Academy of Management Review*, **9**(2), 193–206.

Harland, L., Harrison, W., Jones, J., and Reiter-Palmon, R. (2005). Leadership behaviors and subordinate resilience. *Journal of Leadership and Organizational Studies*, **11**(2), 2–14.

Harrison, D.A. and Klein, K.J. (2007). What's the difference? Diversity constructs as separation, variety, or disparity in organizations. *Academy of Management Review*, **32**(4), 1199–228.

Hayward, M.L.A. and Hambrick, D.C. (1997). Explaining the premiums paid for large acquisitions: Evidence of CEO hubris. *Administrative Science Quarterly*, **42**(1), 103–27.

Hiller, N. and Hambrick, D.C. (2005). Conceptualizing executive hubris: The role of (hyper-) core self-evaluations in strategic decision-making. *Strategic Management Journal*, **26**(4), 297–319.

Hogan, R. and Kaiser, R.B. (2005). What we know about leadership. *Review of General Psychology*, **9**(2), 169–80.

Hui, C. and Lee, C. (2000). Moderating effects of organizational-based self-esteem on organizational uncertainty: Employee response relationships. *Journal of Management*, **26**(2), 215–32.

James, L.R., Demaree, R.G., and Wolf, G. (1984). Estimating within group interrater reliability with and without response bias. *Journal of Applied Psychology*, **69**(1), 85–98.

Judge, T.A. and Bono, J.E. (2001). Relationship of core self-evaluations traits – self-esteem, generalized self-efficacy, locus of control, and emotional stability – with job satisfaction and job performance: A meta-analysis. *Journal of Applied Psychology*, **86**(1), 80–92.

Judge, T.A. and Piccolo, R. (2004). Transformational and transactional leadership: A meta-analytic test of their relative validity. *Journal of Applied Psychology*, **89**(5), 755–68.

Judge, T.A., Erez, A., and Bono, J.E. (1998). The power of being positive: The relationship between positive self-concept and job performance. *Human Performance*, **11**(2/3), 167–87.

Judge, T.A., Bono, J.E., Ilies, R., and Gerhardt, M. (2002a). Personality and leadership: A qualitative and quantitative review. *Journal of Applied Psychology*, **87**(4), 765–80.

Judge, T.A., Erez, A., Bono, J.E., and Thoresen, C.J. (2002b). Do the traits self-esteem, neuroticism, locus of control, and generalized self-efficacy indicate a common core construct? *Journal of Personality and Social Psychology*, **83**(3), 693–710.

Judge, T.A., Erez, A., Bono, J.E., and Thoresen, C.J. (2003). The core self-evaluations scale (CSES): Development of a measure. *Personnel Psychology*, **56**(2), 303–31.

Judge, T.A., Higgins, C., Thoresen, C.J., and Barrick, M.R. (1999a). The Big Five personality traits, general mental ability, and career success across the life span. *Personnel Psychology*, **52**(3), 621–52.

Judge, T.A., Thoresen, C.J., Pucik, V., and Welbourne, T.M. (1999b). Managerial coping with organizational change: A dispositional perspective. *Journal of Applied Psychology*, **84**, 107–22.

Kearney, E. and Gebert, D. (2009). Managing diversity and enhancing team outcomes: The promise of transformational leadership. *Journal of Applied Psychology*, **94**(1), 77–89.

Knight, D., Durham, C.C., and Locke, E.A. (2001). The relationship of team goals, incentives, and efficacy to strategic risk, tactical implementation, and performance. *Academy of Management Journal*, **44**(2), 326–38.

Kozlowski, S.W.J. and Klein, K.J. (2000). A multilevel approach to theory and research in organizations: Contextual, temporal, and emergent processes. In K.J. Klein and S.W.J. Kozlowski (eds), *Multilevel theory, research, and methods in organizations: Foundations, extensions, and new directions*. San Francisco, CA: Jossey-Bass, pp. 3–90.

Larson, C.E. and LaFasto, F.M.J. (1989). *Teamwork: What must go right, what can go wrong*. Newbury Park, CA: Sage.

Lee, C., Tinsley, C.H., and Bobko, P. (2002). An investigation of the antecedents and consequences of group-level confidence. *Journal of Applied Social Psychology*, **32**(8), 1628–52.

LePine, J.A., Colquitt, J.A., and Erez, A. (2000). Adaptability to changing task contexts: Effects of general cognitive ability, conscientiousness, and openness to experience. *Personnel Psychology*, **53**(3), 563–94.

Lim, B.C. and Ployhart, R.E. (2004). Transformational leadership: Relations to the Five Factor Model and team performance in typical and maximum contexts. *Journal of Applied Psychology*, **89**(4), 610–21.

Luthans, F. (2002). The need for and meaning of positive organizational behavior. *Journal of Organizational Behavior*, **23**(6), 695–706.

Luthans, F., Avey, J.B., and Patera, J.L. (2008). Experimental analysis of a web-based training intervention to develop positive psychological capital. *Academy of Management Learning and Education*, **7**(2), 209–21.

Luthans, F., Vogelgesang, G.R., and Lester, P.B. (2006). Developing the psychological capital of resiliency. *Human Resource Development Review*, **5**(1), 25–44.

Luthans, F., Youssef, C.M., and Avolio, B.J. (2007a). *Psychological capital: Developing the human competitive edge*. Oxford, UK: Oxford University Press.

Luthans, F., Avolio, B.J., Avey, J.B., and Norman, S.M. (2007b). Positive psychological capital: Measurement and relationship with performance and satisfaction. *Personnel Psychology*, **60**(3), 541–72.

Luthans, F., Avolio, B.J., Walumbwa, F., and Li, W. (2005). The psychological capital of Chinese workers: Exploring the relationship with performance. *Management and Organization Review*, **1**(2), 247–69.

Morgeson, F.P. (2005). The external leadership of self-managing teams: Intervening in the context of novel and disruptive events. *Journal of Applied Psychology*, **90**(3), 497–508.

Moynihan, L.M. and Peterson, R.S. (2001). A contingent configuration approach to understanding the role of personality in organizational groups. *Research in Organizational Behavior*, **23**, 327–78.

Pawar, B.S. and Eastman, K.K. (1997). The nature and implications of contextual influences on transformational leadership: A conceptual examination. *Academy of Management Review*, **22**(1), 80–99.

Peterson, R.S., Smith, D.B., Martorana, P.V., and Owens, P.D. (2003). The impact of CEO personality on top management team dynamics: One mechanism by which leadership affects organizational performance. *Journal of Applied Psychology*, **88**(5), 795–808.

Peterson, S.J. and Byron, K. (2008). Exploring the role of hope in job performance: Results from four studies. *Journal of Organizational Behavior*, **29**(6), 785–803.

Peterson, S.J. and Luthans, F. (2003). The positive impact and development of hopeful leaders. *Leadership and Organization Development Journal*, **24**(1), 26–31.

Peterson, S.J., Walumbwa, F., Byron, K., and Myrowitz, J. (2009). CEO positive psychological traits, transformational leadership, and firm performance in high-technology start-up and established firms. *Journal of Management*, **35**(2), 348–68.

Ployhart, R.E., Lim, B.C., and Chan, K.Y. (2001). Exploring relations between typical and maximum performance ratings and the five factor model of personality. *Personnel Psychology*, **54**(4), 809–43.

Priem, R.L., Lyon, D.W., and Dess, G.G. (1999). Inherent limitations of demographic proxies in top management team heterogeneity research. *Journal of Management*, **25**(6), 935–53.

Quinn, R.E. (2000). *Change the world: How ordinary people can achieve extraordinary results*. San Francisco, CA: Jossey-Bass Inc.

Rotter, J.B. (1954). *Social learning and clinical psychology*. Englewood Cliffs, NJ: Prentice-Hall.

Schaubroeck, J., Lam, S.S.K., and Cha, S E. (2007). Embracing transformational leadership: Team values and the impact of leader behavior on team performance. *Journal of Applied Psychology*, **92**(4), 1020–30.

Schulman, P. (1999). Applying learned optimism to increase sales productivity. *Journal of Personal Selling and Sales Management*, **19**(1), 31–7.

Seligman, M.E.P. (1998). *Learned optimism*. New York: Pocket Books.

Seligman, M.E.P. and Schulman, P. (1986). Explanatory style as a predictor of productivity and quitting among life insurance sales agents. *Journal of Personality and Social Psychology*, **50**(4), 832–8.

Shamir, B., House, R.J., and Arthur, M.G. (1993). The motivational effects of charismatic leadership: A self-concept based theory. *Organizational Science*, **4**(4), 577–94.

Simon, M. and Houghton, S.M. (2003). The relationship between overconfidence and the introduction of risky products: Evidence from a field study. *Academy of Management Journal*, **46**(2), 139–49.

Snyder, C.R., Irving, L., and Anderson, J. (1991). Hope and health: Measuring the will and the ways. In C.R. Snyder and D.R. Forsyth (eds), *Handbook of social and clinical psychology*. Elmsford, NY: Pergamon, pp. 285–305.

Stajkovic, A.D. (2006). Development of a core confidence higher-order construct. *Journal of Applied Psychology*, **91**(6), 1208–24.

Stajkovic, A.D. and Luthans, F. (1998). Self-efficacy and work-related performance: A meta-analysis. *Psychological Bulletin*, **124**(2), 240–61.

Waldman, D.A. and Yammarino, F.J. (1999). CEO charismatic leadership: Levels-of-management and levels-of-analysis effects. *Academy of Management Review*, **24**(2), 266–85.

Walumbwa, F.O., Luthans, F., Avey, J., and Oke, A. (2009). Authentically leading groups: The mediating role of positivity and trust. *Journal of Organizational Behavior*, available at: http://www3.interscience.wiley.com/cgi-bin/fulltext/122581343/PDFSTART; accessed 22 July 2010.

Wanberg, C.R. and Banas, J.T. (2000). Predictors and outcomes of openness to change in a reorganizing workplace. *Journal of Applied Psychology*, **85**(1), 132–42.

West, B.J., Patera, J.L., and Carsten, M.K. (2009). Team-level positivity: Investigating positive psychological capacities and team-level outcomes. *Journal of Organizational Behavior*, **30**(2), 249–67.

Wunderley, L.J., Reddy, W.P., and Dember, W.N. (1998). Optimism and pessimism in business leaders. *Journal of Applied Social Psychology*, **28**(9), 751–60.

Yammarino, F.J., Dionne, S.D., Schriesheim, C.A., and Dansereau, F. (2008). Authentic leadership and positive organizational behavior: A meso, multi-level perspective. *Leadership Quarterly*, **19**(6), 693–707.

Youssef, C.M. and Luthans, F. (2007). Positive organizational behavior in the workplace: The impact of hope, optimism, and resiliency. *Journal of Management*, **33**(5), 774–800.

Zaccaro, S.J., Blair, V., Peterson, C., and Zazanis, M. (1995). Collective efficacy. In J.E. Maddux (ed.), *Self-efficacy, adaptation, and adjustment: Theory, research, and application*. New York, NY: Plenum Press, pp. 305–28.

7 Top management team confidence
Kevin D. Clark and Patrick G. Maggitti

A critical success factor for firms facing today's turbulent and competitive environment is the action of an able executive team. Top management teams (TMTs) affect the performance of their firms in many ways, the most direct being through the strategic decisions they make (Child, 1972; Finkelstein and Hambrick, 1996). Indeed, the decisions TMTs make, and the timeliness with which they make them, are arguably the most important determinants of success or failure for the firm. Despite the importance of the topic, TMT research has been limited because of unique methodological challenges that exist in attaining access to and information from top managers. The strategic context is also problematic for researchers because it is very complex, ambiguous, and involves decisions that unfold over long periods of time. In this chapter, we briefly discuss the state of research on top management teams and call for more varied approaches to knowledge creation in this area. We offer suggestions about new methodologies to uncover important relationships in the hopes of better understanding TMT functioning. In an effort to model our recommendations, we present a study of TMT confidence (potency) in which we use a dual design. Specifically, a positivist theory-testing approach is first used to establish the importance of top management team potency for decision speed followed by an inductive outlier analysis, which we use to develop propositions concerning functional vs. dysfunctional potency.

TMT RESEARCH METHODOLOGY AND THE CREATION OF KNOWLEDGE

Three main characteristics of the strategic context serve as significant inhibitors to the creation of knowledge concerning TMT functioning: (1) TMTs are amongst the most secretive organizational phenomena; (2) strategic decisions occur infrequently and unfold over long periods of time; and (3) outcomes of the strategy process are notoriously difficult to measure. One of the earliest attempts at overcoming the problem of access originated in the upper echelons stream when articles by Pfeffer (1983) and Hambrick and Mason (1984) provided compelling logic for the need to broaden CEO research to include members of the "dominant coalition." Upper echelons theory proposed a way to investigate top management teams that negated the need for primary data collection. Demographic proxies for group processes were proposed and a robust stream of research demonstrated the power of the demographic methodology. However, demographic approaches proved to have limitations – for example, without speaking with the CEO even the ability to accurately determine who was truly on the team could be an issue. Moreover, some of the commonly used proxy variables seemed to measure more than one construct. A classic case involved the ability to interpret the role and functionality of team heterogeneity

(Hughes-Morgan, Ferrier, and Labianca present an alternative viewpoint of TMT heterogeneity in Chapter 11).

Beginning in the early 1990s, several researchers questioned the efficacy of demographic proxies requesting that future research investigate the "black box" of demography (Pettigrew, 1992; Smith et al., 1994; West and Schwenk, 1996; Lawrence, 1997; Priem et al., 1999). Smith and colleagues (1994) demonstrated that the direct measurement of process added explained variance to demographic models. The ensuing TMT process studies further showed the importance of directly measuring process (Isabella and Waddock, 1994; West and Anderson, 1996; Amason and Sapienza, 1997; Carroll and Harrison, 1998; Knight et al., 1999; Simons et al., 1999; Barsade et al., 2000; Simons and Peterson, 2000; Pitcher and Smith, 2001; Simsek et al., 2005). Interestingly, the seminal article in the demographic stream holds out "the possibility of questionnaires administered to top management teams" (Hambrick and Mason, 1984, p. 203) and acknowledged right from the beginning that demographic approaches were a limited but an important step in building a knowledge base necessary to advance the field.

Although we have learned much about TMT functioning from the demographic and process studies, glaring gaps remain. Several researchers have argued for greater attention in TMT research to mediators of the relationships between distal antecedents and decision-making outcomes (Smith et al., 1994; West and Schwenk, 1996; Lawrence, 1997). Specifically, while the groups literature has examined issues of affect, very little is known about *affective* processes in the strategic decision-making context. Indeed, Hiller and Hambrick (2005, p. 297) argue that "scholars still only possess a fragmented understanding of the origins and implications of executive self-potency." One approach suggested by these authors is to focus attention once again on the CEO as there may be an enhanced ability to garner direct measurement of psycho-social properties of one key decision maker. Importantly, Hiller and Hambrick suggest several interesting methods by which greater insights into CEO confidence can be derived. We believe this approach is valuable. However, we also believe in the original premise of an "upper echelon" or team that is responsible for the strategy-making function in the firm. Thus, we argue for the need to overcome methodological challenges and to push the state of TMT research. Peterson and Zhang, in work related to executive confidence, test the effects of various TMT psychological characteristics on transformational leadership and performance in Chapter 6.

At about the time researchers were beginning to look for approaches to supplement the rather fruitful, but limited, demographic methodology, Eisenhardt and Bourgeois were engaging in rich inductive approaches to the study of TMTs (Bourgeois and Eisenhardt, 1988; Eisenhardt, 1989). These studies relied on small samples and a repeated case methodology to develop propositions that could be tested by future research. The rationale for these approaches was that processes like politics, emotion, and conflict are difficult to uncover using traditional theory-testing methods. Qualitative methodologies and specifically the interplay between inductive theory building and normal science theory-testing methods are much more likely to build knowledge of organizational phenomena.

While TMT research can be further advanced through the use of multiple methodologies, including an inductive component, in the intervening 20 years since Eisenhardt's seminal article few inductive studies have been published. The reason is simple – it is difficult to publish this research in a top management journal. This is indicative of the "normal science straightjacket" described by Daft and Lewin (1990) in the inaugural issue of *Organization Science*. Daft and Lewin advocated the application of new and even "heretical" methods to advance knowledge. Moreover, Hambrick (2007) details how an obsession with theory coupled with a requirement for near perfect theory-testing methods creates a difficult situation for management researchers as compared with those in other business fields. In a recent update to the upper echelons stream, Hambrick (ibid.) calls for the use of sophisticated strategy simulations to model decision-making by using more available non-executive populations. One thing is certain, the study of TMTs is at a crossroads and the ability to push knowledge in this area will be predicated on the courage of dedicated researchers to use ingenuity in the application of borrowed methodologies. In this research, we apply a normal science approach to discern whether TMT potency mediates relationships between demography and process and decision speed and then employ one such "heretical" technique (outlier analysis) to develop insights and questions that can be tested in future research. We begin with a discussion of the strategic decision-making context.

THE STRATEGIC DECISION-MAKING CONTEXT

Researchers have outlined at least six ways strategic decisions differ from other types of decisions: importance, urgency, complexity, duration, uncertainty, and the composition of the decision-making team (Eisenhardt, 1989; Amason, 1996; Finkelstein and Hambrick, 1996; Nutt, 2001). Strategic decisions are high stakes decisions. Strategic decisions are of critical importance to the firm, often involving the mobilization of a significant proportion of the firm's resources and as such place considerable stress on decision makers. Strategic decisions are also more difficult to reverse than many tactical and day-to-day decisions made in the organizational core (Chen, 1988; Smith et al., 1992). Thus, top management teams are wont to take more time, and use more resources, than lower-level teams in order to avoid poor outcomes. However, the pervasiveness of hypercompetitive conditions across a variety of industry segments, and especially in high-technology firms, has increased the urgency of strategic decision making (D'Aveni, 1994). First-mover advantages are significant, and high-quality but late decisions often result in poor outcomes. As noted above, strategic decision speed has been linked to performance (Bourgeois and Eisenhardt, 1988; Baum and Wally, 2003) and has been considered a critical area of research interest (Judge and Miller, 1991; Wally and Baum, 1994; Baum and Wally, 2003; Forbes, 2005). Thus, the strategic context requires TMTs to make critically important decisions quickly.

Strategic decisions often involve a broad and significant set of organizational resources. Moreover, strategic decisions tend to involve external parties (Thompson, 1967) either directly (e.g., acquisitions, alliances), or indirectly (e.g., entry to a new market, introduction of a new product or service) and are thus subject to greater uncertainty. According to the view of firms as open systems, a critical task of the top management team is to buffer the organizational core from environmental distractions (ibid.). While buffering provides teams in the core with an environment relatively conducive to decision making, the opposite is true for top management teams. The complexity introduced by the openness of the system, and breadth of resources involved differentiates strategic from other types of decision processes. Similarly, Jehn's (1995) work illustrated that highly complex decision contexts differed in comparison to more routine environments.

In a seminal study of strategic decision-making speed, Eisenhardt (1989) found that the fastest TMTs made decisions in under four months, whereas most teams took at least six months and often more than one year to come to a decision. Decisions of such long duration provide unique hazards for the decision-making process. When decisions unfold over many months, the potential for misunderstandings to occur increases (Mason and Mitroff, 1981). Teams may have difficulty staying current on issues in the environment or even on the state of the decision process (Eisenhardt, 1989). Moreover, turnover in the composition or leadership of the team is more likely to occur. Eisenhardt (ibid.) documents the mid-decision departure of important members of several TMTs she studied. Finally, when decisions typically occur over several months or more, formal structure (e.g., tracking mechanisms, decision rules, etc.) may be required in order to ensure an efficient and effective decision process.

Because strategic decisions typically unfold over a long period, involve external parties, and require the evaluation of broad sets of resources in a rapidly changing environment they are the exemplar of decision making under uncertainty. Information search for such far-reaching decisions is a difficult task especially when the environment shifts (Galbraith, 1973; Tushman and Nadler, 1978). TMTs face high rates of environmental turbulence and the ability to leverage increased vigilance and creativity while regulating the application of heuristics may be the key to decision effectiveness.

In addition to characteristics of the decision environment, differences in the position and composition of the TMT affect its functioning. Most teams are directly accountable through a formalized hierarchy. TMTs reside at the top of the organization and are accountable to a board of directors who represent ownership. Seminal work on governance and managerial discretion highlight the high variance in the degree to which a given TMT is accountable to its board of directors (Finkelstein and Hambrick, 1996). Under circumstances where a CEO also serves as the board chairperson (CEO duality) and a high proportion of board members are also TMT members (captive board) the TMT may have few constraints on its decision-making ability. This situation is quite dissimilar to the limits faced by other types of teams and because some TMTs face little oversight of their decisions, susceptibility to overconfidence is greater.

Finally, the composition of TMTs differs greatly from that of other decision-making teams (Finkelstein and Hambrick, 1996; Hiller and Hambrick, 2005). TMTs are comprised of highly successful executives, whereas most decision-making teams in the organizational core consist of middle-level managers or technical personnel (Hayward and Hambrick, 1997). Individual characteristics, coupled with the disproportionate benefits of being CEO, can lead to a tournament atmosphere where members compete for the top job. Moreover, in the TMT the CEO has positional power over the rest of the team, some of whom may owe their jobs to him or her. In many operational teams, members may come from various areas of the firm and the assigned leader may not be the "boss" in any substantive sense. Indeed, members of the TMT often owe their position to the CEO who usually selects and evaluates TMT members. We now turn from elements of the strategic decision context and characteristics of the TMT to focus more intently on a key affective state that we propose affects decision outcomes: confidence.

WHAT IS TEAM CONFIDENCE AND WHY DOES IT MATTER?

Confidence can be defined as the faith or belief that one will act in a right, proper, or effective way (*Merriam-Webster's Online Dictionary*, 2009). As a key affective state, confidence can influence numerous individual and group outcomes. In TMTs where the primary task is strategic decision-making, positive affect, and particularly confidence, plays a critical role in outcomes. The interplay between affect and decision making has been shown in non-executive contexts (Isen, 1993; Isen and Labroo, 2003; Baron, 2008). More specifically, positive affect is associated with decision speed (Erez and Isen, 2002), vigilance of search (Baron, 2008), creativity (Isen, 1993; Estrada et al., 1997), and decision effectiveness (Isen and Labroo, 2003) particularly in unpredictable and changing environments (Baron, 2008).

   Confidence at the individual level is core to the notion of self-efficacy within social cognitive theory (Bandura, 1986). Self-efficacy refers to "people's judgments of their capabilities to organize and execute courses of action required to attain designated types of performance" (p. 391). Indeed, individual self-efficacy has been empirically tested in a wide range of contexts and has been shown to have a significant impact on individual behavior, motivation, and performance. Specifically, individual confidence plays a major role in the display of vigilant decision making, increased effort, and persistence of individuals and these behaviors affect performance (Stajkovic, 2006). Emerging cognitive and neuro-science research suggests functional effects of positive affective states on important outcomes such as creativity, search, and decision-making generally (Estrada et al., 1997; Isen, 2000, 2002; Erez and Isen, 2002; Baron, 2008). Baron (2008) summarizes this work nicely and suggests three ways positive affective states, like potency, impact the effectiveness of decision makers facing novel and uncertain situations. First, positive affect stimulates the decision maker such that they become more attuned to their environment attending to a "broader array of events and stimuli" (p. 330). Second, though work in this area is still emerging, positive affect is generally associated with increased creativity (Estrada et al., 1997; Isen, 2000). Finally, positive affect has been linked to the increased use of heuristics in decision making (Mackie and Worth, 1989; Wegener and Petty, 1994; Park and Banaji, 2000). Use of heuristic rules of thumb can confer significant benefits in routine environments, but can lead to mistakes when decision makers fail to realize that the environment has shifted.

TMT STRATEGIC DECISION-MAKING CONTEXT AND CONFIDENCE

Research suggests a heightened role for affect in decision making under conditions of uncertainty and stress (Forgas, 1995; Forgas and George, 2001; Baron, 2008). The degree of ambiguity faced by TMTs makes the strategic decision-making process an especially inviting context within which to study the impact of confidence. Recent work on the role of positive affective states in team decision making point to two very different outcomes: teams may become more sensitive to environmental stimuli (e.g., relevant shifts) and be more able to develop and apply creative solutions; or they may become more susceptible to the habitual application of decision rules based on past experience.

Studies of work groups have found potency to mediate relationships with performance (e.g., Sivasubramaniam et al., 2002). While there is reason to suspect that confidence plays an important role in TMT functioning, the strategic decision context is distinct from that of most small groups (Mintzberg et al., 1976; Hambrick, 1994; Nutt, 2001). Thus, research in this area fails to examine the uncertain, stressful, and ambiguous nature of the TMT strategic decision context. These contextual distinctions suggest that the TMT strategic decision-making process provides an important and under-researched context in which to study the effects of group potency.

Concepts of Confidence

As highlighted by the example studies shown in Table 7.1, a number of constructs have been used to represent and capture confidence across both individual and group levels. For the most part, differences between these conceptualizations focus on the scope of confidence and aggregation issues. For example, whereas collective efficacy, like self-efficacy at the individual level, is defined as a team's belief in its ability to perform a specific task (Zaccaro et al., 1995; Bandura, 1997, 2000), team potency refers to the shared belief members have about the team's general effectiveness when faced with a broad set of tasks in a complex environment (Guzzo et al., 1993; Gully et al., 2002). Gully et al. (2002) used an example of a team of engineers to demonstrate the difference between the two concepts. The team might strongly believe they can design a particular product, thereby exhibiting a high degree of collective efficacy, but might have low potency because they do not believe they can effectively produce, market, and sell that product. Therefore, while a key distinction between collective efficacy and team potency constructs concerns task scope, we expect potency to be largely the result of group composition and the social interactions among those group members (Bandura, 1997).

Though potency and affiliated constructs of efficacy such as team certainty have become theoretical fulcrums of small group research in industrial psychology, strategic management researchers are only now beginning to explore affective states and have not empirically investigated confidence in true top management teams. For example, Hmieleski and Baron (2008) found that high performance led to over-optimism among entrepreneurial CEOs/founders. Similarly, Amason and Mooney (2008) found that the mindset of CEOs and TMTs varies along with firm performance. Hiller and Hambrick (2005) advocate the investigation of CEO core self-evaluations over concepts of hubris, overconfidence and narcissism and observe CEO efficacy is the only CSE component not yet studied in the executive context. While the CEO is arguably the most important individual in the firm, research in the upper echelons literature has consistently demonstrated the increased predictive power of measuring the entire team when explaining group or organization-level outcomes such as decision speed (Finkelstein and Hambrick, 1996).

In the following section, we offer two studies of TMT potency to advance our understanding of the role and importance of confidence in the TMT context. In both studies, we operationalize TMT confidence as potency – the assessment of TMT members about their confidence in the TMT's ability to be successful. This approach highlights our belief in the value of adopting the upper echelons approach for studying the confidence of the entire top management team versus an aggregation of the individual-level confidence of the TMT members.

Table 7.1 *Examples of empirical confidence research on non-TMT groups, individual TMT members, and TMTs*

Author	Year	Journal	Construct	Sample	Method	Relevant Findings
Non-TMT group-level research						
Isabella & Waddock	1994	JOM	Team certainty	40 teams of grad students	Simulation	Environmental beliefs and strong team orientation lead to team certainty
Sivasubramaniam et al.	2002	GOM	Group potency	41 teams of undergraduate students	Lab study	Perceptions of team transformational leadership leads to potency
Taggar & Seijts	2003	Hum. perf.	Collective efficacy	59 teams of undergraduate students	Lab study	Leader and staff role efficacy lead to collective efficacy
Mulvey & Klein	1998	OBHDP	Collective efficacy	Teams of undergraduate students: 59 in Study 1; 101 in Study 2	Lab study	Collective efficacy related to performance
Lester et al.	2002	AMJ	Firm potency	23 high school junior achievement "companies"	Field experiment	Potency mediates the leadership–performance relationship
Clarkson et al.	2009	JESP	Certainty	Teams of undergraduate students: 66 in Study 1; 50 in Study 2	Lab study	General certainty amplifies specific certainty
Clarkson et al.	2008	JPSP	Certainty	Teams of undergraduate students: 95 in Study 1; 62 in Study 2; 99 in Study 3	Lab study	Certainty amplifies other attitudes
Tasa et al.	2007	JAP	Collective efficacy	50 teams of undergraduate students	Lab study	Performance, functional teamwork behaviors, and collective efficacy over time influence collective efficacy
Tasa and Whyte	2005	OBHDP	Collective efficacy	54 teams of undergraduate students	Simulation	Moderate efficacy leads to performance

TMT research at individual level						
Amason & Mooney	2008	SO!	Mindset	51 CEOs and 45 TMTs	Survey	Performance is associated with framing issues as threats rather than opportunities
Hmieleski & Baron	2008	AMJ	Optimism	201 entrepreneurial CEOs/ founders	Survey	High performance can lead to over-optimism
TMT research						
Amason & Mooney	2008	SO!	Mindset	51 CEOs and 45 TMT	Survey	High performance is associated with less comprehensiveness in decision making

Source: Authors.

TMT Potency and Strategic Decision Making in High-tech Firms

Two factors are necessary in order to achieve effective decision-making, particularly in a strategic context: quality and timeliness (Eisenhardt, 1989). Accordingly, we first study the role of potency in the pace of strategic decision making and follow this with a second inductive study that focuses on how different forms of potency affect decision quality. In high-technology firms, decision speed is a critical outcome since early-mover advantages become more important across a wide variety of industry segments where rates of change and levels of uncertainty increase (Eisenhardt, 1989; D'Aveni, 1994; Talaulicar et al., 2005). Upper echelons researchers have shown a relationship between the pace of strategic decision making and organizational performance for firms facing turbulent environments (Judge and Miller, 1991; Baum and Wally, 2003). Studies in adjacent fields have also demonstrated the link between decision-making speed and firm performance (e.g., Barnett and McKendrick, 2004; Baumol, 2004; Derfus et al., 2008).

Researchers in the "upper echelons" stream (Hambrick and Mason, 1984) have linked top management team composition, such as educational background and experience (Judge and Miller, 1991; Wally and Baum, 1994; Finkelstein and Hambrick, 1996; Bluedorn et al., 1999; Forbes, 2005) to strategic decision-making speed. Team interaction processes such as centralization, formalization, and the level and type of conflict have also been linked to strategic decision speed (Eisenhardt, 1989; Judge and Miller, 1991; Wally and Baum, 1994; Bluedorn et al., 1999; Baum and Wally, 2003). In her seminal study, Eisenhardt (1989) found that the introduction of rational and structured process (e.g., decision rules and tactics) increased the speed of decision making in some teams she studied. In this research, we adopt and test a "black box" model whereby demographic composition and process are relatively distal antecedents of decision speed that work primarily through TMT potency.

STUDY 1: TMT POTENCY AND STRATEGIC DECISION SPEED

Group process constructs like participation, consensus, and conflict address questions of who is involved in group discussions and how these interactions play out. An affective state, such as potency, refers to how the team feels about itself, for example does the team believe it will be successful? As Eisenhardt points out "the view emerging from this research program is that emotion is critical for understanding strategic decision-making" (1989, p. 573). Our focus on potency is consistent with Hiller and Hambrick's (2005) call to include components of the core self-evaluations (CSE) meta-construct into TMT research since "scholars still only possess a fragmented understanding of the origins and implications of executive self-potency" (2005, p. 297). Moreover, Guzzo et al. (1993) suggest that potency is particularly important for teams operating in complex and challenging environments. Thus, we expect that potent teams will be more confident in their ability to make good-quality decisions, creating an atmosphere in which team members are ready and willing to "pull the trigger" on a given decision.

Team potency has been shown to influence decision making in work groups. Lester and colleagues found that potent teams are likely to be confident in their ability to make good decisions and perform high-quality work such as strategy formulation and implementation (Lester et al., 2002). More potent teams tend to use more efficient and well-developed problem-solving strategies in dealing with team goals, compared with those with a lower level of potency (Guzzo et al., 1993; Lester et al., 2002). In particular, a high level of TMT potency stimulates arousal, discovery, and integration of task-relevant knowledge and skills in the process of formulating strategies to achieve goals (Bandura and Locke, 2003). A more potent TMT, as opposed to a less potent TMT, can more effectively integrate organizational resources and knowledge to formulate a well-developed strategy. Finally, teams with a high level of potency respond faster to negative feedback demonstrating greater effort and more persistence toward goal accomplishment in comparison to low-potency teams, which can flounder in the face of challenge (Mulvey and Klein, 1998; Lester et al., 2002). Since strategic decision-making is one of the primary responsibilities of TMTs (Bantel and Jackson, 1989; Finkelstein and Hambrick, 1996), we expect more potent TMTs to spend greater effort and persist in formulating and implementing strategies. Especially under adverse conditions of uncertainty, the interdependent nature of the strategic decision-making task should enhance the relationship between potency and decision speed (Mischel and Northcraft, 1997). Thus we propose:

Hypothesis 1: TMT potency is positively related to strategic decision speed.

Demographic Antecedents to TMT Potency

Demography has been used as a proxy for both the capabilities and interaction processes of TMTs. However, since we measure process directly our choice of demographic antecedents was driven by the desire to capture team knowledge and capabilities rather than the potential for (dys)functional interaction. Teams having a high level of capability will be more confident about their ability to perform (Guzzo et al., 1993). Accordingly, two important factors that influence team potency are the quality and breadth of work and educational experiences of the people comprising the team. (Bandura, 1997). This is especially important since the work of team members is often interdependent (Jehn, 1995).

Because of the novel nature of strategic decision making we expect that teams having diverse experience, and thus "requisite variety" (Ashby, 1956), will be better able to deal with the inherent uncertainty represented in the competitive environment. Early TMT studies relied on functional heterogeneity with mixed results (West and Schwenk, 1996; Carpenter et al., 2004). In their review of the "upper echelons" stream, Carpenter et al. (2004) point out that functional heterogeneity may be less relevant to TMT functioning, as opposed to those in the early stages of a career, than are firm and industry experiences. Moreover, Smith et al. (1994) found that TMT functional diversity did not affect outcomes, while heterogeneity of industry experience did. Accordingly, we include a measure of diversity of industry experience present in the TMT. Exposure to many contexts allows executives to develop flexible and creative approaches to problem solving (Bantel and Jackson, 1989). Broad industry experience should also affect team potency directly. Senior executives have been successful throughout their careers; however, those having experienced success in a variety of industry contexts should develop even greater feelings of effectiveness in novel and uncertain circumstances. Such varied and successful backgrounds can reasonably be expected to result in team potency for TMTs facing turbulent environments.

We also expect that teams comprised of more highly educated members will be more confident in their collective capability to make good and timely decisions. Hitt and Tyler (1991) argued that formal education imbues standard tools and approaches to decision making. Highly educated teams are more likely to draw upon these similar decision-making frameworks especially in novel circumstances. The application of tried and true approaches to decision making is likely to lead to greater team confidence in the comprehensiveness of the team's decision-making process (Fredrickson and Mitchell, 1984; Eisenhardt, 1989). Education level has also been associated with cognitive complexity, the ability to process ambiguous and complex information, and consideration of multiple alternatives (Wally and Baum, 1994). This enhanced processing should lead to greater team confidence to act and in the belief that these actions will be successful (Eisenhardt, 1989). Thus:

Hypothesis 2a: TMT experience breadth is positively related to TMT potency.

Hypothesis 2b: TMT education level is positively related to TMT potency.

TMT Process Antecedents to TMT Potency

In this research, we adopt the view that TMT process impacts how the team feels about itself and its prospects for success (Eisenhardt, 1989; Isabella and Waddock, 1994) thus, we expect potency will be affected by process (Gibson, 1999; Tasa et al., 2007). Indeed, our perspective is congruent with the behavioral integration meta-construct, which is comprised of both social and task dimensions of team functioning (Simsek et al., 2005), as well as Isabella and Waddock's (1994) team orientation construct. Consistent with this prior work, we examine a core set of TMT processes that includes consensus, participation, process rationality, affective conflict, and cognitive conflict.

Consensus is the ability of the team members to agree on and accept a course of action. In TMTs that value and are willing to work toward agreement, members are likely to experience increased communication and cooperation, factors that have been shown in work groups to lead to team potency (Bandura, 1997; Lester et al., 2002). Such teams will experience enhanced belief in decisions because of this inherent agreement, which serves as a form of reinforcement (Bandura, 1997). Experience with achieving consensus will also provide members with actual proof that the team can reach agreement on different issues. Successful cooperation has been shown in work groups to be related to increased potency (Stevens and Campion, 1994; Campion et al., 1996). Moreover, based on shared cooperative experiences, group members will be more confident in the group's ability to reach consensus on important decisions in the future. Therefore, we propose:

Hypothesis 3a: TMT consensus is positively related to TMT potency.

Participation has been shown to positively impact the confidence team members have in the team's ability to successfully complete tasks (Latham et al., 1994; Phillips, 2001). Lester et al. (2002) demonstrated that team potency increases when members believe they will play a central role. Moreover, through shared responsibility over time, team members become familiar with the individual strengths and skills of others on the team (Shea and Guzzo, 1987; McGrath, 1997; Gibson, 1999) and recognition of the actual capabilities of team members also allows for more appropriate assignment of tasks. Thus, in decentralized teams, the enhanced opportunity to observe team-mate behaviors leads to increased confidence and trust in the abilities of team members as "Team members' collective efficacy may increase (or decrease) if they observe their colleagues demonstrating (or failing to demonstrate) performance-relevant teamwork behaviors" (Tasa et al., 2007, p. 20).

Forbes (2005) found that decentralized strategic decision making in entrepreneurial firms led to greater levels of self-efficacy regarding the team's performance. Conversely, where tasks are centralized in one or a few members, team potency will depend on the improbable circumstance where the few are able to adequately perform in the face of increasing complexity and uncertainty. Participation also enables TMTs to handle greater levels of complexity and uncertainty because information processing is shared among a larger number of individuals (Baum and Wally, 2003). Based on the preceding arguments, we propose:

Hypothesis 3b: Participation is positively related to TMT potency.

Potency will also be related to the extent to which TMT's activities are rationally structured. Though overly formal systems have been seen as a constraint on creativity (Shaw, 1981), the presence of some level of rational structure within the team should lead to TMT member perceptions of a careful and organized approach (Dean and Sharfman, 1996). Rational structure is especially useful for TMTs because the strategic decision-making process is highly complex and unfolds over a longer time-frame, usually several months, as compared with workgroup decisions (Eisenhardt, 1989). Moreover, because of the complexity involved, TMT strategic decision making is likely to be a highly interdependent task. Research in group effectiveness suggests that a certain level of structure is required to coordinate effort and facilitate information flow (Gladstein, 1984; Stasser, 1992), especially in interdependent tasks. Rational structure allows team members to track their interactions, increasing confidence in the process. Indeed, Eisenhardt's (1989) seminal study of fast decision making focused largely on the incorporation of rationality in the form of tactics and procedures TMTs could use to speed up decisions. Finally, TMTs will feel potent to the extent that they believe they have comprehensively evaluated alternative courses of action. Thus:

Hypothesis 3c: Process rationality is positively related to TMT potency.

Intra-team conflict has also been identified as a critical determinant of team outcomes (Jehn, 1995; Amason, 1996; Amason and Sapienza, 1997; Jehn et al., 1999; Gully et al., 2002). Research suggests that team performance will increase as a result of fact-based (e.g., cognitive) conflict, but that team members are likely to have little or no confidence in outcomes where affective conflict has occurred (Jehn, 1995; Amason, 1996). Cognitive conflict is a process of critical debate whereby the various skills and knowledge bases of team members are displayed. As previously mentioned, the observance of functional teamwork behaviors such as reasoned debate, increases group confidence (Tasa et al., 2007). Importantly, cognitive conflict implies an objective truthful process of debate where individual needs are subordinated to the group goal (Amason and Schweiger, 1994). As Amason points out (1996), however, the advent of personal or affective conflict destroys any perception of truthful and objective inquiry. Team members may lose faith in the ability of the team to perform, since individual motives may detract from the team's ability to succeed (Campion et al., 1993). Specifically, personal conflict may result in the withholding of critical information from the team if such information is counter to one's individual objectives (Bourgeois and Eisenhardt, 1988). Moreover, personal conflict turns the decision-making process into a game where the ability to force adoption of one's position may result in an inferior team outcome. Personal conflict is poisonous to group process and in particular to team potency (Jehn, 1995; Amason, 1996).

Given the potential impact of conflict on group decision-making outcomes, management of conflict would appear an extremely important teamwork and leadership skill (Sivasubramaniam et al., 2002; Taggar and Seijts, 2003). Teams that have managed conflict successfully will exhibit a high level of cognitive conflict coupled with a low level of affective conflict. TMTs that strike this balance will acquire confidence in their ability to do so in the future and will, therefore, have increased potency (Gully et al., 2002). Interestingly, and in line with our arguments, Shea and Guzzo (1987) point out that potency in teams will often be associated with more assertive participation by team members. Based on the preceding arguments, we propose:

Hypothesis 3d: Cognitive conflict is positively related to TMT potency.

Hypothesis 3e: Affective conflict is negatively related to TMT potency.

Potency as Mediator

Importantly, and in line with Locke's (1991) "motivational hub," we expect that TMT demographic composition and TMT process work primarily through their collective impact on TMT potency in affecting the rate of strategic decision making. Therefore, we predict the following:

Hypothesis 4: TMT potency mediates the relationship between TMT demography, TMT interaction process, and strategic decision-making speed.

Sample and Data Collection

Because access is difficult, primary data collection from true TMTs is unusual (Finkelstein and Hambrick, 1996; Hiller and Hambrick, 2005). However, the nature of strategic decision making is high stakes, unfolds over longer time-frames, and involves considerable novelty, thus we adopted a grounded field-study methodology whereby data was collected through on-site structured interviews with each firm's corporate-level CEO and through questionnaires completed by the CEO and members of the firm's TMT. Because we were interested in studying the antecedent conditions of potency and its effects on decision speed we focused on a set of high-technology firms for whom speed is paramount and environmental uncertainty pervasive.

We initially identified 211 high-technology companies using two sources: a regional trade almanac and a high-technology council. To obtain access we first sent a package to the CEO outlining the study and including the endorsements of three entities influential in the regional high-technology community. Second, we conducted an on-site CEO interview, during which we collected company information, obtained a list of other members of the TMT, and gained their support for the research. Finally, we distributed surveys to all of the TMT members, including the CEO.

A number of firms were no longer in business and several others did not conform to a common definition of "high technology" from Milkovich (1987). Of the remaining 180 firms, we obtained full responses from 73 firms for a participation rate of 41 percent. On average, 3.22 top executives (average team size = 5.6) responded for an internal response rate of 58 percent. Participant firms were not significantly different from others contacted in terms of the number of employees ($t = 1.22$, $p > 0.05$), total revenue ($t = 1.49$, $p > 0.05$), and R&D spending ($t = 1.03$, $p > 0.05$).

Measures

- *TMT decision speed.* Previous research has operationalized decision speed primarily in absolute terms (Eisenhardt, 1989; Judge and Miller, 1991; Baum and Wally, 2003; Forbes, 2005) and, in fewer cases, relative measures have been used (Wally and Baum, 1994). Schumpeterian views of competitive advantage (Smith et al., 1992; Wally and Baum, 1994) advocate measuring speed relative to rivals. Moreover, a long tradition within organization theory (Thompson, 1967; Galbraith, 1973; D'Aveni, 1994) suggests that decision speed at least match and preferably exceed the rate of change in the external environment. Accordingly, we asked three questions of respondents regarding: the absolute speed of decision making, speed relative to rivals, and speed relative to the rate of change in the environment. We used a five-item Likert response format where 1 = "strongly disagree" and 5 = "strongly agree." We aggregated responses across the members of the TMT and calculated the arithmetic team-level mean to provide an index of decision speed for each team. Consistent with our expectations for the turbulent environment of technology firms, we found agreement ($\alpha = 0.74$) across the three components of decision speed (see Appendix for scale items).
- *TMT potency.* Guzzo et al. (1993) suggested that researchers should measure potency by asking team members of their perception of the team's capability to perform effectively and successfully. We measured TMT potency with five items adapted from Guzzo et al. (1993) on a scale from 1 = "strongly disagree" and 5 = "strongly agree" ($\alpha = 0.86$). Although team potency is similar to the concept of collective efficacy, there is an important distinction. Whereas collective efficacy, like self-efficacy at the individual level, is defined as a team's belief in their ability to perform a specific task (Zaccaro et al., 1995; Bandura, 1997, 2000), team potency refers to the shared belief members have about the team's general effectiveness when faced with a broad set of tasks in a complex environment (Guzzo et al., 1993; Gully et al., 2002).

- *TMT industry breadth*. Carpenter et al. (2004) argued that executive teams having broad industry experiences would be more important than the commonly measured but more distal functional heterogeneity. We measured TMT industry breadth as the sum of the number of industries members of the TMT have worked in during their career.
- *TMT education*. We measured TMT education as the average number of years of post-high-school education of the TMT (Wally and Baum, 1994).
- *Consensus*. To measure consensus we developed a four-item scale that asked respondents to assess the value that TMT members place on agreement and acceptance of strategic decisions ($\alpha = 0.84$).
- *Participation*. We measured participation with a four-item scale ($\alpha = 0.91$) assessing the degree to which decision-making tasks are shared throughout the team.
- *Process rationality*. A five-item scale adopted from Smith et al. (1994) assessing the degree to which TMT interactions and processes are formally structured and rational ($\alpha = 0.81$).
- *Affective conflict*. Measured using a four-item scale adapted from Jehn (1995) ($\alpha = 0.89$) assessing the degree to which there are personal differences and discord within the TMT.
- *Cognitive conflict*. Measured using a three-item scale adapted from Jehn (1995) ($\alpha = 0.77$) assessing the degree to which there are disagreements of fact within the TMT.

Common Method Variance

We took several procedural steps in order to mitigate the possibility of common method variance, a problem that can occur with perceptual survey data. First, in addition to using existing pre-validated scales where possible, when adapting those scales or developing our own we followed the general prescriptions of Tourangeau et al. (2000) by reducing method biases through the careful construction of the items themselves. Specifically, where possible, we defined ambiguous and unfamiliar terms, provided examples when we thought concepts in our items were vague, attempted to keep questions simple, specific, concise, and uncomplicated. Next, we interspersed questions of different types in an effort to minimize the potential that respondents would fall into a pattern linked to the use of repetitive Likert scales (Aulakh and Gencturk, 2000; Podsakoff et al., 2003). We also mixed the order of items for various scales and included reverse-coded items to reduce question-to-question priming effects that can lead to bias (Aulakh and Gencturk, 2000; Podsakoff et al., 2003). Finally, we assured respondents about the anonymity of their responses to reduce apprehension and make them less likely to answer in a way they deemed socially desirable (Podsakoff et al., 2003).

Consistent with a number of similar studies (Andersson and Bateman, 1997; Aulakh and Gencturk, 2000; Becerra et al., 2008), we used Harman's single factor test to examine the effectiveness of our survey procedure for reducing potential common method bias. Harman's single factor test is one of the most widely used techniques to assess issues of common method variance (Podsakoff et al., 2003). In order to perform the test, all seven scaled variables from our study were loaded into an exploratory factor analysis. The results indicated that there are seven factors present and that they account for

71.9 percent of the total variance explained, the highest loading factor accounted for 21.2 percent of the total variance explained. Harman's test assumes that if a significant amount of common method variance is present, either one factor will emerge from the factor analysis or one factor will account for a majority of the variance among measures (Aulakh and Gencturk, 2000; Podsakoff et al., 2003). Since neither of these conditions was present in our analysis, it appears that potential problems with common method variance were not significant in our study (Andersson and Bateman, 1997; Aulakh and Gencturk, 2000; Becerra et al., 2008).

Aggregation Statistics

As reported above, the Cronbach alphas of the constructs in our study indicate a sufficient level of convergent validity. In addition, our analysis of common method bias indicates that it is not of substantial concern. As a final check of our data, it is necessary to ensure that aggregation to the team level is justified (Klein et al., 1994). In order to do this we used intraclass correlation coefficients ICC(1) and ICC(2) (Bliese, 2000) and within-group interrater agreement (r_{wg}) (James, 1982; James et al., 1984). In all cases, variables appeared to be justifiably aggregated. Specifically, mean r_{wg} values for all variables were above 0.70, ranging from 0.72 for participation to 0.96 for potency, an indication of agreement (James, 1982). In addition, with ICC(1) values that ranged from 0.19 for decision speed to 0.35 for potency, all teams exhibited substantial between-group variance in excess of the threshold value of 0.12 that is often cited as sufficient for testing hypotheses based on team aggregated measures (James, 1982; Bliese and Halverson, 1998). ICC(2) scores provide evidence of reliability of group means. Because ICC(2) is a function of ICC(1) and team size, it is not unusual to have lower ICC(2) values in studies with small team size (e.g., Hofmann and Jones, 2005; Morgeson, 2005; Salanova et al., 2005). In our case, all variables had ICC(2) values above 0.50 providing evidence that the group means are reliable and that group-level relationships will be detected (Bliese, 2000). Thus, we believe our measures provide strong support for aggregation to the team level.

Results

Table 7.2 contains a correlation matrix of all variables used in the analysis. Consistent with our expectation and the findings of most process studies, several variables are correlated. Since some bivariate correlations were in the medium to high range, we conducted multicollinearity tests. The variance inflation factor (VIF) scores were all well within the acceptable range, with the highest being 3.6, indicating that the results of the regression were not adversely affected by intercorrelation (Neter et al., 1996). Of particular note is the high correlation between TMT potency and strategic decision speed. Social cognitive theory predicts a strong relationship between efficacy and performance and provides a conceptual basis for distinctions between feelings of confidence, or potency, and action (e.g., decision speed, Bandura, 1997; Tasa et al., 2007). Moreover, research has consistently found (Gully et al., 2002), that confident groups act quickly. Finally, in circumstances requiring high levels of cooperation and task interdependence, like strategic decision making, Mischel and Northcraft (1997) find that the relationship between

Table 7.2 Correlations and descriptive statistics

	Mean	S.D.	1	2	3	4	5	6	7	8	9
1. Potency	3.92	0.54	1.00								
2. Decision pace of TMT	3.63	0.72	0.85	1.00							
3. Mean no. of industries worked in during career (TMT)	2.32	0.72	-0.29	-0.22	1.00						
4. Mean yrs post-high school education of TMT	5.73	1.56	0.32	0.27	-0.24	1.00					
5. TMT consensus	3.14	0.67	0.50	0.43	-0.03	0.04	1.00				
6. Centralization of TMT decision making	2.82	0.73	-0.58	-0.47	0.24	-0.16	-0.70	1.00			
7. TMT process rationality	2.00	0.40	-0.28	-0.30	0.26	-0.34	-0.23	0.35	1.00		
8. TMT affective conflict	2.71	0.68	-0.62	-0.58	0.30	-0.02	-0.64	0.68	0.47	1.00	
9. TMT cognitive conflict	3.46	0.49	-0.20	-0.17	0.18	0.31	-0.42	0.53	0.15	0.58	1.00

Note: Correlations greater than 0.234 significant at $p < 0.05$; values greater than 0.301 at $p < 0.01$.

Source: Authors' calculations.

Table 7.3　*Regression of TMT potency on demography and process; regression of TMT strategic decision speed on TMT demography, process, and potency*

	Model 1 TMT Potency	Model 2 Decision Speed	Model 3 Decision Speed
TMT number of industries	−0.231†	−0.174	0.040
TMT education level	0.237*	0.194†	−0.009
Demography block	$\Delta R^2 = 0.135$ $F = 5.247**$	$\Delta R^2 = 0.084$ $F = 3.065*$	
TMT consensus	0.031	0.026	0.000
TMT decentralization	0.315*	0.166	0.096
TMT process rationality	0.209†	0.115	0.058
TMT affective conflict	−0.607**	−0.623**	−0.119
TMT cognitive conflict	0.298*	0.271*	0.024
Process block	$\Delta R^2 = 0.414,$ $F = 11.367***$	$\Delta R^2 = 0.330$ $F = 6.971**$	
TMT potency			0.830***
Mediation test			$\Delta R^2 = 0.311$ $F = 68.737***$
Full model	Adj. $R^2 = 0.498***$	Adj. $R^2 = 0.347***$	Adj. $R^2 = 0.688***$

Note: † $p > 0.10$, * $p < 0.05$, ** $p < 0.01$, *** $p < 0.001$.

Source: Authors' calculations.

potency and team outcomes is stronger. Accordingly, and in strong support of our Hypothesis 1, Model 3 of Table 7.3 indicates that TMT potency is positively related to strategic decision speed ($\beta = 0.830$, $p < 0.001$).

Because prior research has demonstrated the impact of demographic and process variables on decision speed, we did not offer formal hypotheses. We observe, however, that both demography and process do affect decision speed. Thus, our results are consistent with prior research findings. We predicted that TMT demography is positively related to TMT potency. In Model 1 of Table 7.3 the TMT demography block was positively related to TMT potency ($R^2 = 0.135$, $F = 5.247$). Both demographic measures were related to TMT potency, however, the finding for number of industries was in the opposite direction from our hypothesis ($\beta = -0.231$, $p = 0.053$). Educational level was significant and in the predicted direction ($\beta = 0.237$, $p < 0.05$). Thus, we find support for the relationship between demography and potency, but the link is complex.

We predicted that TMT process would be related to TMT potency. We find the process block was significantly related to TMT potency even controlling for demography variables ($\Delta R^2 = 0.414$, $F = 11.367$). Specifically, participation (Hypothesis 2b, $\beta = 0.315$, $p < 0.05$), process rationality (Hypothesis 2c, $\beta = 0.209$, $p < 0.05$), and cognitive conflict (Hypothesis 2d, $\beta = 0.298$, $p < 0.05$) increase TMT potency, while affective conflict (Hypothesis 2e, $\beta = -0.607$, $p < 0.001$) is associated with lower TMT potency. TMT consensus (Hypothesis 2a) was not related to potency. Thus, four of the five process hypotheses were supported.

Hypothesis 4 predicts that TMT potency mediates the relationship between TMT demography, TMT process, and the strategic decision-making speed of the TMT. Consistent with Baron and Kenny's (1986) three-step procedure, we first examined the relationships between the independent and the mediator variables. As Smith et al. (1994) suggest, we tested the effects of a block of demography first, then we tested for the incremental effect of a block of process variables. In the second of the three steps, we demonstrated the significant relationships between the independent variables and dependent variable. Finally, to test for mediation, we examined changes in the effect of the independent variables when the mediator was added to the regression. Models 2 and 3 of Table 7.3 provide the test of this hypothesis. As shown in Model 2, both TMT demography ($R^2 = 0.084$, $F = 3.065$) and TMT process ($R^2 = 0.330$, $F = 6.971$) are related to TMT decision speed. In column three, TMT potency is entered in to the equation. The mediation hypothesis (Hypothesis 4) is confirmed when the TMT potency measure is both significant and the antecedents to potency drop below statistical significance in the same regression. As shown in Model 3, the addition of TMT potency resulted in an R^2 change of 0.311 ($F = 68.737$), and each of the TMT demography and process variables become non-significant. Thus, we observe a strong mediation effect for TMT potency such that demographic and process variables appear to work primarily through TMT potency.

Discussion of Study 1 Results

The main purpose of Study 1 was to examine demographic and process antecedents to TMT potency and the role of TMT potency in the speed of strategic decision making. Though potency and affiliated constructs of efficacy have become theoretical fulcrums of small group research, strategic management researchers are only now beginning to explore affective states and have not investigated TMT potency. Hiller and Hambrick (2005) advocate the investigation of CEO core self-evaluations over concepts of hubris, overconfidence, and narcissism and observe that CEO efficacy is the only CSE component not yet studied in the executive context. While the CEO is arguably the most important individual in the firm, research in the upper echelons literature has consistently demonstrated the increased predictive power of measuring team characteristics when explaining group or organization-level outcomes such as decision speed (Finkelstein and Hambrick, 1996). We adopt an upper echelons approach by studying the potency of the entire top management team.

TMT potency and decision-making speed
Our expectation was that potency would be an important affective characteristic of TMTs, and specifically that potent teams would be able to make strategic decisions quickly. Accordingly, we found potency to be strongly related to decision speed and that potency fully mediates the relationships between demography and speed and process and speed. Thus, we establish the need for TMT researchers to consider potency and its impacts on important TMT outcomes.

TMT composition and potency
Hypotheses 2a and 2b dealt with the relationship between breadth of industry experience and education level and TMT potency. Experience and education level have been argued

to be important predictors in past research on potency, strategic decision making, and upper echelons (Smith et al., 1994; Wally and Baum, 1994; Carpenter et al., 2004). We add to our understanding of the mechanism through which education level affects speed, however, by showing that the effect is mediated fully through TMT potency. Thus, while education level of the team is expected to directly impact decision quality, the impact on speed of decision making appears to act mainly by increasing the confidence of team members in the team's ability to be successful. We also predicted that breadth of industry experience would be positively related to potency but found that these variables were significantly and negatively related. We expected broad experience to bolster potency in our sample of high-technology firms since exposure to a variety of competitive contexts might increase the adaptability of executives of firms facing uncertain environments. An alternative view is that in highly complex environments executives place more credence on specific, deep knowledge of the industry context. Moreover, we observe that broad industry experience is correlated in our sample with affective conflict and centralization, both found to have deleterious effects on potency. In sum, TMT demography does impact potency though the links are complex and merit further study.

TMT structure and interactional process and potency
The decision-making literature generally supports the functionality of participation, but this is not always the case. Centralized teams are generally thought to be quicker since fewer interactional processes (e.g., consensus-seeking, discussion of alternatives) need to occur for the decision to be made. Similarly, more formal teams are thought to be slower since they adopt additional structure and procedure that can impede progress toward reaching consensus. Hiller and Hambrick (2005) proposed that hyper-CSE CEOs will engage in centralized, non-comprehensive, and fast decision making. In a team context, Eisenhardt (1989) suggested a counter-view; based on case studies of eight TMTs of semiconductor firms the fastest teams actually adopted a somewhat decentralized decision-making process. Moreover, by adopting a more rational decision-making structure, reflected in decision-making procedures and tactics, these teams were able to simultaneously make fast and high-quality strategic decisions. Accordingly, we hypothesized that participation (Hypothesis 3b) and process rationality (Hypothesis 3c) would be associated with increased decision speed. The results of our analysis lend support to the emerging idea that increased participation does not necessarily result in a speed penalty, and that some level of rational structure can be functional – even for speed.

We also find that fact-based (cognitive) conflict increases and personal (affective) conflict decreases decision speed. While this is consistent with the expectations of Amason (1996), his research did not hypothesize the link through potency. We find that fact-based conflict is associated with increased TMT potency (Hypothesis 3d), and that personal conflict has a deleterious effect on TMT potency (Hypothesis 2e). Moreover, and consistent with our other results, the impact of conflict on decision speed is mediated by TMT potency. Thus, conflict is critically important to the strategic decision-making process, but the relationships are more complex than prior research would suggest, extending beyond implications for search and rationality to include the team's affective state.

We hypothesized that TMT consensus would be related to potency (Hypothesis 3a), and through potency to decision speed (Hypothesis 3). Contrary to our expectation, consensus was neither associated with potency nor with decision speed (either directly or indirectly). Confronting a similar result, Isabella and Waddock (1994) focused on the operationalization of consensus. During our review of the consensus literature, we were also struck by the varying ways in which researchers have thought about and measured the construct. Indeed, our operationalization of consensus displays a pervasive confound: consensus as obligation versus consensus as demonstrated capability. The most common measurement approach is to ask respondents how easily they reach consensus – consensus is an occurrence, it either happens or it does not. Upon reflection, the more important questions may be: (1) what happened on the path to achieving consensus and (2) how does the team frame attitudes toward consensus (e.g., is reaching a consensus a task that must be achieved, or is consensus a state that tends to happen as a natural and positive outcome of other interaction processes)? The effects of consensus on team affect (e.g., potency) and on performance (e.g., decision speed) are almost certainly impacted by how consensus is framed by the team. Teams that view consensus as an obligation to be fulfilled may approach the decision process with more than a little dread, preoccupied with an agreement imperative. These are the teams Eisenhardt (1989) may have had in mind when she proposed the functionality of tie-breaker tactics such as "consensus with qualification." At the other extreme, teams that have experienced consensus in the past as a result of functional (and perhaps enjoyable) interaction processes (e.g., cognitive but not affective conflict, participation, and inclusion, etc.) may not dwell on the need for consensus, having faith that they will somehow reach agreement. Moreover, in the context of such well-functioning teams, the act of having easily reached consensus in the past will result in an increase in potency. Thus, it is not surprising that researchers have viewed consensus as both a facilitator and impediment to speedy decision making. Certainly, Eisenhardt's proposals for dealing with dysfunctional consensus resonate most strongly with teams experiencing a consensus as an obligation, rather than an indicator of capability. Future research must address the sources and implications of consensus in teams if we are to offer actionable prescriptions for effective team decision making.

STUDY 2: DECISION SPEED AND DECISION QUALITY

There are at least three views on the link between decision speed and decision quality. Most management research suggests an implicit tradeoff between the speed at which decisions are made and the quality of such decisions (Fredrickson and Mitchell, 1984). Hiller and Hambrick (2005) argue that speedy decisions will result in extremes of performance, both low and high. Eisenhardt (1989) suggested that TMTs could make both quick and high-quality decisions by employing rational decision tactics. In this research, we demonstrated that demography and process affect TMT potency, which in turn affects decision speed. Perhaps the more important observation is that certain demographic and process variables affect potency in different ways. For example, education is positively associated with potency, but teams with diverse industry experience are less confident than those with focused experience in the current industry. Moreover, participation and cognitive conflict enhance potency while affective conflict has a deleterious effect. We suspect that the association between decision speed and decision quality may very well depend on which factors are driving potency in the team. Potent TMTs make quick decisions; however, it is possible that the manner in which a given team's potency developed will determine decision quality. Some TMTs likely make speedy high-quality decisions because their potency is associated with interactional processes that simultaneously improve speed and quality, and thus based on justifiable confidence. Others may tend to make mistakes because the factors driving potency lead to hubris.

Outlier Analysis: Potency or Hubris?

Organizational researchers are ultimately concerned with decision effectiveness, or the ability to make timely and high-quality decisions. We have shown that potent TMTs make quick strategic decisions, but what about the quality of these decisions? Potency researchers have viewed the level of team confidence as primarily linear and functional (Guzzo and Shea, 1992; Bandura, 1997; Gully et al., 2002). Though not focused on decision speed, Tasa and Whyte (2005) identified overconfidence as a key factor leading to decreased decision rationality and quality. Specifically, in simulated TMTs the relationship between the level of collective efficacy and decision quality is curvilinear – too much or too little confidence can actually have a negative impact on decision quality, whereas moderate levels of potency lead to more vigilant problem solving and higher-quality decisions (ibid.). Though instructive, Tasa and Whyte (2005) did not account for potential differences in the origins of the confidence felt by the teams they studied. Moreover, very little research has simultaneously examined decision speed and quality though balancing these is clearly the tension felt by high-technology TMTs as they strive to be effective.

Potency and Decision Quality

Affect has been found to be a consistent predictor of team performance in research on small groups (e.g., Bandura and Locke, 2003; Kirkman et al., 2004). Potency may improve decision quality by influencing: (1) the comprehensiveness of information search; (2) the evaluation of alternative courses of action; (3) the extent to which teams form well-developed and appropriate strategies; (4) the amount of effort teams exert in pursuing tasks; and (5) the persistence teams demonstrate in the face of difficulties (Guzzo and Shea, 1992; Bandura, 1997; Gibson, 1999; Gully et al., 2002; Lester et al., 2002). Moreover, emerging neuro-science research suggests functional effects of positive affective states on important outcomes such as creativity, search, and decision making generally (Estrada et al., 1997; Isen, 2000, 2002; Erez and Isen, 2002; Baron, 2008). Baron (2008) suggests three ways positive affective states, like potency, impact the effectiveness of decision makers facing novel and uncertain situations. First, positive affect stimulates the decision maker such that they become more attuned to their environment attending to a "broader array of events and stimuli" (2008, p. 330). Second, though work in this area is still emerging, positive affect is generally associated with increased creativity (Estrada et al., 1997; Isen, 2000). Third, however, positive affect is linked to increased use of heuristics in decision making (Mackie and Worth, 1989; Wegener and Petty, 1994; Park and Banaji, 2000). Use of heuristic rules of thumb can confer significant benefits in routine environments, but can lead to mistakes when decision makers fail to realize that the environment has shifted.

Thus, recent work on the role of positive affective states in decision making point to two very different outcomes: teams may become more sensitive to environmental stimuli (e.g., relevant shifts) and be more able to develop and apply creative solutions; or they may become more susceptible to the habitual application of decision rules based on past experience. In the context of TMTs facing high rates of environmental turbulence, the ability to leverage increased vigilance and creativity while regulating the application of heuristics may be the key to decision effectiveness.

Based on the above arguments, we conducted an outlier analysis of the most potent TMTs in the sample. Outlier analysis has been championed by organizational researchers for its ability to provide insights that normal science cannot (Teece and Winter, 1984; Daft and Lewin, 1990; Day et al. 1990, Van de Ven and Huber, 1990). Outlier analysis is an inductive method useful for raising research questions that can then be tested in future normal science research. Daft and Lewin (1990) make a strong case for the inclusion of such methods as a complement to normal science because the fuzziness of organizational phenomena does not lend itself to investigation of average conditions alone. They state that "significant insights can be gained from studying the best or worst of a given population" (p. 6). We defined the outlier group by identifying breakpoints in the data. The seven teams in the top decile for potency were clustered tightly and there appeared to be a meaningful breakpoint delineating this outlier group from the rest of the sample. The potency scores of the outliers ranged from 4.87 to 5.00, with three TMTs scoring 4.87 and two each scoring 4.90 and 5.00. The next three most potent TMTs scored 4.60, 4.60, and 4.47 respectively.

We next confirmed that these outliers were also among the speediest decision makers in the sample with even the slowest TMT in the top decile. Decision quality is difficult to measure as one cannot know what outcomes would have resulted from decisions not undertaken. However, it is reasonable to expect that timely quality decisions, as opposed to quick but poor ones should be associated with higher firm performance. Accordingly, we next checked to determine whether there were differences in firm performance for the potent speedy decision-making teams. We found that four of the seven TMTs were in firms achieving high performance (double-digit sales growth, strong profitability), while three were in firms experiencing performance difficulties (flat or negative sales growth, flat or negative profit). Apparently there are two subgroups within the high-potency outliers: speedy high performers and speedy low performers. This is consistent with Hiller and Hambrick's (2005) proposition that confidence (e.g., hyper-CSE) will result in performance extremes, but somewhat in contrast to Tasa and Whyte's (2005) directional finding:

Proposition 1: Potency level has positive effects on decision speed, but no predictable effect on decision quality.

We next assessed the antecedents to potency for each of the two subgroups. We found that the drivers of potency for the high performers included education, high consensus ability, high cognitive conflict, and low affective conflict (see Figure 7.1). We found that potency in the low-performing subgroup was driven by a different combination of antecedents. While consensus ability was also high, the low performers experienced an extreme absence of conflict of either type. The resultant potency appears to be of differing types for each subgroup. Although the levels were nearly identical, we suspect

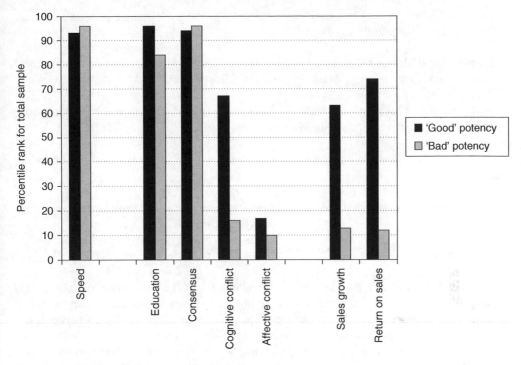

Source: Authors' calculations.

Figure 7.1 Outlier analysis of high potency TMTs

that the way in which potency affects each team differs considerably. This is a critically important point as virtually all research on potency has focused on the level rather than the type (Hiller and Hambrick, 2005; Tasa and Whyte, 2005).

The antecedents of functional potency should reasonably lead to a decision-making process where differences of opinion are aired and resolved through a rational process of reasoned inquiry. Multiple alternatives are developed and assessed leading to the selection of a very high-quality solution. Though such a process can be time-consuming, Eisenhardt (1989) demonstrated that teams can compensate for this by implementing decision rules and tactics. We expect that such teams place bounds around their potency, whereby confrontation of novel circumstances signals the team to pause, reflect, and engage in active problem solving and debate. These teams may be experiencing the increased awareness and creativity positive affect can confer (Baron, 2008).

The antecedents of dysfunctional potency may lead to an abbreviated decision process where the first reasonable solution, and particularly a solution that has worked in the past, is readily adopted. As Baron (2008) suggests, in these teams positive affect may result in the overuse of heuristics even when the situation facing the team has changed. Dissent, indeed debate of factual differences of any type, is unlikely to occur in such a team. These teams may possess a form of unbounded potency, such that even when facing extreme novelty and uncertainty, the team applies an abbreviated process suitable for routine circumstances:

Proposition 2a: Potency is a multidimensional construct consisting of level and type (bounded and unbounded).

Proposition 2b: Bounded potency originates in a gestalt of education level, high consensus ability, high cognitive conflict, and low affective conflict.

Proposition 2c: Unbounded potency (hubris) originates in a gestalt of high consensus ability, low cognitive conflict, and low affective conflict.

Proposition 2d: Bounded potency is associated with both quick and high-quality decisions.

Proposition 2e: Unbounded potency is associated with quick, but low-quality decisions.

DISCUSSION OF STUDY 1 AND STUDY 2

Our research in Studies 1 and 2 demonstrates both support and a critique of the TMT demography stream. On the one hand, we find that composition matters. Clearly, more educated teams were also more potent and this resulted in the ability to make quick decisions. On the other hand, these results are consistent with those of Smith et al. (1994) in demonstrating that process is also important and needs to be measured separately from demography. Indeed, a comparison of the coefficients of determination for the demography and process blocks of variables shows that even when controlling for demographic effects, process adds three times the explanatory power for predicting TMT potency ($\Delta R^2 = 0.135$ vs. 0.414), and nearly four times the impact on decision speed ($\Delta R^2 = 0.084$ vs. 0.330). Early calls for more focus on direct measurement of process (Smith et al., 1994; West and Schwenk, 1996; Lawrence, 1997; Priem et al., 1999) have been joined by influential demography researchers (Hiller and Hambrick, 2005) and it is imperative to begin the hard work of directly measuring a variety of TMT processes and especially the role of affect, if we are to consolidate and advance the gains made by 20 years of upper echelons research.

The cross-sectional nature of this research precludes us from making definite statements of causality. This may be a particularly important issue because some of our variables may be mutually reinforcing. For example, in their theory of efficacy spirals, Lindsley et al. (1995) proposed the reinforcing nature of efficacy and experience, noting that it almost impossible to adequately understand efficacy without explicitly considering the dynamic and recursive effects of experience. Moreover, the interpretation of experience is likely impacted by efficacy levels. TMT demography research has focused on the impact of composition, through cognition, on group process (Hambrick and Mason, 1984). We expand this line of thinking by proposing that group process is affected not only by demography, but by other group characteristics. Furthermore, we recognize that group processes should be thought of in terms of interaction process (e.g., how do group members interact with one another) and affective state (e.g., how do group members feel about the team). Given the results of our research, we fully suspect that the link between process and affective state is mutually reinforcing. Longitudinal research is required to untangle the directionality, or which construct affects which more, of the causal links between TMT processes on the way to explaining decision effectiveness. Taken together with the need to separate "good" and "bad" drivers of TMT potency, we can think of no greater gap in the strategic decision-making literature. The lesson for managers is fairly straightforward: confident teams can make very fast decisions. However, the quality of these decisions may well rest on the source of the confidence.

While this research certainly has weaknesses, there are several strengths inherent in the design. First, unlike most prior research on strategic decision speed, we sample the top management team of the entire enterprise, including the CEO. Additionally, instead of relying on an arbitrary definition of the team based on position or title, we ask the CEO to define the team. These procedures allow us to be confident that we have included only those executives who are actually directly and intimately involved in strategic decision making. A cause for concern is the potential for bias when relying on self-reports emanating from CEOs and other top executives. As discussed in our methodology, we took numerous steps in our study to reduce the possibility of, and indeed found no evidence to indicate, this type of common source bias. In addition, the multiple-respondent design of this study provides added confidence in the results since interrater reliability can be assessed. Ours is one of the very few TMT studies to use a primary data collection technique, namely an intensive on-site field study. Finally, given the recognized importance of decision speed across a variety of industry contexts, it is extraordinary how few studies actually measure it. Moreover, those that do seldom approach the operationalization of decision speed in a manner comprehensive enough to capture the complexity of the construct. Specifically, of the small number of studies we found that purport to measure decision speed, two-thirds used absolute measures such as the number of months or days for a decision to be made (Eisenhardt, 1989; Judge and Miller; 1991; Bluedorn et al., 1999; Forbes, 2005), one-third used measures that allow for some relative operationalizations of speed vis-à-vis a particular context (Wally and Baum, 1994; Baum and Wally, 2003), and only one used multiple measures (Wally and Baum, 1994). We have attempted to redress this deficiency of the literature by measuring speed in both absolute and relative terms. Additionally, taking our cue from seminal organizational theory research (i.e., Thompson, 1967; Galbraith, 1973), we also pay heed to the notion that the aspect of speed that may be most critical is whether the firm can make decisions quickly enough to match the rate of change present in the environment.

Finally, through the use of outlier analysis, we have developed propositions concerning the multidimensional nature of potency. Specifically, we argue that functional (bounded) potency results from education level, high consensus ability, and high cognitive conflict, but low affective conflict. Teams possessing potency based on these conditions are able to both make quick and high-quality strategic decisions. Teams whose potency is based in consensus ability and the absence of both cognitive and affective conflict run the risk of making quick but poor-quality strategic decisions, especially in changing environments. We propose that such teams do not engage in vigilant decision processes and thus fall victim to hubris. Finally, we propose that potency should be thought of both in terms of level, and also in terms of the breadth of domain over which the team feels potency. We propose that the development of hubris, and the consequent lack of debate, stems from the failure of some teams to place bounds around their feelings of potency.

FUTURE RESEARCH AGENDA

In this chapter we have begun to demonstrate the critical impact confidence has on important TMT outcomes. However, the relationship is almost certainly more complex than what we have represented. Three areas of inquiry merit particular attention if we are to advance our understanding: (1) what are the different forms of confidence and in which combinations of antecedents do they originate; (2) what is the nature of the link between forms of confidence and outcomes; and (3) can confidence be calibrated or directed in a purposeful manner? Within each of these larger questions lie several elements worth investigating.

In this chapter we have introduced the notion that different forms of confidence likely exist and presented evidence that their effects on outcomes differ widely. We have focused on the boundedness of confidence, or how generalizable a TMT's confidence appears to be. Unbounded confidence appears to have deleterious effects on firm performance and we propose that the harmful effects occur when a TMT unknowingly encounters circumstances it is ill-equipped to resolve. Researchers have long studied similar concepts of hubris, overconfidence, and certainty but have had a singular focus on the level rather than type of confidence. In each case, the conclusion is that the effects of confidence follow an inverted U-shaped curve whereby confidence beyond some level results in poor outcomes (see Figure 7.2). We have shown that at least in some outlier cases, extreme levels of confidence can have positive effects on performance. Specifically, we suggest that an important distinction must be made between confidence that is justifiably based on characteristics of the team and its process that increase the chance for success and false confidence based on distal and/or irrelevant factors. In this research we have shown that the rare ability of a TMT to experience high cognitive conflict while controlling personal animosity can lead to increased confidence and ultimately to high performance. We identified other factors such as education level (a proxy for cognitive ability and skill levels), organized process, and decentralized participative climate as important ingredients in functional confidence. It is likely there are other factors on which justifiable confidence is based and probable that these factors work by ensuring that confidence results in the display of behaviors appropriate to the circumstances confronted by the TMT at a particular point in time. We believe this is an important oversight in the literature and one that could be resolved through further study.

It is possible that additional dimensions of confidence exist. For example, the durability of confidence would seem an important factor. Durable confidence might provide benefits to firms facing uncertain and turbulent environments, but may be less important in other contexts. On the other hand, there may be reason to believe that short-lived confidence, or confidence bursts, provides advantages to firms. Perhaps the ability to ramp up or mobilize confidence when an unexpectedly severe challenge arises confers advantage. Certainly, if we take a cue from sports and military arenas, inspiring speeches delivered proximally to a task have been known to produce bravery and resolve in the face of daunting odds. Of course, it is unlikely that any such pep talk would have much impact if there weren't already some minimal and latent level of confidence present. Thus, perhaps the layering of different forms and types of confidence leads to the appropriate aggregate resolve to meet a given challenge.

Are some forms of confidence deeper than others such that they are intransigent and

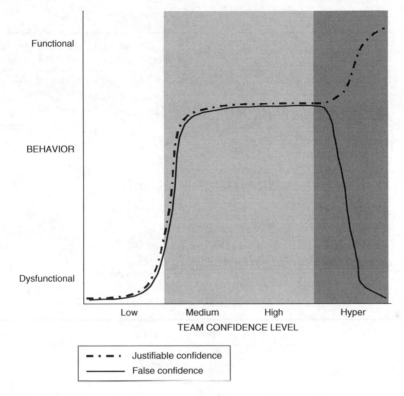

Functional

BEHAVIOR

Dysfunctional

Low   Medium   High   Hyper

TEAM CONFIDENCE LEVEL

- · - · Justifiable confidence
——— False confidence

Source: Authors' calculations.

Figure 7.2   Confidence level, behavior, and justifiability

relatively immutable? If so, deep confidence would provide resilience during challenging times, but could also lead to an inability to regulate confident feelings when caution and reflection is warranted. We expect that confidence originating in personality characteristics, company or country culture, and/or in long experience of shared success might be less malleable. Moreover, there is some evidence that some long-successful (or otherwise high-profile) TMTs are susceptible to the negative effects of celebrity (Hayward et al., 2004; Rindova et al., 2006). In other words, external affirmation of their status can reinforce and even shift perceptions by the team as to its competence, ultimately leading to hubris. An important area for study is what forms and duration of positive experience lead to deep confidence. In particular, is experience-based confidence developed primarily through the passage of considerable time, or are streaks of several repeated "wins" (even in a short period) more likely to engender such confidence? One approach that might lend insight into this would be to study TMTs that have been intact for a long time and compare them to similar TMTs having recently experienced the departure of key executives. Does the loss of key human capital and/or the decisions around what sort of replacement is made impact the confidence of the TMT? If so, then these sorts of succession decisions should be made with an eye toward (re)calibrating the confidence of the team.

In our models, demography and team process lead to confidence, which in turn

Table 7.4   Objective and subjective bases of TMT confidence

	Individual Factors	Team Factors	Organizational Factors	External Factors
Objective factors	Knowledge, skills, and abilities	Human capital	Absolute past performance	Environmental munificence
	Past experience	Demographic composition	Culture and climate	Environmental dynamism
	Individual personalities	Experience as a team		
		Structure		
Subjective factors	Perceptions of objective factors	Perceptions of objective factors	Perceptions of objective factors	Perceptions of objective factors
	Individual confidence	Functionality of team processes	Relative past performance	Media accounts and celebrity
			Repetitiveness of past performance (streaks)	
			Durability of past performance	

Source: Authors.

affects decision speed and different combinations of antecedents determine the quality of these decisions. As detailed above, it is almost certainly the case that these effects are recursive. Thus, a considerable opportunity exists to delineate exactly how confidence affects decision speed and quality. To be sure, some work has focused on the confidence–performance link. However, very few if any empirical investigations in TMTs have taken place. The commonly proposed links are of two types: (1) confidence can lead to clipped process and thus poor outcomes, and (2) confidence leads the team to be more creative, persistent, and vigilant in its approach, thus leading to improved outcomes. The current state of knowledge on TMT functioning does not allow us to predict a priori how confidence will play out in a given TMT. However, an intriguing model from psychology could help guide future research efforts. Clarkson et al. (2008) propose that attitude certainty, a form of confidence, serves as a catalyst or amplifier of behaviors already exhibited by teams. That is, confidence does not change the behavioral proclivities of a team, rather it activates and accentuates them. Thus, if a TMT is predisposed to use functional group process, increased confidence will cause them to be even more dedicated to this approach, displaying even more of the behaviors that have proven effective in the past. Under this theory, we would expect high-confidence teams facing severe challenges (high stakes, time-constrained decisions under uncertainty) to be more creative, more vigilant, more organized, and to engage in vigorous debate. Consistent with this, we would expect other TMTs whose confidence is based on nonprocess factors (personality, celebrity, winning streaks) to forge ahead in the same nonreflective manner, perhaps even more quickly. The important point here is that if different forms of confidence originating in different gestalts exist, what is most important is the behaviors these produce.

Finally, while it is important to better understand forms and consequences of confidence, the real gold resides in an understanding of whether and how confidence can be manipulated to achieve desired end states. We believe there are different forms of confidence, some of which are relatively stable over time and others that wane and wax depending on a variety of factors. Some factors are deeply rooted in personality, experience, and even culture while others, like expectations regarding the future and group structure and process, are susceptible to change in the short term. The strategic decision-making literature often casts the CEO as the person ultimately responsible for calling the shots. While the upper echelons stream touts that the role of the entire team is shaping responses to strategic challenges, the CEO is still recognized as the single most important team member. We believe this depiction of the team as a consultative body that influences the CEO's decision can lead to dysfunction in TMTs. We propose that the primary task of the CEO is to understand the demands of the current task environment and to calibrate TMT confidence to meet the decision challenge. In this role, the CEO is primarily responsible for putting the TMT in the correct emotional frame of mind to do the hard work ahead. In line with some conceptualizations of leadership as mentorship, the CEO takes on the role of master coach. In this way, the CEO is able to manipulate the level and type of team confidence such that the TMT is sufficiently motivated and cognitively "in the game" while avoiding the pitfalls of hubris.

REFERENCES

Amason, A. (1996). Distinguishing the effects of functional and dysfunctional conflict on strategic decision-making: Resolving a paradox for top management teams. *Academy of Management Journal*, **39**(2), 123–49.

Amason, A.C. and Mooney, A.C. (2008). Icarus' paradox revisited: An examination of the relationship between past performance and strategic decision making. *Strategic Organization*, **6**(4), 407–34.

Amason, A.C. and Sapienza, H.J. (1997). The effects of top management team size and interaction norms on cognitive and affective conflict. *Journal of Management*, **23**(4), 495–516.

Amason, A. and Schweiger, D.M. (1994). Resolving the paradox of conflict, strategic decision making, and organizational performance. *International Journal of Conflict Management*, **5**(3), 239–53.

Andersson, L.M. and Bateman, T.S. (1997). Cynicism in the workplace: Some causes and effects. *Journal of Organizational Behavior*, **18**(5), 449–69.

Ashby, W.R. (1956). *Introduction to cybernetics*, London, UK: Chapman and Hall.

Aulakh, P.S. and Gencturk, E.F. (2000). International principal–agent relationships: Control, governance and performance. *Industrial Marketing Management*, **29**(6), 521–38.

Bandura, A. (1986). *Social foundations of thought and action: A social cognitive theory*. Englewood Cliffs: Prentice Hall.

Bandura, A. (1997). *Self-efficacy: The exercise of control*. New York, NY: Freeman.

Bandura, A. (2000). Cultivate self-efficacy for personal and organizational effectiveness. In E.A. Locke (ed.), *Handbook of principles of organizational behavior*. Oxford, UK: Blackwell, pp. 120–36.

Bandura, A. and Locke, E.A. (2003). Negative self-efficacy and goal effects revisited. *Journal of Applied Psychology*, **88**(1), 87–99.

Bantel, K.A. and Jackson, S.E. (1989). Top management and innovations in banking: Does the demography of the team make a difference? *Strategic Management Journal*, **10**(S1), 107–24.

Barnett, W.P. and McKendrick, D. (2004). Why are some organizations more competitive than others? Evidence from a changing global market. *Administrative Science Quarterly*, **49**(4), 535–71.

Baron, R.A. (2008). The role of affect in the entrepreneurial process. *Academy of Management Review*, **33**(2), 328–40.

Baron, R.M. and Kenny, D.A. (1986). The moderator–mediator variable distinction in social psychological research: Conceptual, strategic, and statistical considerations. *Journal of Personality and Social Psychology*, **51**(6), 1173–82.

Barsade, S.G., Ward, A.J., Turner J.D.F., and Sonnenfeld J.A. (2000). To your heart's content: A model of affective diversity in top management teams. *Administrative Science Quarterly*, **45**(4), 802–36.

Baum, J.R. and Wally, S. (2003). Strategic decision speed and firm performance. *Strategic Management Journal*, **24**(11), 1107–29.

Baumol, W.J. (2004). Red-queen games: Arms races, rule of law and market economies. *Journal of Evolutionary Economics*, **14**(2), 237–47.

Becerra, M., Lunnan, R., and Huemer, L. (2008). Trustworthiness, risk, and the transfer of tacit and explicit knowledge between alliance partners. *The Journal of Management Studies*, **45**(4), 691–713.

Bliese, P.D. (2000). Within-group agreement, non-independence, and reliability: Implications for data aggregation and analysis. In K.J. Klein and S.W.J. Kozlowski (eds), *Multilevel theory, research, and methods in organizations: Foundations, extensions, and new directions*. San Francisco, CA: Jossey-Bass, pp. 349–81.

Bliese, P.D. and Halverson, R.R. (1998). Group consensus and psychological well-being: A large field study. *Journal of Applied Social Psychology*, **28**(7), 563–80.

Bluedorn, A.C., Turban, D.B., and Love, M.S. (1999). The effects of stand-up and sit-down meeting formats on meeting outcomes. *Journal of Applied Psychology*, **84**(2), 278–85.

Bourgeois, L.J. and Eisenhardt, K.M. (1988). Strategic decision processes in high velocity environments. *Management Science*, **34**(7), 816–35.

Campion, M.A., Medsker, G.J., and Higgs, A.C. (1993). Relationships between work group characteristics and effectiveness: Implications for designing effective work groups. *Personnel Psychology*, **46**(4), 823–50.

Campion, M.A., Papper, E.M., and Medsker, G.J. (1996). Relations between work team characteristics and effectiveness: A replication and extension. *Personnel Psychology*, **49**(2), 429–52.

Carpenter, M.A., Geletkanycz, M.A., and Sanders, W.G. (2004). Upper echelons research revisited: Antecedents, elements, and consequences of top management team composition. *Journal of Management*, **30**(6), 749–78.

Carroll, G.R. and Harrison, J.R. (1998). Organizational demography and culture: Insights from a formal model. *Administrative Science Quarterly*, **43**(3), 637–67.

Chen, M.J. (1988). Competitive strategic interaction: A study of competitive actions and responses. Unpublished doctoral dissertation, University of Maryland.

Child, J. (1972). Organization structure, environment and performance: The role of strategic choice. *Sociology*, **6**(1), 1–22.

Clarkson, J.J., Tormala, Z.L., and Rucker, D.D. (2008). A new look at the consequences of attitude certainty: The amplification hypothesis. *Journal of Personality and Social Psychology*, **95**(4), 810–25.

Clarkson, J.J., Tormala, Z.L., DeSensi, D.L., and Wheeler, S.C. (2009). Does attitude certainty beget self-certainty? *Journal of Experimental Social Psychology*, **45**, 436–39.

Daft, R.L. and Lewin, A.Y. (1990). Can organizational studies begin to break out of the normal science strait-jacket? An editorial essay. *Organization Science*, **1**(1), 1–9.

D'Aveni, R.A. (1994). *Hyper-competition: Managing the dynamics of strategic maneuvering*. New York, NY: Free Press.

Day, D., Farley, J., and Wind, J. (1990). The state of art in theory and method in strategy research. *Management Science*, Special Issue.

Dean, J.W.J. and Sharfman, M.P. (1996). Does decision process matter? A study of strategic decision-making effectiveness. *Academy of Management Journal*, **39**(2), 368–96.

Derfus, P.J., Maggitti, P.G., Grimm, C.M., and Smith, K.G. (2008). The red queen effect: Competitive actions and firm performance. *Academy of Management Journal*, **51**(1), 61–80.

Eisenhardt, K.M. (1989). Making fast strategic decisions in high velocity environments. *Academy of Management Journal*, **32**(3), 543–76.

Erez, A. and Isen, A.M. (2002). The influence of positive affect on the components of expectancy motivation. *Journal of Applied Psychology*, **87**(6), 1055–67.

Estrada, C.A., Isen, A.M., and Young, M.J. (1997). Positive affect facilitates integration of information and decreases anchoring in reasoning among physicians. *Organizational Behavior and Human Decision Processes*, **72**(1), 117–35.

Finkelstein, S. and Hambrick, D.C. (1996). *Strategic leadership: Top executives and their effects on organization*. St. Paul, MN: West Publishing Company.

Forbes, D.P. (2005). Managerial determinants of decision speed in new ventures. *Strategic Management Journal*, **26**(4), 355–66.

Forgas, J.P. (1995). Mood and judgement: The affect infusion model (aim). *Psychological Bulletin*, **117**(1), 39–66.

Forgas, J.P. and George, J.M. (2001). Affective influences on judgments and behavior in organizations: An information processing perspective. *Organizational Behavior and Human Decision Processes*, **86**(1), 3–34.

Fredrickson, J.W. and Mitchell, T.R. (1984). Strategic decision processes: Comprehensiveness and performance in an industry with an unstable environment. *Academy of Management Journal*, **27**(2), 399–423.

Galbraith, J. (1973). *Designing complex organizations*. Reading, MA: Addison-Wesley.

Gibson, C.B. (1999). Do they do what they believe they can? Group efficacy and group effectiveness across tasks and cultures. *Academy of Management Journal*, **42**(2), 138–52.

Gladstein, D. (1984). Groups in context: A model of task group effectiveness. *Administrative Science Quarterly*, **29**(4), 499–517.

Gully, S., Incalcaterra, K.A., Joshi, A., and Beaubien, J.M. (2002). A meta-analysis of team efficacy, potency, and performance: Interdependence and level of analysis as moderators of observed relationships. *Journal of Applied Psychology*, **87**(5), 819–32.

Guzzo, R.A. and Shea, G.P. (1992). Group performance and intergroup relations in organizations. In M. Dunnet and L. Hough (eds), *Handbook for industrial and organizational psychology* (2nd edition). Palo Alto, CA: Consulting Psychologists Press, pp. 269–313.

Guzzo, R.A., Yost, P.R., Campbell, R.J., and Shea, G.P. (1993). Potency in groups: Articulating a construct. *British Journal of Social Psychology*, **32**(1), 87–106.

Hambrick, D.C. (1994). Top management groups: A conceptual integration and reconsideration of the "team" label. In B.M. Staw and L.L. Cummings (eds), *Research in organizational behavior*. Greenwich, CN: JAI Press, pp. 171–214.

Hambrick, D.C. (2007). The field of management's devotion to theory: Too much of a good thing? *Academy of Management Journal*, **50**, 1346–52.

Hambrick, D.C. and Mason, P. (1984). Upper echelons: The organization as a reflection of its top managers. *Academy of Management Review*, **9**(2), 193–206.

Hayward, M. and Hambrick, D.C. (1997). Explaining the premiums paid for large acquisitions: Evidence of CEO hubris. *Administrative Science Quarterly*, **42**(1), 103–27.

Hayward, M.L.A., Rindova, V.P., and Pollock, T.G. (2004). Believing one's own press: The antecedents and consequences of chief executive officer celebrity. *Strategic Management Journal*, **25**(7), 637–53.

Hiller, N.J. and Hambrick, D.C. (2005). Conceptualizing executive hubris: The role of (hyper-) core self-evaluations in strategic decision-making. *Strategic Management Journal*, **26**(4), 297–320.

Hitt, M.A. and Tyler, B.B. (1991). Strategic decision models: Integrating different perspectives. *Strategic Management Journal*, **12**(5), 327–51.

Hmieleski, K.M. and Baron, R.A. (2008). When does entrepreneurial self-efficacy enhance versus reduce firm performance? *Strategic Entrepreneurship Journal*, **2**(1), 57–72.

Hofmann, D.A. and Jones, L.M. (2005). Leadership, collective personality, and performance. *Journal of Applied Psychology*, **90**(3), 509–22.

Isabella, L.A. and Waddock, S.A. (1994). Top management team certainty: Environmental assessments, teamwork, and performance implications. *Journal of Management*, **20**(4), 835–58.

Isen, A.M. (1993). Positive affect and decision making. In M. Lewis and J.M. Haviland (eds), *Handbook of emotions*. New York, NY: Guilford, pp. 261–77.

Isen, A.M. (2000). Positive affect and decision making. In M. Lewis and J. Haviland-Jones (eds), *Handbook of emotions* (2nd edition). New York: Guilford, pp. 417–35.

Isen, A.M. (2002). Role for neuropsychology in understanding the facilitating influence of positive affect on social behavior and cognitive processes. In C. Snyder and S. Lopez (eds), *Handbook of positive psychology*. New York, NY: Guilford.

Isen, A.M. and Labroo, A.A. (2003). Some ways in which positive affect facilitates decision making and judgment. In S.L. Schneider and J.R. Shanteau (eds), *Emerging perspectives on decision research*. New York, NY: Cambridge, pp. 365–93.

James, L.R. (1982). Aggregation bias in estimates of perceptual agreement. *Journal of Applied Psychology*, **67**(2), 219–29.

James, L.R., Demaree, R.G., and Wolf, G. (1984). Estimating within-group interrater reliability with and without response bias. *Journal of Applied Psychology*, **69**(1), 85–98.

Jehn, K.A. (1995). A multi-method examination of the benefits and detriments of intra-group conflict. *Administrative Science Quarterly*, **40**(2), 256–82.

Jehn, K.A., Northcraft, G.B., and Neale, M.A. (1999). Why differences make a difference: A field study of diversity, conflict, and performance in work groups. *Administrative Science Quarterly*, **44**(4), 741–63.

Judge, W.Q. and Miller, A. (1991). Antecedents and outcomes of decision speed in different environmental contexts. *Academy of Management Journal*, **34**(2), 449–63.

Kirkman, B.L., Rosen, B., Tesluk, P.E., and Gibson, C.B. (2004). The impact of team empowerment on virtual team performance: The moderating role of face-to-face interaction. *Academy of Management Journal*, **47**(2), 175–92.

Klein, K.J., Dansereau, F., and Hall, R.J. (1994). Levels issues in theory development, data collection, and analysis. *Academy of Management Review*, **19**(2), 195–229.

Knight, D., Pearce, C.L., Smith, K.G., Olian, J.D., Sims, H., Smith, K.A., and Flood, P. (1999). Top management team diversity, group process, and strategic consensus. *Strategic Management Journal*, **20**(5), 445–65.

Latham, G.P., Winters, D.C., and Locke, E.A. (1994). Cognitive and motivational effects of participation: A mediator study. *Journal of Organizational Behavior*, **15**(1), 49–63.

Lawrence, B.S. (1997). The black box of organizational demography. *Organization Science*, **8**(1), 1–22.

Lester, S.W., Meglino, B.M., and Korsgaard, M.A. (2002). The antecedents and consequences of group potency: A longitudinal investigation of newly formed work groups. *Academy of Management Journal*, **45**(2), 352–68.

Lindsley, D.H., Brass, D.J., and Thomas, J.B. (1995). Efficacy-performance spirals: A multilevel perspective. *Academy of Management Review*, **20**(3), 645–78.

Locke, E.A. (1991). The motivation sequence, the motivation hub, and the motivation core. *Organizational Behavior and Human Decision Processes*, **50**(2), 288–99.

Mackie, D.M. and Worth, L.T. (1989). Processing deficits and the mediation of positive affect in persuasion. *Journal of Personality and Social Psychology*, **57**(1), 27–40.

Mason, R. and Mitroff, I. (1981). *Challenging strategic planning assumptions*. New York, NY: Wiley.

McGrath, R. (1997). Small group research, that once and future field: An interpretation of the past with an eye toward the future. *Group Dynamics*, **1**(1), 7–27.

Milkovich, G.T. (1987). Compensation systems in high technology companies. In D.B. Balkin and L.R. Gomez-Mejia (eds), *New perspectives on compensation*. Englewood Cliffs, NJ: Prentice-Hall.

Mintzberg, H., Raisinghani, D., and Theoret, A. (1976). The structure of unstructured decision processes. *Administrative Science Quarterly*, **21**(2), 246–75.

Mischel, L.J. and Northcraft, G.B. (1997). "I think we can, I think we can . . .": The role of efficacy beliefs in group and team effectiveness. In *Advances in group processes* (Vol. 14). Greenwich, CT: JAI Press, pp. 177–97.

Morgeson, F.P. (2005). The external leadership of self-managing teams: Intervening in the context of novel and disruptive events. *Journal of Applied Psychology*, **90**(3), 497–508.

Mulvey, P.W. and Klein, H.J. (1998). The impact of perceived loafing and collective efficacy on group goal processes and group performance. *Organizational Behaviors and Human Decision Processes*, **74**(1), 62–87.

Neter, J., Kutner, M.H., Nachtscheim, C.J., and Wasserman, W. (1996). *Applied linear statistical models*. Chicago, IL: Irwin.

Nutt, P. (2001). Strategic decision-making. In M. Hitt, R. Freeman, and Harrison (eds), *The Blackwell handbook of strategic management*. Oxford, UK: Blackwell.

Park, J. and Banaji, M.R. (2000). Mood and heuristics: The influence of happy and sad states on sensitivity and bias in stereotyping. *Journal of Personality and Social Psychology*, **79**(6), 1005–23.

Pettigrew, A.M. (1992). On studying managerial elites. *Strategic Management Journal*, **13**(S2), 163–82.

Pfeffer, J. (1983). Organizational demography. *Research in Organizational Behavior*, **5**, 299–357.

Phillips, J. (2001). The role of decision influence and team performance in member self-efficacy, withdrawal, satisfaction with the leader, and willingness to return. *Organizational Behavior and Human Decision Processes*, **84**(1), 122–47.

Pitcher, P. and Smith, A.D. (2001). Top management team heterogeneity: Personality, power, and proxies. *Organizational Science*, **12**(1), 1–18.

Podasakoff, P.M., MacKenzie, S.B., Lee, J.-Y., and Podsakoff, N.P. (2003). Common method biases in behavioral research: A critical review of the literature and recommended remedies. *Journal of Applied Psychology*, **88**(5), 879–903.

Priem, R., Lyon, D., and Dess, G. (1999). Inherent limitations of demographic proxies in top management team heterogeneity research. *Journal of Management*, **25**(6), 935–53.

Rindova, V.P., Pollock, T.G., and Hayward, M.L.A. (2006). Celebrity firms: The social construction of market popularity. *Academy of Management Review*, **31**(1), 50–71.

Salanova, M., Agut, S., and Peiró, J.M. (2005). Linking organizational resources and work engagement to employee performance and customer loyalty: The mediation of service climate. *Journal of Applied Psychology*, **90**(6), 1217–27.

Shaw, M.E. (1981). *Group dynamics: The psychology of small group behavior* (3rd edition). New York, NY: McGraw Hill.

Shea, G.P. and Guzzo, R.A. (1987). Group effectiveness: What really matters? *Sloan Management Review*, **28**(3), 25–31.

Simons, T.L. and Peterson, R.S. (2000). Task conflict and relationship conflict in top management teams: The pivotal role of intragroup trust. *Journal of Applied Psychology*, **85**(1), 102–11.

Simons, T., Pelled, L.H., and Smith, K.A. (1999). Making use of difference: Diversity, debate, and decision comprehensiveness in top management teams. *Academy of Management Journal*, **42**(6), 662–73.

Simsek, Z., Lubatkin, M.H., and Floyd, S.W. (2003). How networks influence entrepreneurial behavior: A structural embeddedness perspective. *Journal of Management*, **29**, 427–42.

Simsek, Z., Veiga, J.F., Lubatkin, M., and Dino, R.N. (2005). Modeling the multilevel determinants of top management team behavioral integration. *Academy of Management Journal*, **48**(1), 69–84.

Sivasubramaniam, N., Murry, W.D., Avolia, B.J., and Juang, D.I. (2002). A longitudinal model of the effects of team leadership and group potency on group performance. *Group and Organization Management*, **27**(1), 66–96.

Smith, K.G., Grimm, C.M., and Gannon, M. (1992). *The dynamics of competitive strategy*. Los Angeles, CA: Sage Publishing.

Smith, K.G., Smith, K.A., Olian, J.D., Sims, H.P., O'Bannon, D.P., and Scully, J.A. (1994). Top management team demography and process: The role of social integration and communication. *Administrative Science Quarterly*, **39**(3), 412–38.

Stajkovic, A.D. (2006). Development of a core confidence–higher order construct. *Journal of Applied Psychology*, **91**(6), 1208–24.

Stasser, G. (1992). Pooling of unshared information during group discussions. In S. Worchel, W. Wood, and J.A. Simpson (eds), *Group process and productivity*. Newbury Park, CA: Sage, pp. 48–67.

Stevens, M.J. and Campion, M.A. (1994). The knowledge, skills, and ability requirements for teamwork: Implications for human resource management. *Journal of Management*, **20**(2), 503–30.

Taggar, S. and Seijts, G.H. (2003). Leader and staff role-efficacy as antecedents of collective efficacy and team performance. *Human Performance*, **16**(2), 131–56.

Talaulicar, T., Grundei, J., and Werder, A.V. (2005). Strategic decision making in start-ups: The effect of top management team organization and processes on speed and comprehensiveness. *Journal of Business Venturing*, **20**(4), 519–41.

Tasa, K. and Whyte, G. (2005). Collective efficacy and vigilant problem solving in group decision making: A non-linear model. *Organizational Behavior and Human Decision Processes*, **96**(2), 119–29.

Tasa, K., Taggar, S., and Seijts, G.H. (2007). The development of collective efficacy in teams: A multilevel and longitudinal perspective. *Journal of Applied Psychology*, **92**(1), 17–27.

Teece, D. and Winter, S.G. (1984). The limits of neoclassical theory in management education. *American Economic Review*, **74**(2), 116–21.

Thompson, J.D. (1967). *Organizations in action*. New York, NY: McGraw-Hill.

Tourangeau, R., Rips, L., and Rasinski, K. (2000). *The psychology of survey response*. Cambridge, UK: Cambridge University Press.

Tushman, M.L. and Nadler, D.A. (1978). Information processing as an integrating concept in organizational design. *Academy of Management Review*, **3**(3), 613.

Van de Ven, A.H. and Huber, G.P. (1990). Longitudinal field research methods for studying processes of organizational change. *Organization Science*, **1**(3), 213–19.

Wally, S. and Baum, R. (1994). Personal and structural determinants of the pace of strategic decision-making. *Academy of Management Journal*, **37**(4), 932–56.

Wegener, D.M. and Petty, R.E. (1994). Mood management across affective states: The hedonic contingency hypothesis. *Journal of Personality and Social Psychology*, **66**(6), 1034–48.

West, C.T. and Schwenk, C.R. (1996). Top management team strategic consensus, demographic homogeneity, and performance: A report of resounding non-findings. *Strategic Management Journal*, **17**(7), 571–6.

West, M.A. and Anderson, N.R. (1996). Innovation in top management teams. *Journal of Applied Psychology*, **81**(6), 680–93.

Zaccaro, S.J., Blair, J., Peterson, C., and Zazanis, M. (1995). Collective efficacy. In J.E. Maddux (ed.), *Self-efficacy, adaptation, and adjustment*. New York, NY: Plenum, pp. 305–28.

APPENDIX 7A   SCALE ITEMS

TMT decision speed

1. This TMT routinely makes important decisions in under three months.
2. Relative to rivals, it take this TMT too long to make important decisions.
3. Given our competitive environment, this TMT moves quickly to make key strategic decisions.

TMT potency

1. Our TMT is known to be successful at the things it tries to do.
2. I believe this TMT's decision-making capabilities will lead this firm to achieve high performance.
3. I feel this TMT can solve any problem we encounter.
4. I have confidence in the TMT's ability to make sound decisions.
5. The quality of this TMT's decisions gives me the confidence to act.

Consensus

1. TMT decisions are not final until all members agree that the decision is acceptable to them.
2. The TMT believes that taking more time to reach consensus on a strategic decision is worth the effort.
3. When final decisions are reached, it is common for at least one member of the TMT to be unhappy with it.
4. When making decisions, the TMT works hard to reach an agreement.

Decentralization

1. There is a high level of delegation for decision making in the TMT.
2. Even tactical issues have to be referred to the CEO for a final decision.
3. All TMT members are actively involved in making important strategic decisions.
4. Our CEO calls the shots on important strategic decisions.

Process rationality

1. Our TMT tends to be very formal in our interactions.
2. Communication between TMT members is always in writing.
3. Our TMT uses rather formal communication channels.
4. Interactions between TMT members are very informal.
5. Our TMT uses procedures like meeting agendas and minutes as an important part of our decision making.

Affective conflict

1. I sense personal friction between members of this TMT.
2. There are personality clashes within this TMT.
3. There is tension between members of this TMT.
4. In this TMT, members are sometimes angry after a decision has been made.

Cognitive conflict

1. In this TMT, there are often disagreements over different ideas about important decisions.
2. There are many different ideas expressed within the TMT when making important decisions.
3. Differences about the factual content of decisions rarely occur in this TMT.

PART III

TMT EXPERIENCE AND STRATEGY

8 How does TMT prior experience shape strategy? A routine-based framework based on evidence from founding teams

Anne S. Miner, Yan Gong, Ted Baker, and Jay O'Toole

The top management team (TMT) literature and upper echelons perspective (Hambrick and Mason, 1984) rest on the premise that executives' influence on their organizations is a product of their experiences (Carpenter et al., 2004; Hambrick, 2007). This body of work argues that executives' experience will influence their fields of vision, selective perceptions, and interpretation of environmental and organizational stimuli. These in turn then drive strategic choices (Hambrick and Mason, 1984). Considerable evidence exists for the link between TMT experiences, strategic choices, and firm performance (e.g., Eisenhardt and Schoonhoven, 1990; Boeker, 1997; Carpenter et al., 2001; Kor, 2003). In this chapter we propose an additional causal pathway for how and why executive experience influences organizational actions and outcomes. Specifically, we propose that prior experience exposes TMT members to specific organizational routines that they automatically or mindfully deploy in ways that shape strategy and outcomes.

Our focus is on organization-level routines, sets of coordinated and repetitive organizational activities (Miner, 1991). To develop our framework, we first report an inductive study of how *founding* top management teams draw on prior experience to create organizational routines. In this study we uncovered that top management teams replicate routines from their own previous experiences in several ways. They integrate routines between TMT members and network partners and use routines from real-time experiences while creating and growing new businesses. We discovered five ways that top management teams shape the creation of organizational routines that directly affect organizational action. Specifically, they (1) automatically import routines from their prior experience, (2) selectively import routines, (3) redeploy prior routines for new purposes, (4) recombine routines from diverse prior organizations, and (5) recombine routines from informal advisory networks.

To begin, we provide a basis for an alternative causal pathway to the standard cognitive assumptions of the upper echelon perspective. Next we report on what we discovered: TMTs draw on their experiences to enact routines. The following section explicates these processes and considers how routines represent an alternative pathway to the cognitive premises of the upper echelons perspective. We clarify specific pathways for prior results from existing research. This chapter then offers several ways to differentiate between the cognitions and organizational routines pathways, describes how the two competing models imply different outcomes, and presents testable propositions to be explored in future research. Lastly, we discuss the implications of our alternative model to the top management team literature and organizational entrepreneurial learning (Kim et al., 2009).

Our chapter seeks to make two important contributions. First we offer a potentially fruitful additional causal pathway by which TMT prior experience shapes crucial strategic actions and outcomes. The existence of this pathway implies different types of effects of prior experience than those already assumed in the TMT literature. More broadly it expands the vision of how TMTs themselves influence change, as well as continuity in organizations. Second, by building on inductive research on founding top management teams in particular, the chapter contributes to the literature on founding teams and builds the case for several ways in which prior experience influences the early years of an organization's life.

THEORETICAL CONTEXTS: TMT EXPERIENCE AND ORGANIZATIONAL ROUTINES

Impact of TMT Prior Experience

Substantial attention has been paid to the upper echelons perspective and the study of the importance of top management teams since Hambrick and Mason (1984) originally emphasized this using observable managerial characteristics to predict organizational outcomes. Figure 8.1, adopted from their classic paper, lists potential observable characteristics that they argue will be correlated with cognitive biases and lenses that will shape important strategic activity. Prior experience of TMT members stands as one important observable feature hypothesized to shape cognition and values and strategic actions. In this paper, we focus specifically on the potential impact of TMT experience.

Broadly speaking, the original upper echelons model proposes that the career experiences of the top management team have a significant effect on strategic choices and organizational outcomes through "their cognitive and emotional givens" (Hambrick and Mason, 1984, p. 200). For example, executives who have already worked in an international firm might take it for granted that international activity is both possible and likely to work out, without this even being the subject of explicit thought. We propose that above and beyond values and perceptions, executive experiences will expose them to specific organizational routines. This then shapes their later action, less from cognitive biases than from automatic importation of such routines without much deliberation, or through the deliberate replication of routines out of convenience rather than primarily cognitive processes. Our framework supplements the traditional cognitive approach, and highlights the additional causal pathway shown in the lower left-hand corner of adapted Figure 8.1.

The most extreme version of our framework would imply that in some cases, executives simply replicate routines from prior settings without any reference to mental processes or values. Prior work in the behavioral theory of the firm tradition emphasizes that considerable organizational activity occurs through enacting routines without strong cognitive involvement. Such action occurs partly on "automatic pilot" with its impact probably underestimated in much management research. Our framework is also consistent, however, with routines encountered in prior settings being used deliberately as tools to implement cognitive approaches also derived from those settings. In this version of our causal framework, the presence of routines in prior experience can enhance other prior experience impact, because they offer immediate tools to use in pursuit of TMT

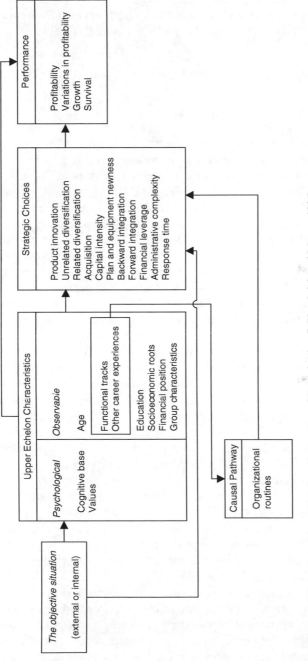

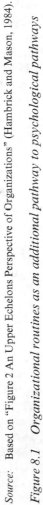

Source: Based on "Figure 2 An Upper Echelons Perspective of Organizations" (Hambrick and Mason, 1984).

Figure 8.1 Organizational routines as an additional pathway to psychological pathways

biases or values. The core idea is that in all cases, exposure to and access to organizational routines gained in prior experience offers a crucial mediating step in the link between experience and strategic action. While this possibility has been noted in prior work, the pervasive causal theory to date in the TMT theoretical framework has emphasized more cognitive processes, making it useful we believe, to develop a routine-based causal pathway.

Organizational Routines

To develop this framework, it's important to start with a clear construct of organizational routines. Over the past decades, organization scholars have built on the intuition behind standard operating procedures (Cyert and March, 1963) to develop multiple versions of organizational routines. Despite the widely varying views on definitions of routines, on close examination, coordination and repetition of behavior have been at the core of most definitions used by evolutionary and learning theorists (e.g., Nelson and Winter, 1982; Miner, 1991; Feldman, 2000). We define organizational routines as coordinated, repetitive sets of activities in organizations (Cyert and March, 1963; Miner, 1991; Ocasio, 1997; Feldman, 2000; Feldman and Pentland, 2003). Crucial features of this definition include that they are *organizational*, something that goes beyond individual beliefs or values or even skills. They can guide collective activity in areas as varied as marketing, manufacturing, acquisition behavior, administration, financial activity, or new product development. They are also not one-time actions devised for a particular context. Prior research on organizational inertia suggests that once in place, routines will often persist even if their origins or even value are no longer clear.

Routines are sometimes characterized as being history dependent and originating as a result of shared organizational experience (Levitt and March, 1988; Phillips, 2002, 2005), although for purposes of our framework their origins are less important than their potential for shaping ongoing behavior. Penrose (1959) argued that organizational resources including organizational routines play a key role in strategies and outcomes, the perspective taken here. Some routines are ceremonial without specific outcomes, but one stream of research sees routines as central to organizational capabilities (Nelson and Winter, 1982; Teece, et al., 1997; Winter, 2000). These capabilities can play a fundamental role in firm performance (Barney and Arikan, 2001; Knott, 2003; Ray et al., 2004). See Martin for a discussion of dynamic capabilities in multi-business teams in Chapter 10 of this volume. Organizational routines are often associated with stored knowledge and organizational memory (Day, 1994; Moorman and Miner, 1997). They embody what the organization has learned from its own prior activities when the organization routinizes activities that appeared to be successful, generating a memory that transcends any individual's memory (Walsh and Ungson, 1991).

Overall then, organizational routines can affect action and in some cases enhance performance in many ways, including when they support capabilities in a specific function, embody lessons from the organization's prior trial and error learning, help establish organizational stability, and boost efficiency under conditions of scarce managerial attention. Our goal here is to consider whether and how the impact of TMT experience involves organizational routines, above and beyond cognitive biases and values.

EVIDENCE FROM THE FIELD: FOUNDING TMTs AND ORIGINS OF ORGANIZATIONAL ROUTINES

Our core notion that TMT prior experience can shape organization behavior through routines springs from an inductive study we conducted on new firms. We explored the simple question of how new firms acquire organization specific routines at all. As a respondent reported in one of our interviews when asked whether his firm has some formal procedures to handle advertising, "Well, I knew that we don't have a. . ., we're new. How do we have a routine in anything?"

By definition, new firms cannot start with organization-specific routines based on their own limited experience. As new firms they do not actually have lengthy histories of experience distinct to themselves. Thus, the standard idea that a routine develops through a firm's institutionalization of apparently useful activities, or even accidental routinization of its own prior actions, does not apply in this setting. We were interested in whether new firms did somehow actually enact routines, and if so, where they came from. As part of a larger study of start-ups, we collected data on young knowledge-based firms' life histories, yielding more than 1725 pages of transcripts in addition to field notes. As described below, we followed standard inductive data analysis procedures to examine data that related to the origins of routines in these organizations. In this section, we report the study itself and its implications for how founding TMTs can shape the routines at work in their own organizations.

The study's core findings imply that the founding team members' own prior experience can have a major influence on routines they implement and there are several different pathways through which this can occur. The routines involve many areas of the organizations and include those with strategic impact. The study implies, then, that these founding TMTs' prior experience shapes their new organizations' strategic action in part through the routines they draw on, from prior experience, in various ways. This is the inductive and theory-building study on which our broader framework for a routine-based TMT causal pathway is built.

Study Sample

Our sample of 60 young knowledge-based firms in a specific region was drawn from three archival sources: the Dun and Bradstreet database (D&B), *Creating High-Tech Business Growth*, a list of firms published by an important local group, and the *2001 Directory of High Technology Companies* published by the local utility company. We also reviewed our list with local experts who had information about new, knowledge-based firms at their earliest stages. We used a stratified random sampling approach to pick firms to interview, using several filters. The goal was to generate a sample of knowledge-based young firms operating in the same geographic area, with a mixture of firms with and without direct roots to the nearby research university, a type of firm we wanted in our sample for the larger study of which this was a part. Our sample contains firms that were in the focal county, began operating no earlier than 1 January, 1995, with at least three employees as of November, 2001, and operating within the drug, biotech, or IT industries (SICs 283, 737, 873). These filters generated a sample that included 147 firms.

From these 147 firms, we interviewed founding top management team members from

60 companies. No firm refused our request that they participate in the study, and every firm allowed us to tape our interviews. During the interview process, we discovered that two firms actually started before 1 January, 1995, and two other firms operated in a line of business different from their SIC description. Table 8.1 provides a descriptive summary of our sample.

Data and Analysis

Our data collection and analysis followed standard grounded theory-building techniques (Ragin, 1989; Denzin and Lincoln, 1998; Strauss and Corbin, 1998). A project team member contacted a member of the founding TMT by phone and introduced us as university researchers investigating management practices in knowledge-based firms, and scheduled a time to visit the firm and conduct interviews. We conducted pilot interviews, which permitted us to improve our protocol and study how the interview materials and interview style affected respondents' reporting behavior. We developed refined protocols for formal semi-structured interviews that began with open-ended questions but then moved toward standardized probes. These included written instruments completed during and after the interviews.

At least two and sometimes more members of the project team conducted each interview. The typical interview lasted two-and-a-half to three hours, with some lasting much longer. All interviews were taped and transcribed by a professional transcription service. An advantage of studying firms of this type is that members of the founding TMT are typically involved in all key aspects of the business and consequently have first-hand knowledge of the firm's day-to-day activities. Our respondents were generally able to offer very detailed responses to our questions, and to provide detailed timelines and histories for their firms. We encouraged respondents to refer to their own archival records for clarification and documentation when necessary.

We collected detailed information on employee hiring, and on specific individuals who were not employed by the firms, but whom the members of the founding TMT reported as having influenced the top management team in the strategic development or day-to-day operations of the firm. The interview and documentation process generated over 1725 pages of transcripts, plus detailed field notes.

The possibility of retrospective bias by informants is a potential threat to the quality of our data. However, because we studied young firms and because we asked our respondents to describe specific events without providing them with a framework with which to evaluate and interpret their answers, we believe that this threat is minimized.

None of our systematic questions explicitly asked informants to reflect on the processes through which the firms acquired routines or flagged this as an important issue in the research. This helps protect our work from several possible sources of bias. Our interviews did not ask informants to provide their own informal theories about where organizational routines come from or how their experience influences them. In addition, as the informants described firm histories, it is very unlikely they were framing their reports in ways designed to match ideas about possible interviewer expectations related to organizational routines. It also seems unlikely they would have shaped their reports to match ideas about what "good" managers would do or not do related to routines, thereby distorting the factual reports of organizational histories. Overall then, we

Table 8.1   Descriptive summary of sample

Type	Year of Founding	No. of Employees	No. of Founders	No. of Interviews	Length of Transcripts	University Start-up
Software	1999	5	1	1	45	N
Internet	1998	5	2	1	43	N
Electronics	1996	7	1	1	29	N
Software	1999	7	1	1	23	Y
Instrument	1980	3	1	1	16	Y
Biotech	1997	2	2	1	12	Y
Biotech	1984	7	4	1	16	Y
Biotech	2000	5	2	1	41	Y
Software	1996	5	4	1	37	Y
Recycling	1999	9	2	1	24	Y
Coating	1996	5	1	1	34	N
Internet	1996	14	4	1	31	N
Software	1996	4	1	1	18	Y
Biotech	2001	8	2	1	16	Y
Engineering consulting	1997	4	6	1	26	Y
Internet	1999	7	1	1	28	Y
Internet	1995	6	3	1	30	N
Engineering consulting	1997	13	1	1	27	Y
Software	1997	3	1	1	30	Y
IT consulting	1996	22	1	1	36	N
Engineering consulting	1998	2	2	1	16	N
Engineering consulting	1996	6	6	1	11	Y
Software	1999	5	1	1	33	N
Internet	1999	3	3	1	36	N
Internet	1999	10	2	1	19	N
Biotech	1998	35	4	1	31	N
Internet	1998	6	2	1	23	N
Internet	1998	18	3	1	42	N
Biotech	1997	30	3	1	20	N
Internet	1995	6	1	1	41	N
Internet	2000	22	5	1	44	N
Software	1996	7	3	1	52	N
IT consulting	1998	3	3	1	27	N
IT consulting	1999	1	1	1	33	N
Biotech	1998	6	1	1	26	Y
IT consulting	2001	4	3	1	27	N
IT service	1998	3	2	1	26	N
Biotech	1990	1	1	1	16	Y
IT consulting	2000	4	4	1	37	N
Biotech	1998	4	4	1	21	Y
Biotech	1997	4	4	1	20	Y

Table 8.1   (continued)

Type	Year of Founding	No. of Employees	No. of Founders	No. of Interviews	Length of Transcripts	University Start-up
Biotech	1995	36	3	1	17	Y
IT consulting	1999	52	1	1	27	N
Optical fiber	1999	3	1	1	27	N
Internet	1996	8	1	1	39	N
Internet	2000	3	3	1	31	N
IT consulting	1995	2	2	1	20	N
IT consulting	1999	3	3	1	42	N
Biotech	1997	11	3	1	31	Y
Software	1996	2	3	1	42	N
Biotech	1997	3	3	1	18	Y
Software	1996	12	2	1	31	Y
Biotech	1996	11	3	1	40	Y
IT consulting	1996	54	2	1	26	N
Electronics	1995	55	1	1	12	Y
Engineering consulting	2000	10	1	1	36	N
Internet	1997	17	5	1	36	N
IT consulting	1997	49	1	1	42	N
Biomedical equipment	1991	135	2	1	21	Y
Software	1996	5	2	1	24	N
TOTAL				60	1725 (pages)	

believe that interview demand effects related to routines are extremely unlikely in our data.

Although we did not systematically ask about routines, our initial reviews of transcripts revealed a wealth of data on a variety of processes and patterns that appeared to strongly influence the presence of routines. These data were ancillary to the primary research questions of the original study, but are central to our current focus on patterns and processes of routine development by founding top management teams.

We studied the transcripts, starting with the basic research question of where routines come from in young firms. Through discussions among members of the project team and with colleagues outside the team, we developed an initial framework for organizing the relevant data and characterizing the events and processes. Through multiple iterations between our developing theoretical framework and the data, we first generated a large number of themes and apparent patterns. We compiled and reviewed individual descriptions for each type of process we hypothesized might be at work. We then subjected these apparent themes and patterns to stringent scrutiny, re-reading transcripts, and challenging whether the data consistently supported the proposed observation. Eventually, a limited number of themes and patterns withstood this scrutiny and were demonstrated to have robust support in our data. We described the findings in the section below, drawing on transcript materials as illustrations.

Findings

We observed five primary sources of routines in our sample: (1) automatic importation from experience with prior employers, (2) selective importation from prior employers, (3) redeployment of prior routines for distinctly different purposes, (4) recombination of routines based on TMT prior experience, and (5) recombination based on experience with external networks. These pathways are illustrated in Figure 8.2.

Automatic importation from experience in prior organizations

We found instances in which founding teams transferred organizational routines from their repertoire of routines gained through experience with prior employers by exact replication or automatic importation. In many cases, automatic importation was a quick, simple, and effective solution to enact organizational routines in the new ventures. For example, we observed that one founding team member drew from his experience working with insurance salespeople to establish clear expectations and goals with new salespeople hired for the marketing firm he started. This was very effective and led to better human resources strategies and marketing outcomes. The enactment of this routine in the new setting was not accompanied by explicit theories of what to do, or values about how to do things. Instead, it was a way of doing things in terms of written procedures, timing of interactions, reporting requirements, and other subroutines that made up a higher-level routine of accountability imported into the new firm.

We observed, however, that automatic importation of organizational routines across very different operating environments could also trigger unexpected organizational outcomes. For example, members of one founding team had worked as employees of a music business entrepreneur and later founded a software consulting firm. Following a routine that they had learned and taken for granted in the music business, they used a potential partner's intellectual property on their website. This automatic importation of a standard organizational routine from a different setting resulted, to their great surprise, in a devastating lawsuit by that partner.

In another case, we noted that founding TMT members with prior experiences in university settings often imported university-based, non-profit organizational routines into their for-profit business setting. One such university organizational routine involved a pattern of following a research path wherever it seemed to lead and the pursuit of multiple technical and research objectives simultaneously. One academic scientist described his automatic importation of this routine in a new start-up during the founding process:

> So I started the process essentially by myself, sitting at a desk and a computer and just typing out five or six, seven concepts basically of products. What would be things that we were working on that could be products. They were agricultural, they were pharmaceuticals, they were nutraceuticals, etc. And I made a binder that was divided up into seven. And each one was a product that had a description what it was, a description of what kind of patent protection either we had or would be required.

The diffused product development planning execution routine stood in stark contrast with the value of having focus in new venture development. In this instance, the scientist's eyeing six or seven "one billion dollar markets" drained limited resources and stretched the company to the brink of bankruptcy. He simply imported a standard and

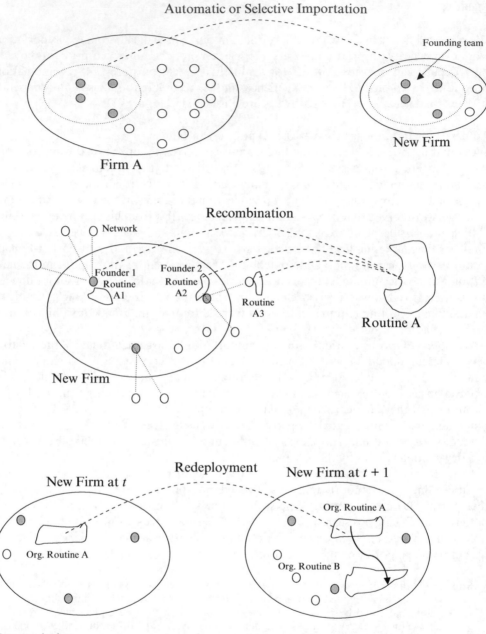

Source: Authors.

Figure 8.2   Sources of organizational routines in new ventures

fruitful organizational routine from his prior experience into the new venture, but in this case the imported routine was destructive.

Selective importation of routines based on prior experience
In contrast to the automatic carryover of procedures and routines from prior settings, some founding teams made use of mindful knowledge of prior routines to engage in a very calculated process of selection during which some organizational routines were imported while others were explicitly rejected. We label this process "selective importation," a more deliberate and selective process of importing routines from prior experience to a new firm. Selective importation sometimes appeared to be a slower process than automatic importation.

In one case, two of the three founders of an IT firm became unhappy with their experiences of how organizational routines focusing specifically on human resource practices had evolved in the old firm. Because of this, they left with three employees to found another firm offering competing services. Early experiences with their old firm were engineer-centered, aiming "to have fantastic engineers and we're going to make sure that they are growing and have a great place to thrive." However, gradually the organizational routine for attracting and nurturing engineers was supplanted by routines focusing explicitly on generating short-term financial returns and an IPO. The previously nurturing environment for engineers became an environment in which engineers were tightly managed, with routines that engineers are required to fill out spreadsheets for tracking working hours and activities, and with rewards closely tied to these tracking sheets.

With their deep experience of the prior firm's organizational routines, and a desire to avoid replicating the prior firm's failure, the five future founders met on a weekly basis and carefully planned which routines they would and would not transplant, even before embarking on the new venture. As one member of the founding TMT of the new firm put it:

> And then (we) got together and talked about, you know, what are we going to do with our company? And we looked at a lot of, at what G (the previous company) had done right in the beginning and then we used a lot of examples of what G had started doing wrong. And so we had a great, it's like we'd all been involved since almost the beginning at G and seeing them go from, you know, a few people to 120 people. And so we got to ride in that cycle and be part of it. And we got to see it then go wrong. So it was a great lab for us.

With deliberation and planning, the founders selectively imported the early engineer-centered organizational routines and stayed away from the set of routines on close monitoring and controlling. The founders believed that they had been able to learn about possible routines and practices from their experience with failures of their prior firm. This, they felt, allowed them to build a business that not only fit their values better, but was also able to out-compete the old firm. The old firm eventually entered bankruptcy, and the new firm was able to take over and retain most of the old firm's accounts. Essentially, prior experience served as a source of trial-and-error learning of the nature and impact of various organizational routines. The TMT picked out the organizational routines from their prior experience that they concluded had the most value.

Radical redeployment

New firms in our sample also extended existing routines to new domains, which we label "redeployment," as illustrated by Figure 8.2. For example, in some cases, members of the founding TMTs started their businesses with technical or scientific expertise but little or no business experience and/or few useful business contacts. In such cases, the founding team sometimes relied on the crude redeployment of existing routines from a very different context, but with which they were familiar, as a way to deal with business challenges. While this failed in some cases, in other cases such redeployment seemed to create idiosyncratic and useful routines.

In one case, a firm, founded by a group of software engineers with little business experience, faced a new challenge of how to bill customers efficiently in cases where they had no substantial relationship with a customer, but the customer called up and requested small or simple services. The founders had no experience with billing systems or common business routines for billing. Instead of asking someone to help them develop a billing routine, or buying an off-the-shelf billing and accounts receivable package, they used their experience in web design to develop their own web-based system for billing minor customers for minor requests, drawing on organizational routines from web design in other contexts.

The founders believed that their approach allowed them to optimize customer management during a time when they really couldn't afford to say "no" to any customer. One founder explained it this way:

> But on the profit side of things, we would never have said that if a client's going to call you once a month for $200, that's not worth your time. Instead we developed a system to make it very efficient to capture that $200 . . . right, they call you . . . on their web page. You know, you talk to them. You do what they need, hit a button on their web page. They get billed, period, end of story.

They were later able to further extend this innovative billing routine to other business domains. They believe that the information generated by their system – an unintended outcome – has allowed them to do much better systematic strategic planning. As one founder put it:

> We have records from, god, 1990, mid-1997 to the present, of every single hour billed, of every single minute billed to every single client and what was being done (for) that client. And we used that in our analysis last year to restructure the business. And we said, big . . . okay. What's our work really worth? What's the part of the work that we want to do among various classes and things we've been doing? And what's that part really worth? What will the market bear? How much of it will come? You know, if you do a $20 000 project for somebody, how much more could you get in the next year, and who can do it, you know? What does that person need to get paid?

Thus, the initial redeployments based on their technical expertise in web designs created a ripple effect across multiple business domains, and helped build organizational capabilities on billing system and strategic planning as well.

Recombination of routines from founding team experience

In some cases firms generated routines by combining elements of routines brought to the firm by different founders or by members of its external network, including for example, advisors, bankers, suppliers, and customers. We label this process "recombination," as illustrated in Figure 8.2.

In some instances, this process seemed to work quite smoothly. For example, founding TMT members of an applied genetics company recombined organizational routines associated with cloning cows learned through prior experiences to enact routines to clone pigs. These new technical routines had very important strategic value to the firm, and represented valuable capabilities that supported the firm's prosperity and survival.

In other cases, however, the recombination process generated confusion and even struggle. For example, when business people and scientists jointly formed a new start-up, the scientists frequently had no intellectual knowledge on a sound business model, while the business people had no or little familiarity with the nature of scientific development. As a result, the recombination was often characterized by a lack of a common conceptual framework, which can erect significant barriers to an effective recombination of splintered routines from individual founders. In these cases, substantial give and take and adjustments took place and the members of the founding TMT engaged in substantial evaluation and adjustment of their diverse knowledge structures before the adoption of collective routines.

In one instance, a scientist had a single patent for which he perceived multiple potential product applications in the pharmaceutical industry, including a promising cancer drug. His three business partners proposed a routine they had followed before, which involved focusing their resources on exploiting one relatively easy application and using this to generate cash flow for financing the development of other applications. However, the scientist continued to insist on following his previously successful routine of pursuing multiple simultaneous research paths, though couching his preferences in business terms. In the scientist's words, "So I thought well, okay, so maybe, I'm not a table slammer or anything like that, but I continued to be fairly strongly, we need to develop these. This product right here, you're telling me this is a billion dollar market. We can't just let that sit." For four years, the scientist continued investing resources in multiple projects simultaneously but none of the projects reached the stage where it might be commercialized. The product that eventually showed the most promise was not the one that any of the other three founders would have chosen to focus upon initially. Over time, the scientist began to appreciate the potential value of focused business routines, while the business partners started to see some value in keeping multiple scientific options open. The firm ended up with a firm-level development routine in which the most promising short-term projects would become the primary scientific focus, while other applications would be given less immediate attention. Instead of developing multiple potential drug development lines, the firm concentrated on applying its patent to treating a specific medical condition resulting from chemotherapy while keeping some work on other possibilities alive. Overall, the difficult and lengthy process of evaluating and integrating founders' knowledge of very different routines resulted in a new "recombination" routine that the founders viewed as contributing to their firm's success.

Recombination of routines known through advisors or partners
The members of the founding TMT were not limited to their own experience as sources of routines. Young firms rely on a wide variety of outside advisors and stakeholders as they emerge, and these same groups represent potential sources for the new firm's routines. Among all potential network members, an advisor plays an integral role in facilitating routine development in new firms. The network of advisors can be very informal, but nonetheless provide a support and governance function much like a formal board of directors in an established corporation. As one member of the top management team for an academic-based firm put it: "I never do things on my own, simply because I don't know it all. I make decisions with my five mentors. There are times where three people will say yes and two people will say no, I being one of the two people. It's kind of like a marriage. Sometimes you can lose on a one-to-one vote."

In this instance, the academic scientist founding team member had limited experience on most aspects of business operation, so she relied heavily on the experience of her five business advisors for developing new routines in her areas of responsibility. Whenever she attempted to build new routines in the young firm, she always went to the five advisors for their inputs. For example, the founding team member hired her best friend for marketing, but it turned out to be a total failure: her friend met only two potential customers in six months and spent most of her work time on private emailing and vacation. Entangled in the cross-fire of personal and professional relationship, she brought the issue to her advisors for a solution. By piecing together inputs from her five mentors, she successfully set up new routines on recruiting, which included, but were not limited to, a formal background check and group job interviews. This produced a general overall hiring routine, which was made up of lower-level subroutines for recruiting, evaluation, selection, and formal appointment. The recombination of routines drawn from her advisor network experiences, she believes, brought consistency to the new firm, "When I fired her, [the friend hired for marketing] it was objective, versus when I hired her, it was subjective."

SUMMARY: PRIOR TMT EXPERIENCE AS INFLUENCE ON ROUTINES IN NEW FIRMS

Taken as a whole, the data from the histories of these new firms suggested that prior experience represented a crucial source of routines for the organizations we studied. Founding TMT prior experience influenced firm strategies in product mix, sales force management, human resources strategies, strategic planning, and product development strategies.

Qualitative data of the sort we developed cannot test theories of causality, but can provide important evidence of the existence of a given phenomenon, and can reveal different types of a focal process. In this instance, the field data not only revealed that prior experience could lead to routines in a new organization, but also revealed several different pathways through which this can occur. The impact of prior experience, then, does not represent a single replication process in which routines simply move across organizational boundaries. At one extreme, it involves a quite automatic and relatively fast process in which TMT members enact routines with little reflection in new settings.

At another, it involves deliberate choices to pull in routines from prior settings into a new context.

Declarative and procedural knowledge and processes through which prior TMT experience impacts routines in a focal organization

Our data show different pathways through which prior experience affects the organizational routines enacted in the focal firm. However, they cannot answer the question of why different processes unfold at different times. We speculate that one important factor relates to the type of knowledge founders accumulated in their prior experience, relative to the routines in question. In some cases, members of the founding TMT had actually been the people responsible for performing routines at prior workplaces, rather than the people responsible for developing routines or deciding how or when to implement them. In other cases, members of the founding TMT had participated primarily in decision making or oversight of specific routines at prior firms, but had little actual "hands-on" knowledge of the performance of the routines.

In this situation, one would predict that the TMT members previously involved in implementation would have acquired considerable procedural knowledge. This type of knowledge can be seen as "know how" and involves an ability to carry out specific actions. Procedural knowledge differs from declarative knowledge, sometimes seen as "know why." It involves theoretical and informational knowledge, or the "understanding of the principles that govern a domain and of the interrelations between units of knowledge in a domain" (Rittle-Johnson et al., 2001, pp. 346–7). One key difference between these two types of knowledge is that procedural knowledge is typically tied to specific problem types and therefore is not widely generalizable, while declarative knowledge is more flexible and generalizable.

Procedural knowledge is closely associated with skills and habits, and it becomes automatic or accessible unconsciously over time (Cohen and Bacdayan, 1994; Moorman and Miner, 1998). When the members of the founding TMT have only procedural knowledge, routines from previous employers can be automatically activated with a simple cue from the environment. In the cases of automatic importation of organizational routines, we often observe the presence of a high level of procedural knowledge, combined with a lack of declarative knowledge within the founding team. In other words, if founding team members had strong procedural knowledge, simple cues might prompt them to enact a routine in a new setting, without strong links to cognitive activity or frameworks. Importation could be triggered by some weak, or even wrong, cues from the operating environment. This in turn implies that prior TMT experience influences later strategic behavior by the firm in some cases relatively automatically.

In summary, we conclude that evidence from TMT founding teams provides considerable support for the claim that one way prior experience shapes organizational strategic action is through the importation of organizational routines, enacted by both deliberate and emergent or automatic processes. These processes, we suggest, supplement and are not the same as the traditional TMT focus on cognitive biases and frameworks. Further, we suggest that the same core processes unfold not just in new firms, but in existing organizations. TMT members, we propose, accidentally and deliberately import routines (and combinations of routines) from prior organizational contexts in ways that shape firm strategies and outcomes. In the following section, we illustrate how our framework would interpret evidence about the impact TMT prior experience in top large-scale systematic research on TMTs with an eye to checking the plausibility of our framework given the rich existing literature on TMT impact.

COMPATIBILITY WITH EVIDENCE ON THE IMPACT OF TMT PRIOR EXPERIENCE

Substantial attention in the TMT literature has been paid to the importance of executives' international experiences on globalization (e.g., Reuber and Fischer, 1997; Tihanyi et al., 2000; Carpenter and Fredrickson, 2001; Carpenter et al., 2001). The results from these studies provide considerable support for the link between TMT international experience and firm performance (Carpenter et al., 2001), degree of internationalization (Reuber and Fischer, 1997), and firm global strategic posture (Carpenter and Fredrickson, 2001).

In this section we describe specific evidence that prior TMT experience shapes later firm-level behavior, flag more traditional explanations, and describe how the routines perspective would predict the same results. In addition, we suggest that the routines perspective is consistent with some of the apparent anomalies in these prior studies. We focus on the link between prior international experience and later outcomes because it is a well established area of strong work with fairly robust findings.

Evidence that International TMT Experience Shapes Later International Firm Behavior in Existing Firms

In an examination of 54 US-based Fortune 500 multinational manufacturing corporations, the mean number of years each executive on the TMT spent abroad on assignment was shown to relate positively to both the percentage of foreign sales to total sales (FSTS) and the percentage of foreign assets to total assets (FATA; Sambharya, 1996). The proportion of TMT members with some international experience was also found to relate positively to both FSTS and FATA. Another study of 126 firms operating in the US electronic industry between 1986 and 1988 provided further support for the positive link between top management team international experience and key international organizational outcomes. The average degree of international experience of the TMT members, based on an executive's international education and work experience, predicted the degree of international diversification, a composite of a firm's average FSTS and average number of foreign countries with subsidiary operations, after controlling for other important firm (size, prior performance) and TMT (average age, tenure, elite education, and various aspects of TMT heterogeneity) variables (Tihanyi et al., 2000).

Similarly, an examination of 49 Canadian software product firms found that TMTs for which CEOs had experience working outside of Canada and/or other TMT members possessed experience selling outside Canada, predicted the number of nonCanadian headquartered strategic partners and the firm's degree of internationalization, a composite of FSTS, percentage of employees who spend over half their time on international activities, and the geographic distance of sales (Reuber and Fischer, 1997). In another important study, Carpenter and Fredrickson (2001) studied 207 US industrial firms from 1984 to 1996 and examined the effects of TMT demographic characteristics on firms' global strategic posture, a composite measure varying slightly from Sullivan's (1994) measure and incorporating FSTS, FATA, and the presence of subsidiaries in cultural zones. The analyses support previous research demonstrating positive associations between international experience and internationalization.

Evidence Concerning New Firms

The link between international experience of top management teams and internationalization is not constrained to existing firms. In a sample of 61 venture capital-backed IPO firms from 1991, the number of TMT members with international work experience positively related to percentage of primary value chain activities (Porter, 1998) that a firm at least partially engaged in internationally (Bloodgood et al., 1996). McDougall et al. (1994) reported results that indicate firms characterized as international from birth are more often founded by management teams with international experience.

Causal Processes

Early upper echelons perspective research typically assumes that TMTs influence organizational outcomes through the cognitive biases, values, and perceptions developed over time through past experience (Hambrick and Mason, 1984). This traditional perspective offers rich possibilities about cognitive or individual-level processes through which prior experience shapes observed later actions. For example, TMT members can develop general cognitive frameworks in which they are aware of the possibility of international activities. It can also make international action seem more natural, feasible, and likely to have positive value.

Our framework differs because it focuses on organizational routines as a key potential pathway between executive experiences and organizational outcomes that can be distinguished from the cognitive influences. The organizational routines framework suggests that in addition to mental or personal cognitive assumptions or values, prior international experience exposed the TMT members to organizational routines specifically related to firm-level internationalization. In this causal pathway, the same types of processes described in our report of founding teams will shape firm behavior through different forms of importation and deployment of international-related activity. This idea is not foreign to the TMT literature, of course. For example, prior work has suggested that prior experience helps build knowledge related to coordination of routines in alliance-based international strategies (Barkema et al., 1997). However, prior work does not tend to clearly separate these processes, and does not differentiate between different pathways through which routines are imported or deployed.

The routine-based approach, however, offers an additional palette of different ways in which prior experience can shape future behavior, and would also explain the results described above. For example, a TMT member can automatically import international-related routines from prior experience into a new setting. Even micro-routines may affect firm-level behavior. A manager with prior experience may have standard marketing analysis software tools or reporting formats that include international issues and data sources, have communication patterns that automatically contact international sales outlets, have recruiting sources that involve international sources, or accounting processes that are set up to deal with international manufacturing partners. The TMT member can automatically use these micro-routines in executing various tasks, which will in turn enhance the chances of international action by the firm, even with no special mental biases. The existence of these routines might not only change the chances that the firm would take international action, but speed up its chances, since the operation of the new routines would not require thinking and planning. These processes could operate with relatively little linkage to deliberate higher-level planning in some cases.

In addition, selective importation of international routines offers another causal pathway. TMT members might more deliberately replicate subroutines within areas such as international marketing, production, shipping and sales routines that seemed to work in prior settings, while leaving behind others that did not. The existence of the original, apparently successful routines would shape behavior by offering immediate tools for taking action that look field tested. This behavior clearly could often take place after a decision to pursue international goals has occurred. We suggest, however, that the prior involvement with such routines can also trigger action, whether through automatic action or through increasing the chances of a positive international decision. Again, the routine-based part of the process would also affect the pace of action, because to assemble a combination of prior routines would presumably take less time than constructing completely new sets of systems.

Finally, TMT members could combine routines from their varied experience or networks with which they interact. For example, a TMT might move into certain countries with certain market sequencing strategies by combining country choice routines from one prior setting with market entry routines from another prior firm or setting. Or, the combined routines could come from interaction with advisors. The final action in these instances would not look like the automatic importation of a given routine, but a bundle of actions that combines routines from prior experience. The combination could involve subroutines within a given area – for example, manufacturing or marketing – or could combine routines from different operational areas. The possibility that the TMT draws on external partner routines to compose its own approaches seems consistent with research that indicates that the use of foreign strategic partnerships mediated the relationship between TMT international experience and the firm's degree of internationalization (Reuber and Fischer, 1997),

Moderation for the Effect of TMT International Experience

In addition to offering a potential additional pathway through which TMT experience directly influences firm strategic action, the routines pathway may lead to important moderation processes. Prior findings in these areas may even be more consistent with a routines-based pathway in some cases than a pure cognitive viewpoint.

For example, Hambrick and Mason (1984) argued that executive cognitions should influence organizational outcomes more when uncertainty is greater than when it is lower. Carpenter and Fredrickson (2001) examined the role uncertainty plays in the relationship between top management team characteristics and global strategic posture. Environmental uncertainty moderated the relationship between TMT demographics such as functional experience, educational and firm tenure heterogeneity, and global strategic posture. However, TMT international experience failed to display patterns consistent with the cognitive underpinnings of the upper echelons perspective. The pattern of results may be more consistent with a routines-based causal process in which the impact of the prior international experience occurred heavily through routines-based processes.

Summary

The routines-based pathway provides an alternative and additional set of micro-processes through which prior TMT international experience should enhance later international firm-level actions. From that viewpoint, the routines pathway provides a plausible rival interpretation of the prior literature on the impact of TMT experience on firm-level action. In addition we suggest that the routines pathway offers a window for interpreting some apparent anomalies in prior work, an area for further depth of inquiry.

We note that the cognitive and routines pathways are not mutually exclusive. As shown in our field reports, in some cases the routines pathway can dominate and trigger action. In others, routines and cognition intertwine in terms of core causality. In other cases, decision making follows standard patterns of goals and planning, and routines appear primarily as potential tools at hand. In these cases, the impact of prior routines known to TMT members may have greater impact through their influence on the timing or nature of specific actions. In theory one might even see the two pathways as potentially interactive themselves: it seems theoretically possible that the presence of prior routines and cognitive frameworks in combination might enhance each other's impact, so that their presence would be more than additive.

Importantly, however, at this point one cannot truly rule out either a cognitive or routines-based causal pathway as a major driver for the existing findings about TMT experience and strategic action and outcomes. Thus, we cannot falsify either approach through the findings reported above. This, we suggest, points to the importance of developing propositions grounded in the routines-based framework for two reasons. First it will be important to look for areas in which the cognitive and routines-based approaches will generate contrasting predictions. Second, it will be important to explore ways that the routines framework has nonobvious implications for important strategic issues such as the speed of strategic action.

SAMPLE PROPOSITIONS FOR RESEARCH ON THE ROUTINES-BASED FRAMEWORK

In this section we offer six propositions based on the routines framework. We do this for two reasons. First, testing these propositions should help tease out the relative contribution of routines-based processes versus a purely cognitive approach. Second, these propositions should help probe the potential theoretical value of the routines framework to generate different predictions based on which type of importation process is involved (automatic, selective, redeployment, recombination from prior employment or recombination from networks). We relate each proposition to the two general types of processes (primarily cognitive versus routines-based) and then develop implications of different routine-based pathways.

Similarity Between Routines in New and Prior Firms

If prior experience shapes general attitudes and goals, one would expect that the specific routines used in later contexts would match the specific demands of those contexts. The early experience would work through the goal of internationalization. The TMT members would pick action routines that reflect current aspirations or rational analysis of what should work best in a specific setting. In contrast, routines-based pathways should lead the later firm to enact specific routines imported or recombined from a prior setting. This similarity might be visible in artifacts such as handbooks, checklists, vendor directories, required operational procedures in manufacturing, and other quite distinct features of operational routines. If the impact of prior experience is broader, these specific artifacts would not be expected to closely resemble the prior setting's routines, but rather the functional demands of the new one. The routine-based viewpoint implies, then:

> *Proposition 1:* TMTs enact identifiable specific routines used in prior settings in a focal firm.

Type of Routine Importation Process and Degree of Similarity in New and Prior Firms

The degree of similarity between the focal firm's international activities, such as using the same partners for foreign strategic alliances, should vary depending on whether the organizational routines are automatically or selectively imported from past experiences, redeployed, or recombined. Organizational routines automatically or selectively imported are most likely to be similar to firms that previously employed members of the focal firm. Organizational routines recombined or redeployed are less likely to be similar, because the actions executed will combine parts of prior routines. They are still more likely to be similar, however, than if prior experience worked solely through cognitions. Therefore, the similarity between firm behavior of the focal firm and firms that previously employed TMT members will likely be moderated by how the organizational routine is enacted:

> *Proposition 2:* Automatically and selectively imported routines have greater similarity to routines in the site of prior TMT experience than routines involving recombination or redeployment.

Speed of Implementation

If a firm has a new TMT member with international experience, both cognitive and routines-based pathways predict greater chances of international action. This may also occur of course, because the executive was put on the team precisely to promote internationalization, not because of the prior experience itself.

There is little reason to believe however, that having *more* international experience will necessarily amplify an executive's cognitive urgency to attend to issues of globalization. However, strategic decisions to internationalize likely will be implemented faster when top management teams have more international organizational routines to consider and the time to the first international sale should decrease accordingly. As discussed in the section on founder importation, procedural knowledge embedded in routines typically can have faster execution than other types of knowledge. Having more experience increases the breadth of organizational routines available to the TMT. Notice our prediction differs from prior studies linking international experience to the speed at which a first international sale occurs (e.g., Reuber and Fischer, 1997) because we focus on the length of exposure to international experience. Therefore:

Proposition 3: The degree of international experience of new top management team members enhances the speed at which a first international sale occurs.

Type of Routine Importation Process and Speed of Implementation

Depending on whether or not the organizational routines are automatically or selectively imported from past experiences or recombined or redeployed, the time to the first international sale should vary. Decisions to automatically import organizational routines require less time and are easier than recombining or redeploying organizational routines. Selectively importing organizational routines requires more decision-making time than automatically importing organizational routines, which is the fastest way to use routines to solve problems. Recombining and redeploying organizational routines takes more time to implement than selectively importing because they require more coordination. Therefore:

Proposition 4: The type of organizational routine enacted affects the speed to the first international sale: firms with automatically and selectively imported routines have the shortest time to first international sale and recombined and redeployed routines have the longest times.

Impact of Variation in Prior Employment Affiliation

If prior experience merely influences the attention and field of vision of top management team members, the firm backgrounds of the TMT members would not affect the specific routines implemented in the new firm. Routines used would match the unique demands of the new context without regard to prior knowledge with the simple goal of internationalization. However, routines are embedded in prior managerial experiences and employee mobility is a key mechanism by which routines are passed from one firm to another (Phillips, 2005). TMT members are likely to carry with them organizational routines from their prior employers that are implemented in their existing firm.

TMT members with common firm backgrounds possess a shared understanding and knowledge of how to get things done. The common prior experience at the same firm provides TMT members with procedural knowledge of specific organizational routines. The routines-based pathways should lead TMT members with common firm backgrounds to enact organizational routines by automatically and selectively importing routines from their prior common employment with little to no need to make any adjustments because of the shared experience. Firms with TMT members possessing common prior company affiliations often adopt exploitative behaviors by utilizing their shared firm-specific knowledge including available routines (Beckman, 2006).

In contrast, TMT members that come from different firm backgrounds are more likely to possess a broader repertoire of routines from which to draw upon when implementing routines in the new firm. TMT members with international experience, but without common firm backgrounds, may have shared declarative knowledge regarding internationalization. When routines are implemented it will be more difficult for the TMT to automatically and selectively import routines. Rather, the TMT will likely implement routines that represent a recombination of existing routines from their varied employment experiences. Therefore:

> *Proposition 5a:* Given that there is prior international experience in the top management team, the degree to which the top management team shares the same firm background increases the likelihood that they automatically or selectively import routines.

> *Proposition 5b:* Given that there is prior international experience in the top management team, the degree to which the top management team comes from different firm backgrounds increases the likelihood that they recombine routines.

Impact of Variation in Prior Employment Affiliation and Speed of Implementation

If Proposition 5 is supported, TMTs with common firm backgrounds are more likely to automatically and selectively import routines, which requires less time and are easier to implement than recombining routines. The shared procedural knowledge gained from the common employment experiences allows for easier and faster routinization of activities in the new firm, which leads to shorter times to the first international sale. TMT members with a variety of firm backgrounds are more likely to recombine routines to develop new routines. This process of recombination requires more coordination, decision making, and time for implementation. Therefore:

> *Proposition 6:* Given that there is prior international experience in the top management team, the degree to which the top management team shares the same firm background increases the speed to the first international sale: firms with top management teams that share firm backgrounds have shorter times to first international sale than firms with top management teams from a variety of firm backgrounds.

DISCUSSION AND CONCLUSION

This chapter contributes to the top management team literature by proposing a distinct theoretical causal pathway through which TMT experience shapes organizational strategies and outcomes. We argue that executives' experiences can spur the use of organizational routines that in turn alter key firm outcomes. This process can work in addition to and even separately from cognitive biases and dispositions. We first report a study of founding top management teams that revealed five specific ways in which prior experience led to organizational routines in new firms. We then argued that such processes provide a plausible causal pathway consistent with important empirical results in the TMT literature. Finally, we developed six testable propositions that point to ways in which our proposed causal mechanisms can generate distinct outcomes that either complement or contrast with the results predicted by standard cognitive pathways. Different routines-based processes will generate different strategic actions and – through these – predictably different outcomes. In work in progress, we are developing additional implications for outcomes in terms of strategic actions taken, speed of action, and performance implications of routine-based causal pathways.

Contributions to Other Literature

Research exploring these processes will contribute to strategy research that emphasizes path dependence and the role of routines (Phillips, 2005; Beckman, 2006; Beckman and Burton, 2008). If our routine-based framework has explanatory power, it implies *cross-organizational* path dependence in the development of key firm actions. In addition, the routines perspective has implications for the important outcomes of speed of strategic action. More broadly, the routine-based causal processes can be seen as forms of bricolage – defined as using and combining resources at hand (Baker et al., 2003; Baker and Nelson, 2005). The routines and TMT prior experience framework implies that bricolage may occur when a TMT combines routines across time, from varied prior settings, in addition to combining routines from varied members of a current network (Baker et al., 2003). Unlike prior work in bricolage, this perspective portrays bricolage as a process that may be actively *negotiated* among stakeholders – in the current case among members of the TMT. The routine-based causal processes can also be seen as forms of improvisation, "making it up as you go along" formally defined as "the deliberate and substantive fusion of the design and execution of novel production" (Miner et al., 2001, p. 314). It is easy to envision improvisation as a tactical activity designed to pursue larger goals. The routine-based framework developed here implies that improvisational action may have lasting and strategic impact. This advances prior work that proposed strategic improvisation in young firms but did not develop the strategic viewpoint at length in the context of existing firms (Miner et al., 2001; Baker et al., 2003; Gong, 2007).

The routines framework has practitioner value in addition to theoretical promise. If the propositions are supported, for example, they would have implications for a focal firm hiring new members of a TMT to promote internationalization. They imply that when firms consider new TMT candidates, they should inquire about a candidate's experience and knowledge of specific implementation practices (routines) encountered in prior settings, not just about general international experience. A firm seeking to internationalize rapidly could be better off adding new TMT members coming from a single prior employer, rather than from varied employers, to enhance the chances of shared routines being deployed without negotiation or other delays. Beyond issues of internationalization, the implications would hold more generally any time a firm sought to move into any new area or set of tasks and was considering new TMT members.

CONCLUSION

Our speculation regarding the potential impact of different forms of importing routines from prior settings offers a promising line of work, we hope, for the TMT literature. We see the work as theory building and exploratory, and invite others to both challenge and deepen the framework as it develops.

REFERENCES

Baker, T. and Nelson, R. (2005). Creating something from nothing: Resource construction through entrepreneurial bricolage. *Administrative Science Quarterly*, **50**(3), 329–66.
Baker, T., Miner, A., and Eesley, D. (2003). Improvising firms: bricolage, account giving and improvisational competencies in the founding process. *Research Policy*, **32**(2), 255–76.
Barkema, H., Shenkar, O., Vermeulen, F., and Bell, J. (1997). Working abroad, working with others: How firms learn to operate international joint ventures. *The Academy of Management Journal*, **40**(2), 426–42.
Barney, J. and Arikan, A. (2001). The resource-based view: Origins and implications. In M.A. Hitt, E.Freeman, and J.Harrison (eds), *The Blackwell handbook of strategic management*.
Beckman, C. (2006). The influence of founding team company affiliations on firm behavior. *Academy of Management Journal*, **49**(4), 741–58.
Beckman, C. and Burton, M. (2008). Founding the future: Path dependence in the evolution of top management teams from founding to IPO. *Organization Science*, **19**, 3–24.
Bloodgood, J., Sapienza, H., and Almeida, J. (1996). The internationalization of new high-potential US ventures: Antecedents and outcomes. *Entrepreneurship: Theory and Practice*, **20**(4), 61–76.
Boeker, W. (1997). Strategic change: The influence of managerial characteristics and organizational growth. *Academy of Management Journal*, **40**(1), 152–70.
Carpenter, M. and Fredrickson, J. (2001). Top management teams, global strategic posture, and the moderating role of uncertainty. *Academy of Management Journal*, **44**(3), 533–45.
Carpenter, M., Geletkanycz, M., and Sanders, W. (2004). Upper echelons research revisited: Antecedents, elements, and consequences of top management team composition. *Journal of Management*, **30**(6), 749–78.
Carpenter, M., Sanders, W., and Gregersen, H. (2001). Building human capital with organizational context: The impact of international assignment on multinational firm performance and CEO pay. *Academy of Management Journal*, **44**(3), 493–511.
Cohen, M. and Bacdayan, P. (1994). Organizational routines are stored as procedural memory: Evidence from a laboratory study. *Organization Science*, **5**(4), 554–68.
Cyert, R. and March, J. (1963). *A behavioral theory of the firm*. Englewood Cliffs, NJ: Prentice-Hall.
Day, G. (1994). The capabilities of market-driven organizations. *Journal of Marketing*, **58**(4), 37–52.
Denzin, N. and Lincoln, Y. (1998). *Collecting and interpreting qualitative materials*. Thousand Oaks, CA: Sage Publications Inc.
Eisenhardt, K. and Schoonhoven, C. (1990). Organizational growth: Linking founding team, strategy, environment, and growth among US semiconductor ventures, 1978–1988. *Administrative Science Quarterly*, **35**(3), 504–29.
Feldman, M. (2000). Organizational routines as a source of continuous change. *Organization Science*, **11**(6), 611–29.
Feldman, M. and Pentland, B. (2003). Reconceptualizing organizational routines as a source of flexibility and change. *Administrative Science Quarterly*, **48**(1), 94–121.
Gong, Y. (2007). Dancing around improvisation: Advisor network and improvisation migration in new firms. Unpublished doctoral dissertation, University of Wisconsin–Madison.
Hambrick, D. (2007). Upper echelons theory: An update. *Academy of Management Review*, **32**(2), 334–43.
Hambrick, D. and Mason, P. (1984). Upper echelons: The organization as a reflection of its top managers. *Academy of Management Review*, **9**(2), 193–206.
Kim, J., Kim, J., and Miner, A. (2009). Organizational learning from extreme performance experience: The impact of success and recovery experience. *Organization Science*, **20**(6), 958–78.
Knott, A. (2003). The organizational routines factor market paradox. *Strategic Management Journal*, **24**(10), 929–43.
Kor, Y. (2003). Experience-based top management team competence and sustained growth. *Organization Science*, **14**(6), 707–19.
Levitt, B. and March, J. (1988). Organizational learning. *Annual Reviews in Sociology*, **14**(1), 319–38.
McDougall, P., Phillips, P., Shane, S., and Oviatt, B. (1994). Explaining the formation of international new ventures: The limits of theories from international business research. *Journal of Business Venturing*, **9**, 469–87.
Miner, A. (1991). Organizational evolution and the social ecology of jobs. *American Sociological Review*, **56**(6), 772–85.

Miner, A., Bassoff, P., and Moorman, C. (2001). Organizational improvisation and learning: A field study. *Administrative Science Quarterly*, **46**(2), 304–37.

Moorman, C. and Miner, A. (1997). The impact of organizational memory on new product performance and creativity. *Journal of Marketing Research*, **34**, 91–106.

Moorman, C. and Miner, A. (1998). Organizational improvisation and organizational memory. *Academy of Management Review*, **23**(4), 698–723.

Nelson, R. and Winter, S. (1982). *An evolutionary theory of economic change*. Cambridge, MA: Belknap Press.

Ocasio, W. (1997). Towards an attention-based view of the firm. *Strategic Management Journal*, **18**(S1), 187–206.

Penrose, E. (1959). *The theory of the growth of the firm*. New York, NY: John Wiley and Sons.

Phillips, D. (2002). A genealogical approach to organizational life chances: The parent–progeny transfer among Silicon Valley law firms, 1946–1996. *Administrative Science Quarterly*, **47**(3), 474–508.

Phillips, D. (2005). Organizational genealogies and the persistence of gender inequality: The case of Silicon Valley law firms. *Administrative Science Quarterly*, **50**(3), 440–72.

Porter, M. (1998). *Competitive advantage: Creating and sustaining superior performance: With a new introduction*. New York: Free Press.

Ragin, C. (1989). *The comparative method: Moving beyond qualitative and quantitative strategies*. Berkeley and LA, CA: Univ. of California Press.

Ray, G., Barney, J., and Muhanna, W. (2004). Capabilities, business processes, and competitive advantage: Choosing the dependent variable in empirical tests of the resource-based view. *Strategic Management Journal*, **25**(1), 23–37.

Reuber, A.R. and Fischer, E. (1997). The influence of the management team's international experience on the internationalization behaviors of SMEs. *Journal of International Business Studies*, **28**(4), 807–25.

Rittle-Johnson, B., Siegler, R., and Alibali, M. (2001). Developing conceptual understanding and procedural skill in mathematics: An iterative process. *Journal of Educational Psychology*, **93**(2), 346–62.

Sambharya, R. (1996). Foreign experience of top management teams and international diversification strategies of US multinational corporations. *Strategic Management Journal*, **17**(9), 739–46.

Strauss, A. and Corbin, J. (1998). *Basics of qualitative research: Techniques and procedures for developing grounded theory*. Thousand Oaks, CA: Sage Publications.

Sullivan, D. (1994). Measuring the degree of internationalization of a firm. *Journal of International Business Studies*, **25**(2), 325–42.

Teece, D., Pisano, G., and Shuen, A. (1997). Dynamic capabilities and strategic management. *Strategic Management Journal*, **18**(7), 509–33.

Tihanyi, L., Ellstrand, A., Daily, C., and Dalton, D. (2000). Composition of the top management team and firm international diversification. *Journal of Management*, **26**(6), 1157–77.

Walsh, J.P. and Ungson, G.R. (1991). Organizational memory. *Academy of Management Review*, **16**(1), 57–91.

Winter, S. (2000). The satisficing principle in capability learning. *Strategic Management Journal*, **21**, 981–96.

9 Corporate elite career experiences and strategic preferences: the case of the Chinese corporate governance reform

Wm. Gerard (Gerry) Sanders and Anja Tuschke

In the past several decades, research on top executives has grown steadily, largely as a result of Hambrick and Mason's (1984) influential upper echelons framework (Carpenter et al., 2004; Finkelstein et al., 2009). At a theoretical level, top managers process stimuli through filters comprised of values and cognition. They make strategic choices based on how they process these stimuli, and those choices affect important organizational outcomes. Top management's values and cognitive base are developed in numerous ways, such as through indigenous culture, education, and work experiences. As Carpenter et al. (2004) note, the upper echelons perspective is also a methodological orientation that proposes that demographic characteristics serve as useful proxies for unobserved cognitive and psychological properties of top managers. Such a perspective generally assumes that the observed proxies tap into relatively stable managerial properties. However, a number of cognitive properties are developed over time through experience, and thus even mature managers may develop along different pathways from colleagues who otherwise appear to be homogeneous on a number of the dimensions that upper echelons research typically focuses on (e.g., tenure, age, functional background).

Only recently have scholars started to analyze the evolution of demographic distributions among the firm's upper echelons (Beckman and Burton, 2008). Consistent with this recent work, we assume that managerial values and preferences develop over time through foundational experiences. However, these foundational experiences may also play important roles in preparing and qualifying managers for positions at the pinnacle of organizations (Carpenter et al., 2001). Moreover, it is important to recognize that individuals with certain background experiences and capabilities may be more attractive to certain companies and certain types of companies may be more attractive to them as places of employment. The formation of the corporate upper echelons is an endogenous and dynamic formative process. In this chapter we focus on particular aspects of managerial experience that are developed over time and which may uniquely qualify managers for positions at the top. Consequently, we take steps to explicitly account for the endogeneity of these experiences and investigate how such experiential pathways affect the values and preferences of the corporate elite decision-making body as evidenced by the choices they make regarding corporate governance reform.

Our empirical context is novel and relevant to such an inquiry. We examine how governmental work experiences and western experiences of the Chinese corporate elite[1] influence the propensity of Chinese publicly traded firms to adopt western-style corporate governance mechanisms. We focus specifically on the evolution of the composition of the corporate board of directors through the appointment of independent (outside) directors. Stock markets re-emerged in China in 1990 in Shanghai and Shenzhen and since that time corporate governance practices have gradually evolved as investors have sought greater protections. Prompted by corporate scandals, the China Security and Regulatory Commission (CSRC) released a Code of Corporate Governance for Listed Companies in 2002. The Code largely follows the US regulatory system by tightening the supervision of the firm's top management, elevating requirements related to the disclosure of information, and introducing independent directors (Rajagopalan and Zhang, 2008). Thus, the context provides an interesting natural experiment to investigate how top management's formative experiences affect the evolution of firms' governance choices.

The upper echelons perspective, like most theories of management, had its genesis in western culture. Because of its collectivist and authoritarian culture, research suggests that individual career experiences among the Chinese corporate elite may have less influence on values and cognition, and thus less influence on strategic choices (Crossland and Hambrick, 2007). Consequently, using the Chinese corporate elite as an empirical context imposes both an interesting context and conservative constraint on our empirical tests.

RECENT UPPER ECHELONS RESEARCH – AND BEYOND

The upper echelons perspective proposes that organizational actions and outcomes are fundamentally a function of managerial characteristics and experiences (Hambrick and Mason, 1984). Research on the corporate elite has capitalized on early empirical studies linking top management characteristics and experiences to firm strategies (e.g., Bantel and Jackson, 1989; Finkelstein and Hambrick, 1990; Smith et al., 1991) and firm performance (e.g., D'Aveni, 1990; Haleblian and Finkelstein, 1993). In addition, upper echelons research has documented that characteristics of the corporate elite help explain numerous firm phenomena such as interfirm rivalry (Lyon and Ferrier, 2002), alliances (Eisenhardt and Schoonhoven, 1990), internationalization (Sambharya, 1996; Sanders and Carpenter, 1998), and achieving early milestones in entrepreneurial firms (Beckman and Burton, 2008). More recently, Miner, Gong, Baker and O'Toole, in Chapter 8 of this volume, explore how prior experiences of founding TMTs influence firm outcomes through the routines deployed in new firms.

An important trend in recent research involves the extension of the original upper echelons model to the global arena. A number of studies link top management characteristics to various aspects of firm globalization like international involvement (Sambharya, 1996), international partnerships (Reuber and Fischer, 1997), firm global strategic posture (Sanders and Carpenter, 1998; Tihanyi et al., 2000), globalization strategies of IPOs (Carpenter et al., 2003), and multinational firm performance (Carpenter et al., 2001). A significant advance emanating from this focus on international contexts is the identification of critical job experiences, such as formative international work assignments. Specific career experiences, particularly those that are relatively rare and rich in opportunities to learn and extend personal networks, infuse the top management team with perspectives lacking in teams absent executives with such experiences (ibid.). Alternatively, individuals deeply embedded in their domestic institutional environment can develop cognitive patterns, values, and biases that result in favoring local strategies and resisting outside pressures (Kraatz and Moore, 2002; Sanders and Tuschke, 2007).

Research on international and domestic managerial experience effects, like most management research, has been primarily documented in western contexts (see Wiersema and Bird, 1993 for a notable exception). Consequently, little is known about the experience distributions of Chinese managers. Yet, Chinese firms are embedded in a cultural, legal, and economic environment far different than those in which most published research in management is conducted (Tsui, 2006). Given the scant direct empirical evidence of upper echelons effects in China (Gu, 2008; Li and Tang, 2010), the extent to which the upper echelons perspective describes strategic decision processes and outcomes in China is not clear. Therefore, the first purpose of this study is to identify and document the level and types of international and domestic professional work experiences that might be formative among the Chinese corporate elite.

In contrast to the predominant view of extant upper echelons research, we assume that relevant and influential managerial experiences within the Chinese corporate elite may not be exogenous. Specifically, managers may ascend to the ranks of the elites because they possess some unobserved traits, characteristics, or connections. Moreover, executives and directors with particular skills and experiences may be drawn to organizations that have particular need for these skills. Thus, the second purpose of this study is to account, to the degree possible, for the endogenous nature of the developmental experiences and the "matching" of individuals with firms.

The third purpose of our study is to extend research on the upper echelons perspective by integrating it with coercive isomorphism, resource dependence theory (Pfeffer and Salancik, 1978), and the concept of familiarity that is closely linked with imprinting of experiences (Lay and Verkuyten, 1999) and cognitive schema theory (Fiske and Taylor, 1984; DiMaggio, 1997). From the perspectives of coercive isomorphism and resource dependency, managers are responding to requirements and wishes of important constituents in order to manage the firm's external dependencies (Lester et al., 2008). Due to the cultural tendencies of authoritarianism, Chinese managers may be more likely to willingly conform to directives issued by regulators than managers in the West. However, certain types of career experiences may influence this tendency to follow the lead of the central government. Work experience in the government may make elites more susceptible to coercive pressures. Alternatively, an increasing familiarity with western-type corporate governance policies is likely to influence the cognitive base of Chinese managers, thereby making them more open towards governance mechanisms that those without similar experience may overlook or misinterpret (cf., Hargadon and Douglas, 2001). We expect that both types of career experiences – governmental experience and western – will not only help managers on their way to the firm's upper echelons but also will shape their cognitive predispositions and will thus influence subsequent decision making.

Our preliminary field work in China led us to focus on two types of experience that are likely to be important sources of heterogeneity across Chinese corporate elites: governmental experience (e.g., through party membership and government positions) and western experiences (e.g., through birth, educational, and work assignment experiences). These types of life experiences represent very formative backgrounds relative to those lacking them and may have significant influence on managers' cognition and choices. Whereas governmental experience in China reflects closeness to the accustomed collectivist and authoritarian culture, western experience may increase the corporate elite's willingness to accept foreign ideas and practices. Against the background of this unique setting the fourth purpose of our study is to link upper echelons research to choices regarding the firm's corporate governance. We examine the effects of the Chinese corporate elite's heterogeneous career experiences in the context of restructuring boards with more independent directors.

CORPORATE GOVERNANCE REFORM IN CHINA[2]

China's Company Law, passed in December 1993 (and amended in 1999), initiated the modern evolution of China's corporate governance reforms. The law stipulates the rights and responsibilities of shareholders, the board of directors, and managers (Rajagopalan and Zhang, 2008). All limited liability companies were required to set up a board of directors, and large companies were required to implement an additional oversight group known as the board of supervisors, consisting of at least three independent (i.e., non-company) supervisors. The law also gives shareholders the right to appoint and to remove directors and supervisors, and to decide their remuneration. In this study, we do not focus on the supervisory board because they are not part of the main decision-making bodies and because research has suggested that they are dysfunctional and not effective at monitoring (Xi, 2006; Jia et al., 2009)

Corporate scandals in 2001 prompted officials of the CSRC and other state regulatory bodies to further improve Chinese firms' governance. In January 2002, the CSRC released its Code of Corporate Governance for Listed Companies in China, which aims to establish solid corporate governance in stock market listed companies by, among other things, introducing independent director systems, and tightening the supervision of corporate management (Shi and Weisert, 2002). The code also expands the rights of shareholders, mandating that minority shareholders should have equal status with other shareholders and giving shareholders the right to protect their interests through civil litigation and other legal actions. On the other hand, the code gave institutional investors more weight in the decision-making process, including the nomination of directors. In an attempt to strengthen the roles of the board of directors the code required that listed companies have at least two independent (i.e., outside) directors on or before 30 June, 2002, increasing to a ratio of one-third independent directors on or before 30 June, 2003 (Zhang, 2007).

HYPOTHESES DEVELOPMENT

Formal education and work experiences help to form managerial skill sets and distinctive worldviews, along with networks of personal and professional ties. For those reasons, Hambrick and Mason (1984) argued that important organizational outcomes would reflect characteristics of firms' "upper echelons." Extending this view, we believe that relevant and influential managerial experiences within the corporate elite may not be exogenous. Specifically, managers may ascend to the ranks of the upper echelons because they possess particular traits, characteristics, or experiences. Moreover, firms and managers/directors likely engage in a mutual matching process whereby firms proactively look for certain types of human and social capital and individuals look for organizations where their experiences will be more valuable. Thus, while traits, characteristics, and experiences are likely to shape management's values and cognition, thereby influencing firm choices, it is important to account for the selection process.

In contrast to the western context that predominates upper echelons research China was a geographically isolated and closed nation, until relatively recent times. Isolation leads to the evolution of homogeneous societies that exhibit high degrees of insularity and particularism (Clark, 1979). Under these circumstances, the values and cognition of Chinese managers are developed through a uniform cultural environment and rather similar educational and work assignment experiences.

Based on preliminary field interviews and anecdotal evidence, we expect that the Chinese corporate elite is not as homogeneous as one might first assume. Reform in China has led to significant growth of for-profit corporations, opening up thousands of managerial opportunities. Likewise, the opening up of China and the relaxed controls on Chinese citizens seeking foreign education, and particularly education in the West, has infused the managerial labor pool with more heterogeneity than existed pre-reform. Nevertheless, despite these market and societal reforms, China is still unique in the relative strong hand of central control. Consequently, career experiences within the corporate hierarchy that allow firms to manage the resource dependency with the state might be critical. Yet not all Chinese firms are on equal footing with respect to corporate elites with these experiences.

We expect that the Chinese corporate elite will reflect heterogeneity in their degree of western experience and their subsequent familiarity with western-type corporate policies and practices. Likewise, organizations are likely to vary in the degree to which their elites possess significant governmental experiences. Based on an upper echelons framework, we theorize that both western experience and governmental experience will affect the degree to which corporate elites are receptive to making changes in the organization's corporate governance.

Western Experience

We consider three types of experiences that familiarize the Chinese corporate elite with the West: being born in the West, western education, and work assignments in the West. Chinese managers who have had major life experiences in the West have been exposed to western ideas and philosophies in ways that those without this specific experience cannot attain. One of the relevant philosophies that Chinese confront when living, studying, and working in West, is the capitalist economic ideology. Against a western cultural background characterized by a strong tendency towards individualism and relatively low power distance (Hofstede and Hofstede, 2005), Chinese students and managers gain first-hand experience with the working of the free market. Specifically, they learn about the benefits and pitfalls of the separation of ownership and control (Jensen and Meckling, 1976) and how to efficiently govern companies in a capitalist society.

Chinese who are born in the West have significant developmental and imprinting experiences that alter the way they view the world and themselves (Rosenthal and Feldman, 1992; Lay and Verkuyten, 1999). And while western-born Chinese retain a strong Chinese identity, they also develop an identity with the West (Lay and Verkuyten, 1999). Consequently, their personalities and values tend to differ from those of native Chinese.

The corporate elite's values, beliefs, and abilities, as well as their resulting actions, are also shaped by their educational experiences (Hambrick and Mason, 1984). A degree from a western university, for instance, may influence how members of the corporate elite handle complex information, engage in boundary-spanning activities, and receive the adoption of innovations (cf., Young et al., 2001).

A western education introduces Chinese managers to new ways of thinking about work, economics, and corporate strategies. It also gives them the tools to acquire a deep understanding of corporate policies and practices around the world. Application of these analytical processes and tools is likely to help shape the executives' cognitive base. As a consequence, they are more likely to possess the cognitive structures that they need to become aware of new business practices and to assess their potential economic efficiency. Cognitive schema theory helps explain this phenomenon. A schema is a "cognitive structure that represents organized knowledge about a given concept or type of stimulus" (Fiske and Taylor, 1984, p. 140). It directs specific individual action and understanding (DiMaggio, 1997), helps actors to become aware of new information in their environment, and guides the understanding and interpretation of this information. In the absence of a link to an existing cognitive structure, however, a new practice or policy is likely to go unnoticed or to be misunderstood.

Executives with a western education develop the absorptive capacity to scan the global environment for best practices. Therefore, western education not only influences executives' values, beliefs, and abilities but also serves as an informal link to other institutional contexts. Consistent with this logic, Sanders and Tuschke (2007) found that large German firms managed by executives with a graduate business education (which exposed them to business practices from the US and UK) were more likely to adopt US-styled stock option plans, which were actually illegal in Germany until 1996.

Theoretical and anecdotal evidence also suggests that executives with international assignment experience develop unique sets of skill to the extent that such experiences among CEOs and TMTs is associated with higher levels of firm performance (e.g., Sanders and Carpenter, 1998; Tihanyi et al., 2000; Carpenter et al., 2001, 2003). Roth (1995) found, for instance, that among medium-sized firms in global industries, CEO international assignment experience was positively related to income growth in companies with high levels of international interdependence (i.e., internal coordination needs across borders). Carpenter et al. (2001) reported that US MNCs achieved higher levels of firm performance when their CEOs and TMTs possessed international assignment work experiences.

Independent of the type of western experience (i.e., early life experiences, formal education, work assignment), the cognitive predispositions of Chinese managers will be influenced by an increasing familiarity with western-type corporate governance policies. Becoming familiar with norms and values that vary in fundamental ways from those of their home environment is likely to broaden the cognitive base of Chinese managers. They learn that some corporate practices and policies, although uncommon in their home environment, are accepted in the western world and are widely used by prestigious firms. As a result, these managers may weaken the historical cultural bias against western practices and policies and re-evaluate previous homogeneous values and beliefs rooted in their home culture. In addition, the likelihood of an unbiased assessment of the economic consequences of respective corporate governance mechanisms should increase.

Chinese managers who are familiar with western policies and practices are likely to be more open towards perceiving, assessing, and adopting novelties that those without similar experience may never have been exposed to (cf., Hargadon and Douglas, 2001). Acquiring a deep familiarity with western corporate policies and practices through early life experiences, formal education, or work assignments, Chinese managers possess knowledge that is valuable and still rare in the home environment. If corporate elite western experience truly results in a broadened worldview and superior professional network relationships, then its presence should be reflected in different strategic behaviors. This relationship is summarized in the following hypothesis:

> *Hypothesis 1:* The propensity of large Chinese firms to add outside directors to the board is positively associated with the level of the upper echelon's western experience.

The preceding hypotheses addressed how familiarity with western corporate policies and practices should influence Chinese corporate elites to be more receptive to adopting western governance conventions, specifically the addition of outsider board members that increase the independence of the board of directors. We now turn our attention to the influence of governmental experiences and ties that help the Chinese corporate elite to manage their resource dependencies and increase their likelihood of answering requests of governmental authorities.

Government Affiliations and Experience

In the Chinese authoritarian culture, government affiliations and experiences are likely to be of importance for the corporate elite. There are a number of ways for Chinese managers to establish these affiliations and experiences. Managers can, for instance, be employed by a government agency, have a seat on the company's Communist Party committee, be a member of the Chinese Communist Party (CCP), the National People's Congress (NPC), or the Chinese People's Political Consultative Conference (CPPCC). Although we don't expect that these affiliations are equally strong, they are all likely to help shape the cognitive base of Chinese managers and influence their subsequent decision making.

Without western experience, Chinese upper echelons are mostly embedded in traditional Chinese governance norms and values that leave little room for independent firm oversight. Left to their own preferences, Chinese elite managers cannot be expected to be prominent adopters of western governance practices. However, one key mechanism that encourages firms to break from historical patterns is coercive isomorphism (DiMaggio and Powell, 1983). In the context of Chinese corporate governance reform, the central government has enacted revised policies dictating at least nominal increases in board independence (nominal by western standards, monumental by Chinese historic norms Rajagopalan and Zhang, 2008). Tight affiliations with the local institutional environment increase pressure to conform to government standards. Although all Chinese firms are subject to the same governance laws and regulations, the pressure to conform is especially strong when mechanisms embed the firm in the socio-political institutional environment. This should particularly be the case in a strong institutional environment like that of the PRC. As a result, governmental experience and affiliations should influence the Chinese corporate elite towards being more predisposed to accept an otherwise distasteful western-style oversight mechanism (cf., Fligstein, 1991).

Corporate upper echelons with affiliations and ties to the government possess social capital in the form of "actual and potential resources embedded within, available through, and derived from the network of relationships possessed by an individual or social unit" (Nahapiet and Ghoshal, 1998, p. 243). According to Pfeffer and Salancik (1978), firms need to access and exploit these resources, which are also being sought by rival organizations, in order to ensure profitability and survival. Consequently, Chinese upper echelons that have established network ties to the government may be better able to manage their resource dependencies. However, these network ties come at a cost. In order to develop and maintain government affiliations, Chinese managers are likely to be under pressure to answer the requests of government officials. In the early 2000s, one of these requests was to improve governance through adding independent directors to the management board and the supervisory board.

To adopt practices that deviate significantly from what was previously taken for granted in the home institutional environment, organizations require mechanisms to help educate them about alternative norms, customs, and even the potential economic efficiency of a particular practice (Sanders and Tuschke, 2007). Absent ties to other institutional environments where a practice is already taken for granted, rules and regulations may exert pressure on an organization to adopt a practice that still lacks legitimacy. Especially those organizations that are deeply embedded in an institutional environment will be more likely to follow the lead of the institutional rule makers (D'Aunno et al., 1991). Therefore, we expect Chinese firms managed by corporate elites with strong affiliations with the Chinese government to more swiftly adhere to new governance rules and regulations including the adoption of independent directors.

We argue that organizations assess the desirability and legitimacy of new practices not only on the basis of how those practices are perceived from a practical business perspective, but also in relation to how the practice is perceived in its home institutional environment. Consequently, the likelihood that a western strategy will be adopted is a function of just how embedded the corporate elite is within the local institutional environment. Firms deeply embedded in the socio-political hierarchy will be most subject to the coercive pressures to conform to the governance reform regulations.

Taken together, our arguments suggest that strong ties to the Chinese socio-political environment will increase the likelihood that a firm will adopt government-directed corporate governance reform. Thus, we propose:

Hypothesis 2: The propensity of large Chinese firms to add outside directors to the board will be positively associated with the level of the upper echelon's government experience (e.g., work and political positions).

METHOD

Sample and Data

The China 100 was our sampling frame; a list compiled annually by *Fortune* magazine detailing the largest publicly traded Chinese firms. We attempted to collect data on these firms between 2000 and 2006. Our collection efforts yielded complete data on

74 firms. A means test indicated that the 26 excluded firms were somewhat smaller on average than those for which we had complete data. Data were compiled from company annual reports, stock exchange filings, company websites, and GTA, a data warehousing company located in Shenzhen, China.

Dependent Variables

The hypotheses address the evolution of the board of directors of Chinese public companies and the shift toward more independent boards. Thus, the dependent variable, *outside board additions*, was measured as the number of independent outside board members added to the board of directors between 2001 and 2006.

Independent Variables

The independent variables in our hypotheses relate to the career experiences of members of the Chinese firms' upper echelons, including both members of the TMT and the board of directors. We coded the corporate elite resumés in several ways to capture the extent and nature of their backgrounds, exposure to western markets, and experience within the Chinese socio-political system.

   Corporate elite *western experience* was assessed by gauging the degree of experience along three dimensions: western work assignment experiences, western educational experiences, and western living experiences due to being born overseas. We first coded experiences variables at the level of the individual member of the corporate elite. As indicated above and described in detail below, formative life experiences may not be random, exogenous events and may have a bearing on which executives are recruited to (or self-selected to) specific companies. We used an indicator variable to reflect whether a member of the corporate elite had western assignment experience. The variable was coded 1 if said member had western experience, 0 otherwise. A member of the corporate elite was coded as having western assignment work experience if she or he spent at least one year of their career assigned to an operation in the West. We coded work experiences as being western if they were located in Hong Kong, Australia, North America, and Western European countries.[3] We attempted to collect data on the number of years and breadth of experience represented by these western assignment experiences, but this data was missing in most instances. The second indicator of western experience was western education. We coded an elite's *western education* as 1 if the individual obtained at least one degree from a western university, 0 otherwise. In addition, we also collected data on the country of origin of all executives. Some Chinese corporate elite are foreign-born Chinese and they may have developed similar worldviews and western bias before moving back to the PRC. Foreign-born Chinese were coded as 1 if they were born in the West, 0 otherwise.

   To transform individual-level data to group-level data, we explored several means of aggregation, including summation and factor analysis. In the end, the results were consistent regardless of the method employed. For ease of interpretation, we report the results with the simple and straightforward summation measures. *Western experience* was thus measured as a sum of sums. We summed western assignment experience, western education, and western-born indicators at the level of the individual, and then aggregated these individual values at the firm level to form a composite measure of western experience.

There are several ways that the corporate elite may have experiences with the social political establishment. For instance, a member of the corporate elite may have a seat on the company's Communist Party committee. In addition, the elite may be members of the Chinese Communist Party (CCP), members of the National People's Congress (NPC), or members of the Chinese People's Political Consultative Conference (CPPCC). Finally, a member of the corporate elite may be currently or previously (or concurrently) employed by a government agency. While potentially varying in strength, each of these types of experiences should result in the members of the elite to be more exposed to and affected by the values of the central government.

To gauge the extent to which the corporate elite has work experience in the socio-political milieu of China, we again followed the routine of coding the experiences of individual members of the corporate elite, and then aggregating these measures. An individual was coded 1 if she or he was a member of the firm's communist party committee (*CP committee*), 0 otherwise. This indicator was then aggregated at the level of the team. Second, we coded individual members of the corporate elite who were affiliated in some way with the Chinese government and political system (*govt. position*). This includes members of the Chinese Communist Party (CCP), members of the National People's Congress (NPC), or members of the Chinese People's Political Consultative Conference (CPPCC). This indicator was coded 1 if the individual was a member of one of these bodies, 0 otherwise. The indicator was then summed at the level of the team. Third, members of the corporate elite may have previous (or concurrent) *government work experience*. We coded this indicator as 1 if the individual had such experience, 0 otherwise. Again, the indicator was summed at the level of the team. The aggregate measure of the firm's government experience was then the summation of the three indicators.

Control Variables

We included a number of control variables that may have an effect on the adoption of western-styled governance reform. Large firms attract more attention from institutional investors and governments and may be more likely to adopt new governance innovations. Consequently, we control for *firm size*, measured as number of firm employees, log transformed. Firm performance can attract attention from investors and analysts. Poor-performing firms may receive more pressure to improve their governance. Therefore, we controlled for firm performance, measured as industry-adjusted *return on sales* (ROS). It could be that governance innovation starts in some industries before migrating elsewhere. Therefore, we created dummy variables corresponding to the broad industry categories utilized by *Fortune* in the China 100 (similar to industry sectors in the US). Using all these dummy variables in our analysis is infeasible due to the small N. Consequently, we first ran each model including industry dummies to see if any were significant, we then retained only those that are found in the subsequent analyses.

We controlled for firm ownership structure by including controls for institutional ownership and blockholder ownership. *Institutional ownership* was measured as the percentage of shares owned by institutional investors. *Blockholder ownership* was the percentage of shares owned by the largest owner (usually an SOE – state-owned enterprise).

The listing of a Chinese firm on a western exchange is a major strategic move that can have implications for the governance choices firms make. Listing on western exchanges requires the approval of the board of directors and the Chinese government. The variable *US exchange* was coded 1 if the firm had listed ADRs (American Depositary Receipts) on NASDAQ or the NYSE, 0 otherwise, and the variable *HK exchange* was coded 1 if the firm was listed on the Hong Kong exchange, 0 otherwise. Listing on these exchanges is attractive for several reasons, including the endowment of institutional legitimacy and access to the world's largest capital markets. However, the decision to list in these exchanges is not an easy one for a Chinese firm because of the level of disclosure and compliance required by the respective regulatory agencies associated with both exchanges.

We controlled for a number of factors related to the board specifically and the firms' upper echelons generally. We controlled for *board size* as the number of board members in 2000. We controlled for the extent of pre-existing outsider participation on the board, by including the *number of outsiders* on the board in 2000. The age of members of the upper echelons may affect the propensity to add outsiders for at least two reasons. First, older teams may be less prone to adopt new innovations. However, older teams are also the most likely to experience retirements and have an opportunity to appoint new members of the board. Thus, we control for the *average age* of the members of the firms' upper echelons. For similar reasons as age, tenure may affect the propensity to add new outside board members. Consequently, we control for the *average tenure* of members of the firms' board of directors and TMT. Finally, the education level can affect how people approach new problems. Consequently, we control for the *average education level* possessed by members of the firms' TMT and board of directors. No university degree was coded as 1, college degree as 2, masters degree as 3, and doctoral or other terminal degree as 4. Table 9.1 reports the descriptive statistics and correlations of the variables used in our analysis.

Analysis

The dependent variable is a count measure. Consequently, we used negative binomial regression. Negative binomial regression is used to estimate count models when the Poisson estimation is inappropriate due to overdispersion. In a Poisson distribution the mean and variance are equal. When the variance is greater than the mean the distribution is said to display overdispersion. In our data the variance was slightly greater than the mean. The estimation parameter α, which is an estimate of the degree of overdispersion, was 1.13 and the chi-square test that the parameter was different from zero was 58.60 ($p < 0.001$) indicating that the distribution was not Poisson. When there is overdispersion the Poisson estimates are inefficient with standard errors biased downward yielding spuriously large z-values. The negative binomial distribution is given by:

$$\Pr(y|x) = \frac{\Gamma(y + \alpha^{-1})}{y\Gamma(\alpha^{-1})}\left(\frac{\alpha^{-1}}{\alpha^{-1} + \lambda}\right)^{\alpha^{-1}}\left(\frac{\lambda}{\alpha^{-1} + \lambda}\right)^{y}$$

Like many problems in management, the question of how the firm is affected by the TMT and board is subject to the concern of endogeneity. We had two separate concerns

Table 9.1 Descriptive statistics and correlation matrix

Variable	Mean	Std. Dev.	Min	Max	1	2	3	4	5	6	7	8	9	10	11	12	13
Additions	3.31	3.66	0	14													
Firm size	9.29	1.19	5.70	12.94													
ROS	-0.01	0.07	-0.17	0.24													
US listing	0.38	0.49	0	1													
HK listing	0.15	0.36	0	1													
Blockholders	0.54	0.37	0.00	1													
Inst. ownership	0.24	0.28	-0.03	1													
Board size	10.07	4.20	1	19													
Prior ind directors	1.60	1.78	0	6													
Avg age	49.02	3.73	38.93	63													
Avg bd tenure	2.59	2.19	0.20	17													
Avg educ level	2.42	0.33	1.86	3.5													
Govt experience	4.00	3.42	0	23													
West experience	2.96	5.67	0	24													
1 Additions																	
2 Firm size					0.13												
3 ROS					-0.09	0.10											
4 US listing					-0.14	0.46	0.06										
5 HK listing					0.23	0.32	0.03	0.31									
6 Blockholders					0.32	0.15	0.01	-0.42	-0.06								
7 Inst. ownership					-0.27	0.10	0.00	0.59	0.08	-0.77							
8 Board size					-0.21	0.10	0.23	0.28	0.01	-0.33	0.46						
9 Prior ind directors					0.37	0.07	-0.07	-0.23	0.12	0.26	-0.30	0.28					
10 Avg age					0.13	0.25	0.04	-0.04	0.04	0.27	-0.15	-0.02	0.08				
11 Avg bd tenure					-0.25	0.07	0.03	-0.10	0.05	0.00	0.00	-0.20	-0.30	0.32			
12 Avg educ level					0.04	-0.06	0.01	0.14	-0.25	-0.11	0.17	-0.20	-0.15	-0.15	0.08		
13 Govt experience					0.31	0.32	0.10	0.06	0.07	0.21	-0.12	0.32	0.53	0.36	-0.26	-0.12	
14 West experience					-0.23	0.01	-0.06	-0.12	0.06	0.07	-0.14	-0.13	0.08	0.05	0.16	0.13	-0.03

Note: Coefficients greater than 0.24 and 0.29 are significant at $p < 0.05$ and $p < 0.01$, respectively.

Source: Authors.

225

regarding endogeneity. First, it is possible that there is something about the firms and members of the upper echelons that draws them together in the first place. For instance, some firms, knowing that they are on a trajectory of certain types of change, may systematically recruit and promote managers with idealized backgrounds. In our case, firms that are becoming more global may be more likely to recruit and promote managers with western experience. The same can be said about other types of experience, like government ties and experience. The second problem is different in nature, but results in the same estimation problem. This problem is that individuals who gain western experience or who are selected into government political and work positions may be fundamentally different from their colleagues who do not have such experiences. Consider, for instance, individuals who were allowed to move to the West to pursue their education. These individuals are likely different than their counterparts on several dimensions. First, to receive permission to move to the West, the Chinese government will have carefully screened them. This is especially true during the early years of reform. In addition, they likely scored exceptionally well in earlier exams and degree programs. Similar screening and selection likely transpires before individuals are able to receive the types of government experiences we study.

Consequently, to account for this possible endogeneity, before estimating our main models, we conducted exploratory tests to see if those with government and or western experience were systematically different from their peers on objective, convenient, and unobtrusive measures. We conducted these tests by estimating logistic regressions that predicted the likelihood that an individual received any or multiple western and government experiences outlined above. We used several demographic indicators as predictors in these models, including: age, gender, and level of education. In addition, when temporally appropriate, we used other experience indicators as predictors. For instance, having a western education may affect later receiving a western assignment experience. But, having a western assignment experience cannot affect being western born. As these models were exploratory in nature, we ran several iterations to find the best fitting models. Because the likelihood for each of these experiences is unlikely to be independent, after estimating the logistic regressions for each experience, we then estimated the suest (seemingly unrelated estimation) command in STATA, which uses all the data to adjust for the simultaneity.

Because the results of the suest revealed that the experience paths were not random, we then estimated probit models that predicted whether a firm's corporate elite was one that was likely to attract individuals with western or government experience. To do so, we created dummy variables for a firm's western and government experience within the corporate elite. Inspections of the distributions of experience within the corporate elites revealed that the distribution was bimodal. There were many firms with no or very little experience and others with moderate to very high levels of experience. Consequently, we coded firms as 1 if they had experience levels above the median, 0 otherwise. In the models, the left-hand side is western experience and government experience, respectively. On the right-hand side, we included several firm and corporate elite predictor variables (firm size, blockholder ownership, institutional ownership, average age of the firm's corporate elite, average education level, and industry dummies). Because our main purpose was to control for endogeneity and not test hypotheses about the specific nature of its causes, we iterated these models to find the best fitting estimates. From these models we saved the predicted value and then generated the inverse Mills ratio. The inverse Mills ratio was then included in the subsequent negative binomial regression models as a control for the possible endogenous process of TMT/board composition and firm evolution toward western practices.

RESULTS

The results for the suest estimations predicting which managers/directors receive different types of foundational experiences are reported in Table 9.2. As reported there, in each case the findings suggested that receiving these types of experience, both western and government, were not random and likely not exogenous to the overall theory.

Table 9.3 reports the results of the hypotheses tests. The table reports the estimated negative binomial regression coefficients for the model. Recall that the dependent variable is a count variable and the model models the log of the expected count as a function of the predictor variables. We can interpret the negative binomial regression coefficient as follows: for a one unit change in the predictor variable, the difference in the logs of expected counts of the response variable is expected to change by the respective regression coefficient, given the other predictor variables in the model are held constant. This can be written as $\beta = \log(\mu_{x0+1}) - \log(\mu_{x0})$, where β is the regression coefficient, μ is the expected count and the subscripts represent where the predictor variable, say x, is evaluated at x_0 and x_{0+1} (implying a one unit change in the predictor variable x).

Model 1 reports the effects of the control variables. Larger boards were less likely to add new independent directors. Firms with more independent directors in the first place were more likely to add additional independent directors. Firms with boards that are more entrenched as evidenced by their average tenure were less likely to add independent directors.

The key independent variables were added in Model 2. Contrary to Hypothesis 1, western experience was negatively associated with firms' likelihood of adding independent directors to the board. The coefficient was -0.20 ($p < 0.0001$). Exponentiating the coefficient reveals that every increase in one additional increment in western experience decreases the likelihood of adding an independent directly by 22 percent. However, consistent with Hypothesis 2, the coefficient for government experience was 0.12 ($p < 0.05$). Exponentiating this coefficient indicates that every additional increment of government experience increases the likelihood of adding an independent directly by 13 percent.

DISCUSSION

Top management's values and cognitive bases are developed in numerous ways, such as through indigenous culture, and education. However, a number of cognitive properties are developed over time through experience. We contribute to the recent work in upper echelons by examining how managerial values and preferences are a function of foundational experiences. In doing so, we explicitly account for the likelihood that these foundational experiences may be endogenous. We examined how governmental work experiences and western experiences of the Chinese corporate elite influenced the

Table 9.2   Simultaneous estimations for individual experience tracks

	Coef.	Robust Std. Err.	z	P>z
CP committee				
Age	0.03	0.01	3.26	0.001
Female	−0.01	0.54	−0.02	0.987
Educ level	−0.28	0.18	−1.55	0.121
Western ed	0.19	0.56	0.33	0.74
West assignment	−2.21	0.58	−3.84	0
_cons	−3.54	0.65	−5.48	0
Govt political position				
Age	0.10	0.02	4.28	0.00
CP comm	3.10	0.43	7.15	0
Educ level	0.66	0.25	2.68	0.007
West ed	−0.38	0.55	−0.69	0.491
West assignment	1.39	0.60	2.31	0.021
_cons	−10.87	1.60	−6.81	0
Govt work exp				
Age	0.10	0.02	6.3	0
Female	−1.56	1.01	−1.54	0.123
Educ level	0.49	0.20	2.47	0.013
West assignment	0.78	0.42	1.87	0.061
_cons	−8.58	1.02	−8.42	0
West assignment				
Age	−0.03	0.01	−3.06	0.002
Female	0.48	0.27	1.78	0.075
Educ level	−0.26	0.13	−2.02	0.044
West ed	1.18	0.27	4.36	0
_cons	1.37	0.58	2.36	0.018
Western educ				
Age	0.00	0.02	0	0.999
Female	−1.46	0.71	−2.05	0.04
Educ level	1.59	0.18	8.61	0
Foreign born	3.74	0.32	11.57	0
_cons	−7.11	1.17	−6.07	0

Source: Authors' calculations.

propensity of Chinese publicly traded firms to adopt western-style corporate governance mechanisms in the form of the appointment of independent (outside) directors.

Our theory suggested that governmental experience within the corporate elite would make the elite more predisposed to being open to adopting more rigorous corporate governance standards. Having Chinese corporate elites that are composed of members with many and a variety of experiences in the government gives the firm many advantages

Table 9.3   Negative binomial regression: no. of independent directors added to the board of directors

	Model 1	Model 2
_cons	25.91*	33.65***
Firm size	−0.27	−0.46
ROS	−1.47	−1.99
US listing	−0.81	0.23
HK listing	0.85	0.36
Blockholder ownership	−5.34	−6.44
Institutional ownership	5.64	6.45**
Board size	−0.16**	−0.22****
Prior no. ind directors	0.22†	0.40***
Avg age	−0.08	−0.17†
Avg board tenure	−0.50***	−0.26**
Avg education level	2.75	3.58
Govt exp inverse mills ratio	−30.86	−36.64**
West exp inverse mills ratio	−9.23*	−10.97**
Government experience		0.12*
Western experience		−0.20****
Log likelihood	−142.79	−133.43
LR chi^2	37.01***	53.93***
Psuedo R^2	0.12	0.17

Note: †$p < 0.10$, *$p < 0.05$, **$p < 0.01$, ***$p < 0.001$.

Source: Authors' calculations.

managing its resource dependencies. However, these experiences create network ties and they come at a cost. In order to develop and maintain government affiliations, Chinese corporate elites are likely to be under pressure to comply with requests of government regulators even more so than other Chinese firms. Our findings indicate that with respect to adopting more stringent corporate governance in the form of western-styled independent boards, government work experience among the elite significantly increased compliance with the government directive.

Contrary to our hypothesis, our findings suggested just the opposite with respect to western experience. We suggested that western experience results in the elite being more familiar with western practices and more amenable to emulating them. If the familiarity effect were operating, then we would expect that as Chinese elite come to know more about the West they should become more comfortable with adopting western governance mechanisms. As the theory goes, familiarity should breed liking and acceptance. But our findings suggested just the opposite. This requires revisiting the familiarity logic used to formulate the hypothesis. Recent research by Norton et al. (2007) may provide some insight into this unexpected finding.

Norton and colleagues conducted a number of experiments to better understand the familiarity attraction phenomenon. They surveyed two groups of people that are generally actively looking for dating partners: members of an online dating site and undergraduate students. They asked them whether they generally preferred someone they knew little about, or someone they knew more about, and consistent with the familiarity hypothesis, 81 percent of the online daters and 88 percent of the undergraduates said they would prefer the person they knew more about. However, in a series of follow up experiments when they carefully controlled how much information potential daters knew about their dating partners the results showed that, contrary to the familiarity-attraction hypothesis, the more information people had about others the less they liked them. Norton and colleagues hypothesized that the reason for this finding was that the more people find out about others, the more likely it is a trait will be uncovered to which they take a dislike. Further investigation revealed that what was driving the connection between knowledge and dislike was a lack of similarity. Effectively, the more traits participants knew about another person, the more likely they were to find dissimilarities with themselves, and so the more likely they were to dislike them.

In our context, it may be that the more elites are exposed to western governance norms, the more they come to understand the dark side of governance. Managers and directors with broad-based western experiences may be more attuned to the costs of monitoring. This is not to suggest that elites with western experience are more likely to avoid monitoring because they are more prone to engage in empire building or pursue private benefits at the expense of shareholders than any other managers or directors. Rather, they are more likely to understand the costs of monitoring in terms of questioning authority and limiting managerial discretion.

Our findings suggest several potentially fruitful avenues for future research. First, we explicitly controlled for the possible endogenous nature of the experiential variables of interest in our study. It is interesting to note that had we not taken the steps to control for endogeneity, the findings would have significantly overstated the effects of western experience and significantly understated the effects of governmental experience, though the direction of effects would not have changed.[4] There are likely a number of other situations in which upper echelons researchers may be advised to carefully consider the potentially endogenous processes. For instance, it is not uncommon in upper echelons and managerial social capital studies to include measures of elite education. The factors that lead some individuals to get advanced degrees from elite institutions may be the same factors that cause certain managers and firms to be attracted to one another. Failing to account for this may overattribute or incorrectly specify the effects of elite education.

Another avenue for future research suggested by our study is to turn attention to the developmental pathways that senior managers follow. Some types of experiences are likely to be much more influential on cognitive predispositions than others. Prior research has shown that western managers that are given the opportunities to have foreign assignment experience earlier in their careers tend to manage firms differently (and in the case of MNCs, they seem to manage them better) than their counterparts who lack such experience (Roth, 1995; Carpenter et al., 2001). What is it about these managers that enables them or leads them to pursue such experiences in the first place? Are the same factors at play with young potential managers in China (and other emerging economies)?

Our research was cast in the context of evolving corporate governance practices in

China. Governance practices are not only evolving in China, but indeed in the rest of the world; firms and investors seek governance solutions that will better protect them from some of the corporate governance failures that have transpired recently around the globe (e.g., Tyco, Enron, and WorldCom in the US, Satyam Computer Services in India, Sanlu Group in China). Our findings reveal that the choices firms make with respect to new governance changes they implement is strongly influenced by who occupies the current positions in the top management team and board of directors. Perhaps the most practical implication of the findings with respect to governance change is that the results seem to indicate what types of factors make directors and managers more likely to support the adoption of mechanisms that may be in the best interest of the firm's shareholders but may not be in the best interests of management.

Of course, our research says nothing about how effective these changes in governance have been or will be in China. Such performance implications are beyond the scope of this study and additional research is needed to see if western-styled governance (i.e., increased shareholder protections) has any meaningful effect on the decisions firms make or on their financial and market performance.

NOTES

1. Consistent with prior research in the Western context, we define corporate elite as the board and top management team of the largest Chinese corporations (Davis and Greve, 1996).
2. For a detailed discussion of corporate governance reform in China, see Zhang (2007) and Rajagopalan and Zhang (2008).
3. While Australia and Hong Kong are not geographically in the West, their socio-political systems are based on British law and Chinese managers working in divisions based in these locations were exposed to radically different philosophies than those of mainland China.
4. Results available from authors.

REFERENCES

Bantel, K.A. and Jackson, S.E. (1989). Top management and innovations in banking: Does the composition of the top team make a difference? *Strategic Management Journal*, **10**(S1), 107–24.

Beckman, C.M. and Burton, M.D. (2008). Founding the future: Path dependence in the evolution of top management teams from founding to IPO. *Organization Science*, **19**(1), 3–24.

Carpenter, M.A., Geletkanycz, M., and Sanders, W.G. (2004). The upper echelons research revisited: Antecedents, elements, and consequences of top management team composition. *Journal of Management*, **30**(6), 749–78.

Carpenter, M.A., Pollock, T.G., and Leary, M.M. (2003). Testing a model of reasoned risk-taking: Governance, the experience or principals and agents, and global strategy in high-technology IPO firms. *Strategic Management Journal*, **24**(9), 803–20.

Carpenter, M.A., Sanders, W.G., and Gregersen, H.B. (2001). Bundling human capital with organizational context: The impact of international assignment experience on multinational firm performance and CEO pay. *Academy of Management Journal*, **44**(3), 493–511.

Clark, R. (1979). *The Japanese company*. New Haven, CT: Yale University Press.

Crossland, C. and Hambrick, D.C. (2007). How national systems differ in their constraints on corporate executives: A study of CEO effects in three countries. *Strategic Management Journal*, **28**(8), 767–89.

D'Aunno, T., Sutton, R.I., and Price, R.L. (1991). Organizational isomorphism and external support in conflicting institutional environment: The case of drug abuse treatment units. *Academy of Management Journal*, **34**(3), 636–61.

D'Aveni, R.A. (1990). Top managerial prestige and organizational bankruptcy. *Organization Science*, **1**(2), 121–42.

Davis, G.F. and Greve, H.R. (1997). Corporate elite networks and governance changes in the 1980s. *American Journal of Sociology*, **103**(1), 1–37.

DiMaggio, P.J. and Powell, W.W. (1983). The iron cage revisited: Institutional isomorphism and collective rationality in organizational fields. *American Sociological Review*, **48**(2), 147–60.

DiMaggio, W.W. (1997). Culture and cognition. *Annual Review of Sociology*, **23**(1), 263–87.

Eisenhardt, K.M. and Schoonhoven, C.B. (1990). Organizational growth: Linking founding team, strategy, environment, and growth among US semiconductor ventures, 1978–1988. *Administrative Science Quarterly*, **35**(3), 504–29.

Finkelstein, S. and Hambrick, D.C. (1990). Top management team tenure and organizational outcomes: The moderating role of managerial discretion. *Administrative Science Quarterly*, **35**(3), 484–503.

Finkelstein, S. Hambrick, D.C., and Cannella, A.A. (2009). *Strategic leadership: Theory and research on executives, top management teams, and boards.* New York, NY: Oxford University Press.

Fiske, S.T., and Taylor, S.E. (1984). *Social cognition.* New York, NY. Random House.

Fligstein, N. (1991). The structural transformation of American industry: An institutional account of the causes of diversification of the largest firms, 1919–1979. In W.W. Powell and P.J. DiMaggio (eds). *The new institutionalism in organizational analysis.* Chicago, IL: University of Chicago Press, pp. 311–36.

Gu, J. (2008). An empirical study on the relation between characteristics of enterprise top management team and strategic decision in industry cluster of China. *International Journal of Human Resource Development and Management*, **8**(1/2), 96–110.

Haleblian, J. and Finkelstein, S. (1993). Top management team size, CEO dominance, and firm performance: The moderating roles of environmental turbulence and discretion. *Academy of Management Journal*, **36**(4), 844–63.

Hambrick, D.C. and Mason, P. (1984). Upper echelons: The organization as a reflection of its top managers. *Academy of Management Journal*, **9**(2), 193–206.

Hargadon, A.B. and Douglas, Y. (2001). When innovation meets institutions: Edison and the design of the electric light. *Administrative Science Quarterly*, **46**(3), 476–501.

Hofstede, G. and Hofstede, G.J. (2005). *Cultures and organizations: Software of the mind* (revised and expanded 2nd edition). New York, NY: McGraw-Hill.

Jensen, M.C. and Meckling, W.H. (1976). Theory of the firm: Managerial behavior, agency costs and ownership structure. *Journal of Financial Economics*, **24**(3), 305–60.

Jia, C., Ding, S., Li, Y., and Wu, Z. (2009). Fraud, enforcement action, and the role of corporate governance: Evidence from China. *Journal of Business Ethics*, **90**(4), 561–76.

Kraatz, M.S. and Moore, J.H. (2002). Executive migration and institutional change. *Academy of Management Journal*, **45**(1), 120–43.

Lay, C. and Verkuyten, M. (1999). Ethnic identity and its relation to personal self-esteem: A comparison of Canadian-born and foreign-born Chinese adolescents. *Journal of Social Psychology*, **139**(3), 288–99.

Lester, R.H., Hillman, A., Zardkoohi, A., and Cannella Jr., A.A. (2008). Former government officials as outside directors: The role of human and social capital. *Academy of Management Journal*, **51**(5), 999–1013.

Li, J. and Tang, Y. (2010). CEO hubris and firm risk taking in China: The moderating role of managerial discretion. *Academy of Management Journal*, **53**(1), 45–68.

Lyon, D. and Ferrier, W. (2002). Enhancing performance with product market innovation: A note on the influence of the top management team. *Journal of Managerial Issues*, **14**(4), 452–69.

Nahapiet, J. and Goshal, S. (1998). Social capital, intellectual capital, and the organizational advantage. *Academy of Management Review*, **23**(2), 242–66.

Norton, M.I., Frost, J.H., and Ariely, D. (2007). Less is more: The lure of ambiguity, or why familiarity breeds contempt. *Journal of Personality and Social Psychology*, **92**(1), 97–105.

Pfeffer, J. and Salancik, G. (1978). *The external control of organizations: A resource dependence perspective.* New York, NY: Harper & Row.

Rajagopalan, N. and Zhang, Y. (2008). Corporate governance reforms in China and India: Challenges and opportunities. *Business Horizon*, **51**(1), 55–64.

Reuber, A.R. and Fischer, E. (1997). The influence of management team's international experience on the internationalization. *Journal of International Business*, **28**(4), 807–25.

Rosenthal, D.A. and Feldman, S.S. (1992). The nature and stability of ethnic identity in Chinese youth: Effects of length of residence in two cultural contexts. *Journal of Cross-Cultural Psychology*, **23**(2), 214–27.

Roth, K. (1995). Managing international interdependence: CEO characteristics in a resource-based framework. *Academy of Management Journal*, **38**(1), 200–231.

Sambharya, R. (1996). Foreign experience of top management teams and international diversification strategies of U.S. multinational corporations. *Strategic Management Journal*, **17**(9), 739–46.

Sanders, W.G. and Carpenter, M.A. (1998). Internationalization and firm governance: The roles of CEO compensation, top team composition, and board structure. *Academy of Management Journal*, **41**(2), 158–78.

Sanders, W.G. and Tuschke, A. (2007). The adoption of institutionally contested organizational practices: The emergence of stock option pay in Germany. *Academy of Management Journal*, **50**(1), 33–56.

Shi, S. and Weisert, D. (2002). Corporate governance with Chinese characteristics. *China Business Review*, **29**(5), 40–44.

Smith, K.G., Grimm, C.M., Gannon, M.J., and Chen, M.-J. (1991). Organizational information processing, competitive responses, and performance in the U.S. domestic airline industry. *Academy of Management Journal*, **34**(1), 60–85.

Tihanyi, L., Ellstrand, A.E., Daily, C.M., and Dalton, D.R. (2000). Composition of the top management team and firm international diversification. *Journal of Management*, **26**(6), 1157–77.

Tsui, A.S. (2006). Contextualization in Chinese management research. *Management and Organization Review*, **2**(1), 1–13.

Wiersema, M. and Bird, A. (1993). Organizational demography in Japanese firms. *Academy of Management Journal*, **36**(5), 996–1026.

Xi, C. (2006). In search of an effective monitoring board model: Board reforms and the political economy of corporate law in China. *Connecticut Journal of International Law*, **22**, 1–46.

Young, G.J., Charns, M.P., and Shortell, S.M. (2001). Top manager and network effects on the adoption of innovative management practices: A study of TQM in a public hospital system. *Strategic Management Journal*, **22**(10), 935–51.

Zhang, A. (2007). Legal deterrence: The foundation of corporate governance – evidence from China. *Corporate Governance: an International Review*, **15**(5), 741–67.

PART IV

HOW EXECUTIVE ACTIONS AFFECT STRATEGY, RIVALRY, AND ENTREPRENEURSHIP

10 A practice theory of executive leadership groups: dynamic managerial capabilities and the multi-business team
Jeffrey A. Martin

Multi-business organization is arguably one of the most significant organizational innovations in the history of firms (Fligstein, 1985; Freeland, 1996) and continues to be a subject of significant scholarly research (e.g., Gulati and Singh, 1998; Eisenmann and Bower, 2000; Bowman and Helfat, 2001; Galunic and Eisenhardt, 2001; Gilbert, 2005) and practical importance (Goold et al., 1994; Campbell and Luchs, 1998; Eisenhardt and Galunic, 2000). There continues to be persuasive empirical evidence that gathering multiple business units together can have significant effects on outcomes for the organization as a whole as well as the individual business units (e.g., Palich et al., 2000; Bowman and Helfat, 2001; Galunic and Weeks, 2001; Hough, 2006). In particular, studies on the sources of variances in firm performance show a significant relationship between corporate effects on variances in firm performance. This indicates that firm value can be created or diminished by gathering multiple business units together under the same organizational umbrella (Roquebert et al., 1996; Bowman and Helfat, 2001; Hough, 2006). This "corporate effect" has been identified as being distinct from industry and individual business unit effects (Brush and Bromiley, 1997; Bowman and Helfat, 2001). Yet, as Bowman and Helfat (2001) argue, the corporate effect remains a relative "black box" that provides little direct understanding of the relationship between the structures, processes, and individual actions that contribute to the corporate effect. This chapter focuses on individual actions as it relates to dynamic managerial capabilities (Martin, 2010).

In this chapter I use a practice theory lens to describe dynamic managerial capabilities in executive leadership groups as an element of the corporate effect. Practice theory provides a lens that integrates aspects of organizational theories of agency, resource dependence, and dynamic managerial capabilities. In practice theory, resource decisions are decidedly political in that they typically involve plans within plans that take into account memory of the past, imagination of the future, and the affordances and constraints of present circumstances (Emirbayer and Mische, 1998; Feldman, 2003). Practice theory thus brings "agency, and therefore, subjectivity, intent, and power back into the picture" (Feldman, 2003, p. 95). Most executive leadership resource actions reproduce the system of organizational relationships necessary for the firm to earn a living in the present. However, when the environment responds in an unexpected way to the results of resource actions, executives can either respond with actions similar to the past (inertia), or formulate and choose a decidedly different resource action. Decidedly different actions can result in changes within the firm and at times even the environment and thereby position the firm to earn a living in an uncertain future. The capacity for executives to take such resource actions is the essence of dynamic managerial capabilities.

Thus, a practice theory lens considers inertia and adaptability to be two sides of the same coin.

There is persuasive evidence in the literature that the resource actions of executive leaders, individually and collectively, can produce significant firm outcomes (Martin, 2010). Such resource actions include diversification into new product markets (Jensen and Zajac, 2004), the acquisition or divestiture of a business unit (Boeker, 1997; Hambrick et al., 2005), and the formation of alliances. Much of our understanding of executive leadership groups focuses on top management teams (TMTs). However, in multi-business organizations there are at least two distinct levels of executive leaders (Martin, 2010) – the TMT and the multi-business team (MBT). This study focuses on the latter as a means to contribute to a greater understanding of how executive leadership groups actually operate. For a discussion of the configurations of the TMT, see Jones and Cannella in Chapter 1 of this volume.

The MBT, illustrated in Figure 10.1, is comprised of the set of executive leaders that each head one of the firm's business units (sometimes referred to as "divisions" or "strategic groups") (Martin, 2010). In this chapter I refer to these executive leaders as "general managers" or "GMs." Business unit general managers run semi-autonomous business units that have annual sales that typically range from tens to hundreds of millions of dollars. They have authority and control over their business unit's resources and direct accountability for their business unit's performance. They also expect significant autonomy and discretion in the conduct of their affairs and operate in a task environment without a beginning or end. Thus, their role is analogous to that associated with conceptualizations of TMT members, but decidedly different than the role of middle managers – those managers that head up subunits within businesses. Because the MBT is an executive leadership group, it is also an essential component of a multi-business organization's dynamic managerial capabilities. In this study I ask: "What are the affordances and constraints on executive leadership group resource actions and how do these differences relate to important firm outcomes, such as performance, in dynamic markets?" In addressing this research question, I add new insight into the nature of managerial dynamic capabilities (Adner and Helfat, 2003; Martin, 2010), practice theory (Bourdieu, 1977; Giddens, 1984; Martin and Carlile, 2000), and understandings of how executive leadership groups operate (Martin, 2010; Martin and Eisenhardt, 2010).

BACKGROUND

Practice theory provides a framework that integrates several seminal organization theories that have long been used to motivate studies of executive leadership groups. These include theories of multi-business organization, resource actions, and executive decision making, upper echelon approach, and capabilities along with practice theory provide the context for interpreting the results and theoretical contributions of this study. A central assumption of this study is that the affordances and constraints of executive resource actions are a significant factor of interest in firm competitive advantage and ultimately survival.

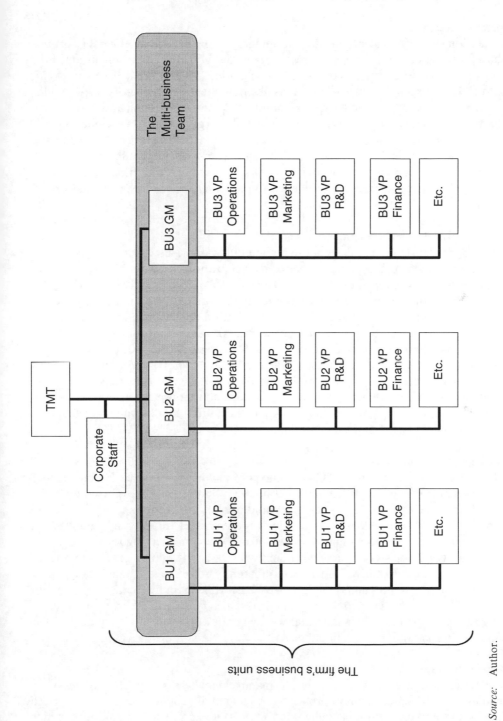

Source: Author.

Figure 10.1 The multi-business group

239

Multi-business Organization, Resources, and Executive Decision Making

Population ecology

A population ecology conceptualization to understanding executive leadership groups emphasizes resources and changes in resources in the industry environment and how they in turn determine firm outcomes (Campbell, 1969; Hannan and Freeman, 1977; Aldrich, 1979). Executive leaders are considered to be rational actors with similar information and skills. The underlying assumption is that two organizations that have similar resource endowments are likely to have similar organizational outcomes regardless of their executive leaders. If the environment changes, firms are viewed as being unlikely to adapt their resources to such change because they are subject to inertia. In a population ecology world the environment selects which firms succeed and which firms fail. Executive leaders have little effect on whether or not firms succeed or fail over time.

Resource dependence and evolutionary economics

Resource dependence theory takes a more granular view of organizations by focusing on how the extent of resource dependence between organizations provides both affordances and constraints to organizational actors (Jacobs, 1974; Pfeffer and Salancik, 1978). Executive leadership groups are viewed as effectual actors who will proactively seek to reduce their organization's dependence on others within and outside the organization. Evolutionary economics begins to bridge the organization–environment relationship by arguing that changes in the environment result in disequilibrium in the market that entrepreneurial managers can exploit (Nelson and Winter, 1982). Evolutionary economics embraces a Schumpeterian (1934, 1942) approach that suggests that executive leader initiative in identifying emerging opportunities, formulating novel resource actions to seize these opportunities, and then deciding and executing these resource actions is an essential factor in organizational adaptation.

Transaction-cost economics

The transaction-cost economics (TCE) of Oliver Williamson (1975) builds on theories of information processing (March and Simon, 1958; Simon, 1982), the costs of transactions (Coase, [1937] 1991), efficiency (Berle and Means, 1932), and agency (Fama and Jensen, 1983; Eisenhardt, 1989a) by focusing on the cost of formulating, monitoring, and controlling transactions within or between firms. Williamson also goes a step further than Simon's (1982) thesis of bounded rationality by asserting that at least some organizational actors (e.g., executive leaders) are inherently self-interested and may pursue "self-interest seeking with guile" (1975, p. 26). Thus, while executive leadership plays an essential role in achieving firm outcomes, they must also be subjected to various governance mechanisms to limit their potential to engage in opportunistic behavior in their pursuit of personal and organizational goals.

Upper echelons approach

Executive leadership groups, especially top management teams, have been extensively studied using an upper echelons approach (Carpenter et al., 2004). Much of the research on TMTs has built on Hambrick and Mason's (1984) upper echelons framework, which is at once both a theory and a methodology (Carpenter et al., 2004). The theory is that organizations are reflections of their top managers. The methodology is that observable "managerial characteristics are reasonable proxies for underlying differences in cognitions, values and perceptions" of top managers (ibid., p. 750). These differences will in turn determine individual and collective strategic decision making and thus be related to significant organizational outcomes. The results of empirical studies employing this approach provide persuasive support that observable characteristics of the TMT members are associated with differences in firm performance. In addition, discussions in the literature suggest that group characteristics such as structure, process, and psychosocial characteristics are mediating variables that affect performance. However, these variables are inferred from observable characteristics rather than directly measured (Priem et al., 1999; Carpenter et al., 2004). Because of this, some scholars have suggested that the upper echelons approach is stretched too far when it is used to explain the causal logic of how demography influences firm outcomes, and this has in turn resulted in somewhat ambiguous understanding of how executive leadership groups actually operate (West and Schwenk, 1996; Priem et al., 1999).

Operational and Dynamic Capabilities

A more recent managerial view of how firms operate comes from theories of organizational capabilities (Eisenhardt and Martin, 2000; Helfat et al., 2007b; Teece, 2007). Following Helfat and colleagues (2007b, p. 121), capabilities are defined as the organization's capacity "to perform a particular task, function, or activity in at least a minimally acceptable manner." Two categories of capabilities have been defined in the literature – operational and dynamic. "Operational capabilities" refer to the capacity of an organization to exploit its resource base through learning and refining the processes, procedures, skills, and incentive systems necessary to repeat, leverage, and sustain past successes (Collis, 1994; Winter, 2003). Superior operational capabilities can help a firm sustain competitive advantages and create the inertia necessary to maintain technical fitness with the organization's technologies, product market demands, and competitor situations (Hannan and Freeman, 1984; Dosi et al., 2000; Benner and Tushman, 2003). Technical fitness expresses how well a capability performs its function (Helfat et al., 2007b; Teece, 2007), or in other words, it is about doing things right (whether or not it is the right thing to do).

In contrast, "[a] **dynamic capability** is the capacity of an organization to purposefully create, extend, or modify its resource base" (Helfat et al., 2007a, p. 5, bold text in original). Dynamic capabilities enable both small incremental adjustments in resource actions as well as novel resource actions that are decidedly different than past actions (Eisenhardt and Martin, 2000). Since novel resource actions are not formulated from a direct experience base, it is difficult for managers to assign probabilities to the possible outcomes of these resource actions or in some cases even know what the set of possible outcomes might even be. Thus, their outcomes are decidedly uncertain (Knight, 1921). Dynamic capabilities are the essential means by which an organization maintains evolutionary fitness (Teece, 2007, p. 1321). Dynamic managerial capabilities adds a Kirznerian (Kirzner, 1973) perspective to the above organization theories by arguing that while executive leaders are subject to the internal and external environment, their resource actions can also at times shape the environment in which they compete (Eisenhardt and Martin, 2000). Moreover, in contrast to TCE, empirical results suggest that executive self-interest is not necessarily suboptimal but rather can lead to decisions that enhance overall firm performance, especially in high-dynamic contexts (Martin, 2010; Martin and Eisenhardt, 2010).

"Dynamic managerial capabilities" are a particular type of dynamic capability that refers to the "*capacity of **managers** to purposefully create, extend, or modify the resource base of an organization*" (Adner and Helfat, 2003; Helfat et al., 2007b, p. 24, italics in original, bold added). They differ from typical conceptions of dynamic capabilities in that they are distinctly non-routine. That is, while they contain elements of practiced behavior, they are not rote in nature and therefore the performance of dynamic managerial capabilities cannot be separated from the manager(s) who carry them out (Martin, 2010). Managerial intent is thus a crucial element in the effectiveness of dynamic managerial capabilities and firm performance outcomes.

Practice theory
Practice theory (Bourdieu, 1977; Giddens, 1984; Feldman, 2003) provides a means to integrate these diverse conceptualizations of executive leadership group resource actions by adding a sociological dimension to a phenomenon that has long been dominated by economic reasoning. Building on earlier work in the tradition of practice theory (Bourdieu, 1977) and structuration theory (Sewell, 1992), members of executive leadership groups can be conceptualized as employing their individual agency and judgment in choosing particular resource actions at specific times and in specific places, within systems of organizational relationships (e.g., Bourdieu, 1977; Giddens, 1984; Emirbayer and Mische, 1998; Feldman and Pentland, 2003). The system of organizational relationships includes group structure, process, and psychosocial characteristics that have been employed in studies of executive leadership group performance (e.g., Cohen and Bailey, 1997; Carpenter et al., 2004; Martin, 2010).

Group structures in this chapter represent those "durable" social relationships like group composition, hierarchy, incentive systems, and autonomy. Such structures provide a framework within which executive leaders act with resources. Group processes are regular and repeated behaviors like monitoring and control, knowledge transfer, and decision making. Group processes are an essential means by which the organization reproduces its capacity to regularly and predictably repeat past successes and increase efficiency. Group "psychosocial [characteristics] include, but are not limited to, shared beliefs, understandings, or emotional tone" (Cohen and Bailey, 1997, p. 244). In particular, a practice theory conceptualization views the decisions of executive leadership groups as decidedly political (e.g., Fligstein, 1990). That is, their decisions often involve plans within plans rather than simply being reactions to discrete events. Likewise, the web of social relationships within which executive leadership groups operate results in affordances and constraints on the capacity of such groups to sense and seize opportunities in a changing and uncertain market environment. Overall, a practice theory lens extends understanding of organizations by considering reproduction (inertia), transformation (adaptation), and individual agency (human action) in relation to each other, rather than as separate areas of theoretical interest.

METHODS

This study is based on an ongoing research program that explores how multi-business organizations create value in high-dynamic markets. This particular study utilizes the empirical results of my prior published studies on cross-business-unit collaboration (Martin and Eisenhardt, 2010) and dynamic managerial capabilities (Martin, 2010) and integrates unpublished results that shed greater light on the effects of executive leadership demography and incentives. The research design is a multiple case study. Multiple cases enable a replication logic, in which a series of case studies are treated as a set of experiments, with each serving to confirm or disconfirm the inferences drawn from the others (Eisenhardt, 1989b). The results are typically more robust and generalizable than those of single case studies (Yin, 2003). This research also employs an embedded design in which the multiple levels of analysis are: business unit general managers (GMs), business unit (BU), cross-business collaboration, within business unit informants (BUI), and the corporation. While complex, such an embedded design improves the likelihood of richer and more accurate emergent theory (Yin, 1989, 1993). The research setting is six publicly held multi-business software organizations, a highly dynamic industry. There are two organizations in each of three industry segments: consumer, enterprise, and infrastructure. These six organizations also vary by founding date, ranging from 1965 to 1995. This combination of multiple industry segments within a single industry and range of founding dates should improve the robustness and generalizability of the results.

The primary data source is over 80 semi-structured interviews conducted over eight months, supplemented by internal documents and publicly available records collected during the interview period as well as over the next several years (e.g., subsequent annual and financial reports). The interviews are semi-structured with both open and closed-ended questions. I began by asking informants about their competitive environment (e.g., rate of market change), their organization (e.g., strategic challenges), and the relationships among business units and with the corporate center. Interview data were supplemented with follow-up emails and phone conversations and archival data from annual reports, Compustat® Data, company websites, press releases, popular media, and industry analyst reports. Comparisons were made between interview and archival data, where possible, to provide a further check that informants were accurate and competent sources (Jick, 1979; Kumar et al., 1993).

Two types of case analysis were used: within-case and cross-case (Miles and Huberman, 1984). There were no a priori hypotheses. The within-case analysis focused on the focal multi-business team, particularly the events experienced during each of the collaborations. Preliminary constructs and relationships were developed and similarities and differences noted. However, further analysis was postponed until all case write-ups were completed to maintain the independence of the replication logic. The cross-case analysis involved developing constructs and relationships across all cases (Eisenhardt, 1989b). I used tables, graphs, and heuristics for cross-case comparisons (e.g., comparison of successive pairs of cases for similarities and differences) to develop the emerging constructs and relationships (Miles and Huberman, 1994). I also used multiple combinations of case-pairings based on relationships of interest to refine conceptual insights. Once the cross-case analysis was underway, I cycled among emergent theory, data, and literature until a strong match between data and theory emerged. The major results from this research program have been theoretical insights of how multi-business teams operate and cross-business-unit collaborations occur.

RESULTS

Multi-business Team Composition

Following the upper echelons perspective proposed by Hambrick and Mason (1984), I collected data on MBT composition from several sources. First, I asked informants to describe their background and asked them for a resumé or personal biography if one was available. I also collected data from publicly available sources such as press releases, industry articles that reported on informants' backgrounds, company websites, financial reports such as 10-Ks and annual reports, and Internet searches on the informants' names. These data were used to construct a demographic profile of each of the MBT members.

An upper echelons perspective would predict that differences in MBT composition should be associated with differences in organizational outcomes, like performance. Yet, an analysis of the composition of the MBTs in this study, which is summarized in Table 10.1, suggests that there is no apparent pattern of association between MBT composition and performance. The compositions of the MBTs in this study are surprisingly similar. Yet there were clear distinctions in firm performance among the organizations in this study.

Why do these results differ from prior executive leadership group studies that have employed an upper echelons approach? One reason might be the higher turnover that these executive leadership groups have relative to executive leadership groups that operate in less dynamic environments. In high-dynamic environments it might well be that turnover, rather than being an indicator of lower performance, may in fact be an important source of renewal in these executive leadership groups. When the environment is constantly changing, it may well be that different skills and capabilities are required in executive leadership groups in order for firms to create new competitive advantages. Another reason could be due to the robust market there is for executives who are able to effectively run business units. Yet another reason is that executive leaders are also motivated by emotion (e.g., "fun") in addition to pecuniary benefits. Executive leaders are constantly recruited by other organizations and thus have many options to obtain similar earnings in other organizations. Because of this, if satisfaction with their work in the organization diminishes, they are likely to be able to move to another organization with little effort and without loss of income or responsibility. Finally, the high rate of turnover in the MBT executive leadership groups relative to most studies may also be a factor in the lack of differences in the extent of heterogeneity between these executive leadership groups – which is likely amplified by the highly dynamic market context. In summary, there was no association between demography of the MBT executive leadership groups and performance in this study, suggesting that other factors explain the observed differences in firm performance.

Table 10.1   Multi-business team demography

	Year Focal Organization Founded	% of GMs Listed as Corporate Officers	Average GM Group Tenure (in years)	Average Tenure in Focal Organization (in years)	Average Number Firm's BU GMs Worked in	Average Years of Industry Experience
Higher-performing organizations						
DataCo	1967	33	2.0	12.0	3.0	18.0
Adlib	1982	33	2.0	7.7	3.7	19.3
Vertical	1990	33	3.0	5.0	4.7	24.7
Lower-performing organizations						
Symbol	1982	17	2.2	3.8	4.8	14.6
Autumn	1982	100	4.7	4.7	4.0	20.0
Bean	1995	33	2.0	7.7	3.7	19.3

	% GMs w/ Technical Education	% GMs w/ Graduate Education	% GMs w/ Output Function Experience[†]	% GMs w/ Throughput Function Experience[†]	% GMs w/ Peripheral Function Experience[†]	% GMs w/Prior Corporate Officer Experience
Higher-performing organizations						
DataCo	100	100	67	100	33	0
Adlib	100	33	100	100	33	33
Vertical	100	100	100	100	67	67
Lower-performing organizations						
Symbol	100	50	100	50	50	67
Autumn	100	33	67	100	33	33
Bean	100	33	100	100	33	33

Notes: Unless otherwise noted, data is reported as of the time of the study, which is 2001. Averages across groupings are not reported as this violates the method.
† Following Hambrick and Mason (1984), functional expertise is categorized as follows:
Output functional experience: marketing, sales, and product research & development (growth & search functions).
Throughput functional experience: production, engineering process, accounting (improvement of transformation process).
Peripheral function experience: finance, law (activities not integrally involved with core activities).

Source: Author.

Executive Leadership Group Structures

Organization and strategy theory has long emphasized the importance of developing structural relationships that increase stability and efficiency in firms (Chandler, 1962; Child, 1972; Galbraith, 1977; Williamson, 1996). Following work by Blau (1977), Pfeffer (1991), and Sewell (1992), structure is defined in this study as "durable" organizational relationships that empower and constrain resource actions. Some perspectives of multi-business organization argue that centralized structures that facilitate exploitation or efficiencies are required in relatively stable environments and that decentralized structures are required in changing and/or uncertain environments where adaptation is essential to the creation of firm value (Thompson, 1967; March, 1991; Hill et al., 1992). However, in Martin's (2010) study of multi-business teams such a distinction between efficient and adaptive structural relationships did not appear. Rather, a pattern of structural relationships, which he named "recombinative structures," emerged that was associated with higher firm performance. Recombinative structures are indicated by a pattern of essential resource autonomy, social equivalence, and reciprocal interdependence (Martin, 2010). These structures facilitated the use of judgment by executive leaders in formulating and pursuing individual and collective resource actions. In contrast, more stable structures were associated with lower firm performance. Such stable structures appear to have constrained possible resource actions and limited firms' capacity to adapt to changing markets. This is similar to the paradox of core rigidities (Leonard-Barton, 1992) in that the same structures that produce the greatest efficiency are also those that are most likely to limit the capacity of an organization to adapt.

Self-enhancing incentives

The role of incentives is central to theories of coordination, control, and motivation in organizations. Providing a more nuanced understanding of incentives is a contribution of this chapter. Some scholars have argued that incentive schemes that emphasize group-based rewards are essential to motivating collaborative behavior in multi-business organizations; otherwise GMs will make decisions that will benefit their own individual BUs in ways that ultimately will be at the expense of overall firm performance (e.g., Williamson, 1975, 1985; Hill et al., 1992). Other scholars have argued that shared meanings, norms, and values (i.e., a strong culture) within groups are most important to organizational effectiveness (Pettigrew, 1979; Kunda, 1992). However, what emerged from the data was a pattern that combined internal incentive factors with elements of incentives that are external to the organization. I call this pattern of relationships "self-enhancing incentives" and found that they were associated with higher firm performance. Building on work by Pfeffer and Fong (2005), I define self-enhancing incentives as structures that provide GMs with opportunities to see themselves, and by extension, their actions, traits, and attitudes, in the most positive light.

I determined self-enhancing incentives by asking informants direct questions and from the interview narratives. Specifically I asked each GM to describe the metrics that they used to monitor their respective business units and to describe their financial incentives. While all of the MBTs had financial compensation schemes that combined significant group-based and individual-based elements, there was, as summarized in Table 10.2, an association between a higher extent of individual-based financial compensation and higher performance. Most interesting, though, were the narratives that accompanied GM depictions of their measurement and incentive schemes. This suggests that a much more nuanced perspective is called for to understand the motivations of GMs. That is, while financial incentives were important, such incentives seemed to be more of a necessary rather than sufficient aspect of GM motivation. Surprisingly, what also emerged from the data was the importance to GMs of having opportunities to be influential in their industry. For example, GMs at Adlib, DataCo, and Vertical

Table 10.2   Self-enhancing incentives in the multi-business teams

	Incentives†		Difference	Incentive autonomy	External presence	Self-enhancing incentives
	Corporate % (group)	BU % (individual)				
Higher-performing organizations						
DataCo	43	57	14	TRUE	HIGH	TRUE
Adlib	50	50	0	TRUE	HIGH	TRUE
Vertical	42	59	17	TRUE	HIGH	TRUE
Lower-performing organizations						
Symbol	55	45	−10	FALSE	LOW	FALSE
Autumn	73	27	−50	FALSE	MOD	FALSE
Bean	58	42	−16	FALSE	LOW	FALSE

Note: † Percentage of financial incentives allocated to group (corporate) verse individual (BU) performance.

Source: Author.

all had a noticeable public presence during the study period as indicated by the extent of their individual association with conference events and press releases. This was discovered during the process of obtaining GM background information through means like Internet searches on GM informant names. GMs in high-performing MBTs also expressed an "external" focus when describing what motivated them as individuals. As a GM at Adlib related: *"So to me, what is most important is the ability to influence the industry at large, but at the same time to be able to deliver [in my organization]" (GM, Vertical).*

In contrast, the GMs in lower-performing BUs appeared to have a much lower public presence, as indicated by little if any association with company press releases or industry conferences. Furthermore, GMs in the lower-performing BUs were characterized by a more organizational focus. For example, when asked about what motivated him, an Autumn GM emphasized that:

> It's the stock price, absolutely. Everybody on executive staff and my staff is highly driven by the stock price, because of stock options. Well you know, certainly my salary and bonus are tied to specific BU objectives and my performing based upon those objectives. But, that's only on an annual basis. The stock price is what really drives me. . . I mean don't get me wrong, I have three objectives for the year and then a revenue objective that drive my behavior, but my thinking in the company is around how are we going to drive shareholder value and how are we going to drive the stock price up. (GM1, Autumn)

Specifically, GMs at Symbol and Bean rarely appeared in their firms' press releases or in industry conference agendas or news articles, even though their BUs' products often were considered leaders in their particular product markets by analysts. One exception was Autumn, where two GMs did have several public listings as conference speakers and appeared occasionally in company press releases, while the third GM had no apparent public presence – suggesting an overall "moderate" public presence among members of the set of GMs. There was also surprising ambiguity in the perceived linkage between

GM financial incentive schemes and individual financial outcomes in all of the MBTs. For example, as GMs at DataCo and Adlib related when asked to describe their financial incentives:

> I, Tom, or Fred can sway revenue a lot. It's not really cut and dry. If I over-achieved my revenue and DataCo didn't, I'd probably get 90 percent of my compensation plan. If both DataCo and my BU over-achieve, I'd get well over 100 percent, probably close to 200 percent (GM3, DataCo)

> . . .day to day the group performance is sort of distant. It's not something I can pull directly the levers on. Then there's the MBO system, which is based on a quarterly set of objectives. They tend to be goal oriented . . . complete this product, launch this business initiative, and each carry 10–15 percent attached to my bonus pool . . . we get close to 100 percent pay up on the base. So we are not a company that sort of tightly manages to a set of objectives where the average bonus payout is 50 to 60 percent. (GM1, Adlib)

Incentive scheme ambiguity was also apparent in several of the interviews with corporate executives (CEs). For example, when I asked the CEO of Bean how he constructed GM financial incentives, his initial reaction was puzzlement at the relevance of my question, followed by the following statement: *"I hire people who want to build businesses, and then figure out how to pay them right. Some years it might be with stock options, other years it might be with cash bonuses" (CEO, Bean)*. By and large, questions regarding the percentage group verses individual financial incentives were surprisingly difficult for GMs and CEs to answer with any real degree of clarity.

The importance of self-enhancement to GMs is also suggested by the surprisingly high MBT turnover that was discovered. Two years after the study period (2001), 11 of the 21 GMs in this study had transitioned to other organizations, seven to head BUs of similar significance and four to become CEOs of new ventures. This suggests that organizations (or stakeholders involved in the formation of new ventures) are likely to recruit GMs who they perceive to have a track record of significant accomplishment and who can also function autonomously. Such perceptions are formed from information available through means that extend beyond the individual GM's organization. For GMs to be mobile, they must create a presence in the environment that is external to their current organization. Those GMs who are most successful at creating a positive external presence will have the greatest mobility. This presence is produced in part by intentionally framing their activities inside and outside the organization in the most positive light to others. Therefore, a high extent of inter-organizational mobility suggests that being in an organization that provides opportunities to be acknowledged in the external environment is likely to be very important to GMs. Overall, structures that provided opportunities for self-enhancement, like individually based financial incentives and opportunities to be acknowledged in the external environment, appear to be associated with higher performance. Consequently, discussions as to whether or when individual or group-based GM rewards are effective (e.g., Kerr, 1985; Hoskisson et al., 1993; Zenger and Hesterly, 1997) may be less relevant than understanding how to provide GMs with structures that provide GMs with self-enhancing opportunities. GMs in the lower-performing firms also appeared to have a much lower public presence, as indicated by little, if any, individual association with company press releases or industry conferences. In summary, self-enhancing incentives provided a foundation for the motivation, coordination, and control within the MBT executive leadership group.

Executive Leadership Group Processes

Organizational theory emphasizes the importance of process to accomplishing predictable outcomes (e.g., Fredrickson, 1983; Chandler, 1991; Pettigrew, 1992) and in adapting the organization to changing environments (e.g., Nelson and Winter, 1982; Burgelman, 1983; Teece et al. 1997; Eisenhardt and Martin, 2000; Feldman and Pentland, 2003). While process can arguably be subsumed under the definitions of structure, I separate them here in order to draw attention to those regular and predictable behavioral patterns that are related to reproduction and adaption in organization. Martin's (2010) study of the relationship between executive leadership groups and performance and Martin and Eisenhardt's (2010) study of cross-business collaboration provide illustrations of such processes of reproduction and adaptation at the firm and business unit levels of analysis respectively.

My study (Martin and Eisenhardt, 2010) of cross-business collaborations observed a process that we named "rewiring" that described the relationship between how the sequence of actions in the formation of cross-business-unit collaboration unfolds. These process steps are the origin, shaping, choice, and implementation steps of the creation of cross-business collaboration. In my (2010) study of the multi-business teams, I extended the forementioned collaboration study by providing an empirical example of the relationship between differences in executive leadership group dynamic managerial capabilities and performance outcomes. In my analysis of these differences, I inducted a construct named recombinative group processes. Recombinative group processes are those regular patterns of behavior that facilitate executive leader resource actions that increase efficiency (i.e., reproduction of the system of social relationships) and adaptation – the collective sensing and seizing of opportunities to reconfigure their subunit resources. These resource patterns resulted in the creation of new resource positions from which business units, and likewise the firm, were able to adapt to compete in an uncertain future. Moreover, my results suggest that the extent of managerial agency and intent were crucial factors in a firm's dynamic managerial capabilities and, likewise, firm performance outcomes.

Social Relationships

There are extensive literatures that examine social relationships within groups and their effect on outcomes (for review see Cohen and Bailey, 1997). While considerable progress has been made, much of the focus continues to be at the work group or project level. Understandings of TMTs have been inferred using an upper echelons perspective, rather than being observed directly (e.g., Hambrick and Mason, 1984; Carpenter et al., 2004). Because of this, studies of executive leadership groups typically examine variables like power or interpersonal perceptions as mediators or moderators through variables like TMT composition and performance (Carpenter et al., 2004). In addition, psychosocial characteristics of executive groups have been shown to differ in important ways from work groups or project teams and argue that research in these lower-level groups should not be generalized to executive leaders (Hambrick and Mason, 1984; Cohen and Bailey, 1997). In my (2010) study of multi-business teams I observed a pattern of power relationships and peer perceptions that were associated with performance that led me to induct another construct that I named "social equivalence." Social equivalence is the material and perceptive reality among GMs that they are similarly effectual in their capability to effectively act with resources. Specifically, I found that when MBT members viewed each other as socially equivalent, the result was higher performance relative to firms with MBTs that did not.

Social relationships among MBT members that exhibit social equivalence suggest a greater motivation of GMs to collectively formulate possible resource actions together versus simply focusing solely on their possible within-business-unit actions. Moreover, social equivalence also enabled GMs to access resources beyond those contained in their own BUs. This can at times then lead to the formulation of collective resource actions that are decidedly different than past actions in response to changes in their market environments. Such actions are particularly important in highly dynamic contexts where adapting firm resource configurations is necessary for continued success (Eisenhardt and Galunic, 2000; Eisenhardt and Martin, 2000; Benner and Tushman, 2003). In addition, my (2010) observation of the relationship between social equivalence and higher firm performance suggests that social equivalence in executive leadership groups can stave off the "centrifugal forces" that Hambrick (1994, p. 188) theorized would inevitably lead to the disaggregation of executive leadership groups as firms succeed and grow.

TOWARD A PRACTICE THEORY OF EXECUTIVE LEADERSHIP GROUPS

My goal in this chapter is to contribute new understandings of how executive leadership groups operate that retains the valuable insights of prior work while accounting for the empirical observations in this and several other recent studies. In doing this I seek to begin to provide a more comprehensive framework, summarized in Figure 10.2, within which a deeper understanding of the link between the resource actions of GMs that stem from their motivation, agency, and intent, and the reproduction and transformation of the system of organizational relationships in the firm. A practice theory approach implies that resource actions are the medium of reproduction and transformation in organizations (Bourdieu, 1977; Giddens, 1984; Ortner, 1984). Thus, a practice theory of executive leadership groups focuses on the system of organizational relationships that empower and constrain strategic resource actions by group members, the consequence of such actions tending to reproduce the system with little alteration such that the firm can develop ever greater efficiencies in competing in its current product markets (i.e., structural inertia). But at times, when the environment responds to executive leadership group resource actions in an unexpected way, then an occasion occurs in which they may exercise their agency and choose subsequent resource actions that are decidedly different than before. A consequence of such novel resource actions may be a transformation of those parts of the system of social relationships in the organization that are no longer efficacious. Thus, a practice theory of executive leadership groups views organizational inertia and adaptability as two sides of the same coin – the ability to effectively respond to the current environment while at the same time positioning the firm to compete in an uncertain future – rather than separate and distinct attributes of particular sets of relationships, like structure or process, within an organization.

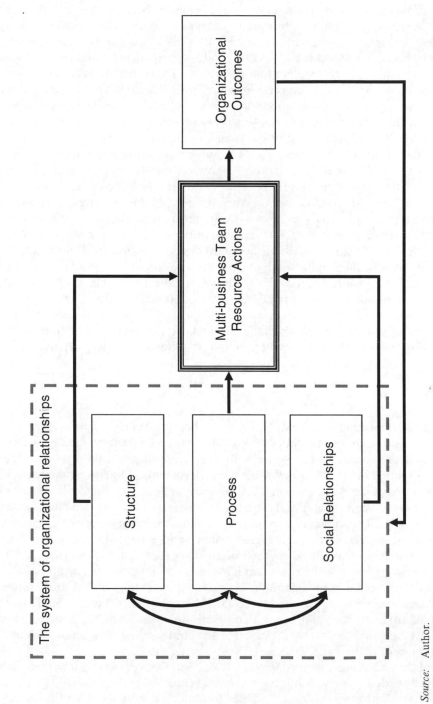

Source: Author.

Figure 10.2 Practice theory model of dynamic managerial capabilities in executive leadership groups

DataCo provides an illustration of how the development of GM resource actions within a system of organizational relationships can produce adaptive as well inertial consequences. From DataCo's inception, GMs shared engineers between their BUs, advised each other in structuring solutions to product market problems, shared infrastructure resources as appropriate, considered each other's BUs in planning and executing significant market moves, developed complementary industry experiences, and co-developed technologies relevant to each other's product markets. This contributed to several successful generations of each BU's respective products with little apparent alteration of the organization's overall structural relationships. However, in 2001 the DataCo customers began to complain that the price of complementary products (software tools) necessary to use DataCo's BU products effectively was making the overall cost of using DataCo BU products prohibitively expensive. This was an unexpected response from the environment. Fortunately, DataCo's GMs were empowered enough by the DataCo system of organizational relationships to make decidedly different resource actions than they had in the past. The GMs collaborated together and entered the software tools business with the goal of driving down the price of software tools by increasing competition in a product market that had been consolidating and, at the same time, generate additional profitable revenue. The consequence of these GM resource actions was ultimately the formation of a new business unit within DataCo to focus on the software tool product market – clearly a transformation of the system of organizational relationships. While DataCo GMs naturally sought corporate executive consent in taking such significant resource actions, it was GM initiative in the development of resource actions that was paramount to producing the transformation in DataCo. In other words, transformation was brought about in part by resource actions that were developed within the same organizational system that reproduced past successes.

Contributions

I make three key contributions. First, I contribute theory that helps explain why multi-business organizations pursuing strategies of relatedness and autonomy among business units in high-dynamic environments may require different organizational relationships than firms operating in relatively low-dynamic environments. Clearly, economic value can be gained or lost from gathering multiple business units together under a single corporate umbrella (i.e., corporate effect) (Brush and Bromiley, 1997; Bowman and Helfat, 2001; Hough, 2006). Theories of agency, information processing and coordination argue that multi-business organizations in high-dynamic markets should be decentralized and pursue strategies of unrelated diversification (Chandler, 1962; Thompson, 1967). This same received wisdom also argues that if a firm does pursue related diversification, centralized control and a clear separation of strategy formulation and strategy implementation are most efficient (Williamson, 1975; Hill et al., 1992). Yet, my study (with Eisenhardt, 2010) found that business unit autonomy, relatedness among business units, and an intertwining of firm strategy formulation and strategy implementation were associated with higher firm performance.

Why might these findings differ from received wisdom? One reason might be that while such received wisdom may well be true for multi-business organizations that operate in relatively stable manufacturing economies (on which prevailing theory rests, e.g.,

Chandler, 1962; Rumelt, 1974; Williamson, 1975), it does not appear to be so for firms operating in more dynamic information- or knowledge-based economies – like the software firms in this study where the need for adaptation is heightened. Yet another reason is that strategies of related diversification appear to provide an opportunity for developing a unique context in which business heads can be more motivated and willing to consider collective resource action between their business units than would likely be the case for business heads contracting with organizational entities outside their firm. The better information inside the firm suggests that such internal collaborations are likely to have higher quality than those with outside entities.

Second, using a practice theory lens, I integrate elements of structure, process, and social relationships in executive leadership groups to provide insight through a practice theory lens that explains the association of these features with managerial resource actions and likewise firm outcomes. In particular, I add an empirical example of the notion of "self-enhancing incentives" introduced by Pfeffer and Fong (2005) to better explain executive leader motivations, agency, and intent. Third, my non-findings of any relationship between executive leadership group demography stands in contrast to the large body of prior research that has focused on the relationships between executive leadership group composition and important firm outcomes like performance (cf. Carpenter et al., 2004). As an alternative, my research program brings elements of structure, process, and social relationship to the forefront through direct observation, and then considering these elements in relationship to each other, rather than examining these elements as separate areas of theoretical interest.

A practice theory of executive leadership groups
A practice theory of executive leadership groups considers the organizational relationships that make up an organization to be at once a system of structures, processes, power relationships, norms of behavior, and so on – rather than a set of separate causal elements – within which GMs can exercise their personal and collective judgment and initiative in developing possible resource actions. The system of organizational relationships is regarded as constraining, but not totally so. That is, in any given circumstance the system provides a framework within which the "productivity set" (Penrose, 1959) of possible resource actions are developed by GMs exercising their individual initiative (agency).

GM resource actions are thus inherently improvisational. But, like adjustments to cadence and dynamics in the popular Jazz Band metaphor (e.g., Eisenberg, 1990; Weick, 1998; Miner et al., 2001), such actions still tend to reproduce the system. That is, it is still jazz. Since the audience (environment) is likely to respond back in the expected way to the music, with its anticipated divergences from the musical scores, the resulting and subsequent performances are clearly a reproduction of the system. To carry the music metaphor a step further, transformation of the system is more analogous to Ray Charles's integration of gospel music with blues-based lyrics to produce an entirely new genre of music called soul. Transformative consequences to actions are rare.

GM resource actions shape the system of organizational relationships in two primary ways. The first of these involves the everyday activities of GMs, similar to those described in Mintzberg's (1973) seminal study of managerial life. These are those regular GM resource actions that reproduce and incrementally improve the system of relationships that make possible the reproduction of past success. This reproduction of the system is likely to continue as long as feedback from the environment remains within the boundaries of predictable expectations. This is the administrative dimension of business general management. However, since all environments have some extent of dynamism, at some point resource actions will produce novel feedback from the environment. When this occurs, it calls into question the current resource configurations within and among the BUs. GMs, as knowledgeable organizational actors, are likely to reconsider the efficacy of some past resource actions, and likewise consider the possibilities of different productivity sets (i.e., resource combinations) for possible resource actions individually and in collaboration with sister BUs. This possibility of new resource configurations, following scholars like Schumpeter (1934, 1942), Penrose (1959), Nelson and Winter (1982), and Stevenson and Jarillo (1990), can be considered the essence of entrepreneurial management. The theory of business general management presented here thus includes both the entrepreneurial and administrative roles of top managers.

Motivations of executive leaders

Executive leader resource actions are decidedly political, as they take place as plans within plans that exist in systems or organizational relationships, rather than as "ad hoc" responses to a particular stimulus (cf. Ortner, 1984). Power permeates the relationship between the organizational system and the motivations of GMs to consider resource actions. GMs are highly knowledgeable organizational actors with significant track records of accomplishment, who also have authority and control over strategic organizational resources. Therefore, GMs have the cognitive capacity and material reality necessary to consider the immediate consequences of their resource actions as well as several possible scenarios that subsequent resource actions might lead to. In addition, GM resource action appears to be motivated by opportunities for personal development rather than simply economic incentives. The extent of GM turnover suggests that GMs have ready access to similar economic rewards in other organizations, and therefore such rewards may be a necessary rather than sufficient source of motivation. That is, what appears to be more variable, idiosyncratic, and somewhat fleeting are the developmental aspects that membership in a particular MBT might offer a particular GM during a particular time-frame. In addition, the opportunity to form trusting (or distrusting) relationships through repeated group interactions appears to be salient as well (cf., Granovetter, 1985; Gulati, 1995; Tsai and Ghoshal, 1998). This suggests that traditional understandings of motivation in groups might not be sufficiently explanatory in coalitions of powerful organizational actors.

There are three fundamental assertions that I am making in the theory development: First, social systems are subject to the extent of environmental dynamism; second, social systems within organizations differ in their reproductive and transformative efficacy; third, transformative efficacy will be associated with outcomes in high-dynamic environments. I summarize a preliminary practice theory of executive leadership groups with the following central axioms:

1.   Organizational outcomes are a consequence of strategic resource actions within a system of organizational relationships. Resources are defined as anything that can be used as a source of power in an interaction.

2. Strategic resource actions are performed by powerful organizational actors. Powerful organizational actors are knowledgeable social beings that have agency, motivations, emotions, and social relationships. Powerful organizational actors are typically either TMT members (but not all members) and, in the case of multi-business organization, include the business unit GMs.

3. Resource actions take place within a system of organizational relationships that include structure, process, resources, and group interactions that empower and constrain action. The consequences of resource actions tend to reproduce the existing system of organizational relationships. However, in some cases, resource actions can have the consequence of transforming the system relationships.

4. All organizations need structures that reproduce past success, otherwise they will not persist once they survive the liabilities of newness. When the extent of environmental dynamism is low, reproduction is most salient to organizational outcomes. When the extent of environmental dynamism is high, then systems that facilitate transformation as well reproduction will be associated with successful outcomes

5. Significant organizational outcomes will be associated with the practice of executive leadership. Executive leadership is explained by the relationship between observable organizational elements like interdependence, autonomy, incentives, behaviors, group interactions, power relationship, interpersonal perceptions and the agency of general managers. Overall, the preliminary outline of a practice theory of executive leadership groups presented offers a more "socialized" view of organizational actors as a counterpoint to an "under-socialized" view of the individual as an economic actor or the "over-socialized" view that individual actions are determined by path-dependent norms, values, and culture (e.g., Granovetter, 1985).

Multi-business team members, individually and collectively, provide an exemplar of entrepreneurial management within firms previously articulated by Schumpeter (1934), Penrose (1959) and Kirzner (1973). That is, executive leader intent is a means by which firm resources are reconfigured in novel ways so that they can be put to more productive use in changing product market environments. Likewise, if general managers are not familiar with sister business units and do not communicate or develop trusting relationships with peer general managers, then few new synergies will be realized – and "dissynergies" may even result. This does not suggest that the top management team should yield their crucial role in assembling the businesses, setting long-term strategy and vision, and mediating the financial relationship between the corporation and market stakeholders. Rather, it calls for a more thoughtful approach regarding the locus of authority and control of particular resources, especially in high-dynamic markets, where novel resource actions are a primary means of firm adaptation. For example, the mixing in some prior studies of high- and low-power organizational actors (e.g., those TMT members that control strategic resources and those that do not), as well as omitting other powerful organizational actors (e.g., the MBT), may well be a factor in weak or conflicting results in many studies using an upper echelons approach (e.g., Priem et al., 1999; Martin and Eisenhardt, 2010).

CONCLUSION

This preliminary outline of a practice theory of business general management extends all three sides of the Berger and Luckmann (1966) triangle to an organizational context. That is, an organization is a system. Organizations are powerful and constraining (and we want them to be!). Yet, organizations can be made, adapted, and unmade through human action and interaction, particularly those actions and interactions that involve strategic resources. Thus, by considering theories of organization through a practice theory lens, an understanding of inertia and adaptive forces emerges that is far more intertwined than articulated in past research. That is, organizations that survive are systems of organizational relationships that tend to be reproduced through business general management. However, if change in the environment creates a different response to an organization through such things as decreases and/or increases in sales and/or profits, then the validity of the current alignment of the business unit resource configurations and the configuration of the relationships among the business units themselves are called into question. If the system of organizational relationships enables the possibility of novel resource actions, then managers may be able to take actions that reconfigure the organization's resources in a more optimal way. However, if the structures and processes constrain action in a way that maintains the "status quo," then the organization will likely begin to decline as the environment changes. More broadly, resource actions in the environment may also have the consequence of shaping the environment itself by changing rents or, more interestingly, behavior itself. For example, buying behaviors of individuals who use services like Amazon's online marketplace continue to be shaped by online commerce, and the nature of online commerce is in turn shaped by individual behaviors as to what they are willing to or not willing to purchase online. This study thus extends practice theory to an organizational level as a complement to more micro-level studies of how technology structures individual and project work (e.g., Barley, 1986; Orlikowski, 2000; Carlile, 2002) and macro-level studies that focus on the reproduction of society through political and social processes (e.g., Bourdieu, 1977; Giddens, 1984).

This study also has several practical implications for managers. First, this study provides clarity in understanding the leverage points that corporate-level executives can use to create an effective MBT. For example, corporate-level executives can alter the power relationships by shifting product market rights (charters) among the business, expeditiously removing GMs who are under-performing or who fail to "fit" with the team, or facilitate group interactions by creating occasions for such interactions through internal and external gatherings. Likewise, they can increase GM commitment to the organization by encouraging and supporting GM participation in roles that are external to the organization. Second, the value of closely related diversification in high-dynamic markets comes to the forefront as such diversification increases the likelihood of collaborative resource actions among the businesses and potential for co-evolutionary transformations. Third, a more nuanced portrait of corporate leadership is suggested. Sometimes corporate executives should lead the way (e.g., board relationships, repatching the business portfolio, shaping organizational identity), while at other times they should step back. More broadly, the foremost challenge of corporate leadership may lie in knowing what behaviors to constrain and what behaviors to empower given the organization's particular environmental constraints. In summary, this research provides corporate executives with practical insight into actions that they can take to improve the realization of value from gathering multiple businesses together under one organizational umbrella.

ACKNOWLEDGMENTS

This research has been generously supported by the Stanford Technology Ventures Program, Ewing Marion Kauffman Foundation, and the Herb Kelleher Center for Entrepreneurship and the IC2 Institute of the University of Texas at Austin. I would like to thank Kathleen Eisenhardt, Kyle Lewis, Filipe Santos, and participants at the McCombs School research paper series for their comments on earlier drafts of this paper.

REFERENCES

Adner, R. and Helfat, C.E. (2003). Corporate effects and dynamic managerial capabilities. *Strategic Management Journal*, **24**(10), 1011–25.

Aldrich, H. (1979). *Organizations and environments*. Englewood Cliffs, NJ: Prentice-Hall.

Barley, S.R. (1986). Technology as an occasion for structuring: Evidence from CT scanners and the social order of radiology departments. *Administrative Science Quarterly*, **31**(1), 78–108.

Benner, M.J. and Tushman, M.L. (2003). Exploitation, exploration, and process management: The productivity dilemma revisited. *Academy of Management Review*, **28**(2), 238–56.

Berger, P.L. and Luckmann, T. (1966). *The social construction of reality; a treatise in the sociology of knowledge* (1st edition). Garden City, NY: Doubleday.

Berle, A.A. and Means, G.C. (1932). *The modern corporation and private property*. New York, NY: Commerce Clearing House.

Blau, P.M. (1977). *Inequality and heterogeneity: A primitive theory of social structure*. New York, NY: Free Press.

Boeker, W. (1997). Executive migration and strategic change: The effect of top manager movement on product market entry. *Administrative Science Quarterly*, **42**(2), 213–36.

Bourdieu, P. (1977). *Outline of a theory of practice*. Cambridge, UK: Cambridge University Press.

Bowman, E.H. and Helfat, C.E. (2001). Does corporate strategy matter? *Strategic Management Journal*, **22**(1), 1–23.

Brush, T.H. and Bromiley, P. (1997). What does a small corporate effect mean? A variance components simulation of corporate and business effects. *Strategic Management Journal*, **18**(10), 825–35.

Burgelman, R.A. (1983). A process model of internal corporate venturing in the diversified major firm. *Administrative Science Quarterly*, **28**(2), 223–44.

Campbell, A. and Luchs, K.S. (1998). *Strategic Synergy* (2nd edition). London, UK; Boston, MA: International Thomson Business Press.

Campbell, D.T. (1969). Variation and selective retention in socio-cultural evolution. *General Systems: Yearbook of the Society for General Systems Research*, **14**, 69–85.

Carlile, P.R. (2002). A pragmatic view of knowledge and boundaries: Boundary objects in new product development. *Organization Science*, **13**(2), 442–55.

Carpenter, M.A., Geletkanycz, M.A., and Sanders, W.G. (2004). Upper echelons research revisited: Antecedents, elements, and consequences of top management team composition. *Journal of Management*, **30**(6), 749–78.

Chandler, A.D. (1962). *Strategy and structure: Chapters in the history of the industrial enterprise*. Cambridge, MA: MIT Press.

Chandler, A.D. (1991). The functions of the HQ unit in the multibusiness firm. *Strategic Management Journal*, **12**(S2), 31–50.

Child, J. (1972). Organizational structure, environment and performance: The role of strategic choice. *Sociology*, **6**(1), 1–21.

Coase, R.H. (ed.) [1937] (1991). *The nature of the firm*. New York, NY: Oxford University Press.

Cohen, S.G. and Bailey, D.E. (1997). What makes teams work: Group effectiveness research from the shop floor to the executive suite. *Journal of Management*, **23**(3), 239–90.

Collis, D.J. (1994). How valuable are organizational capabilities? *Strategic Management Journal*, **15**(S1), 143–52.

Dosi, G., Nelson, R.R., and Winter, S.G. (2000). *The nature and dynamics of organizational capabilities*. New York, NY: Oxford University Press.

Eisenberg, E.M. (1990). Jamming: Transcendence through organizing. *Communications Research*, **17**(2), 139–64.

Eisenhardt, K.M. (1989a). Agency theory: An assessment and review. *Academy of Management Review*, **14**(1), 57–74.

Eisenhardt, K.M. (1989b). Building theories from case study research. *Academy of Management Review*, **14**(4), 532–50.

Eisenhardt, K.M. and Galunic, D.C. (2000). Coevolving: At last, a way to make synergies work. *Harvard Business Review*, **78**(1), 91–101.

Eisenhardt, K.M. and Martin, J.A. (2000). Dynamic capabilities: What are they? *Strategic Management Journal*, **21**(10/11), 1105–21.

Eisenmann, T.R. and Bower, J. (2000). The entrepreneurial M-Form: Strategic integration in global media firms. *Organization Science*, **11**(3), 348–55.

Emirbayer, M. and Mische, A. (1998). What is agency? *American Journal of Sociology*, **103**(4), 962–1023.

Fama, E.F. and Jensen, M. (1983). Separation of ownership and control. *Journal of Law & Economics*, **26**(2), 301–25.

Feldman, M.S. (2003). A performative perspective on stability and change in organizational routines. *Industrial & Corporate Change*, **12**(2), 727–51.

Feldman, M.S. and Pentland, B.T. (2003). Reconceptualizing organizational routines as a source of flexibility and change. *Administrative Science Quarterly*, **48**(1), 94–118.

Fligstein, N. (1985). The spread of the multidivisional form among large firms, 1919–1979. *American Sociological Review*, **50**(3), 377–91.

Fligstein, N. (1990). *The transformation of corporate control*. Cambridge, MA: Harvard University Press.

Fredrickson, J.W. (1983). Strategic process research: Questions and recommendations. *Academy of Management Review*, **8**(4), 565–75.

Freeland, R.F. (1996). The myth of the M-Form? Governance, consent, and organizational change. *American Journal of Sociology*, **102**(2), 483–27.

Galbraith, J.R. (1977). *Organization design*. Reading, MA: Addison-Wesley Pub. Co.

Galunic, D.C. and Eisenhardt, K.M. (2001). Architectural innovation and modular corporate forms. *Academy of Management Journal*, **44**(6), 1229–49.

Galunic, D.C. and Weeks, J. (2001). Interorganizational ecology. In J.A.C. Baum (ed.), *Companion to organizations*. London, UK: Blackwell, pp. 75–97.

Giddens, A. (1984). *The constitution of society*. Berkeley, CA: University of California Press.

Gilbert, C.G. (2005). Unbundling the structure of inertia: Resource versus routine rigidity. *Academy of Management Journal*, **48**(5), 741–63.

Goold, M., Alexander, M., and Campbell, A. (1994). *Corporate-level strategy: Creating value in the multibusiness company*. New York, NY: J. Wiley.

Granovetter, M. (1985). Economic action and social structure: The problem of embeddedness. *American Journal of Sociology*, **91**(3), 481–510.

Gulati, R. (1995). Social structure and alliance formation patterns. *Administrative Science Quarterly*, **40**(4), 619–52.

Gulati, R. and Singh, H. (1998). The architecture of cooperation: Managing coordination costs and appropriation concerns in strategic alliances. *Administrative Science Quarterly*, **43**(4), 781–815.

Hambrick, D.C. (1994). Top management groups: A conceptual integration and reconsideration of the team label. In B.M. Staw and L.L. Cummings (eds), *Research in organizational behavior* (Vol. 15). Greenwich, CT: JAI Press, pp. 171–214.

Hambrick, D.C. and Mason, P.C. (1984). Upper echelons: The organization as a reflection of its top managers. *Academy of Management Review*, **9**(2), 193–207.

Hambrick, D.C., Finkelstein, S., and Mooney, A.C. (2005). Executive job demands: New insights for explaining strategic decisions and leader behaviors. *Academy of Management Review*, **30**(3), 472–91.

Hannan, M.T. and Freeman, J. (1977). The population ecology of organizations. *American Journal of Sociology*, **82**(5), 929–64.

Hannan, M.T. and Freeman, J. (1984). Structural inertia and organizational change. *American Sociological Review*, **49**(2), 149–64.

Helfat, C.E., Finkelstein, S., Mitchell, W., Peteraf, M.A., Singh, H., Teece, D.J. et al. (2007a). Dynamic capabilities: Foundations. In Helfat et al., *Dynamic capabilities: Understanding strategic change in organizations*. Malden, MA: Blackwell Pub., pp. 1–18.

Helfat, C.E., Finkelstein, S., Mitchell, W., Peteraf, M.A., Singh, H., Teece, D. J. et al. (2007b). *Dynamic capabilities: Understanding strategic change in organizations*. Malden, MA: Blackwell Pub.

Hill, C.W.L., Hitt, M.A., and Hoskisson, R.E. (1992). Cooperative versus competitive structures in related and unrelated diversified firms. *Organization Science*, **3**(4), 501–21.

Hoskisson, R.E., Hitt, M.A., and Hill, C.W.L. (1993). Managerial incentives and investment in R&D in large multiproduct firms. *Organization Science*, **4**(2), 325–41.

Hough, J.R. (2006). Business segment performance redux: A multilevel approach. *Strategic Management Journal*, **27**(1), 45–61.

Jacobs, D. (1974). Dependency and vulnerability: An exchange approach to the control of organizations. *Administrative Science Quarterly*, **19**(1), 45–59.

Jensen, M. and Zajac, E.J. (2004). Corporate elites and corporate strategy: How demographic preferences and structural position shape the scope of the firm. *Strategic Management Journal*, **25**(6), 507–24.

Jick, T.D. (1979). Mixing qualitative and quantitative methods: Triangulation in action. *Administrative Science Quarterly*, **24**(4), 602–11.

Kerr, J.L. (1985). Strategies and managerial rewards: An empirical study. *Academy of Management Journal*, **28**(1), 155–80.

Kirzner, I.M. (1973). *Competition and entrepreneurship*. Chicago, IL: University of Chicago Press.

Knight, F.H. (1921). *Risk, uncertainty and profit*. Boston, MA: Hart, Schaffner & Marx; Houghton Mifflin Co.

Kumar, N., Stern, L.W., and Anderson, J.C. (1993). Conducting interorganizational research using key informants. *Academy of Management Journal*, **36**(6), 1633–51.

Kunda, G. (1992). *Engineering culture: Control and commitment in a high-tech corporation*. Philadelphia, PA: Temple University Press.

Leonard-Barton, D. (1992). Core capabilities and core rigidities: A paradox in managing new product development. *Strategic Management Journal*, **13**(S1), 111–25.

March, J.G. (1991). Exploration and exploitation in organizational learning. *Organization Science*, **2**(1), 71–87.

March, J.G. and Simon, H.A. (1958). *Organizations*. New York, NY: Wiley.

Martin, J.A. (2010). Dynamic managerial capabilities and the multi-business team: The role of episodic teams in executive leadership groups. *Organization Science*, in press.

Martin, J.A. and Carlile, P.R. (2000). Designing agile organizations: Organizational learning at the boundaries. In R.E. Quinn, R.M. O'Neill, and L.S. Clair (eds), *Pressing problems in modern organizations: Transforming the agenda for research and practice*. New York, NY: Amacom, pp. 129–52.

Martin, J.A. and Eisenhardt, K.M. (2010). Creating cross-business-unit collaborations in multi-business organizations. *Academy of Management Journal*, **53**(2), 265–301.

Miles, M.B. and Huberman, A.M. (1984). *Qualitative data analysis: A sourcebook of new methods*. Beverly Hills, CA: Sage Publications.

Miles, M.B. and Huberman, A.M. (1994). *Qualitative data analysis: A sourcebook of new methods* (2nd edition). Beverly Hills, CA: Sage Publications.

Miner, A.S., Bassoff, P., and Moorman, C. (2001). Organizational improvisation and learning: A field study. *Administrative Science Quarterly*, **46**(2), 304–37.

Mintzberg, H. (1973). *The nature of managerial work*. New York, NY: Harper & Row.

Nelson, R. and Winter, S. (1982). *An evolutionary theory of economic change*. Cambridge, MA: Belknap Press.

Orlikowski, W.J. (2000). Using technology and constituting structures: A practice lens for studying technology in organizations. *Organization Science*, **11**(4), 404–28.

Ortner, S.B. (1984). Theory in anthropology since the sixties. *Comparative Studies in Society and History*, **26**(1), 126–66.

Palich, L.E., Cardinal, L.B., and Miller, C.C. (2000). Curvilinearity in the diversification–performance linkage: An examination of over three decades of research. *Strategic Management Journal*, **21**(2), 155–74.

Penrose, E.T. (1959). *The theory of the growth of the firm*. New York, NY: Wiley.

Pettigrew, A.M. (1979). On studying organizational cultures. *Administrative Science Quarterly*, **24**(4), 570–82.

Pettigrew, A.M. (1992). The character and significance of strategy process research. *Strategic Management Journal*, **13**(S2), 5–11.

Pfeffer, J. (1991). Organization theory and structural perspectives on management. *Journal of Management*, **17**(4), 789–803.

Pfeffer, J. and Fong, C. (2005). Building organization theory from first principles: The self-enhancement motive and understanding power and influence. *Organization Science*, **16**(4), 372–88.

Pfeffer, J. and Salancik, G.R. (1978). *The external control of organizations: A resource dependence perspective*. New York, NY: Harper & Row.

Priem, R.L., Lyon, D.W., and Dess, G.G. (1999). Inherent limitations of demographic proxies in top management team heterogeneity research. *Journal of Management*, **25**(6), 935–53.

Roquebert, J.A., Phillips, R.L., and Westfall, P.A. (1996). Markets vs. management: What "drives" profitability. *Strategic Management Journal*, **17**(8), 653–64.

Rumelt, R.P. (1974). *Strategy, structure, and economic performance*. Boston, MA: Harvard University Press.

Schumpeter, J.A. (1934). *The theory of economic development* (R. Opie, Trans. 7th edition). Cambridge, MA: Harvard University Press.

Schumpeter, J.A. (1942). *Capitalism, socialism, and democracy*. New York, NY: Harper.

Sewell, W. (1992). A theory of structure: Duality, agency, and transformation. *American Journal of Sociology*, **98**(1), 1–29.

Simon, H.A. (1982). *Models of bounded rationality*. Cambridge, MA: MIT Press.

Stevenson, H.H. and Jarillo, J.C. (1990). A paradigm of entrepreneurship: Entrepreneurial management. *Strategic Management Journal*, **11**, 17–27.

Teece, D.J. (2007). Explicating dynamic capabilities: The nature and microfoundations of (sustainable) enterprise performance. *Strategic Management Journal*, **28**(13), 1319–50.

Teece, D.J., Pisano, G., and Shuen, A. (1997). Dynamic capabilities and strategic management. *Strategic Management Journal*, **18**(7), 509–33.

Thompson, J. (1967). *Organizations in action: Social science bases of administrative theory*. New York, NY: McGraw Hill.

Tsai, W. and Ghoshal, S. (1998). Social capital and value creation: The role of intrafirm networks. *Academy of Management Journal*, **41**(4), 464–76.

Weick, K.E. (1998). Improvisation as a mindset for organizational analysis. *Organization Science*, **9**(5), 543–55.

West, C.T. and Schwenk, C.R. (1996). Top management team strategic consensus, demographic homogeneity and firm performance: A report of resounding nonfindings. *Strategic Management Journal*, **17**(7), 571–676.

Williamson, O.E. (1975). *Markets and hierarchies*. New York, NY: Free Press.

Williamson, O.E. (1985). *The economic institutions of capitalism: Firms, markets, relational contracting*. New York and London: Free Press, Collier Macmillan.

Williamson, O.E. (1996). *The mechanisms of governance*. New York, NY: Oxford University Press.

Winter, S.G. (2003). Understanding dynamic capabilities. *Strategic Management Journal*, **24**(10), 991–5.

Yin, R.K. (1989). *Case study research: Design and methods* (rev. edition). Newbury Park, CA: Sage.

Yin, R.K. (1993). *Applications of case study research* (2nd edition). Newbury Park, CA: Sage.

Yin, R.K. (2003). *Case study research: Design and methods* (3rd edition). Newbury Park, CA: Sage.

Zenger, T. and Hesterly, W. (1997). The dissaggregation of corporations: Selective intervention, high-powered incentives, and molecular units. *Organization Science*, **8**(3), 209–22.

11 The joint effect of top management team heterogeneity and competitive behavior on stock returns and risk

Margaret Hughes-Morgan, Walter J. Ferrier, and Giuseppe (Joe) Labianca

Members of the top management teams (TMTs) of competing firms are responsible for executing an unending series of competitive moves and countermoves meant to attract customers, keep rivals off balance, and make their own firms profitable. These competitive actions and responses, including price cutting, introducing new products, marketing campaigns, capacity expansions, and customer service improvements, are the overt manifestations of the TMT's cognitive and experiential breadth and its strategic decision-making process. Indeed, effectively implementing a series of competitive moves depends on the ability of the TMT to monitor the environment, navigate obstacles, define and exploit opportunities, develop and select potential competitive moves, and deftly pilot the firm through the currents of competitive rivalry and retaliation.

As suggested by a substantial body of empirical research on upper echelons, the TMT influences a wide range of organizational processes and outcomes (Finkelstein and Hambrick, 1996; Carpenter et al., 2004). With specific regard to the TMT's influence on competitive actions, the burgeoning stream of research in strategic management known as competitive dynamics has found, for example, that TMTs characterized by high levels of cognitive and experiential heterogeneity are more likely than their heterogeneous counterparts to proactively initiate competitive actions and quickly respond to rivals' actions (Hambrick et al., 1996). This research has also found that heterogeneous TMTs typically carry out complex (as opposed to simple) attacks against rivals that consist of many types of competitive actions (Ferrier, 2001). Further, socially integrated TMTs were found to carry out more competitive actions and do so with greater speed and frequency than socially disconnected TMTs (Lin and Shih, 2008). Yet, firms led by heterogeneous TMTs were less competitively aggressive under conditions of financial distress than firms led by more homogeneous TMTs (Ferrier et al., 2002). These studies underscore the importance of accounting for managerial cognitive and experiential breadth because research in competitive dynamics has found robust empirical support for the link between the intensity, pace, and patterns of competitive behavior and a wide range of organizational performance outcomes, such as sales growth, market share, profitability, and stock returns (Smith et al., 1991; Young et al., 1996; Ferrier et al., 1999; Ferrier, 2001; Ferrier and Lee, 2002; Lyon and Ferrier, 2002; Ferrier and Lyon, 2004).

The full range of TMT and competitive dynamics research notwithstanding, we believe that two serious gaps exist. First, much of the upper echelons and competitive dynamics research has relied on annualized, longer-term accounting-based measures of performance. This leaves open the possibility that a wide variety of potential confounding factors (e.g., changing industry conditions, changing consumer preferences, etc.) unrelated to either TMT heterogeneity or competitive actions could impact long-term performance. To avoid these potential confounds and to tease out the impact of TMT characteristics on a measure of firm performance that is contemporaneous with competitive actions carried out over time, we use stock returns and risk as our dependent constructs. In so doing, we respond to the call for more research on how organizational factors and strategy impact short-term performance, such as stock returns and measures of competitive risk (McNamara and Bromiley, 1999; Bromiley et al., 2001). Moreover, within the behavioral finance stream of research there is a growing recognition of human capital as one among many determinants of stock performance and risk (Goyal and Santa Clara, 2003). Because a firm's human capital – the knowledge, skills, abilities and experience of management and employees – cannot be traded or easily duplicated, it uniquely determines the firm's overall strategic posture and shapes the competitive actions that ultimately influence performance. Unfortunately, only a few studies to date in the competitive dynamics literature have explored how competitive action influences stock-market-related outcomes (e.g., Bettis and Weeks, 1987; Ferrier and Lee, 2002).

Second, much of the extant research in upper echelons and competitive dynamics has explored how TMT characteristics *directly* influence competitive action and, in turn, performance (Hambrick et al., 1996; Ferrier, 2001; Lin and Shih, 2008). However, the idea that managerial characteristics and processes are both antecedent to and, more importantly, *dynamically interactive* with competitive strategy and other factors has gained greater traction among TMT scholars (Tihanyi et al., 2000; Carpenter and Fredrickson, 2001; Carpenter, 2002; Carpenter et al., 2004; Certo et al., 2006; Lester et al., 2006). Yet, surprisingly few studies have explored the contingent relationship between various aspects of the TMT and competitive action and performance (cf., Ferrier et al., 2002; Lyon and Ferrier, 2002; Ferrier and Lyon, 2004).

We firmly believe that managerial cognition and choice and the observed patterns of competitive behavior carried out among head-to-head rivals cannot be theoretically or empirically disentangled from another. We argue that a firm's human capital and observed competitive actions jointly drive its ability to meet strategic challenges. More specifically, firms that are led by top managers who collectively possess and engender diversity in perspective and an alertness to opportunity, strategic experience, and engender decision-making skills that enable them to carry out a set of competitive actions that investors believe will lead the firm to future profitability will experience higher stock returns and lower levels of stock risk (Ang et al., 2006). Hence, the question our study explores is: in the context of head-to-head rivalry between firms, how do the firm's human capital and observed competitive behavior jointly influence stock returns and risk?

BACKGROUND AND HYPOTHESES

TMT Heterogeneity and Firm Performance

As noted above, upper echelons theory posits that top management team heterogeneity influences the firm's strategic choices and competitive behavior that ultimately affects firm performance. Generally, demographically heterogeneous TMTs are thought to possess a broad variety of cognitions and experiences that the team brings to bear in developing and executing strategy. Thus, high levels of TMT heterogeneity lead to "diversity, novelty, and comprehensiveness in the set of recommended solutions" (Wiersema and Bantel, 1992, p.96). Such TMTs have more potential "socio-cognitive horsepower" than teams with homogeneous backgrounds and experiences (Carpenter, 2002, p.277). Studies indicate, for example, that cognitive and experiential diversity among TMT members is associated with technical innovation (West and Anderson, 1994), a higher likelihood of alliance formation (Eisenhardt and Schoonhoven, 1996), and higher levels of corporate diversification (Wiersema and Bantel, 1992). Most relevant to our study, heterogeneous TMTs are better equipped than homogeneous TMTs to carry out aggressive, quick, and complex competitive attacks against rivals, which prior research shows to have a strongly positive influence on performance (e.g., Hambrick et al., 1996; Miller and Chen, 1996; Ferrier et al., 1999; Ferrier, 2001).

Consistent with prior research, we believe that TMT characteristics and background serve as important signals of managerial competence, skills and prestige to investors in the stock market who implicitly recognize that human capital is a driver of both strategy and future performance (D'Aveni, 1990; D'Aveni and Kesner, 1993; Lester et al., 2006). Indeed, Lester et al. (2006) found that firms with TMTs characterized as having high levels of managerial prestige, based on factors such as education, corporate board affiliations, and political experience, had higher valuations when issuing their initial public stock offerings (IPOs). Similarly, Cohen and Dean (2005) found that TMT demographics – age, education, and firm tenure – influence IPO under-pricing. Further, Higgins and Gulati (2006) found that TMT capabilities impact the quantity and the quality of the pool of investors, as indicated by underwriter prestige, who participate in the firm's IPO. Other studies have, for instance, examined how the level of cultural fit between the TMTs of merging firms, as perceived by investors, influences post-merger valuation (Chatterjee et al., 1992). Also, corporate creditors were less likely to support firms led by TMTs viewed as having low prestige, which, in turn, led to a higher likelihood of bankruptcy for those firms (D'Aveni, 1990). These studies strongly suggest that equity and credit markets are influenced by the firm's human capital. Although the preponderance of research in management and behavioral finance has focused on the influence of the human capital of new-to-market firms on performance (see Simsek, Heavey, Prabhakar and Huvaj in Chapter 12 of this volume for a more in-depth analysis of strategic leadership and entrepreneurship), the relationship between TMT characteristics and investment performance is also relevant among large, market-leading firms (D'Aveni, 1990; D'Aveni and Kesner, 1993; Lester et al., 2006).

As noted above, our aim is to explore the contingent relationship between human capital, competitive behavior, and performance. Yet, we offer the following direct-effects hypothesis as a baseline:

Hypothesis 1: TMT heterogeneity is positively related to stock returns and negatively related to stock risk.

Stock Returns and Risk as a Function of TMT Heterogeneity – Competitive Strategy "Fit"

The upper echelons perspective views the TMT as a storehouse of cognitive and experiential resources that the team brings to bear to solve problems and make decisions manifest in the strategy carried out by the firm (Finkelstein and Hambrick, 1996; Carpenter et al., 2004). Prior studies have also acknowledged and explored the potential negative repercussions of demographic heterogeneity. For example, TMT diversity is related to slower decision making, lower levels of team cohesiveness, and potentially fruitful informal communication, decision-making dysfunction, and lower levels of strategic consensus (Smith et al., 1994; Amason, 1996; Knight et al., 1999). Thus, extant research suggests an important trade off; namely, that heterogeneous TMTs are better at *creating*, whereas homogeneous TMTs are better at *deciding* (Hambrick et al., 1996).

Our study aims to flesh out the boundaries and contingencies of this trade off, insofar as which TMT characteristics are supportive of competitive novelty or complexity, and which support competitive aggressiveness and speed. More specifically, as evidenced by a firm's stock market returns and levels of risk, we believe that the stock market is sensitive to the (in)congruence between the TMT's collective experiences and capabilities and the competitive actions that the firm carries out against rivals. Indeed, research on the TMT heterogeneity–performance relationship has increasingly moved toward examining issues of "fit," with the central argument being that a requisite level of TMT heterogeneity is necessary to maximize organizational performance. These contingency arguments describe fit between TMT heterogeneity and important dimensions of the strategic contexts. For example, Keck (1997) found that short-tenured TMTs were most effective in complex, turbulent environments (i.e., rivalry characterized by performance risk and demand instability), whereas long-tenured TMTs were most effective in stable environments. Similarly, Haleblian and Finkelstein (1993) found that demographically diverse TMTs outperformed their homogeneous counterparts in turbulent environments. Carpenter (2002) found that the positive relationship between TMT heterogeneity and firm performance was stronger for firms with high levels of globalization – which implies high levels of geographic, cultural, and greater complexity – than those firms whose operations were confined to domestic markets.

In the context of head-to-head rivalry and the dynamics of strategic decision making, we argue that certain patterns of competitive actions are reflective of a greater or lesser cognitive load that exerts pressure and risk upon the TMT in the decision-making process. In other words, the TMT's cognitive and experiential capabilities should match the complexity and instability of the competitive actions carried out by the firm. More specifically, we argue that a firm's entire set – or *repertoire* – of competitive actions carried out in a relevant period of time is reflective of this cognitive load. From the perspective of organizational information processing theory (Galbraith, 1973; Fairbank et al., 2006), the firm's repertoire of competitive actions relates to the greater or lesser information processing needs of the TMT that is manifest in and vary along two important dimensions of the firm's *competitive strategy*: strategic complexity and strategic volume.

Consistent with prior research in competitive dynamics, we characterize a firm's competitive strategy as the set or repertoire of competitive actions carried out in a given window of time (Miller and Chen, 1994, 1996; Ferrier et al., 1999; Deephouse, 1999;

Ferrier and Lyon, 2004). From an information processing perspective, a firm's competitive repertoire exhibits the following dimensions: internal strategic complexity (the range of different types of competitive actions), external strategic complexity (the extent to which the firm's repertoire of competitive actions is distinct from a referent rival), and strategic volume (the number of competitive actions carried out). These three dimensions have received robust conceptual refinement and empirical validation in the competitive dynamics literature (see Smith et al., 2001 for a comprehensive review) and determine the extent of the cognitive load placed upon the firm's top management team.

One of the few studies to explore the moderated relationship between TMT heterogeneity, competitive action, and performance found that competitive repertoire simplicity – carrying out a narrow range of competitive actions, such as engaging in only pricing or marketing actions – was positively related to profitability for firms with heterogeneous TMTs at the helm and negatively related for homogeneous TMTs (Ferrier and Lyon, 2004). Similarly, we believe that a firm's stock performance and stock risk is also a function of the fit between the information processing capabilities of the TMT and the characteristics of the firm's competitive repertoire. In other words, as the firm's strategy unfolds and these characteristics come into view, the stock market reconciles the TMT's information processing capabilities with the cognitive load placed upon the team inferred by the observable pattern of competitive actions carried out by the firm. Here, the firm's stock returns increase and risk decreases accordingly when there is good fit, and vice versa when the fit is poor.

Internal strategic complexity
A simple competitive repertoire consists mainly of a few types of strategic actions, such as using only marketing actions and new product introductions. A complex competitive repertoire, by contrast, consists of several types of actions, such as pricing actions, marketing actions, product actions, capacity actions, service actions, and signaling actions in various combinations, but exhibit a relative representative balance among the possible action types. One of the most fundamental ideas of competitive interaction posits that firms should execute strategy in an effort to diminish the ability of competitors to respond (e.g., Smith et al., 2001). Prior research has found that very simple competitive repertoires will be easily understood and unraveled by rivals, thereby leaving the attacking firm vulnerable to aggressive competitive response (Miller and Chen, 1996; Ferrier et al., 1999).

The performance benefits of a complex competitive strategy notwithstanding, such a strategy is difficult to conceive of and carry out. For example, a simple series of pricing actions will be easier to carry out and monitor than a continual complex series consisting of a wide range of different action types, such as new products, carefully executed price cuts, clever marketing campaigns, and capacity expansion actions. TMT members that come from different backgrounds, such as having worked in dissimilar industries or having a variety of functional backgrounds, gives the TMT a greater capacity for generating the variety of competitive moves that comprise a complex strategic repertoire. Indeed, heterogeneous TMTs possess a broader set of cognitive and experiential resources, generate a wider range of alternatives for strategic action, and engage in a comprehensive strategic decision-making process (Eisenhardt and Schoonhoven, 1990; Simons et al., 1999).

Consequently, TMTs with diverse backgrounds will be more effective at carrying out a complex set of competitive actions than homogeneous TMTs. This TMT–strategy combination will yield higher stock returns and lower risk:

Hypothesis 2: Firms with heterogeneous TMTs that attempt to carry out internally complex strategies experience higher stock returns and lower stock risk than firms with homogeneous TMTs.

External strategic complexity

In the context of head-to-head rivalry, managers must take full account of the actions of other firms in formulating strategy. When competing firms' competitive strategies are similar to one another, strategic decision making becomes a rather straightforward task. However, as the variance or complexity in the patterns of competitive actions carried out by rivals increases, so too does the complexity of the strategic environment faced by the firm's TMT. Consequently, when a firm's competitive strategy differs greatly in terms of the composition, pattern, and pacing of competitive actions relative to rivals, the stock market responds negatively (Ferrier and Lee, 2002). This would suggest that the stock market implicitly considers the characteristics of a referent rival's competitive repertoire as an anchor (Kahneman and Tversky, 1979) or strategic reference point (Fiegenbaum, 1990) against which the focal firm's strategic deviations carry higher or lower levels of risk. This means that as the focal firm's pattern of competitive behaviors deviate further and further from that of its principal rival – a form of exogenous risk – the stock market responds negatively.

We believe, however, that the stock market will react *jointly* to both external competitive complexity and the firm's human capital. More specifically, a firm led by a homogeneous TMT that carries out a set of competitive actions that increasingly deviates from the tried-and-true somewhat familiar strategies that the stock market has observed and valued in the past will garner a sharp negative market response and higher risk. Indeed, owing to their lack of experiential breadth and perspective, homogeneous TMTs are less capable of generating and carrying out a complex set of competitive behaviors. Homogeneous TMTs are less likely to engage in comprehensive decision making and avoid challenging one another as to the best course of action (Cosier and Rose, 1977; Simons et al., 1999). These features of the decision-making process are essential when the firm attempts to carry out strategies that have no proven track record of success and greatly differ from the strategies of its principal rival.

Examples of this from industry abound. For instance, led by a famously homogeneous TMT, Home Depot undertook a strategy that differed greatly from its competitors (Roush, 1999). At a time when most other firms in the industry were small and carried a limited product line at higher prices, Home Depot engaged in a series of innovative and aggressive pricing moves, implemented its "one stop shop" store concept by building astoundingly large retail units, and stocked tens of thousands SKUs (store keeping units). Such competitive aggressiveness is usually rewarded (cf., Smith et al., 2001). Yet, although Home Depot was a success story in the long term, its stock price in its early years suffered greatly. During the period 1987–95, Home Depot's average abnormal stock returns were 40 percent lower than that of its principal referent rival, Lowe's. The firm's lower stock returns were also accompanied by 12 percent higher firm-specific risk than Lowe's. Thus, it appears that investors feared that the firm's homogeneous TMT was not fully capable of deviating so radically from strategic norms in the hardware industry.

As we argue above, a sharp deviation from a tried and true set of competitive actions represents a significant cognitive load placed upon the TMT. We predict that the extent to which a TMT can effectively carry out a repertoire of competitive actions that differs from that of rivals will be contingent upon the heterogeneity of its members. More specifically, externally complex competitive strategies with heterogeneous TMTs at the helm, so to speak, will lead to positive outcomes in the form of higher stock returns and lower levels of risk:

> *Hypothesis 3:* Firms with heterogeneous TMTs that attempt to carry out externally complex strategies experience higher stock returns and lower stock risk than firms with homogeneous TMTs.

Strategic volume

An important principle of competitive rivalry posits that a firm that is able to initiate and sustain an aggressive series of competitive actions when attacking rivals will keep its rivals off balance and on the defensive (D'Aveni, 1994; Ferrier, 2001). This aptly describes the third dimension of competitive action that we believe is reflective of the information processing needs of the TMT – strategic volume. This is defined as the total number of competitive actions that a firm carries out in a given time period (in our study, one month). Prior research strongly supports the idea that the number of competitive actions carried out by a firm is related to better performance (Young et al., 1996; Ferrier et al., 1999).

These studies underscore the possibility that the firm's ability to carry out complex combinations of competitive actions is not always necessary to defeat an opponent. Sometimes round after round of a continuous, aggressive attack comprised of the repeated use of a given type of competitive action can overwhelm and weaken a rival to the point where the rival cannot carry out responding actions necessary to regain its competitive position.

The much-publicized demise of the British motorcycle industry at the hands of Japanese competition aptly describes the debilitating effects of strategic volume. The Japanese aggressively entered the motorcycle industry with a flurry of new product introductions and novel marketing campaigns that came in constant and rapid-fire succession over several years. While the Japanese strategy was rather simple, the British companies could not react in time to the Japanese firms' repeated blows. Companies like Honda introduced new products (e.g., the CB 750 motorcycle) that were bigger, faster, and better than the British products, and repeatedly unleashed marketing campaigns targeting teens and young adult consumers. Consequently, the rapid decline in market share experienced by the British manufacturers was, in part, due to their inability to respond to the Japanese's competitive moves quickly enough. They could not introduce new models of their own or counter the Japanese manufacturers' marketing campaigns effectively. As a result, several British motorcycle firms withdrew from the US market.

Prior research suggests that *heterogeneous* TMTs are less able to (re)act quickly to competitors' challenges (Hambrick et al., 1996) because they engage in a longer decision-making process (Simons et al., 1999) and are less likely to arrive at strategic consensus (Knight et al., 1999). This suggests that owing to their more "efficient" decision-making processes, *homogeneous* TMTs, by contrast, will be able to quickly and more aggressively carry out competitive attacks of longer duration that consist of more competitive actions as compared with heterogeneous TMTs.

The implications from both prior research and the lesson learned from industry experience suggest that high-volume strategies need to be developed and carried out in rapid succession and the attack sustained for longer duration. We predict that firms with heterogeneous TMTs that carry out high-volume strategies represents a serious misfit between observed competitive behaviors and the TMT's relative inefficiency of making quick decisions for a sustained period of time:

Hypothesis 4: Firms with heterogeneous TMTs that attempt to carry out high-volume strategies experience lower stock returns and higher stock risk than firms with homogeneous TMTs.

METHOD

Sample

Our sampling procedure and measures are similar to those used in prior research in competitive dynamics (cf., Ferrier, 2001; Ferrier and Lyon, 2004) and strike a delicate balance between theoretical fidelity, measurement precision, and generalizability. Given our focus on the influence of competitive actions on stock performance and risk, we tested our hypotheses on a sample of publicly traded, market-leading firms that were unambiguously engaged in head-to-head rivalry with one another in their respective industries.

We initially grouped and ranked all publicly traded members of the Fortune 500 in terms of each firm's total sales within their "primary industry" (the designator used by Compustat at the four-digit SIC level). Next, we retained only those industries in which the leading firms were non-diversified or at least dominant business firms – those having Rumelt's (1974) specialization ratios greater than 0.70. This provides assurance that these firms are highly (if not solely) dependent on their primary industry and that the top two firms in a given industry unambiguously view one another as head-to-head rivals (Chen, 1996; Ferrier et al., 1999; Ferrier, 2001; Chen et al., 2007). Further, the competitive actions carried out within a diversified firm's other lines of business, for example, may confound the potential relationship between competitive actions and performance in the focal industry. Then, we retained only those firm-industry groupings in which the leading firms had annual sales of at least $500 million. Prior research on corporate reputation and visibility suggests that the largest competing firms receive a disproportionate share of attention from the media (Fombrun and Shanley, 1990; Deephouse, 2000). Since we used content analysis to capture competitive actions found in various published news sources, our focus on large, market-leading firms helps us avoid the biases due to differences in firm size that are inherent in the depth of news coverage of competing companies. Our final sample is a pooled, cross-sectional data panel that consists of 70 firms representing 35 different four-digit SIC industries with an overall N of 5880 firm-months (12 months × 7 years × 70 firms).

Dependent Variables

We tested our hypotheses using two interrelated dependent variables: cumulative abnormal stock returns and firm-specific unsystematic risk. Ang et al. (2006) found that greater firm-specific risk substantially depresses stock performance. Specifically, while price and unsystematic risk change daily, the average return for a portfolio of stocks with the highest unsystematic risk lags the average return on the portfolio of stocks with the lowest unsystematic risk by over 1 percent per month. Their results showed that stocks with high levels of firm-specific risk have an average return that is 12 percent less per year, or 84 percent lower average return over the seven-year period in their study, than firms with low levels of firm-specific risk. As firm-specific risk increases, shrewd investors will realize that the riskiness of the investment has increased without a corresponding increase in returns, and sell the stock.

Cumulative abnormal stock returns

We used event study methodology to measure the abnormal stock price returns associated with the occurrence of each of the focal firm's competitive actions (McWilliams and Siegel, 1997). Abnormal returns capture the stock market's reactions to unanticipated and new information associated with each competitive action as it is announced in the business press. Rather than use average monthly stock market returns, we were careful to exclude confounding events and broad market-level influences on stock price and risk by measuring only the stock returns associated with a two-day window (the day of the announcement and the day after) for each competitive action in our study. This minimizes the potential for information "leakage" that sometimes occurs prior to the public announcement of a particular competitive action.

The rate of return of a share price from stock i on day t is estimated as follows:

$$R_{it} = \alpha_i + \beta_i + R_{mt} + \varepsilon_{it}$$

where R_{it} = the rate of return on the share price of firm i on day t; R_{mt} = the rate of return on the Standard & Poor's 500 day t; α = the intercept term; β = the systematic risk of stock i; ε_{it} = the error term.

To calculate the cumulative abnormal returns (CARS) associated with the focal firm's entire repertoire of competitive actions carried out in a given month, we simply summed the abnormal returns associated with each individual action for the month. Thus, each firm's monthly CARS served as one of our dependent variables for the study. The higher the value of CARS, the better the stock performance associated with the firm's monthly repertoire of competitive actions.

Firm-specific, unsystematic risk

Unsystematic risk is measured for each firm as the standard deviation of the residual (ε_{it}) from the CARS estimation model described above. It is a widely used measure of firm-specific risk in the behavioral finance literature and has been gaining acceptance in the strategy literature as well (Miller and Bromiley, 1990; Alessandri and Khan, 2006). The higher the value, the greater the stock performance risk associated with firm-specific factors (including competitive actions) beyond broader market influences.

Independent Variables

Top management team demographics
To capture the full range of skills, experiences, competence, and prestige of each firm's TMT, we drew data from *Dun & Bradstreet Reference Book of Corporate Managements* from 1987 to 1993. This source provides information about each TMT member's background, including managerial title, organizational tenure, functional position, industry background, age, educational background, military service. Using these data, we adopted the basic methodological approach described by Wiersema and Bantel (1992) and measured the degree of TMT heterogeneity along a composite of these demographic variables in two different ways. First, for the continuous demographic TMT variables, we used the coefficient of variation defined as the standard deviation divided by the mean. The relevant TMT variables using this measure are: *age heterogeneity, firm tenure heterogeneity, industry tenure heterogeneity*, and *educational years heterogeneity*. Second, for the categorical demographic variables – *educational degree heterogeneity, functional background heterogeneity, value chain (positional) heterogeneity, military service heterogeneity*, and *elite school heterogeneity* – we used Blau's (1977) index of heterogeneity. Educational background categories consist of six different degree categories – business, science, liberal arts, engineering, law, and other. Functional background categories included engineering/R&D, finance/accounting, legal, human resources management, manufacturing, logistics, purchasing, public relations, and general management. Value chain position categories were inbound logistics, operations/manufacturing, outbound logistics, marketing and sales, service, procurement, technology development, human resources management, and general management and supporting services. Military service was a binary variable coded "1" for military service, and "0" for none. Similarly, an individual's attendance at an elite college or university (i.e., Ivy League schools, plus a select group of other top-tier universities and military service academies) was a binary variable coded "1" for elite school, and "0" for other.

Prefatory note – competitive repertoires as strategy
Competitive actions are defined as externally directed, specific, and observable competitive moves initiated by a firm to enhance its relative competitive position (Smith et al., 2001). Extending beyond the study of individual competitive actions, responses, and/or action–response dyads, research in competitive dynamics has found robust support for the idea that specific characteristics of a firm's *repertoire* of competitive actions impacts performance (Miller and Chen, 1994, 1996; Ferrier et al., 1999; Deephouse, 1999; Ferrier and Lyon, 2004;). Indeed, one of the key tenets of competitive dynamics and hyper-competition theory posit that competitive advantage must be achieved by aggressively and cleverly outmaneuvering rivals in the marketplace with a range or series of multiple competitive actions (D'Aveni, 1994).

We used the competitive actions and the resultant action categories developed in previous competitive dynamics research for our competitive action data (Ferrier et al., 1999;

Ferrier, 2001). Using structured content analysis, these authors identified and categorized the competitive actions of each firm into six specific action categories – pricing actions, marketing actions, new product actions, capacity-related actions, service actions, and overt signaling actions – based on the appearance of a set of reliability-tested keywords listed in the headlines and abstracts of news reports found in the US series of F&S Predicasts. Using Perrault and Leigh's (1989) index of reliability, we attained an index of 0.91 for these set of different action types. These action types serve as the building blocks to measure the important dimensions of a firm's monthly competitive repertoire, defined as the entire set of competitive actions carried out by a firm in a given time period.

Our study represents a very important departure from previous studies in competitive dynamics in that the competitive repertoires were analyzed at the *monthly* as opposed to the *annual* level. This is important when measuring how investors react to firm strategy because investors' shorter-term focus generally makes the annual level of analysis less meaningful.

Internal strategic complexity

To measure the extent to which a firm's monthly competitive repertoire consists of a broad range (as compared with a narrow range) of different action types, we used a Herfindahl-type index that accounts for the weighted diversity among all six action types (Ferrier et al., 1999; Ferrier and Lyon, 2004). For example, a competitive repertoire composed solely of a series of advertising campaigns (i.e., marketing actions) is considered a *simple* repertoire because it lacks action-type diversity. By contrast, a competitive repertoire that exhibits a representative balance among a wide range of possible action types is more *complex*. Thus, firms with high internal strategic complexity scores carry out a repertoire of competitive actions each month that typically consists of a broad range of action types; low scores indicate that a firm typically carries out competitive repertoires consisting of just a few action types.

External strategic complexity

We measured external strategic complexity using a Euclidean distance score calculated as the weighted, summed difference between the proportion of actions of each type (pricing, marketing, product, etc.) carried out by the focal firm to the proportion of actions of each type carried out by the referent rival firm in the same time period (Ferrier et al., 1999). Here, for example, Nike's three marketing actions carried out in June 1991 represented 33 percent of the nine total actions the firm carried out in that month. The difference between the focal firm's percentage and the percentage of marketing actions that Reebok carried out in the same month (i.e., 50 percent, representative of Reebok's two marketing actions among four total actions) was computed. We computed a similar difference score for each of the other action categories by squaring and summing these differences to arrive at an overall score for competitive action heterogeneity between the focal firm and the referent rival for the month of June 1991, for example. High scores indicate that the focal firm and its referent rival carry out very different competitive strategies (i.e., high external strategic complexity from the TMT's point of view); whereas low scores indicate that the rivals carry out a set of competitive actions very similar to one another (i.e., a similarity-reduces-external-complexity situation for the TMT).

Strategic volume

Consistent with prior research, we measured the extent to which a firm sustains competitive repertoires of considerable volume by tallying the number of competitive moves the firm carried out each month (Young et al., 1996; Ferrier et al. 1999).

Control Variables

We included a variety of relevant controls in our analyses. We included the Herfindahl index for *industry concentration* for each four-digit SIC industry for each year over the seven-year time panel. We also included the *industry growth* rate for each industry-year (year t) calculated as the percentage change in industry gross sales from that of the previous year (year $t - 1$) for each four-digit SIC industry. Because different industries are likely to possess different entry barrier characteristics, we included industry-level *capital intensity* and *R&D intensity*. We also included total assets as a measure of *firm size*. To measure *firm age*, we tracked each firm's first appearance in Compustat, which dates back 37 years, and calculated a difference (age) score from the year indicator in our time panel. All left-censored firms were given the maximum score for firm age. To measure *past performance*, we used Altman's Z-score, which is a weighted composite of financial indicators relating to profitability, revenue, debt/equity, slack resources, and market return (Chakravarthy, 1986). High Z-scores indicate a condition of strong financial health; low Z-scores indicate financial distress or a risk of bankruptcy.

Analysis

We used a mixed, fixed-effects regression to test our hypotheses. Given that our data is a cross-sectional time panel, this technique controls for firm- and industry-specific effects, as well as accounts for autocorrelation across time periods by using each observation's month-year as a fixed effect. To test our moderated hypotheses, we ran three models that included the interaction terms separately. This reduces the potential for multicollinearity due to a four-fold presence of the TMT heterogeneity measure in a single regression model – that is, TMT heterogeneity appearing once as direct effect and three times in the three interaction terms. To aid in the interpretation of the regression coefficients, the main variables of interest were centered. The sample means, standard deviations, and correlations are reported in Table 11.1.

RESULTS

As stated in our baseline Hypothesis 1, we predicted that TMT heterogeneity would be positively related to stock returns and negatively related to firm-specific risk. As evidenced by the non-significant regression coefficients for TMT heterogeneity reported in Models 1 and 5 found in Table 11.2, we did not find support for this hypothesis. Thus, it appears that the stock market is not influenced in any direct way by the demographic composition of each firm's top management team.

Although we did not articulate any hypotheses about the direct effects of the characteristics of firm's competitive repertoire on risk and stock performance, we found that

Table 11.1 *Descriptive statistics and correlations*

	Mean	S.D.	1	2	3	4	5	6	7	8	9	10	11	12
1. Firm size	7.61	1.75												
2. Firm age	31.54	11.81	0.11											
3. Past performance	4.46	3.37	-0.12	-0.07										
4. Industry concentration	0.21	0.15	0.13	-0.07	-0.01									
5. Industry growth	0.22	0.36	0.06	-0.20	0.04	0.15								
6. R&D intensity	0.04	0.04	0.11	-0.14	0.23	-0.35	0.10							
7. Capital intensity	0.93	0.41	0.10	0.12	-0.25	-0.15	-0.04	0.36						
8. TMT heterogeneity	0.56	0.25	0.05	0.14	0.03	0.01	-0.05	0.11	-0.10					
9. Internal strategic complexity	0.79	0.19	0.24	0.04	-0.18	-0.01	0.04	-0.25	-0.12	-0.09				
10. External strategic complexity	0.88	0.50	-0.04	0.03	-0.01	-0.11	-0.02	0.01	-0.05	0.01	0.16			
11. Strategic volume	2.07	0.82	0.20	-0.01	0.39	-0.08	-0.02	0.31	0.14	0.14	-0.72	-0.17		
12. Stock returns	0.01	0.07	-0.04	-0.01	-0.07	0.01	-0.01	-0.01	0.01	-0.01	0.03	-0.06	0.02	
13. Unsystematic risk	0.02	0.01	-0.36	-0.28	-0.04	-0.01	0.09	0.16	-0.07	-0.08	-0.17	0.01	-0.10	0.01

Note: All pair-wise correlations above 0.04 are significant at the $p < 0.05$ level or better.

Source: Authors' calculations.

Table 11 2 *Regression results – stock returns and unsystematic risk on TMT heterogeneity and strategy*

	Stock Returns				Unsystematic Risk			
	Model 1	Model 2	Model 3	Model 4	Model 5	Model 6	Model 7	Model 8
Intercept	0.0356				0.0233			
Firm size	−0.0030				−0.0003			
Firm age	0.0001				−0.0001			
Past performance	−0.0020*				−0.0002			
Industry concentration	0.0179				0.0050			
Industry growth	−0.0028				0.0003			
R&D intensity	0.1069				0.0224			
Capital intensity	−0.1394				−0.0037			
TMT heterogeneity	−0.0247				0.0001			
Internal strategic complexity	−0.0183				0.0001			
External strategic complexity	−0.0134†				−0.0002			
Strategic volume	0.0035				0.0001			
TMT heterogeneity × internal strategic complexity		0.1343†				−0.0052***		

274

TMT heterogeneity × external strategic complexity				−0.0040			−0.0023***	
TMT heterogeneity × strategic volume				−0.0574***				0.0007***
−2 Log likelihood	−896.8	−910.8	−892.4	−937.8	−4043.5	−4205.9	−4205.6	−4043.9

Note: Non-standardized regression coefficients are reported; one-tailed hypothesis tests: † $p < 0.10$, * $p < 0.05$, ** $p < 0.01$, *** $p < 0.001$.

Source: Authors' calculations.

only external strategic complexity exhibited a marginally significant negative impact on stock returns (Model 1: $b = 0.1034$, $p < 0.10$).

Hypothesis 2 was partially supported for stock returns (Model 2: $b = 0.1343$; $p < 0.10$) and fully supported for firm-specific unsystematic risk (Model 6: $b = -0.0052$; $p < 0.01$). Firms with heterogeneous TMTs that carry out competitive strategies characterized by a broad range of action types exhibit both higher stock returns and lower levels of risk than firms with homogeneous TMTs attempting to carry out similarly complex strategies.

In Hypothesis 3, we predicted that firms with heterogeneous TMTs that carry out a repertoire of competitive actions that differ significantly from that of the referent rival will experience higher stock returns and low levels of unsystematic risk. We found only partial support for this hypothesis. The significant interaction term for TMT heterogeneity and external strategic complexity (Model 7: $b = -0.0023$; $p < 0.001$) suggests that this condition is related to lower levels of firm-specific unsystematic risk, but not higher stock returns.

We found strong support for Hypothesis 4. Here, we predicted and found that firms with heterogeneous TMTs that carry out a large number of strategic moves in a given month experience both lower stock returns (Model 4: $b = -0.0574$; $p < 0.001$) and higher levels of unsystematic risk (Model 8: $b = 0.0007$; $p < 0.001$) than firms with homogeneous TMTs attempting to be equally aggressive.

We also ran models like those described above that included the three TMT × competitive action interaction terms together in the same model for each dependent variable. The results mirrored those reported above. But, multicollinearity diagnostics indicated that this analytical approach was mildly problematic. Hence, we used separate models for each interaction term.

Post Hoc Analyses

We ran several alternative models that account for more nuanced relationships than we hypothesized. First, because it is possible that the costs of implementing competitive actions increases as the number (volume) of competitive actions carried out in a given month increases, we added the squared term for strategic volume to two post hoc regression models similar to Models 1 and 5. We found neither the squared terms for strategic volume nor the linear terms to be statistically significant.

Second, it is possible that strategic complexity and strategic volume interact across all levels of TMT heterogeneity. Indeed, prior research in marketing, for example, found that the interaction of product broadening (complexity) and product versioning (volume) leads to a lower probability of firm survival than does focusing on one product strategy or the other (Fosfuri and Giarratana, 2007). Relevant to our study, firms that carry out highly complex repertoires consisting of a large volume of competitive actions may generate an unbearably large cognitive load on the TMT, which may affect stock performance and risk. To test for this potential effect, we conducted post hoc analyses that added three-way interactions to Models 2–3 and 6–7 that included both types of strategic complexity, strategic volume, and TMT heterogeneity. The results for these three-way interactions were not significant.

DISCUSSION AND CONCLUSIONS

This study stands among the first that we know of that empirically tests the moderating role of a firm's competitive strategy on the relationship between a firm's TMT heterogeneity and stock market performance and firm-specific risk. Drawing from core ideas in upper echelons theory, information processing, and competitive dynamics, we predicted that the risk and stock returns influenced would be influenced by the (in)congruence between TMT characteristics and the firm's set of competitive actions. More specifically, our findings suggest that higher unsystematic risk and lower returns are not directly influenced by the level of TMT heterogeneity, but that the interaction of TMT heterogeneity and three characteristics of a firm's competitive strategy – internal strategic complexity, external strategic complexity, and strategic volume – influence the stock market's reactions manifest in higher stock returns and lower firm-specific risk.

Consistent with prior research in management and finance, our findings suggest that the stock market does indeed react to human capital; but *only* in joint consideration with the firm's competitive strategy. More specifically, we did not find a direct effect for TMT heterogeneity in either our model for stock returns or the model for unsystematic risk. This "non-finding" is common to many previous studies that tested the relationship between TMT characteristics (with measures of competitive actions also present in these models) and various measures of firm performance (Ferrier, 2001; Lyon and Ferrier, 2002; Ferrier and Lyon, 2004).[1]

Given the uncertainty and complexity associated with head-to-head rivalry, the stock market values the fit between TMT heterogeneity and both internal and external strategic complexity. TMTs with sufficient breadth of experience and perspective that give rise to high-quality decisions and the resultant strategic complexity experience higher stock returns and lower stock risk. By contrast, firms with homogeneous TMTs that carry out complex strategies that consist of a large number of a diverse range of competitive actions of different types experience lower stock returns and higher levels of risk. Here, the market appears to favor decision-making speed and the more rapid formation of strategic consensus manifest in a simple repertoire of competitive actions over decision-making comprehensiveness that often gives rise to a complex set of actions.

Implicit in our findings is the general notion that due to their impact on performance, both a given firm's human capital and competitive maneuvering among rivals in the marketplace should be directly incorporated in the risk management analyses and schemes used by investors and managers alike. Unfortunately, "very few firms [and strategy scholars] have actually embraced risk management as an integral part of strategic management – a core competence they can utilize to generate competitive advantage as well as influence market perceptions of income stream uncertainty" (Chatterjee et al., 2003 p. 74, note in brackets added). Indeed, risk has such a strong theoretical basis in the finance literature that it has been the subject of some of the discipline's pre-eminent papers – including Markowitz (1952), Sharpe (1964), Fama and MacBeth (1973), and Lakonishok et al. (1994). Thus, we find it puzzling that strategy researchers have not thoroughly investigated this phenomenon. Despite early strides in the finance literature, the strategy literature has lagged behind, which prompted Lubatkin and O'Neill (1987) to argue: "very little is known about the relationship between corporate strategies and corporate uncertainty, or risk" (p. 685). While a handful of strategy scholars have since provided linkages between firm risk, managerial choice, and organizational performance (e.g., Miller and Bromiley, 1990; Bromiley, 1991; Miller and Leiblein, 1996; Wiseman and Bromiley, 1996; Chatterjee et al., 1999; Alessandri and Khan, 2006), this gap persists today. Consequently, it is difficult to assess the cumulative contributions of this research (Bromiley et al., 2001).

We address this gap by following suggestions articulated by strategy scholars who study risk (cf., McNamara and Bromiley, 1999; Bromiley et al., 2001). First, given our focus on stock market performance, we adopted the appropriate measures that enable us to test for the fit between a firm's visible competitive behavior and the limited range of outcomes associated with the market's reaction. Second, our study makes the distinction between the effects of the exogenous factors that drive risk (i.e., observed competitive actions; strategic risk) and stock market risk itself (i.e., the outcome of strategy). Third, our study adopts the appropriate time-frame within which dynamic strategy and performance are contemporaneously interrelated.

The body of findings from previous research that explores the relationship between internal strategic complexity-simplicity and performance is itself quite complex. On one hand, early studies found that competitive repertoire complexity gives rise to higher performance (Miller and Chen, 1996; Ferrier et al., 1999). On the other hand, competitive repertoire simplicity was found to lead to better long-term performance if the competitive repertoire was conceived of and carried out by heterogeneous TMTs (Ferrier and Lyon, 2004). Moreover, one study found that heterogeneous TMTs were more likely to carry out competitive strategies, yet complexity exhibited a U-shaped relationship with performance (Ferrier, 2001). Owing to our use of daily stock market data and the conceptualization of competitive strategy that occurs in real time (i.e., actions carried out on a given day), our findings differ from these studies and suggest that the relationship between organizational factors, strategy, and performance is indeed conditioned on the time-frame in question (Bromiley et al., 2001). This suggests that more research is needed to flesh out the complex, interactive relationship between characteristics of the TMT, patterns of competitive strategy at various levels of aggregation, and measures of performance captured at different time-frames.[2]

Our findings that relate to between-firm "differences" in the pattern of competitive actions that rival firms carry out are generally supportive of Ashby's (1956) law of requisite variety (Buckley, 1968) and hypercompetition theory (D'Aveni, 1994). More specifically, in the context of fierce competitive rivalry, a firm's ability to *effectively* out-maneuver rivals through strategic deviation or novelty (carrying out a pattern of actions different than rivals) is contingent on the make up of the top management team. Firms with heterogeneous TMTs who possess the diversity in cognition and experience to get the job done are rewarded with lower firm-specific risk by the marketplace. So, to paraphrase Buckley (p. 495; material in brackets added), it indeed appears "that only variety [among TMT members] can regulate variety [in carrying out complex and differentiated competitive repertoires]."

Our findings pertaining to the number of strategic moves carried out by a firm seem to indicate that while the main effect of more, rather than fewer, strategic moves is positively related to stock market response (only in the case of stock returns, not risk), more is not always better. As a follow-up, we pondered the possibility of increasing marginal costs due to limited managerial talent and other resources. Specifically, we wanted to investigate whether the main effect of volume and the interaction with TMT is curvilinear, implying that at some point TMT heterogeneity no longer matters because the firm is carrying out too many strategic actions and exhausting its cognition and resources, which could lead to negative outcomes. To test for this effect, we conducted post hoc analysis by running our models using polynomial regressions. We did not find any curvilinear or polynomial results.

Our theory and findings are congruent with the emergent awareness-motivation-capability (AMC) perspective of competitive interaction (cf., Chen, 1996; Chen et al., 2007; Ferrier, 2001; Yu and Cannella, 2007). Here, TMT cognitive and experiential heterogeneity (along with its attendant social and decision-making team processes not directly part of our study) is dynamically interactive with competitive behavior because such TMTs possess a greater awareness of competitive opportunities (and pitfalls), a nuanced understanding of the need to balance and temper the firm's motivations for competitive aggressiveness with competitive action breadth, and a superior capability to more insightfully and purposefully design, decide on, and carry out an effective set of competitive actions.

Our findings also have strong managerial implications. With respect to the market for managerial talent, managers (and management teams) that are able to control risk will command a premium for employment as they can potentially have a greater impact on stock price than those that do not control risk. Indeed, the overall quality of the management team is generally lower in high-risk firms (Jacobson and Aaker, 1987). Thus, stockholders may further value reductions in risk because they are a signal of the ability of a firm to attract better managers (Miller and Bromiley, 1990).

Our study is limited in a number of possible ways. First, we acknowledge that our use of demographic proxies may obscure several unobserved or latent managerial attitudes, cognition, group dynamics, and social phenomena. Indeed, as evidenced by explicit tests of the relationship between TMT demography, team processes, and organizational performance (e.g., Smith et al., 1994), Priem et al. (1999) rightly note that studies using TMT demography, like ours, may be limited by a variety of intrinsic trade offs. These concerns notwithstanding, we side with Carpenter et al. (2004) who support the continued, but careful use of TMT demography. Accordingly, we remain confident in our findings principally because prior empirical research suggests that the relationship between TMT demography on organizational outcomes is only partially mediated by group processes (Smith et al., 1994), which suggests that some direct effect of TMT demography on organizational outcomes remains. In our study, we test how this residual direct effect interacts with competitive behavior in predicting performance. We also take comfort in the congruence between our research question and research design; namely, that our model of stock returns and risk accounts for the joint influence of organizational and strategic factors that investors are clearly and unambiguously able to observe and monitor. In other words, the stock market reacts to overt visible competitive behaviors and overt, visible characteristics of the top management team, not unobservable or latent group processes or other firm-specific resources. However, future research should indeed account for managerial cognition and team processes that result in competitive action, as well as the decision process that investors use in actually evaluating competitive strategy.

Second, owing to our focus of the role of "observables" – competitive actions and

TMT demographics – we necessarily ignored differences in rival firms' unique resource profiles that may, in part, facilitate competitive behavior, competitive advantage, and performance. This is not to say that the core principles and concepts within the resource-based view (RBV) are irrelevant in competitive dynamics research. Indeed, as noted by Grimm et al. (2005), RBV concepts such as resource inimitability, causal ambiguity, and so on, are important parts of the "strategy as action" model of competitive advantage. These authors argue that "competitive actions should be designed on the basis of the principle of resource strength" and that "firm resources make action possible, but they also flow from action" (ibid., pp. 69 and 90). We view resources and actions as two sides of the same coin (Wernerfelt, 1984). Yet, acknowledging the importance of resource-based rivalry (Peteraf, 1993), we do make the inference that ex post limits to competition are manifest in competitive actions, in general, and that resource heterogeneity gives rise to competitive repertoire complexity and heterogeneity among competing firms, in particular. Future research could indeed measure resources more explicitly and link them to specific patterns of competitive behavior exhibited by head-to-head rivals.

Third, our theory and empirical reasoning implies that members of the investment community actively and systematically evaluate the firm's human capital when they assess the future profit potential of the firm's observed competitive behaviors as they unfold over time. In our exploratory study, we test for the stock market's *reactions* – measured as stock returns and firm-specific unsystematic risk – as evidence of this process. Future research could measure investors' actual evaluative and decision processes more directly by using surveys or techniques adopted from ethnographic research disciplines.

In sum, our paper sheds new light on the complicated relationship between competitive behavior, managerial perspective and capabilities, and performance. We tested our predictions on a multi-industry sample of firms over a seven-year time period. When investors assign firm-specific stock risk and estimate its future competitive advantage and performance, our findings provide robust support for the notion that investors jointly consider both a given firm's competitive strategy and the cognitive and experiential capabilities of its top management team. As such, we believe that the firm's human capital and competitive behaviors cannot be disentangled from one another as scholars endeavor to better understand the multiplex drivers of firm-level stock risk and return.

NOTES

1. Although Hambrick et al. (1996) indeed found a direct relationship between TMT characteristics and the firm's growth in market share and profit, their model did not account for the firm's competitive actions.
2. As reviewed and explained by Smith et al. (2001), competitive actions have been studied at three levels of aggregation: *action–reaction dyad*, a firm-year *competitive action repertoire*, and a time-indifferent *competitive attack*.

REFERENCES

Alessandri, T. and Khan, R. (2006). Market performance and deviation from industry norms: (Mis)alignment of organizational risk and industry risk. *Journal of Business Research*, **59**(10–11), 1105–15.

Amason, A.C. (1996). Distinguishing the effects of functional and dysfunctional conflict on strategic decision making: Resolving the paradox for top management teams. *Academy of Management Journal*, **39**(1), 123–48.

Ang, A., Hodrick, R., Xing, Y., and Zhang, X. (2006). The cross-section of volatility and expected returns. *Journal of Finance*, **61**(1), 259–99.

Ashby, W.R. (1956). *An introduction to cybernetics*. Englewood Cliffs, NJ: Prentice Hall.

Bettis, R. and Weeks, D. (1987). Financial returns and strategic interaction: The case of instant photography. *Strategic Management Journal*, **8**(6), 549–63.

Blau, P.M. (1977). *Inequality and heterogeneity*. New York, NY: Free Press.

Bromiley, P. (1991). Testing a causal model of corporate risk taking and performance. *Academy of Management Journal*, **34**(1), 37–59.

Bromiley, P., Miller, K., and Rau, D. (2001). Risk in strategic management research. In M.A. Hitt, R.E. Freeman, and S.J. Harrison (eds), *The Blackwell handbook of strategic management*. Oxford, UK: Blackwell Publishers Ltd.

Buckley, W. (1968). Society as a complex adaptive system. In W. Buckley (ed.), *Modern system research for the behavioral scientist*. Chicago, IL: Aldine.

Carpenter, M.A. (2002). The implications of strategy and social context for the relationship between top management team heterogeneity and firm performance. *Strategic Management Journal*, **23**(3), 275–84.

Carpenter, M.A. and Fredrickson, J. (2001). Top management teams, global strategic posture, and the moderating role of uncertainty. *Academy of Management Journal*, **44**(3), 533–45.

Carpenter, M.A., Geletkanycz, M., and Sanders, W.G. (2004). Upper echelons research revisited: Antecedents, elements, and consequences of top management team composition. *Journal of Management*, **30**(2), 749–78.

Certo, S.T., Lester, R., Dalton, C., and Dalton, D. (2006). Top management teams, strategy and financial performance: A meta-analytic examination. *Journal of Management Studies*, **43**(14), 813–39.

Chakravarthy, B. (1986). Measuring strategic performance. *Strategic Management Journal*, **7**(5), 437–59.

Chatterjee, S., Lubatkin, M., and Schulze, W. (1999). Toward a strategic theory of risk premium: Moving beyond CAPM. *Academy of Management Review*, **24**(3), 556–67.

Chatterjee, S., Lubatkin, M., Schweiger, D., and Weber, Y. (1992). Cultural differences and shareholder value in related mergers: Linking equity and human capital. *Strategic Management Journal*, **13**(5), 319–34.

Chatterjee, S., Wiseman, R., Fiegenbaum, A., and Devers, C. (2003). Integrating behavioral and economic concepts of risk into strategic management: The twain shall meet. *Long Range Planning*, **36**(1), 61–79.

Chen, M.J. (1996). Competitor analysis and interfirm rivalry: Toward a theoretical integration. *Academy of Management Review*, **21**(1), 100–134.

Chen, M.J., Su, K.H., and Tsai, W. (2007). Competitive tension: The awareness-motivation-capability perspective. *Academy of Management Journal*, **50**(1), 101–18.

Cohen, B. and Dean, T. (2005). Information asymmetry and investor valuation of IPOs: Top management team legitimacy as a capital market signal. *Strategic Management Journal*, **26**(7), 683–92.

Cosier, J. and Rose, G. (1977). Cognitive conflict and goal conflict effects on task performance. *Organizational Behavior and Human Performance*, **19**(2), 378–91.

D'Aveni, R. (1990). Top managerial prestige and organizational bankruptcy. *Organization Science*, **1**(2), 121–42.

D'Aveni, R. (1994). *Hypercompetition: Managing the dynamics of strategic maneuvering*. New York, NY: The Free Press.

D'Aveni, R. and Kesner, I. (1993). Top managerial prestige, power and tender offer response: A study of elite social networks and target firm cooperation during takeovers. *Organization Science*, **4**(2), 123–51.

Deephouse, D. (1999). To be different, or to be the same? It's a question (and theory) of strategic balance. *Strategic Management Journal*, **20**(2), 147–66.

Deephouse, D. (2000). Media reputation as a strategic resource: An integration of mass communication and resource-based theories. *Journal of Management*, **26**(6), 1091–112.

Eisenhardt, K.M. and Schoonhoven, C.B. (1990). Organizational growth: Linking founding team, strategy, environment, and growth among U.S. semiconductor ventures. *Administrative Science Quarterly*, **35**(3), 504–29.

Fairbank, J., Labianca, G., Steensma, K., and Metters, R. (2006). Information processing design choices, strategy, and risk management performance. *Journal of Management Information Systems*, **23**(1), 293–319.

Fama, E. and MacBeth, J. (1973). Risk, return, and equilibrium: Empirical tests. *Journal of Political Economy*, **81**(3), 607–36.

Ferrier, W. (2001). Navigating the competitive landscape: The drivers and consequences of competitive aggressiveness. *Academy of Management Journal*, **44**(4), 858–77.

Ferrier, W. and Lee, H. (2002). Strategic aggressiveness, variation, and surprise: How the sequential pattern of competitive rivalry influences stock market returns. *Journal of Managerial Issues*, **14**(22), 162–80.

Ferrier, W. and Lyon, D. (2004). Competitive repertoire simplicity and firm performance: The moderating role of TMT heterogeneity. *Managerial & Decision Economics*, **25**(6–7), 317–27.

Ferrier, W., Smith, K., and Grimm, C. (1999). The role of competition in market share erosion and dethronement: A study of industry leaders and challengers. *Academy of Management Journal*, **43**(4), 372–88.

Ferrier, W., MacFhionnlaoich, C., Smith, K., and Grimm, C. (2002). The impact of performance distress on aggressive competitive behavior: A reconciliation of competing views. *Managerial & Decision Economics*, **23**(4–5), 301–16.

Fiegenbaum, A. (1990). Prospect theory and the risk–return association: An empirical examination of 85 industries. *Journal of Economic Behavior & Organization*, **14**(2), 187–204.

Finkelstein, S. and Hambrick, D. (1996). *Strategic leadership: Top executives and their effects on organizations.* Minneapolis, MN: West.

Fombrun, C. and Shanley, M. (1990). What's in a name: Reputation building and corporate strategy. *Academy of Management Journal*, **33**(2), 233–58.

Fosfuri, A. and Giarratana, M. (2007). Product strategies and survival in Schumpeterian environments: Evidence from the US security software industry. *Organization Studies*, **28**(6), 909–29.

Galbraith, J. (1973). *Designing complex organizations.* Reading, MA: Addison-Wesley Publishing Co.

Goyal, A. and Santa-Clara, P. (2003). Idiosyncratic risk matters! *Journal of Finance*, **58**(1), 975–1008.

Grimm, C., Lee, H., and Smith, K. (2005). *Strategy as action: Competitive dynamics and competitive advantage.* Oxford, UK: Oxford University Press.

Haleblian, J. and Finkelstein, S. (1993). Top management team size, CEO dominance, and firm performance. *Academy of Management Journal*, **36**(4), 844–63.

Hambrick, D., Cho, T., and Chen, M.J. (1996). The influence of top management team heterogeneity on firms' competitive moves. *Administrative Science Quarterly*, **41**(4), 659–84.

Higgins, M. and Gulati, R. (2006). Stacking the deck: The effect of upper echelon affiliations for entrepreneurial firms. *Strategic Management Journal*, **27**(1), 1–26.

Jacobson, R. and Aaker, D. (1987). The strategic role of product quality. *Journal of Marketing*, **51**(4), 31–44.

Kahneman, D. and Tversky, A. (1979). Prospect theory: An analysis of decision under risk. *Econometrica*, **47**(2), 263–90.

Keck, S. (1997). Top management team structure: Differential effects by environmental context. *Organization Science*, **8**(2), 143–56.

Knight, D., Pearce, C., Smith, K.G., Olian, J., Sims, H., Smith, K.A., and Flood, P. (1999). Top management team diversity, group process and strategic consensus. *Strategic Management Journal*, **20**(5), 445–65.

Lakonishok, J., Shleifer, A., and Vishny, R. (1994). Contrarian investment, extrapolation and risk. *Journal of Finance*, **49**(5), 1541–78.

Lester, S., Certo, T.S., Dalton, C., Dalton, D., and Cannella, A. (2006). Initial public offering investor valuations: An examination of top management team prestige and environmental uncertainty. *Journal of Small Business Management*, **44**(1), 1–26.

Lin, H. and Shih, C. (2008). How executive SHRM systems links for firm performance: The perspectives of upper echelon and competitive dynamics. *Journal of Management*, **34**(5), 853–81.

Lubatkin, M. and O'Neill, H. (1987). Merger strategies and capital market risk. *Academy of Management Journal*, **30**(4), 665–84.

Lyon, D. and Ferrier, W. (2002). Enhancing performance with product-market innovation: A note on the influence of the top management team. *Journal of Managerial Issues*, **14**, 452–69.

Markowitz, H. (1952). Portfolio selection. *Journal of Finance*, **7**(1), 77–91.

McNamara, G. and Bromiley, P. (1999). Risk and return in organizational decision making. *Academy of Management Journal*, **42**(3), 330–39.

McWilliams, A. and Siegel, D. (1997). Event studies in management research: Theoretical and empirical issues. *Academy of Management Journal*, **40**(3), 626–57.

Miller, D. and Chen, M.J. (1994). Sources and consequences of competitive inertia: A study of the U.S. airline industry. *Administrative Science Quarterly*, **39**(1), 1–23.

Miller, D. and Chen, M.J. (1996). The simplicity of competitive repertoires: An empirical analysis. *Strategic Management Journal*, **17**(6), 419–40.

Miller, K. and Bromiley, P. (1990). Strategic risk and corporate performance: An analysis of alternative risk measures. *Academy of Management Journal*, **33**(4), 756–79.

Miller, K. and Leiblein, M. (1996). Corporate risk–return relations: Returns variability versus downside risk. *Academy of Management Journal*, **39**(1), 91–122.

Perrault, W. and Leigh, L. (1989). Reliability of nominal data based on qualitative judgments. *Journal of Marketing Research*, **26**(2), 135–48.

Peteraf, M. (1993). The cornerstones of competitive advantage: A resource-based view. *Strategic Management Journal*, **14**(3), 179–92.

Priem, R., Lyon, D., and Dess, G. (1999). Inherent limitations of demographic proxies in top management team heterogeneity research. *Journal of Management*, **25**(6), 935–53.

Roush, C. (1999). *Inside Home Depot.* New York, NY: McGraw Hill.

Rumelt, R.P. (1974). *Strategy, structure and economic performance.* Boston, MA: Harvard University Press.

Sharpe, W. (1964). Capital asset prices: A theory of market equilibrium under conditions of risk. *Journal of Finance,* **19**(3), 425–42.

Simons, T., Pelled, L., and Smith, K. (1999). Making use of difference: Diversity, debate, and decision comprehensiveness in top management teams. *Academy of Management Journal,* **42**(6), 662–73.

Smith, K.G., Ferrier, W., and Ndofor, H. (2001). Competitive dynamics research: Critique and future directions. In M.A Hitt, R.E. Freeman, and J. Harrison (eds), *Handbook of strategic management.* Oxford, UK: Blackwell, pp. 315–61.

Smith, K.G., Grimm, C., Gannon, M., and Chen, M.J. (1991). Organizational information processing, competitive responses, and performance in the U.S. domestic airline industry. *Academy of Management Journal,* **34**(1), 60–85.

Smith, K.G., Smith, K.A., Olian, J., Sims, H., O'Bannon, D., and Scully, J. (1994). Top management team demography and process: The role of social integration and communication. *Administrative Science Quarterly,* **39**(3), 412–38.

Tihanyi, L., Ellstrand, A., Daily, C., and Dalton, D. (2000). Composition of the top management team and firm international diversification. *Journal of Management,* **26**(6), 1157–77.

Wernerfelt, B. (1984). A resource-based view of the firm. *Strategic Management Journal,* **5**(2), 171–80.

West, M. and Anderson, N. (1994). Innovation in top management teams. *Journal of Applied Psychology,* **81**(6), 680–93.

Wiersema, M.F. and Bantel, K.A. (1992). Top management team demography and corporate strategic change. *Academy of Management Journal,* **35**(1), 91–121.

Wiseman, R. and Bromiley, P. (1996). Toward a model of risk in declining organizations: An empirical examination of risk, performance and decline. *Organization Science,* **7**(5), 524–43.

Young, G., Smith, K.G., and Grimm, C. (1996). "Austrian" and industrial organization perspective on firm-level competitive activity and performance. *Organization Science,* **7**(3), 243–54.

Yu, T. and Cannella, A. (2007). Rivalry between multinational enterprises: An event history approach. *Academy of Management Journal,* **50**(3), 863–84.

12 Romeo, Juliet, and Shakespeare: thematizing the nexus of strategic leadership and entrepreneurship

Zeki Simsek, Ciaran Heavey, Smriti Prabhakar, and M. Nesij Huvaj

Strategic entrepreneurship (SE), broadly conceived as entrepreneurial action with a strategic perspective, has emerged as an exciting construct for strategic management and entrepreneurship researchers (Schendel and Hitt, 2007). SE involves the integration of entrepreneurial and strategic perspectives in developing and taking actions designed to create and sustain wealth (Hitt et al., 2001). SE thus, at its core, seeks to combine opportunity-seeking behavior and advantage-seeking behavior (Monsen and Boss, 2009). While research on the conceptualizations, antecedents, and consequences of SE is still evolving, strategic leadership (SL), which focuses on the people who have overall responsibility for the organization, is viewed as an essential fulcrum for developing significant understanding (Ireland et al., 2003). Strategic leaders are a guiding force in determining a vision for entrepreneurship, managing resources strategically, fostering an entrepreneurial culture, and establishing control systems (Ireland and Hitt, 1998). Strategic leaders also shape SE by nourishing an entrepreneurial capability, protecting innovations, making sense of opportunities, and questioning the dominant logic within the firm and industry (Covin and Slevin, 2002).

The study of SL, which was significantly stimulated by the upper echelons theory (Hambrick and Mason, 1984), generally focuses on the impact of the characteristics of strategic leaders on the form, fate, and fortunes of firms by shaping what strategic choices they make, and why and when they make those choices. The people who are the subjects of SL research can be individual executives (CEOs), top management teams (TMTs), or other governance bodies (BODs). (See Jones and Cannella as well as Mooney and Amason in Chapters 1 and 2 of this volume for alternative viewpoints on the composition of TMTs/SLs). In broad terms, strategic leaders determine the overall direction and vision for an organization, manage resources and capabilities strategically, foster an entrepreneurial culture and mindset throughout the organization, and emphasize balanced organizational controls (Ireland and Hitt, 1999). Strategic leaders are the linking pin between strategy and entrepreneurship, mediating between internal resources/capabilities and market opportunities (Bass, 2007). Indeed, implicit in most examinations of entrepreneurial firms is the role of strategic leaders, "as these are the individuals responsible for the creation of goods and services and the leveraging of market opportunities" (Daily et al., 2002, p. 388). Metaphorically, if Romeo is "entrepreneurship" and Juliet is "strategy," then Shakespeare is "strategic leadership," which brings together strategy and entrepreneurship.

Despite this central role of SL in SE behaviors and outcomes, there has to date been no systematic thematization of the SL–SE nexus in terms of central constructs, research evidence, and an overall organizing framework. We suspect that efforts toward this end may have particularly been hobbled by a lack of theory concerning SE's underlying conceptual forms. Although Ireland and colleagues (2003) expounded a broad framework of SE and others discussed its potential types (e.g., Kuratko and Audretsch, 2009), the core dimensions of SE (advantage- and opportunity-seeking behavior) and their juxtaposition have remained opaque. Consequently, our chapter begins by developing a theoretically informed, deductively derived typological view of SE, articulating and juxtaposing the advantage-seeking and opportunity-seeking dimensions to yield four archetypal forms – refinement, replication, rejuvenation, and revolution. Using this typology as the foundation, we then survey extant research findings by undertaking a comprehensive review of relevant literature on SL (CEO, TMT, and BOD – board of directors) and empirical manifestations of four SE forms, over a 30-year period (1978–2008), spanning 12 high-quality management journals (*ASQ, AMJ, AMR, SMJ, JOM, JMS, OS, MS, LQ, JBV, ETP, SEJ*). Synthesizing our typology and review, we finally develop a conceptual framework and discuss promising avenues for future research on the SL–SE nexus. Taken together, our chapter aims at a holistic thematization of the SL–SE nexus by conceptualizing, surveying, and linking central constructs, influence mechanisms, and relationships. We begin by introducing and developing our typology.

A TYPOLOGICAL PERSPECTIVE OF STRATEGIC ENTREPRENEURSHIP

Given that wealth creation is at the heart of both entrepreneurship and strategic management theory (Hitt et al., 2001), research at their nexus has thrived over the past two decades. For Meyer et al. (2002, p. 33) "it would be illogical to look at creation without looking at the outcome of such creation whether this is wealth creation, job creation, profitability, or sales growth." From this perspective, strategy and entrepreneurship represent two sides of the same coin, the coin of value creation and capture (Venkataraman and Sarasvathy, 2001). It naturally follows that "entrepreneurial and strategic perspectives should be integrated to examine entrepreneurial strategies that create wealth," an approach that Hitt and colleagues (2001, p. 480) coined as SE. Defined in formal terms, SE seeks to combine and synthesize opportunity-seeking behavior and advantage-seeking behavior to promote wealth creation (Monsen and Boss, 2009). By focusing on both of these dimensions, SE scholars suggest that firms create and sustain wealth by exploiting current competitive advantages while also identifying opportunities that will create future competitive advantages (Ketchen et al., 2007).

In constructing our typology, we thus first identified two distinct dimensions of SE that underlie its various conceptualizations in the literature, namely opportunity-seeking and advantage-seeking dimensions (Hitt et al., 2001; Ireland et al., 2003). The role of the first dimension, opportunity-seeking behaviors, is well established in the entrepreneurship literature. Most definitions of entrepreneurship identify the discovery/creation and exploitation of opportunities as essential to entrepreneurial activity (Kirzner, 1973; Stevenson et al., 1985; Stevenson and Jarillo, 1990; Shane and Venkatraman, 2000; Brown et al., 2001). Where scholars fundamentally differ in portraying opportunity-seeking behaviors, is whether the pursuit of opportunities involves *exploiting* existing resources, competences, and knowledge, versus *exploring* new resources, competences,

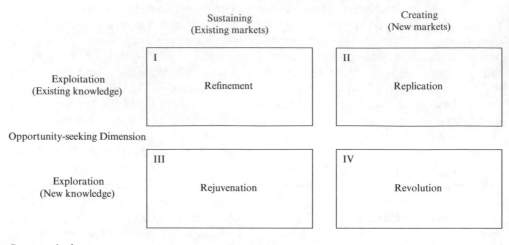

Source: Authors.

Figure 12.1   A typology of strategic entrepreneurship forms

and knowledge, a widely drawn distinction in organization theory (March, 1991). Although both types of opportunities exist (exploitative versus explorative), research suggests that firms tend to pursue one type at the expense of the other (Levinthal and March, 1993).

The role of the second dimension, advantage-seeking behaviors, is also widely discussed in the strategy literature. Advantage-seeking behaviors vary fundamentally as to whether they involve sustaining existing advantages in current markets or creating new sources of competitive advantage in new markets. An emphasis on sustaining is typically concerned with improving competitive positioning within existing markets, whether through the execution of a strategy that differentiates the firms from its rivals (Porter, 1996), or through the unique configuration of hard-to-imitate resources and capabilities (Barney, 1991). While a focus on sustaining is invariably anchored in existing markets, creating competitive advantages takes place in the context of adjacent, related, or entirely new market spaces. Juxtaposing these two dimensions and levels, our resultant typology (Figure 12.1) suggests four archetypes of SE: refinement, replication, rejuvenation, and revolution.

Refinement entails using existing resources, knowledge, and competences to improve positioning within existing markets; for example, introducing new products or adopting new processes. Refinement does not involve developing new knowledge, nor does it involve venturing into new markets. Rather, it primarily involves product line extensions in which firms introduce new products that are variations of existing current products or brands, a process that Normann (1977) labels "repeated replications." Essentially, refinement entails a process of expansion around an underlying core technology or brand knowledge base (Kazanjian et al., 2002), and is fundamentally driven by efforts at increasing efficiency and proficiency (March, 1991). For example, product refinement is primarily concerned with the introduction of new, modified, or improved products to serve existing customer markets. Likewise, process refinement principally involves the adoption of technical and administrative innovations and changes (Bantel and Jackson, 1989).

Replication involves using existing knowledge, resources, and competences to enter new market arenas. In essence, replication refers to a type of entrepreneurial activity, in which firms innovate in a new product market domain, yet are firmly anchored in existing knowledge. With replication, firms leverage their existing knowledge and expertise to develop and introduce products or markets outside their current domain (Helfat and Peteraf, 2003). Although replication can involve entering new product (Boeker, 1997a), geographic (Barkema and Shvyrkov, 2007), and international markets (Sanders and Carpenter, 1998), its main manifestations typically include product and international replication.

With *rejuvenation*, the third form of SE, firms seek to sustain or improve their competitive standing within existing product market domains by pursuing opportunities involving the creation and development of new knowledge and expertise. That is, firms seek to strengthen their basis of competitive advantage by creating new knowledge, which serves as a foundation for the revitalization and development of core competences. For example, with strategic rejuvenation, the focal firm seeks to redefine its position within its markets, by fundamentally changing how it competes (Covin and Miles, 1999), either in terms of transforming business models, structural architectures, or core competencies. These initiatives transform organizations by renewing the core ideas on which they are built and are fundamentally concerned with building the skills needed to promote sustainable growth (Stopford and Baden-Fuller, 1990).

Finally, *revolution* involves the creation and development of new knowledge to seize opportunities in new market arenas. Revolution places a joint emphasis on the development of new knowledge, resources, and competences, and the creation and development of, or entry to new market arenas. This form of SE essentially focuses on proactively identifying new markets that have not yet been recognized or sought (Covin and Miles, 1999). Since it often takes place in unoccupied competitive space, revolutionary behavior may lead to changes in the boundaries of existing industries or even give rise to creation of new industries, which can provide first mover advantages. Corporate entrepreneurship, which at its core involves a concurrent emphasis on the birth of new businesses within existing organizations, and the transformation of organizations through the renewal of key ideas on which they are built (Guth and Ginsberg, 1990) is a key manifestation of revolution. Indeed, two of the key components of corporate entrepreneurship are venturing (emphasizing new market arenas) and renewal (emphasizing new knowledge, resources, and competences). Although corporate entrepreneurship also involves innovation, it tends to be of a radical nature, requiring considerable new knowledge about products, markets, and technologies.

To recap, although we acknowledge the possibility of alternative forms and manifestations of SE, we believe our theory-driven typology provides a comprehensive and parsimonious foundation upon which new insights and knowledge on the nexus of SL and SE can be developed. While previous categorization schemes, like those proposed by Miller (1983), Zahra (1995), Covin and Miles (1999) and most recently Kuratko and Audretsch (2009), are useful heuristics, they don't specify the underlying theoretical dimensions that give rise to different forms of SE. Our typological approach might confer several advantages to SE researchers by providing a parsimonious framework for describing complex organizational phenomena (Mechanic, 1963; McKelvey, 1975), enabling a more robust basis for explanation and allowing researchers to move beyond the limitations of the current empirical world through envisaging new conceptual forms (Doty and Glick, 1994). However, as with any typology, ours can be criticized for collapsing meaningful distinctions in the interests of parsimony (Bacharach, 1989). Our intention is not to capture every nuance of SE, but to elucidate the archetypal forms, which would enable more comprehensive and cumulative understanding.

A REVIEW OF RESEARCH ON THE INTERSECTION OF STRATEGIC LEADERSHIP AND STRATEGIC ENTREPRENEURSHIP

As noted, while there has certainly been a burgeoning stream of research on the effects of CEOs, TMTs, and BODs on various elements, dimensions, and measures of SE, there has been no systematic attempt to synthesize, integrate, or thematize these streams of research into a unifying understanding of the multiplex effects of strategic leaders. To that end, we undertake a comprehensive review of the theoretical and empirical literature dealing with the nexus of SL (CEOs, TMTs, and BODs) and SE (refinement, replication, rejuvenation, and revolution). To focus the scope of our review, we first limit our attention to studies concerned with CEOs, members of the TMT, and BOD, consistent with Hambrick's (1989) original conceptualization of SL. Second, consistent with most definitions of SE, we selected articles that focused on entrepreneurship in established organizations, and not early stage or nascent entrepreneurial activity. Third, we focused on studies published between 1978 and 2008. We chose 1978 as our starting point since it was the year that Miles and Snow published their seminal treaty on the entrepreneurial organization. Using this time period, we attempted to exhaustively review articles published in major management outlets [*ASQ, AMJ, AMR, SMJ* (1980–), *JMS, JOM, OS,* and *MS*], major leadership journals [*LQ* (1990–)], and major entrepreneurship journals [*SEJ* (2007–), *JBV, ETP*]. From our comprehensive review of each issue of each these 12 journals, we identified 72 articles covering the nexus of SL and SE. We examined each article in three key dimensions central to the conceptual development of our chapter: (1) SL (CEO, TMT, and BOD) focus [(a) central question(s), (b) characteristics, and (c) construct]; (2) SE [(a) theoretical forms and (b) empirical manifestations]; and (3) theory/ testing [(a) design, (b) relationships, and (c) conclusions]. Below we discuss our review grouped by SL level beginning with the CEO.

The Nexus of CEOs and Strategic Entrepreneurship Forms

CEOs occupy a position of unique influence in organizations, serving as the locus of control and decision making (Begley and Boyd, 1987; Daily et al., 2002), and playing both a substantive and symbolic role in organizations. Not only do CEOs shape organizational processes, strategies, and outcomes, they are also central members of the TMT (Jackson, 1992; Finkelstein et al., 2009). Given their prominence in the firm, it is not surprising that research suggests that they exert direct shaping influences on SE forms as summarized in Table 12.1.

Researchers studying the influence of CEOs on refinement have particularly emphasized the role of demographic characteristics of CEOs, such as tenure, educational background, and incentives, notably stock ownership (Barker and Mueller, 2002). For example, Barker and Mueller (2002) investigated the impact of CEO demographic and incentive characteristics on R&D spending patterns, a key manifestation of refinement, focused on improving existing products and developing product line extensions. Coupled with a technical and functional background, and young age, the amount of CEO stock ownership determines the extent of R&D spending. Consistent with agency theory, the alignment of interests of the CEO with those of owners, via stock ownership, incentivizes the CEO to engage the firm in pursuit of refinement-type innovations.

As can be seen from Table 12.1, both CEO leadership and incentives are important antecedents to replication, both product and geographic. In a study of the product market entry activities of 26 firms over a five-year period, Eggers and Kaplan (2009) observed that CEO attention to emerging technology and affected industries is associated with faster entry into new product markets. By contrast, greater attention to existing technologies is associated with slower entry into new product markets. Thus, the effect of CEOs differs depending on their focus of attention – replication seems to be most likely when CEOs are focused on events and developments in adjacent market areas. However, our review suggests that incentives are also important for replication. In particular, Sanders and Carpenter (1998) found that internationalization, a key form of geographic replication was positively associated with the percentage of CEO compensation paid in long-term forms, as well as the total level of CEO compensation.

Research dealing with CEO influences on rejuvenation has predominantly studied the dispositional and leadership characteristics of CEOs, as well as changes in leadership vis-à-vis succession events (Table 12.1). It has been particularly argued that whether CEO is a craftsperson-type (characterized by narrow education, low social awareness and involvement, external locus of control, and a lack of futurity in orientation) as opposed to an opportunistic type (characterized by broad education, high social awareness and involvement, internal locus of control, and futurity in orientation) shapes organizational structure and environment, which in turn, promotes or hampers organizational renewal efforts (Smith and Miner, 1983). Beyond personality, the CEO's tenure is an important antecedent to rejuvenation. In a study of 67 semiconductor producers over a 15-year period, Boeker (1997b) observed that the length of a CEO's tenure was negatively associated with the incidence of strategic change. This suggests that long-tenured CEOs engage in more restricted information processing, become more committed to a paradigm, and are less receptive to new ideas and opportunities (Hambrick and Fukutomi, 1991). Research focusing on rejuvenation has also considered the influence of CEO succession (Romanelli and Tushman, 1994; Boeker, 1997b). In a study of 25 minicomputer firms, Romanelli and Tushman (1994) predicted and found that CEO succession, even in the absence of performance declines and environmental jolts, was associated with revolutionary transformation in organizations. By contrast, in a study of 67 semiconductor producers, Boeker (1997b) found that CEO succession had no effect on strategic change. Additionally, changes in CEO pay have also been suggested to be reflected in rejuvenation since incentives create reinforcements of the status quo or inducements to change

Table 12.1   CEOs and strategic entrepreneurship

Authors (Year), Journal	CEO Focus			SE Conceptualization		Design	Theory/Testing	
	Central question(s)	Character-istic(s)	Construct(s)	Theoretical form(s)	Empirical manifestation(s)		Relationship(s)	Conclusion(s)
Miller et al. (1982), *AMJ*	The relationship between top executive's personality and strategy-making behavior	Composition	CEO personality	Refinement	Product market innovation	33 CEOs of Canadian firms in multiple industries (Survey)	CEO's locus of control → CEO's strategy-making behavior and innovation	CEO's locus of control bears a direct relationship to the nature of corporate strategy. CEOs with an internal locus of control tend to pursue more product market innovations and undertake greater risks than other competitors
Balkin et al. (2000), *AMJ*	Whether CEO pay is related to innovation in high-technology firms	Incentive	CEO short-term and long-term compensation	Refinement	Innovation (number of patents)	90 high-technology firms and 74 non high-technology firms compared (Archival)	Firm innovation → CEO compensation	In high-technology firms, executives should be rewarded for sustaining innovation. Incentives are likely to induce executives to take higher risks, such as making investments in innovation
Barker and Mueller (2002), *MS*	The association of CEO characteristics with R&D spending	Disposition Leadership	CEO tenure, age, stock ownership, functional experience, amount and type of formal education	Refinement	R&D spending	172 firms from the Business Week 1000 list (Archival)	CEO tenure, age, stock ownership, career experiences, amount and type of formal education → R&D spending	CEO preferences for higher vs. lower spending on R&D are reflected more in R&D spending patterns as CEO tenure increases (i.e. relationship gets stronger)

Reference	Research question	Category	Construct	Type	DV/Aspect	Sample	Relationship	Findings
Jung, Wu, and Chow (2008), *LQ*	How transformational leadership by top managers can affect firm innovativeness	Leadership	CEO transformational leadership	Refinement	Aspects of innovation including R&D expenditures and patents filed	50 Taiwanese companies in electronics and telecommunications industry (Survey)	CEO's transformational leadership → firm innovation	There is a direct and positive effect of CEO on firm innovativeness. This is further moderated by the attributes of the organization, climate and empowerment, organization structure, uncertainty and competition
Sanders and Carpenter (1998), *AMJ*	How firms manage complexity arising from internationalization by making changes to its governance	Incentives	Long-term CEO pay	Replication	Internationalization	258 large US firms (Archival)	Internationalization → CEO compensation	The difficulty of board monitoring increases with internationalization. In response, boards increase the use of long-term and total CEO pay, thereby aligning their incentives with interests of shareholders
Eggers and Kaplan (2009), *OS*	How managerial cognition affects the timing of entry into a radical new technological market	Leadership	CEO attention to i) emerging technology, ii) existing technology, iii) the industries affected by new technologies	Replication (product market)	Timing of entry into a radical new technological market	Product market entry activities of 26 firms between 1976–81 (Archival)	CEO attention → earlier/later entry into a new product market	The focus of managerial cognition and attention to existing vs. emerging technology has a significant influence on firm responsiveness to new technical opportunities

Table 12.1 (continued)

Authors (Year), Journal	CEO Focus			SE Conceptualization			Theory/Testing		
	Central question(s)	Character-istic(s)	Construct(s)	Theoretical form(s)	Empirical manifestation(s)	Design	Relationship(s)	Conclusion(s)
Smith and Miner (1983), *SMJ*	The role of entrepreneur's bureaucratic orientation during the course of growth of firm	Disposition	CEO entrepreneurial type	Rejuvenation (of organizational structure)	Organizational structure change	38 founder-CEOs and 294 mid- and lower-level managers (Survey)	Type of the entrepreneur (craftsperson vs. opportunistic) ➚ rigid vs. adaptive organizational structure	Succession of a craftsperson-type CEO with an opportunist one during the course of growth of the firm leads to higher organizational renewal, adaptability, and subsequent growth.
Romanelli and Tushman (1994), *AMJ*	How organizations accomplish transformation	Leadership	CEO succession	Rejuvenation	Organizational transformation: organizational culture, strategy, structure, power distributions, and control systems	Life histories of 25 mini-computer producers founded in US from 1967–69 were examined (Case Studies)	CEO succession ➚ likelihood of organizational transformation	Revolutionary transformation, by which organizations fundamentally alter their systems, strategies, and structures, are influenced by major changes in environmental conditions and successions of CEOs

292

Study	Research focus	Perspective	Independent variable(s)	Dependent variable		Sample	Relationship	Findings
Simons (1994), *SMJ*	How top managers use formal control systems to formulate and implement new business strategies	Leadership	CEO usage of organizational control systems	Rejuvenation (strategy)	Strategic change	10 newly appointed top managers (longitudinal, semi-structured interviews)	Using management control systems as levers of strategic change → strategic turnaround and evolution	Management control processes can be used to achieve revolutionary change in turnaround contexts (e.g., to overcome organizational inertia, structure and communicate performance expectations, and gain organizational allegiance to the new agenda) or to align financial targets and incentives with the new strategic direction in successful businesses
Boeker (1997b), *AMJ*	How CEO and TMT characteristics interact with organizational performance to influence strategic change	Disposition/ Composition Leadership	CEO tenure, CEO succession, TMT tenure, TMT heterogeneity	Rejuvenation	Strategic change	67 US semi-conductor producers (Interviews and Archival)	CEO tenure, CEO succession, TMT tenure, TMT heterogeneity → strategic change	CEO tenure, TMT tenure and TMT tenure homogeneity have a negative relationship with strategic change. Further, successful organizations with long tenured CEOs and TMTs, and homogeneous TMTs exhibit less strategic change

Table 12.1 (continued)

Authors (Year), Journal	CEO Focus		SE Conceptualization				Theory/Testing		
	Character-istic(s)	Construct(s)	Theoretical form(s)	Empirical manifestation(s)		Design	Relationship(s)	Conclusion(s)	
Carpenter (2000), *JOM*	Incentive	CEO compensation	Rejuvenation	Strategic change (variation and deviation)		Sample of 314 US firms (Archival)	Increases in CEO pay → strategic change	Changes in the level, form, and structure of CEO pay influence a firm's propensity to deviate from past organizational practices and industry-level strategic norms
Eisenmann and Bower (2000), *OS*	Process	CEO activism (adoption of a top-down approach by the CEO with increased involvement in strategic actions of the firm along with decreased delegation of authority to subordinates)	Rejuvenation	Expansion through strategic integration		3 large media groups (Case Study)	The scale of integration efforts, relative to the corporation's total asset base → successful strategic integration	CEO activism and effective usage of the top-down approach is crucial for the success of strategic integration efforts

Central question(s):
- Carpenter: The relationship between CEO pay and strategic change
- Eisenmann and Bower: The implications of CEO activism during major strategic integration efforts

Young et al. (2001), *SMJ*	CEO factors that influence the adoption of innovative management practices	Disposition	CEO's age, tenure, education, prior exposure to TQM	Rejuvenation (structure)	Adoption of innovation (TQM)	171 Veteran's Health Administration hospitals (Event History Analysis)	CEO's age, tenure, possession of a graduate degree, having had prior exposure to TQM at another hospital → a hospital's likelihood and timing of adopting TQM	CEO effects are more important factors in influencing TQM adoption during early stages of the diffusion process
Gupta et al. (2004), *JBV*	Developing the construct of entrepreneurial leadership	Leadership	Entrepreneurial leadership (leadership that creates visionary scenarios that are used to assemble and mobilize entrepreneurial initiatives)	Rejuvenation (structure and strategy)	Organizational renewal	GLOBE (15000 middle managers from 62 countries) (Archival)	Scenario enactment (reorienting the business model towards the vision of an entrepreneurial opportunity) and cast enactment (assembling a cast of individuals to act as agents of change) → organizational renewal	Effectiveness of entrepreneurial leadership is generally perceived to be less effective in high power-distance societies (e.g., Middle Eastern and Confucian) but more effective in egalitarian societies (e.g., Anglo and Nordic)

Table 12.1 (continued)

Authors (Year), Journal	CEO Focus			SE Conceptualization			Theory/Testing	
	Central question(s)	Character-istic(s)	Construct(s)	Theoretical form(s)	Empirical manifestation(s)	Design	Relationship(s)	Conclusion(s)
Wu et al. (2005), *AMJ*	The relationship between CEO tenure and firm invention under differing levels of technological dynamism	Leadership	CEO tenure	Rejuvenation	Firm invention as measured by number of new patents filed in a single year	84 US-based, publicly traded biotech companies (Archival)	CEO tenure; technological dynamism → firm invention	CEO tenure has an inverted U-shaped relationship to firm's invention success. Further, this relationship is moderated by technological dynamism, such that short-tenured CEOs spur more invention than do long-tenured CEOs in technologically dynamic environments, and vice versa

| Ling et al. (2008), *AMJ* | The mechanisms underlying the transformational CEOs' effect on pursuit of corporate entrepreneurship | Structure Processes Incentives Composition Leadership | Transformational CEOs; TMT behavioral integration, risk propensity, decentralization of responsibilities, long-term compensation | Revolution | Corporate entrepreneurship | 152 SMEs (Survey) | CEO transformational leadership: TMT behavioral integration; TMT risk propensity; TMT decentralization of responsibilities; TMT long-term compensation → corporate entrepreneurship | Transformational CEOs play a significant, though indirect role in shaping corporate entrepreneurship, by positively impacting TMT long-term compensation, decentralization of responsibilities, and risk-taking propensity |

Source: Authors.

(Carpenter, 2000). Demonstrating this effect, Carpenter (2000) observed that changes in the level, form, and structure of CEO pay influence a firm's propensity to deviate from past practices and industry-level strategic norms.

Finally, as might be expected, engaging in revolutionary entrepreneurial activities, concurrently entering new arenas, and exploring new opportunities, requires a special leadership style on the part of CEOs. Research has suggested that a transformational leadership style among CEOs is conducive to the pursuit of revolutionary entrepreneurial actions, such as corporate entrepreneurship. Transformational leaders are drawn by the need to transform individuals, teams, and firms by going beyond the status quo and in doing so, influence their firms' ability to innovate and adapt. In a study of 152 small-to-medium-sized firms, Ling et al. (2008) found that CEOs with a transformational leadership style enabled corporate entrepreneurship, by creating a TMT context that emphasizes decentralization of responsibility, risk-taking propensity, and long-term incentives.

The Nexus of TMTs and Strategic Entrepreneurship Forms

TMTs, which refer to the relatively small group of most influential executives at the strategic apex of the organization, have been the central focus of SL research since the early 1980s (i.e., Hambrick and Mason, 1984). Known also as the "dominant coalition" (Cyert and March, 1963) or "inner circle" (Thompson, 1967), TMTs wield a pivotal shaping influence on most aspects of firm strategy, behavior, and outcomes (Hambrick and Mason, 1984). A TMT has five central conceptual elements: composition (collective characteristics of TMT members), structure (size, role differentiation), process (consensus, cognitive processes, and interaction among TMT members), incentives (compensation and rewards), and leadership (collective leadership styles) (Hambrick, 1994). As with CEOs, our review of the literature on the nexus of TMTs and SE suggests that TMTs, their composition, processes, and leadership styles exert a salient impact on all SE forms (as summarized in Table 12.2).

Our review of the literature suggests that the composition and leadership style of the TMT are important antecedents to refinement, and its various manifestations, such as product and administrative innovation. In an early study of product and administrative innovation, Hoffman and Hegarty (1993) found that executive characteristics explain variance in innovation even after contextual variables have been controlled for. In particular, general management, externally oriented expertise, and scanning activity were found to influence product innovation, whereas general management, internally oriented expertise, access to resources, and planning/control activities influence administrative innovations. And in a more recent study, Srivastava and Lee (2005) found that the size, educational diversity, and collective tenure of the TMT influenced the order and timing of product moves. The collective leadership climate and style of the TMT also emerged as an important predictor of refinement. In a study of innovation in 12 European countries, Elenkov and Manev (2005) found that top managers' influence on product and administrative innovation was a function of their leadership style, which in turn is shaped by the sociocultural context. Both transactional and transformational leadership styles of top managers were found to positively influence product and organizational innovations. In a similar study, Elenkov et al. (2005) reported that the SL behaviors (transactional and

Table 12.2 TMTs and strategic entrepreneurship

Authors (Year), Journal	TMT Focus			SE Conceptualization		Design	Theory/Testing	
	Central question(s)	Character-istic(s)	Construct(s)	Theoretical form(s)	Empirical manifesta-tion(s)		Relationship(s)	Conclusion(s)
Miller and Friesen (1982), *SMJ*	The determinants of innovation in conservative and entrepreneurial firms	Process	Proactiveness	Refinement (product)	Product innovation	52 Canadian firms (Survey)	Entrepreneurial vs. conservative management style measured using information processing (scanning and control) and decision making (analysis, futurity, consciousness of strategy) variables correlate with the type of innovation in conservative and entrepreneurial firms	Entrepreneurial managers continuously engage in innovation, unless resources are expended too much; whereas conservative managers engage in innovation when i) there are environmental challenges or threats, ii) they are aware of them, and iii) resources are available
Bantel and Jackson (1989), *SMJ*	The relationship between the social composition of TMT and innovation adoptions	Composition	TMT age, tenure, education, functional background	Refinement	Adoption of technical and administrative innovation	TMTs of 199 banks (Survey)	TMT age, organizational tenure, education level, fields of study, and functional backgrounds → innovation	Innovation is greater in banks headed by more educated managers coming from diverse backgrounds. Team heterogeneity does not lead to dysfunctional conflict that hampers innovation

Table 12.2 (continued)

Authors (Year), Journal	TMT Focus			SE Conceptualization		Theory/Testing		
	Central question(s)	Character-istic(s)	Construct(s)	Theoretical form(s)	Empirical manifesta-tion(s)	Design	Relationship(s)	Conclusion(s)
Hoffman and Hegarty (1993), JOM	The influence of top management team characteristics on product, market and administrative innovations	Composition	Executive characteristics: expertise and access to resources	Refinement	Changes in product and markets and administrative systems and processes	361 top managers from 97 manufacturing units (Survey)	TMT expertise, scanning, and culture → product and market innovations	TMT's influence on innovation is explained by executive characteristics rather than organizational or environmental factors. Culture moderates TMT influence for administrative innovations but not product/market innovations
Mezias and Glynn (1993), SMJ	Corporate change and renewal in large, established organizations	Leadership Composition	TMT commitment to innovation, TMT tolerance for ambiguity	Refinement	Innovative search	Simulation	Intentional vs. less conscious efforts to encourage innovation → possibility, cost, and success of search; performance relative to aspirations; variance in search process	Strategic leadership can foster innovation actively (i.e. by intentionally guiding innovative efforts through institutional or revolutionary strategies with explicit TMT commitment to innovation), or passively (by creating an organizational structure and culture that encourages and facilitates emergent innovation, which can be achieved with a high TMT tolerance for ambiguity)

Reference	Focus	Type	Construct(s)	Category	Field	Relationships	Sample/Method	Findings
Heller (1999), *ETP*	Management actions that determine the degree of independence between innovation projects and their host corporations	Process	TMT attention	Refinement	New product development	Top management Team attention → more or less independence between innovation projects and host corporations	13 innovation projects in 2 large firms (Interviews)	Top management teams' attention to an innovation project is an important mechanism in creating more or less independence between innovation projects and host organizations
Hitt et al. (1999), *ETP*	Cross-functional new product design team characteristics and processes over time	Process	TMT support	Refinement	Innovation, new product design	Communication in functional team, TMT support, involvement of supplier, customer → effectiveness of cross-functional team, new product design	Longitudinal study over a period of 18 months (Case Study)	Top management team support influences cross-functional team success in terms of design and development of new products and innovation
Kickul and Gundry (2001), *JOM*	The influence of top management team diversity and creativity on the assessment of opportunities and on innovative internal and external managerial relationships and practices	Composition	TMT diversity; managerial creativity	Refinement		TMT diversity, managerial creativity, opportunity assessment → new products and services, external business relationships, internal business relationships	120 CEOs of ecommerce firms (Survey)	Diverse TMTs capitalize on differences in backgrounds and perspectives within the TMT and channel these differences into creative discussion and debate in the assessment of ecommerce opportunities for their organization

Table 12.2 (continued)

Authors (Year), Journal	TMT Focus			SE Conceptualization			Theory/Testing		
	Central question(s)	Character-istic(s)	Construct(s)	Theoretical form(s)	Empirical manifesta-tion(s)	Design	Relationship(s)	Conclusion(s)
Jung et al. (2003), *LQ*	How top managers' leadership style directly and indirectly affects firm's innovation	Leadership	Transfor-mational leadership	Refinement	Organiz-ational innovation: new product, service, process	32 Taiwanese firms (Survey)	Top managers' transformational leadership style ↗ organizational innovation	The results suggest that transformational leadership has a direct and positive relationship with organizational innovation. Transformational leadership is positively related to empowerment and innovation supporting climate
Atuahene-Gima and Li (2004), *AMJ*	The contingent effect of strategic decision comprehen-siveness on new product development and product quality	Process	Decisional comprehen-siveness	Refinement	New product performance	373 Chinese new technology ventures (Survey)	Strategic decision comprehen-siveness → new product performance and quality	Strategic decision comprehensiveness hurts new product performance in technologically uncertain environments in which information is perceived to be unanalyzable. By contrast strategic decision comprehensiveness enhances product performance in environments with high demand uncertainty

Study	Focus	Category	Variables	Type	Dependent variable	Sample	Relationship	Findings
Chen et al. (2005), *JMS*	Whether the degree to which top management teams contribute to their effective leadership of organizational innovation	Process	TMT conflict (cooperative vs. competitive, and conflict avoidance)	Refinement	Organiza-tional innovation	105 CEOs and 378 executives from 105 organizations in China (Survey)	TMT cooperative approach to conflict (as opposed to competitive approach or avoiding conflict) → innovation	TMT's cooperative approach to conflict leads to productive conflict, which, in turn, is an important antecedent of innovation
Elenkov et al. (2005), *SMJ*	The influence of strategic leaders on innovation processes in organizations	Leadership Composition	Strategic leadership behaviors, TMT tenure heterogeneity and TMT social culture	Refinement (product and process)	Product market and administrative innovation	227 firms or business units in six countries (Survey)	Strategic leadership behaviors, TMT heterogeneity → product market and administrative innovations	Strategic leadership behaviors are positively associated with executive influence on innovation processes, beyond the effects of organizational size and the CEO's personality traits
Elenkov and Manev (2005), *JOM*	A model of top management team influence on innovations	Leadership	Top management leadership	Refinement	Product and market innovations	468 European firms (Survey)	TMT influence → product and market innovation	Top managers' leadership is positively associated with TMTs' influence on product and market innovations

Table 12.2   (continued)

Authors (Year), Journal	TMT Focus			SE Conceptualization			Theory/Testing	
	Central question(s)	Character-istic(s)	Construct(s)	Theoretical form(s)	Empirical manifesta-tion(s)	Design	Relationship(s)	Conclusion(s)
Smith et al. (2005), *AMJ*	The influence of TMT knowledge and knowledge creation capability on introduction of new products and services	Composition	TMT experience, education, functional heterogeneity, number of contacts, network range, strength of ties	Refinement	Rate of new product and service introductions	TMTs of 72 technology firms (Survey)	TMT experience, education, functional heterogeneity, number of contacts, network range, strength of ties, organizational climate, climate for teamwork, knowledge creation capability → number of new products and services	TMT knowledge, by virtue of experience and education, and by virtue of access through networks, impacts knowledge creation capability, which is then positively related to the number of new product introductions
Smith and Tushman (2005), *OS*	How TMTs manage strategic contradictions to manage innovation	Structure Leadership	TMT structure, leader coaching	Refinement (product)	Product innovation	Theoretical	Leader-centric vs. team-centric team structure and process → innovation performance	Contradictions in TMTs are managed through coaching by the CEO in leader-centric TMTs or through a higher degree and frequency of team interactions in team-centric TMTs. In both cases, contradictions need to be sorted out and strategic contradictions have to be balanced for successful innovation performance

Study	Focus	Type	Variables	Refinement	Outcome	Method	Relationship	Findings
Srivastava and Lee (2005), *JBV*	The relationship between TMT characteristics and order and timing of new product moves	Composition	TMT education, organizational tenure, and size	Refinement (process)	New product innovation	223 new product introductions (Archival)	Average education level, organizational tenure, and size of the TMT → order and timing of the move, the likelihood of the firm being a first mover versus an imitator	Firms with larger TMTs that are more heterogeneous in terms of tenure are more likely to be first movers with respect to new product introductions
Smith and Cao (2007), *SEJ*	The potential for top management teams to shape and influence their environment	Leadership	TMT belief systems and expectations	Refinement	New products and service creation	Theoretical	TMT belief systems, firm actions → environment changes	Top managers have certain beliefs and expectations about what best products or services are and how they evolve. When these expectations are disconfirmed, they engage in aspirational search and undertake new firm-level actions to learn and shape the environment
Hornsby et al. (2009), *JBV*	Examining TMT support, for entrepreneurial action, to managers at different levels in the organization	Leadership	TMT support	Refinement (process)	Number of new ideas implemented	458 first-, middle-, and senior-level managers (Survey)	TMT support → number of entrepreneurial ideas implemented by senior and mid-level managers (as opposed to first-level managers)	The higher the level of manager within the hierarchy, the more effective received support becomes (i.e. higher-level managers are better able to make the most of TMT support)

Table 12.2 (continued)

Authors (Year), Journal	TMT Focus		SE Conceptualization			Design	Theory/Testing	
	Central question(s)	Character-istic(s)	Construct(s)	Theoretical form(s)	Empirical manifesta-tion(s)		Relationship(s)	Conclusion(s)
Roth (1992), *JOM*	Identifies decision-making character-istics of top management as related to strategic archetypes for competing in a global industry	Process	TMT risk taking, openness in decision making, and group consensus	Replication	International strategy types, for competing in a global industry	Senior managers of 82 business units competing in global industries (Survey)	TMT risk taking, openness in decision making, group consensus → strategy types in global industry	A fit between international strategy, TMT risk taking, openness, and consensus is positively associated with business unit performance
Bloodgood et al. (1996), *ETP*	The antecedents and outcomes of internationali-zation	Composition	TMT international education and work experience	Replication	Internationali-zation	61 venture capital backed US firms (Archival)	TMT international work experience, product differentiation → internationali-zation → performance	Internationalization is higher in ventures in which top management teams have international work experience
Sambharya (1996), *SMJ*	The impact of foreign experience of TMT members on firm's internationali-zation	Composition	TMT international experience	Replication (geographic market)	Strategic posture (international diversifi-cation)	54 US corporations (Survey)	International experience of the TMT (mean and heterogeneity) and proportion of managers with international experience in the TMT are associ-ated with the focal firm's internationalization	TMTs with international experience are associated with firm internationalization

Study	Research question	Leadership/Composition	Variables	Replication	Dependent variable	Sample	Relationship	Key findings
Boeker (1997a), *ASQ*	The impact of executive migration on entry into new product markets	Leadership	Executive migration	Replication (product market)	Firm entry in new product markets	67 semiconductor firms in US (Archival)	Functional background, industry tenure and managerial tenure of the externally recruited top manager; TMT tenure heterogeneity; TMT size → likelihood of product market entry	Background and experience of individual top executives recruited from outside the organization play an important role in product market entry decisions, especially when their functional backgrounds are in R&D or engineering
Sanders and Carpenter (1998), *AMJ*	How firms manage complexity arising from internationalization by making changes to its governance	Composition	TMT size	Replication	Internationalization	258 large US firms (Archival)	Internationalization → TMT composition	In order to manage the complexity arising from internationalization firms employ larger TMTs as they have greater information-processing capacity
Tihanyi et al. (2000), *JOM*	The relationship between top management team characteristics and firm international diversification	Composition	TMT age, tenure, education, elite education, international experience, team heterogeneity	Replication	International diversification, diversification of business activities across national borders	126 firms in US electronics industry (Archival)	Lower average age, higher average tenure, higher average elite education, higher average international experience, and higher tenure heterogeneity → international expansion	Teams with younger managers, greater tenure on TMT, members with elite educational backgrounds, and teams with greater international experience were associated with greater levels of firm international diversification

Table 12.2 (continued)

Authors (Year), Journal	TMT Focus			SE Conceptualization			Theory/Testing		
	Central question(s)	Character-istic(s)	Construct(s)	Theoretical form(s)	Empirical manifesta-tion(s)	Design	Relationship(s)	Conclusion(s)
Carpenter and Fredrick-son (2001), *AMJ*	The impact of the top management team characteristics on the firm's global strategic posture and the moderating role of uncertainty	Composition	TMT international experience, TMT educational heterogeneity, TMT tenure heterogeneity, TMT functional heterogeneity	Replication	Global strategic posture	207 US firms (Survey)	TMT international work experience, TMT educational heterogeneity, TMT functional heterogeneity, TMT firm tenure heterogeneity, environmental uncertainty → global strategic posture	Firms with diverse TMTs in terms of breadth of international experience and heterogeneity of educational backgrounds and firm tenures tend to be highly global. Functional heterogeneity has a negative relationship with global posture. The association between TMT educational heterogeneity and global posture is stronger in uncertain environments

Study	Title	Category	Variables	Type	Dependent variable	Sample	Relationship	Findings
Carpenter and Sanders, (2004), JOM	The impact of TMT compensation and firm internationalization on firm performance	Incentive	TMT pay	Replication	Internationalization	224 US MNCs (Archival)	TMT pay; firm internationalization → firm performance	TMT total pay and use of long-term incentive pay are positively associated with subsequent performance while CEO–TMT pay gap has negative effects on performance. Further, CEO pay has no relationship with performance and TMT pay effects are much stronger in MNCs with high degree of internationalization
Barkema and Shvyrkov (2007), SMJ	The impact of TMT diversity and subgroups on geographic market entry	Composition	TMT tenure and educational diversity, existence of strong fault lines within the TMT, overlapping TMT tenure	Replication (geographic market)	Geographic market entry	2159 expansions of 25 companies in three decades (Archival)	TMT tenure and educational diversity, strong fault line settings, overlapping team tenure, overlapping tenure of TMT members → novelty of the geographic location of new investments	Strong fault lines within the TMT hamper strategic innovations. Overlapping tenure of TMT members, i.e., TMT members' gaining experience of working with each other, decreases this negative effect over time
Allen (1979), AMJ	Why TMTs opt for a particular type and direction of reorganization	Leadership	CEO succession; TMT philosophy	Rejuvenation	Reorganization: retain or adopt particular types of divisionalized organization	30 firms (Surveys and Archival)	Decision to appoint new CEO; whether CEO was career employee; TMT philosophy → pattern of reorganization	CEO succession and TMT philosophy about autonomy and proactive information gathering are significantly related to reorganization

Table 12.2 (continued)

Authors (Year), Journal	TMT Focus		SE Conceptualization		Theory/Testing		
	Character-istic(s)	Construct(s)	Theoretical form(s)	Empirical manifesta-tion(s)	Design	Relationship(s)	Conclusion(s)
Burgelman (1983b), *AMR*	Leadership	TMT support for strategic initiatives	Rejuven-ation	Corporate entrepreneur-ship	Theoretical	TMT influence → autonomous and induced strategic activities	Top management teams play a predominant role in influencing strategic initiatives by providing support to initiatives
Van de Ven (1986), *MS*	Structure Process	Tolerance for ambiguity, fostering an entrepreneurial organization culture	Rejuven-ation (of strategy)	Organiza-tional innovation	Theoretical	Maintenance of diversity, order, and balance among innovative subunits by top management; fostering an innovation culture within the organization → organizational innovation	A supportive institutional leadership (i.e. top management) is critical in creating a cultural context that fosters innovation, and in establishing organizational strategy, structure, and systems that facilitate innovation
Hurst et al. (1989), *SMJ*	Composition	TMT cognitive characteristics	Rejuven-ation (strategy)	Strategic renewal	Theoretical	Composition of the TMT, on the basis of Jungian personality types (intuitive, feeler, thinker, sensor) → strategic renewal	In order for the firm to successfully engage in the creative management process, from idea inception to strategy implementation, all four Jungian personality types should be represented in the top management team

Barr et al. (1992), *SMJ*	The relationship between the change in mental models of top managers and changes in organizational action	Leadership Processes	Managerial learning and cognition	Rejuven-ation (strategy)	Strategic renewal	Top managers of a matched pair of railroad firms (Content Analysis, Archival)	TMT's ability to detect substantial change in the environment, delay in TMT learning process → rapid succession or change in mental models of TMT members that leads to organizational renewal	Managers who can recognize the change in the environment and the prospective impact of these changes on their organization can alter their mental models rapidly, which, in turn, facilitates organizational renewal
Dougherty (1992), *SMJ*	A model of organizational renewal through product innovation	Leadership	TMT cognitive process	Rejuven-ation (strategy)	Product innovation, strategic renewal	Theoretical	Identification of i) emerging technological and marketing trends in the market, ii) the fit between these trends and firm capabilities, iii) feasibility of the business opportunity, iv) visceralization → strategic renewal through product innovation	For a more holistic approach to strategic renewal via product innovation, top managers need to have a deep understanding of the daily use of their products by their customers, and the skill necessary to i) identify market trends, ii) find a fit between them and organizational capabilities, and iii) discern whether a viable opportunity exists

Table 12.2 (continued)

Authors (Year), Journal	Central question(s)	TMT Focus		SE Conceptualization		Design	Theory/Testing	
		Characteristic(s)	Construct(s)	Theoretical form(s)	Empirical manifestation(s)		Relationship(s)	Conclusion(s)
Lant et al. (1992), *SMJ*	The role of managerial learning in strategic renewal	Process Composition	TMT demography, environmental awareness, managerial learning, CEO/TMT turnover	Rejuvenation (strategy)	Organizational dimensions of change	Publicly held 40 furniture and 40 software companies (Content Analysis, Archival)	Managerial awareness, external attributions for poor performance → likelihood of strategic reorientation	Top managers' interpretation of their experiences, vis-à-vis evaluating causal relations between their past decisions and firm performance, play a critical role in actively leading entrepreneurial initiatives, rather than hampering them
Wiersema and Bantel (1992), *AMJ*	The relationship between demography of TMTs and corporate strategic change	Composition	TMT demography	Rejuvenation	Corporate strategic change, absolute change in diversification level	87 manufacturing firms (Archival)	TMT traits (low age, short organizational tenure, short team tenure, high educational level, technical specialization), TMT heterogeneity (age, organizational tenure, team tenure, educational specialization) → corporate strategic change	Firms most likely to undergo changes in corporate strategy have TMTs characterized by lower average age, shorter organizational tenure, higher team tenure, higher educational level, higher educational specialization heterogeneity, and higher academic training in the sciences

West and Meyer (1997), *ETP*	The characteristics and behaviors related to future time orientation and their association with the pursuit of entrepreneurial opportunity	Composition Process	TMT future orientation, communication pattern	Rejuven-ation	Strategic change, challenging status quo	CEOs and TMTs of 22 technology-based firms (Survey)	Future-oriented TMTs, communication patterns → strategic change and growth	Strategic change in young technology ventures is associated with top management teams who are perceived as being more future oriented. Communication patterns linking future-oriented and present-oriented managers are also associated with strategic change
Floyd and Lane (2000), *AMR*	When and where strategic role conflict occurs and how organizational controls may be used to alleviate it	Structure	Strategic role conflict	Rejuven-ation	Strategic renewal: competence definition, deployment, and modification	Theoretical	Top management roles (ratifying, directing, and recognizing) → strategic renewal	Strategic role conflict within TMT, related to disagreement on need for strategic change, is likely to be associated with increased strategic role conflict at the middle and operating levels of management. Environmental change may create role conflicts when individual managers are required to play multiple strategic roles

Table 12.2 (continued)

Authors (Year), Journal	TMT Focus		SE Conceptualization			Theory/Testing		
	Central question(s)	Character-istic(s)	Construct(s)	Theoretical form(s)	Empirical manifesta-tion(s)	Design	Relationship(s)	Conclusion(s)
Gordon et al. (2000), *JOM*	The antecedents of strategic reorientation	Leadership Composition	CEO turnover, TMT turnover, TMT heterogeneity	Rejuven-ation	Strategic reorientation	120 firms in stable furniture and turbulent computer software industries (Archival)	CEO turnover, TMT turnover, TMT heterogeneity → strategic reorientation	Industry turbulence and CEO turnover are important precursors to strategic reorientation. Industry turbulence conditions managers' external attributions for negative financial performance such that stable environments are associated with strategic reorientation. Also, TMT turnover is negatively related to strategic reorientation

Cho and Hambrick (2006), *OS*	The role of attentional orientation of TMTs	Composition Incentive	TMT composition, incentives and attention towards environmental orientation (EO)	Rejuvenation (strategy and structure)	Entrepreneurial strategy	30 publicly traded airlines (1973–86) (Archival)	TMT composition, incentives, interaction between composition and incentives, and attention to EO (following substantial deregulation in the industry) → shift in managerial attention toward more of an entrepreneurial orientation (relative to an engineering orientation)	TMT structure, composition, process, and compensation have an interaction effect, suggesting that the critical impact of upper echelons of the organization on SE is not decomposable to its individual dimensions. Rather, they constitute an integrated and encompassing TMT effect on EO
de Bettignies and Chemla (2008), *MS*	The relationship between corporate venturing and attracting/retaining star managers	Incentive	Executive migration	Rejuvenation	Corporate venturing	Theoretical	Returns from venturing, competition for talent → corporate venturing	In addition to pursuing high returns firms may also engage in corporate venturing activities to incentivize their star managers for exceptional performance, and to recruit or retain key talent. Competition for talent is a key factor in determining corporate venturing investments

Table 12.2 (continued)

Authors (Year), Journal	TMT Focus			SE Conceptualization		Theory/Testing		
	Central question(s)	Characteristic(s)	Construct(s)	Theoretical form(s)	Empirical manifestation(s)	Design	Relationship(s)	Conclusion(s)
Agarwal and Helfat (2009), *OS*	The important characteristics of strategic renewal and its critical impact on entire economies, as well as individual firms and their industries	Process	TMT communication of and commitment to strategic intent	Rejuvenation (strategy and structure)	Strategic renewal	IBM (Case Study)	Top management reshaping of organizational cognition (through constant communication), top management's provision of economic incentives and social status for managers associated with strategic renewal → strategic renewal	The critical role of strategic leadership is not actively leading entrepreneurial efforts, but rather establishing the structure, implementing the system, and striving to build a culture
Burgelman (1983a), *ASQ*	The interlocking key activities of top and middle managers as part of the process of transforming R&D activities into new businesses through internal corporate venturing	Process	TMT support for internal ventures	Revolution	Corporate entrepreneurship (CE)	Qualitative study of a a large, US-based, high-technology firm	Top management support for viable corporate entrepreneurial initiatives → change in corporate strategy	Top management's direct influence on CE is through the manipulation of structural context

Study	Purpose	Category	Key variables	Theme	Type	Method	Relationships	Conclusions
Burgelman (1983c), *MS*	A model of the strategic process concerning entrepreneurial activity in large, complex organizations	Process	TMT tolerance for ambiguity and autonomous behavior, TMT commitment to entrepreneurial activity	Revolution	Corporate entrepreneurship	Theoretical	TMT tolerance for ambiguity and autonomous behavior, TMT commitment to entrepreneurial activity → internal corporate venturing	TMT should mainly be concerned with balancing the emphasis on diversity (i.e., experimentation-and-selection) and order (i.e., planning and structuring) over time. TMT should control the level and the rate of change rather than the specific content of entrepreneurial activity
Shortell and Zajac (1988), *SMJ*	The structuring, development, and performance of internal corporate joint ventures (ICIVs)	Process	Autonomy (provided by the TMT)	Revolution	Forming new internal corporate joint ventures	53 internal corporate joint venture projects in an industry (Archival)	Operating autonomy and strategic integration of the ICIJV, TMT commitment → performance	Success of ICIVs are determined, in part, by the degree of their integration to the corporate strategy, and the extent to which they are provided support and autonomy by top management
Covin and Slevin (1991), *ETP*	A model of entrepreneurship specifying the antecedents and consequences	Leadership	TMT risk taking, TMT values and philosophies	Revolution	Corporate entrepreneurship	Theoretical	TMT beliefs, value structures, and management philosophies; individual level, organizational and environmental variables → entrepreneurial posture	Top management teams, by virtue of their risk taking and philosophies, have a significant influence on organizational-level entrepreneurial behavior among larger, established firms

Table 12.2 (continued)

| Authors (Year), Journal | Central question(s) | TMT Focus | | SE Conceptualization | | Theory/Testing | | |
		Character-istic(s)	Construct(s)	Theoretical form(s)	Empirical manifesta-tion(s)	Design	Relationship(s)	Conclusion(s)
Zahra (1993), *ETP*	Extends the Covin-Slevin entrepre-neurship model specifying antecedents and consequences	Composition Process	TMT background, values and experience, managerial process	Revolution	Corporate entrepre-neurship	Theoretical	External environment, internal variables, strategic variables, firm-level entrepreneurship → firm-performance	Managerial values and background (including age, past experience, functional experience), and managerial process (including participation and fairness) are associated with corporate entrepreneurship
Stopford and Baden-Fuller (1994), *SMJ*	The bundles of attributes shared by managerial, firm-level, and industry-level entrepre-neurship	Process	CEO and TMT attention to the need for change, TMT process (teamwork)	Revolution	Implemen-tation of entrepre-neurial changes in the organization structure and processes	10 firms in 4 European industries (Archival)	Proactiveness, aspirations beyond current capability, team-orientation, capability to resolve dilemmas, learning capability → corporate entrepreneurship	Cultivation of entrepreneurial attributes can only be achieved through top management drive and support over long periods of time

Birkinshaw (1997), *SMJ*	The types of initiatives exhibited by subsidiary TMTs of multinational firms that impact corporate entrepreneurship at the MNC level	Process	Subsidiary TMT initiatives (discrete, proactive undertakings that advance new ways for the corporation to use or expand its resources)	Revolution	Corporate entrepreneurship	39 separate subsidiary initiatives by 6 subsidiaries of multinational corporations (Semi-structured interviews, Survey, Archival)	Local, internal, global market, and hybrid initiatives pursued by subsidiary TMTs → corporate entrepreneurship	Execution of strategic leadership at the local market level has the potential to drive local responsiveness, global integration and worldwide learning capabilities of the MNC, a much broader role than previously recognized. Top management of the MNC should provide the autonomy to TMT of subsidiaries for pursuit of initiatives and actively facilitate the proliferation of successful initiatives in the internal market of the MNC (i.e., among other subsidiaries)
Dess et al. (1997), *SMJ*	The nature of entrepreneurial strategy making (ESM) and its relationship with strategy, environment and performance	Process	TMT styles	Revolution	Entrepreneurial strategy making	32 diversified firms (Survey)	TMT entrepreneurial style → entrepreneurial strategy making	TMT's entrepreneurial style impacts organizational-level entrepreneurial strategy making, a distinct strategy-making process, characterized by experimentation, innovativeness, risk taking, and proactive assertiveness

Table 12.2 (continued)

Authors (Year), Journal	Central question(s)	TMT Focus		SE Conceptualization		Theory/Testing		
		Characteristic(s)	Construct(s)	Theoretical form(s)	Empirical manifestation(s)	Design	Relationship(s)	Conclusion(s)
Barringer and Bluedorn (1999), *SMJ*	The relationship between corporate entrepreneurship intensity and strategic management practices	Process	TMT strategy making	Revolution	Corporate entrepreneurship intensity	169 US manufacturing firms (Survey, Archival)	Scanning intensity, planning flexibility, planning horizon, locus of planning, strategic controls, financial controls → corporate entrepreneurship intensity	Alertness and adaptability to the environment are the main tenets of an entrepreneurial organization. To that end, top management plays a dual role by i) scanning the environment, and ii) nurturing an entrepreneurial culture within the organization by institutionalizing flexibility in and soliciting participation of employees to planning processes
Simsek et al. (2007), *JMS*	How a firm's competitive environment influences the firm's pursuit of entrepreneurial activities	Process Incentives	TMT discretionary slack, TMT incentives	Revolution	Corporate entrepreneurship	495 SMEs (Survey)	Discretionary slack, TMT outcome-based incentives → corporate entrepreneurship	TMT's perceptions of discretionary slack mediate the relationship between environment characteristics (dynamism, complexity, and munificence) and the pursuit of corporate entrepreneurship

Source: Authors.

transformational) were significantly related to both product and administrative innovations, and this impact was moderated by the heterogeneity of the TMT. Beyond leadership style, in a study of 458 managers at different levels, Hornsby and colleagues (2009) found that top management support, defined as the extent to which lower-level managers perceive that top-level managers support entrepreneurial behavior is an important determinant of the number of entrepreneurial ideas implemented, particularly among middle-level managers.

Most TMT studies dealing with replication focus primarily on the relationship between TMT compositional factors and internationalization, particularly the international expertise and experience of the team. Sambharya (1996) reported that the extent and diversity of TMT international experience is positively related to the amount of international diversification. In a similar study of internationalization, Tihanyi et al. (2000) found that TMTs with lower average age, higher average tenure, higher average elite education, higher average international experience, and higher tenure heterogeneity are more likely to pursue international diversification. Similarly, Carpenter and Fredrickson (2001) found that firms with TMTs that had a breadth of international expertise, coupled with educational and experiential diversity, displayed a global strategic posture. Most recently, Barkema and Shvyrkov (2007) studied the effects of TMT composition and configuration (in terms of fault lines and overlap) on the novelty of geographic location. Studying 2159 expansions across 25 companies, Barkema and Shvyrkov (2007) found that while tenure diversity within TMTs increased the novelty of geographic investment, strong fault lines dampened geographic novelty. However, the extent of overlapping team tenure (reflecting continued interaction among TMT members) was found to negate the positive impact of tenure diversity, and negative impact of fault lines on this novelty.

Beyond the effects of composition, some scholars have begun to examine the effects of other conceptual elements of TMTs on replication. In a study of decision-making characteristics of managers, Roth (1992) emphasized the need for a close alignment between decision-making characteristics (risk taking, decision-making openness, and group consensus) and international strategy (multi-domestic, global). And in terms of incentives, Carpenter and Sanders (2004) found that total pay and use of long-term incentives among TMTs was associated with the subsequent performance of multinational corporations (MNCs), but that the effect of compensation on performance was stronger at high levels of internationalization.

TMT research on compositional antecedents of rejuvenation has primarily emphasized demographics (Lant et al., 1992; Wiersema and Bantel, 1992; Gordon et al., 2002), but also collective personality (Hurst et al., 1989). In regard to demographics, Lant and colleagues (1992) found that the diversity of the TMT, in terms of functional expertise, was associated with an increased likelihood of strategic reorientation. In a highly cited study of manufacturing firms, Wiersema and Bantel (1992) demonstrated that a TMT's cognitive perspectives, as reflected by traits (young age, short tenure, high educational level, and technical specialization) and diversity (age, company tenure, team tenure, and educational specialization), were linked to the TMT's propensity to change corporate strategy. And in a follow-up to Lant et al.'s (1992) study, Gordon and colleagues (2000) found that changes in TMT composition, vis-à-vis turnover, are negatively related to the incidence of strategic reorientation. Finally, in a study of managerial attention and strategic change in the deregulated airline industry, Cho and Hambrick (2006) observed that following deregulation, compositional changes in the TMT (increases in proportion of executives with output-oriented functional experience, decreases in average focal industry tenure of executives, and increases in demographic diversity of executives) were associated with a shift in managerial attention to an entrepreneurial orientation, and subsequent strategic changes towards an entrepreneurial orientation.

Cognition and cognitive processes within TMTs have also been argued to play a special role in supporting rejuvenation. Barr et al. (1992), for example, reported that managers who can recognize change in the environment and the prospective impact of these changes on their organization can change their mental models rapidly, in a way that supports strategic renewal. In a study of the time orientations of top managers (future vs. present), West and Meyer (1997) found partial support for their hypothesis that communication intensity between future-oriented managers and present-oriented managers would be positively related to strategic change. In a case study of IBM, Agarwal and Helfat (2009) also demonstrated the pivotal role of communication processes in reshaping organizational cognition to support strategic renewal, by changing organizational routines, and structures, cultures, and systems. Finally, TMT incentives also matter for rejuvenation. In a conceptual exposition, Hoskisson and Turk (1990) (see Table 12.3) argued that an emphasis on short-term incentives among top managers is positively related to corporate diversification, by altering the managers' risk profile.

Investigations of TMT antecedents of revolutionary forms of SE emphasize the importance of a supportive managerial context (Shortell and Zajac, 1988) and set of managerial beliefs and values (Covin and Slevin, 1991). Senior managers create a structural context that is conducive to autonomous strategic initiatives (those that depart significantly from induced initiatives), and in doing so must demonstrate a tolerance for ambiguity (Burgelman, 1983b). According to Stopford and Baden-Fuller (1994), such a context should be characterized by proactiveness, aspirations beyond current capability, a team orientation, a capability to resolve dilemmas, and a learning capability. Beyond providing a supportive context, TMT composition and processes are also salient antecedents to revolution. In terms of composition, Zahra (1993) argued that age, experience, and functional background of TMTs is related to the pursuit of corporate entrepreneurship. Ling and colleagues (2008) similarly found that a risk-taking propensity, coupled with decentralized decision processes, and long-term compensation were pivotal predictors of corporate entrepreneurship in a study of small and medium enterprises (SMEs).

The Nexus of BODs and Strategic Entrepreneurship Forms

Finally, boards of directors, although not responsible for the day-to-day management of the firm, are subsumed within the purview of SL theory. From both resource dependence and agency perspectives, boards fulfill two important roles in organizations: they act as buffers or boundary spanners, linking organizations to critical resources, knowledge, and networks, and they shape strategic choice, by selecting, controlling, and sanctioning senior managers. The main conceptual elements of boards that account for the vast majority of research are composition and structure (Zahra and Pearce, 1989). Board

Table 12.3   BODs and strategic entrepreneurship

Authors (Year), Journal	Board Focus			SE Conceptualization		Theory/Testing		
	Central question(s)	Characteristic(s)	Construct(s)	Theoretical form(s)	Empirical manifestation(s)	Design	Relationship(s)	Conclusion(s)
Baysinger et al. (1991), *AMJ*	The effect of board and institutional ownership on R&D spending	Composition	Ownership concentration; percentage of insider directors	Refinement	R&D spending	176 Fortune 500 firms (Archival)	Levels of stock ownership; percentage of insiders on companies board of directors → corporate R&D spending	Higher insider representation on a board and concentration of equity among institutional investors positively impacts corporate R&D spending
Hoskisson et al. (2002), *AMJ*	The relationship between governance and corporate innovation strategies	Incentives Composition	Types of institutional owners; inside/outside directors; incentives	Refinement	Developing new products by either acquiring through external means or developing in house	234 industrial manufacturing firms (Archival)	Institutional ownership; inside/outside board of director representation; incentives → corporate innovation strategies	While inside directors prefer internal innovation, outside directors prefer external innovation

Table 12.3 (continued)

Authors (Year), Journal	Board Focus		SE Conceptualization			Theory/Testing		
	Central question(s)	Character-istic(s)	Construct(s)	Theoretical form(s)	Empirical manifesta-tion(s)	Design	Relationship(s)	Conclusion(s)
Kor (2006), *SMJ*	The direct and interactive effects of TMT and BOD composition on R&D investment intensity	Composi-tion Structure	TMT tenure, shared experience, functional heterogeneity; separation of CEO and chair; ratio of outsiders on board	Refine-ment	R&D investment intensity	77 entrepre-neurial firms that completed IPO (Archival)	TMT tenure, shared team-specific experience, functional background heterogeneity, separation of CEO and chair duties, ratio of outsiders on board → R&D investment intensity	Separating CEO and chair duties and TMT's shared experience has a direct and positive impact on R&D investment intensity while TMT tenure has a negative effect. Effect of outside members board monitoring weakens as TMT tenure lengthens. Further a combination of teams with high levels of shared experience and outsider-rich boards may hurt R&D investments. Functional heterogeneity in TMTs reduces effectiveness of outside directors in promoting R&D investments since such efforts may be objected to by non-R&D executives

Study	Purpose	Composition / Structure		Replication	Internationalization	Sample	Relationships	Findings
Sanders and Carpenter (1998), *AMJ*	How firms manage complexity arising from internationalization by making changes to its governance	Composition	Structure — CEO duality; board size	Replication	Internationalization	258 large US firms (Archival)	Internationalization → CEO duality; board size	Complexity arising from internationalization requires that firms delegate authority and divide responsibilities, thus a preference for the separation of CEO and chair positions. Complexity is also managed by increasing the size of the board. Additionally, in highly international firms with large boards, inside directors facilitate exchange of information
Tihanyi et al. (2003), *AMJ*	The roles of institutional investors and board of directors in relation to international diversification	Composition — BOD: outside directors, inside directors		Replication	International diversification: measured by combining firm sales from foreign operation, foreign assets, and number of subsidiaries	197 large US firms (Archival)	Institutional ownership; BOD structure; technological opportunity ↗ international diversification	Institutional investors are even more interested in international diversification when the appropriate form of monitoring is in place through its board of directors. Professional investment funds support international diversification when outside director representation is high. Pension funds support international diversification when insider director incentives are high

Table 12.3 (continued)

Authors (Year), Journal	Board Focus		SE Conceptualization			Theory/Testing		
	Central question(s)	Character-istic(s)	Construct(s)	Theoretical form(s)	Empirical manifesta-tion(s)	Design	Relationship(s)	Conclusion(s)
Hoskisson and Turk (1990), *AMR*	Specifies governance, diversification, control, and performance limits of the internal capital market that result in corporate restructuring	Composi-tion Incentive	BOD: outside directors, inside directors executive compensation	Rejuvena-tion	Restructuring: major change in composition of firm assets along with major change in firm strategy	Theoretical	Ownership, board composition, executive compensation → diversification, restructuring, performance	Dispersed ownership and ratio of outside to inside members on board, positively influences diversification. Further, short-term executive incentive compensation is positively associated with diversification. Following restructuring, there is an increase in ownership concentration and use of strategic controls, and a decrease in the ratio of outside to inside directors on the board
Goodstein and Boeker (1991), *AMJ*	The effects of changes in board structure on strategic change	Composi-tion	BOD turnover; outside, inside BODs, change of CEO	Rejuvena-tion	Strategic change: altering market position	327 US hospitals (Survey)	Ownership, BOD turnover, outside/inside BOD, change of CEO, degree of market competition → strategic change	Ownership and board changes can directly influence strategic change independent of CEO succession

Study	Title	Focus	Variables		Outcome	Sample	Hypothesis	Findings
Goodstein et al. (1994), *SMJ*	The influence of board size and diversity on strategic change	Structure	BOD size, diversity	Rejuvenation	Strategic change	334 US hospitals (Survey)	BOD size, diversity → strategic change	Large and diverse boards limit strategic change, such that their effectiveness is limited in directing strategic change
Golden and Zajac (2001), *SMJ*	The influence of the board of directors on strategic change	Composition Structure Process	BOD size, tenure, age, occupational heterogeneity; attention, comprehensiveness, power	Rejuvenation	Strategic change	3000 US hospitals (Archival and Survey)	BOD size, tenure, age, occupational heterogeneity, proportion of members from business occupations, attention to strategic issues, comprehensiveness of board evaluation process, power → strategic change	BOD demography impacts strategic change curvilinearly such that smaller boards, boards with lower levels of tenure, younger boards, and occupationally less heterogeneous boards are associated with strategic change. Further boards with a business orientation are related to strategic change. All these effects are further magnified under conditions of high board power
Zahra (1996), *AMJ*	The impact of ownership on corporate entrepreneurship	Composition	Executive stock ownership; institutional ownership	Revolution	Corporate entrepreneurship	127 CEOs (Survey)	Ratio of inside and outside directors; executive ownership; short- and long-term institutional ownership → corporate entrepreneurship	While executive ownership and long-term institutional ownership enhance corporate entrepreneurship, short-term institutional ownership has a negative impact on corporate entrepreneurship

Table 12.3 (continued)

Authors (Year), Journal	Board Focus			SE Conceptualization		Design	Theory/Testing	
	Central question(s)	Character-istic(s)	Construct(s)	Theoretical form(s)	Empirical manifesta-tion(s)		Relationship(s)	Conclusion(s)
Zahra et al. (2000), *JOM*	Factors that influence managerial support for corporate entrepreneurship	Composition Incentive	Executive stock ownership; BOD composition and incentives	Revolution	Corporate entrepreneur-ship	239 US medium-sized manufacturing firms (Survey)	CEO duality; compensation; BOD size; inside/outside directors; BOD stock ownership → corporate entrepreneur-ship	Managers owning a stock in medium-sized firm may feel that promoting CE programs will have greater impact on firm's bottom line. Outside directors' representation on the board has a negative impact on corporate entrepreneur-ship while outside directors' stock ownership has a positive impact. CEO nonduality is positively associated with corporate entrepreneur-ship.

Source: Authors.

328

composition refers to the affiliations of each director, as well as the demographic background and expertise that each director brings to the board (Finkelstein et al., 2009). Board structure, on the other hand, refers to the formal organization of the board of directors; and more specifically its size, the division of labor between the chair and the CEO, and board committees. Like CEOs and TMTs, our review of the literature on the nexus of board of directors and SE as summarized in Table 12.3 suggests that board of directors have a salient impact on SE forms.

The composition of the board of directors is an important factor contributing to refinement activity. In a study of 176 Fortune 500 firms, Baysinger et al. (1991) reported that higher insider representation on a board coupled with a concentration of equity among institutional investors positively affects R&D spending. In a more recent study of manufacturing firms, Hoskisson and colleagues (2002) similarly examined the influence of board composition on a firm's innovation strategies. Specifically, they found that inside representation on the board of directors was related to internal innovation (R&D, product development), whereas external representation was more related to external innovation (acquisitions, new ventures). It appears that inside directors may be more inclined towards internal innovation and new product innovations since they have relevant information to make strategic decisions. And, in a longitudinal study of technology-based entrepreneurial firms, Kor (2006) found a positive influence of CEO and chair separation on R&D investment intensity. She further found that outsider board representation along with a TMT with high levels of shared experiences also hurt R&D investments since such TMTs may have high levels of confidence, distracting them towards maintaining power relative to the board. Outsider board representation was also found to be less effective in promoting R&D investments when the TMT was functionally heterogeneous.

Researchers studying the impact of boards on replication have emphasized the compositional aspect of the board. For example, Tihanyi et al. (2003) studied 197 firms to examine the moderating role of board composition on the relationship between institutional investors and international diversification. They found that while both types of institutional investors, professional investment funds and pension funds, might favor international diversification, the former support such efforts when more outside directors are present on the board while the latter support such efforts in the presence of more inside directors. In another study, Sanders and Carpenter (1998) found that internationalization is associated with complexity, which can be effectively met by the separation of CEO and chair positions, by increasing the size of the board of directors, and by increasing outsider representation on boards.

SE literature that focuses on BOD influences on rejuvenation predominantly studies board composition and structure. For example, Hoskisson and Turk (1990) develop a model examining the influence of governance structure on corporate restructuring. Following an agency perspective, they argue that the role of the board is to maintain the efficient separation of risk bearing and managerial control and to the extent that outside directors shift risk to managers, managers are likely to reduce such risk through diversification. Goodstein and colleagues (Goodstein and Boeker, 1991; Goodstein et al., 1994) explore the influence of board composition and structure on rejuvenation activities as manifested by strategic change. These studies show that changes in the board can bring about strategic change independent of the influence of CEO succession (Romanelli and Tushman, 1994). Golden and Zajac (2001) also found that small, young, and short-tenured boards, particularly those with low levels of job diversity, were most likely to instigate strategic change. They also found attention to strategic issues and comprehensiveness of evaluation to be associated with strategic change.

Finally, our review suggests that composition, in concert with incentives, is an important antecedent to revolutionary forms of SE. Zahra (1996) suggests that although the proportion of outside directors on the board has a negative impact on corporate entrepreneurship, this impact is dampened to the extent that outside directors have an ownership stake in the corporation. With ownership in the corporation, outside directors are more inclined to monitor the actions of key decision makers, and consequently more informed of corporate entrepreneurship. In a follow-up study, Zahra et al. (2000) also found that outsider representation on the board, in combination with stock ownership, positively impacted corporate entrepreneurship. Additionally it was found, perhaps owing to the intense leadership demands of revolution, that separating the roles of CEO and chair, had a further positive impact on corporate entrepreneurship.

A CONCEPTUAL FRAMEWORK FOR RESEARCH AND FUTURE DIRECTIONS

Our review of 30 years of research has revealed a predominant focus on modeling the unidirectional effects of SL variables and varying empirical manifestation of SE at a single level of analysis. While some studies have begun to examine more dynamic effects between CEOs and top management teams (e.g., Ling et al., 2008) and boards of directors, this type of research has not yet gained sufficient momentum. Using our typology and synthesizing review as a guide, we here move towards the development of a guiding framework on the SL–SE nexus. This comprehensive framework encompasses five potential influences that might exist *within*, *between*, and *across* each level of SL and SE forms (see Figure 12.2): main influences (MI), interactive influences (II) interface influences (IFI), cascading influences (CI), and reverse influences (RI). Our framework recognizes, consistent with an open-system view of the firm, that all these influences take place in certain organizational and environmental contexts even though we here hold these contextual effects constant, operating under the ceteris paribus assumption to parsimoniously elucidate each influence.

Additionally, we summarize the research implications of our framework in Table 12.4. To more directly guide future research efforts on the SL–SE nexus, this table conceptually defines each influence and provides a set of exemplary research foci that might be associated with each. Clearly, these are not meant to be mutually exclusive, comprehensive, or exhaustive research areas, but rather reflect what we consider as promising first steps in taking the "thousand-mile" journey toward creating consensus on the SL–SE nexus. Importantly, in Table 12.4, we also advance a set of representative hypotheses to demonstrate the conceptual benefits of taking such a pluralistic approach to this nexus, as well as to directly help instigate the next generation of theory-testing research. For the sake of parsimony, we advance one representative hypothesis per research focus but next more fully discuss these issues.

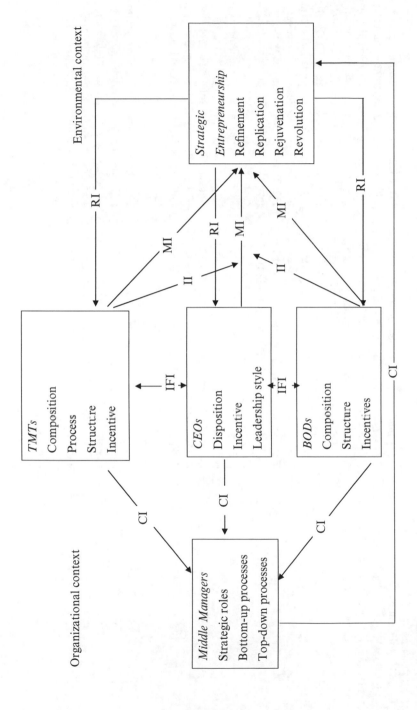

Environmental context

Organizational context

Source: Authors.

Figure 12.2 A conceptual framework on the nexus of SL and SE

Table 12.4 Future research directions on the nexus of SL and SE

Direction	Exemplary Research Focus	Representative Hypotheses
Main influences The study of the main effect or unidirectional impact (positive, negative, or curvilinear) of single strategic leadership constructs on different forms of strategic entrepreneurship	*CEO influences*: What effect does CEO persona have on different forms of SE? What leadership styles are conducive to different forms of SE? What kinds of executive experiences, values, beliefs, etc. are conducive to different forms of SE? *TMT influences*: What are the implications of different aspects of tenure (quantitative, qualitative) for SE? What types of TMT compositions impact SE? What role structures (CEO vs. COO; extent of differentiation and integration) are most conducive to different forms of SE? What is the relationship between TMT size and SE? What types of decision-making and behavioral processes support different forms of SE? *Board influences*: What types of board compositions, processes, structures, and incentives are conducive to different forms of SE? What are the influences of board human and social capital on different forms of SE? How does board involvement in strategy making impact different forms of SE?	H1: CEO core-self evaluation is associated with the pursuit of different forms of SE, such that CEOs with high levels of core self-evaluation engage in more rejuvenation and revolution compared with CEOs with low levels of core self-evaluation. CEOs with low levels of core self-evaluation will more likely engage in replication and refinement H2: TMT size is associated with the firm's pursuit of different forms of SE, such that smaller TMTs are more apt engage in replication and refinement while larger teams are more apt to engage in rejuvenation and revolution compared with smaller teams. Moreover, the latter influence is likely to be a curvilinear function H3: The proportion of outsiders (relative to insiders) on the board of directors is associated with the pursuit of different forms of SE, such that boards with a high proportion of outsiders are more apt to pursue replication and revolution, whereas boards with a low proportion of outsiders are more apt to pursue refinement and rejuvenation

Interactive influences

The interactive influences of CEO, TMT, and board constructs on strategic entrepreneurship, particularly the moderating influences of TMT and board constructs on the main effect of CEO constructs on different forms of strategic entrepreneurship, and vice-versa

CEO-by-board: Do boards empower or constrain the influence of CEOs on SE? How do board composition, structure, and incentives moderate the effects of CEOs and TMTs on SE? What are the implications of CEO-board coherence for different forms of SE?

CEO-by-TMT: Are TMTs most impactful in terms of SE when they provide access to novel, nonredundant sources of expertise, experience, and social networks (supplementary fit), or alternatively when their expertise, experience, and social networks overlap with that of the CEO (complementary fit)? What effect do different types of fit have on different forms of SE? How do TMT composition, structure, processes, and incentives moderate the effects of CEOs on SE? What influences do emergent states between the CEO and TMT have on SE?

H4: Board size moderates the impact of hyper-CEO core self-evaluation on replication and revolution, such that larger-sized boards dampen the influence of CEOs on replication and revolution

H5: The use of long-term (as opposed to short-term) TMT incentives moderates the impact of hyper-CEO core self-evaluation on replication and revolution, such that use of long-term incentives strengthens CEOs' positive effect on replication and revolution

Table 12.4 (continued)

Direction	Exemplary Research Focus	Representative Hypotheses
Interface influences The intermediary role of TMT constructs in the relationship between CEO constructs and strategic entrepreneurship, particularly the various ways in which CEOs and boards can influence SE forms by first influencing numerous TMT characteristics	*CEO–TMT interface:* How does CEO disposition and personality shape the collective personality, and overall functioning and effectiveness of the TMT? How does CEO succession impact TMT composition, structure, and processes? How do CEOs and TMTs fundamentally interact, and how does the pattern of interactions in turn impact SE and its different forms? *BOD–CEO interface:* How does BOD composition impact SE forms through its effects on the CEO behavior, discretion etc.?	H6: TMT potency (or shared efficacy) mediates the relationship between CEO transformational leadership and the pursuit of rejuvenation and revolution H7: The portion of outside directors appointed after a given CEO's appointment will be negatively associated with *board* monitoring of the CEO, thus reducing the board's impact on all four SE forms
Cascading influences The intermediary role of middle (and possibly operational) managers in the relationship between CEO/TMT/board effects and strategic entrepreneurship forms	*CEO–middle management cascades:* How does CEO leadership style, transformational vs. transactional, impact different SE forms by first influencing middle managers' perception of empowerment and managerial support? *TMT–middle management cascades:* How does SL composition, structure, processes, incentives, and leadership style impact different levels of middle manager involvement (and type of involvement) for the effectiveness and outcomes of SE?	H8: Middle manager perceptions of TMT empowerment and support mediate the relationship between CEO transformational leadership and the pursuit of rejuvenation and revolution H9: Middle manager involvement in strategic decision making mediates the relationship between TMT behavioral integration and the pursuit of rejuvenation

334

Reverse influences
The main or interactive effects of strategic entrepreneurship forms/manifestations on strategic leadership

SE-to-CEO: Do different forms of SE lead to different succession events (external, relay, contender, etc.)?

H10: The pursuit of replication and revolution is positively associated with the succession of external CEOs; the pursuit of refinement is associated with the succession of heir apparent CEOs; and the pursuit of rejuvenation is associated with the succession of internal contender CEOs

SE-to-TMT: Do different forms of SE explain/predict TMT composition, size, incentives, and structure? Do different forms of SE impact the human capital, social networks, and overall configuration of the board of directors?

H11: The pursuit of multiple forms of SE concurrently is positively associated with TMT conflict and negatively to TMT social integration

SE-to-BOD: How does the pursuit of different SE portfolios impact board process and dynamics?

H12: The pursuit of replication is positively associated with the proportion of outsiders (relative to insiders) on the board of directors

SE-to-interface: What are the impacts of positive and negative SE outcomes on interactions among upper echelon actors (centrality of decision making, behavioral integration, board involvement, CEO duality)?

H13: Positive SE outcomes are associated with more frequent interactions between the CEO and the board and less frequent interactions between the CEO and the TMT (and vice versa)

Source: Authors.

335

Main Influences (MI)

By MI, we refer to the study of the main effect or unidirectional impact (positive, negative, or curvilinear) of single strategic leadership constructs on different forms of strategic entrepreneurship. Our review of the literature on the main effects of SL on SE revealed several potential avenues for future research. Research on the CEO's impact on SE has predominantly focused on demographic attributes, and to a lesser extent incentive systems and leadership style. This research has not examined the effects of the CEO's persona on the pursuit of different forms of SE. For us, future investigations on the impact of CEO persona on SE would be particularly intriguing, given the recent interest in such constructs as the basis of strategic choice, notably core self-evaluations (Hiller and Hambrick, 2005), and narcissism (Chatterjee and Hambrick, 2007). For example, core self-evaluation, one's overall evaluation of self-worth and competence, is a concept that has gained much traction recently, and that has been linked to firms' entrepreneurial proclivity (Simsek et al., 2010). Yet, it would be interesting to untangle the relationship between core self-evaluation and different forms of SE. For example, CEOs with low core self-evaluation might confine entrepreneurial activities to refinement and replication, forms of SE that entail less risk and more predictable returns, compared with rejuvenation and revolution, which might be endorsed by CEOs with hyper core self-evaluation. Additionally, further research is needed on the leadership styles and skills of CEOs, and how these promote and/or inhibit different forms of SE. Given the potential "dark side" of transformational leadership (Kark et al., 2003), we implore researchers to adopt other, perhaps skills-based models, to complement the emphasis on the visionary perspective of leadership. For example, the "leaderplex" model of leadership (Hooijberg et al., 1997), which focuses on the cognitive, behavioral, and social skills of leaders, could provide a useful starting point for understanding the skills and competences required for different forms of SE. And finally, further research into the alignment of CEOs' beliefs, values, cognitions, and paradigms with different forms of SE would also be worthy of investigation.

Beyond the CEO, we suggest several research directions involving TMT effects on SE. Beginning with composition, we encourage future researchers to adopt a more complete conceptualization of tenure (see Zhang in Chapter 14 of this volume for one model of CEO tenure), and examine the implications of each dimension and component for different forms of SE. Tenure is an inherently multidimensional construct with both a quantitative dimension consisting of quantity (number of jobs an individual has held) and time (length of time working in a position), and a qualitative dimension capturing the variety, challenge, and complexity of experience (Hackman and Oldham, 1976; Tesluk and Jacobs, 1998). Aside from tenure, we also encourage researchers to examine the impact of the personological characteristics of TMTs (core self-evaluation, narcissism, etc.) on different forms of SE, similar to Peterson and Zhang's study in Chapter 6 of this volume regarding the effects on performance of TMT core self-evaluations and psychological capital.

In addition to compositional variables, researchers might study alternative compositional models that go beyond averages and diversity. For example, there has been no investigation of fault lines, subgroupings, or different types of fit (complementary, supplementary) within TMTs. Moreover, most models of composition have thus far been static in nature, while in reality the composition of TMTs is fluid and dynamic, with ongoing membership changes that undermine stability, and that bear implications for strategic behavior, and hence SE. Beyond composition, we encourage additional investigations into the structure, processes, and incentives of TMTs, and their impact on different forms of SE. Concerning structure, examinations of different role structures on the pursuit of SE forms would be illuminating. For example, does the division (or not) of labor across TMT members have significant consequence for different SE forms? In terms of team process, an important research question is to what extent different decision-making processes and styles lead to different types of SE? For example, a rational-synoptic approach to decision making might be appropriate for forms of entrepreneurial behavior within current markets (refinement and rejuvenation), but may be less appropriate for venturing into new arenas (replication and revolution) where information is limited and ill-structured (Forbes, 2007).

Finally, with the increasing involvement of boards in all aspects of strategic decision making and choice, more research is needed on the effects of board composition and structure of SE forms. In terms of composition, studies of the influence of director affiliations on the firm's proclivity towards SE forms would be intriguing. What effects would having a board consisting mainly of outsiders (vs. insiders) have on the firm's overall SE propensity, as well as emphasis on different SE forms? What effect does having intra- versus extra-industry board members have on different forms of SE? We might expect, for example, that a board composed of members inside the focal industry to have a positive impact on refinement and rejuvenation, whereas boards composed of extra-industry members might have a more positive effect on replication and revolution. In addition to composition, future research is called for on the implications of board structure on SE. As in TMT research, we anticipate that board size has an important influence on SE. Large boards provide a conduit to a wide repertoire of cognitive resources, social networks, and resources, but may constrain SE by slowing down decision making and increasing the incidence of political behavior . Whether the CEO enjoys duality may also have some implications for different forms of SE. With the power to determine the board agenda, dual CEOs might be more apt to pursue revolutionary forms of SE.

Interactive Influences (II)

IIs refer to the interactive influences of CEO, TMT, and board constructs on strategic entrepreneurship, particularly the moderating influences of TMT and board constructs on the main effect of CEO constructs on different forms of strategic entrepreneurship, and vice versa. In this regard, we particularly advance two areas of inquiry: (1) how CEOs and boards interact in shaping SE, and (2) how CEOs and TMTs interact in shaping SE. Regarding the first area of inquiry, whether board governance empowers or constrains the influence of CEOs on SE is an important question for future research. Well-composed and organized boards might empower CEOs in their pursuit of SE by providing them with a wealth of expertise, resources, and referrals needed to pursue different forms of SE. We also encourage studies that examine the moderating role of board composition (insider, related outsider, and outsider) and characteristics (size, duality, and use of committees) on the effects of CEO personality and leadership style on SE.

Studies of the overlap or fit (supplementary vs. complementary) between CEO and

TMT expertise (i.e., education, experience, functional expertise) would be particularly instructive. Are TMTs most useful when they provide access to novel, nonredundant sources of expertise, experience, and social networks (supplementary fit), or alternatively when their expertise, experience, and social networks overlap with that of the CEO (complementary fit)? Supplementary fit provides a strong basis for social interaction and communication, in accordance with the principle of homophily, but provides limited, or even no access to new expertise. Perhaps supplementary fit between CEOs and TMTs is more appropriate for refinement, where CEOs have little need for outside expertise, but where frequent social interaction and communication deepens existing knowledge. By contrast, other forms of SE, those that depend on new sources of expertise, might benefit more from a complementary fit. Other possible areas of inquiry could include studies of the moderating role of TMT structure (size, interdependence), process (behavioral integration, cognitive processes), and incentives in tying CEO variables (disposition, leadership style, incentives) to different forms of SE.

Interface Influences (IFI)

IFIs capture the intermediary role of TMT constructs in explaining the relationship between CEO constructs and strategic entrepreneurship, particularly the various ways in which CEOs and boards can influence SE forms by first influencing numerous TMT characteristics. The "interface" refers to the various ways that "leadership and team processes become intertwined so as to influence collective performance" (Zaccaro and Klimoski, 2002, p. 6). Recent studies have demonstrated that CEOs impact SE by shaping the composition, structure, processes, and incentive structures of the TMT (Ling et al., 2008). While these preliminary investigations have been insightful, they are only a first step in our understanding of the interface of CEOs and TMTs, and how that interface shapes SE, and its various forms. We also encourage investigations of how the CEO's individual personality shapes the collective personality and functioning of the TMT, for example, studies of the effect of CEO core self-evaluation or narcissism on the collective cognitive (e.g., cognitive processing), motivational (e.g., potency), and affective (e.g., affective tone, regulatory focus) characteristics of the TMT. Likewise, investigations into the effects of CEOs on the collective potency would be useful, given that potency is an important antecedent to the pursuit of entrepreneurial initiatives (McMullen and Shepherd, 2006). Studies examining the influence of CEO succession (e.g., internal vs. external) on SE might be improved by delineating the effects of succession on the dynamics and functioning of the TMT.

Beyond these, much more needs to be known about how CEOs and TMTs fundamentally interact, and how this interaction promotes or hampers different forms of SE. Very little attention has been devoted to different patterns or models of CEO–TMT interaction, with some notable exceptions (Arendt et al., 2005). In a conceptual exposition of the role of TMTs' involvement in strategic decision making, Arendt and colleagues outlined three models of managerial involvement in decision making: a CEO model (in which top managers gather information, but the CEO processes and assimilates the information and makes the decision), a TMT model (in which top managers are involved in all stages of decision making), and a CEO-advisor model (in which top managers gather information, process and assimilate information, and recommend a decision). An interesting question is whether different models of decision-making involvement are more conducive or appropriate to different forms of SE? Given the intense demands of revolution, one might expect a more involved pattern of decision making (i.e., CEO-advisor model), whereas the stable, predictable nature of refinement might require less TMT involvement (i.e., CEO model). In the case of refinement, for instance a product line extension, TMT involvement in processing/assimilating information and making decisions might actually be counterproductive, by slowing decision making and entrepreneurial action.

Cascading Influences (CI)

By CIs, we specifically mean the intermediary role of middle (and possibly operational) managers in the relationship between CEO/TMT/board effects and strategic entrepreneurship forms. It would be naive to believe that CEOs, TMTs, and boards alone influence SE in organizations. Many other important players are involved, most notably middle managers, who play key strategic roles in SE (Floyd and Lane, 2000; Wooldridge et al., 2008). Middle managers play a key role in endorsing, refining, and shepherding entrepreneurial initiatives, as well as identifying, acquiring, and deploying entrepreneurial resources (Kuratko, 2005). Yet, very little attention has been devoted to the relationship between upper echelon actors (CEOs, TMTs, and boards) and middle managers, particularly in the context of SE. Although other types of influence are possible, we particularly focus on the cascading influence of SL on middle managers, and how this cascading effect impacts SE, as an important direction for future research. For example, with refinement, strategic leaders might play a directing role (i.e., planning, deploying resources, commanding), whereas middle managers play an implementation role (i.e., executing, revising/adjusting, motivating/inspiring). By contrast, perhaps, with replication, strategic leaders recognize (i.e., strategic potential, set strategic direction, and endorse/support), whereas middle managers facilitate (i.e., nourish adaptability and shelter activity, share information, guide adaptation, and facilitate learning). With rejuvenation and revolution, we envisage middle managers playing a championing role, and strategic leaders a ratifying role (i.e., articulating strategic intent, monitoring, and endorsing/supporting). In addition, we urge researchers to study how middle managers' top-down vs. bottom-up processes are impacted by TMTs and in turn impact different forms of SE.

Reverse Influences (RI)

With few exceptions, most research on the intersection of SL and SE has exclusively considered the influence of SL on SE. However, it is equally plausible, and likely, that the form and portfolio of SE being pursued might in turn exert shaping influences on the composition and other conceptual elements of the CEO, TMT, and boards. Starting with the CEO, SE forms might influence succession decisions, which in turn shape the behavior and leadership style of the CEO. A firm consistently pursuing refinement or rejuvenation (i.e., staying within existing market arenas) for example, is probably more likely to choose an internal successor to reinforce commitment to current markets and to maintain the status quo (Shen and Cannella, 2003). By contrast, a firm pursuing rejuvenation might choose an internal contender to instigate strategic and administrative changes. Firms primarily pursuing replication and revolution (i.e., moving into new market arenas) on the other hand might be more apt to choose an external successor to graft expertise needed to enter new market areas (Huber, 1991). The form of SE being pursued by firms might also influence the appropriateness and effectiveness of different leadership styles. Revolutionary forms of SE might call for a greater repertoire of cognitive, behavioral, and social skills on the part of the CEO, as well as the need for a transformational leadership style, whereas with refinement, a transactional style might be most appropriate.

Turning to the influence of SE on TMTs, we expect that pursuing replication and revolution results in larger, more diverse TMT membership than does the pursuit of refinement and rejuvenation. As firms enter new market arenas, they require a larger, heterogeneous stock of expertise and resources, consistent with the principle of requisite variety. As to structure, we encourage investigations into the relationship between different forms of SE and role differentiation and interdependence within the TMT. Given the complexity and intense need for communication, collaboration, and continual negotiation with replication/revolution forms of SE, we would expect greater role differentiation and interdependence, as well as behavioral integration, as compared with refinement/ rejuvenation.

And finally, different forms of SE might shape the composition, human, and social capital of the board of directors. As with TMTs, entering into new market arenas might call for extra-industry board representation, to tap resources, human capital, and social networks in new markets. The pursuit of rejuvenation and revolution might call for change agents on the board of directors, given the need to change and reform strategy, structure, and administrative systems.

IMPLICATIONS AND CONCLUSION

We began by developing a typology of the fundamental forms of SE to organize and structure our review. Juxtaposing the advantage-seeking and opportunity-seeking dimensions recognized in past research (Ireland et al., 2003), we specified four fundamental forms of SE: refinement, replication, rejuvenation, and revolution. Using this typology as an organizing framework, we then undertook a comprehensive review and synthesis of research on the intersection of SL and SE. Integrating this typology and review, we finally outlined an integrative framework for guiding future research, as well as several promising directions for future inquiry.

Our typology, review, and framework enriches understanding of the role played by CEOs, TMTs, and boards in guiding SE efforts, initiatives, and activities within firms. Importantly, we set the stage for future research on the SL–SE nexus, by offering an integrative framework for comprehensively considering the multitude of theoretical influences that connect SL and SE. As well as recognizing that CEOs, TMTs, and boards impact SE, our framework suggests that different forms of SE may give rise to different CEO, TMT, and board configurations, as well as influencing their leadership style, structure, processes, and incentives. Our framework particularly highlights the salience of two linkages typically underplayed in SL research, namely interface and cascading influences. Only recently have scholars begun to study the interface of CEOs and TMTs in shaping firm behavior and outcomes, yet this interface maybe a pivotal force in guiding SE behaviors in firms. Our framework also posits the cascading influences of strategic leaders on middle managers as a further promising direction for future research. The interface of top and middle managers is an important but neglected piece of the puzzle when it comes to understanding the origins of SE. We have suggested that top and middle managers might perform complementary strategic roles in the pursuit of entrepreneurial initiatives, and that the exact configuration of these roles differs depending on the form of SE being pursued. Further research, however, is needed to untangle the roles and effects of strategic leaders and middle managers in shaping various SE forms. We also contribute to the literature by developing a theoretically informed deductive typology of SE, which might prove a robust approach for integrative theory development, measurement, and testing on SE.

In conclusion, research on SE has come of age in the past five years, with the birth of a new journal, and the emergence of a new set of research questions and constructs. In this chapter, we have attempted to contribute to this nascent but burgeoning field of inquiry by systematically reviewing the intersection of SL and SE, and providing a typology and integrative framework to guide future efforts to study this intersection. While we recognize that this is only a first step, we believe it is an essential fulcrum upon which future insights and knowledge about strategic entrepreneurial leadership can be developed and tested.

ACKNOWLEDGMENTS

This work was supported, in part, by a grant from the Connecticut Center for Entrepreneurship & Innovation (CCEI).

REFERENCES

Agarwal, R. and Helfat, C.E. (2009). Strategic renewal of organizations. *Organization Science*, **20**(2), 281–93.
Allen, S.A. (1979). Understanding reorganizations of divisionalized companies. *Academy of Management Journal*, **22**(4), 641–71.
Arendt, L.A., Priem, R.L., and Ndofor, H.A. (2005). A CEO-adviser model of strategic decision making. *Journal of Management*, **31**(3), 680–99.
Atuahene-Gima, K. and Li, H. (2004). Strategizing throughout the organization, managing role conflict strategic decision comprehensiveness and new product development outcomes in new technology ventures. *Academy of Management Journal*, **47**(1), 583–97.
Bacharach, S.B. (1989). Organizational theories, some criteria for evaluation. *Academy of Management Review*, **14**(4), 496–515.
Balkin, D.B., Markman, G.D., and Gomez-Mejia, L.R. (2000). Is CEO pay in high-technology firms related to innovation? *Academy of Management Journal*, **43**(6), 1118–29.
Bantel, K.A. and Jackson, S.E. (1989). Top management and innovations in banking, does the composition of the top team make a difference? *Strategic Management Journal*, **10**(S1), 107–24.
Barkema, H.G. and Shvyrkov, O. (2007). Does top management team diversity promote or hamper foreign expansion? *Strategic Management Journal*, **28**(7), 663–80.
Barker, V.L. and Mueller, G.C. (2002). CEO characteristics and firm R&D spending. *Management Science*, **48**(6), 782–801.
Barney, J.B. (1991). Firm resources and sustained competitive advantage. *Journal of Management*, **17**(1), 99–120.
Barr, P.S., Stimpert, J.L., and Huff, A.S. (1992). Cognitive change, strategic action, and organizational renewal. *Strategic Management Journal*, **13**(S1), 15–36.
Barringer, B.R. and Bluedorn, A.C. (1999). The relationship between corporate entrepreneurship and strategic management. *Strategic Management Journal*, **20**(5), 421–44.

Bass, B.M. (2007). Executive and strategic leadership. *International Journal of Business*, **12**(11), 33–52.

Baysinger, B.D., Kosnik, R.D., and Turk, T.A. (1991). Effects of board and ownership structure on corporate R&D strategy. *Academy of Management Journal*, **34**(11), 205–14.

Begley, T.M. and Boyd, D.P. (1987). Psychological characteristics associated with performance in entrepreneurial firms and smaller businesses. *Journal of Business Venturing*, **2**(1), 79–93.

Birkinshaw, J. (1997). Entrepreneurship in multinational corporations: The characteristics of subsidiary initiatives. *Strategic Management Journal*, **18**(2), 207–29.

Bloodgood, J.M., Sapienza, H.J., and Almeida, J.G. (1996). The internationalization of new high-potential U.S. ventures: Antecedents and outcomes. *Entrepreneurship, Theory and Practice*, **20**(4), 61–76.

Boeker, W. (1997a). Executive migration and strategic change: The effect of top manager movement on product-market entry. *Administrative Science Quarterly*, **42**(2), 213–36.

Boeker, W. (1997b). Strategic change, the influence of managerial characteristics and organizational growth. *Academy of Management Journal*, **40**(11), 152–70.

Brown, T.E., Davidsson, P., and Wiklund, J. (2001). An operationalization of Stevenson's conceptualization of entrepreneurship as opportunity-based firm behavior. *Strategic Management Journal*, **22**(10), 953–68.

Burgelman, R.A. (1983a). A process model of internal corporate venturing in the diversified major firm. *Administrative Science Quarterly*, **28**(2), 223–44.

Burgelman, R.A. (1983b). A model of the interaction of strategic behavior, corporate context, and the concept of strategy. *Academy of Management Review*, **8**(11), 61–70.

Burgelman, R.A. (1983c). Corporate entrepreneurship and strategic management: Insights from a process study. *Management Science*, **29**(12), 1349–64.

Carpenter, M.A. (2000). The price of change, the role of CEO compensation in strategic variation, and deviation from industry strategy norms. *Journal of Management*, **26**(6), 1179–98.

Carpenter, M.A. and Fredrickson, J.W. (2001). Top management teams, global strategic posture, and the moderating role of uncertainty. *Academy of Management Journal*, **44**(3), 533–45.

Carpenter, M.A. and Sanders, W.G. (2004). The effects of top management team pay and firm internationalization on MNC performance. *Journal of Management*, **30**(4), 509–28.

Chatterjee, A. and Hambrick, D. (2007). It's all about me: Narcissistic chief executive officers and their effects on company strategy and performance. *Administrative Science Quarterly*, **52**(3), 351–86.

Chen, G., Liu, C., and Tjosvold, D. (2004). Conflict management for effective top management teams and innovation in China. *Journal of Management Studies*, **42**(2), 277–300.

Cho, T.S. and Hambrick, D.C. (2006). Attention as the mediator between top management team characteristics and strategic change: The case of airline deregulation. *Organization Science*, **17**(4), 453–69.

Covin, J.G. and Miles, M.P. (1999). Corporate entrepreneurship and the pursuit of competitive advantage. *Entrepreneurship Theory and Practice*, **23**(3), 47–63.

Covin, J.G. and Slevin, D.P. (1991). A conceptual model of entrepreneurship as firm behavior. *Entrepreneurship, Theory and Practice*, **16**(1), 7–25.

Covin, J.G. and Slevin, D.P. (2002), The entrepreneurial imperatives of strategic leadership. In M.A. Hitt (ed.), *Strategic entrepreneurship: Creating a new mindset*. Oxford, UK: Blackwell Publishing, pp. 309–27.

Cyert, R.M. and March, J.G. (1963). *A behavioral theory of the firm*. Englewood Cliffs, NJ: Prentice Hall.

Daily, C.M., McDougall, E.E., Covin, J.G., and Dalton, D.R. (2002). Governance and strategic leadership in entrepreneurial firms. *Journal of Management*, **28**(3), 387–412.

de Bettignies, J.E. and Chemla, G. (2008). Corporate venturing, allocation of talent, and competition for star managers. *Management Science*, **54**(3), 505–21.

Dess, G.G., Lumpkin, G.T., and Covin, J.G. (1997). Entrepreneurial strategy making and firm performance: Tests of contingency and configurational models. *Strategic Management Journal*, **18**(9), 677–95.

Doty, D.H. and Glick, W.H. (1994). Typologies as a unique form of theory building: Toward improved understanding and modeling. *Academy of Management Review*, **19**(2), 230–51.

Dougherty, D. (1992). A practice-centered model of organizational renewal through product innovation. *Strategic Management Journal*, **13**(5), 77–92.

Eggers, J.P. and Kaplan, S. (2009). Cognition and renewal: Comparing CEO and organizational effects on incumbent adaptation to technical change. *Organization Science*, **20**(2), 461–77.

Eisenmann, T.R. and Bower, J.L. (2000). The entrepreneurial M-form: Strategic integration in global media firms. *Organization Science*, **11**(3), 348–55.

Elenkov, D.S. and Manev, I.M. (2005). Top management leadership and influence on innovation: The role of sociocultural context. *Journal of Management*, **31**(3), 381–402.

Elenkov, D.S., Judge, W., and Wright, P. (2005). Strategic leadership and executive innovation influence: An international multi-cluster comparative study. *Strategic Management Journal*, **26**(7), 665–82.

Finkelstein, S., Hambrick, D.C., and Cannella A.A. (2009). *Strategic leadership: Theory and research on executives, top management teams, and boards*. New York, NY: Oxford University Press.

Floyd, S.W. and Lane, P.J. (2000). Strategizing throughout the organization: Managing role conflict in strategic renewal. *Academy of Management Review*, **25**(1), 154–77.

Forbes, D.P. (2007). Reconsidering the strategic implications of decision comprehensiveness. *Academy of Management Review*, **32**(2), 361–76.

Golden, B.R. and Zajac, E.J. (2001). When will boards influence strategy? Inclination × Power = Strategic Change. *Strategic Management Journal*, **22**(12), 1087–111.

Goodstein, J. and Boeker, W. (1991). Turbulence at the top: A new perspective on governance structure changes and strategic change. *Academy of Management Journal*, **34**(2), 306–30.

Goodstein, J., Gautam, K., and Boeker, W. (1994). The effects of board size and diversity on strategic change. *Strategic Management Journal*, **15**(3), 241–50.

Gordon, S.S., Stewart, W.H., Sweo, R., and Luker, W.A. (2000). Convergence versus strategic reorientation: The antecedents of fast-paced organizational change. *Journal of Management*, **26**(5), 911–45.

Gupta, V., Macmillan, I.C., and Surie, G. (2004). Entrepreneurial leadership: Developing and measuring a cross-cultural construct. *Journal of Business Venturing*, **19**(2), 241–60.

Guth, W.D. and Ginsberg, A. (1990). Guest editors' introduction: Corporate entrepreneurship. *Strategic Management Journal*, **11**(special issues), 5–15.

Hackman, J.R. and Oldham, G.R. (1976). Motivation through the design of work: Test of a theory. *Organizational Behavior and Human Performance*, **16**(2), 250–79.

Hambrick, D.C. (1989). Guest editor's introduction: Putting top managers back in the strategy picture. *Strategic Management Journal*, **10**(S1), 5–15.

Hambrick, D.C. (1994). Top management groups: A conceptual integration reconsideration of the "team" label. In B.M. Staw and L.L. Cummings (eds), *Research in organizational behavior*. Greenwich, CT: JAI Press, pp. 171–214.

Hambrick, D.C. and Fukutomi, G.D.S. (1991). The seasons of a CEO's tenure. *Academy of Management Review*, **16**(4), 719–42.

Hambrick, D.C. and Mason, P.A. (1984). Upper echelons: The organization as a reflection of its top managers. *Academy of Management Review*, **9**(2), 193–206.

Helfat, C.E. and Peteraf, M.A. (2003). The dynamic resource-based view: Capability lifecycles. *Strategic Management Journal*, **24**(10), 977–1010.

Heller, T. (1999). Loosely coupled systems for corporate entrepreneurship: Imagining and managing the innovation project/host organization interface. *Entrepreneurship, Theory and Practice*, **24**(2), 25–31.

Hiller, N.J. and Hambrick, D.C. (2005). Conceptualizing executive hubris: The role of (hyper-) core self-evaluations in strategic decision-making. *Strategic Management Journal*, **26**(4), 297–319.

Hitt, M.A., Ireland, R.D., Camp, S.M., and Sexton, D.L. (2001). Guest editors' introduction to the special issue: Strategic entrepreneurship, entrepreneurial strategies for wealth creation. *Strategic Management Journal*, **22**(6–7), 479–91.

Hitt, M.A., Nixon, R.D., Hoskisson, R.E., and Kochhar, R. (1999). Corporate entrepreneurship and cross-functional fertilization: Activation, process and disintegration of a new product design team. *Entrepreneurship, Theory and Practice*, **23**(3), 145–67.

Hoffman, E.C. and Hegarty, W.H. (1993). Top management influence on innovations: Effects of executive characteristics and social culture. *Journal of Management*, **19**(3), 549–74.

Hooijberg, H., Hunt, G.H., and Dodge, G.E. (1997). Leadership complexity and development of the leaderplex model. *Journal of Management*, **23**(3), 375–408.

Hornsby, J.S., Kuratko, D.F., Shepherd, D.A., and Bott, J.P. (2009). Managers' corporate entrepreneurial actions: Examining perception and position. *Journal of Business Venturing*, **24**(4), 236–47.

Hoskisson, R.E. and Turk, T.A. (1990). Corporate restructuring: Governance and control limits of the internal capital market. *Academy of Management Review*, **15**(3), 459–77.

Hoskisson, R.E., Hitt, M.A., Johnson, R.A., and Grossman, W. (2002). Conflicting voices: The effects of institutional ownership heterogeneity and internal governance on corporate innovation strategies. *Academy of Management Journal*, **45**(4), 697–716.

Huber, G.P. (1991). Organizational learning: The contributing processes and literatures. *Organization Science*, **2**(1), 88–115.

Hurst, D.K., Rush, J.C., and White, R.E. (1989). Top management teams and organizational renewal. *Strategic Management Journal*, **10**(S1), 87–105.

Ireland, R.D., Hitt, M.A., and Sirmon, D.G. (2003). A model of strategic entrepreneurship: The construct and its dimensions. *Journal of Management*, **29**(6), 963–89.

Jackson, S.E. (1992). Consequences of group composition for the interpersonal issue dynamics of strategic issue processing. *Advances in Strategic Management*, **8**, 345–82.

Jung, D.I., Chow, C., and Wu, A. (2003). The role of transformational leadership in enhancing organizational innovation: Hypotheses and some preliminary findings. *Leadership Quarterly*, **14**(4–5), 525–44.

Jung, D., Wu, A., and Chow, C. (2008). Towards understanding the direct and indirect effects of CEOs' transformational leadership on firm innovation. *Leadership Quarterly*, **19**(5), 582–94.

Kark, R., Shamir, B., and Chen, G. (2003). The two faces of transformational leadership: Empowerment and dependency, *Journal of Applied Psychology*, **88**(2), 246–55.

Kazanjian, R.K., Drazin, R., and Glynn, M.A. (2002). Implementing strategies for corporate entrepreneurship: A knowledge-based view. In M.A. Hitt, R.D. Ireland, S.M. Camp, and D.L. Sexton (eds), *Strategic entrepreneurship: Creating a new integrated mindset*. Oxford, UK: Blackwell.

Ketchen, D.A., Ireland, R.D., and Snow, C.C. (2007). Strategic entrepreneurship, collaborative innovation, and wealth creation. *Strategic Entrepreneurship Journal*, **1**(3–4), 371–85.

Kickul, J. and Gundry, L. (2001). Breaking through boundaries for organizational innovation: New managerial roles and practices in e-commerce firms. *Journal of Management*, **27**(3), 347–61.

Kirzner, I.M. (1973). *Competition and entrepreneurship*, Chicago, IL: University of Chicago Press.

Kor, Y.Y. (2006). Direct and interaction effects of top management team and board compositions on R&D investment strategy. *Strategic Management Journal*, **27**(11), 1081–99.

Kuratko, D.F. and Audretsch, D.B. (2009). Strategic entrepreneurship: Exploring different perspectives of an emerging concept. *Entrepreneurship, Theory and Practice*, **33**(1), 1–16.

Kuratko, D.F., Ireland, R.D., Covin, J.G., and Hornsby, J.S. (2005). A model of middle-level managers' entrepreneurial behavior. *Entrepreneurship Theory and Practice*, **29**(6), 699–716.

Lant, T.K., Milliken, F.J., and Batra, B. (1992). The role of managerial learning and interpretation in strategic persistence. *Strategic Management Journal*, **13**, 585–608.

Levinthal, D.A. and March, J.G. (1993) The myopia of learning. *Strategic Management Journal*, **14**(special issue), 95–112.

Ling, Y., Simsek, Z., Lubatkin, M., and Veiga, J.F. (2008). Transformational leadership's role in promoting corporate entrepreneurship: Examining the CEO–TMT interface. *Academy of Management Journal*, **51**(3), 557–76.

March, J.G. (1991). Exploration and exploitation in organizational learning. *Organization Science*, **2**(1), 71–87.

McKelvey, B. (1975). Guidelines for the empirical classification of organizations. *Administrative Science Quarterly*, **20**(4), 509–25.

McMullen, J.S. and Shepherd, D.A. (2006). Entrepreneurial action and the role of uncertainty in the theory of the entrepreneur. *Academy of Management Review*, **31**(1), 132–52.

Mechanic, D. (1963). Some considerations in the methodology of organizational studies. In H.L. Leavitt (ed.) *The social science of organizations*. Englewood Cliffs, NJ: Prentice Hall.

Meyer, G.D., Neck, H.M., and Meeks, M.D. (2002). The entrepreneurship, strategic management interface. In M.A. Hitt, R.D. Ireland, S.M. Camp, and D.L. Sexton (eds), *Strategic entrepreneurship: Creating a new integrated mindset*. Oxford, UK: Blackwell.

Mezias, S.J. and Glynn, M.A. (1993). The three faces of corporate renewal, institution, revolution, and evolution. *Strategic Management Journal*, **14**(2), 77–101.

Miles, R.E. and Snow, C.C. (1978). *Organizational structure, strategy, and process*. New York, NY: McGraw-Hill.

Miller D. (1983). The correlates of entrepreneurship in three types of firms. *Management Science*, **29**(7), 770–91.

Miller, D. and Friesen, P.H. (1982). Innovation in conservative and entrepreneurial firms: Two models of strategic momentum. *Strategic Management Journal*, **3**(2), 1–15.

Miller, D., Vries, M.F.R.K., and Toulouse, J.M. (1982). Top executive locus of control and its relationship to strategy-making, structure, and environment. *Academy of Management Journal*, **25**(2), 237–53.

Monsen, E. and Boss, R.W. (2009). The impact of strategic entrepreneurship inside the organization: Examining job stress and employee retention. *Entrepreneurship, Theory and Practice*, **33**(1), 71–104.

Normann, R. (1977). *Management for growth*. Chichester, UK: John Wiley and Sons.

Porter, M.E. (1996). What is strategy? *Harvard Business Review*, **74**(6), 61–78.

Romanelli, E. and Tushman, M.L. (1994). Organizational transformation as punctuated equilibrium: An empirical test. *Academy of Management Journal*, **37**(5), 1141–666.

Roth, K. (1992). Implementing international strategy at the business unit level: The role of managerial decision-making characteristics. *Journal of Management*, **18**(4), 769–89.

Sambharya, R.B. (1996). Foreign experience of top management teams and international diversification strategies of U.S. multinational corporations. *Strategic Management Journal*, **17**(9), 739–46.

Sanders, W.G. and Carpenter, M.A. (1998). Internationalization and firm governance: The roles of CEO compensation, top team composition, and board structure. *Academy of Management Journal*, **41**(2), 158–78.

Schendel, D. and Hitt, M.A. (2007). Introduction to Volume 1. *Strategic Entrepreneurship Journal*, **1**(1–2), 1–6.

Shane, S. and Venkataraman, S. (2000). The promise of entrepreneurship as a field of research. *Academy of Management Review*, **25**(1), 217–26.

Shen, W. and Cannella, A.A. (2003). Will succession planning increase shareholder wealth? Evidence from investor reactions to relay CEO successions. *Strategic Management Journal*, **24**, 191–8.

Shortell, S.M. and Zajac, E.J. (1988). Internal corporate joint ventures: Development processes and perform-ance. *Strategic Management Journal*, **9**(6), 527–42.
Simons, R. (1994). How new top managers use control systems as levers of strategic renewal. *Strategic Management Journal*, **15**(3), 169–89.
Simsek, Z., Heavey, C., and Veiga, J.F. (2010). The impact of CEO core self-evaluation on the firm's entrepre-neurial orientation. *Strategic Management Journal*, **31**(1), 110–19.
Simsek, Z., Veiga, J.F., and Lubatkin, M.H. (2007). The impact of managerial environmental perceptions on corporate entrepreneurship: Towards understanding discretionary slack's pivotal role. *Journal of Management Studies*, **44**(8), 1398–424.
Smith, K.G. and Cao, Q. (2007). An entrepreneurial perspective on the firm–environment relationship. *Strategic Entrepreneurship Journal*, **1**(3–4), 329–44.
Smith, K.G., Collins, C.J., and Clark, K.D. (2005). Existing knowledge, knowledge creation capability, and the rate of new product introduction in high-technology firms. *Academy of Management Journal*, **48**(2), 346–57.
Smith, N. and Miner, J.B. (1983). Type of entrepreneur, type of firm, and managerial motivation, implications for organizational life cycle theory. *Strategic Management Journal*, **4**(4), 325–40.
Smith, W.K. and Tushman, M.L. (2005). Managing strategic contradictions: A top management model for managing innovation streams. *Organization Science*, **16**(5), 522–36.
Srivastava, A. and Lee, B.H. (2005). Predicting order and timing of new product moves: The role of top man-agement in corporate entrepreneurship. *Journal of Business Venturing*, **20**(4), 459–81.
Stevenson, H.H. and Jarillo, J.C. (1990). A paradigm of entrepreneurship: Entrepreneurial management. *Strategic Management Journal*, **11** (special issue), 17–27.
Stevenson, H.H., Roberts, M.J., and Grousbeck, H.I. (1985). *New business ventures and the entrepreneur*. Homewood, IL: Richard D. Irwin.
Stopford, J.M. and Baden-Fuller, C. (1990). Corporate rejuvenation. *Journal of Management Studies*, **27**(4), 399–415.
Stopford, J.M. and Baden-Fuller, C.W.F. (1994). Creating corporate entrepreneurship. *Strategic Management Journal*, **15**(7), 521–36.
Tesluk, P.E. and Jacobs, R.R. (1998). Toward an integrated model of work experience. *Personnel Psychology*, **51**(2), 321–55.
Thompson, J.D. (1967). *Organizations in action*. New York, NY: McGraw-Hill.
Tihanyi, L., Ellstrand, A.E., Daily, C.M., and Dalton, D.R. (2000). Composition of the top management team and firm diversification. *Journal of Management*, **26**(6), 1157–77.
Tihanyi, L., Johnson, R.A., Hoskisson, R.E., and Hitt, M.A. (2003). Institutional ownership differences and international diversification: The effects of boards of directors and technological opportunity. *Academy of Management Journal*, **46**(2), 195–211.
Van de Ven, A.H. (1986). Central problems in the management of innovation. *Management Science*, **32**(5), 590–607.
Venkataraman, S. and Sarasvathy, S.D. (2001). Strategy and entrepreneurship: Outlines of an untold story. In M.A. Hitt et al. (eds), *Handbook of strategic management*. Oxford, UK: Blackwell Publishers, pp. 650–68.
West, G. and Meyer, G.D. (1997). Temporal dimensions of opportunistic change in technology-based ven-tures. *Entrepreneurship, Theory and Practice*, **22**(2), 31–52.
Wiersema, M.F. and Bantel, K.A. (1992). Top management team demography and corporate strategic change. *Academy of Management Journal*, **35**(1), 91–121.
Wooldridge, B., Schmid, T., and Floyd, S. (2008). The middle management perspective on strategy process: Contributions, synthesis, and future research. *Journal of Management*, **34**(6), 1190–221.
Wu, S., Levitas, E., and Priem, R.L. (2005). CEO tenure and company invention under differing levels of tech-nological dynamism. *Academy of Management Journal*, **48**(5), 859–73.
Young, G.J., Charns, M.P., and Shortell, S.M. (2001). Top manager and network effects on the adoption of innovative management practices: A study of TQM in a public hospital system. *Strategic Management Journal*, **22**(10), 935–51.
Zaccaro, S.J. and Klimoski, R.J. (2002). The nature of organizational leadership: An introduction. In S.J. Zaccaro and R.J. Klimoski (eds), *The nature of organizational leadership*. San Francisco, CA: Jossey-Bass, pp. 3–41.
Zahra, S.A. (1993). New product innovation in established companies: Associations with industry and strategy variables. *Entrepreneurship, Theory and Practice*, **18**(2), 47–69.
Zahra, S.A. (1996). Governance, ownership, and corporate entrepreneurship: The moderating impact of indus-try technological opportunities. *Academy of Management Journal*, **39**(6), 1713–35.
Zahra, S.A., Neubaum, D.O., and Huse, M. (2000). Entrepreneurship in medium-size companies: Exploring the effects of ownership and governance systems. *Journal of Management*, **26**(5), 947–76.
Zahra, S. and Pearce, J. (1989). Boards of directors and corporate financial performance: A review and integrative model. *Journal of Management*, **15**(2), 291–324.

PART V

THE CONTEXT SURROUNDING CHANGES IN THE EXECUTIVE SUITE

13 The scapegoating premium: a rational view of new CEO compensation

Andrew Ward, Allen C. Amason, Peggy M. Lee, and Scott D. Graffin

Objectively, it's a great achievement for any of us to attract a superstar CEO to one of our companies. If nothing else, it gives peace of mind that our investments are in good hands.
Ravi Chiruvolu, *Venture Capital Journal*, 1 November, 2004

Twas the night before Christmas, and all through the shop
The board of directors was ready to drop. . .
Four years of bad business had laid them quite low,
And then came a surprise third-quarter blow.
Shareholders were angry; they grumbled with disdain.
They wanted a scapegoat to shoulder their pain.
The board knew they'd have to appease the masses
(And still find a way to save their own a****.)
Which led this grim board, though hard to believe
Into firing their CEO . . . on Christmas Eve.
M.M. Picoult and J. Picoult, 22 December, 2003

Chester Barnard explained that accepting symbolic responsibility for the organization was the single most important function of the top executive (Barnard, 1938). This symbolic responsibility for the organization and its performance is reflected in the chief executive's hiring (Khurana, 2002) and firing (Grusky, 1963; Gamson and Scotch, 1964). As the quotations above suggest, top executives are often credited with the successes and failures of their organizations. Hence, they are catapulted to superstar CEO status when the firm outperforms expectations and scapegoated when the firm underperforms. This ability to use a top manager as a symbol of hope for future performance or as a scapegoat for past performance is a valuable function in communicating expectations to stakeholders (Gamson and Scotch, 1964) and as such constitutes a critical component of corporate governance. Indeed, the hiring and firing of the CEO is often argued to be the most important function of the board of directors (Lorsch and MacIver, 1989; Khurana, 2002). Beck and Wiersema discuss the role of the board as well as external governance mechanisms in CEO dismissal in Chapter 15 of this volume.

We propose that executive compensation, at least in part, reflects the symbolic responsibility that the CEO takes for corporate performance and the accompanying risk of being scapegoated for underperformance. Our study tests this assertion, arguing that top managers accept responsibility for stakeholder expectations about future performance. In so doing, they agree to shoulder the blame and to act as a scapegoat in the event of poor results (Gamson and Scotch, 1964). In essence, top managers provide the collateral, in the form of their own human capital, to insure the expected value of the firm. In return, the firm pays a premium related to the value of the collateral risked and the insurance received. Finally, the value at which this exchange occurs is driven by the organization's expectations of future performance, what we define as the "Expectations Index" of the firm.

Using prospect theory and ritual scapegoating theory, we develop a model where executive compensation is driven by this Expectations Index. We then test our model in two samples, Fortune 500 CEOs and head coaches in National Collegiate Athletic Association (NCAA) Division I football programs.

SCAPEGOATING AND PROSPECT THEORIES

The Scapegoating Function of the Top Executive

Gamson and Scotch (1964) introduced ritual scapegoating to explain the replacing of managers in professional baseball. When performance declined, managers were replaced "as an anxiety reducing act which the participants in the ceremony regard as a way of improving performance, even though . . . real improvement can come only through long range organizational decisions" (Gamson and Scotch, 1964, pp. 70–71). Thus, regardless of actual effects on performance, scapegoating worked to renew the expectations of the relevant stakeholders, all of whom wanted to believe that a new manager would produce better results.

To be credible in this role, managers had to have the ability to succeed; they had to have sufficient human capital to offer legitimate hope and to shoulder the symbolic blame should the team perform poorly. Hiring a good manager then transferred responsibility away from the owners. In effect, once the owners had hired a credible manager they had done all they were expected to do. If the team performed poorly, key stakeholders blamed the manager. Owners, who had fulfilled their obligation of hiring a good manager, were blameless and avoided the wrath of fans by simply firing the current manager and hiring a new one.

If scapegoating can work in baseball, it should work just as well in business. In baseball, it is the owners who typically make the key strategic decisions while the visibility of the managers makes them good scapegoats (Gamson and Scotch, 1964). In business, however, it is the CEO that typically drives strategy. As a result, CEOs can be legitimately held responsible for performance. However, unlike the merry-go-round world of baseball, where managers may be quickly rehired after being dismissed, CEOs dismissed for poor performance rarely regain similar positions (Ward et al., 1995). Thus, by accepting the responsibility for performance, and agreeing to act as a scapegoat, a CEO accepts substantial risk, particularly in situations where performance expectations are high. The CEO is, thus, putting his or her human capital at risk in taking on the job, yet it is this very human capital that enables the board to credibly blame the CEO if performance fails to match expectations.

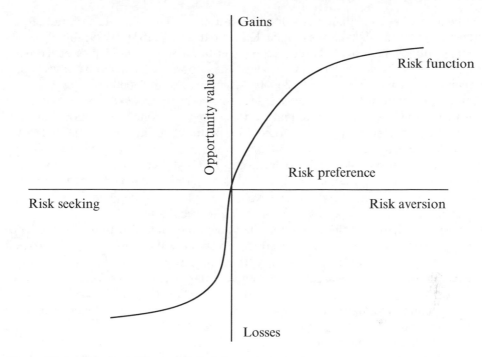

Figure 13.1   Prospect theory risk function

Performance Expectations and the Value to the Organization of the Scapegoating Function

Studies show that CEO turnover relates more to performance expectations than to actual performance (Puffer and Weintrop, 1991). This underscores the reality that what is acceptable performance in one organization may not be in another. Moreover, higher expectations increase the risk of a performance shortfall.

For example, consider Tyrone Willingham, formerly the head football coach at Notre Dame, who was fired three years into a five-year contract, with a record of 21-15. This record would have been adequate for many programs but was not good enough for Notre Dame. Indeed, Notre Dame's Athletic Director, Kevin White, explained, "We simply have not made the progress on the field that we need to make. Nor have we been able to create the positive momentum necessary to return the Notre Dame program to the elite level of the college football world" (ESPN, 2004). It is clear that it was the failure to satisfy expectations that led to the Willingham's departure.

Prospect Theory

How do expectations affect a manager's value to the firm? The answer lies in how performance expectations drive risk propensity. According to prospect theory (Kahneman and Tversky, 1979), individual risk functions are nonmonotonic (see Figure 13.1), concave for gains, convex for losses, and steeper for losses than for gains. Thus, people generally fear losses more than they value comparable gains. As a result, sure and certain gains tend to be overvalued. For example, Kahneman and Tversky (1979) found that 80 percent of subjects preferred a certain $3000 gain to an 80 percent chance of receiving $4000. For losses, however, the result was just the opposite: 92 percent of subjects preferred an 80 percent chance of losing $4000 to a certain loss of $3000.

Expectations of the future, then, are a reflection of a starting reference point and future performance is judged in relation to that reference point. Absolute values notwithstanding, good performance improves upon and poor performance falls below that reference point, the value that is expected. Consider again the example of Notre Dame. Winning at Notre Dame is an assumed reality, a birthright that is all but taken for granted. Given Notre Dame's historical tradition and all-time winning percentage of 0.750, stakeholders have a reference point of eight or nine wins a year. Thus, Willingham's performance, which averaged seven wins per year, failed to meet expectations.

Using a prospect theory lens, those in the "domain of gains" with a high reference point view marginal gains as being worth relatively little but view avoiding marginal losses as being very important. Conversely, those in the "domain of losses" with a low reference point view marginal gains as being very important but view marginal losses as less costly. Consider another example; the Ohio State University (OSU), with an all-time winning percentage of nearly 70 percent and several national championships is among the most respected programs in the NCAA. As such, OSU is in the domain of gains. In contrast, Kent State University (KSU) has an all-time winning percentage of 39 percent and no major championships. With little winning tradition, the KSU program is in the domain of losses. Given the differences in the two programs, consider how each would react to the same season, where the team finished 6-5. At KSU, a six-win season might be seen as a success. At OSU, a six-win season would be a disaster. Based upon their different reference points, the two programs would view the same performance differently.

These programs would also react differently to the same deviation from expectations. Consider that OSU expects to win eight games a year while KSU expects to win four games a year. Suppose both finished two wins below expectation, six wins for OSU and two wins for KSU. While a two-win season is worse than a six-win season, the reaction at OSU might still be worse. For OSU, being in the domain of gains means that virtually any loss is hard to accept. The opposite is true of gains. For OSU, being in the domain of gains means that marginal gains are under-appreciated, despite being harder to achieve as upside potential is limited.[1] For KSU, in the domain of losses, marginal gains are highly appreciated, and marginal losses are more easily accepted. Thus, for OSU, losses are feared more than gains are valued, whereas for KSU, gains are valued more than losses are feared.

Translating these principles to business, firms with a track record of strong performance and continued high expectations are in the domain of gains. Such firms have good reason to be cautious. Good returns are the norm against which marginal changes are measured. Losses are feared and the punishment for falling short is severe. For example, in September 2004 Coca-Cola announced that third-quarter earnings would fall short of expectations by $150 million. On that very day $4.6 billion was wiped from Coca-Cola's market value. Indeed, Skinner and Sloan (2002) report that stock market reaction to earnings surprises are asymmetric – companies are punished for falling short more than they are rewarded for exceeding expectations. Thus, companies like Coca-Cola are actually quite rational in their risk aversion, as they are judged by a high standard. Meeting expectations, and not falling short, is critical, whereas exceeding expectations, while good, is much less critical. Thus, firms in the domain of gains are rationally less inclined to take risks to exceed expectations, but rather more risk-averse in protecting those expectations. However, for a company with more moderate expectations the calculation is different. Such firms tend to view marginal gains and losses more symmetrically. Marginal losses are certainly feared but marginal gains are also valued. As a result, such firms will be more risk-neutral in seeking future returns. This suggests that firms define their risk position by their reference point. Firms with high expectations have much to lose and so much to protect. Firms with low expectations have little to lose and so little to protect.

Insuring the Risk

Those organizations with much value to protect will seek assurance, while those with more moderate expectations will be willing to accept some risk. Finally, those with little value to protect will accept considerable risk in return for the prospect of future gains.

CEO selection is one means by which firms seek to manage this risk. When a board selects a CEO, the board members are making a risky decision (Khurana, 2002), with considerable potential for adverse selection due to the lack of information. Put differently, boards simply do not know how a given CEO will perform, regardless of apparent qualifications. Nonetheless, the selection and compensation of the new leader is among the board's principal responsibilities.

Consider the risk a board takes in hiring a new leader. Suppose the board selects someone who is unknown and unproven, but who they believe will do a good job. If the organization performs well, then the directors will be credited with making a good decision. However, if the organization does not perform well, the directors will look foolish for hiring an unproven individual. In other words if the directors pick someone who lacks credibility in the eyes of relevant stakeholders, that person cannot serve as an effective scapegoat, who can shoulder the blame for failing to perform up to expectations. Rather, the directors themselves will be blamed as they were the ones who selected the inferior CEO. This could result in the directors being fired (Ward et al., 1999) or losing status among the corporate elite, reducing their chance at other directorships (Farrell and Whidbee, 2000). At a minimum, the perception would be that the directors did their jobs poorly and that some of the firm's value was squandered by the board's poor decision.

Alternatively, if the board selects someone proven, the likelihood of negative repercussions for the board and the organization diminishes *regardless* of the actual outcome. If the new leader succeeds, the organization performs well and the board looks wise for making the right selection. However, if the organization fails, the board is held blameless because they did all they could be expected to do; they hired the best candidate, someone with sufficient human capital to perform well. Once the board has done that, the blame for the failure shifts to the CEO, and the CEO can then be scapegoated for the poor performance. Moreover, the perception of the organization's underlying value, or future expectations, remains intact, ready to be restored by the selection of the right leader.

Thus, selecting a CEO with sufficient human capital effectively provides the board and the organization insurance against the consequences of adverse selection. By choosing the "right" candidate, with all the requisite skills and capabilities who will be seen as a good choice, the board protects itself and the organization against the consequences of failure. If the CEO fails, he or she suffers a loss of reputation and future opportunity. The organization and the board, however, suffer little and the underlying expectations for the future remain largely intact.

CEO Compensation as an Insurance or "Scapegoating" Premium

The cost of insurance reflects the value being insured. A firm with high expectations has much to lose and the board of that firm would want to shift as much of the risk as possible to the CEO. To shoulder that risk, the CEO would have to have substantial capital in the form of personal reputation and standing, enough to be considered capable of meeting the performance expectations of the organization, and able to act as a credible scapegoat if performance fails to meet expectations. In this way the CEO underwrites the risk to the firm. Similarly, a prominent football program would need to hire a head coach who is recognized as a top candidate. In both cases, the caliber and size of the candidate pool is driven by the performance expectations of the organization. Viewed in this way, the initial compensation is the premium paid to the person who accepts the responsibility for the firm's expectations and protects that value by risking his or her own reputation.

In essence, it is a market where performance expectations determine demand and human capital determines supply. Expectations represent the size of the risk and the collateral required to cover it; human capital is the collateral that insures the risk. And guaranteed compensation is the price at which the transaction occurs. Organizations will seek collateral commensurate to the risk. Over-insuring would mean paying too large a premium for the protection received. Under-insuring does not provide sufficient coverage in the event of loss. Thus, we would not expect a small organization to pay the premium required for a high profile leader nor would we expect an organization with high expectations to select an unproven leader to save money. Rather, performance expectations determine the amount of human capital needed and the compensation reflects the cost of that human capital.

Viewed in this way, the process of compensating a new CEO appears rational. The salary guaranteed a new CEO reflects the expectations stakeholders hold for the organization. In hiring a new CEO or a new head football coach the board assesses the expected value at risk. It then hires someone with sufficient capital to act as a scapegoat should performance not live up to expectations. The guaranteed compensation is an insurance premium paid to the new leader for accepting the responsibilities of the position and placing his or her personal capital at risk. Thus:

Hypothesis 1: The fixed compensation guaranteed to a CEO or head coach at the time of hiring, is positively related to the performance expectations of the firm or institution.

Hypothesis 2: The human capital of the new CEO or head coach will be positively related to the performance expectations of the firm or institution.

Performance expectations drive the range of candidates an organization will consider – those with sufficient human capital to insure the risk, without excess. Once the selection is made, the price at which the transaction occurs reflects an interaction of the performance expectations of the firm and the human capital risked by the individual:

Hypothesis 3: The fixed compensation guaranteed to a CEO or head coach at the time of hiring, is positively related to the interaction of performance expectations of the firm or institution and the human capital of the individual.

This perspective also explains the pay gap between the top leader and the other upper-level managers. When a person is promoted to the top position, they may not gain any additional human capital in terms of skills and expertise. However, by right of their position, they assume responsibility for the organization's performance expectations. Thus, the human capital that they possess is being deployed differently and subject to an increased amount of risk. If the firm performs badly, then they suffer the greatest consequences in terms of standing and reputation. Second-tier managers suffer less harm and so retain their options for the future. While Boeker (1992) found that second-tier managers are sometimes used as scapegoats by powerful CEOs, the spotlight remains on the chief executive if performance continues to decline. Moreover, second-tier managers can avoid lasting reputational damage by attributing failure to the top leaders (Sonnenfeld and Ward, 2007). Thus, the pay gap represents a "scapegoating premium." Indeed, the increase in pay that a manager might receive upon being promoted from executive vice-president to CEO, or from assistant coach to head coach, reflects almost entirely the responsibility that he or she now has for the performance expectations of the organization. Hence:

Hypothesis 4: The gap between the compensation guaranteed to a new CEO and that guaranteed to the other top managers is positively related to the performance expectations of the firm or institution.

Finally, viewing the process in this way provides a better understanding of how the guaranteed and incentive elements in the total compensation package function. Organizations with lower performance expectations risk less in hiring a new leader. For example, a young, fast-growing organization may face an uncertain future but have tremendous "up side" potential. That firm would have more to gain than to lose. Because it had little to lose, it would need less insurance and so could afford to pay less in guaranteed compensation. However, it would still want to provide strong incentives for the CEO to realize its upside potential. Those incentives could come in the form of variable compensation. Without having to protect high expectations, this firm could hire a candidate with "up side" but unproven potential, to match the nature of the opportunity. For this individual, because the expectations are low and the situation uncertain, the risk of failure is less devastating and the risk to personal capital is smaller. Thus, the individual can accept a smaller amount of guaranteed compensation, in favor of greater incentives.

This effect is even more evident as the expectations fall. In some cases, there is nowhere to go but up. An organization in this situation might be inclined to take a considerable risk in hiring a new CEO. Given that this new leader faces low expectations and modest risk to their reputation in the event of failure, he or she would receive very little guaranteed compensation. However, because gains would be so highly valued, the organization would provide substantial incentives for improved performance. By offering such a package, the organization would be free to search for an up-and-coming, yet unproven, candidate, who lacks the personal capital to demand high guaranteed compensation and would be willing to accept some risk for the prospect of large gains. On the other hand, when an organization has extremely high performance expectations, there is much to lose, and further gains are not valued as highly as protecting current expectations. Accordingly, we would expect that the firm would structure compensation to reflect this rational risk-aversion and pay a high level of guaranteed compensation to pay for a proven candidate to protect the risk driven by high expectations, but less in the way of variable compensation such that risk-seeking behavior is not encouraged. Thus:

> *Hypothesis 5:* The proportion of total compensation guaranteed to a new CEO will relate positively to the performance expectations of the organization.

In sum, we contend the selection and compensation of new leader is a rational process within a well-functioning market, where selection and compensation reflect a deliberate transfer of risk. Organizations with high performance expectations have much to lose and protect. When they do not perform up to expectations, someone must bear the cost of the disappointment, someone must shoulder the blame. To avoid bearing this risk alone, the board "purchases" insurance in the form of the human capital of a recognized leader. In taking the job, that manager recognizes the risks. Doing well simply may not be enough; the manager must live up to or exceed the expectations of the organization. If he or she fails, then he or she bears the cost of that failure in the loss of reputation and future options. In return, the manager receives a premium, in the form of guaranteed compensation, related directly to the size of the risk underwritten. The guaranteed portion of a new leader's compensation then should reflect the performance expectations of the firm. In turn, the performance expectations should determine the level of human capital required of the person selected to fill the role. Compensation then reflects the match between the performance expectations and the human capital of the leader. Moreover, the gap in guaranteed compensation between the CEO and the other top managers also reflects these expectations. Finally, because expectations relate to risk aversion, the guaranteed portion of compensation, as a proportion of total compensation, should also reflect the performance expectations of the firm.

DATA AND METHODOLOGY

To test our hypotheses, we employed two samples: Fortune 500 firms and National Collegiate Athletic Association (NCAA) Division I Football Programs. While the organizations in these two samples are very different, they face similar pressures and scrutiny when hiring new leaders. Thus, our model should hold across both. For the Fortune 500 sample, we examined CEO changes between 1995 and 2002. There were 434 such changes during the period examined. We excluded changes due to firms being taken over or merged, or that were subsidiaries of other firms, and firms for which complete compensation and financial data were unavailable on Execucomp and Compustat. This resulted in a final sample of 255 CEO changes.

The NCAA sample initially consisted of 119 head coaching changes in Division I football programs between 1998 and 2004. Data on this sample was more difficult to gather as much of it is not publicly available or standardized in any fashion. As a consequence, we were able to get all the necessary information for only 67 cases, 56.3 percent of the total. We checked for bias by comparing universities in our sample to those that were eliminated. In general, private and smaller schools are under-represented. This reflects the fact that the needed information is more commonly reported by public schools and more often the subject of press reports for larger schools.

Fortune 500 Sample

Dependent variables
All salary data was obtained from Execucomp. *Fixed compensation* was the base salary paid to the executive. *Human capital* is measured as the highest base salary paid to the individual in their position immediately prior to their hiring by the focal firm. *Compensation gap* was the difference between the base salary of the CEO and the base salary of the next highest paid executive. *Proportion of guaranteed compensation* was the ratio of base salary to the total compensation paid.

Independent variable
Expectations Index (EI): Miller and Modigliani (1961) and Myers (1977) observed that a firm's value depends not only on the value of future revenues that are likely to come from the assets in place, but also from future investment options in other growth opportunities. This value has been discussed in the accounting literature as the firm's investment opportunity set (Myers, 1977; Gaver and Gaver, 1993; Baber et al., 1996). In the management literature, Myers (1977) and Myers and Turnbull's (1977) definition of the firm's value as being comprised of productive capacity from existing assets and the "options to purchase additional units of productive capacity in future periods" (pp. 331–2) has led to the development of real options theory and the use of options reasoning as a heuristic for strategy (McGrath et al. 2004).

Investment opportunity set is a term used to describe the present value of a firm's future investment options. That present value reflects the return potential of the investments, as well as the likelihood of realizing those returns successfully. In other words, the investment opportunity set should reflect the performance expectations of key stakeholders, such as the board who are aware of the investments being made by the firm to develop and capitalize upon future options. As such, we term this construct the Expectations Index (EI). Over time, EI is the present value of the future returns, if the firm makes the right decisions and executes as necessary to realize the potential of those opportunities.

EI then is somewhat similar to Tobin's q, which is the market value of the firm divided by the replacement cost of its assets (Lindenberg and Ross, 1981; Chung and Pruitt, 1994). Both measures capture the value-added by the firm's strategies, management, and opportunities. Indeed, our data showed the correlation between EI and Tobin's q to be 0.75, a proportional overlap of 56 percent. Where the measures differ is that EI includes data on the firm's investment intensity, acquisition activity, and research and development efforts, rather than relying only on market assessments. EI then reflects the enduring value of the firm, without the influence of systematic market variance. In essence, EI is the value that insiders believe the firm represents; it is the value that, over time, they expect the firm to realize.

Variance in EI reflects the fact that the responsibility of which Barnard (1938) spoke is simply larger for some firms than for others. Firms with a high EI represent strong potential and are expected to do well. Firms with low EI represent less or less certain potential and so are not expected to do as well. To calculate EI, we followed Baber et al. (1996). We first calculated four intermediate indicators:

1. Investment intensity:

$$\frac{\sum_{i=t-2}^{i=t} [\text{Capital expenditure} + \text{R\&D} + \text{Acquisitions}]}{\sum_{i=t-2}^{i=t} \text{Depreciation}} \, i$$

2. Geometric mean annual growth rate of market value of assets:

$$\sqrt[n]{\frac{\text{Market value of assets}_t}{\text{Market value of assets}_{t-n}}}$$

3. Market-to-book value of assets:

$$\frac{\text{Market value of assets}}{\text{Book value of total assets}}$$

4. R&D expenditure to total assets:

$$\frac{\text{R\&D expense}}{\text{Book value of total assets}}$$

Each indicator reflects some aspect of potential value-added over and above the appreciated book value of a firm's assets. Factor analyzing the indicators allows us to extract the principal component of common variance. That principal component was used as an empirically derived "weight" indicating the importance or contribution of each indicator value to overall EI. We used these loadings to weight the indicator values and the weighted values were then summed to form a single, continuous index representing a firm's EI at a particular moment in time. Further detail on the procedure and measurements are provided in Appendix 13A.

As conditions and expectations change, so too will a firm's EI value at different points in time. Because we studied firms in the years in which new CEOs were hired and because some firms hired more than one CEO during the nine-year window of our study, several firms appear more than once and with different EI values. We examined this information to gauge the face-validity of the index and found it be consistent with expectations. For example, The Gap had an EI value of 3.43, in 1995. By 2002, however, that value had fallen to 2.39. Home Depot had an EI value of 6.30 in 1997 but 8.25 in 2000. The highest EI value in the sample was for 13.59, for EMC Corporation in 2000. The lowest EI value was 0.789 for Unumprovident, in 2003.

Control variables
Research has shown a relationship between company size and CEO compensation (Agarwal, 1981); thus, we controlled for firm size, measured as sales in the year of the CEO succession. We also controlled for the *Fortune 500 rank* as an ordinal measure of size. This measure may also act as an indicator of reputation and prestige, as organizations frequently tout their Fortune ranking as signal of status. We controlled for the departing CEO's *reason for exit*, creating a dummy variable, 1 for a forced departure and 0 otherwise. If the departing CEO was fired, this may shift the balance of power in negotiations towards the new CEO (Khurana, 2002). Khurana (2002) also suggests that CEOs hired from outside command a compensation premium. Thus, we controlled for the new CEO's status as an *outsider* (defined as joining the organization within two years of becoming CEO). Finally, when testing Hypothesis 4, we controlled for the base salary of the next highest paid executive in the firm and for Hypothesis 5 we controlled for the proportion of guaranteed to total compensation paid to the next highest paid executive. Our thinking was that these variables captured an element of the overall compensation philosophy of the firm, both in terms of the overall level in the case of base salary and incentive structure in the case of proportion of guaranteed to total compensation.

NCAA Sample

Dependent variables
The compensation paid to head coaches is somewhat different from that paid to corporate CEOs. Typically, the "salary" is relatively small. Supplementing that salary, however, is additional money from endorsements, media broadcasts, and summer training camps. These additional payments are guaranteed, however. Variable compensation, which for CEOs includes things like bonuses, stock, and stock options, is less common for coaches. Some have modest incentives associated with bowl game appearances, conference or national championships, or graduation rates. Most, however, are rewarded for extraordinary performance with new contracts, with higher levels of guaranteed compensation.

What we attempted to capture for *fixed compensation* was the total compensation guaranteed to the head coach at the time of hiring – before the first game had been played. That is, even if the university fired the coach after the first game, this was the total amount that the university had committed itself to pay. This information was derived primarily from media reports at the time of the head coach's hiring. Similarly, *human capital* was measured as the coach's fixed compensation in their job immediately prior to their hiring by the focal institution.

To get salary data on assistant coaches, we looked to a report that NCAA member schools are required to file. In this report, schools are required to provide the average salary of all assistant coaches. While not quite the same as the "next highest salary" this number still has a consistent meaning across the universities, and does relate directly to our theory regarding the salary gap. Thus, the *compensation gap* was the difference between head coach guaranteed compensation and the average compensation paid to the assistant coaches. As mentioned, variable compensation is somewhat unusual, generally modest, and not obtainable from public sources. Thus, we were unable to test Hypothesis 5 in this sample.

Independent variable
Expectations Index (EI). While there was no way in this sample to reproduce EI perfectly, we created a measure that parallels the construct and embodies the expectations of performance a university would hold. The measure was constructed from the following components:

1. *Historical position*, determined by the team's all-time winning percentage. This provides an indication of the historical baseline for expectations of future performance for the organization.
2. *Four-year winning percentage* provides a measure of recent performance of the team, which, in conjunction with *historical position*, is likely to guide performance expectations.
3. *Bowl appearances in past five years* provides a second measure of recent performance and current expectations for team performance.
4. *Four-year preseason rank*. For each of the four seasons prior to the coach being hired, we measured whether the team was included in the Associated Press preseason Top 25. A value of 0 was given for any year the team did not appear in the Top 25, and a value of 26-*n* was given for each year the team appeared in the Top 25, where *n* is the ranking of the team.
5. *Stadium size* is a measure of the expected fan-base for the team, and the importance of the team to the university in terms of investment, revenue, and symbolism.
6. *Recruiting budget*. Similar to R&D expense, this variable provides a measure of the investment in future capabilities.
7. *Athletic budget* is an indicator of the importance university's place on athletics and the football program.

We factor-analyzed these seven indicators and used the weighting derived from the first principal component to create a single continuous variable representing EI. Additional details are provided again in Appendix 13B. The program with the highest EI value (13.70) was the University of Nebraska in 2004. The Ohio State University was second, with an EI value of 13.18 in 2001. The programs with the lowest EI values were Navy in 2002 (1.52) and Louisiana-Lafayette in 2002 (1.73). Again, some programs may appear more than once as they hired new head coaches more than once during the period of the study.

Control variables
We used *undergraduate enrollment* to control for university size. Most schools belong to an athletic conference and these conferences vary in terms of strength and reputation. Thus, we controlled for *average conference athletic budget*, which calculated the average athletic budget for all universities within a conference. We controlled for whether the

departing coach was *fired* (1 = fired, 0 = other reason). Finally, we controlled for *public or private university* status (0 = public, 1 = private).

RESULTS

Tables 13.1 and 13.2 contain the zero-order correlations and descriptive statistics for the variables in the study. In the Fortune 500 sample (Table 13.1) a number of relationships stand out. New CEO salary relates strongly to organizational size and the salary of the next highest paid executive. In addition, the Expectations Index (EI) relates positively to new CEO salary and to the guaranteed proportion of that salary. Interestingly, EI is not related to size or Fortune rank, suggesting that performance expectations are independent of size and reputation.

A similar pattern appears in the NCAA sample (Table 13.2). New head coach salary is correlated with enrollment and average conference athletic budget. Head coach salary is also correlated (0.999) with the gap between head coach salary and assistant coach salary, suggesting that assistant coach salary is relatively constant across the sample. EI is correlated with head coach salary and with the gap between head coaches and assistants. However, in this sample, EI is correlated with size (enrollment) and wealth (average conference athletic budget).

Each hypothesis was tested with regression analysis. Our procedure was to create first a model containing the control variables. We then created a second model that includes EI. This allowed us to measure the marginal contribution of the Expectations Index, while testing the statistical significance of that contribution. We also performed standard diagnostic analyses to check for multicollinearity. We found all the correlations and variance inflation factors to be within accepted tolerances.

Hypothesis 1 stated that the fixed compensation, guaranteed a CEO or head coach, would relate positively to performance expectations. As shown in Table 13.3 (Model 1), the control models were significant, with adjusted R^2 values of 0.283 for the Fortune 500 sample and 0.515 for the NCAA sample. Adding EI to the models resulted in an adjusted R^2 of 0.304 for the Fortune 500 and 0.611 for the NCAA sample. In both samples, the expected relationship between EI and guaranteed salary was positive and significant ($p < 0.001$). Thus, Hypothesis 1 is supported.

Hypothesis 2 predicted that the human capital of the new CEO or coach would be positively related to performance expectations. Stated differently, performance expectations would determine the caliber of the person who would be considered for the job. Table 13.4 shows the results for this hypothesis. Model 1 shows the effects of the control variables. These were significant in the Fortune 500 sample (adjusted $R^2 = 0.167$), but insignificant in the NCAA sample. With EI added (Model 2), the Fortune 500 sample has an adjusted R^2 of 0.177 and the relationship between EI and human capital was positive and significant ($p < 0.05$). However, the model remained insignificant in the NCAA sample. Thus, we had mixed support for Hypothesis 2.

Hypothesis 3 stated that the fixed compensation, guaranteed a CEO or head coach, would be a product of the interaction of human capital and performance expectations. In Table 13.3, Model 4 captures this result. Both models are significant with adjusted R^2 of 0.582 (Fortune 500 sample) and 0.745 (NCAA sample). The interaction is also significant

Table 13.1 Fortune 500 sample correlations

	Mean	S.D.	1	2	3	4	5	6	7	8	9
1. New CEO's salary	886.61	326.38									
2. New CEO's salary proportion	0.5381	0.2305	-0.016								
3. Next highest paid exec salary	603.91	343.03	0.630**	-0.074							
4. Next highest salary proportion	0.5981	0.2163	-0.029	0.751**	0.046						
5. Salary gap	281.91	289.14	0.383**	0.074	-0.475**	-0.085					
6. New CEO an outsider?	0.28	0.451	0.074	-0.114†	-0.020	-0.124*	0.102				
7. Reason	0.13	0.336	-0.034	0.024	-0.004	0.083	-0.032	0.199**			
8. Fortune rank	225.6	140.4	-0.418**	0.052	-0.342**	0.030	-0.069	0.049	0.034		
9. Sales	13883.7	21081.6	0.506**	-0.091	0.359**	-0.057	0.146*	-0.037	-0.002	-0.555**	
10. Expectations Index	3.249	1.707	0.197**	0.112†	0.127*	0.073	0.071	-0.087	-0.007	-0.080	0.098

Notes:
** Correlation is significant at the 0.01 level (two-tailed).
* Correlation is significant at the 0.05 level (two-tailed).
† Correlation is significant at the 0.10 level (two-tailed).

Source: Authors' calculations.

362

Table 13.2 NCAA sample correlations

	Mean	S.D.	1	2	3	4	5	6	7
1. Public/Private institution	0.10	0.308							
2. Conference ave budget	25327725	9265429	0.064						
3. Undergraduate enrollment	17035	8176	−0.205†	0.444***					
4. Old coach fired	0.64	0.483	−0.050	−0.018	0.093				
5. Ave assistant coach salary	58249	14767	0.105	0.607***	0.315*	0.153			
6. New coach salary	623351	353877	0.200	0.662***	0.344**	0.257*	0.653***		
7. Salary gap between head coach/assistant coach	567709	344054	0.198	0.650***	0.330**	0.264*	0.628***	0.999***	
8. Expectations Index	5.5791	2.9299	0.108	0.543***	0.433***	−0.101	0.587***	0.610***	0.594***

Notes:
*** Correlation is significant at the 0.000 level (two-tailed).
** Correlation is significant at the 0.01 level (two-tailed).
* Correlation is significant at the 0.05 level (two-tailed).
† Correlation is significant at the 0.10 level (two-tailed).

Source: Authors' calculations.

Table 13.3   *Regression analyses with new CEO salary as dependent variable (Hypotheses 1 and 3) for both Fortune 500 firms and NCAA football programs*

Variable	Model 1	Model 2	Model 3	Model 4
Fortune 500 Sample				
Sales	0.398***	0.386***	0.232***	0.232***
	(6.232)	(6.127)	(4.380)	(4.403)
Fortune rank	−0.201***	−0.196***	−0.098*	−0.114*
	(−3.144)	(−3.105)	(−1.878)	(−2.179)
Old CEO fired?	−0.048	−0.049	0.019	0.019
	(−0.880)	(−0.924)	(0.427)	(0.442)
New CEO outsider?	0.108*	0.121*	0.171***	0.166***
	(1.986)	(2.250)	(3.833)	(3.760)
Expectations Index		0.153**	0.079*	0.053
		(2.904)	(1.810)	(1.174)
New CEO's human capital (prior salary)			0.595***	0.577***
			(12.333)	(11.89)
Interaction (EI × human capital)				0.102*
				(2.236)
Adjusted R^2	0.283	0.304	0.575	0.582
F	26.120***	23.205***	52.169***	46.239***
Df (regression, residual)	4, 250	5, 249	6, 221	7, 220
NCAA sample				
Conference average Budget	0.617***	0.460***	0.402***	0.406***
	(6.343)	(4.817)	(4.602)	(5.104)
Public/Private institution	0.191*	0.138*	0.114†	0.118*
	(2.147)	(1.705)	(1.563)	(1.775)
Undergraduate enrollment	0.084	−0.031	−0.008	−0.017
	(0.841)	(−0.327)	(−0.101)	(−0.226)
Old coach fired?	0.270**	0.314***	0.267***	0.240***
	(3.127)	(4.023)	(3.772)	(3.683)
Expectations Index		0.390***	0.344***	0.082
		(4.019)	(3.906)	(0.756)
New coach's human Capital (prior salary)			0.299***	−0.109
			(4.141)	(−0.833)
Interaction (EI × human capital)				0.578***
				(3.613)
Adjusted R^2	0.515	0.611	0.693	0.745
F	18.542***	21.691***	25.415***	28.100***

Notes:
Standardized regression coefficients shown (t statistics in parentheses).
*** Significant at 0.001 level (one-tailed).
** Significant at 0.01 level (one-tailed).
* Significant at 0.05 level (one-tailed).
† Significant at 0.10 level (one-tailed).

Source: Authors' calculations.

Table 13.4   Regression analyses with human capital (the new CEO's or new head coach's prior salary) as dependent variable for Fortune 500 firms and NCAA football programs (Hypothesis 2)

Fortune 500 Firms			NCAA Football Programs		
Variable	Model 1	Model 2	Variable	Model 1	Model 2
Sales	0.276***	0.268***	Conference	0.225†	0.158
	(3.835)	(3.747)	average budget	(1.602)	(1.019)
Fortune rank	−0.150*	−0.147*	Public/Private	0.106	0.085
	(−2.071)	(−2.048)	institution	(0.829)	(0.658)
Old CEO fired?	−0.104*	−0.107*	Undergraduate	−0.022	−0.068
	(−1.691)	(−1.746)	enrollment	(−0.155)	(−0.454)
New CEO	−0.110*	−0.102*	Old coach fired?	0.134	0.154
outsider?	(−1.768)	(−1.658)		(1.084)	(1.234)
Expectations		0.117*	Expectations		0.162
Index		(1.933)	Index		(1.042)
Adjusted R^2	0.167	0.177	Adjusted R^2	0.018	0.019
F	12.346***	10.745***	F	1.300	1.258
Df (regression, residual)	4, 223	5, 222	Df (regression, residual)	4, 61	5, 60

Notes:
Standardized regression coefficients shown (*t* statistics in parentheses).
*** Significant at 0.001 level (one-tailed).
** Significant at 0.01 level (one-tailed).
* Significant at 0.05 level (one-tailed).
† Significant at 0.10 level (one-tailed).

Source: Authors' calculations.

in both samples ($p < 0.05$ in Fortune 500 sample, $p < 0.001$ in NCAA sample). Thus, Hypothesis 3 was supported.

Hypothesis 4 related the gap between the new CEO's (head coach's) guaranteed compensation and that of the other top managers to performance expectations. As shown in Table 13.5, the control models for the two samples are significant, with R^2 values of 0.350 in the Fortune 500 sample and 0.545 in the NCAA sample. Adding EI produced a significant model for the Fortune 500 sample (NCAA sample) that was significant, with an R^2 of 0.363 (0.604). The relationship between EI and salary gap was positive and significant ($p < 0.01$) in both models, providing support for Hypothesis 4.

Hypothesis 5 stated that the proportion of total compensation guaranteed a new CEO would be positively related to performance expectations. Because the nature of head coach compensation precluded a test of this hypothesis, the results from the Fortune 500 sample are reported in Table 13.6. The control model had a significant R^2 of 0.560. Adding EI increased the R^2 to 0.562. EI is positively and marginally significantly ($p < 0.10$) related to the proportion of guaranteed compensation. Thus, there is marginal support for Hypothesis 5.

Table 13.5   Regression analyses with gap between CEO's salary and next highest paid executive's salary (head coach's salary and average assistant coach's salary) as dependent variable (Hypothesis 4) for Fortune 500 firms and NCAA football programs

Fortune 500 Firms			NCAA Sample		
Variable	Model 1	Model 2	Variable	Model 1	Model 2
Sales	0.311***	0.305***	Conference	0.418***	0.359***
	(4.990)	(4.933)	average Budget	(3.645)	(3.303)
Fortune rank	−0.114*	−0.113*	Public/Private	0.173*	0.146*
	(−1.844)	(−1.836)	institution	(1.935)	(1.737)
Old CEO fired?	−0.054	−0.055	Old coach fired?	0.223**	0.274***
	(−1.037)	(−1.072)		(2.544)	(3.290)
New CEO	0.117*	0.128**	Undergraduate	0.081	0.010
outsider?	(2.271)	(2.490)	enrollment	(0.811)	(0.103)
Next highest	−0.623***	−0.636***	Average assistant	0.297**	0.156†
exec. salary	(−11.300)	(−11.593)	coach salary	(2.706)	(1.397)
Expectations		0.124**	Expectations		0.330**
Index		(2.446)	Index		(3.104)
Adjusted R^2	0.350	0.363	Adjusted R^2	0.545	0.604
F	28.355***	25.100***	F	16.065***	16.987***
Df (regression, residual)	5, 249	6, 248	Df (regression, residual)	5, 58	6, 57

Notes:
Standardized regression coefficients shown (*t* statistics in parentheses).
*** Significant at 0.001 level (one-tailed).
** Significant at 0.01 level (one-tailed).
* Significant at 0.05 level (one-tailed).
† Significant at 0.10 level (one-tailed).

Source: Authors' calculations.

DISCUSSION

Two things about our results are especially noteworthy. The first is the size and significance of the effects. Across the nine tests, excluding the one that was not significant, the R^2 values ranged from a low of 0.177 to a high of 0.745 and, in all of these cases, the EI contributed significantly over and above the variance explained by the control variables. The second is the consistency of the effects across the samples. Fortune 500 firms and NCAA football programs are very different, yet, the size and pattern of results were very similar. This suggests a robust and meaningful effect.

But what does that really mean for top leader compensation and for the various theories that have been used to explain it? Most immediately, it suggests that the guaranteed portion of the compensation serves a different purpose than the variable portion. As discussed previously, the guaranteed portion of initial compensation is unrelated to

Table 13.6   *Fortune 500 sample regression analyses with CEO's salary as a proportion of total compensation as dependent variable (Hypothesis 5)*

Variable	Model 1	Model 2
Sales	−0.045	−0.050
	(−0.903)	(−1.002)
Fortune rank	0.006	0.008
	(0.125)	(0.168)
Old CEO fired?	−0.036	−0.036
	(−0.833)	(−0.839)
New CEO outsider?	−0.016	−0.011
	(−0.370)	(−0.263)
Next highest exec. proportion	0.749***	0.745***
	(17.714)	(17.612)
Expectations Index		0.062†
		(1.477)
Adjusted R^2	0.560	0.562
F	65.572***	55.266***
Df (regression, residual)	5, 249	6, 248

Notes:
Standardized regression coefficients shown (t statistics in parentheses).
*** Significant at 0.001 level (one-tailed).
** Significant at 0.01 level (one-tailed).
* Significant at 0.05 level (one-tailed).
† Significant at 0.10 level (one-tailed).

Source: Authors' calculations.

performance. A CEO or coach could accept a position, deliver nothing in terms of results, and still get the full balance of the guaranteed pay. How then is that pay rationally justified? The answer is that the guaranteed compensation insures the firm against adverse selection and compensates the CEO for the potential down-side risk of the position.

There is an old saying that one should never follow a legend; there is simply no way to look good in comparison. Doug Ivestor found this to be the case at Coca-Cola, where he had to live up to the expectations built during the term of his predecessor, Roberto Gouzieta. The same was true at the Home Depot, where Robert Nardelli took over from the founders, Bernie Marcus and Arthur Blank, in 2000. When performance lagged, stakeholders questioned Nardelli's style and strategy (Sellers, 2002), and ultimately forced him out. Leading large, well-known, and profitable firms like Coca-Cola and Home Depot involves some risk. Expectations are high; there is much to lose with little room for improvement.

Just ask Ron Zook, who took over the head coaching job at the University of Florida following the departure of Steve Spurrier. In three seasons, Zook recorded 23 wins and 15 losses; yet he was fired. While his performance was good, it was not good enough; the expectations were just too high. Those expectations raised the bar for success, increasing the likelihood of failure while limiting the chances for improvement.

Knowing this, why would anyone accept such a position? The answer is that they probably would not, at least not without a substantial guarantee. Thus, it is the guarantee that insures the CEO against the down-side risk of not meeting expectations. So, as the performance expectations increase, so too must the guarantee. In return for the guarantee, the leader provides insurance to the firm and its board, by placing their own human capital at risk. If the new leader does poorly, he or she shoulders the blame. Using the CEO as a scapegoat allows the board to shift the responsibility for poor performance and so avoid sharing in the blame itself (Ward et al., 1999). Finally then, because high expectations increase the likelihood of failure, they also increase the risk to the board and the organization, increasing the need for a suitable scapegoat.

For example, consider Coca-Cola, which with its considerable reputation and wealth, should be able to hire the CEO of its choice. Yet in its last search, the company had difficulty attracting top talent as several qualified candidates declined to be considered. In the same way, Notre Dame, with its tradition and support, should be able to hire any coach it wants. Yet, here again many notable candidates withdrew from consideration during the last search. Given the advantages held by organizations like these, there is great pressure to hire good leaders, who can continue the tradition of success. The boards then must find candidates with enough legitimacy to carry the weight of that responsibility and to serve as credible scapegoats when performance falls short.

Hiring a new leader then involves an exchange of liabilities. The leader accepts that he or she will be a scapegoat if things go poorly and the organization accepts guaranteed payments to the leader, performance notwithstanding. Finally, the value of the exchange reflects the value of the expectations. High expectations necessitate a CEO who can shoulder a heavy burden. To be held harmless in the event of loss, the organization must be able to claim that it hired the best available candidate. Such a candidate, by taking a position where there is much to lose, places his or her own reputational and capital at risk and so will demand substantial guaranteed compensation.

While new and exciting, this explanation does not replace other theories of executive compensation. Rather, our model complements these theories. For example, consider the human capital view (Hogan and McPheters, 1980; Finkelstein and Hambrick, 1989; Belliveau et al., 1996; Carpenter et al., 2001). Our work adds to this view by showing that the pay jump an executive receives in moving from the second level to the top level relates to the expectations of the organization and the risks associated with them. It is the CEO who covers these symbolic risks. Thus, the increase reflects the additional deployment of the human capital, not just in the functional sense but also as symbolic collateral, insuring the organization's expectations.

The data provide further evidence of efficiency in this market for symbolic collateral. The findings in Table 13.5 show negative relationships between human capital and the control variables. When a previous CEO is fired, the human capital of the new CEO tends to be lower. In addition, new CEOs who are outsiders tend to have lower human capital than those who are insiders. Both findings reflect market adjustments to the value of specific CEOs in specific jobs. In the first case, a fired CEO represents a balance in power favoring the board (Khurana, 2002). Such conditions may make the CEO position less attractive. To attract a new CEO, the board must either pay more or select candidates with less human capital. Either way the result is the same: the new CEO is compensated above the level of his or her human capital in return for accepting a position that is considered less attractive and more risky. In the second case, hiring an outsider reflects greater risk as outsiders are less familiar and are more likely to make changes. As a result, a firm may seek candidates who are less expensive, with less human capital, and in a position to demand less guaranteed compensation.

Interestingly, this pattern did not emerge in the NCAA sample. Firing the previous coach did not affect the human capital of the new coach. The lack of an effect associated with the firing of the previous coach suggests differences in the two markets. For instance, most coaches are eventually fired. Indeed, the mean for firings in the NCAA sample is 0.64 but only 0.13 in the Fortune sample. Thus, a firing in the NCAA sample likely conveys less negative information about the position than it does in the corporate sample. Additionally, as noted earlier, assistant coach salary tends to be quite uniform across schools. Thus, for assistant coaches, salary may not adequately reflect the differences in human capital that exist between individuals in similar roles. Indeed, this equality may also reflect suppression of salaries at the second tier explained by tournament theory.

Tournament theory is another popular model for CEO compensation (Lazear and Rosen, 1981; O'Reilly et al., 1988) that provides a competing explanation to the classical economic notion that marginal pay differences reflect marginal differences in contribution. In tournaments, marginal differences in performance produce dramatic differences in reward. This approach then involves viewing the process of CEO selection as a competition. Managers in the running compete for the job and the winner receives a large reward (Bognanno, 2001; Conyon et al., 2001; Henderson and Fredrickson, 2001).

Here again, our results are complementary. We believe it is the desire to divert the risks associated with hiring and being a new CEO that drives guaranteed compensation. Those risks and the process of insuring against them generalize across firms, industries, and organizational types. Indeed, there are many examples of executives who earned their reputations in one firm or industry, only to use that capital in another firm or industry. Robert Nardelli, for instance, was passed over for the top job at General Electric following Jack Welch's retirement before taking the top job at the Home Depot. What this suggests is that the tournament is less about winning than it is about qualifying for the race. Becoming a top leader requires first cultivating the human and reputational capital that will serve as collateral for the position. Moreover, the extra compensation is more than just a reward for winning, it also motivates candidates to try, as failure in the top job can be terminal to future career prospects.

Our findings in the NCAA sample also reflect tournament theory logic. Indeed, the gap between head coach and assistant coach salaries is very large, much larger than in the corporate sample. This reflects a system where assistant salaries are suppressed by the hope of eventually becoming a head coach. Assistants accept lower salaries as investments in their future, paying dues into a system that will reward them handsomely when they become head coaches.

Our study also builds on the symbolic view that CEOs are compensated for more than just the work they perform. In this view, CEO pay illustrates the status of the organization and communicates the value of the CEO to external constituents. We argue that the CEO insures against the costs of potential losses and that those costs vary with the performance expectations of the firm. To provide adequate insurance, the CEO must have sufficient legitimacy and human capital to shoulder the symbolic responsibility for the organization. Thus, expectations drive the level of human capital needed, and the combination of human capital and expectations drives the compensation. Thus, we believe that there is a rational computation using the Expectations Index that can determine the amount of symbolic value a firm needs from a new CEO.

Indeed, we tested this application by applying the regression equation used to test Hypothesis 1 to predict the salaries of a number of head football coaches who were hired at the end of the 2004 season. Our predictions were very accurate. At some point, a similar application could allow boards to determine the appropriate level of compensation for CEOs of their own firms.

Finally, we contribute to the theoretical discourse on CEO pay with the introduction of the EI construct. Drawing from the accounting literature (Gaver and Gaver, 1993; Baber et al., 1996), we calculated an EI to capture the expectations a firm has for future performance, and translated the index into an altogether different context: NCAA football programs. While the EI value performed exactly as we expected, it is interesting to note that it was not highly correlated with organizational size. We also examined the correlation between EI and profit ($r = 0.138$; $p < 0.10$) and return on sales ($r = 0.223$; $p < 0.01$) in the Fortune sample. While significant, the correlations in both cases are modest. Baber et al. (1996) reported similarly modest correlations with return on equity and revenue growth. Thus, this measure appears to capture information that is substantively different from that provided by other measures of performance.

Furthermore, our study offers substantial potential to inform practice. Analysts and members of the press might use our model as a benchmark for evaluating CEO salaries. Much attention is given to CEO pay by the investment and governance communities. Unfortunately, that attention can spread more confusion than understanding because the underlying reasons for CEO pay are never made explicit. Our model could be a tool for gauging the rationality of the package and for assessing the value of the inducements, relative to the contributions.

Limitations

We would be remiss not to detail our study's limitations. While we have discussed this study with several CEOs, board members, and executive recruiters, and while our contentions are consistent with the in-depth work on CEO recruitment by Khurana (2002), we are nevertheless drawing inferences from secondary data about real human thoughts and intentions. Our arguments and theory were supported. Nonetheless, we believe that additional qualitative work would enhance our understanding. We also acknowledge the limitations of our second sample. We included NCAA football programs because they provided helpful illustrations and allowed us to test the generalizability of our theory. Also, research on scapegoating has often been set in the context of sports. Still, the differences between coaches and Fortune 500 CEOs and between college football programs and Fortune 500 firms are substantial. Thus, while our findings are consistent and encouraging, we should not assume that this would necessarily be generalizable to other very different contexts. Finally, additional refinement of our empirical procedures could prove beneficial. The control variables we used seemed reasonable and appropriate but there could be others that we overlooked. While our EI for the Fortune 500 sample came directly from a previously tested construct in the accounting literature, our operationalization of EI in the NCAA sample might provide better understanding with further refinement.

CONCLUSION

These limitations notwithstanding, we are very encouraged by these results and by their implications. CEO compensation is a complicated issue and an issue that has vexed researchers and practitioners for years. We believe that our study provides a simple, yet powerful lens though which the phenomenon may be viewed, and which could generate powerful theoretical models and practical applications. We encourage others to examine CEO compensation in terms of performance expectations.

ACKNOWLEDGMENTS

We wish to thank Daniel Feldman, Ann Buchholtz, Jill Brown, Amy Hillman, and the participants in the Wharton O.B. conference (2004) for helpful comments on earlier drafts of this manuscript.

NOTE

1. In the case of football, at the extreme end of the domain of gains, marginal gains may be highly valued as an extra win may mean a national championship or significant bowl victory. In such a case the marginal value of the extra win becomes huge and valued more than any single win over the course of the season. At such a point, the perception of risk shifts because the reference point shifts. When the possibility of a national championship or similar achievement becomes realistic, expectations shift such that anything less may be perceived of as a loss.

REFERENCES

Agarwal, N.C. (1981). Determinants of executive compensation. *Industrial Relations*, **20**(1), 36–46.

Baber, W.R., Janakiraman, S.N., and Kang, S.H. (1996). Investment opportunities and the structure of executive compensation. *Journal of Accounting and Economics*, **21**(3), 297–318.

Barnard, C. (1938). *The functions of the executive*. Cambridge, MA: Harvard University Press.

Belliveau, M., O'Reilly, C.A., and Wade, J.B. (1996). Social capital at the top: Effects of social similarity and status on CEO compensation. *Academy of Management Journal*, **39**(6), 1568–93.

Boeker, W. (1992). Power and managerial dismissal: Scapegoating at the top. *Administrative Science Quarterly*, **37**(3), 400–421.

Bognanno, M.L. (2001). Corporate tournaments. *Journal of Labor Economics*, **19**(2), 290–315.

Carpenter, M.A., Sanders, W.G., and Gregersen, H.B. (2001). Bundling human capital with organizational context: The impact of international assignment experience on multinational firm performance and CEO pay. *Academy of Management Journal*, **44**(3), 493–511.

Chiruvolu, R. (2004). The myth of the superstar CEO: When VCs invest, should replacing the founder CEO really be the first order of business? *Venture Capital Journal*, **44**(1).

Chung, K.H. and Pruitt, S.W. (1994). A simple approximation of Tobin's q. *Financial Management*, **23**(3), 70–74.

Conyon, M.J., Peck, S.I., and Sadler, G.V. (2001). Corporate tournaments and executive compensation: Evidence from the U.K. *Strategic Management Journal*, **22**(8), 805–15.

ESPN (2004). AD cites lack of on-field progress. 1 December, 2004. Available at: http://sports.espn.go.com/ncf/news/story?id=1935138; accessed 31 July, 2010.

Farrell, K.A. and Whidbee, D.A. (2000). The consequences of forced CEO succession for outside directors. *Journal of Business*, **73**(4), 597–627.

Finkelstein, S. and Hambrick, D.C. (1989). Chief executive compensation: A study of the intersection of markets and political processes. *Strategic Management Journal*, **10**(2), 121–34.

Gamson, W.A. and Scotch, N.A. (1964). Scapegoating in baseball. *The American Journal of Sociology*, **70**(1), 69–72.

Gaver, J.J. and Gaver, K.M. (1993). Additional evidence on the association between the investment opportunity set and corporate financing, dividend, and compensation policies. *Journal of Accounting and Economics*, **16**(1–3), 125–60.

Grusky, O. (1963). Managerial succession and organizational effectiveness. *The American Journal of Sociology*, **69**(1), 21–31.

Henderson, A.D. and Fredrickson, J.W. (2001). Top management team coordination needs and the CEO pay gap: A competitive test of economic and behavioral views. *Academy of Management Journal*, **44**(1), 96–117.

Hogan, T.D. and McPheters, L.R. (1980). Executive compensation: Performance versus personal characteristics, *Southern Economic Journal*, **46**(4), 1060–70.

Kahneman, D. and Tversky, A. (1979). Prospect theory: An analysis of decision under risk. *Econometrica*, **47**(2), 263–92.

Khurana, R. (2002). *Searching for a corporate savior: The irrational quest for charismatic CEOs*. Princeton, NJ: Princeton Press.

Lazear, E.P. and Rosen, S. (1981). Rank-order tournaments as optimum labor contracts. *Journal of Political Economy*, **89**(5), 841–64.

Lindenberg, E.B. and Ross, S.A. (1981). Tobin's q ratio and industrial organization. *Journal of Business*, **54**(1), 1–32.

Lorsch, J. and MacIver, E. (1989). *Pawns or potentates: The reality of America's corporate boards*. Cambridge, MA: Harvard Business School Press.

McGrath, R.G., Ferrier, W.J., and Mendelow, A.L. (2004). Real options as engines of choice and heterogeneity. *Academy of Management Review*, **29**(1), 86–101.

Miller, M.H. and Modigliani, F. (1961). Dividend policy, growth, and the valuation of shares. *Journal of Business*, **34**(4), 411–33.

Myers, S. (1977). Determinants of corporate borrowing. *Journal of Financial Economics*, **5**(2), 147–75.

Myers, S.C. and Turnbull, S.M. (1977). Capital budgeting and the capital asset pricing model: Good news and bad news. *Journal of Finance*, **32**(2), 321–33.

O'Reilly, C.A., Main, B.G., and Crystal, G.S. (1988). CEO compensation as tournament and social comparison: A tale of two theories. *Administrative Science Quarterly*, **33**(2), 257–74.

Picoult, M.M. and Picoult, J. (2003). Nearly defunct CEO leaves his position to pursue other opportunities. *Business Insurance*, December.

Puffer, S. and Weintrop, J. (1991). Corporate performance and CEO turnover: A comparison of performance indicators. *Administrative Science Quarterly*, **36**(1), 1–19.

Sellers, P. (2002). Home Depot: Something to prove. *Fortune*, **145**(13), 68.

Skinner, D.J. and Sloan, R. (2002). Earnings surprises, growth expectations and stock returns or don't let an earnings torpedo sink your portfolio. *Review of Accounting Studies*, **7**(2–3), 289–312.

Sonnenfeld, J.A. and Ward, A. (2007). *Firing back. How great leaders rebound after career disasters*. Cambridge, MA: Harvard Business School Press.

Ward, A., Bishop, K., and Sonnenfeld, J.A. (1999). Pyrrhic victories: The cost to the board of ousting the CEO. *Journal of Organizational Behavior*, **20**(5), 767–81.

Ward, A., Sonnenfeld, J., and Kimberly, J.R. (1995). In search of a kingdom: Determinants of subsequent career outcomes for chief executives who are fired. *Human Resource Management*, **34**(1), 117–39.

APPENDIX 13A   CALCULATING THE EXPECTATIONS INDEX FOR FORTUNE 500 FIRMS

The Expectations Index is derived from four values, (1) investment intensity, (2) annual growth of the market value of assets, (3) market to book value of the assets, and (4) R&D expenses to book value of assets (Gaver and Gaver, 1993; Baber et al., 1996). Each of these values reflects a form of investment in future options. Investment intensity is the sum of expenses for capital items, R&D, and acquisitions, as a proportion of depreciation. Thus, it reflects true growth in capital and research-related investment. Annual growth in the market value of assets reflects the market assessment of the change in asset value. Thus, it captures both marginal investment by the firm and changing assessments of those investments by the market. Market to book value reflects the market assessments of the value-added by the firm's management and strategic positioning, in relation to the depreciated value of the assets. Finally, R&D, as a proportion of asset book value, reflects the tangible investment in new products and services, as a proportion of the actual investment in assets. Across the sample, the means and standard deviations of these values were:

1.   2.40 / 1.82 – investment intensity;
2.   1.02 / 1.39 – growth in asset value;
3.   1.91 / 1.58 – market to book asset value;
4.   0.02 / 0.02 – R&D expense to book value.

Each of these measures is an indicator of the option value that a firm is creating. By combining these measures, we get a robust estimate of that underlying future value. The procedure involves factor analysis and the extraction of the principal component of common variance. That shared variance among the measures is the common indicator of future value. The principal component loadings are provided below:

1.   0.609 – investment intensity;
2.   0.367 – growth in asset value;
3.   0.781 – market to book asset value;
4.   0.732 – R&D expense to book value.

The loadings represent the correlation between the measures and the common factor. Thus, the loadings were used as weights, to adjust each measure. The measures were first adjusted for variance in the scale, by dividing each firm's value by the sample mean. The adjusted values were then multiplied by the appropriate weights and the resulting products were summed to form an index of expected future value.

APPENDIX 13B   CALCULATING THE EXPECTATIONS INDEX FOR NCAA FOOTBALL PROGRAMS

To calculate the Expectations Index for the NCAA sample, the procedure was virtually the same. The measures, however, had to be different. The challenge was to find measures that could indicate the development of option value for the future. We chose seven measures that seemed to satisfy the criteria. They were: (1) historical winning percentage, (2) four-year winning percentage, (3) bowl appearances in the past five years, (4) preseason rank for the past four years, (5) stadium size, (6) recruiting budget, and (7) athletic budget. These measures all reflect resource and reputation generating actions that could benefit the program in the future or that, in their absence, would constrain the program in the future. In athletics, success facilitates better facilities, greater publicity, better recruiting, and healthier budgets. Thus, our measures were designed to capture recent and general levels of success and reputation, along with the flow of resources into the program. As these indicators increased, a program would have greater capability into the future. As such, these measures served the same purpose as the measures in the previous sample. Across the sample, the means and standard deviations of these values were:

1.   0.562 / 0.075 – historical winning percentage;
2.   0.469 / 0.165 – four-year winning percentage;
3.   01.79 / 1.66 – five-year bowl appearances;
4.   11.16 / 17.73 – four-year average preseason rank;
5.   57.59 / 19.88 – stadium size (in thousands);
6.   0.389 / 1.73 – recruiting budget (in millions);
7.   25.6 / 11.01 – athletic budget (in millions).

Because each measure is an imperfect indicator of the underlying option value, we again used factor analysis to extract the principal component of common variation. The principal component loadings were:

1.   0.794 – historical winning percentage;
2.   0.775 – four-year winning percentage;
3.   0.821 – five-year bowl appearances;
4.   0.849 – four-year average preseason rank;
5.   0.794 – stadium size;
6.   0.788 – recruiting budget;
7.   0.793 – athletic budget.

After correcting for scale variation by dividing each measure by the sample mean, we weighted the measures according to these loadings. We then summed the products to yield an index value for each program.

14 CEO leadership: a research agenda
Yan (Anthea) Zhang

The question of "how do CEOs matter" has attracted significant scholarly attention in the past decades (e.g., Hambrick and Mason, 1984; Hambrick and Fukutomi, 1991; Shen and Cannella, 2002a, 2002b; Zhang and Rajagopalan, 2004; Zhang, 2008). Previous studies on this topic can be divided into two broad groups based upon their treatment of time. The first group focuses on the snapshots typically at the time when CEO leadership changes: either when a CEO is newly appointed or when a CEO leaves office. Studies in this group have examined associations between executive characteristics and behaviors, and organizational and environmental contexts (e.g., Gupta and Govindarajan, 1984; Datta and Rajagopalan, 1998; Zhang and Rajagopalan, 2003, 2004). Beck and Wiersema discuss how the governance context affects CEO dismissal in Chapter 15 of this volume.

Inspired by Hambrick and Fukutomi (1991), the second group has focused on how the length of CEO tenure in office can affect organizational outcomes. Hambrick and Fukutomi (1991) divided a CEO's tenure into five seasons: response to mandate, experimentation, selection of an enduring theme, convergence, and dysfunction. They argue that a CEO's leadership in terms of his/her commitment to a paradigm, task knowledge, information diversity, task interest, and power changes over the course of his/her tenure. Based upon this argument, previous studies have examined the impact of CEO tenure and found that CEO tenure can have a significant impact on firm strategy and performance (e.g., Miller and Shamsie, 2001; Wu et al., 2005; Henderson et al., 2006; Simsek, 2007).

With few exceptions (e.g., Bertrand and Schoar, 2003; Zhang and Rajagopalan, 2009), these two groups of research have remained isolated from each other. Studies in the first group have focused only on the snapshots of when CEO leadership changes and have largely ignored how CEO leadership may change over time. On the other hand, studies in the second group have mainly focused on the effect of CEO tenure per se and have largely ignored the initial differences among the CEOs. In other words, these studies have implicitly assumed that all CEOs are the same when they assume the CEO position and examine how their impact on organizational outcomes may change as their tenure in office increases.

As one exception, Bertrand and Schoar (2003) conducted a manager–firm matched panel data set to track the top managers across different firms over time. They found that manager fixed effects matter for a wide range of corporate decisions. Their findings suggest that managers have their specific "styles" that persist over time and across contexts. In a recent study, Zhang and Rajagopalan (2009) examined how the initial differences between outside CEOs and inside CEOs may vary across CEO tenure. They found that the differential relationship between strategic change and performance between outside CEOs and inside CEOs does not exist in the early stage of the CEOs' tenure, but exist in the later stage of the CEOs' tenure. Their findings suggest that the initial differences between outside CEOs and inside CEOs can have an imprinting effect over the course of CEO tenure. Overall, these two studies suggest that the pre-existing differences among CEOs and the effect of CEO tenure should be considered jointly rather than in isolation. On the one hand, the initial differences among CEOs can affect the dynamism of CEO leadership during CEO tenure. On the other hand, the dynamism of CEO leadership during his/her tenure can affect their differences when and after they leave office.

Based upon this premise, in this chapter, I review recent developments in the CEO leadership literature and develop a research agenda for CEO leadership. First, I divide the CEO career into five major stages: appointing a new CEO, taking charge, tenure as CEO, departure, and post-departure. I identify key issues at each of the stages and examine the connections between these stages, assuming that what happens in an earlier stage can affect what happens in a later stage.

The framework is depicted in Figure 14.1. At the first stage of "appointing a new CEO," the critical issue is to identify the key characteristics of the new CEO and to answer the question of "why did the firm appoint this CEO?" At the second stage of "taking charge," the critical issues are twofold: how does the new CEO affect the firm's organizational outcomes post-succession and can the new CEO survive this initial stage? The CEO's characteristics can affect what will happen to the firm and to the CEO at this stage. After passing the "taking charge" stage, the CEO continues his/her tenure as CEO. In this stage, it is important to understand how the length of CEO tenure in office can affect organizational outcomes. There are two other critical issues: when the CEO takes the board chair title (some CEOs assume the board chair title at the time of taking the CEO position) and when the CEO appoints an heir apparent. A CEO's experience as CEO can be affected by his/her characteristics and his/her actions and performance at the "taking charge" stage.

At the fourth stage of "departure," the critical issues are when the CEO will leave office and whether the CEO will voluntarily leave office or be dismissed. The CEO's disposition can be affected by his/her performance as CEO as well as the CEO's characteristics (such as firm insider versus outsider). The CEO's disposition (voluntary turnover versus dismissal) can further affect the choice of the successor CEO and how the successor CEO fares in the "taking charge" stage. In a normal succession, the incumbent CEO passes the CEO position to the successor CEO and the cycle starts again. However, some firms have an interim CEO before appointing a permanent successor CEO. This raises two questions: under what conditions will a firm have an interim CEO instead of appointing a permanent CEO and how does the appointment of an interim CEO affect the firm's organizational outcomes (a question also raised by Beckman and Burton in Chapter 3 of this volume)? When a CEO steps down from the top post, his/her career is not necessarily over – leading to the "post-departure" stage. Some former CEOs remain to serve on their firm's board, typically as the board chair, and/or serve as outside directors of other firms. The former CEO's remaining as the board chair can influence the level of managerial discretion of the successor CEO and thus the successor's strategic choice and performance. In some cases, when the firm does not perform well and/or the successor CEO does not meet the firm's expectations, the former CEO retakes the CEO position to replace the successor CEO. Then the questions are: under what conditions will a former CEO return to the CEO position and how can a "returning king" affect the firm's organizational outcomes?

This chapter differs from Hambrick and Fukutomi (1991) in an important way.

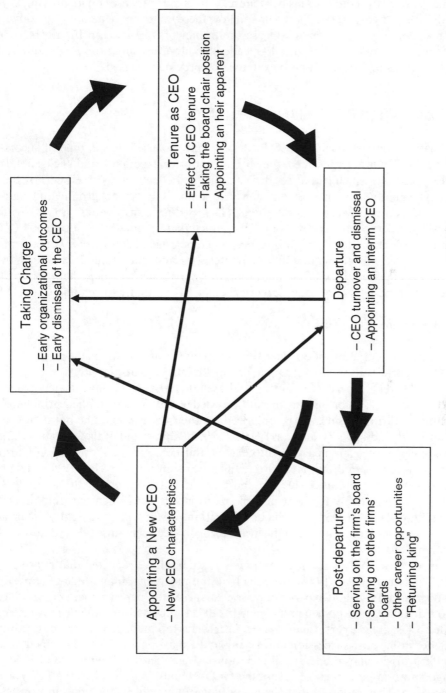

Source: Author.

Figure 14.1   Key issues at various stages of CEO career

Hambrick and Fukutomi (1991) examined how a CEO's leadership in terms of his/her commitment to a paradigm, task knowledge, information diversity, task interest, and power changes over the course of his/her tenure. This chapter focuses on identifying key issues at different stages of a CEO's career and how these issues are related to each other. In the remainder of this chapter, I will use the framework depicted in Figure 14.1 to review the recent development of the CEO leadership literature and propose hypotheses for important links that have not been examined by previous studies.

THE STAGE OF APPOINTING A NEW CEO

As noted earlier, most studies on CEO leadership have focused on the time of succession. When new CEOs are appointed, they bring their prior experience and backgrounds to the CEO position, which can affect their actions and effectiveness as CEO. For this reason, previous studies are interested in newly appointed CEOs' background and characteristics and examine two broad questions: (1) why does a firm choose a CEO with such characteristics (i.e., antecedents of CEO characteristics) and (2) how do the CEO's characteristics affect the firm's organizational outcomes such as strategy and performance post-succession? The major CEO characteristics and background examined by previous studies include the CEO's firm origin (insider versus outsider), heir apparent experience, prior industry experience, experience as CEO of another firm, and so on.

A Newly Appointed CEO's Firm Origin

A CEO's firm origin in terms of outsider versus insider status is perhaps the most examined CEO characteristic in the CEO leadership literature. Outside CEOs and inside CEOs bring different experiences (Harris and Helfat, 1997; Zhang and Rajagopalan, 2003). While inside CEOs bring firm-specific knowledge and skills from their prior experience within the firm, outside CEOs are prized for their nonfirm-specific but relatively novel knowledge and skills (Harris and Helfat, 1997; Zhang and Rajagopalan, 2003). Existing studies have examined the antecedents and consequences of a CEO's firm origin. It has been reported that intra-firm CEO succession is positively associated with firm size and prior performance (Dalton and Kesner, 1983; Guthrie and Datta, 1997, 1998). It is also more likely to occur in firms where inside constituencies are powerful (Boeker and Goodstein, 1993; Cannella and Lubatkin, 1993), when the pool of internal managerial talents is large, and when the firm's prior strategy remains stable (Zhang and Rajagopalan, 2003).

In terms of succession's consequences, previous studies have reported that relative to an inside CEO, an outside CEO is more likely to initiate a large magnitude of strategic change (Wiersema, 1995) and experience poor post-succession performance (Zajac, 1990; Shen and Cannella, 2002a). Shen and Cannella (2002a) reported that the negative effect of outside CEOs on firm performance is stronger when top management team turnover rate is higher in the post-succession era. Zhang and Rajagopalan (2009) examined how a CEO's firm origin may moderate the relationship between the magnitude of strategic change and firm performance across the CEO's tenure instead of in the few years after succession. They reported that the magnitude of strategic change has an inverted

U-shaped relationship with firm performance and outside CEO origin can amplify this relationship so that the positive effect of strategic change on firm performance at lower levels of change and the negative effect of strategic change on firm performance at higher levels of change will both be stronger in firms led by outside CEOs than in firms led by inside CEOs.

A Newly Appointed CEO's Prior Industry Experience

Zhang and Rajagopalan (2003) divided newly appointed CEOs into three categories based upon their firm and industry origins: intra-firm succession, intra-industry (but outside-firm) succession, and outside-industry succession. They proposed and supported the argument that the supply and demand conditions of the industry-level managerial labor market can affect the industry origin of a newly appointed CEO. Specifically, relative to an outside-industry new CEO, an intra-industry new CEO is more likely to be selected when the supply of managerial talents in the industry is abundant as indicated by a large number of similarly sized or larger firms in the industry and a high level of strategic homogeneity among firms in the industry. Further, an intra-industry new CEO is more likely to be selected when the firm's demand of industry-specific knowledge is high as indicated by a high level of the firm's strategic conformity to the industry's central tendency.

Most studies on CEO firm and industry origins have treated them as dichotomy variables. Finkelstein and Hambrick (1996) suggested conceptualizing new CEO's "outsiderness" as a continuum, referring to the extent to which a new CEO brings different leadership style, knowledge, skills, and perspective to a firm based on his/her previous experience in other firms and industries. As a response to this suggestion, Karaevli (2007) measured a new CEO's "outsiderness" as an index variable by summing the inversed standardized (Z-score) firm and industry tenure of the new CEO and found that a new CEO's "outsiderness" has no direct relationship with the firm's post-succession performance. However, a new CEO's "outsiderness" is associated with positive performance under certain conditions such as lower pre-succession firm performance, lower post-succession strategic change, and higher post-succession executive team turnover.

A Newly Appointed CEO's Heir Apparent Experience

A CEO's heir apparent experience occurs when a newly appointed CEO has been in the COO and/or president position and worked with the predecessor CEO in advance of the actual succession event (Vancil, 1987; Cannella and Shen, 2001; Zhang and Rajagopalan, 2004). Vancil (1987) noted that "passing the baton" to an heir apparent is the most common mode for CEO succession in Corporate America. Zhang and Rajagopalan (2004) theorized that the learning benefits of an heir apparent experience accrue to the heir as well as to the firm. On the one hand, the heir has the opportunity to carry out some of the tasks of the CEO position and to thereby acquire and enhance position-specific knowledge and develop broader leadership skills consistent with the position. On the other hand, the firm can conduct a focused assessment of the heir's capabilities (cognitive and interpersonal) and continuously update its evaluation of whether the heir's capabilities fit the CEO position. The firm then can use this evaluation to subsequently decide whether or not to promote the heir apparent. Thus, a CEO's heir apparent experience can reduce the performance risks after succession.

Zhang and Rajagopalan (2004) examined both the antecedents and performance consequence of a CEO's heir apparent experience. They found that a CEO with the heir apparent experience – that is, relay CEO succession – is more likely to occur when the number of internal candidates for the CEO position is small and when pre-succession firm performance is good. They also found that a CEO with heir apparent experience outperforms an inside CEO without heir apparent experience and an outside CEO. This effect is particularly stronger under more "challenging" succession contexts as characterized as lower pre-succession firm performance, higher post-succession strategic instability, and higher post-succession industry instability.

A Newly Appointed CEO's Prior CEO Experience

A newly appointed CEO's prior CEO experience refers to whether the CEO has been a CEO of another firm before assuming the CEO position in the focal firm. Khurana (2001) argued that new CEOs who have been CEOs in other firms have a track record that may equate to an understanding of the function and duties of a CEO. For this reason, a newly appointed CEO's prior CEO experience may reduce this CEO's performance risk after succession. Zhang (2008), however, found that a newly appointed CEO's prior CEO experience does not affect the likelihood that the newly appointed CEO will be dismissed with a short tenure (e.g., within three years after succession).

In the era when CEOs were typically promoted from within the firm and stayed in office till their retirement age, a CEO's prior CEO experience was not an important issue because few CEOs had prior CEO experience. However, it has been a global trend in recent years that the rate of CEO dismissals is increasing and the mean CEO tenure is declining (Lucier et al., 2005). According to a recent Booz Allen Hamilton study of the world's largest 2500 publicly traded corporations, the rate of CEO dismissals escalated to the point that they represented nearly one-third of all CEO turnovers in 2004, which was a 300 percent increase over 1995 – the earliest year benchmarked (Lucier et al., 2005). Meanwhile, the mean tenure of departing CEOs has declined from 11.4 years in 1995 to 8.8 years in 2004 in North America, and from 8.8 years in 1995 to 6.6 years in 2004 globally (ibid., p. 8). As an increasing number of CEOs leave office with a short tenure and with a young age, they likely will become candidates for other firms' CEO positions. Thus, hiring a CEO with prior CEO experience becomes a more common phenomenon. Future research may further examine this interesting question. In general, new CEOs hired from outside the firm are more likely to have prior CEO experience than those promoted from within the firm. While outside CEOs typically suffer from the liability of being an outsider relative to inside CEOs, outside CEOs with prior CEO experience should be better off than those without prior CEO experience. This is because prior CEO experience offers important opportunities for them to learn the task that is specific to the CEO position so that even though they lack knowledge about the focal firm, they have a good understanding of the CEO's job. Moreover, previous studies have suggested that new CEOs tend to enter the job with a relatively high commitment to a paradigm, which is built upon their prior experience (Gabarro, 1987; Hambrick and Fukutomi, 1991). Thus, a new CEO with prior CEO experience tends to copy his/her prior strategy as CEO if his/her prior CEO experience was successful. In contrast, if his/her CEO experience was not successful, he/she tends to deviate from his/her prior strategy:

> *Proposition 1:* Compared with outside CEOs without prior CEO experience, outside CEOs with prior CEO experience are associated with better performance and lower performance variation in the post-succession period.

> *Proposition 2:* If a CEO with prior CEO experience voluntarily left his/her prior CEO position, his/her strategic choices tend to be consistent with his/her prior strategic choices; if a CEO with prior CEO experience was dismissed from his/her prior CEO position, his/her strategic choices tend to deviate from his/her prior strategic choices.

Other Backgrounds of a Newly Appointed CEO

Datta and Rajagopalan (1998) examined a broad range of background characteristics of newly appointed CEOs including age, firm tenure, educational level, and functional background. The authors found that industry structure – that is, industry product differentiation and industry growth rate – plays an important, but not pervasive, role in explaining variations in newly selected CEOs. However, they found very limited support for the normative view that firms that match CEO successor characteristics to industry structure realize better post-succession performance than those with lower levels of fit. Datta et al. (2003) created an index measure of "new CEO openness to change" by combining multiple characteristics (age, firm tenure, and educational background) and found that it was negatively related to the firm's strategic persistence in the post-succession era and this relationship was stronger in industries with greater managerial discretion.

THE STAGE OF TAKING CHARGE

The stage of taking charge (Gabarro, 1987) is the early stage in a CEO's tenure in which he/she takes actions to "develop an early track record, legitimacy, and a political foothold" (Hambrick and Fukutomi, 1991, p.728). In this stage, the CEO's actions tend to reflect his/her going-in mandate (Gabarro, 1987) and his/her going-in credentials (Hambrick and Fukutomi, 1991). Based on these arguments, previous studies have focused on a firm's post-succession strategic change and performance, linking them to important succession contexts (e.g., pre-succession firm performance) and the characteristics of the CEO. A larger magnitude of strategic change is more likely to occur if pre-succession firm performance has been poor. Also, as discussed in the earlier section, previous studies have shown that the new CEO's characteristics and background (e.g., firm and industry origins, heir apparent experience, etc.) can affect the firm's strategic change and performance in the post-succession period.

In a recent study, Zhang (2008) identified a new issue that is important at this stage: the dismissal of newly appointed CEOs. Zhang (2008) defined the dismissal of a newly appointed CEO as a dismissal of a CEO with tenure in office of three years or less. The dismissal of newly appointed CEOs differs from the dismissal of CEOs with relatively long tenure in that the dismissal of newly appointed CEOs is likely the outcome of information asymmetry between the firm's board of directors and the CEO at the time of succession, while for CEOs of relatively long tenure, information asymmetry should be less of an issue (ibid.). She argued that a new CEO selection decision is usually made under conditions of information asymmetry because the CEO candidates typically possess more information about their true competencies than the board, and thus, they may misrepresent such competencies, which makes the board incapable of selecting a new CEO whose competencies fit the firm's task contingencies (Zajac, 1990). However, after the succession, the board can update its estimate of the new CEO's ability as it observes and evaluates how the new CEO applies his or her existing knowledge and skills and develops new task knowledge and skills required for the successful execution of the position. A board of directors may dismiss the newly appointed CEO based on updated information after the succession (Zhang, 2008). Based upon these arguments, Zhang (2008) proposed that the higher the level of information asymmetry between the CEO and the board at the time of succession, the larger the likelihood that the CEO will be dismissed with a short tenure after succession. In support of this argument, she found that the likelihood of new CEO dismissal is positively related to the CEO's outside origin, the dismissal of the predecessor CEO, and board composition.

As the rate of CEO dismissals increases and the mean CEO tenure declines (Lucier et al., 2005), the dismissal of newly appointed CEOs becomes an increasingly important issue. Future studies can examine its other antecedents and its consequences to both the firm and to the dismissed CEO. For example, the pay gap of the newly appointed CEO with the predecessor CEO and/or to other top management team members may explain the dismissal of a newly appointed CEO. If the new CEO's pay is significantly higher than that of the predecessor CEO or other top management team members, that creates a high expectation on the new CEO, which increases the chance of disappointment. Also, a large pay gap between the CEO and other top management team members separates the CEO from other top management team members. If something undesirable happens, the CEO is easily identified as target for the blame (see Ward, Amason, Lee, and Graffin in Chapter 13 of this volume for a discussion of CEO scapegoating). For these reasons, a new CEO with significantly higher pay is more likely to be dismissed with a short tenure:

Proposition 3: The pay gap between a newly appointed CEO and the predecessor CEO is positively related to the likelihood that the CEO will be dismissed with a short tenure.

Proposition 4: The pay gap between a newly appointed CEO and other top management team members is positively related to the likelihood that the CEO will be dismissed with a short tenure.

As for the consequences, the dismissal of a newly appointed CEO will lead to poor firm performance and also increase the likelihood that the subsequent CEO will be dismissed with a short tenure. This is because the dismissal of a newly appointed CEO can result in organizational disruption that can lead to lost opportunities (Khurana, 2001). Moreover, the dismissal of a newly appointed CEO often makes a firm bypass a normal succession process and forces the firm to select another new CEO in an unplanned manner, which may lead to a vicious cycle in the firm's successions (Wiersema, 2002; Zhang, 2008):

Proposition 5: Firms that dismissed their newly appointed CEOs have lower subsequent performance.

Proposition 6: The dismissal of a newly appointed CEO is positively related to the likelihood that the successor CEO will be dismissed with a short tenure.

TENURE AS CEO

The Effect of the Length of CEO Tenure in Office

Hambrick and Fukutomi (1991), based upon their five-season model, proposed that "On average, CEOs whose tenure span all five seasons will experience their peak performance at some intermediate point in their time in office. Performance very early and very late in the tenure will be lower" (p. 732). Based upon this argument, a number of empirical studies (e.g., Miller and Shamsie, 2001; Wu et al., 2005; Henderson et al., 2006; Simsek, 2007) have examined how CEO tenure may affect firm strategic change and performance. Miller and Shamsie (2001) found that (1) top executive tenure has a negative effect on product line experimentation, (2) top executive tenure has an inverted U-shaped effect on firm performance, and (3) top executive tenure moderates the relationship between product line experimentation and firm performance. Wu et al. (2005) found that CEO tenure has an inverted U-shaped relationship with firm invention performance and that this relationship varies with the level of technological dynamism in the environment. Henderson et al. (2006) found that (1) in a dynamic environment, CEO tenure has a negative relationship with firm performance; and (2) in a stable environment, CEO tenure has an inverted U-shaped relationship with firm performance. Simsek (2007) found that CEO tenure is positively related to the top management team's risk-taking propensity.

As noted earlier, these studies have solely focused on the effect of CEO tenure and largely ignored the initial differences among the CEOs. As shown by Bertrand and Schoar (2003) and Zhang and Rajagopalan (2009), further research on CEO tenure needs to simultaneously consider the pre-existing differences between CEOs and the impact of CEO tenure in order to examine what pre-existing differences between CEOs may persist or change over the course of CEO tenure. We may conceptualize the initial differences between CEOs as the differences in their pre-succession learning experience (does the CEO have firm-specific, industry-specific, and CEO-position experience?), while CEO tenure captures the CEO's post-succession learning experience (how long has the CEO learned on the job?). It is important to examine how pre-succession and post-succession learning experience can jointly affect a CEO's actions and performance in office.

Assuming the Board Chair Position

For a CEO, taking the position of the chair of the board of directors is a milestone event in his/her tenure. Most previous studies on this topic focusing on the organizational consequences of CEO duality – that is, a person holds both the CEO and board chair positions – have yielded no consistent findings. As Daily and Dalton (1997, p. 11) concluded, research on CEO duality is "much ado about nothing." The lack of consistent findings on the performance impact of CEO duality is probably because CEO duality is a double-edged sword (Finkelstein and D'Aveni, 1884). On the one hand, the consolidation of these two most important positions in a firm can entrench the CEO and thus reduce a board's ability to effectively monitor and discipline the CEO (ibid.). On the other hand, the consolidation of the two positions establishes a unity of command at the top of the firm that can clarify decision-making authority (ibid.). As these two effects may offset each other, CEO duality has no consistent impact on a firm's performance.

In comparison, previous studies have found relatively consistent evidence that CEOs who are also the board chair are more powerful than those who are not, thus CEO duality can affect results related to the CEO – his/her disposition and the choice of his/her successor. For example, Ocasio (1994) found that a separate board chair increased the rate of CEO turnover. Cannella and Lubatkin (1993) found that CEO duality is negatively related to the likelihood of choosing an outside successor. Zajac and Westphal (1996) found that a CEO who is the board chair is more likely to have a successor who is similar to the CEO in age, functional background, degree type, and educational affiliation. Therefore, the best way to understand CEO duality probably is not from the efficiency perspective (i.e., is the consolidation or the separation of the CEO and the board chair positions better for firm performance?) but instead from the perspective of CEO power consolidation (i.e., duality enhances a CEO's power regardless of its performance impact).

From this CEO power consolidation perspective, there is an important question worthy of examination: what factors can prompt or prohibit a CEO's taking the board chair position? Zhang (2001) examined this issue. She found that inside CEOs are more likely to have a separate board chair in the first year of their tenure than in the later years of their tenure and that firm performance does not affect whether inside CEOs are awarded the board chair position. In contrast, an outside CEO's taking the board chair position is best explained by firm performance. Outside CEOs of better-performing firms are more likely to have the board chair position. These results suggest that outside CEOs and inside CEOs follow different power consolidation processes. For inside CEOs, their power consolidation is a process of routine: at the beginning, the predecessor CEO passes the CEO position to him/her but remains as the board chair for a short time period to guarantee a smooth transition; over time, the CEO will assume the board chair position, independent of the firm's performance. In contrast, outside CEOs' power consolidation is the result of bargaining. Some outside CEOs, who are in a more powerful bargaining position, can negotiate the board chair title as a condition of accepting the CEO position. Thus, there is no difference between the first year and the later years of their tenure in the likelihood of having a separate board chair. Also, outside CEOs of high-performing firms are more likely to have the board chair title because they have "earned" this title.

Appointing an Heir Apparent

Appointing an heir apparent is another milestone event in a CEO's tenure. Vancil (1987) observed that many firms identified an heir apparent in the COO and/or president position in advance of the actual succession event and used this position to groom the next CEO. As noted by Hambrick and Cannella (2004, p. 959):

the decision to have a COO represents a major structural choice: it explicitly divides between two people a set of top-level roles that are typically fulfilled by one person; it draws a structural distinction between strategy formulation and implementation; it adds an organizational layer; and it adds a highly-paid executive position to the organization's costs.

Previous studies on this topic have examined the antecedents of having an heir apparent (Zhang and Rajagopalan, 2002; Hambrick and Cannella, 2004) and the impact of having an heir apparent on the firm (Shen and Cannella, 2003; Hambrick and Cannella, 2004; Zhang, 2006; Marcel, 2009), on the CEO (Zhang, 2006), on the heir (Cannella and Shen, 2001), and on the subsequent successor CEO (Cannella and Lubatkin, 1993; Zhang and Rajagopalan, 2003). These studies in general have followed two different theoretical perspectives: the strategic contingency perspective (Zhang and Rajagopalan, 2003; Hambrick and Cannella, 2004; Marcel, 2009) and the power and politics perspective (Cannella and Lubatkin, 1993; Cannella and Shen, 2001; Zhang and Rajagopalan, 2002; Zhang, 2006).

Taking a strategic contingency perspective, Hambrick and Cannella (2004) examined why some CEOs have COOs while others do not and when it is most beneficial to performance to have a COO. They found that CEOs who lack experience in operational activities and in managing the focal firm are relatively likely to have a COO/president. However, they found no support for the contingency view in explaining when COOs are most beneficial. Instead, they found that CEOs who have COOs deliver lower organizational performance than those who do not. Also taking a strategic contingency perspective, Marcel (2009) proposed that the presence of a COO/president can create TMT-level information-processing benefits by dividing the leadership role between two executives and bringing the perspectives of two executives to strategic decisions. In contrast to Hambrick and Cannella's finding (2004), Marcel (2009) reported that the presence of a COO/president is positively related to subsequent firm performance and this positive relationship is contingent upon some characteristics of the top management team. Shen and Cannella (2003) found that the stock market did not display a significant reaction when an heir apparent was appointed, but reacted negatively when the heir exited from the firm and reacted positively when the heir was promoted to the CEO position.

Taking a power and politics perspective, Cannella and Lubatkin (1993) found that the presence of an heir apparent can decouple the linkage between poor firm performance and the choice of an outside CEO successor. Consistently, Zhang and Rajagopalan (2003) reported that that the presence of a COO/president increases the likelihood of inside CEO succession. Also taking a power and politics perspective, Cannella and Shen (2001) were interested in the tenure outcome of the heir apparent – promotion versus exit. They found that CEO power decreases the likelihood of the heir's promotion to the CEO position, board power increases the likelihood of the heir's exit, and an heir who arises from within the firm is less likely to exit. Zhang (2006) was interested in how the presence of a COO/president may affect the CEO. She proposed that the presence of a COO/president represents a discipline to the incumbent CEO by providing an alternative candidate for the CEO post. In support of this argument, Zhang (2006) found that under conditions of lower firm performance, the presence of a COO/president increases the firm's magnitude of strategic change and the likelihood of CEO dismissal while under conditions of higher firm performance, the presence of a COO/president has no impact on the firm's magnitude of strategic change and the likelihood of CEO dismissal.

From a power and politics perspective, Zhang and Rajagopalan (2002) examined under what conditions a CEO is likely to have an heir apparent. They found that relative to outside CEOs, inside CEOs are more likely to have an heir apparent. Both outside CEOs and inside CEOs are more likely to appoint an heir apparent after taking the board chair position. Moreover, outside CEOs are more likely to appoint an heir apparent under conditions of good firm performance while performance has no impact on inside CEOs' appointment of an heir apparent. These results suggest that the initial differences between outside and inside CEOs affect their appointment of an heir apparent during their tenure. For inside CEOs, appointing an heir is part of the firm's succession routine, in which the CEOs typically first take the board chair position (power consolidation) and then appoint an heir (power sharing), and firm performance has little impact on this power transition. In contrast, for outside CEOs, CEO succession planning is not part of the firm's routine. Also, because outside CEOs generally suffer from a liability of outsideness, they are more vulnerable to potential challenge from an heir apparent (Zhang, 2006). Thus, outside CEOs tend to appoint an heir apparent only when their power is consolidated and the heir's challenge is less a concern – for example, they have the board chair position and the firm has good performance.

THE STAGE OF DEPARTURE

CEO Turnover and Dismissal

An important question at the stage of departure is when a CEO will leave office (turnover versus remain in office). Some studies have further divided CEO turnover into voluntary turnover and dismissal. Because voluntary turnover such as retirement is usually part of a routine, these studies have focused on explaining CEO dismissal. Fredrickson et al. (1988) proposed a comprehensive framework to explain the occurrence of CEO dismissal. In their framework, actual current poor firm performance increases the likelihood of CEO dismissal and this relationship can be moderated by social-political factors such as the board of directors' expectations and attributions, the board's allegiances and values, availabilities of alternative CEO candidates, and the incumbent CEO's power.

Most empirical studies on CEO turnover/dismissal have more or less examined the effect of firm performance and power (the incumbent CEO's power vis-à-vis the board or vis-à-vis other senior executives), and their interactions (e.g., Coughlin and Schmidt, 1985; Boeker, 1992; Ocasio, 1994; Shen and Cannella, 2002b; Zhang, 2006). For example, Ocasio (1994) found that poor firm performance triggers CEO turnover when combined with long prior board tenure of the CEO, large board size, and more inside board members. Boeker (1992) found that while poor firm performance increases the likelihood of CEO dismissal, powerful CEOs can use other executives as scapegoats and save their own position. Shen and Cannella (2002b) found that poor firm performance, the CEO's outside origin, proportion of non-CEO inside directors, and ownership of non-CEO inside directors are positively related to the likelihood of CEO dismissal followed by inside succession. Zhang (2006) found that poor firm performance increases the likelihood of CEO dismissal and this relationship is stronger when there is a separate COO/president present in the firm. In line with the power argument, Ocasio (1994) and Shen and Cannella (2002b) also examined the effect of CEO tenure on CEO turnover/dismissal. Ocasio (1994) found an increasing rate of CEO turnover during the first decade of tenure, followed by a low decline afterward. These findings suggest that a CEO's power faces increasing contestation at the beginning and becomes increasingly legitimate and institutionalized. Similarly, Shen and Cannella (2002b) found that CEOs are more likely to be dismissed in the early years of their tenure because their power has not yet been institutionalized.

While most studies on this topic have focused on "actual firm performance," some scholars argue that it is the gap between performance expectations and actual firm performance that triggers a board's decision to remove the CEO. Consistent with this argument, Farrell and Whidbee (2003) and Puffer and Weintrop (1991), both using analyst earnings forecasts as firm performance expectations, found that the probability of CEO turnover increases when the firm's reported earnings per share fall short of analyst forecasts. Consistent with this logic, Haleblian and Rajagopalan (2006) proposed a cognitive model of CEO dismissal, in which the board's perception and attribution of the firm's performance, along with the board's efficacy assessment of the CEO, determine the board's decision on CEO dismissal.

Recent studies have gone beyond the performance–power paradigm and added new insights into explaining CEO turnover/dismissal. Arthaud-Day et al. (2006), for example, found that firms that have financial restatements are more likely to experience subsequent CEO turnover than firms without financial restatements. They argued that financial restatements represent a serious threat to firm legitimacy so that firms tend to remove the stigmatized CEO to aid the firms to regain legitimacy. Focusing on dismissals of newly appointed CEOs, Zhang (2008) found support for the argument that dismissal of a newly appointed CEO is the outcome of information asymmetry at the time of succession so that the level of information asymmetry at the time of succession affects the likelihood of dismissal of a newly appointed CEO. Wiersema and Zhang (2008) focused on the effect of an external third party on a board of directors' decision on CEO dismissal. They found that negative analyst ratings of a firm's stock (low average analyst rating, downgrade in average analyst rating, and the percentage of sell recommendations) increase the likelihood of CEO dismissal and these effects are stronger when the firm's performance is poor and weaker when the analyst community suffers from a credibility crisis.

Another stream of research has examined the consequences of CEO turnover/ dismissal. Friedman and Singh (1989) conceptualized that CEO succession as an adaptive or a disruptive event and thus the effect of CEO succession on firm performance depends upon the succession's context. Using an event study approach, they found that the stock market reacted favorably to CEO successions if they were associated with poor pre-succession performance and were initiated by the board of directors. Worrell et al. (1986) examined stock market reactions to the death of key executives. They found that sudden death of CEOs led to significantly negative stock market reactions. Wiersema (2002) found that firms experiencing CEO dismissal have lower performance than those that have routine CEO successions. Zajac and Westphal (1996) examined how the departing CEO can affect the choice of the successor CEO. They found that a powerful incumbent CEO is more likely to have a successor who is similar to the CEO in age, functional background, degree type, and educational affiliation.

Appointing an Interim CEO

In a normal succession process, the departing CEO passes the CEO position to the successor CEO and then the cycle described in Figure 14.1 starts again. However, some firms appoint an interim CEO instead of a permanent CEO when the incumbent departs. A recent example is General Motors Inc. On 1 December, 2009, CEO Fritz Henderson was ousted by the board of directors because of disagreements about the future of the firm and the speed of the firm's restructuring after its bankruptcy. The board appointed Ed Whitacre, who was the chairman of the board, as the interim CEO while starting to search for a permanent CEO. After seven weeks, the search for a new CEO stopped and Whitacre was named GM's permanent CEO because "this place needs stability. We don't need any more uncertainty" (MSNBC, 2010).

The choice of an interim CEO and the associated antecedents and consequences represent an interesting new phenomenon. A recent study (Mooney et al., 2009) examined the performance antecedents and consequences of an interim CEO succession relative to other types of CEO succession. They found that interim CEO succession is more likely to occur under conditions of poor firm performance. They also found that after an interim CEO succession, investment analysts tend to rate the firm negatively while the stock market does not react significantly. The finding on poor firm performance leading to the choice of an interim CEO is not surprising. Firms with good performance certainly can attract more candidates, both internal and external ones, interested in the CEO position. What other factors affect the occurrence of an interim CEO succession? Like the GM example suggests, a firm tends to choose an interim CEO when the predecessor CEO was dismissed. The dismissal of the predecessor CEO often leads to the bypassing of a normal succession process (Zhang, 2008) so that when the predecessor leaves office, there is no internal candidate ready to receive the baton. In this situation, choosing an interim CEO can buy the board some time to search for a permanent CEO. The effect will be even stronger if the firm's performance is poor and/or the firm's internal managerial labor pool is small. Dismissal of the predecessor, combined with poor firm performance, creates a challenging task in which few candidates would be interested. Also, if the firm's internal managerial labor pool is small, the firm has to look outside to search for a permanent CEO (Zhang and Rajagopalan, 2003). Since external search takes time, the firm would need an interim CEO during the search time:

Proposition 7: Firms are more likely to choose an interim CEO after the dismissal of the predecessor CEO.

Proposition 8: The positive effect of the dismissal of the predecessor CEO on the likelihood of choosing an interim CEO is stronger if the firm's performance is poor.

Proposition 9: The positive effect of the dismissal of the predecessor CEO on the likelihood of choosing an interim CEO is stronger if the firm's internal managerial labor pool is small.

The performance consequences of interim CEO succession is a more complex issue. Mooney et al. (2009) found mixed evidence: investment analysts downgraded the firm's stock while the stock market did not react significantly. When examining the performance consequences of interim CEO succession, the endogeneity issue needs to be considered. Namely, an interim CEO is typically chosen in a difficult succession context, characterized by poor firm performance and/or dismissal of the predecessor CEO. Therefore, the performance impact of an interim CEO succession should not be directly compared with that of a normal CEO succession. Instead, it should be compared with a firm that was in a similar situation but took different actions.

Under conditions of poor performance and/or dismissal of the predecessor, a firm has two choices: choosing an interim CEO or choosing a permanent CEO. Relative to choosing a permanent CEO, using an interim CEO has both pros and cons. On the positive side, using an interim CEO provides an option for the firm. The firm does not need to commit to a permanent CEO immediately: it can promote the interim CEO or continue its search. As Zhang (2008) found, if the predecessor CEO was dismissed, the selection of the new CEO is likely to be made under conditions of a high level of information asymmetry, which can lead to a poor choice of the new CEO and eventually increase the likelihood that the new CEO will be dismissed with a short tenure. Using an interim CEO may provide additional time for the firm to conduct a more comprehensive search for the new CEO and thus avoid the vicious cycle in CEO succession. On the negative side, however, as the GM example shows, having an interim CEO further increases the uncertainty associated with the firm's prospects, which can further delay the firm's turnaround. Therefore, to understand the performance impact of an interim CEO succession, we need to examine when the value of having an option dominates the cost caused by the uncertainty.

THE STAGE OF POST-DEPARTURE

Post-departure Career Concerns

A CEO's career does not end as he/she steps down from the CEO position. For example, after Jack Welch stepped down from the CEO position at General Electric, he started to offer speeches, seminars, and consulting services and also write a column for *Business Week*. After being forced out from the CEO position at HP in 2005, Carly Fiorina expressed an interest in pursuing a career in politics. In a more common situation, a former CEO may serve on his/her firm's board and/or other firms' boards. Brickley et al. (1999) examined retired CEOs' service on their own firms' boards as well as other firms' boards. They found that both are positively and strongly related to his/her performance while CEO. Retention on the CEO's own board depends largely upon stock returns while service on other firms' boards is better explained by the firm's accounting performance. They argued that because what retired CEOs can do depends upon their performance as CEO, the post-departure career concerns represent an additional source of managerial incentives for CEOs when they are in office (ibid.).

What other factors, in addition to the departing CEO's performance in office, may explain their post-departure career opportunities? The departing CEO's reputation and status as well the firm's reputation and status may matter. In a recent study, Pfarrer et al. (2010; in press) found that firm reputation and celebrity can affect how the stock market reacted to their earnings surprises. Both high-reputation and celebrity firms experience greater rewards for positive earnings surprises and smaller penalties for negative earnings surprises than other firms. These findings suggest that in addition to actual firm performance, firm reputation and status can affect external constituents' perceptions of the firms. Similarly, although firm performance is an overall measure of a CEO's performance, it is usually hard to accurately attribute firm performance to the CEO's leadership versus alternative reasons. Thus, in addition to the firm's actual performance when the CEO was in office, the CEO's and the firm's reputation and status can also influence the CEO's post-departure career opportunities. Other firms may be willing to be associated with these CEOs since status can transfer via association:

Proposition 10: Former CEOs of high reputation/celebrity firms are more likely to serve on other firms' boards or have other career opportunities than other CEOs.

Proposition 11: Former CEOs with high reputation/celebrity are more likely to serve on other firms' boards or have other career opportunities than other CEOs.

On the other side, if a CEO leaves office due to corporate failure or mismanagement, this person can be stigmatized, which can damage his/her social capital as well as the external perceptions of his/her human capital (Wiesenfeld et al., 2008). As a result, the person will be professionally devalued and thus tend to lose career opportunities after they leave the CEO position. For example, Desai et al. (2006) found that 59 percent of the restating firms experienced CEO or president turnover within two years of the restatement, and 92 percent of the managers, who left their positions because of their firms' financial restatement, were unable to secure comparable employment within four years of the restatement announcement. Similarly, Srinivasan (2005) found that outside directors are more likely to leave the board of a company that announces a financial restatement and subsequently to lose directorships at other firms. Applying this logic to the former CEOs, I propose that:

Proposition 12: CEOs who were dismissed from office are less likely to serve on other firms' boards or have other career opportunities than other CEOs.

When the former CEO remains on the firm's board, the former CEO can continuously influence the firm's strategic choice and limit the successor CEO's managerial discretion (Quigley and Hambrick, 2009). If the successor is an insider, the former CEO remaining as the board chair may be less an issue because it is part of a routine and an inside CEO succession typically is associated with little surprise (Zhang, 2008). However, if the successor CEO is an outsider, the former CEO remaining as the board chair represents a threat to the successor CEO. If performance does not meet expectations or the former CEO and the successor CEO disagree on key strategic issues, the outside successor faces an increased chance of dismissal:

Proposition 13: The former CEO remaining as the board chair is associated with smaller strategic change post-succession.

Proposition 14: Under conditions of poor firm performance, an outside CEO is more likely to be dismissed if the former CEO remains as the board chair.

"Returning King"

Another interesting phenomenon in the post-departure stage is that some CEOs resume the CEO position years after leaving office. For example, Michael Dell stepped down from the CEO position at Dell Inc. in 2004 while keeping the board chair position. He resumed the CEO position to replace then CEO Kevin Rollins in January 2007 when the company suffered from slow sales, design glitches, and a rocky start at retail. According to the statement of Dell's board of directors:

> The board believes that Michael's vision and leadership are critical to building Dell's leadership in the technology industry for the long term. There is no better person in the world to run Dell at this time than the man who created the direct model and who has built this company over the last 23 years. (Mingis, 2007)

In another example, Howard Schultz passed the CEO position at Starbucks to Orin Smith in 2000 while keeping the board chair position. Smith retired in 2005 and passed the CEO position to Jim Donald. In January 2008, Howard Schultz took back the CEO position from Jim Donald to turn around the struggling chain of coffee houses. This announcement sent the company's stock up about 9 percent in after-hours trading (MSNBC, 2008). As observed by a security analyst, "Howard Schultz was instrumental in building this business from the ground up, so he is eminently qualified to be the CEO" (ibid.).

In both cases, the returning CEOs have been instrumental in building their companies' strategies[1] and remained in the board chair position after stepping down from the CEO post. Their visions and leadership have not only defined their companies' strategies but also greatly reshaped the landscape of their industries. To a large extent, their images and the images of the companies are closely intertwined. On the one hand, one may argue that since a former CEO who was instrumental in building the company's strategy has close attachment to the strategy, when the strategy no longer works, he/she is the least appropriate person to change the strategy. On the other hand, because a former CEO like that had defined the firm's strategy, any significant change to the firm's strategy can be perceived as a challenge to his/her authority and legacy. It is particularly difficult for another CEO to significantly reshape the firm's strategy if the former CEO is still on the firm's board of directors. Thus, only the former CEO himself/herself has the power to break from the firm's past strategy. Particularly if the former CEO has a large equity stake in the firm, he/she has great interest to turn the firm around. Indeed, both Dell and Schultz have made significant changes since they resumed the CEO position, with some changes more successful than others:

Proposition 15: If a former CEO resumes the firm's CEO position, this tends to be a former CEO who has been instrumental in building the firm's strategy (such as its founder).

Proposition 16: A former CEO who has a large equity stake in the firm is more likely to return when the firm experiences performance problems.

Proposition 17: A returning former CEO tends to initiate greater strategic changes than a new CEO.

THE SYMBOLIC VALUE OF CEOS

So far, I have only discussed the substantive effects of CEOs on the firms they lead. CEOs can also have symbolic value to the firms. Using market signaling theory (Spence, 1973), scholars have examined the signaling role of executive characteristics in conveying firm quality to the financial markets in the initial public offering (IPO) context (e.g., Certo, 2003; Higgins and Gulati, 2003, 2006; Cohen and Dean, 2005). It has been argued that, independent of the effect of the executives' background on their strategic decision making, these observable background characteristics function as signals and are used by critical external constituents to infer the quality of the firm (Certo, 2003). Following this approach, studies have found that the characteristics of the top management team (Higgins and Gulati, 2003, 2006; Cohen and Dean, 2005) provide signals of firm quality, which in turn influences the stock market's valuation of the IPO.

A criticism of this line of research is that it is not possible to ascertain the extent to which the valuation of the IPO is influenced by the signaling role of managerial characteristics or the managerial actions that can be affected by managerial characteristics (Higgins and Gulati, 2006). To address this issue, Zhang and Wiersema (2009) took advantage of a semi-natural experimental setting to examine the signaling role of CEO background that is separated from the substantive effect of CEO background. In response to the wave of corporate scandals (Adelphia, Enron, WorldCom, etc.), in June 2002 the Securities & Exchange Commission (SEC) required chief executive officers (CEOs) and chief financial officers (CFOs) of all publicly traded companies with revenues greater than $1.2 billion to certify their financial statements by 14 August of 2002. In this setting, the attributes of the CEO have no effect on the CEO's action of certifying the firm's financial statement, but they may affect investor perceptions of the credibility of the CEO's certification, which in turn may affect how investors respond to CEO certification. Zhang and Wiersema (2009) found that a CEO's shareholding in the firm, number of the CEO's external directorships, and whether the CEO is associated with the firm's prior financial restatements can significantly affect stock market reaction to the CEO's certification. These findings thus provide strong support to the signaling role of CEO background.

CONCLUSION

In this chapter, I divide the CEO career into five major stages: appointing a new CEO, taking charge, tenure as CEO, departure, and post-departure. I identify key issues at each of the stages and review recent arguments and empirical evidence on these issues. More important, I discuss the connections between these stages in terms of how what happens in an earlier stage can affect what happens in a later stage. With this evolutionary and holistic perspective, I hope this chapter can help us better understand the impact of a CEO on the firm that he/she leads and the impact of the firm on the CEO.

NOTE

1. Schultz was not a founder of Starbucks. He joined Starbucks in 1982 as director of retail operations and marketing, then left three years later to start his own company, Il Giornale. Il Giornale acquired Starbucks in 1987. Schultz then catapulted Starbucks to its global prominence with an ambitious growth agenda that was propelled by its initial public stock offering in 1992.

REFERENCES

Arthaud-Day, M.L., Certo, S.T., Dalton, C.M., and Dalton, D.R. (2006). A changing of the guard: Executive and director turnover following corporate financial restatements. *Academy of Management Journal*, **49**(6), 1119–36.

Bertrand, M. and Schoar, A. (2003). Managing with style: The effect of managers on firm policies. *MIT Press Journals*, **118**(4), 1169–208.

Boeker, W. (1992). Power and managerial dismissal: Scapegoating at the top. *Administrative Science Quarterly*, **37**(3), 400–421.

Boeker, W. and Goodstein, J. (1993). Performance and successor choice: The moderating effects of governance and ownership. *The Academy of Management Journal*, **36**(1), 172–86.

Brickley, J.A., Linck, J.S., and Coles, J.L. (1999). What happens to CEOs after they retire? New evidence on career concerns, horizon problems, and CEO incentives. *Journal of Financial Economics*, **52**(3), 341–77.

Cannella, A.A. and Lubatkin, M. (1993). Succession as a sociopolitical process: Internal impediments to outside selection. *The Academy of Management Journal*, **36**(4), 763–93.

Cannella, A.A. and Shen, W. (2001). So close and yet so far: Promotion versus exit for CEO heirs apparent. *The Academy of Management Journal*, **44**(2), 252–70.

Certo, S.T. (2003). Influencing initial public offering shareholders with prestige: Signaling with board structures. *Academy of Management Review*, **28**(3), 432–46.

Cohen, B.D. and Dean, T.J. (2005). Information asymmetry and investor evaluation of IPOs: Top management team legitimacy as a capital market signal. *Strategic Management Journal*, **26**(7), 683–90.

Coughlin, A.T. and Schmidt, R.M. (1985). Executive compensation, management turnover, and firm performance: An empirical investigation. *Journal of Accounting and Economics*, **7**(3), 43–66.

Daily, C.M. and Dalton, D.R. (1997). CEO and board chair roles held jointly or separately: Much ado about nothing? *The Academy of Management Executive*, **11**(3), 11–20.

Dalton, D.R. and Kesner, I.F. (1983). Inside/outside succession and organizational size: The pragmatics of executive replacement. *The Academy of Management Journal*, **26**(4), 736–42.

Datta, D.K. and Rajagopalan, N. (1998). Industry structure and CEO characteristics: An empirical study of succession events. *Strategic Management Journal*, **19**(9), 833–52.

Datta, D.K., Rajagopalan, N., and Zhang, Y. (2003). New CEO openness to change and strategic persistence: The moderating role of industry characteristics. *British Journal of Management*, **14**(2), 101–14.

Desai, H., Hogan, C., and Wilkins, M. (2006). The reputational penalty for aggressive accounting: Earnings restatements and management turnover. *The Accounting Review*, **81**(1), 83–112.

Farrell, K.A. and Whidbee, D.A. (2003). Impact of firm performance expectations on CEO turnover and replacement decisions. *Journal of Accounting and Economics*, **36**(1–3), 165–96.

Finkelstein, S. and D'Aveni, R.A. (1994). CEO duality as a double-edged sword: How boards of directors balance entrenchment avoidance and unity of command. *Academy of Management Journal*, **37**(5), 1079–108.

Finkelstein, S. and Hambrick, D.C. (1996). *Strategic leadership: Top executives and their effects on organizations*. St. Paul, MN: West Publishing.

Fredrickson, J.M., Hambrick, D.C., and Baumrin, S. (1988). A model of CEO dismissal. *Academy of Management Review*, **13**(2), 255–70.

Friedman, S.D. and Singh, H. (1989). CEO succession and stockholder reaction: The influence of organizational context and event content. *Academy of Management Journal*, **32**(4), 718–44.

Gabarro, J.J. (1987). *The dynamism of taking charge*. Boston, MA: Harvard Business School Press.

Gupta, A.K. and Govindarajan, V. (1984). Business unit strategy, managerial characteristics, and business unit effectiveness at strategy implementation. *The Academy of Management Journal*, **27**(1), 25–41.

Guthrie, J.P. and Datta, D.K. (1997). Contextual influences on executive selection: Firm characteristics and CEO experience. *Journal of Management Studies*, **34**(4), 537–60.

Guthrie, J.P. and Datta, D.K. (1998). Corporate strategy, executive selection, and firm performance. *Human Resource Management*, **37**(2), 101–15.

Haleblian, J. and Rajagopalan, N. (2006). A cognitive model of CEO dismissal: Understanding the influence of board perceptions, attributions and efficacy beliefs. *Journal of Management Studies*, **43**(5), 1009–26.

Hambrick, D.C. and Cannella, A.A. (2004). CEOs who have COOs: Contingency analysis of an unexplored structural form. *Strategic Management Journal*, **25**(10), 959–79.

Hambrick, D.C. and Fukutomi, G.D.S. (1991). The seasons of a CEO's tenure. *The Academy of Management Review*, **16**(4), 719–42.

Hambrick, D.C. and Mason, P.A. (1994). Upper echelons: The organization as a reflection of its top managers. *The Academy of Management Review*, **9**(2), 193–206.

Harris, D. and Helfat, C. (1997). Specificity of CEO human capital and compensation. *Strategic Management Journal*, **18**(11), 895–920.

Henderson, A.D., Miller, D., and Hambrick, D.C. (2006). How quickly do CEOs become obsolete? Industry dynamism, CEO tenure, and company performance. *Strategic Management Journal*, **27**(5), 447–60.

Higgins, M.C. and Gulati, R. (2003). Getting off to a good start: The effects of upper echelon affiliations on underwriter prestige. *Organization Science*, **14**(3), 244–63.

Higgins, M.C. and Gulati, R. (2006). Stacking the deck: The effects of top management backgrounds on shareholder decisions. *Strategic Management Journal*, **27**(1), 1–25.

Karaevli, A. (2007). Performance consequences of new CEO "outsiderness": Moderating effects of pre- and post-succession contexts. *Strategic Management Journal*, **28**(7), 681–706.

Khurana, R. (2001). Finding the right CEO: Why boards often make poor choices. *Sloan Management Review*, **43**(1), 91–5.

Lucier, C., Schuyt, R., and Tse, E. (2005). CEO succession 2004: The worlds' most prominent temp workers. Available at: www.strategy-business.com/press/article/05204; accessed 2 August 2010.

Marcel, J.J. (2009). Why top management team characteristics matter when employing a chief operating officer: A strategic contingency perspective. *Strategic Management Journal*, **30**(6), 647–58.

Miller, D. and Shamsie, J. (2001). Learning across the life cycle: Experimentation and performance among the Hollywood studio heads. *Strategic Management Journal*, **22**(8), 725–45.

Mingis, K. (2007). Michael Dell returns as CEO at namesake company; Rollins out. *Computerworld*, 31 January, 2007.

Mooney, C.H., Semadeni, M., and Kesner, I.F. (2009). Opting for the interim CEO: What is the role of firm performance. Paper presented at the Academy of Management Annual Meeting, Chicago, Illinois, August 2009.

MSNBC. (2008). Starbucks chairman Schultz returning as CEO. 8 January, 2008.

MSNBC. (2010). Whitacre named GM's permanent CEO. 25 January, 2010.

Ocasio, W. (1994). Political dynamics and the circulation of power: CEO succession in U.S. industrial corporations. *Administrative Science Quarterly*, **39**(2), 285–312.

Pfarrer, M.D., Pollock, T.G., and Rindova, V.P. (2010; in press). A tale of two assets: The effect of firm reputation and celebrity on earnings surprises and investors' reactions. *Academy of Management Journal*, **53**(5) (October).

Puffer, S.M. and Weintrop, J.B. (1991). Corporate performance and CEO turnover: The role of performance expectations. *Administrative Science Quarterly*, **36**(1), 1–19.

Quigley, T.J. and Hambrick, D.C. (2009). When the former CEO remains as board chair: Effects on discretion, organizational change, and performance. Paper presented at the Academy of Management Annual Meeting, Chicago, Illinois, August 2009.

Shen, W. and Cannella, A.A. (2002a). Power dynamics within top management and their impacts on CEO dismissal followed by inside succession. *The Academy of Management Journal*, **45**(6), 1195–206.

Shen, W. and Cannella, A.A. (2002b). Revisiting the performance consequences of CEO succession: The impact of successor type, postsuccession senior executive turnover, and departing CEO tenure. *Academy of Management Journal*, **45**(4), 717–33.

Shen, W. and Cannella, A.A. (2003). Will succession planning increase shareholder wealth? Evidence from investor reactions to relay CEO successions. *Strategic Management Journal*, **24**(2), 191–8.

Simsek, Z. (2007). CEO tenure and organizational performance: An intervening model. *Strategic Management Journal*, **28**(6), 653–62.

Spence A. (1973). Job market signaling. *Quarterly Journal of Economics*, **87**(3), 355–79.

Srinivasan, S. (2005). Consequences of financial reporting failure for outside directors: Evidence from accounting restatements and audit committee members. *Journal of Accounting Research*, **43**(2), 291–334.

Vancil, R. (1987). *Passing the baton*. Boston, MA: Harvard University Press.

Wiersema, M.F. (1995). Executive succession as an antecedent to corporate restructuring. *Human Resource Management*, **34**(1), 185–202.

Wiersema, M.F. (2002). Holes at the top: Why CEO firings backfire. *Harvard Business Review*, **80**(12), 70–75.

Wiersema, M.F. and Zhang, Y. (2008). CEO dismissal: The role of investment analysts as an external control mechanism. *Academy of Management Best Paper Proceedings*, Anaheim, CA.

Wiesenfeld, B.M., Wurthmann, K.A., and Hambrick, D.C. (2008). The stigmatization and devaluation of elites associated with corporate failures: A process model. *Academy of Management Review*, 33(1), 231–51.

Worrell, D.L., Davidson, W.N., Chandy, P.R., and Garrison, S.L. (1986). Management turnover through deaths of key executives: effects on investor wealth. *Academy of Management Journal*, 29(4), 674–94.

Wu, S., Levitas, E., and Priem, R.L. (2005). CEO tenure and company invention under differing levels of technological dynamism. *Academy of Management Journal*, 48(5), 859–73.

Zajac, E.J. (1990). CEO selection, succession, compensation and firm performance: A theoretical integration and empirical analysis. *Strategic Management Journal*, 11(3), 217–30.

Zajac, E.J. and Westphal, J.D. (1996). Who shall succeed? How CEO/board preferences and power affect the choices of new CEOs. *The Academy of Management Journal*, 39(1), 64–90.

Zhang, Y. (2001). Three essays on CEO succession. Unpublished dissertation of the Marshall School of Business, University of Southern California, Los Angeles, CA.

Zhang, Y. (2006). The presence of a separate COO/president and its impact on strategic change and CEO dismissal. *Strategic Management Journal*, 27(3), 283–300.

Zhang, Y. (2008). Information asymmetry and the dismissal of newly appointed CEOs: An empirical investigation. *Strategic Management Journal*, 29(8), 859–72.

Zhang, Y. and Rajagopalan, N. (2002). When firms do not designate heirs apparent: Understanding the role of organizational adaptation, power and managerial labor markets. Paper presented at the Academy of Management Annual Meeting, Denver, Colorado, August 2002.

Zhang, Y. and Rajagopalan, N. (2003). Explaining new CEO origin: Firm versus industry antecedents. *Academy of Management Journal*, 46(3), 327–38.

Zhang, Y. and Rajagopalan, N. (2004). When the known devil is better than an unknown god: An empirical study of the antecedents and consequences of relay CEO successions. *Academy of Management Journal*, 47(4), 483–500.

Zhang, Y. and Wiersema, M.F. (2009). Stock market reaction to CEO certification: The signaling role of CEO backgrounds. *Strategic Management Journal*, 30(7), 693–710.

Zhang, Y. and Rajagopalan, N. (2009). Once an outsider, always an outsider? CEO origin, strategic change, and firm performance. *Strategic Management Journal*, 31(3), 334–46.

15 CEO dismissal: the role of the broader governance context

Joseph B. Beck and Margarethe F. Wiersema

While the perquisites of a Chief Executive Officer (CEO) are many, it is increasingly apparent that job security cannot be listed among them. Recent research has shown that the incidence of CEO dismissal (involuntary turnover) has risen significantly not just in the US, but in Germany, France, and Japan as well (Denis and Denis, 1995; Huson et al., 2001; Lucier et al., 2007). The rate of involuntary CEO succession has increased from 13 percent in the 1980s to 39 percent in 2000 (Wiersema, 2002), with one major consequence being that the average tenure of a CEO has dropped from 8.8 years in 1995 to 7.2 years in 2007 (Karlsson et al., 2008).[1] In terms of causal factors, prior research has clearly shown that CEO succession events tend to be preceded by poor financial performance (Coughlan and Schmidt, 1985; Warner et al., 1988; Weisbach, 1988; Murphy and Zimmerman, 1993), and that poorly performing firms are more likely to incur involuntary CEO turnover (Denis and Denis, 1995; Denis and Serrano, 1996; Mikkelson and Partch, 1997; Denis and Kruse, 2000).

However, past financial performance alone cannot explain the increased propensity on the part of corporate boards of directors to undertake an action as drastic as dismissal of the firm's CEO. For example, the credibility of the CEO – whether or not he/she can be trusted – has also been shown to have an impact on CEO turnover: those CEOs of firms that file financial restatements are twice as likely to leave their companies as CEOs of firms that do not (Arthaud-Day et al., 2006). While prior work on CEO dismissal has focused on the effects of firm performance and the nature of the relationship between the CEO and the board (Fredrickson et al., 1988; Cannella and Shen, 2001; Shen and Cannella, 2002; Haleblian and Rajagopalan, 2006; Zhang, 2006, 2008), with few exceptions (Arthaud-Day et al., 2006; Wiersema and Zhang, 2008) the management literature has said little about the influence of the broader governance context on the board's monitoring role and CEO dismissal. The exclusive focus on internal factors (board-driven and performance-related) by management scholars represents an omission in our models of CEO dismissal. Yet, the takeover market (as one dimension of external governance) has been shown to be the second most important driver of CEO turnover (Kaplan and Minton, 2006; Lucier et al., 2007; Karlsson et al., 2008), indicating that the firm's external governance context needs to be incorporated in our models of CEO dismissal. The CEO's increasing visibility, and vulnerability to criticism, is due in large part to the heightened significance of the financial community as a force for corporate accountability. A relentless focus on shareholder wealth maximization, and the greater visibility and influence of the financial community, has created an environment in which the CEO is increasingly held directly accountable for firm performance (see Ward, Amason, Lee, and Graffin in Chapter 13 of this volume for a discussion of CEO scapegoating). The financial community has been shown to be important as a monitor of firm performance in terms of influencing the demand for the firm's stock; however, its role within the context of CEO dismissal merits further scrutiny.

Previous theoretical models of CEO dismissal have focused primarily on internally driven causal factors. Fredrickson et al. (1988), for example, propose a model of CEO dismissal that includes sociopolitical constructs composed of the board's expectations and attributions, the board's allegiances and values, alternatives to the incumbent CEO and incumbent CEO power. The underlying drivers of these constructs, however, are for the most part internal attributes of the corporate environment. Hence we have board characteristics, organization characteristics, and characteristics of the current and previous CEO as proxies for the directly unmeasurable sociopolitical constructs. Even when external factors are considered, in the form of industry characteristics, the objective determinants included in the model do not constitute factors related to external governance; rather they constitute benchmarks by which to assess an internal element of the decision-making process. For example, the life-cycle stage of the industry and the number of firms in the industry establish a context in which boards are supposedly able to more accurately assess the likelihood of finding a suitable replacement for the CEO, which would constitute an internal element of the dismissal decision-making process. Likewise, industry performance constitutes a benchmark by which, in conjunction with prior firm performance, to assess current firm performance: another internal element of the dismissal decision-making process. Thus, internal factors in terms of the board and the firm's financial performance are the primary drivers of CEO dismissal in the Fredrickson et al. model.

Haleblian and Rajagopalan (2006) specifically concentrate on one important segment of the Fredrickson et al. model, illuminating the drivers of the CEO dismissal decision-making process constituted by board characteristics and current firm performance assessments. They extend the Fredrickson et al. model by making explicit the linkages between board composition and (1) how firm performance is assessed; (2) how responsibility for firm performance is placed; and (3) how the CEO's ability to improve firm performance is assessed. This is essentially a model of a decision tree, in which prior performance and board composition first influence whether or not a performance shortfall is perceived to exist. If no problem is perceived, then no dismissal occurs. If, however, a problem is perceived, then responsibility is assessed; an attribution once again influenced by board composition and performance perceptions. When the CEO is deemed responsible, dismissal becomes more likely; however, if responsibility for the performance shortfall is laid on factors beyond the CEO's control, an assessment is made regarding the CEOs ability to improve matters. If the board believes the CEO can turn the situation around, dismissal is less likely; but if the board has little faith in the CEO's efficacy in this regard, then dismissal is probable. This model, again, focuses on internal governance processes and current performance assessments (as benchmarked against the past) to explain CEO dismissal.

Thus, our prevailing models of CEO dismissal are focused on the internal governance of the firm in terms of the board's attributions and expectations regarding the firm's financial performance. However, in order to better understand CEO dismissal, it is important to broaden our model of the firm's governance context to specifically take into account the roles of both internal and external monitors of the firm. External monitors serve an important function because boards, reliant on information from management, can be compromised in their ability to serve as effective monitors (Lipton and Lorsch, 1992; Jensen, 1993; Hermalin and Weisbach, 1998). As previously mentioned, external forces such as the takeover market have been shown to lead to greater executive turnover (Martin and McConnell, 1991; Denis and Serrano, 1996), while merger and acquisition activity, in general, is one of the primary factors associated with executive turnover (Lucier et al., 2007; Karlsson et al., 2008). We propose that the broader financial community plays an important function in influencing the board's perception and assessment of the firm's CEO. In this particular paper, we discuss the roles of two large and important external constituents – investment analysts and institutional investors.

We propose an integrated model of CEO dismissal that incorporates the role of the firm's broader governance context, and thus enables a better understanding of the conditions likely to influence the board's decision to dismiss the CEO. Specifically, we examine investment analysts and institutional investors – important external constituents who, in their respective roles as information intermediaries and investors, have a critical influence on how the board evaluates the CEO. In developing our framework we incorporate prior empirical work in both the finance and management literature on the contextual conditions surrounding CEO dismissal. Theoretically, we extend the Haleblian and Rajagopalan model, in that we incorporate the external monitor as an explanatory factor in CEO dismissal decisions; making explicit the linkages between this element of external governance and (1) the board's perception of performance – current as well as future; (2) the board's assignment of responsibility for performance outcomes; and (3) the board's assessment of the future efficacy of the present CEO in regards to addressing a performance shortfall. In terms of an extension to the Fredrickson et al. model, we incorporate a second set of externally located objective determinants (specifically targeting external governance) to explain the foundations of the sociopolitical constructs (in particular, board expectations and attributions) that are assumed to impact the CEO dismissal decision. Finally, we extend existing theory by incorporating the roles of strategy and leadership assessments into the CEO dismissal process, as well as the role of the financial community in the monitoring role of the board itself. This final extension is related to the consideration of future performance expectations when making a decision to dismiss the CEO, for these expectations are driven by evaluations of the firm's competitive position in the marketplace and of the ability of the CEO to develop and execute an effective strategy. Furthermore, through their sizeable shareholdings, institutional investors can directly influence the board itself. In short, we integrate considerations of the financial community and its assessments of the firm's future financial performance, the efficacy of strategy and leadership, and the effectiveness of the board as an internal monitor, into the existing models based upon considerations of internal governance and current performance measured against past performance, thus making a significant contribution to the research on CEO dismissal.

CORPORATE GOVERNANCE CONTEXT

The focus of prior models of CEO succession on the sociopolitical forces influencing the firm's board stems from an emphasis on board members' fiduciary duties as representatives of the firm's shareholders. These duties and responsibilities entail an obligation to serve in the "best interests" of the firm's shareholders, and to provide oversight of corporate management for the benefit of shareholders. As internal monitors of management, however, boards have not always been all that effective due to a variety of factors associated with the selection of members, the structure of the board, and the power of the CEO (Lipton and Lorsch, 1992; Jensen, 1993; Hermalin and Weisbach, 1998). Furthermore, under an increasing bombardment of calls for improved stewardship of shareholder wealth, the firm has found itself more actively engaged with the various constituents within the financial community. Increasingly, the CEO of a publicly owned firm spends a considerable amount of his/her time interacting with constituents in the financial community; even very large and powerful firms have recognized the need to be aware of institutional investors' concerns. For example, the Coca-Cola Company has established a separate office (the Share-Owner Affairs Department) to handle the task of communicating with its institutional investors (Knowles and Yost, 1999), and Pfizer now has face-to-face meetings between the board and influential institutional investors (Friday and Crum, 2008). Schering-Plough's Engagement Program, touted as a model for successful institutional relations, contains detailed guidelines regarding frequent and regular communications with institutional investors (Russo and Turner, 2009). The changing basis for assessing executive compensation (to an incentive-based system tied to shareholder wealth) has also reoriented management's and the board's attention to how the firm is perceived within the financial community (Friday and Crum, 2008; Millstein et al., 2008). As a result, the sphere of corporate governance influence has expanded, such that external constituents have taken on a more instrumental role, with the firm's board and CEO more dynamically occupied in dialogue with these key constituents.

When internal monitors fail in providing adequate governance oversight, external control mechanisms can take on a more active role as disciplines of last resort (Fama, 1980). In particular, it has been shown that the capital market can serve as an effective monitor of management, forcing exit from an industry with excess capacity over the objections of management, for example, or replacing managers in the face of board inaction (Morck et al., 1989; Jensen, 1993). In their study of the takeover market and management turnover, Mikkelson and Partch (1997) found that management turnover in US companies was far higher during the active takeover market of 1984–88 then in the less active market of 1989–93 (a finding echoed in the work of Denis and Kruse, 2000). Furthermore, hostile takeovers have been found to occur far more frequently in poorly performing firms (Martin and McConnell, 1991; Denis and Serrano, 1996), and these takeovers appear to result in subsequent executive firings. Finally, the market for corporate control appears to discipline managers who make decisions that ultimately damage the firm; managers responsible for acquisitions that resulted in losses for the acquiring firm tend to be replaced following a hostile takeover (Mitchell and Lehn, 1990; Lehn and Zhao, 2006).

In understanding the firm's broader corporate governance context and its role in influencing the board's evaluation of the CEO, we propose that two external constituents play a particularly important role. First, investment analysts, in their role as information intermediaries and external monitors of management, provide an independent assessment of the firm's past performance as well as providing an assessment of the firm's future prospects, and as a result play an important role in influencing the demand for the firm's stock (Givoly and Lakonishok, 1979; Lys and Shon, 1990; Francis and Soffer, 1997; Frankel et al., 2006). Investment analysts' evaluations and recommendations have been shown to have consequences for executive turnover (Wiersema and Zhang, 2008) and thus represent an important addition to our model of CEO dismissal. In addition, institutional investors, as the largest shareholders of public companies, have emerged as a powerful and influential force in the investment community. Their role in influencing demand, and thus the price of the firm's stock, through their trading activity, as well as their increasingly direct involvement in the governance of the firm, is also likely to influence the board's perception and assessment of the firm's CEO. As a result, these two external constituents represent the broader corporate governance context that is likely to influence the board regarding a decision on CEO dismissal.

In the next sections we provide a review and summary of the literature on these two investment community constituents and explain why they are likely to play an important role in influencing the governance context surrounding CEO dismissal.

ROLE OF INVESTMENT ANALYSTS

The assumption that stock prices reflect all information relevant for accurate valuation underlies the hypothetical efficiency of financial markets (Fama et al., 1969). Nevertheless, it is also widely accepted that information asymmetry exists between owners and managers of firms. Investment analysts (research analysts employed by investment banks or brokerage firms) function as necessary information intermediaries by providing research and issuing reports and recommendations (e.g., Strong Buy, Buy, Hold, Underperform, Sell), assessing the firm's future prospects and comparing the firm with its industry peers. Analyst coverage and reports, by influencing demand for the firm's stock and thus the price of the stock, are likely to be noticed by the firm's board of directors (Givoly and Lakonishok, 1979; Lys and Shon, 1990; Francis and Soffer, 1997; Frankel et al., 2006). Just as investors would use investment analysts as an independent source of information regarding future firm performance, so it can be expected that boards of directors would do the same (Wiersema and Zhang, 2008). Although not much prior research has been conducted on the influence of investment analysts on the behavior of managers and boards, some evidence does exist to support the contention that such an influence exists (Yu, 2008; Westphal and Graebner, 2010); and because investment analysts have no vested interest in any particular firm, they have the potential to function as an external control mechanism (Wiersema and Zhang, 2008).

The role of the investment analyst as a source of new information on future firm performance is thus predicated on the assumption of information asymmetry in financial markets (Fama et al., 1969). Investment analysts serve to reduce this information asymmetry through their engagement in activities designed to reveal superior information on the internal conditions of the firm, possessed by managers but not by investors (Healy and Palepu, 2001). Some of the effects of this information provision on the behavior of investors have been documented by prior empirical research. For example, the liquidity of a firm's stock – the ease with which the stock sells – has been shown to improve when analysts provide information regarding the firm's prospects (Brennan and Hughes,

1991). Reductions in costs associated with performing private information searches are realized by investors when a greater number of analysts (analyst coverage) follow a firm, thus providing a service that acts to increase the value of such a firm to investors (Chen and Steiner, 2000). Thus, the more analysts that follow a firm, the greater the savings in search costs realized by investors, increasing the net value of such a firm.

Furthermore, simply by focusing investors' attentions on a particular firm, these analysts can influence the demand for the firm's stock, thus influencing its price (Merton, 1987). For example, when an analyst first initiates coverage of a particular firm's stock (analyst initiation), positive abnormal returns result (Irvine, 2003); and the greater the analyst coverage, the greater the firm's market value (Chung and Jo, 1996). And, as would be expected, the recommendations issued on a firm's stock by investment analysts have an effect on demand, and thus the price of the firm's stock. For example, a Buy recommendation has a significant positive impact on a firm's stock price, while a Sell recommendation has a significant negative effect (Stickel, 1992); and downgrading a stock's recommendation to "Sell" has a negative effect that is greater than the positive effect generated when a stock's recommendation is upgraded to "Buy" (Womack, 1996). Furthermore, the time span during which a downgrade has a price effect is longer (six months) than that (one month) generated by an upgrade. It seems, therefore, that analysts' stock recommendations, especially negative ones, have a strong influence on the way investors evaluate a firm's performance prospects.

In terms of research on the external *monitoring* role played by analysts (as distinct from a simple information-production-and-dissemination role), arguments have been presented that maintain, from an agency-cost perspective, that analysts level the playing field by reducing opportunities for rent-appropriation by managers (Jensen and Meckling, 1976). Owner and agent interests are thus kept more in line with each other. Some evidence has been found that appears to indicate that analysts may be able to pick up on conditions suggesting the presence of agency problems: analyst coverage appears to increase when managerial and shareholder interests are misaligned (Moyer et al., 1989). In addition, some firms are more difficult to monitor than others, firms with a high concentration of intangible assets being an example. These firms have been found to attract greater analyst attention (Barth et al., 2001), supporting the contention that analysts even the odds for investors through the reduction in information asymmetry that would otherwise contribute to agency problems.

Evidence also exists to indicate that investment analysts have an impact on the behavior of managers. The effects on investors of analysts' perceptions and evaluations of companies influenced managerial actions in the de-diversification movement of the late 1980s (Zuckerman, 2000), by explicitly touting the benefits of "coherent image" in the corporate portfolio. Similarly, full service brokerage firms appear to have re-evaluated and revised their strategies and business models on the basis of positive evaluations by analysts of firms with online/discount strategies (Kock, 2006). More extensive analyst coverage appears to reduce the propensity for management to engage in "earnings management" (Yu, 2008) and CEOs of firms with negative analyst evaluations have been shown to manage the impressions of security analysts by appointing independent directors to the board, thus enhancing perceptions about the autonomy of the firm's corporate governance, without actually relinquishing control (Westphal and Graebner, 2010). Quarterly conference calls between top management and investment analysts are now a common occurrence and during these calls, CEOs have been shown to discriminate among analysts by disseminating more information to those analysts whose ratings have been more favorable in the past (Mayew, 2008). This should enhance the reports of these favored analysts in the eyes of the investment community (by virtue of the greater information contained in these reports; yet these reports – through the manipulative process engaged in by managers – would tend to be biased in favor of management. Investment analysts, in short, provide reports and recommendations of considerable informational value to the financial community (Bhushan, 1989; Brennan and Subrahmanyam, 1995; Frankel et al., 2006), and appear to have a real effect on investor decisions and managerial behavior; furthermore, managers are aware of this, and increasingly seek to influence the perceptions of investment analysts.

While investment analysts clearly influence investor demand and the firm's stock price, and have been shown to influence managerial decisions, their influence on the board, and the board's perception and evaluation of the firm's CEO, is less evident. Two studies have shown that a shortfall in reported quarterly earnings per share vis-à-vis analysts' EPS forecasts is associated with an increase in the probability of CEO turnover (Puffer and Weintrop, 1991; Farrell and Whidbee, 2003), which would support the contention that the board looks at the analysts' expected earnings forecasts as a performance benchmark. A failure to meet quarterly earnings targets provides another metric by which the board can assess the performance of the CEO. In addition to evaluating the past performance of the firm, the reports and stock recommendations issued by investment analysts also provide information about the future prospects of the firm, in terms of the firm's strategy and its forecasted financial performance relative to competitors. The assessment of the future prospects of the firm, when negative, has been shown to lead to a higher likelihood of CEO dismissal (Wiersema and Zhang, 2008); indicating that the board utilizes investment analysts' recommendations as a legitimate and reliable assessment of the firm and its leadership.

In addition, apart from the weight placed on the forecasts and recommendations of investment analysts in terms of assessing the firm's past and future performance, missed earnings forecasts and negative analysts' recommendations may contribute to a devaluation of the CEO in a social sense, which has implications for the overall value of the firm itself. Negative assessments of the CEO make their way into the media, for example, to initiate a process of social judgment that galvanizes board action. Wiesenfeld et al. (2008) argue that social arbiters ("those who possess prominent and legitimate platforms for rendering assessments of firms and the individuals associated with them," p. 234), through their judgments regarding the culpability of executives for performance outcomes, engage in a stigmatization process that reduces the value of a CEO to a firm, thus increasing the likelihood that those in charge of the decision-making process (boards) will fire the CEO.

In terms of the actual reliability of analysts' assessment, most studies show them to be optimistically biased (Brown et al., 1985; Chopra, 1988; Stickel, 1992; Sinha et al., 1997; Chan et al., 2007), though a recent study did indicate that analysts were able to reliably predict future unexpected earnings as well as the stock market's reaction to these (Barber et al., 2008). Because of the general optimistic bias, and the fact that analysts issue recommendations to buy much more often than they issue recommendations to sell (Michaely and Womack, 1999; Boni and Womack, 2006), a negative evaluation carries greater weight than a positive one (Chen and Steiner, 2000). Support for the seriousness with which boards view the evaluations of investment analysts has been provided by a recent study by Wiersema and Zhang (2008), in which it was found that lower average investment analyst recommendations, greater investment analyst downgrades of a firm's stock, and greater percentages of analysts issuing sell recommendations were all significantly and positively related to the probability of CEO dismissal. Furthermore, this same study found that negativity of investment analysts' evaluations had a greater effect on the probability of CEO dismissal if the firm's prior financial performance had been poor, indicating that boards utilize a number of analytical frameworks when considering action on a CEO; when the evidence is supportive, action is more likely. However, Wiersema and Zhang (2008) also found evidence that investment analysts are not immune to the scrutiny of their own performance. Following the successful 2002 litigation against investment analysts by then Attorney General Spitzer, the influence of investment analysts' evaluations on CEO dismissal appears to have lessened.

Investment analysts are, therefore, significant external constituents operating within the financial community who influence the broader corporate governance context within which the board evaluates the CEO. As independent providers of information about the firm, its financial performance, and its future prospects, they provide fresh information with which investors and the board can assess both the historical performance of the firm and its future prospects, as well as the ability of the firm's CEO. First, their quarterly earnings-per-share forecasts can be used by the board as a performance benchmark by which to assess the financial results reported by management (Puffer and Weintrop, 1991; Farrell and Whidbee, 2003). Second, investment analysts' stock recommendations can influence investor demand and thus the firm's stock price (Merton. 1987; Stickel, 1992; Chung and Jo, 1996; Womack, 1996; Irvine, 2003); and this in turn is likely to influence the board's evaluation of the firm's CEO. Finally, investment analysts' reports and stock recommendation provide the board with an assessment of the firm's future prospects. This assessment is critical in that it evaluates the firm's strategy relative to its competitors and assesses the future performance implications of that strategy. Since the CEO is the architect of the firm's strategy, the investment analysts' reports and recommendations are in fact an evaluation of the CEO's choice of strategy. Thus, investment analysts are an important external monitor that can influence the board both directly (in their assessment of past and future financial performance and the firm's strategy) and indirectly through their effect on investor demand for the firm's stock. As a result, a model of CEO dismissal must take into account the fact that investment analysts serve an important external monitoring role, by providing objective information with which to assess the financial outcomes of strategic decisions made by management, as well as by providing an assessment of the firm's future prospects under the firm's leadership. These assessments not only influence how the board perceives the firm's historical financial performance and whether or not the board is likely to hold the CEO directly accountable for that performance; but whether or not the board has confidence in the abilities of the CEO to pursue a strategy that will result in a sustainable competitive advantage and thus drive the firm's future financial performance as well. As external constituents, investment analysts thus influence the governance context within which the board determines whether the current CEO should stay or go.

ROLE OF INSTITUTIONAL INVESTORS

Institutional investors (banks; insurance companies; investment companies/mutual funds; investment advisers/brokerage firms; and others, such as pension funds, university endowments, and hedge funds) represent another important constituent in the financial community by virtue of their increasing percentage of ownership in public companies. These investors now control, through ownership, well over half of all public company shares in the United States (Gompers and Metrick, 2001), with recent estimates at over 70 percent (Gillan and Starks, 2007). Moreover, within the ranks of institutional investors, the largest hundred of these entities now possess close to 40 percent of all corporate equity (Gompers and Metrick, 2001), creating through this consolidation of ownership a powerful, legitimate and influential constituent. In addition, the existence of blockholders – investors who hold 5 percent or more of a firm's shares – has governance ramifications for publicly traded companies. Prior to the 1990s, blockholders often represented the founding family and thus were aligned with the firm's management. Increasingly, however, blockholders now consist of independent investors or institutional investors, unaffiliated with, and potentially not allied with, firm management. As a result, by virtue of holding very large ownership positions in public companies, blockholders can be a powerful and influential force in the financial community.

Prior to the 1990s, the primary means by which institutional investors expressed their satisfaction or dissatisfaction with the financial performance of a firm was through the buying or selling of a firm's stock (Lowenstein, 1988; Parrino et al., 2003). Substantial evidence exists to show that the market activity of institutional investors affects both a firm's stock price as well as its volatility. Most studies that have investigated the relationship between the buying and selling of stock by institutional investors and stock price volatility have found that these events are positively associated with each other (Potter, 1992; Sias, 1996), though El-Gazzar (1998) found a negative association. Gompers and Metrick (2001) found that, in comparison with buying and selling activity of other traders, such activity by institutional investors resulted in greater fluctuations in stock prices. The purchase of a company's stock by institutional investors had a greater positive effect on prices than the purchase of said stock by other traders; the sale of a firm's stock had a greater negative effect. It is the significant size of the ownership position, the relatively large fraction of the company's shares that is in play, which drives this impact; when institutional investors sell stock, therefore, the price of said stock tends to drop (Brown and Brooke, 1993). Studies such as those by Gompers and Metrick (2001), and Brown and Brooke (1993) offer a causal argument for the relationship between the buying and selling of company shares by institutional investors and stock prices based on underlying economic theories of supply and demand; Sias, Starks and Titman (2001), on the other hand offer a reflective argument for the association; namely the "informed trading hypothesis." This argues that institutional investors have greater knowledge of which companies' stocks will perform better and which will perform worse. The trading by institutional investors does not, therefore, cause stock prices to change; institutional investors are anticipating the performance of the firms in question, and buying stock in companies that are going to perform well in the future, and selling off equity in those firms whose future performance will decline. The market activity of institutional investors, therefore, merely reflects, but does not cause, the movement of firm stock prices.

Causality is reversed in these two sets of arguments. One (the supply–demand view) argues that institutional investor activity influences stock prices; the other (informed trading) argues that knowledge of future firm performance influences institutional investor activity. These do not, however, contradict each other: knowledge of future performance may influence institutional investor activity, which then influences the demand for company stock, resulting in stock price movement.

Since the early 1990s, however, institutional investors appear to have become more active in their attempts to directly intervene in the internal decision-making processes of the firm (Gillan and Starks, 2000, 2007). The California Public Employees Pension System (CalPERS), the world's largest pension fund, initiated a more active posture among institutional investors by publicly announcing what it considered to be the ten worst-managed companies. While at first CalPERS was considered an outlier in terms of investor behavior, public and union pension funds, in particular, have increasingly engaged in a variety of activist behaviors, ranging from the submission of proxy proposals and attempts to initiate direct dialogues with management and boards, to the use of the media to target firm management with whom dissatisfaction existed (Monks and Minow, 1995; Gillan and Starks, 2007).

Most recently, hedge funds have entered the fray as a highly aggressive form of institutional investor willing to engage in proxy battles to discharge the duties of the external monitoring role and thus bring about desired changes in corporate behavior (Gillan and Starks, 2007; Brav et al., 2008; Greenwood and Schor, 2009; Klein and Zur, 2009). These hedge fund activists have also been characterized as the current version of the corporate raiders – arguably the most aggressive form of institutional investor – who utilized the market for corporate control in the 1980s to exercise the role of external monitor in the disciplining of boards and managers (Gillan and Starks, 2007). In a manner reminiscent of the 1980s' corporate raiders, hedge funds target underperforming firms, as well as those with poor governance practices (Pearson and Altman, 2006); however, rather than then selling off the pieces for more than the value of the whole, hedge funds attempt to intervene with management and the board to unlock the potential value within the firm. In addition to sponsoring shareholder proposals, lobbying of the media, and direct negotiations with management, hedge funds often attempt to place their own nominees on the board, and are willing to engage in proxy contests to reach their goals (Pearson and Altman, 2006; Kahan and Rock, 2007). Thus hedge fund activism seeks to instigate significant strategic change (as opposed to incremental change) within the targeted firms; an approach made possible by the fact that hedge funds tend to focus on individual firms, rather than taking the diversified portfolio tack favored by other institutional investors (Kahan and Rock, 2007).

A number of typologies or categorizations have been proposed or tested in regards to the nature of institutional investors. Hirschman (1971) advocated a response classification for shareholder dissatisfaction, in which dissatisfied investors could either be totally passive – a response type referred to as "loyalty" – or could actively express their dissatisfaction on an implied continuum ranging from "exit," wherein the investors simply divested themselves of the firm's stock, through a variety of increasing aggressive behaviors characterized as "voice." These latter, active investors (shareholder activists) may be viewed as engaging in an array of more or less aggressive forms of external monitoring behavior. The simple market engagement of an institutional investor – the buying or selling of a firm's stock – is an indirect, relatively non-aggressive manner of external governance; whereas the market for corporate control represents a highly aggressive, very direct manner of external governance (Gillan and Starks, 2007). The recent activities of the various pension funds (public, private, labor) and other institutional investors, including hedge funds, fall somewhere along the continuum between these extremes. Public pension funds, as well as union-based pension funds, began to more actively utilize the shareholder proxy proposal as a mechanism of influence over corporate behavior during the early 1990s. Furthermore, the California Public Employees' Retirement System (CalPERS) now publicly identifies the companies it is targeting, thus influencing other investors. Its 2009 Focus List identifies four firms (Eli Lilly, Hill-Rom Holdings, Hospital Properties Trust, and IMS Health) as having both poor market performance and corporate governance practices, as well as the proposed shareholder resolutions CalPERS intends to pursue against these particular firms. For example, CalPERS intends to pursue proposals against Eli Lilly and Hill-Rom Holdings to allow shareholders an opportunity to amend bylaws.

The influence of large investors on the board and firm management through shareholder proposals is currently undergoing a dramatic increase. Though usually unsuccessful in terms of voting approval, the number of shareholder proposals and the percentage of votes cast in favor of shareholder proposals have increased significantly over the past three years. In 2007, public companies received a record number (1169) of shareholder proposals; and a record number of these (269) were withdrawn due to compromises reached as boards attempted to keep the proposals off the ballots (Friday and Crum, 2008). Shareholder proposals increasingly focus on issues of governance and executive compensation. Proposals on greater proxy access, majority voting, an independent chair, and a non-binding vote on executive compensation ("say-on-pay") have become increasingly more frequent, and are likely to gain traction given recent favorable changes in the regulatory environment. In June of 2009, the SEC (Securities & Exchange Commission) formally proposed rules that would allow shareholders with a prescribed minimum percentage (tied to firm size) of the firm's shares to nominate directors for shareholder approval, and have these nominations included on the proxy materials sent to shareholders by the company (SEC Release Nos. 33-9046; 34-60089; IC-28765; File No. S7-10-09). Thus, for the first time, boards would no longer have total control over directors nominated in the proxy materials. Furthermore, the SEC has also adopted changes in how voting occurs for director election, approving in July of 2009 an NYSE rule that prohibits brokers from casting proxy votes without specific instructions from customers. Because brokers tend to vote with management, this ruling effectively makes it more difficult for directors to get the required majority vote. Finally, the Senate Banking Committee is considering HR 3269, a "say-on-pay" bill already passed by the House of Representatives that will provide shareholders with a greater voice in executive compensation. Several countries (e.g., Australia, UK, Sweden, and the Netherlands) have already instituted such shareholder rights, and in the Netherlands the outcome of the vote is binding. While such a vote would be strictly advisory in the US, the board is not likely to dismiss the results of shareholders' input on such a sensitive governance issue, especially given the recent success of director opposition campaigns.

Evidence that shareholders are becoming more active is widespread. In April of 2009, Bank of America shareholders (50.34 percent, or 25 million votes) voted against the continuation of CEO Kenneth Lewis as board chair. Poor strategic decisions, specifically the acquisition of Merrill-Lynch, along with abysmal financial performance led to shareholders communicating their dissatisfaction with the board's oversight role. Furthermore, in May of 2009, Royal Dutch Shell shareholders (59.42 percent) voted down the board's approved executive compensation plan. Although the shareholder vote was non-binding, it sent a strong message to the board regarding investor anger over decisions perceived to reward failure. Many of such shareholder resolutions are initiated by institutional investors, with TIAA-CREF taking on a significant role in influencing other large investors on executive compensation practices. Hedge funds, as mentioned earlier, have also taken on a more active role, and increasingly have sought board representation in order to oversee their investment interests (e.g., Harbinger Capital Partners now controls two board seats at the New York Times Co.). A hedge fund's significant investment in a company can often lead to pressures for board representation.

A variety of other ways in which to distinguish between types of institutional investors have been explored. Bushee and Noe (2000) categorize them as either transient, dedicated, or quasi-indexers. Transient institutional investors buy and sell relatively frequently, preferring firms that are rated highly in terms of information disclosure; short-term financial gain appears to be the incentive. Quasi-indexers have a large portfolio and trade relatively infrequently; however, they tend to do so when disclosure rankings fall, indicating a heavy reliance on such information as an inexpensive monitoring tool for long-term performance. Finally, dedicated institutional investors have a small, stable portfolio of firms in which they hold large ownership stakes, and demonstrate a low level of response to changes in disclosure practices, indicating that they have other means of monitoring behavior and are interested in long-term performance. It would appear, therefore, that not all institutional investors have an interest in performing the role of external monitor: the presence of transient investors within a firm's shareholder base seems to have the negative consequence of high stock price volatility when coupled with an improvement in disclosure practices.

Parrino et al. (2003) examined how institutional investors that correspond to the quasi-indexer class differ in behavior based on constructs of prudence (conservatism or caution) and the degree to which the institutional investor is informed. Bank trust departments are presumed to be more prudent than other investor classes (Del Guercio, 1996; Bennett et al., 2003); these more prudent institutional investors are found to divest more heavily both prior to and following a forced CEO turnover than do other types of institutional investors of the quasi-indexer class. In addition, independent investment advisors emerge as the most well-informed institutional investor type (Jones et al., 1999; Sias et al., 2001); these institutional investors "in the know" appear to eliminate the greatest percentage share of ownership in the year immediately prior to a forced dismissal – supporting the contention that these institutional investors have access to higher-quality information than do others.

In short, institutional investors are not a monotypic class of external monitor; they differ along a number of dimensions such as preferred mode of corporate influence, apparent motivation as shareholder, risk-preference, and access to information (just to mention a few that have been explored). Perhaps due in large part to this heterogeneity among institutional investors, extant research has reported a parallel dissimilarity regarding the impact of institutional ownership on overall firm performance and governance behavior. Hotchkiss and Strickland (2003), for example, categorized institutional investors on the basis of investment style (growth, aggressive growth, value, and income), and found that the magnitude of the market response to earnings announcement was positively associated with the proportion of the firm's stock owned by aggressive growth investors. Woidtke (2002) found that a firm's value, while positively related to institutional ownership by a private pension fund, was negatively related to an ownership position by a public pension fund. Since public pension funds are presumed to exhibit a higher level of shareholder activism, this result suggests that activist shareholders do not perform particularly well in the role of external monitor (Murphy and Van Nuys, 1994; Woidtke et al., 2003). Bainbridge (2005) argues that this result stems from the limited agendas – unfavorably impacting the effectiveness of corporate boards – pursued by shareholder activists.

Performance effects aside, there exists substantial evidence that institutional investors influence the behaviors of boards and managers in a variety of ways. Carleton et al. (1998), for example, investigated the outcomes of negotiated agreements between TIAA-CREF (the largest pension fund, with 1 percent of total US equity) and 45 firms in which it held equity positions. The specific policies that TIAA-CREF wanted implemented were (1) increased diversity in board composition; (2) confidential shareholder voting; and (3) more stringent limits on the issuance of preferred stock as an antitakeover tactic. In more than 95 percent of cases, the desired change was implemented. Institutional investors are usually successful when seeking to dismantle antitakeover devices, such as "poison pills," in poorly performing firms (Bizjak and Marquette, 1998; Akyol and Carroll, 2006). Furthermore, institutional investor concentration has been found to be positively related to performance-based executive compensation and negatively related to the level of that compensation (Hartzell and Starks, 2003). Gillan et al. (2000) present evidence for a more rapid restructuring process on the part of Sears-Roebuck over the 1989–92 time period as a result of institutional investor pressure. Finally, institutional investors are increasingly more willing, as evidenced in an earlier discussion, to use shareholder proposals and proxy voting to enact changes in governance. Institutional investors, in short, significantly shape the strategies and tactics implemented by boards and managers (Huson, 1997; Del Guercio and Hawkins, 1999; Gillan and Starks, 2000; Wu, 2004).

In addition to this evidence pertaining to the general effect on corporate behavior by institutional investor activism, there are a number of studies that specifically address the impact that institutional investors can have on CEO dismissal. Significant shedding of company stock by institutional investors has a disproportionate effect on forced CEO turnovers (Parrino et al., 2003). Wu (2004) found that when CalPERS publicly targeted a firm, the sensitivity of CEO dismissal to performance increased, as well as the probability that a CEO dismissal would occur. Del Guercio et al. (2006) also found that institutional investor activism has a significant and positive impact on both forced CEO and board of director turnovers. The decision by Bank of America CEO Ken Lewis to step down at the end of 2009 was almost certainly directly related to his ouster as board chair which in turn was a direct result of institutional investor displeasure. Similar shareholder anger appears to have been a major factor in the 2007 departure of Citigroup CEO Charles Prince.

Institutional investors, therefore, are another extremely important external constituent group operating within the financial community and exerting influence on the broader corporate governance context within which the board evaluates the CEO.

Trading by institutional investors, representing the bulk of stock ownership, has a significant effect on the firm's stock price as well as on its volatility. Not only does the size of their transactions influence market behavior, but due to the perception of institutional investors as "informed traders," their actions can influence other investors. Moreover, and in addition to their investment activities, institutional investors have in recent years adopted a more aggressive stance by intervening in the internal decision-making processes of the firm. Certain institutional investors have investment strategies that target underperforming firms or those with poor governance practices with the specific goal of seeking significant changes in strategy and leadership. In addition, shareholder resolutions and shareholder proxy proposals have become significant mechanisms through which institutional investors exert their influence and control. Thus, institutional investors, through their shareholder activism and voting, can have a direct effect on internal board processes such as the evaluation of the firm's leadership. Consequently, a model of CEO dismissal must take into account the fact that institutional investors serve an important external monitoring role, influencing how the board reacts to the firm's financial performance; whether or not the board is likely to hold the CEO directly accountable for that performance; and whether or not the board believes the CEO can improve the firm's performance. As the largest shareholders of public companies and as informed investors, institutional investors influence demand for and thus the price of the firm's stock; and in addition, through increased activism, have become directly involved in the monitoring role of the board itself.

ROLE OF THE FINANCIAL COMMUNITY IN CEO DISMISSAL

Previous models of CEO dismissal have focused primarily on internally driven causal factors without giving adequate consideration to the firm's broader governance context. Figure 15.1 depicts our expanded model of CEO dismissal, which postulates that the financial community constitutes a major influence on the board as pertains to the decision to dismiss the CEO. In the following section we will first examine the internal

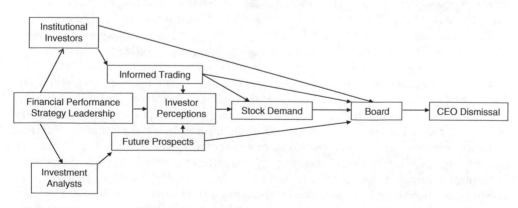

Source: Authors.

Figure 15.1   The role of the financial community in CEO dismissal

relationships of relevance within the financial community, and then make the connection between the financial community and the board, and thus to CEO dismissal.

The heart of this model assumes that investor perceptions of a firm's financial performance, the efficacy of the firm's strategy, and the capabilities of the firm's leadership will influence the demand for the firm's stock, and thus the stock price. Assessments of these primary factors do not, however, depend solely on direct observations by the investors. Investors look to a variety of information sources to facilitate and rationalize the evaluation process. Investment analysts, for example, are also engaged in the evaluation of these primary factors, and generate reports and recommendations that assess the future prospects regarding the profitability of the firm. Investors and potential investors follow these reports and recommendations, and these then have an impact on their perceptions of these primary factors. Similarly, institutional investors are engaged in the same process of evaluation, and other investors perceive their activities as reflective of informed trading. Because institutional investors are assumed to have access to superior information regarding these primary factors of interest, their trading activities are influential in shaping investor perceptions of firm performance, strategy, and leadership (which then impact the demand for and the price of firm stock).

In addition to the indirect influence that the investment analysts and institutional investors have on the board through the shaping of investor perceptions, and thus demand for the firm's stock, there is a more direct link to the board. Obviously, the demand for and the price of firm stock will play a role in shaping the board's perceptions; the board, however, does not exist in an informational vacuum. It, too, will be aware of the reports and recommendations of investment analysts. These will have an effect on the board's perceptions of the firm's future prospects, and these in turn can be expected to influence any decision regarding the fate of the CEO. Similarly, boards are acutely aware of the extent and nature of the institutional ownership of the firm's stock and are equally aware of the distinctions in expectations and investing behavior across different categories of institutional investors. Moreover, many boards now have direct contact with large institutional investors and certain institutional investors have taken on a larger, more direct role through direct intervention in board processes. Through shareholder resolutions, proxy proposals, and voting, institutional investors can now alter the composition of the board, as well as have a direct say on important board decisions including the evaluation of the firm's CEO. As a result, both investment analysts and institutional investors serve as effective external monitors that can increase the diligence and effectiveness of internal governance provided through the board.

Thus, the financial community, as represented by investment analysts and institutional investors, has multiple paths of influence connecting it to the board, and so to CEO dismissal. Both indirectly and directly, these constituents influence the perceptions of the board, as well as the function of the board as an effective internal monitor. Awareness of the information conveyed by investment analysts' ratings and institutional investors' holdings to the wider financial community, and therefore of its influence on investor perceptions, can be expected to influence the behavior of the board. Moreover, these constituents directly provide the board with additional information with which to judge the efficacy of the strategy and leadership of the firm. Finally, institutional investors are also able to directly influence the board, altering its composition as well as influencing its actions; this represents an important leveraging mechanism through which these investors influence the governance of the firm. Consequently the financial community (and in particular investment analysts and institutional investors) functions as an important element of external corporate governance.

NOTE

1. In their examination of Fortune 500 firms from 1992 to 2005, Kaplan and Minton (2006) found that the average tenure of a CEO is now slightly over six years.

REFERENCES

Akyol, A.C. and Carroll, C. (2006). Removing poison pills: A case of shareholder activism. University of Alabama working paper.
Arthaud-Day, M.L., Certo, S.T., Dalton, C.M., and Dalton, D.R. (2006). A changing of the guard: Executive and director turnover following corporate financial restatements. *Academy of Management Journal*, **49**(6), 1119–36.
Bainbridge, S. (2005). Shareholder activism and institutional investors. UCLA School of Law, Law-Economics Research Paper, No. 05–20.
Barber, B.M., Lehavy, R., and Trueman, B. (2008). Ratings changes, ratings levels, and the predictive value of analysts' recommendations. University of Michigan working paper. Available at SSRN: http://ssrn.com/abstract=1077733; accessed 3 August, 2010.
Barth, M.E., Kasznik, R., and McNichols, M.F. (2001). Analyst coverage and intangible assets. *Journal of Accounting Research*, **39**(1), 1–34.
Bennett, J.A., Sias, R.W., and Starks, L.T. (2003). Greener pastures and the impact of dynamic institutional preferences. *Review of Financial Studies*, **16**(4), 1203–38.
Bhushan, R. (1989). Firm characteristics and analyst following. *Journal of Accounting and Economics*, **11**(2–3), 255–75.
Bizjak, J.M. and Marquette, C. (1998). Shareholder proposals to rescind poison pills: All bark and no bite. *Journal of Financial and Quantitative Analysis*, **33**(4), 499–521.
Boni, L. and Womack, K.L. (2006). Analysts, industries, and price momentum. *Journal of Financial and Quantitative Analysis*, **41**(1), 85–109.
Brav, A., Jiang, W., Partnoy, F., and Thomas, R. (2008). Hedge fund activism, corporate governance, and firm performance. *Journal of Finance*, **63**, 1729–75.
Brennan, M. and Hughes, P. (1991). Stock prices and the supply of information. *Journal of Finance*, **46**(5), 1665–92.
Brennan, M. and Subrahmanyam, A. (1995). Investment analysis and price formation in securities markets. *Journal of Financial Economics*, **38**(3), 361–81.
Brown, K. and Brooke, B. (1993). Institutional demand and security price pressure. *Financial Analysts Journal*, **49**(5), 53–63.
Brown, P., Foster, G., and Noreen, E. (1985). *Security analyst multi-year earnings forecasts and the capital market*. Sarasota, FL: American Accounting Association Sarasota.
Bushee, B.J. and Noe, C.F. (2000). Corporate disclosure practices, institutional investors, and stock return volatility. *Journal of Accounting Research*, **38**(Supplement), 171–202.
Cannella, A.A. and Shen, W. (2001). So close and yet so far: Promotion versus exit for CEO heirs apparent. *Academy of Management Journal*, **44**(2), 252–70.
Carleton, W.T., Nelson, J.M., and Weisbach, M.S. (1998). The influence of institutions on corporate governance through private negotiations: Evidence from TIAA-CREF. *Journal of Finance*, **53**(4), 1335–62.
Chan, L.K.C., Karceski, C., Lakonishok, J., and Sougiannis, T. (2007). Investment, financing activities and the predictability of stock returns. Working paper.
Chen, S. and Steiner, T. (2000). Tobin's q, managerial ownership, and analyst coverage: A nonlinear simultaneous equations model. *Journal of Economics and Business*, **52**(4), 365–82.
Chopra, V. (1988). Why so much error in analysts' earnings forecasts? *Financial Analysts Journal*, **54**(6), 30–37.
Chung, K. and Jo, H. (1996). The impact of security analysts' monitoring and marketing functions on the market value of firms. *Journal of Financial and Quantitative Analysis*, **31**(4), 493–512.

Coughlan, A.T. and Schmidt, R.M. (1985). Executive compensation, management turnover, and firm performance: An empirical investigation. *Journal of Accounting & Economics*, **7**(1–3), 43–67.

Del Guercio, D. (1996). The distorting effect of the prudent-man laws on institutional equity investments. *Journal of Financial Economics*, **40**(1), 31–62.

Del Guercio, D. and Hawkins, J. (1999). The motivation and impact of pension fund activism. *Journal of Financial Economics*, **52**(3), 293–340.

Del Guercio, D., Wallis, L., and Woidtke, T. (2006). Do boards pay attention when institutional investors "just vote no"? CEO and director turnover associated with shareholder activism. University of Tennessee working paper.

Denis, D.J. and Denis, D.K. (1995). Performance changes following top management dismissal. *Journal of Finance*, **50**(4), 1029–57.

Denis, D.J. and Kruse, T.A. (2000). Managerial discipline and corporate restructuring following performance declines. *Journal of Financial Economics*, **55**(3), 391–424.

Denis, D.J. and Serrano, J.M. (1996). Active investors and management turnover following unsuccessful control contests. *Journal of Financial Economics*, **40**(2), 239–66.

El-Gazzar, S.M. (1998). Predisclosure information and institutional ownership: A cross-sectional examination of market revaluations during earnings announcement periods. *Accounting Review*, **73**(1), 119–29.

Fama, E.F. (1980). Agency problems and the theory of the firm. *Journal of Political Economy*, **88**(2), 288–307.

Fama, E.F., Fisher, L., Jensen, M.C., and Roll, R. (1969). The adjustment of stock prices to new information. *International Economic Review*, **10**(1), 1–21.

Farrell, K.A. and Whidbee, D.A. (2003). Impact of firm performance expectations on CEO turnover and replacement decisions. *Journal of Accounting Research*, **36**(1–3), 165–96.

Francis, J. and Soffer, L. (1997). The relative informativeness of analysts' stock recommendations and earnings forecast revisions. *Journal of Accounting Research*, **35**(2), 193–211.

Frankel, R., Kothari, S.P., and Weber, J. (2006). Determinants of the informativeness of analyst research. *Journal of Accounting and Economics*, **41**(1–2), 29–54.

Fredrickson, J.W., Hambrick, D.C., and Baumrin, S. (1988). A model of CEO dismissal. *Academy of Management Review*, **13**(2), 255–70.

Friday, N.K. and Crum, T. (2008). Top 10 topics for directors in 2008. *The Corporate Governance Advisor*, **16**(3), 11–21.

Gillan, S.L. and Starks, L.T. (2000). Corporate governance proposals and shareholder activism: The role of institutional investors. *Journal of Financial Economics*, **57**(2), 275–305.

Gillan, S.L. and Starks, L.T. (2007). The evolution of shareholder activism in the United States. *Journal of Applied Corporate Finance*, **19**(1), 55–73.

Gillan, S.L., Kensinger, J.W., and Martin, J.D. (2000). Value creation and corporate diversification: The case of Sears Roebuck & Co. *Journal of Financial Economics*, **55**(1), 103–37.

Givoly D. and Lakonishok, J. (1979). The information content of financial analysts' forecasts of earnings: Some evidence on semi-strong inefficiency. *Journal of Accounting and Economics*, **1**(3), 165–85.

Gompers, P.A. and Metrick, A. (2001). Institutional investors and equity prices. *Quarterly Journal of Economics*, **116**(1), 229–59.

Greenwood, R. and Schor, M. (2009). Investor activism and takeovers. *Journal of Financial Economics*, **92**(3), 362–75.

Haleblian, J. and Rajagopalan, N. (2006). A cognitive model of CEO dismissal: Understanding the influence of board perceptions, attributions and efficacy beliefs. *Journal of Management Studies*, **43**(5), 1009–26.

Hartzell, J.C. and Starks, L.T. (2003). Institutional investors and executive compensation. *Journal of Finance*, **58**(6), 2351–74.

Healey, P.M. and Palepu, K.G. (2001). Information asymmetry, corporate disclosure, and the capital markets: A review of the empirical disclosure literature. *Journal of Accounting and Economics*, **31**(1–3), 404–40.

Hermalin, B.E. and Weisbach, M.S. (1998). Endogenously chosen boards of directors and their monitoring of the CEO. *American Economic Review*, **88**(1), 96–118.

Hirschman, A. (1971). *Exit, voice and loyalty: Responses to decline in firms, organizations, and states.* Cambridge, MA: Harvard University Press.

Hotchkiss, E. and Strickland, D. (2003). Does shareholder composition matter? Evidence from the market reaction to corporate earnings announcements. *Journal of Finance*, **58**(4), 1469–98.

Huson, M.R. (1997). Does governance matter? Evidence from CalPERS interventions. University of Alberta working paper.

Huson, M.R., Parrino, R., and Starks, L.T. (2001). Internal monitoring mechanisms and CEO turnover: A long-term perspective. *Journal of Finance*, **56**(6), 2265–98.

Irvine, J. (2003). The incremental impact of analyst initiation of coverage. *Journal of Corporate Finance*, **9**(4), 431–51.

Jensen, M. (1993). The modern industrial revolution, exit, and the failure of internal control systems. *Journal of Finance*, **48**(3), 831–80.

Jensen, M. and Meckling, W. (1976). Theory of the firm: Managerial behavior, agency costs and ownership structure. *Journal of Financial Economics*, **3**(4), 305–60.

Jones, S.L., Lee, D., and Weis, E. (1999). Herding and feedback trading by different types of institutions and the effects on stock prices. Unpublished working paper, Indiana University, Indianapolis, Kennesaw State University, Kennesaw GA and Merrill Lynch and Company, New York.

Kahan, M. and Rock, E. (2006). Hedge funds in corporate governance and corporate control. *University of Pennsylvania Law Review*, **155**(5), 1021–93.

Kaplan, S.N. and Minton, B.A. (2006). How has CEO turnover changed? Increasingly performance sensitive boards and increasingly uneasy CEOs. NBER working paper No. W12465. Available at: http://ssrn.com/abstract=924751; accessed 3 August, 2010.

Karlsson, P., Neilson, G.L., and Webster, J.C. (2008). CEO succession in 2007: The performance paradox. *strategy + business*, **51**, Reprint 08208, Booz & Co.

Klein, A. and Zur, E. (2009). Entrepreneurial shareholder activism: Hedge funds and other private investors. *Journal of Finance*, **64**(1), 187–229.

Knowles, M.F. and Yost, J. (1999). Share-holder affairs at the Coca-Cola Company: A new approach to institutional investors. *The Corporate Governance Advisor*, **7**, 16–18.

Kock, C. (2006). When the market misleads: Stock prices, firm behavior, and industry evolution. *Organization Science*, **16**(6), 637–60.

Lehn, K.M. and Zhao, M. (2006). CEO turnover after acquisitions: Are bad bidders fired? *Journal of Finance*, **61**(4), 1759–811.

Lipton, M. and Lorsch, J. (1992). A modest proposal for improved corporate governance. *Business Lawyer*, **48**(1), 59–77.

Lowenstein, L. (1988). *What's wrong with Wall Street?* Reading, MA: Addison-Wesley.

Lucier, C., Wheeler, S., and Habbel, R. (2007). The era of the inclusive leader. *strategy + business*, **47**, Reprint 07205, Booz Allen Hamilton Inc.

Lys, T. and Shon S. (1990). The association between revisions of financial analysts' earnings forecasts and security price changes. *Journal of Accounting and Economics*, **13**(4), 341–63.

Martin, K.J. and McConnell, J.J. (1991). Corporate performance, corporate takeovers, and management turnover. *Journal of Finance*, **46**(2), 671–87.

Mayew, W.J. (2008). Evidence of management discrimination among analysts during earnings conference calls. *Journal of Accounting Research*, **46**(3), 627–59.

Merton, R.C. (1987). A simple model of capital market equilibrium with incomplete information. *Journal of Finance*, **42**(3), 483–511.

Michaely, R. and Womack, K. (1999). Conflict of interest and the credibility of underwriter analyst recommendations. *The Review of Financial Studies*, **12**(4), 633–86.

Mikkelson, W.H. and Partch, M.M. (1997). The decline of takeovers and disciplinary managerial turnover. *Journal of Financial Economics*, **44**(2), 205–28.

Millstein, I.M., Gregory, H.J., and Grapsas, R.C. (2008). Rethinking board and shareholder engagement in 2008. *The Corporate Governance Advisor*, **16**, 1–3.

Mitchell, M.L. and Lehn, K. (1990). Do bad bidders become good targets? *Journal of Political Economy*, **98**(2), 372–98.

Monks, R. and Minow, N. (1995). *Corporate governance.* Cambridge, UK: Blackwell Publishers.

Morck, R., Shleifer, A., and Vishny, R. (1989). Alternative mechanisms for corporate control. *American Economic Review*, **79**(4), 842–53.

Moyer, A.C., Chatfield, R.E., and Sisneros, P.M. (1989). Security analyst monitoring activity: Agency costs and information demands. *Journal of Financial and Quantitative Analysis*, **24**(4), 503–13.

Murphy, K. and Van Nuys, K. (1994). State pension funds and shareholder inactivism. Harvard University working paper.

Murphy, K.J. and Zimmerman, J.L. (1993). Financial performance surrounding CEO turnover. *Journal of Accounting & Economics*, **16**(1–3), 273–315.

Parrino, R., Sias, R.W., and Starks, L.T. (2003). Voting with their feet: Institutional ownership changes around forced CEO turnover. *Journal of Financial Economics*, **68**(1), 3–46.

Pearson, R. and Altman, K. (2006). Hedge funds and shareholder activism. *The Corporate Governance Advisor*, **14**(3), 25–7.

Potter, G. (1992). Accounting earnings announcements, institutional investor concentration, and common stock returns. *Journal of Accounting Research*, **30**(1), 146–55.

Puffer, S.M. and Weintrop, J.B. (1991). Corporate performance and CEO turnover: The role of performance expectations. *Administrative Science Quarterly*, **36**, 1–19.

Russo, F.P. and Turner, K.C. (2009). Active shareholder engagement: A model. *The Corporate Governance Advisor*, **17**(6), 10–17.

Shen, W. and Cannella, A.A. (2002). Power dynamics within top management and their impacts on CEO dismissal followed by inside succession. *Academy of Management Journal*, **45**(6), 1195–206.

Sias, R.W. (1996). Volatility and the institutional investor. *Financial Analysts Journal*, **52**(2), 13–20.

Sias, R.W., Starks, L.T., and Titman, S. (2001). The price impact of institutional trading. Unpublished working paper, Washington State University, Pullman and University of Texas, Austin. Available at: http://ssrn.com/abstract=283779; accessed 3 August, 2010.

Sinha, P., Brown, L., and Das, S. (1997). A re-examination of financial analysts' differential earnings forecast accuracy. *Contemporary Accounting Research*, **14**(1), 1–42.

Stickel, S.E. (1992). Reputation and performance among security analysts. *Journal of Finance*, **47**(5), 1811–37.

Warner, J., Watts, R., and Wruck, K. (1988). Stock prices, event prediction and event studies: An examination of top management changes. *Journal of Financial Economics*, **20**(4), 461–92.

Weisbach, M. (1988). Outside directors and CEO turnover. *Journal of Financial Economics*, **20**(1–2), 431–60.

Westphal, J.D. and Graebner, M.E. (2010). A matter of appearances: How corporate leaders manage the impressions of financial analysts about the conduct of their boards. *Academy of Management Journal*, **53**(1), 15–44.

Wiersema, M.F. (2002). Holes at the top: Why CEO firings backfire. *Harvard Business Review*, **80**(12), 70–78.

Wiersema, M.F. and Zhang, Y. (2008). CEO dismissal: The role of investment analysts as an external control mechanism. *Proceedings of the sixty-eighth Annual Meeting of the Academy of Management*, 2008.

Wiesenfeld, B.M., Wurthman, K.A., and Hambrick, D.C. (2008). The stigmatization and devaluation of elites associated with corporate failures: A process model. *Academy of Management Review*, **33**(1), 231–51.

Woidtke, T. (2002). Agents watching agents? Evidence from pension fund ownership and firm value. *Journal of Financial Economics*, **63**(1), 99–131.

Woidtke, T., Bierman, L., and Tuggle, C. (2003). Reining in activist funds. *Harvard Business Review*, **8**, 22–3.

Womack, K. (1996). Do brokerage analysts' recommendations have investment value? *Journal of Finance*, **51**(1), 137–67.

Wu, Y. (2004). The impact of public opinion on board structure changes, director career progression, and CEO turnover: Evidence from CalPERS' corporate governance program. *Journal of Corporate Finance*, **10**(1), 199–227.

Yu, F. (2008). Analyst coverage and earnings management. *Journal of Financial Economics*, **88**(12), 245–71.

Zhang, Y. (2006). The presence of a separate COO/president and its impact on strategic change and CEO dismissal. *Strategic Management Journal*, **27**(3), 283–300.

Zhang, Y. (2008). Information asymmetry and the dismissal of newly appointed CEOs: An empirical investigation. *Strategic Management Journal*, **29**(8), 859–72.

Zuckerman, E. (2000). Focusing the corporate product: Securities analysts and de-diversification. *Administrative Science Quarterly*, **45**(3), 591–619.

Index

charismatic leadership, social networks and
goal setting among US and Chinese
executives study
discussion and future research 112–19,
125–6
introduction 91–3
method 100–103
results 103–12
theoretical background 93–6
theory integration 96–100
Chemla, G. 315
Chen, G. 132, 135, 303
Chen, M.J. 152, 263, 264, 265, 268, 270, 278,
279
Chief Executive Leadership Institute 41
chief executive officers *see* CEOs (chief
executive officers)
chief financial officers (CFOs) 18, 38, 49, 57,
58, 60, 61, 392
chief marketing officers (CMOs) 58, 61
chief operating officers (COOs) 18, 38, 57–8,
379, 385–6, 387
Child, J. 21, 36–7, 118, 150, 245
China *see* charismatic leadership, social
networks and goal setting among US and
Chinese executives study; corporate elite
career experience and Chinese corporate
governance reform study
China Security and Regulatory Commission
(CSRC) 215, 217
Chinese Communist Party (CCP) 220, 223, 228
Chinese People's Political Consultative
Conference (CPPCC) 220, 223, 228
Cho, T.S. 53, 66, 315, 322
Chow, C. 291
Clark, K.D. 3, 5, 11, 127
closed networks 119
CMOs (chief marketing officers) 58, 61
coalition building 117–18
Coca-Cola 352–3, 367, 368, 399
Code of Corporate Governance for Listed
Companies (CSRC) 215, 217
coercive isomorphism 216, 220, 221
cognitive capabilities 39, 40–41, 43–4
cognitive frameworks/schema 205, 206, 207,
208, 215, 216, 219
cognitive processes 310, 311, 312, 315, 316, 322
cohesion 39, 60, 64
Colbert, A.E. 37, 134, 135, 136, 143
collaborative strategic decision making 23, 24,
25, 26, 27, 28, 29
collective goals and objectives 128, 135, 136,
144, 146
collective leadership styles 298, 300, 302, 303,
304, 305, 307, 309–10, 311, 314, 317

collective self-efficacy 133, 134, 155, 156, 161
collectivistic culture 97, 98, 99–100, 107,
109–12, 113, 115, 216
commitment 95, 119, 125–6, 128
common method variance 164–5
communication
and similarity/attraction in inner circles 39,
40, 42, 45
and strategic leadership and
entrepreneurship nexus study 313, 316,
322, 338
compensation *see* assistant coach
compensation; CEO compensation;
compensation gap; executive
compensation; scapegoating premium
and CEO compensation study; second-
tier manager compensation; TMT
compensation
compensation gap 357, 359, 362, 363, 365, 366,
369, 382
competition 54, 56, 153, 261–2, 369
see also competitive strategy 'fit'; TMT
heterogeneity and competitive behavior
study
competitive strategy 'fit' 264–5, 277, 278
complementary 'fit' 252, 333, 336, 337–8
complexity
and strategic decision making 40–41, 43–4,
152–3, 264, 278
and TMT potency 161
see also external strategic complexity;
internal strategic complexity
conference budget size 360, 361, 363, 364, 365,
366
confidence
and collective self-efficacy 133, 134, 155, 161
concept 154, 155, 176–9
and self-efficacy 130, 131, 133
and TMT collective core self-evaluation 133
and TMT collective psychological capital
134, 146
and transformational leadership 128
see also CEO confidence; overconfidence;
potency; team confidence; TMT
confidence studies
conformity 216, 220, 221
Conger, J.A. 93–4, 96–7, 98, 100, 101, 104, 118
connections, and inner circle selection 38–9
conscientiousness 26, 77–8, 81, 82, 83, 84, 85
constraint 237, 238, 240, 242, 245, 246, 250,
253, 255, 256
control 284, 288, 322
cooperation 54, 56
COOs (chief operating officers) 18, 38, 57–8,
379, 385–6, 387